BEHIND THE
DRAGON

BEHIND THE
DRAGON
PLAYING RUGBY FOR
WALES

ROSS HARRIES

POLARIS
PUBLISHING

This edition published in 2021 by

POLARIS PUBLISHING LTD
c/o Aberdein Considine
2nd Floor, Elder House
Multrees Walk
Edinburgh
EH1 3DX

Distributed by
Birlinn Limited

www.polarispublishing.com

ISBN: 9781913538705
eBook ISBN: 9781788851077

British Library Cataloguing-in-Publication Data
A catalogue record for this book is available on request from the British Library.

CONTENTS

ACKNOWLEDGEMENTS

It was while queueing at the bar at Lord's that a well-spoken Scottish gent approached me, and struck up a conversation about rugby. By the end of the evening he'd given me his business card, and asked me to give him a call about a proposition that he had. The next day I was boarding a plane to New Zealand to cover the Wales rugby tour for the BBC, so it wasn't for a few months that I got in touch. I was lounging outside my tent in the foothills of the Pyrenees after a day spent hiking, when the card – which I'd been using as a bookmark – caught my attention. I called Peter Burns, the MD of Polaris Publishing, and listened to him outline his idea: an oral history of Welsh rugby spanning more than a century, from the formation of the Welsh Rugby Union, to the present day. It sounded like an intimidating project, but I was halfway through a bottle of French Malbec, and with a bravado that returned to haunt me on several occasions, I said I'd do it. I'd like to thank Pete for entrusting me with such a monumental undertaking, and for the gentle reassurances and encouragement he offered along the way. As anyone who's written a book will know, it can be a lonely, solitary pursuit, and there are times when you want to take a match to your manuscript and watch it go up in flames. Pete ensured I never acted on such instincts.

It's been an epic journey, and a privilege, to delve deep into the treasure trove of memories shared by those who have proudly worn the three feathers during more than a hundred years of rugby history. In this sense, my role has been that of curator – I was never remotely good enough to play rugby for my country, so the best I could hope for was to write about it. I therefore owe an enormous debt of thanks to all the players and coaches, past and present, who've given so generously of their time and been so candid and entertaining in their recollections. Without their cooperation, this book simply wouldn't exist.

I began in Upper Cwmtwrch with the ebullient, larger-than-life Clive Rowlands. Former player, captain, and coach of Wales, and former president of the Welsh Rugby Union. As the sun shone in through his conservatory windows, illuminating his vast collection of memorabilia, I understood the size of the task ahead. My next port of call was the Cardiff Arms Park trophy room where I spent an enthralling few hours in the company of Gareth Edwards and Gerald Davies – two of the finest practitioners the game has ever seen, yet both were humble to their very core, quick to deflect praise, and engaging with their memories. I spent several hours in Phil Bennett's living room as his wife, Pat, kept us nourished with sandwiches, tea and cake, and I listened to one of rugby's finest raconteurs bring decades-old memories back to life with vivid clarity. And so this continued, through the decades and the generations. In rugby clubs, cafes, living rooms, and bars all over Wales, I spoke with some of the best players to have represented their country, teasing out their memories and listening to their stories. There are tales of triumph and tragedy, of euphoria and misery. It is the latter which were hardest for people to revisit, so I'd like to thank Sam Warburton for patiently fielding yet more questions about 'the red card', and Mike Ruddock and Gareth Thomas for being so honest and open about one of the more painful episodes in recent Welsh rugby history.

Given that this book begins in the nineteenth century, there are clearly those who are no longer with us. That their voices have been brought so vividly back to life is down to the brilliant work of John Griffiths, whose memory for detail, and knowledge of Welsh rugby history is surely unparalleled. John's work on the opening few chapters was critical and helped set this narrative smoothly on its way.

Thanks too to several of my colleagues in the print media for their words of wisdom. To Stephen Jones for his timely advice, and to Tom English who told me – while I was taking a sledgehammer to my unwieldy first draft – that you know you're on to a winner when you're consigning genuinely good bits to the cutting room floor.

Thanks to Jeff Towns, who kindly opened the doors to his stockroom at the sadly defunct Dylan's Books in Swansea. It proved a hugely valuable resource for fact-checking and historical research.

Enormous thanks go to my mum, for always encouraging me to read, and to my dad for fanning the flames of my passion for rugby. I'll never forget my first trip to the national stadium with my dad, ascending the steps to the stand, gazing out upon that seething mass of people, and drinking in the incredible atmosphere. I was intoxicated. There's a photo of my father and I in 1978 watching Wales win the Grand Slam. I was eight months old and oblivious to what was going on. More than twenty years later, I'd resigned myself to the fact that Grand Slam was probably the only one I'd ever witness. As this book goes to publication, I've witnessed four more, and it's been a pleasure to revisit those for this story.

Thanks to my Dadcu, Ken Powell, who also nurtured my interest in rugby. Before that trip to the National Stadium, it was on the terraces of Stradey Park, that I was first entranced by the oval ball game.

And most importantly of all, I'd like to thank my wife, Kathryn and my daughters Isabella and Rosalie. Kath, for always being a reassuring presence on the many occasions when I thought my clumsy, rambling manuscript would never coalesce into something resembling a book. And Izzy and Rosie, for having the patience to wait for their next trip to the pool or the park, while I sat at the kitchen table bashing away furiously at my laptop.

Ross Harries

For my Dadcu, Ken Powell

ONE

THE LEGEND OF BILLY BANCROFT

Welsh rugby's great adventure began as the private scheme of a twenty-nine-year-old Newport printer named Richard Mullock. Late in 1880, Mullock, as secretary of Newport, sent a request to the Rugby Football Union in London for an international match to be played between England and Wales. The challenge was accepted and three months later Wales played their first ever Test and were beaten by a margin equivalent to 82–0 in today's money.

Poor Mullock. He had a lot on his plate. He had to arrange a trial and select a team, he had to finalise the travel and accommodation and then get the kit sorted out – all on his own. He was a one-man committee. Two of his players withdrew because they had their hearts set on playing for England. Two more failed to show on the day because the letters asking for their presence had gone missing in the post. Mullock must have been a nervous wreck long before that first ball had been kicked to signal the beginning of an epic story.

Richard Summers: The game was at Blackheath before a small crowd ranged perhaps three-deep round the ground. I'm not even sure the playing pitch was roped off. We played in ordinary light walking boots with a bar of leather nailed across the sole to help us swerve; jerseys which fitted closely high up round the neck and dark blue knickerbockers fastened below the knee with four or five buttons. The match was a runaway victory for England and Len Stokes was their captain and had most to do with our downfall. He had a most baffling, swerving run. His left-footed kicking broke our hearts. We'd never seen a player who was able to kick with his left foot.

Mullock returned to Wales to a public outcry at the complete absence of men from Neath, Swansea and Llanelli in his team. The battering in Blackheath sparked a flurry of letters to the Welsh press castigating the selection.

On 12 March 1881, the great and the good of Welsh rugby met at the Castle Hotel in Neath. Nearly a dozen clubs sent delegates and helped found the Welsh Football Union (WFU) – it would not officially become the Welsh Rugby Union (WRU) until the mid-1930s. The fledgling body unanimously elected Mullock as its secretary.

Mullock organised a game with Ireland in late January 1882. History was made that day – Wales's first official international match. And they won, by two goals and two tries to nil. Reports from the time suggest that a number of Ireland players were irate at the officiating, particularly some of the decisions made by a touch judge who they claimed had made a series of strange calls against them. The target of their disgruntlement – Richard Mullock.

Later in the year England travelled to Swansea to play in Wales's first official Test in the Principality, and early in 1883 they met Scotland for the first time, in Edinburgh. They were up and running. 'Only one jersey was given to the international players of the 1880s, and it was the wearer's responsibility to keep it in repair and washed to perfection,' said Billy Douglas, one of the men from those early years. 'Three things carried the fair name of Wales to the four corners of the world: coal, singing and rugby football, which is a game truer to life than any other game played by man.'

England and Scotland had enjoyed a ten-year start on the Welsh and Ireland were six years Wales's seniors, but as the Welsh developed it became clear that the youngest of the four Home Unions would lead a tactical evolution in back play. The Welsh clubs, riding the winds of change, felt that the time was ripe to experiment with back formations in order to capitalise on the passing game. First, the back division was tweaked by redeploying one of the two full backs as a third three-quarter and then Cardiff (accidentally at first) began the practice of removing a player from the scrum to experiment with an eight forwards/seven backs split. This Welsh innovation transformed rugby into its modern form.

Giants emerged, none of them more towering than Arthur Gould, the centre and captain on the day in Dewsbury in 1890 when Wales first beat England. Gould would be the automatic choice to lead his nation for the next seven seasons, a run of eighteen Tests and a Welsh record that would stand for close to a century until Ieuan Evans overtook him.

Arthur Gould: I first played with Newport Juniors as a boy of thirteen and went right into the first team at fifteen. The team was short-handed and the groundsman suggested my name to the captain. I was at full back. I got two tries and stayed in the team.

Gwyn Nicholls: Arthur Gould was the most dangerous and cleverest player. He was at top speed in two strides and away almost before one could realise that he was in possession of the ball.

He was the greatest source of anxiety to his opponents; you could never tell what he was going to do. In my early days in the Cardiff–Newport games the instruction was to 'Watch Gould'. The task was about as difficult as trying to catch a butterfly in flight with a hat-pin. He was a quick thinker and could act just as quickly. Stop his progress one way and he was off in a flash in another without scarcely losing his stride; and to vary things he could drop goals. I had some jolly afternoons 'watching' him.

Arthur Gould was Welsh rugby's first celebrity. In 1896 the notion of a testimonial game in his honour was floated by his admirers. Within weeks of the launch of the event there were more than five thousand subscribers from all over the world. The WFU pledged £50, a relative fortune. When the fund reached a sum sufficient to purchase the leasehold on Gould's Newport home, eyebrows were raised. The RFU, still coming to terms with the money-driven crisis that led to the creation of rugby league, complained to their counterparts in Wales about the riches and the dangers of lavishing money on Arthur Gould.

The International Board requested a review of the terms of the testimonial. Fearing a ban from the Test matches of 1897, the Welsh union withdrew their £50 pledge to Gould and Gould, citing advancing age and waiving his right to any benefit that might affect his standing as an amateur, announced his retirement from first-class rugby.

Viv Jenkins: There was Arthur Gould and there was Billy Bancroft. My dad, a born storyteller, regaled me with tales of many a wondrous deed. Billy, the one and only 'Banky', was one of his special heroes. He held undisputed sway in Wales's teams for twelve seasons, from 1890 to 1901.

The tales about him were innumerable – how he used to run opposing forwards off their feet, from one side of the field to the other, or kick goals, in practice, from the corner flag or from a yard in front of the posts, right below the crossbar.

Many years later, when Bancroft was seventy-nine, I accompanied him to Lord's to see his protégé, Gilbert Parkhouse, play his first Test for England, against the West Indies in 1950. Who was the greatest centre he had seen? 'Arthur Gould, without a doubt.' A few years later I met Banky again. Swansea had just played the All Blacks and I asked him what he thought about Bob Scott, the touring team's full back. 'Not bad,' he said, 'not bad at all, though I'd like to see him under a bit more pressure and when you see him next, ask him if he can kick a goal from sixty yards, with either foot.' It was the '*either* foot' that amused me! The implication was that Banky could have done it standing on his head.

Jack Jenkins: In 1893, Wales, for the first time, brought the International Championship home. Who that witnessed that game in January of that year on a frost-bound ground – 500 fire devils had been kept going all through the previous day and night to make the Cardiff Arms Park more or less playable – will ever forget the brilliantly dropped penalty goal of Billy Bancroft which brought the great victory of Gwalia over the Saxon?

Billy Bancroft: It must be a record that during my career I took every free kick awarded to Wales and every conversion. The most important kick of all was that which won the match against England at Cardiff in 1893. England were leading 11–9 a few minutes before the end when we were awarded a penalty thirty yards out and two yards from touch. Arthur Gould as skipper stood on the spot with the ball in his hand. I walked up to take the kick and said, 'Arthur, I'm going to drop kick it.'

To his many remonstrances I merely repeated my statement. The crowd were getting restless and Gould finally threw the ball to the ground and walked away. I retrieved it, took three strides towards an already charging opposition, and drop kicked. Before the ball had travelled ten yards I shouted out to my skipper, now standing in the centre of the field and with his back towards me, 'It's there, Arthur.' Time was called within a matter of seconds with the score Wales 12, England 11.

Wales were outcast by Scotland in 1897 and 1898 and by Ireland in 1898 over what became known as the 'Gould Affair', but the Welsh Union's withdrawal of their pledge and Gould's retirement resolved the matter.

Welsh society had a spring in its step at the start of the twentieth century, with South Wales booming thanks to high employment and record-breaking industrial production. The late-Victorian Education Acts had also improved literacy and numeracy levels among ordinary Welsh children, freeing them to set their career sights beyond the hard grind of manual labour that had beleaguered previous generations. Confidence and optimism were in the air, and Welsh rugby, too, found its swagger as the national side, comprising a democratic mix of working men and aspiring professionals, embarked on a golden era, becoming the leading force among the Home Unions.

The Welsh playing record from when the full rota of International Championship matches resumed in 1899 until the end of the 1905 campaign was fifteen wins and a draw in twenty-one games, including Triple Crowns in 1900, 1902 and 1905. Wales were unbeaten against England, recording a resounding 25–0 victory in 1905 that would stand as their record winning margin against the men in white until the 30–3 triumph that clinched the Six Nations title on points-difference in 2013.

The overture to Wales's first golden era was a virtuoso performance against an English side that spent the afternoon chasing the shadow of young Willie Llewellyn on his fairy-tale debut at Swansea in January 1899. He scored a remarkable four tries as Wales won 26–3 and Llewellyn, who captured the hearts of Welsh supporters, would become a fixture in their most celebrated three-quarter line before retiring with a then-Welsh record of sixteen Test tries to his name in 1905.

Willie Llewellyn: It's a long way back to 7 January 1899, when I first played for Wales against England. The chief obstacle in our path was the great full back, Herbert Gamlin, of Devon, renowned for his octopus tackles, with fourteen-and-a-half stone of weight behind him. As a youngster playing in his first match, I trembled with the thought of coming up against this formidable opponent. However, I managed to score four tries and came off the field feeling very pleased with life. Chief reason for my success was the openings made for me by the famous brothers Evan and David James of Swansea, while the one and only Billy Bancroft was our full back.

Billy Bancroft: I became the first Welshman to hold two Triple Crown medals with the success of 1900, and in my last game for Wales – against Ireland in 1901 on my home ground – I was keen on closing my career with a victory, particularly as I was captain. I was none too happy when at half-time Ireland led us by three tries and with Wales having to face a stiff wind. The Irishmen restarted with great vigour but our forwards came back at them and after fifteen minutes we scored a try near the corner, and I kicked the goal. The Irish simply tore into us and a terrific battle ensued. Our fellows stuck to them grandly and by good all-round teamwork we gradually took the steam out of their pack. We eventually got another try only inches from the corner. The wind was troublesome and I took some little time to decide how I would attempt the kick. I decided to kick right-footed, hard and low, and to a certain extent ignore the wind. In all my experience I have never known a crowd so silent. The ball tore through the wind as straight as a gun barrel, and the crowd went delirious with delight as it sailed between the uprights.

Not only did Wales go unbeaten in 1905, in December they became the only team to beat the Original All Blacks, the first fully representative team from New Zealand to visit Europe. The tourists had won twenty-seven out of twenty-seven, scoring 801 points and conceding only twenty-two before arriving in South Wales for the final stretch of their British journey.

Five of the team Wales selected – Rees Gabe, 'Boxer' Harding, Teddy Morgan, Willie Llewellyn and Percy Bush – had toured New Zealand with the Lions the summer before. Bush had been a revelation, a real bag of tricks whose play was a tantalising mix of audacity and awareness. The New Zealanders held him in high regard – and his fame was to prove the key to a scheme hatched by Dickie Owen, the pint-sized Swansea scrum half. Owen planned to use a dummy pass with Bush as the decoy runner to lure the All Blacks into believing that the fly half was starting one of his teasing blind-side attacks. Once the visitors were wrong-footed and committed to Bush's side of the field, Owen would fire a long reverse pass to Wales's extra back, Cliff Pritchard, who would sweep to the open-side where they could, they hoped, score a try.

The day of the match dawned dry but cold and overcast. Nearly 50,000 were crammed into the Arms Park as the sides filed onto the field wearing numbers, the first time a Welsh XV had done so in a Test. The New Zealanders performed their traditional haka, but Wales had a response up their sleeves. At the time, national anthems were not customarily sung before kick-offs but as the All Blacks finished their war cry the Welsh players gathered near one of the crowded enclosures and began singing *Hen Wlad Fy Nhadau.* The crowd quickly joined in, raising the volume to a crescendo as the chorus rang out around the ground. The atmosphere was electric when referee John Dallas, a recently retired Scottish international player, blew his whistle and the game was on.

Wales mastered the All Blacks up front, stealing the put-in at every scrum. Bert Winfield, the Welsh full back, gave a masterclass with his torpedo-kicking to touch and marvellous positional play, and man-for-man the New Zealand backs were outclassed. Thirty minutes into the game, Dickie Owen sensed the field position was right for him to put his pre-planned scrum move into action. Owen executed it to such perfection that an overlap was created for Teddy Morgan to whizz over the New Zealand line for a try wide out on the left. Wales nursed their lead under intense pressure in the second half and clung on to win 3–0.

Rees Gabe: I had played in all the matches in New Zealand with the 1904 British side. People here could have had no conception of the expertness, the artistry and the enthusiasm of the 1905 side before they arrived; but we knew full well what to expect. I was inclined to the view that they would lose very few matches, if any.

Willie Llewellyn: I was a member of the British team which went to Australia and New Zealand in 1904. We had only twenty-four players in all, including eight from Wales. We won all our matches in Australia and Percy Bush, at outside half, was at his glorious best. We lost two games in New Zealand, one against the All Blacks and the other against Auckland. We knew that when New Zealand came to Wales they would watch Percy Bush very carefully.

Rees Gabe: Percy was one of the most colourful personalities ever capped for Wales. We went to Australia and New Zealand with the British team in 1904 when his displays were so brilliant, so cheeky and so devastating that they even surprised us, who had come to expect extraordinary things from him. The Australian press called him 'will-o'-the-wisp'. His side-stepping was so perfectly done that his opponents were completely baffled. The nearest to approach him in later years, and I use the word 'approach' advisedly, were Cliff Jones and Bleddyn Williams. When he was really at his best and in the mood, he could run through the whole team, as I'd seen him do from a kick-off.

Percy Bush: We have all heard such a lot of blah about the Wales–New Zealand match of 1905 that the mere thought of it is nauseating to those of us who played in it.

Harry Bowen: The scoring of the first try by Teddy Morgan was as smart a piece of work as could be wished for.

Dai Jones: If Teddy Morgan hadn't scored another point during his brilliant career, that try would keep his name green for all time as a rugby player. It started on the blind-side of the scrum. Dicky Owen, Cliff Pritchard and Teddy were there like three ferrets – and Morgan made no mistake.

Bert Winfield: The best game I ever took part in.

Arthur 'Boxer' Harding: The hardest game I ever played.

Harry Bowen: The All Blacks had met what they had never met before on their tour: a team that believed in attack, and one which was acting on that belief. Ten minutes from the finish, and still anybody's game; five minutes, and still the game not safe. We feared; one minute, and still we thought of failing at the finish. But the end came, and Mr Dallas blew his final thrilling shriek, and the greatest of all games ever yet played had been won by Wales.

Welsh fans would bask in the reflected glory of many more Test successes between 1906 and 1910 as new international opponents arrived from Australia, France and South Africa. In 1908, the first Wallabies went down 9–6 to Wales in Cardiff and France were beaten 36–4 on their maiden visit.

The first Springboks succeeded where New Zealand had failed by beating Wales at Swansea in 1906, but national pride was restored by Cardiff a few weeks later. Gwyn Nicholls opened the scoring for his club with a try from a slashing solo effort while Bush was given his head to run the tourists off their feet. He revelled as a free spirit among the backs and inspired Cardiff to a remarkable 17–0 win over the tourists.

Billy Spiller: I always think of the season 1910–11 as one of the most enjoyable of my career, because Wales won the Triple Crown and it was my great privilege to be in the winning XV. The first game was against England at Swansea. In the train down from Cardiff on the way to the ground, Reggie Gibbs said to me, 'Look here, Billy, that fellow Birkett opposite you today is not too safe with his hands and he may drop a pass.' How right he was! There was a scrummage on the English twenty-five, England got the ball and Stoop passed to Birkett. He dropped the ball and it bounced nicely for me to gather and score. Then Reggie Gibbs scored a try after I had flicked a pass on to him. Wales won 15–11.

We really cut loose against Scotland and eventually won 32–10. I scored two tries and Reggie Gibbs three.

The Irish match at Cardiff was important for two reasons. It was the last time Wales won the Triple Crown for thirty-nine years, and Dickie Owen created a new world record for international appearances with thirty-four caps [overtaking Billy Bancroft]. The gates were closed before the kick-off, and five spectators were badly injured at the match, four by falling off a stand and one by falling off a tree. Those were the days. The game wasn't very spectacular, but we won comfortably in the end. After the match the WRU presented us with spirit cases inscribed as 'Winners of the Triple Crown 1910–11'.

Soon after war was declared on Germany in 1914, the WFU urged its clubs to appeal to the 'pluck and patriotism' of its members and rally them to answer Lord Kitchener's call to enlist and serve King and Country. The response from clubs was immediate. Before the war was thirty days old, Cardiff RFC organised a meeting calling sportsmen in the area to get fit with a view to forming a sportsmen's battalion. At Newport, members of the rugby club were quick to swell the numbers of a local sporting platoon which became part of the South Wales Borderers, and many clubs surrendered their grounds to the military for training purposes or, in some cases, for conversion to allotments to sustain the war effort.

Among former Welsh international players, Billy Geen volunteered 'as swiftly into the Army as he used to zig-zag through most defences'. The fair-haired favourite from Newport was also among the first Welsh rugby internationals who were casualties of the war that did not end all wars, but did bring down the curtain on Test rugby for five years. The fallen were spread through every generation, from Richard Garnons Williams of the original 1881 Wales XV to Charlie Pritchard of the famous 1905 pack against New Zealand and on to Dai Watts of the immediate pre-war pack known as the 'Terrible Eight' – not forgetting those whose deaths from wounds sustained on active service fell outside the cut-off date designated by the Commonwealth War Graves Commission for deaths attributable to war service. Men like Hop Maddock, the London Welsh speedster who succeeded Willie Llewellyn in the Welsh team of the golden era. Maddock was severely wounded serving with the Machine Gun Corps and died in Cardiff barely three years after the Armistice. Or Dai 'Tarw' Jones, the magnificent Treherbert bull of the 1905 pack who joined up with the Welsh Guards and served on the Somme until a gunshot wound through his lung left him physically disabled. Jones lingered on bravely until meeting his untimely death, aged fifty-one, on the same day that Wales beat England at Twickenham in January 1933.

The biggest wartime rugby encounter took place in April 1915 when Wales were beaten 26–10 by the Barbarians in a non-cap game arranged to recruit volunteers for the Welsh Guards. It raised more than £200 for military charities. The Welsh XV contained thirteen pre-war caps and was led by Rev. Alban Davies, now an army chaplain, who was reunited with five of his 'Terrible Eight' from 1914. Staged at Cardiff Arms Park and originally advertised as a Forces International between Wales and England, it was the only match played by a team that was representative of the Principality during the war-torn seasons from 1914 to 1918.

ROLL OF HONOUR 1914–1919

GEEN, William Purdon. Killed in action serving with the King's Royal Rifle Corps at Hooge during the Second Battle of Ypres on 31 July, 1915.

LEWIS, Brinley Richard. Killed in action serving with the Royal Field Artillery at Ypres on 2 April, 1917.

PERRETT, Fred Leonard. Wounded while serving with the Royal Welsh Fusiliers. Died in France on 1 December, 1918.

PHILLIPS, Louis Augustus. Killed in action serving with the Royal Fusiliers at Cambrai on 14 March, 1916.

PRITCHARD, Charles Meyrick. Wounded while serving with the South Wales Borderers at the Battle of the Somme. Died in France on 14 August, 1916.

TAYLOR, Charles Gerald. Killed in action serving with the Battle Cruiser Squadron on HMS *Tiger* during the Battle of Dogger Bank on 24 January, 1915.

THOMAS, Edward John 'Dick'. Killed in action serving with the Royal Fusiliers at Mametz Wood during the Battle of the Somme on 7 July, 1916.

THOMAS, Horace Wyndham. Killed in action serving with the Rifle Brigade at Guillemont, France, on 3 September, 1916.

WALLER, Philip Dudley. Killed in action serving with the South African Heavy Artillery at Arras, France, on 14 December, 1917.

WATTS, David. Killed in action serving with the King's Shropshire Light Infantry at Ancre Valley during the Battle of the Somme on 14 July, 1916.

WESTACOTT, David. Killed in action serving with the Gloucestershire Regiment at Zonnebeke in Flanders, Belgium, during the Third Battle of Ypres on 28 August, 1917.

WILLIAMS, John Lewis. Killed in action serving with the Welsh Regiment at Mametz Wood during the Battle of the Somme on 12 July, 1916.

WILLIAMS, Richard Davies Garnons. Killed in action serving with the Royal Fusiliers at the Battle of Loos, France, on 25 September, 1915.

TWO

HAYDN TANNER,
THE NINETEEN-YEAR-OLD VETERAN

There was a decade of decline for Wales when the International Championship was restored after the war. Between 1920 and 1929, Wales played forty-two matches, winning only seventeen. Nine of those victories were against French teams struggling to establish a reputation as a force in Test rugby.

The lure of the north was never greater with rugby league's predatory scouts decimating the union ranks. Nearly fifty of the Welsh Test players capped in the 1920s – and countless more promising club players – signed professional contracts. At first many turned professional in frustration at the fickleness of a dysfunctional selection system which recruited and rejected Test players with alacrity. Then, as the threats of industrial and business uncertainty increased during the depression years, the flow of union players to the north became a flood, with many using it as an escape route from economic hardship.

Dan Jones: Towards the end of my career I was in a Swansea hotel when an Oldham rugby league scout called me outside and showed me £100 in notes which he was willing to give me for playing one game in the North. By that time, I had long passed my best and I told him, 'It won't do your reputation as a successful poacher any good, nor mine as a wing. So forget it.'

Arthur Bowdler: I was earning £3 a week as a collier at Cwmcarn when I was offered £400 to join Leeds in rugby league in 1928. I didn't go – in fact, I paid money out of my own pocket in order to play rugby union.

Rowe Harding: I was privileged to play for Wales and when I toured South Africa with the Lions I had to sell my motorcycle for £40 to help meet the cost of the trip. A first-class rugby player is a public figure, a public entertainer, a public servant, and a part of the national life of the country. It is a heavy responsibility. Not only is his form as a player discussed, but his habits, morals and vices are a subject of universal gossip. Yet he is supposed to be an amateur, who plays for the love of the game, and expects nothing in return except rude health.

It is difficult for me to understand the traditional attitude to amateur sport that exists in this country, that no gentleman should make money by means of his physical prowess, and that a man who makes money out of his physical prowess is no gentleman. The whole attitude towards amateurism is hopelessly illogical. The

English Rugby Union has even indicated that, if a rugby player is so bold as to compete with professional journalists on the subject he knows more about than anyone else, something will be done to stop such shameless money-grabbing. I'm afraid the attitude towards professionalism is purely snobbish. Every amateur who is not a fool or a genius has his price.

Numbers paint a grim picture. In the twenty-one Test matches after the war up to March 1924, ninety-nine players were used by Wales. Thirty-seven of those were capped once and only five appeared ten or more times. Two forwards, Steve Morris of Cross Keys and the leader of the 1922 champion side, Swansea's Tom Parker, were the most-used players, each making fifteen appearances. It was such a shocking attrition rate that, years later, one player recalled (only half in jest) that within a month of making his Wales debut he and several of his erstwhile national team-mates were holding a past-players reunion.

Ivor Jones: I played for Wales against England and Scotland in 1924 and was not picked again. My next game was three years later.

Rowe Harding: After the match against Scotland in 1924, which Scotland won 35–10, largely through Ian Smith's wonderful running [he scored three tries], Codger Johnson, the Welsh left-wing, asked to be introduced to Smith, as he explained that he had not had an opportunity of seeing him during the match. Indirectly, Smith was the cause of a famous remark by one of the Welsh selectors. The day after the match the team was taken to see the Forth Bridge. 'Take a good look at it, boys,' said the selector, 'because it is the last time any of you will see it at the expense of the Welsh Rugby Union.'

Dai Parker: Life was a darn sight more difficult in those days. I was mixing concrete on the morning of my first cap against Ireland in 1924, played in the afternoon, celebrated at night and then walked to work on the Sunday.

Ossie Male: I was banned from playing for Wales in March 1924. I had no idea I had done anything wrong. I boarded the train at Newport for the trip to Paris to play France and had been suspended almost before we had time to cross Newport bridge. I was called out of the compartment and told I would have to leave. I pleaded for a chance to say something in my defence but the decision had already been made. When the train arrived at Paddington I had to turn around and come straight back. My crime? Unwittingly breaking a WRU bye-law stating that no player could take part in a match within six days of an international. I'd made the mistake of playing for Cardiff against Birkenhead Park within five days of the French match. I was anxious to play against Birkenhead Park because I'd been out of action for a fortnight with a broken nose and I wanted to get match fit. I was also confused by the date of the French game which was staged on a Thursday that year.

Tom Lewis: I won my first Welsh cap against England in 1926 when I was told only two hours before the game that I was replacing Steve Lawrence, of Bridgend. A year later I was in the side when we lost 5–0 to Scotland – their last win in Cardiff for years. Conditions were awful. We were ankle deep in mud and you couldn't tell a Scotsman from a Welshman. I've often wondered how the selectors managed to recognise me enough to drop me.

Rowe Harding: Playing for Wales between 1924 and 1928 was, on the whole, a gloomy business. 1926 was probably the least disappointing as we recorded our first victory over Ireland since 1922. It was a vital match for Ireland. If they won, the Triple Crown would be theirs for the first time in thirty years. Swansea was the capital of Ireland that day. The town swarmed with Irish fans who had come to witness their team's triumph. A few had celebrated it beforehand. Windsor Lewis, a mere stripling at nineteen, beat the Irish team on his own – and I say, without hesitation, that no more brilliant display has ever been seen in international rugby, and Wales won by three points after a magnificent game.

Ossie Male: I clashed with the union in 1928 when I skippered Wales at Murrayfield. Arriving in Edinburgh the night before the match, union officials wanted the team to have supper and go to bed early. I had other ideas and marched the team on a five-mile hike to Murrayfield and back to loosen them off and give them the feel for the ground. I tried to get the boys as settled as possible. I told Albert Jenkins to have a pint if he wanted one . . . never mind about the union. They called us 'the old men's team' yet we won 13–0.

Wales finally turned the corner on their path to reviving old glories in 1931 when, for the first time since 1922, they were unbeaten in the Five Nations and finished as outright champions. There would be bumps ahead, but the relief of success was almost tangible.

Viv Jenkins: Watcyn Thomas scored with a broken collarbone against Scotland at Cardiff in 1931. Scotland were leading 8–3 at half-time, and on the re-start he was upended when following up the kick-off and catching the ball. He fell on his left shoulder and knew straight away that his collarbone was gone. But there were no replacements in those days, so Watcyn, who was vice-captain, carried on leading the Welsh pack with his left arm clasped to his chest.

Watcyn Thomas: There was an astonishing sequel to the game. After my shoulder had been strapped up, I took my jersey into the Scottish dressing room to exchange with one of the team – a time-honoured custom – but was ordered out by the stiff-necked Scottish official in charge, because it bordered on professionalism.

Happily, there was the usual intermixing of both sets of players after the game, after which I retired to my hotel bedroom. But I couldn't sleep; I was in such pain that I paced my bedroom throughout the night. Still, it had been worth it as we went on to defeat France and Ireland and carry off the Championship.

After twenty-three years and nine aborted attempts, the day when England's hoodoo over Wales finally ended came on 21 January, 1933. The side that travelled in hope of breaking the infamous Twickenham Bogey, as it was known, comprised a mix of youthful college backs and a hard-core of tough forwards. Seven new caps were blooded, including two young students whose names would reverberate through Welsh rugby for the rest of the decade: Viv Jenkins, the Oxford University centre who, in a gamble by the national selectors, had only recently been converted to full back; and Wilf Wooller, a strapping three-quarter who had just left Rydal School in North Wales.

Ronnie Boon: In those days the players only came together on the Friday before an international, travelling up from Cardiff to Richmond. On Saturday morning the forwards got together to agree on how they would pack down and stand in the lineouts, while we backs threw the ball around for a bit.

Viv Jenkins: On the day before the game I knew I was ill. That night I went to bed with whisky and lemon and Saturday morning the sheets were soaking – I ran onto the field at Twickenham fighting a dose of flu.

Watcyn Thomas: In my pre-game pep talk in the dressing room, I didn't tell my team, as reported in one English newspaper, 'If you see a dark object on the ground, kick it, it might be the ball; or tread on it, and if it squeals say, "Sorry, old chap," and carry on.' What I did say was for all to prepare to inure themselves to the constant Twickenham roar and to regard the game as a hotted-up version of a South Wales club derby game like Llanelli v Swansea. Self-discipline was essential.

Ronnie Boon: Watcyn Thomas was a great captain and in the dressing room he told us to get among them and make them feel uncomfortable. Tackle hard, rattle them around. After he had spoken we felt a sense of freedom and were eager to get out on to the field to play our game. Fifteen minutes before the game was due to start, Walter Rees, secretary of the Welsh Rugby Union and a dominant character in Welsh rugby, came into the dressing room and said: 'Now boys, I want you to remember this: I don't want to see you charging for taxis to Cardiff when you put your expenses in.' Can you believe Walter was worrying about expenses at a time like that?

Watcyn Thomas: England should have scored twice in the opening twenty minutes when Don Burland broke through, but we managed to hold them out. England had wasted chances but the Bogey was still alive – and they went ahead when they scored a controversial try. Lu Booth went racing for the line and passed inside to Walter Elliot, who flung himself over the line when tackled, but the ball had been jerked out of his hands before he could touch it down. The referee awarded the try – maybe he was unsighted.

Ronnie Boon: Shortly after the second half began, Gerrard, the England centre, had to leave the field with an eye injury and Reg Bolton was taken out of their pack. Harry Bowcott, our stand-off half and a magnificent punter of the ball, kept the ball in front of our forwards, who really had their tails up now.

Viv Jenkins: The earth is full of lonely places, but the loneliest of all is the patch of turf occupied by a full back playing in his first international. In a match of many memories, two stand out. One a purely personal one, of horror, when the schoolboy Wooller and myself, both novices, left a high punt to one another in the opening minutes, but somehow managed to scramble out of the mess; the other is of Ronnie Boon dropping a goal when every orthodox canon demanded that he should run for the corner flag. It needed a Boon to get away with it.

Ronnie Boon: An English player fly-kicked off the line. The ball came back to me and I drop-kicked it with my left foot and over the bar it went. It was so straightforward.

It gave us the lead, as a dropped goal was worth four points in those days. The strange thing, though, was that I dropped the ball not on its point but on its side. Wilf Wooller, who was outside me, said I should have passed as he could have scored between the posts and that try and conversion would have given us five points instead of four. 'And have you drop the pass,' I teased him.

Our forwards continued playing a tight, destroying game and carried play back into the English half. A scrum formed, Harry Bowcott feinted to the open-side, Maurice Turnbull served Claud Davey who came blind-side and he made ground brilliantly. I took Claud's pass and the full back could not stop me touching down. It was a piece of cake.

Watcyn Thomas: There was considerable controversy after the score for Viv Jenkins's conversion kick sailed at least a yard outside the posts. The Welsh touch judge raised his flag to indicate a goal, but the English touch judge signalled that the kick had failed, and the referee did not blow his whistle.

Viv Jenkins: The Welsh touch judge was my old friend Willie Llewellyn from

Bridgend. He'd seen me kick countless such goals. It must have been a knee-jerk reaction for him to raise his flag.

Watcyn Thomas: We celebrated, of course, and I remember one of our reserves noting next morning that I was up surprisingly early, when in fact I had just returned to our hotel at 6.45 a.m.

Viv Jenkins: My temperature after the match was 102 and I was confined to my bed. It was the only time in my life that I missed a post-match dinner.

Viv Jenkins returned from injury to make the trip to Murrayfield a month later when several other judicious alterations to the XV resulted in a welcome change of fortunes. Jenkins then created something of a stir in the Irish match at Swansea by scoring a try from the full back position – the first by a Welsh player in a Test match. He was to make his mark again the next season as the match-winner against Scotland at Cardiff with an out-of-the-blue dropped goal. Jenkins and his former Llandovery College schoolmates Cliff Jones and flanker Arthur Rees, together with Idwal Rees, Geoffrey Rees-Jones and Wilf Wooller in the three-quarter line, and solid scrummagers Tom Rees, Trevor Williams and Jim Lang up front, were emerging as a significant leadership group in a Welsh side which was growing in confidence.

Wilf Wooller: I played for North Wales Schools against Cliff Jones, and it was obvious then that he was an exceptional talent. He was a brilliant outside half with a magnificent side-step. I've seen him side-step so quickly that two men moving in to tackle him have collided. He was one of the cleverest, fastest runners I ever saw on a rugby field.

Cliff Jones: No one gets to the top without dedication – I learnt that secret young. For instance, I could side-step off my right foot but not my left, so I went out jinking between a line of stakes, going off my left leg till it came without thinking in matches. The great skill in side-stepping is to accelerate out of it. I practised this at school at Llandovery and at Cambridge University till the balls of my feet were raw and badly cut. There is no substitute for practice. Each day I went out to work at the basic skills, particularly to improve my speed off the mark and my ability to handle the ball in all weathers.

Albert Fear: I was one of the lightest wing-forwards to play for Wales – only eleven stone for my 1934 debut against Scotland at Murrayfield. Following that win, Cliff Jones wrote a kind message on my post-match menu about protecting him: 'How can I thank you enough for looking after me – you are a veritable wizard and have my heartiest congratulations.'

'Don't tell them back home we were beaten because of schoolboys.' That was the remark attributed to New Zealand captain Jack Manchester after his men were beaten 11–3 by Swansea in a history-making game early in the 1935–36 All Blacks tour of Britain and Ireland.

Swansea's win, the first by any club against New Zealand, was the springboard for Wales's most successful season between the wars and made the selection of Haydn Tanner a foregone conclusion. The wiry scrum half was thus awarded his first Welsh cap at the tender age of eighteen and would monopolise the position in the national side until he retired fourteen years later.

The All Blacks, rocked by the unexpected Swansea defeat, had gone on to win twenty tour games on the trot before the day of the Test match in Cardiff. And into the Welsh team came Tanner.

Haydn Tanner: The team was announced on the radio on the previous Saturday night, and, of course, most of the team were established internationals – and legendary figures to me, a schoolboy. The following week passed far too quickly. I had never played with Cliff Jones, so we had two sessions during the week – each lasting approximately an hour-and-a-half. At that time, they were the most exacting training sessions I had ever experienced. I was expected to throw passes from all sorts of positions. One thing that impressed me was Cliff Jones's speed off the mark and the need to redirect the pass for when he was at top speed.

Wilf Wooller: Waiting for a big game is always a nerve-racking experience. You wait, tensed up, for the start. It creeps nearer. You change, make funny comments, laugh nervously, and suddenly you're trotting onto the lush green turf with 60,000 people roaring their welcome. You stand for a brief moment opposite the rival team while the national anthems are played. You look at them, sizing them up: they look big. You tell yourself that they're human, beatable.

Haydn Tanner: The dressing room was electric. To say I was nervous is a masterly understatement. I had to force myself to hide my feelings.

Arthur Rees: When Cyril Gadney turned up at the packed stadium to referee, he was told: 'No ticket, no entry.' When Gadney replied that he was the referee, he was told: 'We've had twelve of them already.'

Wilf Wooller: The weather was perfect. Cold and crisp from the severe overnight frost. The Arms Park was packed to capacity, and the singing rose on the still air in glorious choral harmony. It was both an inspiration to the chosen Welsh XV and a war challenge to the All Blacks. I was selected to play on the wing. A typical oddity of the selectors because, with rare exceptions, I had played all my life in the centre.

Indeed, the first touch on my side found me wondering who was supposed to be throwing in the ball until someone called my name.

Arthur Rees: Before the game I spoke to our forwards about the genius, the strength and skills of our fantastic backs. They could beat the world, I said, so it was to be our privilege and opportunity of unleashing them on the All Blacks through two-handed balls from the lineout, quick heels from the loose and sound, solid scrummaging. No rough stuff unless they start it, I added. We want to play rugby: I'll tell you 'when' if they start it, and then *everybody* in.

Wilf Wooller: Haydn Tanner, not yet nineteen, was playing like a veteran at the base of the scrum and holding Joey Sadler, the All Blacks' scrum half, with some ease. Claud Davey was tackling as though he intended to go right through the opposition and come out on the other side. The crowd were bubbling with excitement although little did they know what fireworks were to explode in the second half.

Arthur Rees: The All Blacks were quicker to settle down than we were, but behind the scrum our players were superb, composed and brilliant. Claud Davey got Charles Oliver with one of his special tackles, Vivian Jenkins tackled George Hart into touch near the corner flag, and already Cliff Jones had twinkle-toed his way right up to the New Zealand line, beating men on a sixpence and disappearing like light, with Wilfred Wooller in support, as always. Only desperate cover stopped a great try.

Wilf Wooller: Almost immediately after the start of the second half, Cliff Jones went away, short-kicked perfectly, and Claud Davey gathered to score under the posts. Jenkins converted, and the crowd went mad. Then I broke clear, kicked ahead and then over-ran the ball on the goal line. But Rees-Jones dashed up in support to touch down and Jenkins again converted. The All Blacks were rattled badly, but Gilbert steadied them with a drop goal, and twenty-five minutes later Hart snapped up a great opportunist try, Gilbert converted and the Arms Park gave a sickening lurch as New Zealand took the lead 12–10.

Arthur Rees: We were taking over up front, and Claud Davey knew that behind we had it all set up for fast, open rugby. We scored ten points in as many minutes in the second half. Haydn Tanner was sending Cliff Jones away on the burst, and Cliff was finding Wooller, whose long, raking strides were eating up space like a robot. I was soon brought to earth when our hooker, Donald Tarr, was carried off with a fractured vertebra, so there we were 10–12 down with ten minutes to play, without a hooker.

Don Tarr: I think it was my own fault. I'd heeled the ball and was looking through my legs as Tanner swept it away. Then the scrum collapsed and my neck went. I never lost consciousness. I said: 'Don't touch me. I've broken my neck.' Gadney would not allow anyone to pick me up.

Wilf Wooller: With the mist coming down and Don Tarr carried off with a broken neck, we somehow rallied: along came the quick heel, the Tanner pass, the Jones burst, and I was through.

Arthur Rees: Wooller was running faster than I had ever seen him run before. The cover was getting to him, but he drew them all, then chipped a little beauty over their full back. We were all in full cry. Wooller missed the bounce and hurtled into the straw, but the happy hunter, Rees-Jones, again swept up the ball and scored. Now it was Wales up 13–12. The game was over, and the heavens opened with caps, bowlers, flags and cushions flying everywhere. We had won a splendid, rip-roaring, sporting game, never to be forgotten. Wales erupted that night, coal output leapt for months, the world was young again.

Viv Jenkins: England went on to beat New Zealand after us. Prince Obolensky was their star. A fortnight after England beat the All Blacks we played them at Swansea and I was selected and naturally wanted to see what these tries of Obolensky's were like. So I went to a news-flick place in The Strand and paid a shilling, sat down and the two tries came – blip, blip like that, quickly, in three minutes. I thought I must see these again. I stayed in another hour through all these awful cartoons to see it again. I stayed there for four hours to see this thing four times before I went. He only had one chance all game at Swansea and I remember putting him down in the straw under the stand.

Wilf Wooller: We met England on 18 January and the result was a pointless draw. It was a typical, hard-fought, England–Wales defensive duel of the thirties. No quarter asked, none given. We still went on to win the Championship.

Cliff Jones: I retired in 1938. I just felt incapable of producing my best form week in, week out. And there were tremendous pressures on me; wing-forwards just stood out of the general play and were often with me long before the ball.

Claud Davey: As far as I am concerned Cliff Jones retired too early.

Wilf Wooller: He'd suffered several broken bones.

Cliff Jones: I broke my leg playing in America in 1934, and then broke my collar-bone in a club game for Cardiff against Swansea in 1937. But I didn't retire in

1938 because of injuries. Really it was to sit my law finals, and the truth is that I was ready to come back in 1939 – I was only twenty-four then – but war came, and that was that. By the time I returned from the war I had had it.

Wilf Wooller: Cliff had many of the characteristics of the prima donna – he only played when he felt he was himself in top form (I would have capped him in spite of this); he inevitably came out of the tunnel on to the field long after the team, and the crowd erupted to greet him – he was one of the all-time greats.

Haydn Tanner: Willie Davies was the better team man, but Cliff Jones was the more brilliant individual. Wilf Wooller was a bloody awful rugby player, but he was a match-winner and you always had to pick him. Idwal Rees, on the other hand, was a marvellous footballer, but you could not compare him with Wilf as a match-winner.

The 1939–40 rugby season in Wales should have been the most intense international campaign for twelve years. France, separated rather than divorced from the Five Nations since 1931 because they were suspected of paying some of their players, had finally been invited to rejoin the International Championship, and a full-scale tour of Europe by the Wallabies was arranged. However, the season turned out to be the shortest on record. After just one first-class match in Wales, between Cardiff and Bridgend played on Saturday 2 September, 1939, Britain declared war on Germany the next day, and for the second time in twenty-five years the WRU suspended organised rugby.

The significant social lesson grasped during the First World War had been the important role sport played in maintaining civilian morale in times of gloom and hardship. By the end of September 1939, an informal season was announced and many fixtures took place between service units, students and even the clubs. Cardiff, in particular, made huge efforts to continue playing, actively recruiting from reserved occupations, including mining, and servicemen stationed nearby. The policy paid off. Emerging talents of the calibre of Bleddyn Williams, Jack Matthews, Maldwyn James, Frank Trott and Billy Cleaver were introduced to senior rugby.

Mercifully fewer were killed in action between 1939 and 1945 than in the First World War, but the three Welsh internationals who were casualties included two who had made their sole appearances among the thirteen new caps at Cardiff in 1934: Cecil Davies and John Evans. The third former Welsh cap who fell in the war was Maurice Turnbull, who had played scrum half in the first Welsh victory at Twickenham in 1933.

Wilf Wooller became Welsh sport's best-known prisoner-of-war. Wooller was commissioned into the Royal Artillery before going out to Java early in 1942. There was no news of his whereabouts for several months and he was officially posted as missing until reports reached Wales that he was being held by the Japanese. When he returned home nearly four years later he was a mere shadow of the strapping three-quarter who owed his rugby fame to those prodigious deeds against the 1935 All Blacks. He never played rugby seriously again.

ROLL OF HONOUR 1939–1945

DAVIES, Cecil Rhys. Killed in action during operations with the Royal Air Force over Brittany, France, on 24 December, 1941.

EVANS, John Raymond. Killed in action serving with the Parachute Regiment near Tunis in North Africa, on 8 March, 1943.

TURNBULL, Maurice Joseph Lawson. Killed in action with the Welsh Guards near Montchamp, Normandy, France, on 5 August, 1944.

THREE

GWILLIAM RAN THE SHOW

Welsh club rugby was quickly back in harness when peace returned. The austerity of ration-book Britain allied to the release from the grave challenges of war brought crowds hungry for entertainment flocking to Saturday-afternoon sport up and down the land. In Wales, rugby enjoyed a post-war boom with Cardiff, Newport, Swansea and Llanelli box-office draws. At the bomb-damaged Arms Park, attendances for Cardiff matches against their main rivals often exceeded 40,000, and when Cardiff played Newport in February 1951, there were officially 48,500 present, a peak for a club match which stood until the professional era more than forty-five years later. Valley clubs flourished, too. Newbridge had built a strong pack around players in reserved occupations during the war and Maesteg were steadily improving. The future looked rosy when Haydn Tanner, a recent Cardiff recruit from Swansea, led Wales against England in Cardiff in January 1947 in the first official Test for eight years in the United Kingdom.

Bleddyn Williams: It was an all-ticket match and because the North Stand seating hadn't yet been repaired after bomb damage, only 43,000 spectators saw the game. Wales were out and away favourites, and I felt a surge of pride as the Welsh national anthem swelled from the thousands of throats and thundered into the still air.

I pulled a thigh muscle in the very first minute as I sprinted to gather a rolling ball. Haydn Tanner saw my look of distress, and quietly understood its meaning. It must have been a big blow to the skipper to know his fly half was now at least a yard slower than expected. However, we hid the fact from the English back row, and I made no attempts to break. It was really galling to see gaps that I could have sped through. Of course, I should have requested Tanner swap me with Billy Cleaver. If I had changed, then Cleaver may well have sliced through and brought Wales victory instead of defeat in that first match of the Championship.

Billy Cleaver: On the morning of my first selection for Wales I was called from the coalface to the mine boss's office. He said: 'Hello, Cleaver. I hear you've been picked for Wales this weekend.' 'Yes,' I replied. 'Congratulations,' he said. 'Take Saturday morning off.' Thanking him, I said that I would, to which he responded: 'Good, good, come in on Sunday instead.'

For the first seventy-odd years of the twentieth century, matches in the International Championship conformed to a fixed pattern. Wales always opened their campaigns against England in mid-January, then played Scotland on the first Saturday of February, and the Irish and French matches were staged in March. Glyn Davies was called up at fly half for Wales's 22–8 win at Murrayfield, with Bleddyn Williams now partnering Billy Cleaver in the centre. Wales also blooded two popular Cardiff forwards who were to play significant roles in the years ahead – Cliff Davies coming in to the front row and Bill Tamplin, a goal-kicking lineout expert entering the second row. The Welsh back division finally realised its potential and the three-quarters scored five tries with Glyn Davies, Bleddyn Williams and Cleaver whipping the small band of Welsh supporters in the crowd into a frenzy by finding countless openings in a porous Scottish defence.

The 1947 Irish match had to be postponed because of a frozen ground so Wales's third opponents that season were the French in Paris where Wales won thanks to a Tamplin penalty goal. But events preceding the game threw the Byzantine political workings of the WRU into sharp focus when George Parsons, the young Newport second row, was withdrawn from the team while on his way to Paris. He had boarded a carriage at Newport station where he was seen engaging in a brief but earnest conversation with Captain Walter Rees, the octogenarian who had been in the thick of the union as its secretary for more than fifty years. Moments later Parsons was back on the platform. It had been rumoured that he had signed for a rugby league club and it was known that he had resigned his position as a policeman. On the strength of the rumour and the circumstantial evidence of his leaving the Monmouthshire force he was summarily dismissed from the Welsh XV, never again played for Wales and eventually threw in his lot with St Helens rugby league club in 1948.

Into the vacancy stepped Newport's Bob Evans for the first of his ten Welsh caps. He positively bristled with energy in Paris and sealed a flying start to his Welsh career a week later when he and his back row colleague Gwyn Evans hounded the life out of the Irish half backs in the re-arranged match at Swansea. Evans scored the only try of the match from a Tanner break and another Tamplin penalty projected Wales to a 6–0 win that secured a share of the Five Nations title with England, who astonishingly had been hammered 22–0 by Ireland in Dublin.

Bleddyn Williams: A marvellous tale is of WG Jones, a great prop and cousin of the incomparable Cliff Davies. WG arrived at Cardiff station to wave goodbye to the Welsh team off to play Scotland at Murrayfield in 1947. Chatting idly to the team before departure, non-international Jones was handed a train ticket by the then WRU secretary, Captain Walter Rees, who must have assumed from WG's cauliflower ears that he was one of the travelling party. The short of it was that he had a wonderful weekend at the expense of the WRU, completely unnoticed by the powers that be, and treasured it as the escapade of a lifetime.

Bob Evans: We had some pretty useful players. Ken Jones was a great athlete and an outstanding defensive wing three-quarter; Haydn Tanner an outstanding scrum half whom I place second only to the great Gareth Edwards, but only because the latter's highlights were repeatedly screened during the television age; and Rees Stephens, a strong forward who knew how to use his elbows and cope with the opponents of his day. He was a dedicated and very fit player.

Handel Greville: My selection for the 1947 Wallabies match was a surprise, because I had not taken part, or even been nominated as a reserve, in any of the trials. I read of my selection on the news placards at Cardiff station on my way to the pre-match run-out. I couldn't believe my eyes. I was flabbergasted at the thought of playing for my country in place of the injured Haydn Tanner. I don't remember much about the training session. I was longing to get home to my family to see their reaction.

No one outside Llanelli had heard of the name Greville. I went for a haircut on the Friday morning and I remember the barber saying as he was cutting my hair, how lucky Greville was to get his cap and how hopeless Wales's chances were without the famous Haydn Tanner.

On the day of the match I travelled up by train from Llanelli and could hear the name Greville mentioned frequently. Everyone was bemoaning the fact that Tanner was not playing. This made me all the more determined to do well. In the dressing room I could hear *Cwm Rhondda*. It sent shivers down my spine and made me tingle with excitement. I always had butterflies before a match, but never like this one – and worse was to come as we stood in the middle of the field listening to the national anthem being sung. I could feel everyone's eyes looking for the chap who was substituting for Haydn Tanner.

I was eager to get the feel of the ball and to get my first pass to my outside half, Glyn Davies. I didn't have to wait very long because we had a scrum straight from the kick-off. I put the ball in – it came out on our side and was I glad to see Glyn taking my pass in his stride and getting the line moving. From that moment the crowd were all rooting for me. When I was chaired off the field I thought what a difference one-and-a-half hours had made. They were still talking of Greville, but now a little kinder.

Clem Thomas: I well remember my first game for Wales in 1949 against France in Paris when my captain, Haydn Tanner, did not speak more than a couple of words to me throughout the weekend. His team talk was of such brevity that I was totally unaware of any tactics to be employed. The result was that we played like a scratch team and lost.

Haydn Tanner: The committee travelled first-class and we, the players, travelled third. At the Paris hotel in 1949, we waited while they and their wives sorted out their rooms, and I went berserk. They also asked us to present a bill and receipts for our expenses, which were about three shillings [15p] a man. I was so angry that I told them of my contempt for them and I believe that I was the first captain to put the players' needs on a decent footing.

Clem Thomas: Such was Tanner's stature in the game at that time, that he was the only person I knew who could get away with it.

Bleddyn Williams: The Wooden Spoon for Wales was the humiliation of the 1948–49 season. It was Tanner's last season and his dearest ambition was to lead a Welsh Triple Crown team. He never did, and I have never forgotten the criticism showered on him for his captaincy of the Welsh team at Murrayfield in 1949. Tanner's shoulders were broad, and he took all the criticism with the same indefatigable outlook with which he bore the brunt of the opponents' offensive on the field. He never flinched in the interests of saving his team under pressure and shouldered criticism with the same stoic outlook.

Welsh rugby enjoyed a golden era between 1950 and 1952, winning two Grand Slams and supplying more than half the tourists for the first British & Irish Lions tour of the post-war era.

The new captain in charge against England at Twickenham in 1950 was John Gwilliam who had served as a lieutenant with the Royal Tank Regiment in the after-waves of the 1944 Normandy landings that set in train the liberation of Western Europe. After demobilisation, he returned to Cambridge to complete his education, won Blues in 1947 and 1948, and became a history teacher. Austere and aloof almost to the point of being remote from his colleagues, he nevertheless commanded the respect of all who came into professional or playing contact with him. The strength of his personality and the magnificent team spirit he engendered were about to pay handsome dividends for Welsh rugby.

Rex Willis, the new scrum half, continued where Haydn Tanner had left off to provide a smooth link between pack and back line, and with eighteen-year-old Llanelli full back Lewis Jones among the six new caps at Twickenham, Wales possessed the initiative to spark success and Jones's genius was encouraged to flourish.

Bleddyn Williams: 'Where will Wales find a scrum half?' was the cry when Tanner departed. Cardiff, too, were worried. They never expected to fill the maestro's boots with a player of the same calibre. Many people claim Rex Willis to be every bit as good as his illustrious predecessor. I played behind both, and found the difference almost imperceptible. Both were brilliant; both received glowing praise in victory; both were subjected to criticism behind a beaten pack. To me, they are synonymous.

Lewis Jones: On a beautifully mild January afternoon in 1950, I followed John Gwilliam and the rest of my teammates out into the babble of noise and excitement that surrounded the verdant green turf of Twickenham to win my first cap for Wales. I savour the thrill of pride that tingled through my whole being as Welsh trainer, Ray Lewis, handed me the scarlet jersey with the three feathers gleaming silvery against the sombre background of the dressing room. I felt that sinking feeling in the pit of the stomach as I stood for the playing of the national anthem. I recall too John Gwilliam – he must have been a psychologist as well as a great captain – handing me the bright yellow ball, with the instruction, 'Far downfield as you can, Lewis.' I took him at his word, kicked deep into the England twenty-five, and the battle was on.

John Gwilliam: At half-time we were losing 3–0 and we were beginning to wonder if there was some magic attached to the English team on their home ground.

Lewis Jones: Murray Hofmeyr [England's full back] failed to make touch in our half, and as I retrieved the ball and shaped to make the angle for my own kick back, I noticed that the England follow-up was slow and disjointed. I moved infield, dummied left, switched right, and raced through a gap right up to the English twenty-five, where I found supporting forwards at my elbow. Chunky Cliff Davies was one of them and he took the final pass and scored, amid a din that seemed likely to lift the roof off the Twickenham stands. I missed the conversion, but early in the second half was able to bang over a penalty and convert a try. I'll never forget the thrill of being chaired off the field along with skipper John Gwilliam.

John Gwilliam: The enthusiasm and ability of our young team were the principal causes of success in this game, but the experience of Jack Matthews was an important factor. At Swansea, in January, 1951, Jack made a straight burst through the centre to score under the posts. The Welsh touch judge stood behind the posts for the conversion and heard one English player consoling another by saying, 'Of course you can't stop him, he's made of iron.'

Lewis Jones: Ireland were now the last obstacle between us and an objective that had eluded Welsh XVs for thirty-nine years – the Triple Crown. John Gwilliam implemented his own ideas of psychological warfare by throwing our dressing-room door wide open so that the Irish team could hear our singing.

Malcolm Thomas: At Ravenhill, the tension was tremendous. Ireland had been Triple Crown champions for the previous two years and were determined not to surrender the Crown lightly. With the final whistle near, Billy Cleaver robbed Jack Kyle, fed Matthews who found Lewis Jones and his pass cleared the way for me to race to the corner.

Billy Cleaver: He was over, but so was the flag. There were a few seconds of agonised waiting. The referee indicated the line for the kick. We were ahead. The next three minutes were the longest any fifteen players ever played. But it was over and the Triple Crown, that mythical prize, was back in Wales.

Celebrations were muted when, the next day, an aircraft carrying Welsh fans back from Ireland crashed near Cardiff with the loss of eighty lives. There was a minute's silence and buglers sounded the Last Post in memory of the air disaster before the French match kicked off at Cardiff a fortnight later.

John Gwilliam: It only remained for us to play France at Cardiff, and here, in beautiful sunshine, Wales celebrated with a carefree win.

Malcolm Thomas: We romped home to a Grand Slam with a 21–0 victory.

Wales opened the 1951 Five Nations by overwhelming England 23–5. It was as powerful and polished a display at Swansea as any seen since the war. Surely nothing could stop Wales from achieving back-to-back Grand Slams?

But the story of Welsh rugby is punctuated by results where seemingly invincible XVs have been inexplicably beaten. Arguably the most famous Welsh setback came out of the blue at Murrayfield in February 1951 when John Gwilliam's Grand Slammers were thumped by the staggering margin of nineteen points without reply. It was a result that stunned the rugby world. A side that had only three weeks earlier beaten England by eighteen points – a huge margin considering the scoring values and laws of the time – had its ambitions to retain the Championship title completely decimated. The attendance was reported as 80,000 – a then record for an international rugby match – and 20,000 of those were Welsh spectators expecting victory.

Glyn Davies: John Gwilliam devoted more thought to the game than any other captain. He also had the ability to needle well-seasoned internationals into giving of their best. That side at Murrayfield in 1951 disintegrated more than any other I have known. Gwilliam was quite unable to rally us.

Lewis Jones: To blame Gwilliam's captaincy in Scotland was unfair because that afternoon the Scottish forwards would have devoured any opposition. For his sin, John was relieved of the captaincy.

Bleddyn Williams: The truth of the Murrayfield Disaster was that the forwards failed. Here was a test for John Gwilliam, and he proved unequal to the demand. Other players, too, were found wanting, and the Welsh illusion of supreme confidence in their ability to conquer, was rudely shattered by the flailing Scotsmen.

Having beaten England 23–5, Wales scoffed at any talk of 'don't underrate the Scots'. We scoffed and we paid the price.

Cliff Morgan: It takes defeat and disappointment to effect change. Disaster in Scotland in February in 1951 brought new ideas and a relatively new-look Welsh team to meet Ireland at Cardiff. My mother was listening to the wireless with her head down near the kitchen copper boiler when the side was finalised. When she heard my name read out she jumped up so excitedly that she hit her head and knocked herself unconscious.

It was Jack Kyle's twenty-first cap for Ireland. It was my first. Ireland had already beaten England and Scotland. I slept little for the five nights before the game. The Welsh selectors couldn't make up their minds about five of the positions until the Monday evening before the big day. Des O'Brien, my friend and colleague in the Cardiff team [and Ireland's number eight], sent me a telegram, 'Congratulations, Cliff bach – is your life insured?'

Still, I had the greatest scrum half of them all, Rex Willis, to care for me and Jack Matthews and Bleddyn Williams were outside to take the attention away from me. I would survive because of them. Kyle scored a beautiful try – big Ben Edwards hit an enormous penalty. A draw satisfied neither side. But I did learn that day that the odd gap was there for a man of courage who would go hard. I sensed the possibility of bringing the blistering Olympic speed of Ken Jones into action.

Ben Edwards: What's it like to line up in the red shirt of Wales? It's all very unreal until the morning of the match, when your stomach suddenly feels weak. In the dressing room you're having a rub down and the trainer cracks a joke. But nothing registers. You are in a daze, you feel a little sick, the shirt is a bit tight.

At last, action. The call for photographs and, as the door opens, the singing of *Cwm Rhondda* by 50,000 Welshmen sends a shiver down your spine. The referee calls the captains together. Then, to a tremendous roar you follow your skipper onto the field. The double-decker stand sends an echo onto the field. You are choking, crying, shivering and sweating. A magnificent moment that will live with you forever.

The tributes over, the crowd roars, the whistle blows and the battle is on. Nothing matters then, only victory.

Cliff Morgan: Wales were again in search of the Triple Crown in 1952 and took as fine a team as any outside half would wish to play in to Twickenham. John Gwilliam had the pack going tremendously well – Rex Willis was playing superbly, and Alun and Malcom Thomas, Lewis and Ken Jones made a fine three-quarter line in front of Gerwyn Williams.

What happened is now history. England scored early on – twice – then came the try! Rex Willis aimed to pass – paused long enough to get his pass behind the back of Don White who thundered towards me. The Willis pass was short and accurate and the gap was made. After forty yards with Alun and Malcolm Thomas blocked, Ken Jones appeared on the right. With only full back Bill Hook to beat, and he was committed to running diagonally for me, Ken called for the reverse pass.

No one could catch the Olympic sprinter over the final fifty yards. I sat on the halfway line and watched. The score came because the move was different, as was Ken's second try, made by the genius of Lewis Jones. It was a notable victory.

The one thing that spoiled the day for me was the WRU's treatment of Jack Matthews. Bleddyn had been forced to cry off, and Jack was called up. Assuming that he was going to play, he travelled up to London overnight on the sleeper and reported to our hotel in Richmond. It was only when we got to Twickenham that he found out he wasn't playing. The selectors had decided to play Alun Thomas in the centre instead of him – they didn't even give him a ticket to watch the match. It was an Englishman, Surgeon-Captain Ginger Osborne, who had been manager of the 1950 Lions, who came to the rescue. He had a spare ticket and they sat together.

I remember Jack coming into the dressing room and asking the selectors angrily, 'Why the hell did you send for me, when you've got a man here already?' He was furious, and because he was a fairly tough character, and as a doctor was used to being treated with a bit of respect, he really told them some home truths. Selectors were a law unto themselves in those days and extremely inconsiderate. They didn't feel they had to explain or apologise. And I suppose we went along with it. We were afraid of speaking out of turn.

The Twickenham game had a terrific effect on our confidence for the rest of the season. John Gwilliam remained our captain. He had strict views on this role and, because his manner was so schoolmasterly, you listened to whatever he said. At that time the Welsh side was an extraordinary combination of labourers, policemen, students and teachers, but he pulled them together as a team.

Ken Jones: John Gwilliam never stopped bullying, cajoling, pleading and praising until our pack was so fired up that it would have taken sledgehammers to subdue them.

Billy Williams: Gwilliam ran the show.

Cliff Morgan: The 1952 side got the reputation of being unorthodox, different and exciting. The match in Dublin has very happy memories for me, even though, as I discovered later, at a certain point during the play I had broken my leg. I didn't pay much attention to it on the field, but back in the dressing room I was in agony. I was lying in the bath when I was wanted at the top of the stand to be interviewed for the BBC by Eamonn Andrews. 'Listen, I can't walk properly. I honestly don't feel like it.'

'Get someone to carry him up,' demanded his producer. So that's what they did, and Eamonn asked me about Jack Kyle and Ken Jones's try in the corner.

I said to Eamonn: 'My father lost his teeth, and he wasn't even playing.' It was true; I'd been talking to him outside the dressing room. I'd given him my one complimentary ticket, and it was an awful seat in the corner of the stand next to Roy John's mother. At least it was an awful seat until Ken Jones scored his try in the corner just below them. They saw it perfectly, Dad jumped up and shouted and spat his top set of teeth fifteen rows in front of him. He never did get them back.

Then followed the most extraordinary night. I struggled into my dinner suit, and after the official meal, I was carried on Lewis Jones's back to the dances. Lewis plonked me on a seat with a beer. When I got home my mother said something that struck me as very acute: 'You're no longer ours. You belong to everyone now.' And it was true. You couldn't lead the same sort of life ever again. Everybody, on the bus and in the street, felt entitled to a few moments of your attention.

Lewis Jones: The stage was now set for a grand Championship finale with the French. What the large crowd at Swansea witnessed was a thoroughly inept and disjointed exhibition – one of my bad days when I missed tackles, passes and even goal kicks.

John Gwilliam: France were always a bit difficult to play against. Their back row came around the edge of scrums to kick the ball. If that wasn't within reach they kicked your shins, or even your ribs. They might even bite you. Basquet once put his teeth into me and bit a chunk of flesh from around my ribs.

Lewis Jones: We won in the end, but only on the strength of a drop goal by Alun Thomas, and two penalty goals belatedly kicked by myself. So ended my international career for Wales in rugby union. I had enjoyed every minute of it.

Terry Davies: Being in the Royal Marines, I found myself on one of the highest points on Dartmoor for a spot of grenade training after the team to face England in the 1953 Five Nations had been finalised. In between the explosions we heard the sound of a jeep making its way up from the valley below. When it arrived, a sergeant jumped out and asked, 'Have you got a Private Davies here? The Commanding Officer wants to see him immediately.' I thought I must have done something wrong.

When we arrived at the barracks I was marched to the CO's office. The CO stood up behind his desk and reached his hand out to shake mine. 'Congratulations Davies, you've been selected to play for Wales.' It was a bit surreal trying to comprehend my call-up while on the base.

I made the long journey home from Plymouth on the Thursday, arriving quietly in Bynea where I enjoyed a little celebration with my family. On the Friday I caught the train to Cardiff to meet up with the team. I got up early the next morning and my mother had been to the market to get me some cockles and laverbread to go with my bacon and egg.

The dressing room was quiet, nobody had much to say, everyone was preoccupied with their own thoughts and rituals. Then came the magic moment when the jersey was handed to me by the trainer. I couldn't take my eyes off it.

I don't remember much about the game because it really did fly by so quickly. I kicked a penalty in the first half but the English ran out 8–3 winners.

Cliff Morgan: Rex Willis and I played for Cardiff at Bath that day. Afterwards we got the train back to Cardiff, and at about nine o'clock met three of the Big Five, the Welsh selectors. 'Where were you two today? We voted for you to play, you know.' Which must have been the first time that three selectors had ever been out-voted by the other two. The incident told me something about the small-mindedness of the selectors. They were already making their excuses; they didn't want to admit they were wrong – as they often were.

John Gwilliam: On my last appearance at Swansea, against Ireland in 1953, I was forced to travel from Worcester on the Saturday morning. I had started on my way on the Friday afternoon but owing to the excitement of the previous night, when our first son was born, I travelled some way without my rugby boots and had to turn back to collect them. I eventually crawled into Swansea station after 2.00 p.m. – with kick-off at 3.00 p.m. A policeman on point duty put things right by stopping the traffic and insisting that the next car took me to the ground.

Terry Davies: The final game of the Championship was away to France. We took the train to Dover and then a boat across the Channel and then on to Paris. It was a wild day and everybody was seasick but none more so than Clem Thomas, who would be sick on a pedalo. I'd never seen anybody be so sick in all my life, but at least it stopped him talking for a while.

One of the biggest characters in our team was policeman Dai Davies. He was the roughest character I'd ever seen. We changed next to each other. I was ready within a few minutes but Dai had to go through a pre-match ritual. First he put a bandana on, then a handful of Vaseline which he smeared all over his forehead, cheeks and knees, then it was the horse liniment. It was an amazing sight altogether.

Cliff Morgan: The French match is shadowy. I played four times for Wales at Stade Colombes, and all that comes back out of the mists of 1953 is what a dreadful place it was to play. You came out of the dressing rooms, which always looked tatty, and up through a tunnel behind the posts. Around the pitch was a running track, which meant the crowd was a long way away from you.

Terry Davies: It was a fast and open game and we won 6–3. I thoroughly enjoyed my first season of international rugby and it was exhilarating playing alongside my heroes: John Gwilliam, Bleddyn Williams, Ken Jones and Billy Williams. We had a good crowd of boys.

The Fourth All Blacks came to Cardiff Arms Park on 19 December, 1953, and the question on everyone's lips was whether Wales had discovered a team capable of beating them for a third time.

Cardiff scrum half Sid Judd scored a first-half try but New Zealand held an 8–5 lead at half-time and the All Blacks were looking comfortably in control as the game entered its final quarter. To add to Wales's woes, Gareth Griffiths had to leave the field with a dislocated shoulder. Griffiths, however, shrugged off medical advice and returned to herald a magnificent Welsh revival. Nine minutes from time Gwyn Rowlands equalised with a penalty from in front of the posts and as the match headed for a draw, Griffiths took the game to the New Zealanders deep in their own half. The ball reached Clem Thomas slightly isolated near the touchline. There had been doubts about whether he would play as he had been involved in a car accident travelling to Cardiff on the eve of the match. But with a stroke of genius the Swansea open-side put in a high-risk, high-reward cross kick to his right. There, Ken Jones, the Newport Express, steamed up to latch on to the bounce of the century and score to the right of the posts. Rowlands converted to make the final score 13–8.

Bleddyn Williams: I can never hope to recapture the excitement of beating New Zealand in 1953 in words. The thunder of the crowd drummed in our ears.

Cliff Morgan: There are only two kinds of bounces, lucky and unlucky, and this one couldn't have been kinder. Ken Jones, steaming up, plucked the ball out of the air and scored under the posts to win the match for us. What makes that story more extraordinary is that Ivor Jones, a great back row forward for Wales in his day, who was working the touchline that afternoon, claimed to have had a hand in that try. I can see Ivor now: blazer, grey trousers tucked into his socks, flag in hand. Ivor always said afterwards, 'I told Clem to cross kick.'

Bryn Meredith: I started off at West Monmouthshire Grammar School as a second-row forward and then as prop. I got my Welsh Secondary Schools cap as a prop. I played for the Royal Navy as a prop and when I left the Navy I went to Rodney Parade and thought if I was going to get a Welsh cap I should play at prop as I would get two chances instead of one. So I decided to ask Newport to consider me as a prop, which they did. I played prop for Newport against the All Blacks and a week later Wales picked me as hooker. I'd have probably still been a prop if I'd not got my cap at that time.

I remember vividly the pride I felt when I was given my first Welsh jersey, I felt ten feet tall and six feet broad, but five minutes after the start of my first game against Ireland in 1954, I was hoping that I was less conspicuous. In the first three scrums I had given away three penalties. I remember thinking in my already exhausted state, 'This is my first and probably my last cap.' However, after these early transgressions everything slipped into gear and went right for me from then on. The first cap is the one you're after. The second is just as important if only to prove that the first wasn't a mistake.

The stand-out performances by Welsh players of the mid-fifties were achieved not in the red shirts of the Principality but in the red shirts of the British and Irish Lions on the high veldt of South Africa in 1955. Front rowers Billy Williams, Bryn Meredith and Courtenay Meredith; Rhys Williams, Russell Robins and Clem Thomas. It was a team of talented backs ignited by Cliff Morgan, the Welsh fly half showing that he was the finest player of his generation.

Morgan was, therefore, the obvious choice to captain Wales when the 1956 Five Nations resumed in January at Twickenham. The six returning members of the Lions pack were his trusty lieutenants, and fresh pace and initiative were injected by the three new caps behind the scrum: Harry Morgan and Lynn Davies in the three-quarter line, and Onllwyn Brace as Morgan's new partner at scrum half.

Cliff Morgan: Captains didn't have any great influence in my day because the selectors kept switching the job around; I know I played under nine of them. I used to give a dressing room talk before the match. There was no brilliant tactical thinking involved; it was all fire and brimstone. We won the Championship outright that year despite losing to Ireland in Dublin.

I was dropped as captain in 1957. I don't know quite why. Perhaps the selectors didn't either, for over the next two seasons, which brought my international career to a close, we were captained first by Malcolm Thomas, then Rees Stephens and finally Clem Thomas. Although we had great continuity in team selection, we had no continuity in captaincy. If I had to choose one game from my last two years in the Welsh side, Stade Colombes in March 1957 would be it. It was no accident that three of our tries came from the pack and two of these from front row forwards: Ray Prosser and Bryn Meredith, the backbone of our team. Rhys Williams was a colossus.

In 1958 France discovered a new leader, Lucien Mias, to motivate a team that found its mojo in an earth-shattering 19–0 defeat of the Wallabies. Now, an unchanged XV enjoyed its finest hour to send Wales's Championship hopes plunging to the depths with a maiden Cardiff victory that brought the curtain down on Cliff Morgan's career. It was not the way Cliff would have wanted to depart from a scene he had graced with distinction during a twenty-nine-cap career which was a new appearance record for the iconic Welsh fly half position. Many, anticipating the huge void his retirement would leave, hoped that he might have second thoughts. He was only twenty-seven.

Cliff Morgan: Some of the press stories on why I had retired were that I was worried I was losing my pace, or that I was jaded after playing too much rugby. The explanation was much simpler. I couldn't afford to go on playing big time rugby. If I had continued, I'd have been in the running for another, bigger tour at the end of the next season: the Lions to New Zealand. I couldn't contemplate another six months off work.

Haydn Morgan: I got my first cap in 1958, against England, and played in a jersey without a Welsh badge, as did all the team on that day. As the only newcomer in the Welsh side, I can claim to be the first player in Welsh rugby history to get a cap before an official Welsh jersey!

I trained twice a week, cross-country running with my boxer dog and in my parachutist's kit, including old army boots, through the bogs and up the slopes of the mountain above Trinant. When you were on top of the mountain you sometimes wondered if it was all worthwhile. And then every time you turned out for Wales you realised it was.

Carwyn James: Our 16–6 defeat by France at the end of the season was a bad day for Wales but a great day for rugby football.

Dewi Bebb: I will always remember my debut against England at Cardiff in 1959. Beforehand I was worried about marking the great Peter Jackson whose reputation as a Lion and try-getter had travelled to Cardiff long before the team arrived. It was a dreadful day and the Arms Park was covered in mud. I was nervous donning my jersey, but proud of the emblem of the Prince of Wales's feathers, and felt much better when the crowd burst forth to sing *Hen Wlad Fy Nhadau*. I threw in at a lineout fifteen yards from the English line. It was said that the ball 'was tapped back to me' for my run inside Peter Jackson for the try. In fact, Rhys Williams admitted he'd tried to catch it, but that it bounced off his hand towards me. My biggest disappointment was that, although my mother and brothers saw me score the try, my late father, who died four years earlier, missed what would have been for him a big thrill.

Terry Davies: Having been a star in New Zealand with the 1959 Lions I was selected by Wales, more on reputation than merit, for the first game, at Twickenham against England in 1960. We lost by 14–6. The game marked the arrival of the English outside half Richard Sharp, who ran rings around our open-side flanker, Haydn Morgan, who had had such a good tour in New Zealand. I wasn't on form either, and never really got into the game. Rhys Williams, who was captain, was the same. The fallout saw all the Lions dropped for the next fixture and that prompted Rhys to retire from the game entirely. I was a spectator for the rest of the season, which really hurt.

Alun Pask: It was not until March 1961, after more than two years as a Welsh reserve, that I got my first cap – against France in Paris. I'd appeared in thirteen Welsh Trials and been a reserve thirteen times – I had almost given up hope. When the team was announced I was sitting in a cinema in Blackwood with my fiancée Marilyn. My mother heard the side on the radio and was so excited she came round to the cinema to tell us.

I was back in the reserves when I went to Twickenham in 1962. I had usually been very careful how much I ate before a match, but this time I was getting down to a good meal, thinking I was certain to sit in the stand. Then Haydn Morgan came up and said, 'Watch it, I think you're in.' And at 1.30 p.m., on the coach to the ground, David Jones of Blaina, a selector, told me, 'You're playing – David Nash has a cold.' I played in borrowed boots. I had always looked after mine carefully but this time I'd forgotten them and had to borrow a pair from John Leleu. My father, sitting in the stand, didn't know until half-time I was playing. We drew 0–0 but I was never dropped after that.

Keith Rowlands: On St David's Day 1962 I discussed with friends my failure to break into the international team. Three weeks later I'd been capped for Wales and picked for the Lions.

I had been called into the game to form a new second row with David Nash after the Ireland match had been postponed due to the smallpox epidemic here. Wales were languishing near the bottom of the table, while France were at the top and unbeaten in nearly a dozen Five Nations games.

As the game went on, we were leading through a Kelvin Coslett penalty goal to nil, forwards could be heard muttering, almost as if to keep themselves going as well as their teammates, 'Come on boys, we can beat this lot,' and, 'We've got them, we've got them!' Alun Pask's unforgettable last-minute tackle on Henri Rancoule ensured that France were beaten and Wales were once more a force in international rugby. Of the pack that destroyed the mighty French that day six were immediately selected to tour with the Lions and Glyn Davidge was to join us later.

Between 1959 and 1962 there had been five different fly halves, five different scrum halves and five different captains in the seventeen XVs fielded by Wales. This was a churn-rate on a par with the dreadful days of the 1920s. In January 1963, five years since Cliff Morgan's send-off, they finally installed a settled pair of half backs in David Watkins, the former Wales Youth fly half, and Clive Rowlands, a teacher from Cwmtwrch. Rowlands, moreover, captained the side with an iron fist throughout their partnership.

Watkins had a glowing reputation as a mesmeric runner cast from the same mould as Cliff Morgan. Early in his career he was often criticised for being too individualistic, but cleverly nursed by his captain he grew in confidence as the Welsh number ten and became the kingpin of the back division. Rowlands was a tactical genius with the mind of a chess-master.

The pair were among six new caps blooded against England in 1963. Two of the freshmen were Denzil Williams and Brian Thomas, who would shore up the Welsh tight five with passion, strength and a wealth of scrummaging and mauling skills for the rest of the decade. Then there was Norman Gale, whose only previous cap had been as a late replacement for Bryn Meredith in Dublin in 1960. The Trostre steelworks fitter proved a worthy successor to the Newport rake and quickly established a reputation as a powerful and technically brilliant hooker.

Clive Rowlands: Because of the awful weather we trained indoors at Rodney Parade before the England game. Dai and I had to use a rolled-up tracksuit top as a ball because we'd been told that using a proper rugby ball was too dangerous in case we broke the windows.

David Watkins: As if anxiety about making my Test debut wasn't enough, the other big fear was that the game might not happen at all because of the weather. Dai Hayward had offered me a lift from Blaina on the Saturday morning but he was delayed by the snow and ice on the roads, so in a panic I begged a lift to the Angel Hotel with a car-load of supporters. Dai made it, but he was a bit white about the gills when he came in.

Clive Rowlands: We drove down in my A35 van to Cardiff, arriving at the team hotel by mid-morning. Lunch was served at midday and it was only then that the prospect of what lay ahead really began to hit home – I was about to lead out the national team in a Test match.

It was so bloody cold. The pipes in the showers were frozen solid and the WRU, not famous for their generosity in those days, bought woollen vests, gloves and shorts to help keep us warm. Kevin Kelleher, the referee, came in and told us that because of the frozen conditions we wouldn't be going out onto the pitch until after the anthems had been sung. I experienced such a bitter sense of disappointment mixed with rage – the Welsh people out there singing the national anthem in unison while we were still trapped in the changing room.

David Watkins: The walk from the changing room was the longest of my life: we had to troop all the way from the north stand and behind the west terrace before running onto the field from underneath the south stand. Most of the benefit gained by delaying our exit from cosy, warm changing rooms was blown away on the bitter wind that sliced into us from the River Taff. Those eighty minutes were the fastest of my life.

Dai Hayward: The game was an anti-climax. As soon as the straw was cleared the ground began to freeze and it appeared that England had picked better skaters than we had. It started snowing again after the game and I must have been the last driver that night to run the gauntlet of icy roads, massive snowdrifts and a howling blizzard. I eventually got back to Newbridge but, after failing to negotiate Pant Hill, I had to abandon my vehicle. I didn't see it again for five days.

England won 13–6, but Rowlands plotted to restore winning ways at Murrayfield, a Test of 111 lineouts. In years to come Rowlands would be hailed as a national treasure, but in February 1963 he was public enemy number one for his playing approach. Still, with Wales winning in Scotland for the first time for a decade, Rowlands felt the end justified the means.

Wales played Ireland at the Arms Park and the Welsh public, disillusioned by poor recent results, disappointed by the monotonous kicking tactics of their captain and deterred by disagreeable weather, had gone AWOL. The official attendance was barely 45,000, the lowest for a Cardiff international for many years.

Clive Rowlands: In Scotland I changed the tactics after ten minutes and it brought us success. People may have criticised all the kicking, but as captain of Wales I wanted to win at all costs *within the laws*. I believed in playing fairly but hard. You could kick directly to touch from anywhere on the field, so that's what I did.

David Watkins: Beforehand he had told us, 'One sure way to beat them is to kick, kick, kick. That's what I'm going to do.' And he did, one of them a fine dropped goal. For the record, the ball went out of play 111 times, I touched it on only five occasions: once to collect the Scottish kick-off, twice to pick up their grubber kicks, and twice to catch passes from my scrum half. But we were happy enough afterwards, and Clive was unrepentant, because winning was all that mattered.

Alun Pask: When I first started playing I believed that it was better to lose a match 25–24 as long as it was a cracking good game. But as a Test player I wanted to win at all costs. I backed Clive for his methods at Murrayfield. Tactically it was a perfect game.

FOUR

WHEN BARRY MET GARETH

A wind of change now blew through 1960s British society. The Beatles had a profound effect on popular culture, Labour leader Harold Wilson came to power to head the first socialist government since the immediate post-war era, and an increasing and socially diverse student population became more politically active. England won football's World Cup and by the end of the sixties televised sport was broadcast in colour. Rugby was not immune to the spirit of the age and the IRB, that most conservative of bodies, did more to modernise the game in the second half of the decade than at any time in the previous seventy years – and Wales were to be at the forefront of exploiting those changes.

The common denominator in Welsh rugby's revival was Clive Rowlands. As tactician, captain and later coach he was the man who called the shots. Even his best friends, though, would be among the first to admit that he was more than a trifle lucky to retain the Welsh captaincy when Wales made a bid for Five Nations laurels in 1964. His record as player and captain was not impressive: played five, lost four; but for sheer drive and force of personality he had no equal. Despite his shortcomings as a scrum half, Rowlands exercised a strong tactical grip and he had clearly imbued an inexperienced XV with a mighty spirit the season before, engendering intense loyalty among his players. Continuity in selection would now play a major part in restoring Wales as a world force.

Clive Rowlands: England at Twickenham were our first opponents in 1964. John Ranson and David Perry scored for England, but Dewi Bebb got two back for us. We had a match-winning penalty shortly before the end, but Grahame Hodgson was unsuccessful. Had I known that Grahame would miss, I would have taken the kick myself.

Grahame Hodgson: That kick was mid-way between the posts and the touchline, and two yards inside the twenty-five, but every year it seems to get closer and closer.

David Watkins: It's a pity that Clive's remembered as a kicking scrum half because he could – and did – play the running game when circumstances warranted it.

I remember Clive having a quiet word to me in Dublin before the start of our match against Ireland. He said, 'If you feel good this afternoon, pull out all the tricks.' I obliged and so did our pack. We won 15–6. John Dawes got a try on his debut, and so did Stuart Watkins, while my own came after a break in which I got around the Irish back row and Mike Gibson. This was a turning point for me: I felt at last that I had established myself. I have to hand some of the credit for that to Clive's style of captaincy.

Welsh rugby's stock was rising, but the young John Dawes had not been impressed by what he saw on his Welsh debut. The son of a coalminer, Dawes had graduated with a chemistry degree from Aberystwyth University before taking a postgraduate diploma in PE at Loughborough College, which was fast becoming recognised as the country's foremost institution for rugby coaching theory. Dawes, a committed rugby analyst, was surprised by the limited tactical direction in the national set-up and made his own contribution to change when he was elected captain of London Welsh a season later, setting up the 'Old Deer Park staff college' which became an invaluable source of Welsh rugby talent.

John Dawes: It's very hard to remember detail from my debut in Dublin in 1964. I think I handled the ball twice. As for tactics, if we learned anything of them from Clive beforehand it could be summarised in one word: 'Kick'.

My Welsh cap arrived by post the following week at my London address in a tattered old box that had once held a pair of shoes. That was all, with no word of thanks and congratulations from the selectors and not even a compliment slip to say where it had come from. I didn't feel I belonged in the Welsh team. We were not adventurous, our style was limited and the traditional excitement of the national game was absent. Don't get me wrong, representing my country was magical, but the way we played in the mid-sixties was so mundane.

Clive Rowlands: When France came to Cardiff that year, Keith Bradshaw supplied the three first-half points for Wales, converted another penalty in the second half but experienced scant reward generally, missing six of eight attempts, but making amends with a wonderful touchline conversion of Stuart Watkins's try, which ensured the first ever drawn encounter between the two countries. After two wins and two draws, we shared the Championship with Scotland.

The summer of 1964 was notable for Wales's first international tour – to South Africa. They lost 24–3 to the Springboks – the worst Welsh performance for nearly sixty years, a loss that set the Principality talking about the state of its national game.

Dai Hayward: The events of the sixties which probably had the most far-reaching effect on the future of Welsh rugby took place in the cold of Cardiff in 1963 and in the heat and humidity of Durban in 1964. In the space of six months Wales had lost to New Zealand for the first time at Cardiff and been crushed by the Springboks. The administrators had to look at how the game was run in Wales because we were being left far behind by the big sides from the southern hemisphere.

David Watkins: Wales got a mauling at the hands of South Africa that summer but out of adversity came triumph and we returned to win a Triple Crown in 1965. It is significant that during the campaign we used a mere seventeen players. In turn Bill Morris and Keith Rowlands replaced Brian Thomas who figured in our victory over England in January, the first time for my generation.

Brian Price: I remember getting anonymous letters back in 1965, when we won the Triple Crown. Bob Rowell, who was playing for England in the second row, was trodden on at one time, and another boy playing in the centre was supposed to have been bitten. I was accused of both these attacks and all these letters started pouring in criticising me. I never had anything to do with either incident.

Clive Rowlands: We went up to Murrayfield next and the lead changed hands on four occasions before Norman Gale thundered over for the match-winning try. Norman told everyone he ran twenty-five yards for that try. It was twenty-five inches.

We were one game away from winning the Triple Crown on home soil for the first time for fifty-four years against Ireland, who also had the chance to capture the mythical Triple Crown.

Dewi Bebb: The atmosphere was electric. We were penalised at the very first lineout, but Tom Kiernan missed with the penalty, as he did with several other attempts that afternoon. I appreciate how lucky we were that he had an off day.

David Watkins: Dewi Bebb and I got tries, but the major contribution to our win came from Terry Price. He kicked a penalty and a conversion besides dropping a monster goal from forty-five yards out.

Dewi Bebb: So to Stade Colombes to meet France, and, as so often happens at Paris, the French were at their brilliant best. Before we knew what had happened they were nineteen points up. This poses a question. How good a side were the 1965 Triple Crown team? Certainly we had limitations. We were primarily a wet weather team and on the dry ground at Stade Colombes the quick-running French exposed our weaknesses to an extent we never thought possible.

David Watkins: It was an absolute nightmare. After forty minutes our hopes of a Grand Slam had gone, and at half-time we looked wide-eyed at each other as if to say, 'How the hell is it going to end?' Thankfully we ran in a try and knocked over two goals for a respectable 22–13 scoreline at the final whistle.

Clive Rowlands: That was the proverbial 'one game too far'.

Brian Price: I remember playing against Scotland in 1966 in Cardiff when I tore my hamstring, and I had to go off the field. I had two injections pumped into the leg, was strapped up and when the doc was asked, 'Is he all right to go back on?' he said: 'Oh he can't do any more damage to it, it's completely ruptured, so he may as well go back on.' So I went on the field with one leg.

Alun Pask: Throughout my rugby career I had my happy moments and also my unhappy moments. The unfortunate thing about my disappointments is that most could have been avoided, because practically every big game I played, where we were defeated, we didn't deserve to lose. In Dublin, in 1966, we would have taken the Triple Crown had we won, and it was a bloody disappointment because we should have pressed home our territorial advantage and could have scored fifteen points in the first twenty minutes.

David Watkins: The years 1965 and 1966 were the high-water mark as far as my international career with Wales was concerned. In both seasons we topped the Championship, though in each season we fluffed the Grand Slam.

Near the end of the 1966 Ireland match, I tried to start a counter-attack from broken play near our try line, considering it better to go down honourably than to throw in the towel before the final whistle. I ended up getting us into more trouble, but at least we'd had a go. Afterwards, however, a selector said bluntly, 'You had no business trying that. Next time we'll pick a man who knows how to find touch.'

Stuart Watkins: Wales had to win to clinch the Championship. We were still trailing late in the second half. Then I managed to make an interception and ran a heck of a long way to score the try which eventually clinched the match. The whole thing happened so quickly it's difficult to remember all the details. There was no thought of an interception in my mind but when Jean Gachassin threw his pass, everything changed. The next thing I recall is having the ball in my hands with an awful lot of field in front of me. I went as far as I could, straight up to full back Claude Lacaze. Haydn Morgan was inside me, but he appeared to be covered by Guy Boniface, so I moved back outside Lacaze. I felt sure someone on the French side would come at me again, but no one did and I just kept running until I reached the line. That put us 9–8 in front, but France were far from beaten and in the last minute they were awarded a penalty out on the touchline. Lacaze took the kick but the wind caught the ball and swung it away outside the posts at the last second.

David Watkins: I remember being in a Cardiff hotel one night in early autumn 1966 with a group of students from Carmarthen. They pointed to this fresh-faced guy in their group and said, 'That's Barry John. He'll have your place in the Welsh team before long.' I laughed it off but sure enough he appeared in the trial as stand-off in a Possibles XV which nobbled the Probables under my captaincy. I thought he was a good player, but didn't have any real fear that he could replace me.

The body-blow came a few days later. I rang a friendly journalist to learn what side the selectors had chosen to play the Wallabies. 'You're not in,' he said. 'They've picked Barry John.'

My first reaction was disbelief. I hung up, feeling sick. I sent off a good-luck telegram to him and then sat with the conundrum that all dropped players face: did I want Wales and Barry to do well against Australia? Did I want Wales to win, with Barry playing poorly? Did I want Wales to lose, with Barry carrying the can for defeat? I never quite worked out the answers to those questions.

Barry John: I'll never forget the moment I reached the turf for the first time in the Welsh jersey. It was everything – and more – that I had dreamed of.

Gerald Davies: I was in a Canton pub with friends to see the announcement of the Welsh team to play the Wallabies. When Bleddyn Williams, who was chairing the programme, gave the news that I had been chosen to play for Wales, my friends felt that the best thing to do with the beer was to shower me with it.

Alun Pask: We should have beaten Australia. We fielded an excellent side but it was a team that missed chances when they mattered. We went on to lose to Ireland in Cardiff, in horrible conditions and we were smashed by the critics. The pressure on an international rugby player is enormous, and I played an average of sixty-five games a season. During ten years I don't think I played a really bad game in an important match. I wasn't enjoying my rugby in 1967, and so I decided to retire. I always wanted to retire while I was at the top.

Barry John: I was picked to play in the trial for the international against Scotland and the scrum half in the Probables was Gareth Edwards. I didn't know him personally, although I knew of his growing reputation. He phoned me and suggested that we get together for a practice session before the trial.

Gareth Edwards: So down I went to the West, and after a bit of a search I found where he was staying. I climbed the stairs, knocked on the door and went in to find him lying on his bed, looking rough. He'd been out at a party all night and had forgotten I was coming. Worse than that, he couldn't remember where he'd put his boots. But he got up anyway and we went out – me in my pristine Cardiff College tracksuit and polished boots, him in a skanky old t-shirt, gym shorts and trainers. The pitch was a soggy bog and I thought the whole thing was going to be a disaster, but I was determined that we'd get used to playing with each other. 'I reckon I can get the ball out to you from pretty much any place,' I remember saying to him. 'How do you want the ball?'

Barry John: It was a bleak Sunday morning with the rain pelting down. I could see that we would get on well and there seemed to be little point in hanging about in the rain, so I said, 'Look, Gareth, you throw 'em – I'll catch 'em. Let's leave it at that and go home.'

Gareth Edwards: That was the BJ plan. But you know what, it worked. He had this incredible easiness of the mind. He backed his own talent and he gave off a constant calm superiority. He was powerful and quick – much more powerful than he looked – and had the ability to accelerate from a standing start, which is so hard to defend against. His kicking was superb and he always had time on the ball. That's something I'll always remember. He always had time. To my shame I have to admit that I was actually quite a poor passer of the ball back then – but as he said that filthy day in Carmarthen, I just had to throw the ball in his direction and he would do the rest. He really was that good.

Barry John: Next Saturday we met at Swansea for the Welsh trial but I badly gashed my knee in the game and had to be helped from the field. During the days that followed my knee was stiff and I was in pain. Three days before the international I had to get around with the aid of a walking stick. I should have withdrawn from the team.

Billy Hullin was chosen as scrum half instead of Gareth – and I didn't play well at Murrayfield. Back in Wales, I didn't feel like going out much, I didn't want to be seen; I felt a failure.

David Watkins: My final season for Wales was a shambles. Barry played his first two matches for Wales in losing sides and I was then restored to the team to play Ireland – and later France and the big victory over England, as captain – when the selectors started Gareth Edwards off on his huge trail of caps.

Gareth Edwards: The England game was my first match in Cardiff and we won 34–21. With virtually the last move, I broke down the blind-side of a scrum deep in England's half before passing to Dewi Bebb, who scored his final try in the same corner I saw him score his first. Having watched him begin his international career, I had helped set up a fitting end to it.

Gerald Davies: There was a lack of cohesion in the team. We all identified with Wales and recognised a common purpose to win the game, and each captain did his best to mould a team spirit, but there was no common strategy as such, no real direction or attempt to establish a style of play. We were, in effect, a collection of individuals who went for a run-out the Friday afternoon before a game in an attempt to mould a team effort. We lacked a conductor – a coach.

FIVE

TWO AND THREE THOUSAND
ON ABERAVON BEACH

As the seventies dawned, a studious and mild-mannered man by the name of Ray Williams was in his third year as the WRU's national coaching organiser, overseeing a coaching revolution that would transform Welsh rugby. His meticulously researched coaching manual was distributed throughout the land to schools, colleges, and clubs from Wrexham to the Rhondda, from Llandrindod to Llanelli. It provided a template for the way rugby should be played. It is no coincidence that Williams's ideas, which encouraged flowing, attacking rugby, found vivid expression in the now legendary Welsh teams of the seventies.

Clive Rowlands: You must realise that a club coaching session in those days was to run around the field ten times, have a massage, have a pint and go home. Suddenly there was this boom for coaches, even in places like Cwmtwrch. We had a coach in Cwmtwrch – Terry Nicholas – who ended up there for twenty years. He would prepare his sessions meticulously, and the players would arrive in their droves. Instead of having six or seven training, you'd have *twenty*-seven, because he made it *interesting*. Ray Williams was the key to it all. He was a pioneer. He realised that if the coaches down at the bottom were really good, then when they were coming through at the other end, they'd be first class. He cast his net wide.

Gerald Davies: Ray was a tough guy, a firm guy, who had to deal with a lot of opposition within Wales. But he survived it, persisted, and made a monumental difference.

Gareth Edwards: Once the wheel had turned, there was no stopping the revolution. But there was firm opposition from some quarters. Roy Bish was the first coach at Cardiff. As a college lecturer he was well respected and knew what he was talking about. But in those early days, the poor bugger had a tough time of it, from players and all.

Gerald Davies: I was captain at Cardiff, and the players would regularly come up to me and question the purpose of Roy Bish. It was the same attitude up and down the country.

Gareth Edwards: 'Do we need it?' That was the prevailing attitude, particularly among senior players. Somebody from the committee once said to me, 'I've heard you're going to start pre-season training a month before the season starts?' They were furious. 'Shouldn't be allowed,' they said. 'You must be mad.'

Clive Rowlands: It didn't go down well with *all* the players. I remember delivering the team talk before one international at Twickenham and just before the players went out, I overheard the captain say, 'Bollocks to that, you all just do as I tell you.'

JPR Williams: When we went out on the field we used to forget what the coaches had said and do things our own way.

Clive Rowlands: It was difficult for some to accept but that's the way the game was going. New Zealand had always done it. South Africa had always done it, and all the great rugby league teams had always done it. If we hadn't embraced it, we'd have fallen behind. The coaching boom and the corresponding rise in standards persuaded many a player to stay in union because they didn't want to miss out on what proved to be a golden era.

Phil Bennett: Ray believed in training with the ball as opposed to aimless running. He'd have us in grids and would time everything with his stop watch. He'd time us passing the ball down the three-quarter line and say, 'That took four seconds to get to Gerald. I want it there in three.' The obvious way to get it to the winger quicker would be to throw a miss-pass. It sounds simple but these were things we hadn't considered. In his book there was no excuse not to score from a two-on-one overlap. This kind of thinking took us out of our comfort zone. Him and Clive were a dream team. Clive would give you the rabble-rousing, chest-thumping *hwyl*. Ray would give you the dispassionate tactical analysis.

Barry Llewelyn: Ray was so technical. He would analyse individual physiques. I always remember him saying to the second rows, 'When you pack down in the scrum, get your shoulders into "nature's niche",' meaning the fold underneath the buttocks. He'd visualised this as the place where the shoulder would actually fit for the maximum advantage.

Clive Rowlands: He was a very good schoolteacher and a master of communication. He didn't overcomplicate things. Whether you're a child or an international, you pass the bloody same, you kick the bloody same, you score tries in the same way. But he put it all *together*. There was a myth about the seventies; that our hard edge was because our team was stacked with steelworkers and colliers. But I say to you – JPR Williams, doctor; Gerald Davies, schoolteacher; John Bevan, schoolteacher; Barry Llewelyn, schoolteacher; Barry John, schoolteacher; Jeff Young, schoolteacher; John Dawes, schoolteacher; Gareth Edwards, schoolteacher; John Lloyd, schoolteacher;

Mervyn Davies, schoolteacher; John Taylor, schoolteacher. And all PE. So not only were they in good physical condition, they were sharp of mind as well. Gareth was sharp as a button. He knew instinctively when to score tries. Gerald – once he moved to wing and didn't have to worry about people bumping him – used to beat people without bloody thinking about it. Ray encouraged them to use their brains.

Barry Llewelyn: I was teaching at Greenhill school in Tenby one day when Ray's coaching manual arrived in the post. It was the hymn sheet, and everybody had it throughout Wales which meant, for a small country, we could coordinate our rugby philosophy from schools through the clubs, right through to Test level. Inevitably, those manuals were gathered up and found their way across the Severn bridge. The English stole Ray's ideas.

JPR Williams: He understood that no two players were the same, and what might stimulate one might bore another.

Barry John: I'm not so sure about this coaching business to be honest. Clive Rowlands was a wonderful influence on us, in that he backed us one hundred per cent. But I can't remember him *telling* me anything, I can't remember Carwyn James *telling* me anything. I can't remember *anyone* telling me anything. Behind the scrum, they recognised the gifts we had and left us to it. It was like a card player being dealt the perfect hand.

JJ Williams: Nobody ever told me how to play. No one ever said do this or do that. John Dawes, Clive Rowlands . . . if I made mistakes, they'd come down on me a bit, but we were encouraged to express ourselves. We were picked to be side-steppers and swervers and that's what we did. They trusted us. They knew we had skills – 'Just go out and do it, boys.' It was the same on the Lions tours. In '74 when I scored all those tries, I didn't speak to Syd Millar once.

Gareth Edwards: Before the introduction of organised coaching, we used to meet at the Angel Hotel in Cardiff on the Friday before the Test match, where the captain would take the training. The backs would go through a few basic moves, and the forwards would go through a few lineout calls. It was as simple as that. No coach, no input, no nothing. After the coaching revolution began, it was like chalk and cheese. We'd meet in Aberavon the weekend *before* the game, which was previously unheard of.

Phil Bennett: The clubs didn't like those Aberavon weekend sessions because they were being deprived of their international players for the Saturday games. On one occasion Llanelli deliberately rescheduled their match against Maesteg for the Friday night so we wouldn't miss it. We went up there on the Friday in the shit and the mud, with their wing-forward, Leighton Davies, trying his level best to knock my head off. We were knackered turning up to the Afan Lido the following day only to be told there was a professor from Aberystwyth University there. Good god, what for? 'We're going to do fitness tests.' It was a real eye-opener. I'd never done pull-ups before. And some of the forwards, who were among the strongest people I'd met, couldn't do it. They didn't have the right technique. You may have one of the strongest maulers I've ever known – Geoff Wheel – who could pull an entire pack on his own, but ask him to pull himself up on bars, and he couldn't do it. That attention to detail made a magnificent player like Geoff even better, by addressing weaknesses he didn't know he had.

JJ Williams: There were athletes in that squad. Gareth Edwards was English Schools hurdles champion, Mervyn was a basketball player, Graham Price used to throw shot for Wales, JPR was junior Wimbledon champion, Allan Martin was an international discus thrower, so we were all very athletic. Combine that with the hardness of some of those forwards. Dai Morris, coalminer, Charlie and Bobby, steelworkers, and it's a lovely combination.

Gerald Davies: We were criticised for doing all this. In Scotland the coach was referred to as the 'adviser to the captain'.

Gareth Edwards: They were so bloody stuck in the mud that they wouldn't call the coach the coach. To call him adviser to the captain was utterly bloody ridiculous. They threatened to cancel fixtures against us.

Phil Bennett: We stole a march on the other unions. There were representatives from Australia, New Zealand and South Africa coming over to speak to Ray Williams, to Clive Rowlands, to Carwyn James, to pick their brains.

Gerald Davies: There was a resentment from other unions towards us for taking the game too seriously, without a shadow of a doubt. They were dead against it.

Gareth Edwards: It was little things. We'd have a new jersey for every match. I think the Scotland players were just given one to last a campaign.

JPR Williams: There was a lot of jealousy from the other unions. Not just because we had coaches, but because we had so many good players at the same time.

JJ Williams: Ray Williams used Bridgend as guinea pigs in the late sixties. He started showing us unopposed rugby which was alien to us at the time. If you speak to Ray and his many disciples, they think they were the sole reason for the success of the seventies. I don't totally agree with that. I think they played their part, but it was mainly down to the schooling we had. We all came out of excellent schools with excellent PE masters who taught us good skills, good values, and how to keep fit. It was a freakish coincidence that we all peaked in pretty much the same era, but the background was there. Ray would talk about the three Ss: speed, strength and stamina. Speed, strength and sexiness I liked to call them.

Clive Rowlands: We'd go to Aberavon beach on a Sunday. There'd be two thousand, three thousand people sometimes, just to watch us train. It raised the standards. Gareth Edwards would be too scared to drop the ball because you'd have a thousand kids going, 'God, did you see Gareth dropping the ball then?' We used to love the beach. It was special. Duw, people from Pontypool had never seen the bloody sea.

JJ Williams: Clive used to say, 'Right, forwards, pick a back,' and my heart would sink. Allan Martin would pick me because I was one of the lightest, like a pimple on his back. He'd carry me up one end of the beach, then we'd have to swap. Clive would say, 'Carry him to the pier.' The pier would be this tiny dot in the murky distance and I'd think, 'What the hell am I doing here on a Sunday morning?' We'd have sandwiches and a bowl of soup underneath the swimming pool in the Afan Lido, then back out for an afternoon session, and we'd all be back in work on Monday. Gerry Lewis, our physio had to work like a trojan, having to see to every player's injuries and niggles, notwithstanding the fact that Gareth hogged the physio table for hours on end with his constant hamstring injuries.

JPR Williams: I'm a great believer in the notion that the strength of a team is not in the players playing, but the players who want to get into the side, because they're the ones who keep you on your toes. Those sessions at Aberavon beach were often harder than international matches because you were up against your rivals for the shirt. Everyone was afraid of having a bad game.

Gareth Edwards: It gave us a chance to gel as a squad. Before those days, you'd never met your hooker until the Friday night before the game. You didn't know how he'd want it put in to the scrum. You inevitably had to do that on a Friday afternoon in a two-hour session before playing the next day in front of seventy thousand people in the biggest match of your career. Gerald wouldn't know his centre from Adam unless he'd played with him at club level.

Barry Llewelyn: We'd sleep in the dorms there at the Afan Lido. Gareth used to challenge everyone to do the Sergeant Jump, where you'd jump as high as you can, and mark your height with a piece of chalk on the wall. Delme Thomas had the highest, and Gareth was a close second. Mine was tiny by comparison. We were doing that one night in bare feet, and Gareth came down and landed on a stray ball, turning his ankle. He wasn't 100 per cent fit going into the game, but he daren't tell Clive he'd injured himself larking about in the dorm.

Gareth Edwards: Having a beer on a Saturday night in the Afan Lido made you feel like a team. The club rivalries melted away.

JJ Williams: We were so successful because it felt like a club team. To me I felt more like a member of a club with Wales than with Llanelli. I was closer to the Welsh boys than the Llanelli boys. We were together for nearly ten years, and the bond was strengthened by the fact we went on Lions tours together.

Clive Rowlands: We used to counter-attack. That doesn't happen anymore. If a member of the opposition kicks us the ball, we kick it back to them. In the seventies, if that happened, the first thing Barry John would say was, 'Thank you. Now try to stop us.' I encouraged everyone to have a go.

JJ Williams: Creativity was in our blood. Think back to Dai Watkins, Cliff Morgan. That was inside us; it just needed to be encouraged. We all grew up playing in the back yard. We were never a big nation. My heroes, like Dai Watkins, were the dazzlers of the rugby world. Even the centres back then were little guys, jinkers who'd look for space rather than contact.

Clive Rowlands: My secret was motivation. I didn't have time to go into other psychological battles. I did my homework with my speeches. I'd use little observations from real life. We were in the Berners hotel at Twickenham before an England game once, and this rusty car pulled up. These guys climbed out carrying a television. I asked what on earth they were doing. 'We haven't got tickets, Clive, so we've brought our own television to make sure we see the game!' So I went to the team talk, and I said, 'Boys, have you seen what I've just seen? To think that you've been given the opportunity to play for Wales against England, and there's these boys carrying a bloody television because they haven't got tickets. What are we going to do? We're going to win it for *them*.' They enjoyed things like that, little stories.

Phil Bennett: He'd pile us all into a single room at the hotel on Saturday morning at eleven o'clock to give his team talk. And he'd be crying his eyes out. He'd have a red tie on with the three feathers. A red pullover with the three feathers. He was Welsh to his very core.

JJ Williams: There he'd be, with his fag in one hand, and froth coming out of his mouth. And twenty-five of us jammed in like sardines.

Clive Rowlands: I insisted on good timekeeping. Eleven o'clock didn't mean five-past, it meant eleven. Five-to, if anything. Nobody would dream of being late, because if they were it would mean they wouldn't play. Discipline is discipline.

JJ Williams: Clive was giving a lecture to the squad at one of those early sessions. It was all a bit new to everyone, especially me as I hadn't broken into the squad yet. Arthur Lewis was captain, and he and his Ebbw Vale teammates weren't in the room. About forty-five minutes into the meeting, they all burst in, red-faced. They'd been stuck in a snowdrift and had had to dig themselves out. Clive asked where they'd been. They explained. 'Get on the floor,' says Clive. It was Arthur, Denzil Williams and Glyn Turner I think. Fifty press-ups, fifty sit-ups. And they did it, while muttering their apologies. The discipline was famous. No one was given special treatment, not even the captain.

Clive Rowlands: And when they were all there, I'd shout 'Gareth!' Gareth would jump up, and he'd know what was coming. He'd pick a shoe up or something. 'We're on the last scrum, and we're ahead. But only just, boys. If we lose this one, we could lose the game.' I'd say, 'Ball coming in . . . NOW!' And I'd expect everyone in that room to shout, '*Now!*' at that exact same moment. No delay, no half measures. Not 'nooowww', because if you do that you've lost the ball.

JJ Williams: He still does that at after-dinner speeches.

Phil Bennett: I was a shy boy, and used to cringe at this. Barry would be trying his best not to laugh. We all had to scream 'NOW!' at the top of our lungs. More than twenty of us, squashed into one little room.

Clive Rowlands: If you don't want to do it, piss off, I don't want you. It was like a pistol going off. BANG!

Phil Bennett: That's how he wanted you – on the edge. He was so *Welsh*, it oozed from every pore. He never once said, 'This is how we're going to play the game.' He just gave us the emotional build-up.

JPR Williams: It worked on the forwards. It appealed to their more brutish sensibilities. Most of us backs would get fed up with it, and spend most of the time stifling yawns.

JJ Williams: Clive was one of the best coaches I ever worked under, but I suppose you can only do something so many times before it becomes a bit stale. But when it worked, it bloody worked. John Lloyd was a big eater, loved his food. One time, Clive was shouting, 'What are we going to do to England, boys? Eh? What are we going to do?' And he was getting fired up and emotional, his voice getting louder, and more tremulous. And he singled out Lloydy. 'What are we going to do, Lloydy? Eh? What are you going to do?' And Lloydy bellows at the top of his lungs, 'I'm gonna fuckin' EAT 'EM!' We all fell about laughing. And all the time, Dai Morris would be sat at the back in his own world listening to the horse racing on his transistor radio.

Clive Rowlands: I paid very little attention to the opposition in those days, and that was my biggest problem. I once received a letter from a vicar in Kent, following a rare defeat, and he very politely said, 'Please, Mr Rowlands, can you pay more attention to the next opposition.' And he was right. I always felt that we were better than them in all positions, whomever they may be. The players may have analysed the strengths of their opposite number, but as a coach, I concerned myself solely with Wales. John Dawes, who succeeded me, was more thorough in that respect. John was a thinking man.

The seventies began with a match against the travelling Springboks in Cardiff. It was the final match of a tour that was played out against a backdrop of hostility and ill-feeling.

Gerald Davies: I didn't play in the Test, but the anti-apartheid demonstrations were vociferous in the extreme. At the Swansea game in particular, there were ugly scenes. They sprinkled nails and broken glass on the pitch. Peter Hain was leading the charge.

Gareth Edwards: They were fighting like hell. The police were throwing students over walls. All we knew about it was what we'd seen on TV. Unless you were politically engaged, the ugly reality of life under apartheid passed you by. We were naive in many ways, but it wasn't like today when mobile phones dictate our lives, and news is available at the touch of a button.

Gerald Davies: There wasn't a great deal of sympathy towards the protestors because most people just wanted to watch the rugby. You've got to draw the line somewhere between politics and sport. Anyone can pick up a reason for not playing another country. What about Eastern Europeans? What about South America? There are difficult regimes in all those countries. If you bring politics into it, would sport even exist? Ultimately, it's between you and your conscience to make up your mind.

Phil Bennett: That was only my second game for Wales, after a four-minute cameo in Paris where I hadn't touched the ball. I was picked on the wing – a position I hadn't played since I was eleven. I pointed that out to the selectors, who brushed it aside, saying I was a good enough footballer to cope. Those were the days when wingers threw the ball into the lineout, and I didn't have the faintest idea what I was doing. After a disastrous practice session with Delme Thomas where I tried underarm, overarm and everything in between, the big man looked at me in exasperation and said, 'Phil bach, just lob the bloody thing in, and may the best man win!' The ball never travelled past the inside centre, because the conditions were so bad. Before the game, Jeff Young had told me to close my eyes during the anthem and to think of all the people that meant so much to me. He promised that when I opened my eyes, the Springboks wouldn't look so big. I was fighting back the tears as the anthem reached its crescendo, and with Jeff's words still in my ears, I opened my eyes, and looked across. They looked just as bloody big as they had before. I learned an important lesson about international rugby that day – they did their analysis, they looked at the opposition. I remember getting the ball, and their number eight, Tommy Bedford, was in front of me. I looked up and thought, 'I can do him.' I stepped inside thinking I'd leave him grasping for air, and he cut me in half. They'd clearly studied me, my running style, and my tendency to step off that foot.

Barry John: The one thing I remember about that game was the weather. The steam was rising off the scrums, and it looked warm enough in there. For us backs standing in the open field, and carrying no fat, it was freezing. I was tapping ice from my jersey after the game. There was whisky in the changing rooms post-match. Not to drink, but to rub into us. Nobody could undo the laces on their boots, so Gerry Lewis, our physio, had to cut them off with scissors. The next day the river Taff flooded its banks. They were the worst conditions ever. It should have been called off.

Gareth Edwards: The 1970 Championship began well enough. The year before had been a learning curve – we'd come within a whisker of a Grand Slam, but had been humbled by New Zealand when we went on tour there. The main reason we beat England was thanks to Chico Hopkins, and his masterclass off the bench. He played so well I was genuinely concerned I'd lose my place.

Gerald Davies: Don't tell Chico that.

Gareth Edwards: He tells me all the time.

Clive Rowlands: It's unbelievable to think that Chico Hopkins had only one cap for Wales. He would have had fifty caps had he been any other nationality.

Chico Hopkins: Gareth had good days and he had bad days, but I never ever felt inferior to him. The man in my day who I would say was the difference was Barry John. Overall, Gareth probably had the edge on me because he was a 440 yards man, but he was a different player behind a beaten pack and he never played in many games when the pack was beaten. Some of the Cardiff players told me they preferred it when he wasn't playing because they were better as a team then. But if the pack was on top he could exploit it more than me.

I got on with him all right, as long as he knew he was the top dog. But when I was out in New Zealand in 1969 and putting him under pressure, they couldn't decide who they were going to play at half back and everybody forgets that. I sound a right big-headed bastard here but I played six times in his place at the top level, for the Lions and on the Welsh tour, and we didn't lose a game because we were such a good side. He didn't play in the provincial games in '69 and Clive Rowlands always said to me he should have picked me in the Test matches because Gareth had a niggling hamstring. I won the man of the match against Wellington before the final Test and everyone thought I was bound to play, but Gareth got in again.

I had a knee injury before that England game and had hardly played for months and was about a stone overweight, but I remember turning to Phil Bennett, who was on the bench with me and saying, 'I've got a feeling I'm going on today.' He said, 'That bastard won't come off.' All of a sudden, Gareth is down. We sat in the stand in those days and I went down the stairs like bloody greased lightning. It was like I was in a trance. You were thankful to be part of a great side, but me and Phil were always under pressure because Gareth and Barry were always pushed to the front so much by the Cardiff papers. We were shitting ourselves that if we went on and made the slightest mistake the first thing they would say was that we missed the other guys.

Things just worked out for me on the day and we got the win after a massive comeback. It was the stuff of dreams. But that was my Test career for Wales – twenty minutes off the bench. Gareth was back in for the next match. He and Barry were disastrous against Ireland and they lost us the Triple Crown. Gareth was still there against France and I thought, 'Well, I am never going to get in the side now.' It would have to be a broken leg or something.

But there are no sour grapes because I had a great time. The game has been a godsend for me. I would have been a bastard recluse without it because I was a bit shy. And now people remember me because the name Chico sticks with them. There were better players than me around and people think 'Who?' when you mention them. What more can a player want than to be remembered after all these years?

Gerald Davies: The manner of playing had changed. With JPR coming into the line, we were less inclined to kick, and more inclined to counter-attack. What always used to strike me about JPR was that he was teak-tough, hard as nails, and nobody ever got the better of him, but when you saw him stripped, he looked as if he had puppy fat. There was no muscle definition at all. Yet he could smash people, shoulder Jean-François Gourdon into touch as he famously did in '76, but when you looked at him compared to say John Bevan, or Gareth Edwards, he had no shape. Stripped, he didn't look the part.

Steve Fenwick: If Gourdon had scored then, they'd have won the game. When JPR hit him into the advertising hoardings, everybody just turned round and thought, 'Thank God he was there.' Nobody else could have managed that.

John Taylor: He wasn't exactly rippling with muscles, but he was big, strong and quick, and he loved the physical side of it. He thought that was a core part of rugby. He'd have thrived in the modern game.

Steve Fenwick: He was the only back that the forwards allowed to drink with them. He had special dispensation because he could hold his own with any of them.

Gareth Edwards: He was never injured, was he? And yet he would throw himself recklessly into any physical confrontation. He was hugely competitive – almost to a fault. And that permeated through the entire squad. People feared him. He wasn't as big as you'd think, but he was so competitive in mind, and his mind could overcome anything. No one would get the better of him, nobody would get past him, and he genuinely believed that. After a while, people realised and stopped kicking to him unless they absolutely had to. First and foremost, he was absolutely *sound* in defence. We all knew that so we never feared that he would drop a high ball. If he ever did, God alive, he'd never admit it. Our confidence stemmed from having him at the back.

Barry John: I wouldn't have swapped JPR for anyone. When it came to the real battles, he never flinched. Never dropped a thing. When the ball went over your head, you knew the master was there. It must have been demoralising for the opposition.

Phil Bennett: He was the bravest player I ever took to the field with. Fearless. What guy gets stamped on, has his face stitched up, and runs back out onto the pitch?

JPR Williams: I played on through broken jaws, fractured cheekbones, and people ask me how I could have withstood such pain. But when the adrenaline is pumping, you can do anything.

Barry John: He had a bit of the 'nut factor' about him. They say that about goalkeepers, don't they? That they're a different breed. JPR was a very select breed. I don't know what kind of category he'd be in at Crufts, but it wouldn't be the poodle class.

JPR Williams: You grow up quickly playing club rugby in Wales. Playing against teak-tough teams in the Gwent Valleys in the pouring rain on a wet winter evening toughens you up pretty quickly. There was a lot of play off the ball, so you had to look after yourself. I always felt that the harder you played, the less likely you were to get injured. That's why I always played flat out in charity games, and friendlies – not because I was taking it too seriously, but because I didn't want to get injured. It was also built into me by my father. He encouraged me to embrace the fundamentals of full back play, the most important aspect being getting under the high ball. Waiting for a ball to descend from the sky, knowing there's any number of marauding forwards hurtling towards you, is the definition of bravery on a rugby field. My father used to take me to the beach at Porthcawl, and pump balls up into the swirling, gusting winds. If I caught every one, I'd get an ice cream. If I dropped one, I'd get nothing. I ate a lot of ice cream back then.

Barry John: JPR had an insatiable hunger for the action. If he didn't get involved every ten minutes, he'd be screaming and shouting for the ball. You'd hear him bellowing at Gareth and me, 'Pass me the bloody ball, I'm getting bloody cold back here.'

Gerald Davies: Clive's great strength was his willingness to give us free rein. He never restricted us. Didn't say 'don't do this, don't do that'.

Phil Bennett: After those victories against Scotland and England in 1970, we lost badly out in Ireland. Barry didn't have such a great game, and that evening he was quarrelling with the selectors. For the final game against France, he dropped out with the flu. To this day, I don't think he had the flu. He just wanted to stick two fingers up to the selectors. That was Barry.

Barry John: I don't remember any quarrel, but I don't think I should have played against Ireland anyway. I was living in Cardiff, and the life I was living wasn't sporty. I'd been down with glandular fever and was feeling low. But I have no excuses. Once you've entered the race, you're all fit.

Gareth Edwards: Ireland was a wake-up call. 14–0. We were going for the Triple Crown. It was like a nightmare from which I couldn't wake up. Barry and I had been surfing the crest of a wave. Nobody thought they had a chance of winning, but it was a typical Irish performance full of fire and brimstone. Ken Goodall, their young number eight, just tore into us.

Barry John: He caught one of my kicks, and raced seventy yards to score. My only saving grace was that I was the only other player visible in the picture when he went over for the try. Evidence that I had at least tried to chase him down.

Gareth Edwards: Cardiff's next game was against Penarth on the Wednesday, a game Barry and I would ordinarily have been rested for. But we both said, 'Pick us.' We needed to get the Irish game out of our systems.

Barry John: We were on a hiding to nothing against Penarth. If we did something well, the Cardiff fans would be shouting, 'Why couldn't you have done that against Ireland?', and if we did something badly, the same fans would be shouting, 'No wonder we bloody lost at the weekend!'

Gareth Edwards: We'd felt invincible before then. Despite being opposites off the pitch, we'd become inseparable on it. Barry was so laid back, nothing seemed to bother him. Maybe things did, but he rarely showed it. Our understanding was telepathic. I'd say to him, 'How did you know I was going to go there then?' 'I just knew,' he'd say. It's hard to bloody explain it.

Barry John: Both Gareth and I used Welsh as a first language, and that helped with our communication. Signals are one thing, but being able to speak in our native tongue, confident that no one in the opposing team could understand, was critical. Gareth would hear the urgency in my voice if I'd spotted a gap, and he'd respond accordingly.

Clive Rowlands: Barry John was outstanding. He kicked with both feet. Beautiful passer, lovely runner. But he was very, very skilful *in mind* as well. He was probably one of the most confident guys I've seen on a rugby field. He knew what he was capable of, and he brought the best out of those around him.

Barry John: I was surrounded by so many gifted players. It was my job to let the greyhounds off the leash, to give the likes of Gerald and JPR the time and space in which to work their magic.

Phil Bennett: After the Ireland debacle, John Dawes sidled up alongside me ten minutes before going out against France and said 'Phil, I don't want to touch the ball today.' I was nineteen or twenty thinking, 'What do you mean John?' The conditions were filthy, the Arms Park was a mudbath. He said, 'Have you seen their back division? Have you seen ours?' We had the slowest back division in history, and they had Pierre Villepreux and all these flyers. We had Roy Mathias winning his first cap on the wing. Jim Shanklin on the other wing. Not the fastest. In the middle, Arthur Lewis – crash ball merchant. And Dawes himself. On the field, I kept asking Dawesy, 'Can we have a go here? Can I have a run here?' And he'd say, 'Just stick it down there, Benny.' We won 11–6. John was right. He came from the London Welsh tradition of mercurial running rugby, but he realised that it would have been suicidal to try to play that way against *that* French team.

Phil Bennett's appearance at fly half in the game against France meant he became just the second Welsh player to play in three different positions in one season. The victory in Cardiff went some way to atoning for the hiding at the hands of Ireland, but John Dawes and his side knew they could do better. The 1971 Championship was to prove an era-defining one for Wales, and it began with a 22–6 victory over England. It was particularly sweet because it meant Wales took the lead in the series between the two fierce rivals for the first time since 1912. Thirty-three wins to thirty-two, with eleven games drawn. Not the result England were hoping for in the RFU's centenary year.

Gareth Edwards: The main tactic was to pepper their full back, Peter Rossborough, with high balls. It went against our attacking ethos, but Clive had targeted him as a weak link. 'Gar,' he'd said before the game, 'I want those kicks to go so high that the ball comes down with snow on it.' It worked particularly well off one lineout. I put the ball up there, Arthur Lewis chased – he wasn't the biggest but he was a hard, nuggety player, typical Ebbw Vale – and he got in, disrupted Rossborough, and Gerald sneaked in for the try.

Clive Rowlands: Before the Scotland game, Gareth got himself in a panic because he'd forgotten his gumshield. There were no spares in those days, so I had to commandeer a police bike to take me back to the hotel to find it. We were snaking through the matchday traffic desperate to get the gumshield on time so the show could go on.

Gareth Edwards: The Scotland game was one of the greatest I ever played in. Murrayfield in those days was like a beautiful carpet, compared to Cardiff Arms Park, which was a quagmire. Murrayfield was pristine, like a bowling green.

Gerald Davies: Easily the best surface to play on. Scotland loved to run the ball in those days. It came from their tradition of seven-a-side in the Borders. Melrose, Gala and Hawick all had sevens tournaments at the end of the year. Wales–Scotland games were always adventurous affairs. In that game the score went back and forth. The lead changed hands six times. We thought we'd won it one minute, and then we fell behind. They were a rugged side, but they could all handle the ball well.

Gareth Edwards: They were tenacious. The Borders are like our South Wales Valleys. They produce hard, abrasive players, always battling. A bit of the old clans-and-dagger mentality. We played some great rugby, scored some great tries, and out of nothing – which was so typical – they started getting the rub of the green. A ball got tapped off a lineout and fell directly into the hands of Sandy Carmichael, and he was over the line. They hadn't been anywhere near the line until then. Similarly, John Bevan ran back and tripped over, a bit of inexperience, and Chris

Rea scored from the fumble. It got him on a Lions tour, that. Thankfully, Peter Brown hit the post with the conversion from bang in front. Barry had done the same thing earlier in the game. His excuse was that he'd been concussed. Brown had no such excuse. He hit the post so hard, it rattled back and forth.

JPR Williams: If he'd hit that, it would have been impossible for us to have won the game.

Gareth Edwards: Despite the missed conversion, our heads dropped. We were still four points behind and ready to throw in the towel. Dawesy jogs up and says, 'Boys, don't worry about it, I've just spoken to the ref, and we've got ten minutes left.' We later discovered there was less than four. There were no clocks in those days, and we blinking believed him.

Gerald Davies: That's great leadership, to have the presence of mind to go to the final whistle. He was calm, he was conscientious, and he was a marvellous captain. That was exactly what we needed, and it won us the game. It all came down to a lineout, on Scotland's throw. All they needed to do was win the ball.

Gareth Edwards: Gordon Brown was twitchy because he hadn't lost a lineout all day, and he knew how good Delme was. The ball came in, Delme palmed it, and the rest is history. If they'd won the lineout, they'd have belted it into touch and the whistle would have gone.

Gerald Davies: When the ball came my way, I was desperate to get as close to the posts as possible. But McHarg, fair play, was there to cover, which made John Taylor's conversion attempt that bit trickier.

Gareth Edwards: I'm on the halfway line, while Baz is lining up the conversion and Delme's going, 'Gar, I can't watch it. I can't bloody watch it.' I'm thinking, 'We've come all this way, played so well, and now we're going to lose.' I was thinking, 'This isn't London Welsh against whoever, Baz. This is Murrayfield in the winter with nearly a hundred thousand raging Scots willing you to miss.'

Gerald Davies: Murrayfield looked much wider than other pitches because it was open-ended. It was an optical illusion, but it made the kick look fiendishly difficult from my perspective.

Gareth Edwards: So I say to Delme, 'I'll watch it, then.' John gives it a right old slog. BUMPH! 'Bloody hell, he's kicked it,' I said. Every time I tell Baz that, he gives me a withering look and says, 'Gar, I knew I was going to get it.' And I reply, 'You're the only one who thought you would.'

JPR Williams: I knew he was going to get it. I had total faith in him.

Gerald Davies: Alun Williams came up with another memorable quote in that commentary. 'When people mention 19–18 in the future, they won't think of the end of the First World War, they'll think of John Taylor's winning kick against Scotland.'

JPR Williams: The greatest conversion since St Paul.

John Taylor: Every dog has his day, that was mine, and it was lovely. I always remember thinking, 'You're either going to be a hero or a villain.' I was saying to myself, 'You can do this, rely on your technique, don't try to over-hit it.' I got it right.

Barry John: Later that summer on the Lions tour, at the end of the training session, some of the Scottish boys – Sandy Carmichael and Gordon Brown – were ribbing JT, telling him it was a bloody fluke, saying he'd never be able to do it again. JT casually picked up one of the balls, placed it in the same spot it had been in Murrayfield, and kicked it straight through the middle of the posts.

Clive Rowlands: That game set the benchmark for what was to follow on the Lions tour that year. I wasn't watching when Basil [John Taylor] took that kick, I'd already left to order the champagne. But the players thought I'd disappeared because I had no faith. I was bundled into the bath fully-clothed as a punishment.

Gareth Edwards: Clive loved it, rolling around in there like a big kid, he was.

Wales followed up their nail-biting win over Scotland with a demolition of Ireland that helped banish memories of the previous year's defeat. It secured the Triple Crown, and restored the reputation of Gareth Edwards and Barry John as the northern hemisphere's pre-eminent half back pairing. The two contributed seventeen points between them, as Wales won 23–9, and both were carried from the field by jubilant fans. Edwards slammed the ball down hard over the line for his second try, an act of defiance that released the frustration he'd held inside since the Dublin debacle. Wales now had the small matter of a Grand Slam match against France in Paris to look forward to.

Gerald Davies: That game cracked the fear we always had about playing France in the Paris springtime. It was always warm, and the way they played in those days was so different from now. It always worried us. Up until then it had always been a struggle, and, by and large, a failure.

Gareth Edwards: It gave us the confidence that we could scrap it out in tight circumstances. They had some world class players. Pierre Villepreux – I still drool over the way he used to play – Roger Bourgarel, Jean-Pierre Lux, Jack Cantoni. They were mesmerising when they were on song.

Gerald Davies: Benoit Dauga, Walter Spanghero, Christian Carrère. All of them ball players.

Gareth Edwards: They were brilliant. To win 9–5, that was a hell of a result for me. The best result of all. It was the improvisation, the confidence we had in each other. Knowing what other guys were capable of doing. That's what that squad preparation was giving us. There was a lot to take on board off the field, but not so much as to clutter the brain. In reality, we only had about three moves. Miss-move, Arthur Lewis coming back on the inside – that one was called 'Arthur coming back' – and JPR coming into the line. He was strong and quick for a full back, and he loved coming into the line. He caused panic. JPR set the victory in motion with an early bone-crunching hit on Roger Bourgarel. The next time he had the ball, he saw JPR in his line of sight, panicked and threw it away in fright. JPR plucked it from the air and was away.

Clive Rowlands: And who was there in support but Denzil Williams. He drew two men because he was running like the clappers. He didn't know where he was running to, but three Frenchmen followed him. That gave Gareth the clear run to the line.

JPR Williams: God knows what Denzil was doing.

Clive Rowlands: The other try came when Jeff Young won the ball against the head underneath the posts. Barry feinted and went wide, and *pssht*, he nipped in between the wing and full back.

Gareth Edwards: He waltzed through the defence. Nobody touched him.

Barry John: That try belonged to Jeff Young. They were standing back because they expected to win the ball and clear it. When Jeff won it against the head, all of a sudden the French backs were out of position, and I knew we were going to score.

Gareth Edwards: Stade Colombes was such an intimidating place. Those French teams could put the fear of God in you, but Barry produced the piece of genius that won us the game.

Gerald Davies: For all the talk about his laid back, insouciant air, Barry was hugely competitive. And a lot quicker than people gave him credit for. His mazy running style was deceptive. The one criticism he endured was that he had no appetite for tackling. But that didn't bother him – he didn't consider it to be in his job description. His role was to be on his feet.

Gareth Edwards: 'John Taylor tackles, Dai Morris tackles. I don't tackle.' That was his attitude.

Barry John: Jeff Young won a scrum against the head, about twenty yards out from the French line. Gareth flipped it up and I ran straight at my opposite man, Jean-Louis Bérot, and then swerved outside him so that I was directly between Bérot and Jean-Pierre Lux. I knew that if Lux came in for me I'd be able to pop the ball to John Dawes, and John would go in; and if Lux stayed on his man, then I knew I had the ability to get past Bérot. And at the crucial moment, I saw Lux was fixed where he was, I slipped about six inches wider and just felt the scrape of Bérot's fingers down my back and I knew I was in. It was a great moment.

Clive Rowlands: Everybody said, 'Great try, Barry.' But Barry was quick to defer praise. 'It wasn't my try,' he said. 'That was Jeff Young's try. He's the one that won the ball.' Great team spirit that. I could pick individuals from other eras, but that '71 side was the best *team* I've ever seen. The off-the-cuff tries they scored were incredible. It was obvious something special was brewing.

Barry John: As much as we knew our own strengths, our success was equally about being aware of our weaknesses. If a player doesn't like going right for example, because he's naturally left-sided, don't put him in a situation where he'll be exposed. Don't pass the ball to someone in danger and expect them to kick off their weaker foot. Exploit your opponents' weaknesses, but protect your teammates from their own. And my mind was like an encyclopaedia of rugby knowledge. I knew intimately every players' habits, foibles, and idiosyncrasies. Down to the way they tied their laces.

Gareth Edwards: Winning the Grand Slam in Paris was almost beyond our comprehension. Triple Crowns rang bells with me as a kid growing up, but Grand Slams were things of myth and legend. Wales hadn't won one since 1952, when I was too young to remember. There was no live TV then so it didn't travel down the generations like our victories have.

SIX

LIFE WAS NEVER THE SAME AGAIN

The Welsh contingent had played starring roles on the 1971 Lions tour to New Zealand, where Barry John broke the points record for a tourist in New Zealand with 191, a record that stands to this day. They began the 1972 Five Nations campaign as undisputed champions, but limped to a routine victory over England at Twickenham on day one. Impressive wins followed over Scotland and France, but history would deny Wales a chance to claim back-to-back Grand Slams as the spectre of the IRA loomed over the 1972 Championship. The WRU and SRU both decided to boycott their fixtures in Dublin, fearing that their players might become targets of an increasingly militant IRA. The decision remains contentious to this day, with many Irish players and fans claiming it was unwarranted and cowardly.

Gareth Edwards: We'd had a good win up in Twickenham, and were looking forward to Scotland. They had good players. Frame, Renwick, Biggar, Steele, Telfer, Paterson, Carmichael, McLauchlan, Brown. They were the better side in the first half, scored some good tries and outplayed us. It took us until midway through the second half to assert our dominance. Barry Llewelyn, who was an outstanding young prop, provided the impetus. He peeled off the back of the lineout, which was his party piece, and he really took some stopping.

Barry Llewelyn: I always pushed myself on the field. If there was a chance to run, I didn't walk. The lineout peel was something I'd done since my school days. I'd come off on an angle towards the outside half. If you went too shallow, you had the back row to worry about, but if you got it right, it was you against the outside half, and I'd always back myself in that scenario. The problem with it was once you'd done it once, you'd get marked more tightly.

Gareth Edwards: He drove and drove and drove to the line and was stopped just short. I said, 'Thank you very much, Barry, you've done all the work,' and I picked up and scored. It was such a contrast to the other try I scored that day – the one that has been played and replayed a million times. But I maintain that that was the more important one, because it came at a time when we needed a boost. It lifted the crowd and got them all going again.

Barry John: Barry Llewelyn was a hell of a player. Carwyn James did everything in his power to try to get him on that '71 Lions tour. He didn't tour for personal reasons, but when we toured New Zealand with Wales in '69, he was the only player of ours the All Blacks would have wanted for their own. When he peeled off the back of the lineout, he was like a thoroughbred. He had a wonderful high running action. It was like having an extra loose forward on the pitch. He was the prototype of the modern prop. He'd have thrived in the modern game.

Gareth Edwards: I knew it was important to maintain that momentum, so when they kicked off deep, I thought I'd try a quick move to keep the crowd on their feet. Mervyn Davies gave me the ball from the lineout, and I looked up and saw the Scottish defence was in disarray and I ran from the twenty-two. I looked to pass inside to Dai 'Shadow' Morris, so called because wherever I went, Dai was always one step behind me. For the first time in my life, Dai wasn't there.

Clive Rowlands: The Shadow. That was my name, I gave him that. I couldn't leave Dai out of my team. He played number eight for Neath, but I picked him on the flank. I couldn't leave him out because of his tank. He was everywhere.

Phil Bennett: I loved Dai. A real gent, he was. He never got on a Lions tour. Not because he wasn't good enough, but because he'd get so homesick. We toured Argentina with Wales in 1968 and it took about nine hours for the bus to pick everyone up, get us to the airport, and through security. As we were boarding the plane, Dai turned to me and said, 'Duw, it's been a long trip hasn't it, Phil?' I remember thinking, 'Dai, we haven't left the bloody country yet, mun!' He loved his Rhigos home so much, he'd never change his watch. Wherever we were in the world, be it Argentina or Canada, he'd always have his watch set to Rhigos time.

Gareth Edwards: I've just gone past the twenty-two thinking, 'The Scottish flankers are going to crush me now.' I'd got away from Rodger Arneil, and because Dai wasn't there I thought I'd better keep going. I wasn't thinking of tries, just of getting as far as I could and keeping the momentum going. So I kicked, hoping for distance. I kicked it again, and was praying it wouldn't dribble over the dead ball line. Seconds later I caught up with it, dived on top of it, and there it was. A dramatic score. I'd jack-knifed in going for the ball, and covered myself in red shale. My mother was panicking in the stands, thinking I'd split my head open. Gerald was the first to arrive, and I said to him, 'Ger, the cameras are on us now, give us a kiss.' Something stupid like that.

Gerald Davies: What he actually said was, 'Bugger off now, and let me milk the moment.'

Barry John: It's amazing how misleading a photo can be. That image of Gareth makes it look as though the game was played in dreadful conditions. But it was actually a perfect day. The rest of us left the field with barely a mark on us. I don't think the jerseys even had to go to the laundry.

Gareth Edwards: It never occurred to me that it would go down in folklore as one of the great tries, immortalised in song by Spike Milligan. But I maintain it wasn't as good as the first one that Barry Llewelyn created, because that one was the springboard to victory.

Barry John: When I retired, I was up at the Grogg Shop, and the owner John Hughes told me I could have anything I wanted as a gift. Anything at all. I chose one of the Welsh front row, with Barry Llewelyn, Jeff Young, and Denzil Williams. That's the only bit of rugby memorabilia I own, and that says it all. Those guys were the foundation, the rock on which our success was based.

Clive Rowlands: And then came the cancelled game in Ireland. I felt the criticism was unjustified. It's all very well saying we should have gone in hindsight. I'm not so bloody sure. What if something had happened?

Gerald Davies: I'd had a letter. I wish I'd kept it. It was one of those where they'd taken letters from newspapers and magazines to make up the sentences, like you see in films. The sentiment was pretty clear. You're putting your life in danger if you come over. I was afraid, and I got rid of it. I assumed that everybody had had one, but perhaps it was just me.

Gareth Edwards: We were all called together. One or two of the committee were senior police officers and they considered the threats real. Even today, the Irish hate the fact we didn't go. England went the following year, and were lauded for doing so. John Pullin famously said, 'We might not be any good, but at least we turn up.' That grates on me to be honest, because it's easy to say it would have been okay after the event.

Clive Rowlands: Player welfare was my concern. Jeff Young was in the air force and was a target. The players all had their say and we decided to put on a united front. It wasn't an easy decision. For a bloke like John Lloyd, it could have been a second Grand Slam in a row. That had never been done before. It would have rankled a bit for him as captain. But the Irish were bloody good in those days. There's no guarantee we'd have won. But you couldn't cater for the clown. In the years after that, we stayed in the same hotel, but we'd have a Garda man on each floor.

Gerald Davies: We accepted the decision, but as players we had little choice in the matter. The union had made up its mind on our behalf.

JPR Williams: The decision was taken from us. The WRU, for once, did the right thing, even if it was just for peace of mind. They took the pressure off us.

Gareth Edwards: It was difficult because we'd made great friends with so many of the Irish boys on the '71 Lions tour. Willie John McBride, Mike Gibson, Sean Lynch and all those boys. They thought we should have come, but it was different for them. They'd grown up with it, lived in its shadow, whereas to us, it was terrifying. We were just kids. I was just about to get married, Gerald had got married the year before. Lots of the boys had children. It was a no-brainer.

JPR Williams: I was living in London, and they were threatening times. You'd be afraid to go into a pub in London because of the IRA. You were always looking over your shoulder.

Barry John: I'd won in most places at least once, but I'd never won in Dublin. As fate would have it, this was to be my last chance, as I'd retire at the end of the campaign. So I was denied that. I was watching the news and heard the newsreader mention that I was one of a number of senior players who'd refused to travel. I'd said no such thing, so I rang the station, and went on air before the end of the programme. I said if fourteen players out there fancied a game in Dublin, I'd go with them. A few people wrote in too. It was a great shame. I never lost in Paris, but I never won in Dublin. Maybe my motivations were a bit selfish, but I felt it was another Grand Slam that perhaps went begging.

Gareth Edwards: The Championship was declared incomplete, but we could have had another Grand Slam, as we finished top of the pile with six points despite having played a game less. Had we travelled to Ireland and won we'd have won another Grand Slam, but in the cold light of day, our safety was more important than a rugby match. We were relieved we didn't have to go.

Clive Rowlands: There was a unity among that squad that was strengthened by situations like that. Welsh players of the seventies were the sons of miners and steelworkers. Their fathers had worked in the factories and the mines, and those boys had entered different professions. In the main, they were schoolteachers. They were all so close. We used to laugh all day. They were good friends.

Phil Bennett: I hope we're still the same country. It doesn't matter whether you're a barrister or a steelworker. There was a real cross section in the seventies. Schoolteachers from London, highly educated men. Steelworkers like myself, although I eventually got a posh job as a sales representative. I worked for a beer company, and if Wales won on a Saturday, the sales would rocket up because all the clubs would be putting big orders in.

Gerald Davies: That was part of Welsh rugby's history, it's always been the case of the clerics and the steelworkers. The white-collar worker and the blue-collar worker. It's always been an easy mix in Wales.

Ask any person our age 'what's your background?' and the answer is 'mining'. We benefited from education after the 1944 Act, but before that, if you looked into our backgrounds, any one of us, I'd put any money on it, it was a mining background.

Barry John: We were all war babies and the one thing that bound the nation together was the rugby team. Richard Burton famously said he'd give up everything he'd achieved to have won just one Welsh cap.

Phil Bennett: We got on great, but that's not to say it was peace and harmony all the time. I've seen fights break out on the training field. Big guys slamming into one another. And they could do some damage.

JJ Williams: The Swansea and the Pontypool boys saw it as a real test of their manhood. Blood was often spilt. Geoff Wheel and Mervyn Davies had a good kicking from some of the Pontypool boys in some training sessions.

Phil Bennett: But as soon as John Dawes or Clive would come in and break it up, they'd behave. It'd be forgotten by the time we were back in the showers.

Clive Rowlands: It sounds like a daft thing to say but a big part of the success was down to the team rituals and camaraderie. The cinema trip on a Friday night was a prime example. Gerry Lewis, the physio, would come down the aisle, and say 'Right. Choc ice for Barry John. Lollipop for Gareth. Tub for Barry Llewelyn.' The whole cinema would be full but no one would bother them, because they knew what they had in store the following day.

Phil Bennett: People would be staring. 'Duw, it's the Welsh team.' Gerry Lewis was the old mother hen. He'd get the ice cream order in. Twenty-four ice creams. And Geoff Wheel would pipe up, 'Any chance of a flake?' 'No, no, Bill Clement [secretary of the WRU] said no flakes.' They were too mean to give us a bloody flake.

Graham Price: Geoff Wheel was a character. We were waiting in the team bus outside the Grand Hotel in Paris once, and it was getting pretty hot and stuffy in there. Somebody told him to open the window. Without hesitation, he threw his elbow into the window, and the entire thing shattered. There was glass everywhere.

Clive Rowlands: Afterwards we'd all go back to the hotel and have sandwiches together, and we'd have the stories of the week. Charlie Faulkner would be holding court. They were all so different, but they were friends, and they would die for each other. In the old Arms Park, there was an advert that said, 'Never forget you're Welsh', and I used to say, 'Boys, if you're struggling have a look up there, and if that doesn't do something for you, you're in trouble.' Small things like that, they mattered.

At the start of December in 1972, Wales had a chance to prove themselves as the greatest team on earth. New Zealand were coming to Cardiff. Victory over the All Blacks would confirm Wales as true rugby royalty, but if they were to upset the odds, they'd have to do it without their King.

Barry John: I wasn't naive enough to think life would be the same after the Grand Slam and the '71 Lions tour, but I had no idea how extreme the change would be. I had to lead three lives. The life of a guy working at Midland Bank, the life of a family man, and the life of a pop star. When I came home from New Zealand, my boss, Gwynne Walters, sat me down and said, 'Right, what are we going to do with you?' I'd been a normal rep going to garages and hauliers and things like that, but it was becoming impossible to do my job. I was on the way to North Wales once, and I stopped at a garage in Newtown to fix a problem with my car. The owner called his mates to tell them Barry John was there, and before you knew it the schoolkids had been given the afternoon off to come and gawp at me. The bank asked me if I wanted a private secretary to handle all the fan mail that was pouring in. I couldn't book a table in a restaurant without the owner telling everyone he knew. It would be overcrowded with fans coming for a glimpse of 'the King' before I'd ordered my main course. I once caused a traffic jam on Queen Street. I was waiting at the lights to cross the road, and somebody left their car idling to come and shake hands. Others joined in, and before long there was a massive tailback. It was funny at times, but ultimately, it was too much. On another trip to Rhyl to open a new branch, a young woman approached me, got a bit excited and curtsied. That's when I knew it was time to get out. I felt alienated from people, and I'm very much a people person. But I also felt as though I wasn't being fair to the boys, because I wasn't as physically fit as I should have been, I wasn't as sharp as I should have been. A week or two of that kind of attention, I could have handled. But it felt like a long marathon with no sign of the finishing line. I once said I was happiest on the pitch because no one could touch me, and it was interpreted as arrogance. What I meant was, I was away from the relentless, cloying attention that eventually became so suffocating.

Clive Rowlands: I didn't know he was going to retire straight after the French game. I thought he was having another year. The next game was Wales against the All Blacks and I'm convinced that they were terrified of facing Barry John. They must have had parties everywhere in New Zealand when Barry retired.

Gareth Edwards: The New Zealand game rankles. I've never forgotten it. We should have beaten them that day.

Gerald Davies: We had them on the back foot in the second half, and you rarely get to say that.

Gareth Edwards: JPR still thinks he scored to this day. The ref claimed it was a double movement. But JPR is adamant. He won't have it any other way.

JPR Williams: I did score. It would be a try now, there's no doubt about that. If he'd awarded that we'd have gone on to win.

Gerald Davies: The ref had awarded a try to Keith Murdoch in the first half in similar circumstances, but he disallowed that one.

Gareth Edwards: He said he'd wriggled over the line. I think Sid Going may have swayed the ref. But New Zealand were on the rack. With the very last kick, Phil Bennett scraped the paint off the upright. It would have drawn the game. It sounds as though I'm having a whinge, I'm not really.

Phil Bennett: I curse myself to this day.

Barry Llewelyn: We'd beaten them the week before while playing for Llanelli. The famous 9–3 game. It's obviously gone down in folklore, given the significance of the win, but people forget it was horrifically violent at times. Five minutes from the end, I was getting up from a ruck. Keith Murdoch ran up behind me, and kicked me up the backside so hard I thought he'd killed me. I collapsed in a heap in absolute agony. My shorts were red, he'd cut me so bad. The ref accused me of playing for time, trying to run the clock down. It was an indication of what Murdoch was capable of.

JPR Williams: They played like thugs in some of those tour games. John Ashworth stamped on me during the Bridgend game, and it was definitely deliberate. You can forgive somebody for doing something once, but to do it twice, it's not accidental.

Steve Fenwick: It was a terrible injury. He split his face, all the way down the length of his jaw. You could literally see through his cheek. He turned to me and said, 'Steve, take charge. I'll be back in two minutes.' And I thought, 'No, you won't. You'll be in hospital.' A few minutes later, I heard the crowd erupt behind me, and there he was, sprinting back on with this grim expression, wearing these horrible stitches in his face. Two big knots in his face. He looked like Frankenstein's Monster. The All Blacks were absolutely gobsmacked that'd he come back. They tested him out immediately with a high ball, he took it and ran straight back over the top of the All Black forwards. He was determined to come back on. If it had been me, I'd have been 'hands up for the ambulance'. That wasn't JPR's style.

Phil Bennett: The Test match a week later put a strain on the relationship between the two countries, because of the whole Keith Murdoch affair. He was sent home for assaulting a bouncer in the Angel, and some of the Kiwis thought it was our fault. He'd been a bit naughty in the Llanelli game. I'd seen the carnage in the dressing room afterwards when the boys stripped off. They were covered in cuts and bruises. He stepped on Roy Thomas's head at one point. Kicking heads is unacceptable. You're talking about people's eyes and brains, or maybe putting someone's lights out for good. He caused some serious damage. I witnessed the fracas in the Angel, and there were bouncers being knocked all over the place. They were ugly scenes. He didn't like authority. It was frightening. He was a big man and he could handle himself. He was getting stuck in and scattering them like nine-pins.

Barry Llewelyn: He was sat opposite me in the post-match dinner. The forwards were all together, and the pretty boys – Gareth, Gerald and JPR – were off on another table with the backs. I tried to make conversation but he was in some kind of trance. One of the other forwards warned me that he was in a dangerous state, whether it was drink or something else, I don't know. He came to his senses, stood up, grabbed the table, and started shaking it violently. A few minutes later he got up to go to the toilet. I saw him trying to return to the dining room, but the security man told him, 'You're not coming in here without a pass.' Murdoch clenched his fist and replied, 'Here's my pass,' before punching the guy square in the face. He went down like a ton of bricks, out cold. Murdoch calmly stepped over him, and walked back in. The New Zealand Rugby Union heard what had happened, called a meeting and sent him home the next day. But he never made it home.

Phil Bennett: His life took a strange turn after that. He was sent home in disgrace, then disappeared into the Australian outback never to be seen again. A reporter tried to track him down, and she was threatened with death. I've been told that successive Kiwi touring parties always have a drink to Keith Murdoch in the Angel Bar, because they think he was unfairly treated. He became a martyr in their eyes. Those incidents overshadowed what happened on the pitch.

Barry Llewelyn: Murdoch aside, that was easily the toughest examination of my scrummaging. I remember being in the scrum thinking, 'One slip here, and my back will break.' There was all this force coming through from behind, and I knew if I'd buckled, I'd snap. The sweat was pouring off me and I was genuinely afraid.

JPR Williams: It was frightening, having these big black-clad beasts thundering towards you. I had to keep reminding myself to take the man with the ball, don't take a dummy. Nobody can criticise you then. They were much bigger than us, their pack was ferocious.

Gerald Davies: 1973–74 were the transition years before the new guys came along. The Pontypool front row, JJ, Gravell, Fenwick. A whole new gang came along, and a transition occurred. All of those helped to continue the success. Merv the Swerve was captain.

JJ Williams: Grav and Fenwick were a hell of a combination. A new breed of hard men who blocked up that midfield. They used to run straight and hard with the ball, and act as a brick wall without it. Fenwick wasn't the fastest or most skilful but he had wonderful timing. He knew when to put his foot on the ball or when to spray it around.

Wales finished top of the pile in the 1972 Championship, but the tournament was declared incomplete because of the cancelled games in Ireland. The following year the Five Nations ended in an unsatisfactory quintuple tie, with all five teams finishing on four points. Wales had the superior points difference, but perversely appeared last in the table as it was shown in alphabetical order. 1974 saw Wales pick up a solitary victory over Scotland, draw with both Ireland and France, and lose – controversially – to eventual wooden spoonists, England. It was their first defeat at the hands of the auld enemy for eleven years, and was arguably orchestrated by the referee, John West. He blew the whistle needlessly when Phil Bennett was en route to the try line, and disallowed a perfectly good JJ Williams try late in the game. It left a sour taste in the mouths of the travelling supporters, and the departing Wales coach.

Clive Rowlands: I went bananas. It still rankles to this day. My last day as coach of Wales . . . I was *so* annoyed. It was a try, I don't care what he says. I felt sorry for JJ, because it was definitely a bloody try. Christ. JPR didn't play, Roger Blyth played at full back. That was the difference. JPR never lost to England. John West came to my club with Clive Norling years later and we presented him with a white stick and a pair of dark glasses. Christ, he wasn't happy at all. But he was a really nice guy, mun. Nice guy, top man. He must have had a brain-freeze. That could have won us the Championship.

JJ Williams: At another dinner, years later, he was asked if, with the benefit of replays, he'd have given it, and he said no. I bloody fell on the ball. I got winded doing so. I remember looking up after scoring the try, and West was still on the bloody halfway line. He sent me Christmas cards for ten years. In the end, I had to tell him, 'Stop sending them, because you're not ever getting one back.'

Barry Llewelyn: I played with Bobby Windsor and Graham Price out in Japan in '75, and Bobby was lobbying hard to get Charlie Faulkner in the team. Bobby claimed he was the best loose-head in the world, and they were desperate to get the Pontypool front row together for Wales. Fair play, Charlie came in and did the business, but he had a big cheerleader in Bobby. That tour was my swansong. Japan's coach, Shiggy Konno, was a failed kamikaze pilot. That was the biggest disappointment of his life. He was scheduled to go in one of these planes, and take out an American destroyer, but the mission was called off. We beat Japan comfortably in the first Test, but the second game was a different proposition altogether. They came at us like banshees. Somebody said he was going to shoot them if they didn't turn up. He used to wear his white bandana with the red dot in the middle of it.

JJ Williams: We were superstars over there. Fifty thousand fans turned up to watch both games and we were mobbed wherever we went. Bobby had been singing Charlie's praises the previous year on the '74 Lions tour. The Welsh boys were discussing our prospects for the next Five Nations, and wondering if we'd have enough ball-winning forwards. Bobby said, 'I've got a mate coming down here. He's in Angola at the moment fighting as a mercenary soldier, and he's a black belt in judo. He'll be in Durban soon to meet up with his brother. I'm telling you now, this boy is the best prop you've ever seen.' A few days later, up turns Charlie, and I thought, 'You're joking.' He looked like an old man. He starts sitting amongst us, laughing, cracking jokes, with that easy manner of his. And he said, 'I'll tell you what, if I get in the Welsh team, we might go up, we might go down, but we'll never go back.' That was music to our ears. The likes of Phil Llewelyn and Glyn Shaw had been good players, but they often struggled against the likes of Fran Cotton of England or Ray McLaughlin of Ireland. Charlie – who'd fought dirty in the jungles of Africa – took no prisoners.

SEVEN

PHIL BENNETT WAS READY

As the second half of the seventies arrived, a subtle shift occurred. A number of stalwarts had retired from Test rugby – Delme Thomas, Dai Morris, and Barry Llewelyn among them. The ebullient Clive Rowlands had passed the coaching baton on to the quiet, introspective John Dawes. Gareth Edwards relinquished the captaincy to Mervyn Davies, a clubmate of Dawes's at London Welsh. Two polar opposites combined to form a formidable midfield partnership, and Phil Bennett continued to emerge from the long shadow of Barry John. In 1975 the Pontypool front row first combined at Test level. Individually, they were world class. As a unit, they were virtually invincible, scrummaging low and making mincemeat of opponents with an irresistible combination of technique and raw power.

Terry Holmes: Considering how hard they were on the pitch, they were hilarious off it. Graham was a bit more serious, but Charlie, Bobby and Geoff Wheel were like a comedy troupe. When we got together on a Friday before an international they'd hold court, and the rest of us would barely say a word. We'd be falling about laughing, and they wouldn't know why. They were hilarious without realising it. But they had hidden depths. Charlie and I got lost in Bordeaux once. We didn't know where the hell we were, and he got us home by following the stars. He's a wise old owl.

Gareth Davies: Geoff Wheel would sit there and recount his stories from the week, talking about the horrors he'd see as a bin man.

JJ Williams: I liked everything about them. The stories of drinking and hell-raising were exaggerated. They were seriously conditioned, you only had to look at their body shapes.

Phil Bennett: The Pontypool front row wouldn't eat meat on a match day because their club coach Ray Prosser had told them it would be bad for their digestion. So you'd see them folding their steaks up in a serviette and popping them in their inside pocket, to save for later.

Graham Price: Prosser always used to say, 'A lion hunts on an empty stomach.'

Phil Bennett: Delme Thomas would just have a glass of milk and a sherry. Gareth Edwards and Dai Morris a big plate of fish and chips. The boys from London Welsh were very sophisticated – honey on toast for them. And then you'd come to Brian Thomas, from Neath – a bunch of grapes was all he'd have. Black grapes, because of Neath. Prince Charles once told him he was surprised that he of all people would be eating *grapes* before a game, and he replied, 'Grapes before, meat during.'

Gerald Davies: Gareth had *two* steaks in a Paris hotel ahead of his Wales debut. As a student he was always hungry and didn't have any money.

Phil Bennett: The steak on a Friday night at the Angel would be the last meal that would pass my lips before Saturday night. I wanted to leave my stomach completely empty, otherwise I'd feel sluggish and bloated. On game day I used to think, 'I haven't eaten since last night, I'm feeling light, I feel good.' Now they're telling you, 'Get some pasta down, get the carbohydrates in.' I'd have nothing, not a morsel. And I used to finish the game with the most splitting headache. I'd get back to the Angel and Pat would immediately order me a large coffee and a steak sandwich. I'd have to take tablets because my head was pounding. I understand now, it was dehydration.

Gareth Edwards: The second wave came in 1975. That kept the impetus going for a good few years. Barry had gone, Phil was maturing. He'd had to live in Barry's shadow for so many years, and now had the confidence to step out of that shadow.

Gerald Davies: Phil was ready.

JJ Williams: Barry was cocky, whereas Phil was full of self-doubt. That was the fundamental difference. I roomed with Phil a lot and he used to get terribly nervous before games. I don't think he really wanted to be there in the early part of his career. And he didn't get properly fit until later on. He was quite small and chubby in his early days, and very quiet. His confidence grew when he became captain, and he became quite the orator in the dressing room. Fundamentally though, he was a shy Felinfoel boy. He had massive natural ability. Sometimes he was bewildering to watch. But the London Welsh boys, JPR and John Taylor, used to criticise him a lot. They'd accuse him of not doing for Wales what he'd do for Llanelli. But, come on, he was one of the greatest rugby players of all time.

Phil Bennett: I knew Barry as a sixteen-year-old. He came from just down the road from me. I loved him, and I loved David Watkins. Those two had a huge rivalry. When Dai went to league, Barry took over. As much as I admired and respected him, I wasn't going to bow down to him. I was playing for Llanelli at eighteen, up against a Cardiff team that had Barry, Gareth Edwards, Gerald Davies, Maurice Richards, DK Jones, a star-studded side. We played them twice in a season, and hammered them both times. Norman Gale would say, 'Look at these ponces coming down here, with their Baa-Baas kit.' So at the same time, Norman taught us, don't ever be frightened of them boys. 'We're the real deal, the miners, the steelworkers. They're the soft city boys from Cardiff.' There wasn't one ounce of jealousy, and I backed myself all the way.

Gareth Edwards: We had to work a bit harder when Phil came in, because he was a different type of player, and we didn't have the advantage of being clubmates like Barry and I had been. Barry liked the ball delivered back far, Phil stood a bit closer. Phil was more of a staccato runner, whereas Barry glided. But Phil arrived to the manor born, and the experience he'd had before becoming first choice stood him in great stead. He was destined for greatness.

Phil Bennett: I must give credit to Gareth. He never went on about his partnership with Barry. He just got on with it. And that's for one simple reason. The team is more important than any one player.

Gerald Davies: People tried to make it a competition, but it was never that way in reality. Barry relinquished his crown, and Phil was the natural successor.

Phil Bennett: For a couple of years I think Barry was happy with his decision to step out of the limelight. But once the adulation started to fade a bit, he began to think, 'What have I got left in life?' He realised then that we carried on winning. I had a pint with him two years after he'd retired, and he admitted to me that he missed it. He missed the boys, and he missed the craic. I thought he was crazy to bow out when he did, but I could understand how the pressure may have told in the end. I played a few charity football matches with him afterwards, and some of the boys were making fun of him for having put on a bit of weight. I don't think he liked that. His pride remained strong.

Gareth Edwards: He finished and Gerald and I went on another six, seven years. Years later I said, 'You do miss it, don't you?' He said, 'Yes.'

Barry John: Do I regret it? Of course I have regrets – big regrets – and I've probably thought about them most days since then. Any top sportsman will tell you that you should carry on playing, particularly at the highest level, until the moment your body tells you that you simply can't do it anymore. But at the time I really felt that it was the decision I had to make. But I have to be honest and admit it took fully three years to come to terms with the fact I wouldn't ever be out on that Arms Park pitch again.

Although Phil Bennett was seen as the natural successor to Barry John, his place in the side was never guaranteed in the way Barry's was. For the opening game of the 1975 Five Nations Championship, John Bevan was preferred at number ten despite Bennett having shone for the Lions on their unbeaten tour of South Africa the previous summer. Bevan was one of six new caps in a Welsh side that travelled to Paris more in hope than expectation.

Phil Bennett: I can take being dropped. It's happened to all of us. What hurt was the way it happened. I'd have expected one of the Big Five selectors to have given me a ring. What would a phone call have cost? But I found out from the journalist, Peter Jackson. Clive Rowlands jokes that he came to Llanelli to tell me in person, but that he got lynched on the way into town. That Sunday my wife and I took our little baby for a walk along the coast, and it occurred to me that there was more to life than running myself ragged at the Afan Lido. It was one of those moments when you have to challenge yourself to be the bigger man. You can win Lions tours, Championships and Grand Slams, but when you come home, you're just a normal bloke.

JJ Williams: He may have been a bit jaded after the Lions tour, and he missed a Sunday squad session [it was actually a trial match]. The following day, he played for Llanelli against South Wales Police. That was frowned upon, and he paid the penalty. He was his own worst enemy at times, and often rebelled against the discipline. Although Phil had recently opened a sports shop in Llanelli, which would have taken a bit of business away from Clive Rowlands' shop in the Swansea Valley, so maybe that had something to do with it. Clive is a very good friend of mine, but if you cross him, you're buggered. Those issues aside, Phil was an amazing player. So skilful, and so talented. He didn't always show it, but when he did, look out. He was very quick, and very powerful, but confidence was his biggest enemy. When it was low, the demons crept into his head.

JPR Williams: We were big underdogs going into that game in Paris. No one gave us a hope. But I've never witnessed a quieter Parc des Princes than towards the end of that match. With fifteen minutes to go, I looked up and the stands were virtually empty. The fans had upped and left.

Gerald Davies: As well as being aggressive scrummagers, the forwards were ball handlers. Formidable opposition. That try Graham Price scored was amazing. Coming at the end of the game, on a heavy, leaden French pitch. He played in the front row against a monstrous and aggressive French pack. The fact he could run seventy metres to score that try at the end was quite incredible. 25–10 against France was a big, big victory.

Graham Price: I thought I'd done pretty well. Running that distance at the start of the game would have been impressive, let alone at the end. Days later, I was back in the Pontypool changing room being congratulated by my clubmates, when Ray Prosser – my mentor – walked over, and put his arm around my shoulder. His praise would have meant more than most, so I leaned in to receive it. 'Pricey,' he said, 'if you had enough energy to run that distance at the end of the game, you obviously weren't pushing hard enough in the scrums.' He then ordered me outside, and put me through one of the most intensive scrummaging sessions of my career.

Phil Bennett: I preferred playing *with* the Pontypool front row. Clubs used to cancel games against Pontypool back in those days. We'd draw them in the cup and I'd be filled with dread. Bobby Windsor would phone me in the week. 'I've booked a room for you in the Royal Gwent Hospital. I'm going to kill you.' We beat them 26–0 in the cup, and they were devastated, but it didn't affect the following Saturday when we'd meet up to play for Wales. Tribalism was important, but it didn't affect national friendships.

JJ Williams: The three of them had a sinister aura. They were ruthless killers on the field. When you looked across the dressing room at those three, you knew that if trouble broke out on the pitch, they'd be the ones dishing out the punishment. Cobner used to divide the squad into those he'd take into the jungle with him, and those he wouldn't. The Pooler front row were his first choice battalion. I remember playing against them in the cup. The previous year, I'd run the length of the field to score an interception against them. This year, they were bollocking us. Smashing us up front. We'd spent most of the match tackling, and I got dragged into a ruck by Charlie. That was one place I did not want to be. You might as well take a shovel and dig your grave. As a sense of terror crept over me, our eyes met, Charlie grinned, and said in his inimitable Gwent accent, 'You're my mate, JJ. I'll let you go.' I've never been more grateful.

Graham Price: We had to be uncompromising, because those French forwards were hard as nails. Vaquerin went for my eyes at the first scrum, and I had to bite him to warn him off.

JJ Williams: Those French teams always had big, hard, nasty forwards that would rattle your bones.

Charlie Faulkner: You'd always have to look out for a stray boot or a wandering finger.

JJ Williams: Raking was a huge thing, and the authorities tried to get rid of it by introducing smaller, shorter studs. As soon as the referee left the changing room after the inspection, the forwards would reach into their bags, and swap their boots for ones with enormous long studs. Perfect for causing maximum damage to anyone who dared lie over the ball.

Graham Price: If a scrum went down in a Welsh club game, your opposite number might 'tickle' you, to let you know they were about and weren't to be messed with, but the French would kick you to maim you.

Charlie Faulkner: Some of them were lunatics. The violence was brutal at times. But we prided ourselves on our technique. We'd rather beat opponents through superior skill than through violence. We had a good snap scrum. Not many teams could handle it. We'd dip low, wait for the call, and go. All eight of us, not just the front five.

Graham Price: The modern players don't have the same intrinsic strength as the players from our era. They're bulked up and they look the part, but they don't have the same wiry strength of guys like Charlie and Bobby – strength that was honed, quite literally, at the coalface. I was a student so I didn't have the same natural strength as those two, but I developed it through competing with and against them.

Gerald Davies: When you talk about contrasts, they didn't come much more stark than Grav and Fenwick in the centres. Grav was passionate, emotional, and fiery. Fenwick was calm as anything. He'd crack a joke in the middle of a Test match, in the heat of the battle. Nothing fazed him. Grav was all nerves and raw energy.

JJ Williams: They were polar opposites. Grav would be charging around, punching down doors and being sick. Fenwick would be chilling out.

Phil Bennett: Ray Grav. We only had two toilets in the dressing room. Grav would go in with the programme, and he'd be in there for twenty minutes singing Dafydd Iwan songs. There was one song, *Carlo*, about Prince Charles and Charlie Faulkner would come up to me in his broad Pontypool accent and say, 'Benny! Who the hell is this "Caaaarlo"? What's he on about? Who the hell is this Dafydd Iwan? Get the bastard off the bog.'

JPR Williams: Grav was *so* insecure. He'd always be haranguing me during a match. 'Doc, how am I doing? Am I playing well?' I'd say, 'Grav, you're doing very well, but I'm trying to concentrate on my own game. Keep doing as you are, and leave me alone.'

Gareth Edwards: Fenwick was dry as a bone. He'd say something funny, but wouldn't laugh. So you didn't quite know where he was coming from. He had nerves of steel kicking goals, and he had the knack of being in the right place at the right time. I attempted a drop goal in that game against France that was nearer to the corner flag than it was to the posts, and everybody stopped in their tracks. But Stevie was after it, and scored a try. He turned a pig's ear into a silk purse.

JPR Williams: He was a fine player, Fenwick. But he'd have been very difficult to coach. He was very much his own man, and that's not necessarily a bad thing.

Phil Bennett: Grav would eventually come out of the bog, and stand in the mirror, appraising himself. Looking at the three feathers emblazoned on his chest. And he'd be ready for battle.

The 25–10 scoreline in Paris was Wales's biggest winning margin in the French capital since 1911, and France's heaviest home defeat since their reversal at the hands of the Springboks twenty-three years earlier.

JJ Williams: We beat England comfortably at Cardiff after the French win, and were halfway to another Grand Slam before disaster struck at Murrayfield. John Bevan broke his shoulder, and Fenwick broke his cheekbone. So Phil came on for Bevan, but he didn't want to be there. He wasn't happy about being on the bench. He had a kick in front of the posts which he initially refused to take. But Merv pulled rank and insisted. He missed. Then Trevor Evans scored a try at the death, and Phil was asked to kick the conversion. Didn't want to. So Allan Martin steps up, and he misses. We lost it 12–10.

Gareth Edwards: So we finished the campaign against Ireland, and with Willie John McBride coming to the end of his fabulous career, we thought Ireland would do it for him.

JJ Williams: They were strong in those days. They may not have been winning things, but their teams were always star-studded. Willie John McBride, Willie Duggan, Fergus Slattery, Mike Gibson, all of whom featured prominently on Lions tours.

Gareth Edwards: Grav and Roy Bergiers were unbelievable that day. Grav was the most insecure man I knew, but a bit of self-belief would do him the world of good. 'How am I playing, Gar?' 'Great, Grav, never looked better.' And he'd roar like a lion. He was possessed that day. Every time he'd tackle Mike Gibson he'd knock him up in the air. Some of those Irish players seemed tired and past it, but we were irresistible. I scored first, then Gerald, then Charlie Faulkner. JJ and Roy Bergiers added tries for good measure, and we were out of sight. We were so much on top that *anything* seemed possible. We were 32–0 up with minutes to play, and found ourselves in our twenty-two. The ball came back very quickly from a lineout, and I threw an audacious reverse pass to Benny. It was after the famous Baa-Baas game, and I had visions of a repeat of *that* try. I felt invincible. The Irish were on their knees, poor buggers, and I thought we would carve through them. Little did I know that Willie Duggan had anticipated this, and was already coming up on the blind-side. He intercepted and scored. Afterwards I said, 'Christ, I never knew you were that quick, Willie!' And he said, 'Thanks, Gar. The only way we were going to score today was if you passed to us.'

Charlie Faulkner: The scrum won us the game that day. Our job was to provide sweet ball for the backs. If we were in trouble, they were in trouble. So it all started up front. A lot of people didn't respect the scrum like we did. They just saw it as a way to restart the game. We saw it as the epicentre of everything. Even *I* got on the scoresheet. Bobby Windsor gave it to me. I didn't have to run very far. It was nice to score a try for Wales, especially against Ireland. I've got relatives out there, so there were a few telegrams going back and forth.

JPR Williams: Charlie was a character. Legend has it that he was thirty-six when he was first capped, but I think he was older than that. Even now, no one knows his real age.

Graham Price: We saw the scrum as sacred, and at Pontypool it bordered on religion. Ray Prosser's standards were higher than anyone's. We'd often return to Pontypool following an international to find Ray had forensically analysed our performances, and come up with ways to rectify any faults or weaknesses. It was an added pressure that drove our standards even higher.

The 32–4 winning margin was Wales's biggest against Ireland since 1907, and Wales's points total was their highest ever against their Celtic cousins. The victory took them to the top of the Championship table. Had it not been for a few wayward kicks against Scotland, they'd have been celebrating another Grand Slam. A record 28–3 win followed against the touring Australians that winter, before Wales began the defence of their title against England in 1976. For the second season running, Felinfoel's finest found himself out of favour with the Big Five selection panel. Not only did Phil Bennett miss out on the starting line-up, he didn't even make the squad. Bennett had missed the Australia Test with a foot injury, and remained injured for the trial match ahead of the Championship. But his decision to play for Llanelli against Bath days afterwards didn't sit well with the selectors, who named John Bevan and Dai Richards as their outside-halves for the opening game.

Phil Bennett: The foot injury I had was genuine. It meant I couldn't kick the ball.

But the style we played with Llanelli didn't require me to kick much, and I could still run like the wind. I'd resigned myself to the start of another Championship on the sidelines, when Rod Morgan called to ask if I could come to training. The first person I saw when I turned up was Gareth Edwards. 'You jammy bastard,' he said. 'John Bevan has pulled his knee ligaments and Dai Richards has done his hamstring, so you're straight back in for Saturday.' We beat England, and life goes on.

Life went on pretty smoothly for Bennett after that. He retained his place for the next match against Scotland, contributing thirteen points in a 28–6 victory, and surpassing Barry John's record of ninety points in international rugby. It was also the match in which Gareth Edwards scored his seventeenth Test try, equalling a record held jointly by Ken Jones, Reggie Gibbs, and Johnnie Williams. The result was sweet revenge after the previous season's narrow defeat. Two weeks later, Wales travelled to Dublin in search of a Triple Crown.

Gareth Edwards: The second half in Dublin was the best forty minutes I've ever played in. It was the day I equalled Ken Jones's record for caps, with forty-four in a row. Not one of the Welsh XV had ever won at Lansdowne Road. The last Welsh win there had been in '64, twelve years previously. To have played like that in Ireland was special, because it was usually tight as hell.

Gerald Davies: Gareth and I were actually vying with one another for the Welsh try record in that game. We didn't realise until the press made a big thing of it during the build-up.

Gareth Edwards: We had a laugh. I'd say, 'Ha ha, you're not having this, I'll give it to Benny instead.' And Benny scored.

Gerald Davies: I still think Gareth paid Phil a tenner for that. I was outside Phil, and in the clear, but he dummied and went himself.

Gareth Edwards: Some of the rugby we played was scintillating. I know defences are better organised these days, but we played some *beautiful* rugby. The Irish crowd were applauding us by the end. It was quite humbling, to be honest. I still get a positive reaction when I'm over in Dublin, even now.

JJ Williams: Ireland had this ferocity up front that needed taming, and the noise at Lansdowne Road only served to ramp up their aggression. We may have got on well on the Lions tour but in the Five Nations, they'd kick you in the head as much as look at you. Maybe they were getting a bit old. Our pack was particularly well-oiled: Mervyn controlling things at the back, Allan Martin tapping the ball down off the top of the lineout, and the sheer might of the Pontypool front row.

Add our star-studded backline, and we were a real handful. We seemed to take it in turns to steal the limelight. One player would always excel, and make the game his own, whether it was me or Gerald or Phil. It was always the turn of one of us to deliver the goods.

JPR Williams: We'd take it in turns as to who would be the match-winner. And we had so many match-winners in that team. We were much better than Ireland. There was never any doubt in our team. We were all quietly confident. We all knew that in the last twenty minutes, something would happen.

JJ Williams: At that point, wherever Wales travelled it was the big game of the season. We were the benchmark, and others were judged on how well they'd done against us. If you beat Wales, well then you'd had a good season. That's the way it was back then. Had there been a World Cup, France, New Zealand and Wales would've been the three teams vying for it. I laugh now, when some suggest Ireland is a bigger rugby nation than Wales. Back then, they were in our shadow, copying our tactics, our coaching, our way of playing. They loved us out there, even their own fans.

Phil Bennett: It was like sevens at one point. We were running them ragged. I scored a try, Grav scored a try. We won a penalty, twenty to twenty-five metres out from the posts and me and Gareth were fighting over the ball, because we both wanted to tap and go. Mervyn Davies strolled over, snatched the ball off the two of us and said, 'Fucking hold on here, boys. Calm down and stick three points on the board.' 'But Merv, we're 26–3 up!' I said. And he said, 'You stick three points over there. Let's cool it down a bit.' It was brilliant captaincy, because we'd lost our heads. We wanted to run from everywhere.

Graham Price: That was Merv's style. So laid back and matter-of-fact. He'd sit there in the changing room before a match puffing away on a cigarette, in his own little world. When the time was right, he'd stub it out on the bench, knock to get everyone's attention, and deliver his team talk.

JPR Williams: He didn't say much, Merv. Very understated. 'Just follow me into battle, boys.' Great player.

JJ Williams: It was 10–9 at half-time, and while we were huddled round on the halfway line sucking our oranges, Merv gave us licence to go out and play. He led by example, but trusted Gareth and Phil to control things tactically. He told them to give us backs the ball, and we'd score the tries. Thank you very much, Mervyn, and off we went. But you can only let loose if you have the platform up front, and boy did we have that.

Phil Bennett: The late, great Mervyn Davies. Didn't say a lot. But he inspired you. Good god, he inspired you. Just before half-time in the Grand Slam decider against France, he was struggling. His leg had been trampled on, and it was bruised and swollen. He said to Gerry Lewis, 'My calf's gone.' Gerry told him to give it five minutes, and he'd have another look at it at half-time. I went up to him and said, 'Merv, stay on. Please stay on.' 'I can't run,' he said. 'Limp through it,' I said. And he did. He played until the bitter end, on one leg, running at three-quarter pace. But he stayed on, and we beat France. He was the inspiration. That kind of spirit permeated through the entire team.

Within a few weeks of leading his side to Grand Slam glory, Mervyn Davies suffered a brain haemorrhage during a Welsh Cup match between Swansea and Pontypool. It may have been fatal were it not for the swift action of the medics. His magnificent career had come to a sad and premature end.

Phil Bennett redeemed himself in the eyes of the selectors, playing a starring role in Wales's seventh Grand Slam, and contributing thirty-eight points overall. In the final game against France, he kicked two penalties and created the game's only try with a trademark jinking run. Victory was secured in the dying moments, when France's final assault on the Welsh goal-line was snuffed out by a thunderous JPR shoulder-charge. Wales's backline may have built its reputation on invention and delicacy, but when the occasion demanded, it could resort to brute force and obstinacy.

Phil Bennett: We were all in that room, that sacred room at the Angel, and Windsor Davies – the actor who'd starred in the brilliant movie *Grand Slam* – was coming up the stairs as I was leaving. 'Hello, lovely boy,' he boomed and gave me a bear hug. I tried to persuade him to come in. 'No, no,' he said, 'that's the holy of holies. I couldn't go in there.' I said, 'Just come in and have a drink.' The boys loved him. And he's always said since, 'Duw, Phil. That room. That night. Best room I've ever been in.'

Wales's Grand Slammers were rock stars. Revered in their own country, envied and admired in others. They had the kind of profiles that could have made them a lot of money. But the game's staunch amateur status meant they weren't able to capitalise on their celebrity. Not only that, they were routinely denied the kind of perks their heroics deserved.

Phil Bennett: How could it be that there are seventy thousand tickets sold at Cardiff Arms Park, with all that money flooding in, and Gareth Edwards and I have to share rooms with our wives on a Saturday night? It was appalling. The committee members' wives had their own rooms with their husbands. Gareth and I would have to shut our eyes when each others' wives were getting dressed.

JJ Williams: Why were they so mean to us? If you were a Welsh rugby administrator, you were getting to travel to places like New Zealand and Australia, and living off *our* glories. Yet if we tried to get a free meal or a free drink, it was denied. Pathetic. We didn't *want* to be paid, but they could have given us the best bedrooms, the best transport, and treated us a whole lot better. Whenever we travelled to Twickenham in the seventies, there'd be a thousand buses heading east. The whole of Wales used to travel across, red shirts everywhere. We'd have the cheapest, oldest, most battered fucking bus. We'd be chugging up the motorway at fifty miles an hour, and these luxury buses carrying fans would be slowing down to beep at us and wave.

Phil Bennett: It got quite frosty with certain members of the hierarchy. Once, eight of the wives got a train from West Wales to Paddington for an England game. It was pouring with rain, and they arrived bedraggled and lost, not knowing where to go. They bumped into Cliff Morgan who asked where they were going. 'We don't really know, Cliff,' they told him. 'Haven't the WRU sorted you rooms?' 'They don't really want us here, Cliff,' they said. He went berserk. He found them somewhere to get shelter and bought them tea. I spoke to the WRU committee on the Saturday night, and asked if, instead of getting the early train home, they could get a lift back on the committee bus that was only three-quarters full. 'Oh no,' they said, '*that* would set a precedent.' *Their* wives were on the bus. I was captain and wasn't willing to back down. They had a bloody meeting about it, and eventually relented on the grounds it was a one-off, and we wouldn't be allowed to ask again in the future.

Barry Llewelyn: Those were the days when the *players* were lucky to get a seat on the team bus, as it was so full of committee men and their wives. We were the ones running out spilling blood, and breaking bones on the field, yet they were reaping the rewards.

JJ Williams: After we lost in Paris in '77, the committee men left us behind in the airport. The announcement that the flight was departing had been in French, and none of us dumb rugby players understood it. Next thing you know, the plane's gone. How the hell are we going to get home? I think Gareth and Gerald managed to sneak on, but the rest of us were stranded. The flight went back half-full. It's like the committee men had gone, 'Ah, fuck 'em. Leave 'em there.' We were having to bum on to these chartered flights going back, a few here, a few there.

Phil Bennett: On another occasion, we stopped on the way back from a game somewhere near the Severn Bridge. The wives and girlfriends came in and they were so shy and embarrassed. They didn't want to sit with us because they felt like they were imposing. We had all been ordered a set meal of roast chicken, and I insisted they come and eat with us. They were our wives for crying out loud. So they did, and we all dined together. The following Wednesday I received a bill through the post for Pat's meal. I thought to myself, we've just beaten England in front of 78,000 people. All of Wales is on a high, and I'm getting this bill for £6.80. We should be bigger than that. If the committee's wives can come up, get dressed up to go to a show on a Friday evening, why the hell can't ours have a measly roast dinner? It's no wonder so many boys went to rugby league. They didn't treat the players with the respect they deserved.

Barry Llewelyn: Even the notion of sponsorship was anathema to the WRU. Adidas came on the scene and wanted us to wear their stuff. Their rep needed someone on the inside to convince us all to wear adidas boots and tracksuits. They were giving them all away, but they wanted us, as a successful side, to be associated with the brand. They found their man on the inside, and that man's name was Gareth Edwards. He virtually filled his house with kit. So a sort of informal deal was struck, but some players were creatures of habit, and didn't want to wear adidas boots. Phil Bennett would only wear GT Law boots. Plain black, hand-made, leather soles. I used to wear them, but they didn't last two minutes in the front row. We got around it by painting three stripes on with white paint. I'm not sure if any money changed hands between the union and adidas, but as long as we were getting a free bit of kit, we weren't that bothered.

Phil Bennett: The Union's innate conservatism is the reason a genius like Carwyn James never became Wales coach. He was simply too progressive for them. He coached the Lions to their only ever series victory in New Zealand, yet the WRU wouldn't touch him. Had he been coach he'd have wanted to pick the team himself without any interference from the Big Five, and they weren't willing to allow that. They'd have become redundant. The union would have been scared stiff. But he was a finer man than any of those in the WRU hierarchy.

JJ Williams: The thinking was that he'd take over from Clive because John Dawes had not long finished playing, but his insistence on the abolition of the Big Five meant the WRU ruled him out. That was Carwyn. He wanted to upset the establishment. Had he been a bit cuter, he'd have got the job.

Phil Bennett: We lost a little baby boy in 1974. It was the worst experience of my life. I saw the little boy in an incubator and he was so pretty. It will live with me forever. He had something wrong with his chest. Two days later, he died. I was overcome with grief. I didn't want to play rugby. It seemed irrelevant. My boss at the steelworks was magnificent, and he gave me time off to come to terms with my grief. Unbeknownst to me, Carwyn had booked a week's holiday for Pat and I in Spain. The club was paying. Carwyn said to me, 'Take her away, and chill out for a bit.' Pat cried for two days, but eventually she got something out of her system. It helped us to cope with our unimaginable loss. Carwyn had thought of that. It was the measure of the man. The WRU could have done with a man of his stature. Most of the committee men thought they were better than the players. He was a great coach, but as a man-manager, he was a genius.

Wales's title defence began strongly in 1977, with a 25–9 victory over Ireland, but hopes of another Grand Slam were dashed in Paris when France won the fiftieth meeting between the two sides. Redemption arrived against England in Cardiff, which meant Wales travelled to Edinburgh with the Triple Crown in their sights. It was a day that another record tumbled – Gareth Edwards won a world record forty-ninth consecutive cap, overtaking the mark previously set by Willie John McBride. But that was destined to become a footnote, as Murrayfield bore witness to the finest match of the Championship, and to a score which – in the eyes of many – is the greatest Welsh try ever.

Phil Bennett: I stood on the balcony of the North British Hotel at 10.30 in the morning, and watched in awe as ten thousand scarlet-clad supporters made their way down Princes Street. Most of them didn't have tickets. Times were hard for manual workers then, with miners and steelworkers facing uncertainty. Yet, they'd all come up for the occasion, and spent all this money. I was captain, and I said to my teammates, 'Boys, we have to win it for these people today.' The connections were personal. We'd walk among them and see people we knew. There'd be conversations like, 'What shift you working on Monday then?' 'Oh, I'm nights all week.' We may have been heroes to many, but the reality was we were all Welsh people. We were the ones lucky enough to pull on the shirt and run out at Murrayfield.

Gareth Edwards: Days earlier, I'd been in Atlanta taking part in the *Superstars* TV tournament. Being that far away made me realise how important that game at Murrayfield was, and I became worried that I'd pull a hamstring, and miss it. I offered my apologies, and told the TV people I wanted to fly home early.

Phil Bennett: It was a hard game because Scotland had guys like McGeechan and Andy Irvine who could run. They were throwing everything at us in attack, and we were being seriously stretched. That famous try of mine came from a lineout Bobby Windsor – who I loved – tapped down badly, and it landed in their scrum half's hands. Bobby was fuming. He launched himself at the scrum half and missed. Then he flew at the fly half, and missed, so then he ran at the centre, trying to get to him. Then they bring it back the other way, and Bobby's all in a tizz tearing his hair out. All he wants to do is hit someone. But then, Andy Irvine decided to chip. And you don't chip to JPR.

Gerald Davies: I was out of position in midfield, filling a gap in defence, when the counter-attack began. I took the pass from Steve Fenwick, and managed to squeeze through the cover before handing off Dougie Morgan. I passed to Phil Bennett, and then stood back to admire the rest.

Phil Bennett: It unfolded perfectly. I made about twenty yards before passing to David Burcher, he lobbed it back inside to Steve Fenwick, who delivered a beautiful split-second pass back to me. The last person I beat was Mighty Mouse McLauchlan. I'm thinking, 'Mouse, what on earth are you doing here? Sixty yards from where the last set piece was?' I remember Mouse from the Lions in '74. He was never one for loose play. It was all about scrums, lineouts, and fighting in the rucks and mauls. When I crossed the line, I felt pure relief. We'd done it for those thousands of travelling fans. We'd won the Triple Crown and made them proud. That's what I was thinking about when I had the ball tucked under my chin, and I took a moment. That would be one of my favourite games. Not because of the try, but because all of Wales seemed to be right there in Murrayfield. These titles really meant something. Years later, I was at an Ireland game, and Fergus Slattery asked me if I'd come to a dinner that weekend. We were on the way over there, me, Fergus and Willie Duggan, and they were dressed to the nines. Proper dinner suits, the works. I said to Fergus, 'What's all this in aid of then?' And he said, 'Phil, we're celebrating our Triple Crown.' I laughed, and he asked what was so funny. I said, 'Sorry Fergus, we've won so many of these, it's boring.' And he told me to fuck off.

On the night of 19 March, 1977, when Phil Bennett and his teammates were celebrating another Welsh success, he received a phone call asking whether he'd be willing to captain the British and Irish Lions on their summer tour to New Zealand. After the ignominy of being left out of the squad the previous two seasons, the former steelworker from Felinfoel was now the man to lead the best of the best to the toughest destination on earth. The tour wasn't a memorable one for the Lions, after their series-winning adventures in '71 and '74. Key players like Gareth Edwards, Gerald Davies and JPR Williams were unavailable, and the rain was so torrential and unrelenting, that many of the matches degenerated into energy-sapping slugfests. The Lions returned defeated from a largely joyless tour.

As the 1978 Championship got underway, Wales – who'd made up the majority of the Lions touring party – were hoping to reignite the spark that had been snuffed out during a wet and dreary New Zealand winter. The conditions that greeted them at Twickenham on 4 February would have felt familiar, as the steady drizzle that fell from breakfast onwards presaged a tryless kickfest. Gareth Edwards, winning his fiftieth consecutive cap, starred again, but not with his usual rambunctious try-scoring menace. Instead it was his masterful kicking display that helped win the day, his raking, tortuous line kicks sapping England's morale, and keeping Wales in the right half of the field.

If the rain was Wales's biggest enemy against England, it was the cold that became their nemesis back in Cardiff when the Scots came to town. The temperature dropped steadily as the match progressed, until snow began to fall, leading to a blizzard that would keep hundreds of Scottish supporters trapped in the Welsh capital for days. Luckily for Wales, a scoring blitz either side of half-time – including a record twentieth Test try for Gareth Edwards – put them in a commanding position, which they wouldn't relinquish.

From the rain of Twickenham to the snow of Cardiff, Wales then entered a seething cauldron of Irish aggression in Dublin. A maniacal Fergus Slattery whipped his fellow forwards into a frenzy, and they very nearly succeeded in battering Wales into submission. But sixteen points from Steve Fenwick and a JJ Williams try saw Wales over the line, and to an unprecedented 'triple-Triple Crown'.

JJ Williams: We were exhausted after that Ireland game. There was champagne popping around, but there was no feeling of elation. Terry Cobner, Derek Quinnell and Allan Martin were just slumped on their seats looking absolutely spent. Ireland had booted the shit out of us. Moss Keane and Slats were running around like madmen kicking everything that moved. A lot of us were thinking that things were getting too hard.

The match which followed was arguably the toughest of the decade. It was a winner-takes-all Grand Slam decider against the defending champions, France. After the bruising, blood-and-thunder encounter in Dublin, most of the Welsh players had returned to their clubs to take part in a round of Welsh Cup ties. They arrived at the Arms Park wondering whether they had anything left in the tank to withstand the inevitable Gallic onslaught.

Phil Bennett: There weren't many times that I was scared on a rugby field. Back in those days, the forwards were the more intimidating ones, and they only really picked on each other. But playing against France, whether in Paris or Cardiff, was intimidating. Standing there in the tunnel, watching their players headbutting the walls, and fighting one another. Even hard men like Graham Price and Bobby Windsor struggled against some of those brutes.

Graham Price: The scrummaging sessions on the sand in Aberavon helped in those days. They were seriously hard.

Charlie Faulkner: Full-on live scrummaging. No machines. Just eight-on-eight on a shifting surface. You'd come back red raw, because once the sand got into your jersey, that was that.

Graham Price: We were all exhausted on the day of the French game. We'd beaten Ireland in Dublin to win the 'triple-Triple', and we felt physically and mentally drained. I'm not sure where we found the reserves to pull off that win, especially when they scored first and everybody's heads dropped. We had to dig in and guts it out. That was the best front row I ever played against. For those three years, the Wales–France game was the Grand Slam decider.

Phil Bennett: We didn't play particularly well. A lot of us were tired from the Lions tour, and there were niggling injuries. But the crowd was incredible. After we went 7–0 down, I called the lads into a huddle, and told them the game was going away from us. I don't know whether the crowd sensed we needed a lift, but at that exact moment they broke into song. The hairs stood up on the back of my neck, and I said, 'Jesus boys, listen to how much it means to them.' Not long after that, I scored my first try. Bobby took a scrum against the head, Allan Martin gave me the ball, and I just had enough speed to make it to the line. When I was lining up that conversion, I had a real feeling that this was the most important moment of my rugby life. I just *had* to kick it. Another two points to peg them back would have changed the complexion of the match. Sometimes the smallest of things take on the biggest significance. It was from the touchline, and I nailed it. I can remember the reaction of the crowd behind the posts; they went *berserk*.

JJ Williams: It was nip and tuck throughout the whole game, but at that point we felt as though we'd quelled the fire. We'd taken the sting out of them. We knew that if we scored next, we'd take the lead. As it happened, France didn't score a single point after that.

A Gareth Edwards drop goal nudged Wales ahead, before Phil Bennett scored a second try to extend the lead. It was another classic team effort, Gravell busting through the first line of defence, a switch of direction from Edwards, a superb bootlace pick-up from JJ, and an instinctive basketball pass inside to Bennett. Another drop goal, this time from Steve Fenwick, sealed the deal. France would have won had they selected a reliable goal-kicker. Between them, Jean-Michel Aguirre and Bernard Vivies missed six attempts on goal.

Gareth Edwards: We were so thrilled to beat France to win the Grand Slam again. Jerome Gallion was the flavour of the month. He was apparently going to show me how to play the game. He was the young pretender, and I was beginning to worry that my time was running out. I didn't want to be remembered as the man who played once too often for Wales. After the game, he approached me and said, 'Today, you were the teacher.' I appreciated that.

JJ Williams: It was a huge achievement, but all we got from it was a commemorative tankard and an ill-fitting blazer. We had a good night in the Angel Hotel, though. My abiding memory is of Geoff Wheel pinning JBG Thomas up against the wall. I can't quite remember the reason, but I had to separate them. Thomas was the all-powerful doyen of Welsh rugby-writing. He almost selected the team. If he said in print that your career was over, it probably was, so Geoff's decision not to harm him probably extended his career. We were all married at this point, so we didn't go out on the town and get pissed, we just stayed in the Angel and enjoyed the moment.

Gareth Edwards: Because you worked in those days, you were conscious of the fact that you were away from your family and always asking for favours from your employer. I was thinking more and more about bowing out. I didn't want to be a burden to the team. I wanted to get out on top. I saw the upcoming itinerary, and it almost made my decision for me. There was an Australian tour in the summer. Then the All Blacks were coming in the autumn. It occurred to me then: there's never an end. You just have to make the decision. It was my third Grand Slam, and as we were leaving the field, the old warrior, Jean-Pierre Rives said to me, 'Gareth, today you were "old foxy". It was your day. Next year, in Paris maybe it'll be my day.' And it was at that moment that it hit me. I knew I wouldn't be in Paris next year.

The only Welshmen for whom his retirement was good news were the scrum halves who'd been denied a run in the jersey by Edwards' once-in-a-generation brilliance. The likes of Ray 'Chico' Hopkins, Clive Shell, and Brynmor Williams may all have won dozens more caps had they been English, Scottish or Irish. Gareth Edwards retired having won fifty-three consecutive caps. For a player so combative, so eager to run at defences, it seems implausible that he enjoyed such an uninterrupted run. To several members of that glorious Welsh side of the seventies, this Grand Slam felt like an end. The competitive flame within them began to flicker and dim, and their creaking limbs were taking longer to recover.

Phil Bennett: I remember people using the boxing analogy – one fight too many, and you've gone from being the world's greatest to being knocked out, and you're remembered for that last fight. I was lucky. I bowed out having been coached by some of the best there's ever been. Ray Williams, Carwyn James, Clive Rowlands, and John Dawes. JPR, if I'm honest, played on too long. He couldn't help himself, and I was worried he'd tarnish his reputation. He lost a couple of yards of pace, and he was never the quickest to begin with. I wanted to go out at the top, hopefully with a Grand Slam, and with the crowd thinking, 'That Phil Bennett, he was okay.'

And so it was without the record-breaking half back pairing of Gareth Edwards and Phil Bennett that Wales travelled down under in 1978. It was an arduous journey at the end of an exhausting season, but the Grand Slam champions thought they had little to fear from an Australian side who'd been well beaten on their previous two visits to Cardiff.

JPR Williams: That was a genuine awakening because we didn't expect any trouble from them. We'd always put twenty-plus points on them in Cardiff. We had some players who in retrospect shouldn't have been picked. Spikey Watkins was one of them. After three days we'd all had enough of him, playing the fool and being the showman. And there were others who were plainly out of their depth.

Gareth Davies: That first Test was my debut, and it was pretty violent. They targeted us physically, because they knew they wouldn't beat us playing rugby. They tried to beat the shit out of us. At one point they had a five-on-one overlap. I turned around to see where my backs were, and they were all fighting. Fenwick, JPR and Grav just going at it.

JJ Williams: We went over there as a favour because they were on the verge of going bankrupt. The money flowed into the coffers as a result of that tour and gave them a lifeline. They won both Tests, and have been beating us ever since. I wish we hadn't bothered.

JPR Williams: I started on the flank in the second Test, and it worked a treat at first. Stuart Lane and myself were both open-sides, and we had the Australian fly half under real pressure. But Alun Donovan tore his cruciate and I had to revert to full back.

Terry Holmes: I had my debut in the second Test, and they won it with a drop goal that was so wide, it was unbelievable.

Gareth Davies: It was at least five yards wide. I went to charge it down, but realised it was well wide, so I started jogging towards the twenty-two for the drop out.

Terry Holmes: We all did.

Gareth Davies: Next thing, the whistle's gone and the ball's back on the halfway line. The ref had bloody given it. There was no such thing as neutral referees in those days. Famously, during the Queensland game, the ref blew up for a scrum and said, 'Our ball.'

JPR Williams: It was the most miserable feeling returning to Cardiff on the back of an unexpected defeat, but some good things came out of it. We saw the emergence of Terry Holmes and Gareth Davies, and I got to know some of the younger generation, because by that point, I was one of the last survivors of the squad that had gone through the seventies. I thought about knocking it on the head, but the team needed me because most of the old guys had gone.

Gerald Davies: I captained Wales for the second Test, but I felt a little detached. I was beginning to repeat myself, and things were losing their lustre. I was never going to make the decision to retire at the end of a season because you're tired and irrational. So at the beginning of the next season, I waited for that first smell of the mown grass and the wintergreen, when you'd normally be raring to go. But this time I knew it was it. I'd done my time. The desire had gone.

One by one, the players that had inspired a generation were stepping away. Gareth, Benny and Gerald had now all joined Barry on the sidelines. Totems of Welsh rugby, they had all been at the beating heart of the side that had danced, shimmied and scorched its way into the history books. A litany of excuses were offered up after the Australian defeats – biased referees, over-confidence, a freakish injury list, exhaustion – but could it have been that the sheen was coming off? That the cogs were beginning to rust? The next challenge could not have been tougher. The All Blacks were coming to Cardiff in November of 1978. They had won their last five encounters against Wales, dating back to 1953. Wales thought they'd been robbed in 1972, but the outcome of this match would provoke far more rancour and debate than any other between the two rivals.

Gareth Davies: The message from John Dawes was: 'You're going to be legends.' He didn't push the same emotional buttons as Clive Rowlands; Dawesy was more of a pragmatist. It was a case of, 'You do your job on Saturday, don't make any mistakes, beat New Zealand, and you'll go down in folklore.'

Gerald Davies: Another game we should have won.

Gareth Edwards: I was doing the commentary. It was the first time in twelve years that I hadn't run out in a Welsh jersey. Geoff did lean on the guy, but every lineout was like that in those days.

Gerald Davies: That was the only lineout penalty he gave that day.

It remains one of the most contentious penalties in Welsh rugby history. As the match approached full time, Wales were leading 12–10. Bobby Windsor threw the ball in to Geoff Wheel in the middle of the lineout, and as he did so, Andy Haden fell theatrically to the floor, followed closely by Frank Oliver. The passage of time has exposed it for what it was – a deliberate act of sabotage. But on the day, without the benefit of replays, or a Television Match Official, the referee was hoodwinked into giving a penalty against Geoff Wheel for 'leaning on' his opposite number.

Charlie Faulkner: They screamed at the top of their lungs to make out they had been pushed.

Gareth Edwards: The fact that Geoff did what he did gave the ref an easy option. I'm big mates with Andy Haden, I go fishing with him in New Zealand and I don't hold it against him. He told me they'd spoken about it the night before, and he admitted that if they were up against it, he'd take a dive. But I'm not totally convinced that that's what the referee gave the penalty for. He was standing next to Geoff when he nudged Frank Oliver, and that's what he may have blown up for. I felt gutted for the boys. They deserved to win that game. We outplayed them.

JJ Williams: I'd played against them the previous week for West Wales. I'd suffered a nasty gash down my thigh, and got myself stitched up in that stinking dressing room in St Helen's. I wasn't really fit, and perhaps that's why I missed out on a try in the Test. Holmesy made a brilliant break, passed me the ball, and I let it bounce too much. Had I been quicker on to it, I could have hacked on and scored. By the time I had it, Mourie smothered me and stopped the try. I regret that, because I didn't do my job. My job was to finish chances. I was the striker, and I failed to do it that day.

JPR Williams: This remains one of my biggest regrets. Not many people have captained Wales to victory against New Zealand, and I could have been one of them. When I saw the tape of the lineout after the game, I felt physically sick. Most things that happen on the field can be forgiven, because they're done in the heat of the moment. But that was cynical, and pre-ordained. It had clearly been practised, yet they still made it look clumsy and obvious.

JJ Williams: It was typical New Zealand thinking. When they're backed into a corner they'll do anything to win. We had them that day.

Graham Price: Malcolm Lewis, one of our assistant coaches, went rushing up to the referee at the end of the game to remonstrate with him. In those days, there were no big screens to consult, and he wanted to know why he'd given the penalty. The referee, Roger Quittenton, explained that there had been so much barging throughout the game that he had to make a stand and do something. It was the last lineout of the game. Geoff Wheel did what he had to do in every other lineout, because Frank Oliver was climbing and barging all over him. He was just trying to fend him off. It had been happening throughout the game, and the ref only decided to penalise him for it during the last lineout.

JJ Williams: I think Bill McLaren even missed it in commentary, because he didn't have all the multi-angle replays we do these days. It was only as time passed that the sense of injustice began to grow. In the immediate aftermath, the feeling was just that we'd thrown it away.

JPR Williams: I see Andy Haden fairly regularly, and he admits full well that it was a tactic. And he's completely unrepentant about it.

Terry Holmes: We could have been legends. New Zealand were at the pinnacle, but their will to win was strong enough that they were prepared to cheat.

Gareth Davies: We were robbed.

Charlie Faulkner: I'm not bitter about 1978, but it's never gone away. I think about it every couple of days, even now.

Barry Llewelyn: In the eighties, I was invited to play in the Bermuda Classics. Wales played New Zealand, and during the first lineout, when New Zealand threw in, all the Welsh players theatrically fell out. It's ingrained in Welsh rugby history.

By the start of the 1979 Five Nations, Terry Cobner had also retired. Between him, Gareth Edwards, Gerald Davies and Phil Bennett, 144 caps' worth of experience had been lost in the blink of an eye. But the front five remained intact, and a powerful pack performance led by the all-action Derek Quinnell saw them to an opening win over the Scots at Murrayfield. A tight victory over Ireland in Cardiff followed in which Steve Fenwick became only the second Welshman to pass through the one hundred points barrier.

In round three, France exacted revenge for the previous year with a narrow 14–13 win in Paris, before Wales handed England their heaviest Cardiff thrashing for more than a decade. Five tries from Dai Richards, Paul Ringer, Mike Roberts, Elgan Rees and JJ Williams saw Wales romp to a 27–3 victory, and defend their title in the process. They'd pulled off an unprecedented run of four successive Triple Crowns. A quadruple-Triple. These truly were the crowning years. The question was, could this be a springboard to another 'decade of the Dragon', or had the curtain fallen on the final act?

EIGHT

WHEN THE TOP DOG FALLS

'They were handing caps out like confetti.' That was the accusation levelled at the WRU by JPR Williams as Welsh rugby began its alarming decline. Becoming a Welsh international no longer felt like joining an exclusive club.

The seventies were about verve and panache, but they were also about consistency and solidity. Wales scored tries that were sent from heaven, but they were crafted by mere mortals.

The onset of the eighties did mark a significant fork in the road for Welsh rugby. 1980/81 was the WRU's centenary season, and they were hoping for a successful Championship to mark the milestone. But the consistency that defined the seventies gave way to chaos.

Welsh rugby lost its swagger. Wales won seven of the ten Five Nations Championships in the seventies, either outright or jointly. Seven years would pass before they mustered a team capable of winning another. For the first six Championships of the eighties, Wales didn't register more than two wins per campaign. They came joint second in 1980 and 1981, although if points difference had been taken into account, they would have finished third and fourth respectively. In 1982 they came last, in 1983 they were fourth. For the next three years running they came third, and in 1987 they were fourth. Where once the three feathers had represented brilliance, now, they represented mediocrity. While Wales was preparing to celebrate its centenary year, results suggested that the party was already over.

Graham Price: Everything happens in cycles. We had good players in the eighties, but never the same concentration of world class players in the same side.

Eddie Butler: It was pure chance that the Gareths, the Geralds and the Barrys were born at the same time, and that they all turned out to be such superb rugby players. That was a lucky stroke, and they maximised it by fulfilling their potential to an extraordinary level. But to think that the next generation was just going to emerge from the womb, well that was never going to happen.

Gareth Davies: The year I was captain – 1981/82 – we began the season by beating Australia and France who were Grand Slam champions at the time. You'd die for that now wouldn't you? Australia had recently won a three-Test series against New

Zealand, and beaten France during the summer, so they were no mugs. But we beat them playing a fairly narrow game, only really scoring penalties and drop goals. Our coach, John Lloyd, and I agreed that we needed to play with a more open style, but we didn't have the personnel to do it. We lost every game after France, culminating in a record defeat to Scotland. As captain, I take some of the responsibility for that, and I didn't feature much in the two seasons that followed. The media played its part as well, because it was critical following our victory over France, drawing attention to the lack of flair in our game. That lodges in the players' minds. Rather than celebrating that win, we were dwelling on the negatives. And it all unravelled after that.

Terry Holmes: Winning is more important than style. You have to play within the parameters of what your skill levels are. The Welsh public know their rugby, and want to be entertained, but winning is the most important thing.

The defeat to Scotland was particularly painful. It was Wales's first home defeat in the Five Nations for fourteen years, but it was the manner of it that was most galling. 34–18 on the scoreboard, five tries to one, and barely a shot fired in anger. The Welsh team of the seventies could barely have contemplated a reversal on that scale. The free-flowing rugby of the previous decade had been replaced by stodge. The rock stars had been replaced by session musicians. The x-factor was gone. Wales had forgotten how to score tries. And never was that more in evidence than in November, when they travelled to Bucharest to face Romania. They were shamed, losing 24–6, conceding four tries.

Gareth Davies: There was probably a bit of arrogance about the Welsh team. That's not a criticism, it's what naturally follows success.

Terry Holmes: Complacency played a big part. Rugby was evolving in other countries, and we didn't keep pace. It became apparent to me during a club match for Cardiff against Bristol. We won well, but the pace of the game was something we weren't used to. We were taking it for granted that we'd keep on winning without needing to evolve. And it wasn't just on the pitch. You'd go to England to play, and they'd have their own rooms with their wives. If our wives wanted to come with us, we'd all have to bunk in together.

Gareth Davies: Before one game at Twickenham, Terry and I were sharing a room with our other halves. I'd roll over and feel an elbow and wouldn't know whether it was Terry or my wife.

Adrian Hadley: I was into football, so I couldn't tell if Welsh rugby was in decline. I barely watched it. The first time I went to the National Stadium was when I made my debut for Wales. Looking back though, it's obvious that the other nations were getting better. We were blessed with the players we had in that era, and good players bounce off each other. It was a once-in-a-generation group in the seventies.

JPR Williams: The decline of the steelworks and the collieries was significant. We didn't have those same naturally hard men coming through. The consistency of selection that defined the squad in the seventies became a thing of the past. There were lots of players who were only there fleetingly. Lots of one-cap wonders.

Eddie Butler: We didn't tour as Wales during my time. We went to Canada and Spain as Wales B, but never as Wales because they were too busy paying off the stadium. Everything was a compromise. We never played against Australia, South Africa or New Zealand on tour, which was a mistake. Ask Warren Gatland now about the importance of testing yourself against the best, and he says it's absolutely essential. We hardly played together outside the Five Nations and the one game in November. It was an aberration, and the strangest of circumstances.

It's difficult to believe that the decline of Wales's national sport wasn't arrested. There were those within the game who despaired at how dramatically Wales's status had fallen. The situation required decisive action, but an amateur game run by an unwieldy committee system isn't conducive to decisive action. The WRU is a union of clubs, and the fact that every club has voting rights, regardless of its size means swift radical change is almost always stymied by those voting according to self-interest, rather than the greater good of the game. Rugby was changing. Suggestions of a first-ever World Cup were being quietly mooted. Other nations were eager to join the party, and Wales were in danger of being trampled underfoot in the race to a new dawn.

Terry Holmes: Timing is everything. Gareth had retired, and Brynmor Williams had moved from Cardiff to Newport, so I became the first-choice scrum half for Cardiff and for Wales. Gareth Davies and I were young, and playing in an exciting club side which allowed our partnership to flourish. I never felt any pressure to live up to Gareth Edwards, because he's the best scrum half that's ever played the game. I did my own thing. As much as I'd have loved to have been as good as him, it was never going to happen.

Eddie Butler: I never thought about standing on the shoulders of giants. Derek Quinnell got injured, so I had my chance. It wasn't as if somebody rolled out the red carpet into the future, and said, 'Now it's yours, Butler.' There followed a period of experimentation, of trying to find a settled team. I don't think anyone felt secure in their position throughout the eighties. They were particularly turbulent times. Nobody had the confidence to say, 'Calm down, we need to rebuild, and we may need to accept a few losses.' Because of what had happened in the seventies, there was little tolerance of anything bar victory. It was a burden.

Gareth Davies: When you're twenty years old, you don't feel pressure; just excitement. I couldn't wait to run onto the park, sing the anthem, and hear Bill McLaren say my name the next day. I was proud to take my place in the pantheon, but I didn't care whether it was Phil Bennett or Barry John wearing the jersey before me. I used to watch both of them from the terraces at Stradey Park, and I never imagined I'd one day take their place. My PE master at school, Ray Williams – who'd played for Wales himself – told me I was better than Barry John had been at the same age. I'm not saying that to be conceited. I think it was a bit of amateur psychology from Ray, because it gave me an inner confidence, that I carried through my youth. By the time I won my first cap, I felt I'd earned it.

Terry Holmes: We came within a whisker of a Grand Slam in our first Five Nations campaign together. The Triple Crown game against England remains vivid in my memory because we won 27–3, which was a huge margin in those days. It's not often in a Test match that you know you've won it with twenty minutes to go. It was the opposite to the game against France which was so fast, and so frenetic that for the first twenty minutes I had no idea where I was or what I was doing.

Gareth Davies: The highlight for me was the following season when France came to Cardiff. We absolutely stuffed them, tore them apart. Elgan Rees gave me a bit of stick because I mentioned afterwards that he'd bombed about four tries which, had he scored them, would have taken us to around forty points. That was unheard of back then.

That handsome victory over France meant Wales travelled to Twickenham with confidence. England had already beaten Ireland and France under the leadership of Bill Beaumont, and their prospects were being talked up. England–Wales matches always came with an extra frisson of excitement, but the press ratcheted up the rhetoric ahead of this one, pushing the tension to dangerous levels. Accusations were levelled at Wales that they were ill-disciplined and barbarous. It was during a period in which several English club sides had cancelled fixtures against Welsh clubs in 'protest at alleged acts of violence'. Just fifteen minutes had passed before Wales flanker Paul Ringer was sent off amid a combustible cocktail of flared nostrils and seething tempers.

Eddie Butler: The social and industrial history of Wales was impossible to ignore. The steelworkers' strike in 1980, and the miners' strike in 1984, contributed to a fairly febrile atmosphere. Having this backdrop of support that was a little hysterical usually worked in Wales's favour, particularly when we played against England. But that match erupted like never before.

Graham Price: That opening quarter of an hour was like World War Three, and Ringer's red card meant we spent sixty-five minutes with just seven men in the pack. We didn't do too badly considering, and by modern scoring methods, we'd have won the game. It was all John Scott's fault. The Englishman who played for Cardiff. He kicked Terry Holmes, his own club teammate, in the head.

Terry Holmes: We should still have won. The way our forwards kept us in the game was heroic. We outscored them two tries to nil. One conversion would have done it.

Gareth Davies: We used four kickers that day. I missed both conversions. Fenwick missed a few, so did Roger Blyth. Allan Martin even tried a few that day.

Terry Holmes: We were winning 8–6 with minutes remaining, when I was penalised for going over the top. It was never a penalty. We were robbed.

Gareth Davies: The seeds for the Ringer match were sown on BBC Wales's *Sports Lineup* programme after the France game, where Carwyn James was the studio analyst. He highlighted a few instances of dirty play from Paul Ringer which had gone unnoticed during the game. One particularly nasty stamp left Alain Paco bleeding heavily. Well, the English press seized upon this, and all the build-up to the game the following Saturday centred on the so-called thuggery of us dirty Welsh bastards. It was my first experience of the power of the press to influence things. That game was destined to turn ugly. There was a horrible atmosphere, it was genuinely nasty, and realistically, there could have been four or five sent off.

Eddie Butler: The stage was set long before the players came out. It was a particularly hostile atmosphere. It just oozed hostility. Things got off to a fairly tempestuous start, and continued in that vein until David Burnett, the referee, issued a final warning. We should have reined it in a bit, but tempers were running hot, and Ringer just couldn't restrain himself. He launched himself into John Horton, and hit him both high and late. Having said that, Horton milked it for all it was worth. Burnett was conscious that he was losing his grip on the game, and knew he could only restore his authority by taking the ultimate sanction. It was obvious he was going to do something given the opportunity, and Paul fell into the trap. England got very theatrical about it, and opened the trap door a little wider.

Terry Holmes: It spilt over into the night as well. There were a lot of English players who weren't celebrating in the right spirit. Contrary to public perceptions,

English and Welsh boys usually mix really well. My experiences socialising with the English players have been overwhelmingly positive. But not that night.

Gareth Davies: If ever there was a cause to send Ringer off it was in the French game. All week John Dawes had been getting inside his head, telling him his only purpose was to scare the shit out of their number ten, Alain Caussade. We were having our team photograph before the game, and France were on the pitch going through their lineout drills. We were in red, France were in white. We looked over, and there was a solitary red shirt among the white. It was Ringer, getting right up in Caussade's face, veins popping, eyeballs bulging, threatening him and all sorts. JPR and Jeff Squire had to sprint the length of the field to drag him back. It nearly all kicked off before the game began.

Eddie Butler: They must have thought he was barking mad, and he probably was a bit. The French game was actually more violent than the England game. Those were my first two internationals, and I thought it was the norm for Test rugby. It was far more violent than what I was used to at Pontypool. There, the rugby was hard and uncompromising, but it was pretty cold-blooded. The violence was administered in a measured way. Those two Test matches were different. They were frenzied. The violence was utterly flagrant.

Gareth Davies: For two years afterwards, the Welsh pack never really fired. The feeling was that the England game had killed us. The forwards were so fearful of the referee's whistle that they lost their bite. The coaches made some changes, and Paul Ringer didn't play again for a while.

JJ Williams: This was the moment the tide turned. People were fed up of Wales being so powerful and winning everything, and Ringer became the scapegoat. Whether it was conscious or subconscious, there was a feeling that the referee was punishing Ringer for Wales having been so good for so long.

Eddie Butler: It was a mark in the sand for Wales. After that it was like we were being told to get back on the horse but they'd taken away our spurs. The press reaction was so hostile, and everybody was on our case. The good name of Welsh rugby was savaged in the press. We were hauled over the coals of scrutiny, and knew we had to be whiter than white from that point onwards.

Gareth Davies: That game affected a lot of people's careers. Ringer didn't make the Lions tour that year, and it may well have been because of his red card. But it's easy to forget that that was a good England side. They went on to win the Grand Slam, and Bill Beaumont went on to captain the Lions.

Eddie Butler: There was a definite sense of glee that Wales were being given their comeuppance, but that's the natural order of things. When the top dog falls, everyone else takes a particular relish in it happening. It was spelt out starkly that no more nonsense would be tolerated. But Welsh rugby at that time *had* to have an edge. We weren't as mighty as some teams. France were huge, England were huge, so we had to have a bit of bite to us to compensate for our lack of size. That was taken away, and suddenly we were exposed. But I never wished I'd been born a decade earlier. You have your own time, and your own generation, your own mates, and you go through it together. Just as that seventies team came together by good fortune, it was bad luck to arrive once so many of them had left the stage. You took it on the chin, and got on with it. We beat Scotland comfortably after the Ringer game, but we had a really tough game out in Ireland. They really piled into us.

It seems far-fetched to suggest that the Ringer game alone triggered the decline, but there are many who claim that the experience emasculated the game in Wales. Afraid of the sanctions, the Welsh forwards, consciously or otherwise, became cowed and lost some of their hard edge. The centenary season was a damp squib. A record 23–3 defeat to New Zealand was followed by a forgettable Championship. The early eighties turned out to be a period during which success eluded Wales. Gareth Davies won the majority of his twenty-one caps during that period, and is currently the guardian of the game in Wales, holding the chairmanship of the Welsh Rugby Union. He may never have believed he'd end up in such a role, given the shabby way his international career came to an end. He was always something of a square peg in a round hole. He was a master tactician, and an astute manager of the game. A conductor rather than a soloist. And in Wales, that didn't fit the romantic ideal. This is a nation that prefers a conjurer to a cool-head, and his talents were never truly acknowledged.

Terry Holmes: Gareth was ahead of his time in the way he controlled the game. He'd kick well and probe the corners, but he'd get criticised because he wasn't a running, jinking fly half. Dan Carter was later lauded for the way he controlled a game. Gareth was criticised for doing the very same thing. He had very high standards. I'd have the scowl if the pass wasn't good enough. There were a few of them. But then I'd get stuck into him for not tackling.

Gareth Davies: I didn't play the game to tackle. I don't think anybody ever told me to. I think my laid-back approach gave some the impression I didn't care. We used to do fitness testing down at St Athan in the Vale of Glamorgan. I was a good 400m runner, and we were running a mile against the clock. At one point, I lapped Adrian Hadley. Adrian was a lazy bastard. He had gas on the field, but was lazy off it. When the results came out the following week, I was bottom of the list. Naturally, I queried this with John Dawes, and he just shook his head and said, 'The clock doesn't lie, Gareth.' I was fuming. Adrian naturally thought it was hilarious. But joking aside, that sort of stuff was fed back to the selectors, who probably took me for a lazy bastard. Whether that influenced selection or not, I don't know.

Terry Holmes: He took a lot of pressure off me tactically, because I didn't have to bother. I could just play what was in front of me. And his mother made the best Welsh cakes, so I couldn't afford to fall out with him. There was no better pre-match snack than a cup of tea and a Welsh cake.

Gareth Davies: I was dropped twice, once for Gary Pearce and once for Malcolm Dacey. But I don't think I had a serious rivalry with either of them. I wouldn't go out of my way to be sociable with them, but I didn't hate them either. I always considered my personal duel to be with the opposing wing-forward rather than my opposite number. The nutcase that would be hunting me down. Most of the ones I feared were in the Welsh club game. Steve Williams once threatened to kill me at the Gnoll before a ball had even been kicked.

The way my Wales career ended still rankles. I sometimes think I should have packed it in after the first game of the 1985 campaign. I'd been recalled after two seasons in the wilderness, and we had a good win against Scotland. I felt as though I'd proved a point. We then lost a game to Ireland that we should've won, but it didn't go too badly for me personally. I *did* play badly against France, but then the whole team did. The coach, John Bevan, handed Paul Thorburn the lineout kicks, which I considered an insult. The day the team for the England game was due to be announced, I had a call from a journalist telling me that 'AN Other' was going to be listed at fly half. The WRU wanted to keep their options open and weren't willing to commit. Malcolm Dacey had been injured and was coming back on the Saturday for Cardiff versus Swansea. So they were effectively using that as a trial for the fly half position. What confidence does that give you?

Terry Holmes: It was a disgrace. What other country would have done that? It summed up the attitude of those in charge.

Gareth Davies: I spoke to Rod Morgan at the WRU, and said if the team was released to the public with 'AN Other' down as fly half, I was out, I was quitting. He tried to talk me down, but I was adamant. They did it anyway. On the Saturday, Cardiff hammered Swansea by forty points. I scored about 25 of them myself, and Dacey played like a complete prat. I had a call the following morning from Rod Morgan asking if I'd reconsider. I said no. He said, 'Well we can't pick Dacey after yesterday,' to which I replied, 'That's *your* bloody problem.' They thought it was a legitimate thing to do, and that if I outplayed Dacey, they could put me in the team. I looked at it the other way – I'd played more than twenty times for my country, captained my country, and they were effectively putting me on probation. It was demeaning. So that's how Jiffy got his start. I quit, and Dacey played himself out of contention, which meant they had to pick the new guy. If I have any regrets, it's that eighteen months later, there was a World Cup, and had I still been good enough, I could've taken part in that.

And so the baton was passed to the next feted Welsh number ten. The man who carries the hopes and dreams of a nation more heavily than any other. Jonathan Davies was a product of the fly half factory at Gwendraeth Grammar School., like Gareth Davies, Barry John and Carwyn James before him. This rural area between Llanelli and Carmarthen in Welsh-speaking West Wales is unusually fertile when it comes to producing fly halves of wit and invention. There was an element of destiny to Davies's elevation. But while Gareth was all poise and elegance, 'Jiffy' was a runner, a jinker, and an impish jester who took pleasure in making others look stupid. He became renowned for his terrifying turn of pace – an attribute that would leave bewildered back rowers swiping at thin air. But it was his speed of thought that marked him out. He knew what he was going to do before the ball had reached his hands. His coach at Neath, Brian Thomas, once likened him to a chess player, always thinking at least three moves ahead. There is a certain romance to the image of a rugged coalminer or steelworker, bringing his strength and fortitude to bear on the rugby field. But if Wales is indeed a nation with music in its blood and poetry in its soul, then it needs its artisans too. Jonathan Davies was among the finest. It was a difficult time for him to step into the breach, notwithstanding Gareth Davies's enforced retirement. Wales were looking to avoid a humiliating fifth consecutive defeat at their once impregnable National Stadium.

Terry Holmes: He looked like a schoolboy when he arrived, all wide-eyed and innocent. But I'd already played against him, and knew what he was capable of. I promised I'd look after him on his debut, and I did so by barely passing him the ball! But he exuded confidence, and was ultra-positive. He scored that day after chasing his own kick. It was a terrible kick, but he didn't give up on it. International rugby was his destiny. He felt he was made for it. From that day on he strutted around like he owned the place.

The Jonathan Davies era began with a 24–15 victory over England, a match in which his brother-in-law, Phil Davies, also made his debut. The following season saw another changing of the guard as Wales began the 1986 tournament with a new coach and captain. John Bevan had stepped down due to illness, and Terry Holmes departed for a lucrative contract with Bradford Northern. Tony Gray and Derek Quinnell took over as coaches; Neath flanker David Pickering took over the captaincy, and Swansea's Robert Jones filled the scrum half berth vacated by

Holmes. It was another unremarkable campaign, with victories over Scotland and Ireland overshadowed by defeats to England and France. If it was memorable for one thing, it was for an astonishing, gravity-defying place kick that remains a world record to this day. During the Scotland game, Wales were awarded a penalty in their own half, more than seventy yards from the posts. The capacity crowd at the National Stadium seemed to a man bewildered when Paul Thorburn told the referee he was going for the posts. But the Neath full back knew what he was capable of, and when the ball sailed between the uprights, the success-starved Welsh fans at least had something unique to savour.

NINE

I'M GOING TO DIE IN TONGA

At around three o'clock on 12 June, 1986, the waterlogged pitch at Teufaiva Stadium in Nuku'alofa resembled a battlefield. Stricken bodies were splayed out on the soggy turf, as a fearsome Tongan prop went on the rampage, swinging his granite fists at anyone within range. A groggy Adrian Hadley had just been unceremoniously slung into an ambulance. Moments earlier his legs had buckled beneath him after he'd been knocked out by a sickening right hook. John Devereux, the teak-tough centre from Bridgend, was one of the few Welsh players still standing, fists clenched like a pugilist, willing his Tongan assailants to try their luck. The Australian referee, Brian Kinsey, had lost control. The Test match between Tonga and Wales had descended into a brutal free-for-all, and scrum half Robert Jones feared for the lives of some of his colleagues. It was a long way from the idyllic ramble around the South Pacific he'd imagined, but with the first World Cup on the horizon, it was an experience that helped sharpen these Dragons' claws. It all began in Fiji, where things weren't quite as ugly as Tonga, but neither were they for the faint-hearted. Captain David Pickering was the first to receive a welcome, Polynesian style.

Robert Jones: Fiji was by far the nicest place in the South Seas. It was hot. Swelteringly hot, and we trained hard every day. We played hard as well, mind. I've got photos of us sitting around after training in our club kit – we didn't have any official Wales kit – tops off, surrounded by about a hundred cans of beer. It was important to get the fluids back in. As hot as it was, the on-field reception wasn't particularly warm. That first Test was physical.

John Devereux: Their captain, Esala Teleni, jumped over a ruck. Dai Pickering was lying there, and he accidentally stepped right on his head.

Adrian Hadley: There was nothing accidental about it. Dai's head was hanging out the side of the ruck. He lined him up and booted him.

Robert Jones: Dai went into convulsions.

John Devereux: He was twitching horribly, and blood was pouring out of his ear. It affected him badly. I genuinely don't think he's been the same since. His personality changed that day.

Jonathan Davies: He had to go to hospital to have a brain scan.

Robert Jones: We didn't see him for the rest of the trip. He hid himself away in his room.

Robert Norster: He sat like Howard Hughes in the hotel for about ten days, with the curtains drawn. It put a mark on him both physically and mentally.

Adrian Hadley: That was the beginning of the end of Dai's rugby career. He became a lot quieter, more introspective, and his rugby never recovered. He was off the pace after that.

Robert Norster: I got hit in that opening match as well. Modern day player that I was, I was trying to jackal or something, and some fella comes in, boots me in the head, and I ended up sparko on the other side of the ruck. The back of my head opened up. Tudor Jones, our physio, tried to fish-hook tack it in a tent at the side of the pitch. I looked like Frankenstein's monster, with a big zip up the back of my head. As soon as I returned to the field, it popped open again. By the end of the game, my white shorts were soaked with blood, as was my white collar. I swapped shirts with my opposite number before being taken to hospital to have my injury seen to, and by the time I got there, my Fiji shirt looked like a Wales shirt. I'd lost so much blood, it was like jelly spilling out. Huw Richards nearly killed a bloke – this big ugly tight-head that was picking on Phil Davies. Pulled his head out of a ruck and booted him with his studs to get him off the pitch.

Phil Davies: Violence was a continuing theme. It was a brutal tour. To be fair to Tudor, he looked after us. He wasn't a qualified doctor, but there were a lot of illnesses, ailments and battle scars. He was kept pretty busy.

Robert Norster: We'd been vaccinated at the start of the tour. We were all lined up outside a grass hut and told to drop our pants. There were just two needles for the entire squad. One for the forwards, one for the backs. This Fijian fella just kept topping it up as he needed to. It became a spectator sport. You'd get yours done, and race around to watch the next victim. I was rooming with Jeff Whitefoot, and he had a mosquito bite on his elbow that swelled up terribly. I got a horrible boil on my hip, which Tudor had to slice off. It was the size of a golf ball, getting bigger and bigger, and going all yellow and tender. He laid me down on a table, with all the boys watching, and plunged his scalpel in. Once it had deflated, he pulled out a cord of something with his tweezers. God knows what it was. It was like he'd squeezed a toothpaste tube.

Phil Davies: It looked like a rawl plug or something.

Robert Norster: I've still got the bullet hole there to show for it.

John Devereux: Off the pitch, the hospitality was great. We were invited to a curry tea on a merchant navy ship docked in Suva harbour. Our hosts were these British navy officers impeccably turned out in their white shorts, white plimsolls and white hats.

Robert Jones: The infamous night on the Cable and Wireless ship.

John Devereux: Rob can't drink on the best of days, so I was looking after him. We were playing drinking games, and he couldn't handle half of his fines so I was helping him out. Every time you got a question wrong, as well as having to drink, you'd have a mark stamped on your face with a burnt cork.

Robert Jones: The more pissed you got, the more black marks you got on your face.

John Devereux: Rob was in a hell of state, and at one stage, he got up and buggered off. Nobody realised he'd gone. As night fell, a bus arrived to collect us and we all piled on. Next morning we woke up, and realised that not only was Rob not at the hotel, he hadn't been on the bus the previous night.

Robert Jones: I'd fallen asleep in the toilet. When I woke up, the ship was on, the engines were running. I opened the door, and the sailors were studiously going about their business. They're literally ten minutes from setting sail. I was trying to be all polite and explain my situation, with my face covered in bloody black spots.

John Devereux: We were all having breakfast, and he turned up in a taxi, with his clothes all crumpled and his face covered in burnt cork. We were rolling with laughter. It was fucking brilliant.

Adrian Hadley: Another day we went shark fishing, caught a bluefin, and sailed to an island to cook it. We all dived off the boat and swam ashore, and had ourselves a hearty banquet. It was a good while later when someone pointed out that Ian Eidman was missing. We looked back at the boat, and there he was looking lonely and forlorn. No one knew he couldn't swim. Tudor Jones got shitfaced that afternoon, and we nicked his false teeth. He used to do the warm-ups, and the next day he could barely speak. He was hungover to hell, and was all lips and gums.

Jonathan Davies: There was a gang of us. Me, Stuart Evans, Phil Davies, Paul Moriarty – a good set of drinkers. On the bus on the way back, we stripped Tudor naked, leaving him in just his trainers. He had no choice but to walk into the hotel buck naked. He was so pissed he started singing in the lobby. His tender rendition of *Are You Lonesome Tonight* was slightly at odds with his lumpy naked appearance, and as he was delivering the final chorus, the committee men – who'd been to an altogether more civilised function – arrived back. The timing couldn't have been better.

Phil Davies: Someone nicked his shoes as well before the flight out. We were all dressed in our number ones at the airport, and he turns up in a suit with a pair of muddy rugby boots on. He walked up and said, 'Do you reckon this plane will take a stud, boys?'

Adrian Hadley: Fiji was fantastic, but it went downhill from there. Tonga and Western Samoa were completely backward.

Robert Jones: They'd told us beforehand that Tonga was amazing. A gorgeous place, with beautiful people. Paradise, apparently. It was anything but. You'd walk out of the hotel onto a dirty cobbled road strewn with rubbish. Within a hundred yards was the Prime Minister's place which was just a shack. Washing on the line, and a rusty hulk of a car out the front.

Jonathan Davies: The 'Friendly Isles', apparently. We didn't see much evidence of that.

Robert Norster: Nuku'alofa is a tip. An ugly old industrial port town.

Adrian Hadley: While we were checking in to the International Dateline Hotel, a rat walked casually across the front desk. It didn't run or scurry across, it just *ambled* across, and none of the staff seemed remotely bothered about it. We were like, 'What the fuck?' Then when we arrived in our room, the first thing we saw was an industrial-sized can of cockroach repellent. The food was terrible. The pitches were terrible. The medical cover was non-existent.

Robert Norster: Because it was the International Dateline, they had a little duty-free shop, with net curtains. We were all sat there in flip-flops, having some beers one night. It was steaming hot, and Jonesey shouted that there was a rat climbing up the net curtain. We ran out to reception to report it, and the man just looked at us as if to say, 'Yes? Your point being?'

Phil Davies: I thought he was going to offer to cook it for us.

Robert Norster: There were holes in the wall where the air-con units were supposed to be, and we'd have to stuff them with pillows to keep the mosquitoes out. There were mice running around the restaurant. I just lived on cheese and tomato toasties for the ten days we were there. There was a hut out by the swimming pool where they had a little toasting machine.

John Devereux: I had to sit my second year college exams out there. Our head coach, Tony Gray, was the invigilator. They allowed him to do it because he'd worked at Bangor University or something. So I was sat on my own in my room, sweating, with Tony looming over me. I could hear all the boys in the pool outside, building human pyramids, jumping in, larking about. And I'm stuck in there bloody working. It was a nightmare.

Robert Jones: Brian Kempson came in for a bit of abuse on that tour.

John Devereux: The secretary of the Welsh Rugby Union. He looked like Arthur Askey. He spent the entire tour lounging by the pool, smoking, with a hanky on his head.

Phil Davies: We'd go off to training, and he'd be on the sun lounger. We'd come back from training, and he'd *still* be on the lounger. 'All right boys!' He'd be steaming drunk by then.

John Devereux: One day he turned to the boys and said, 'Go on then! You've been dying to do it. Chuck me in the pool.' We picked him up, chucked him in the pool, and went back to our loungers. Next thing . . . where's Brian? We look round. *Blub blub blub.* He's at the bottom of the pool.

Robert Jones: He can't swim, can he? Rob Norster had to dive in to save him. He was just bobbling around at the bottom, with bubbles coming out of his nose.

Robert Norster: I saved him, aye. He was drowning, poor dab.

Jonathan Davies: He said afterwards, 'I didn't want to spoil your fun, boys. I didn't want to tell you I couldn't swim.'

John Devereux: The Tonga Test will always be remembered for the mass brawl. Best fight ever in a Test match. Dirtiest game I've ever played in in my life. And you'll never get to see it again, because the tape mysteriously went missing.

Robert Jones: S4C was recording the match, and were planning to send it home before we left for Samoa, but the tape was nicked from the hotel the night before we left. The game itself was bonkers. There was a curtain-raiser going on, and the King arrived. The game stopped, and everyone just waited for him to make his way to the top of this stand that held about twenty people.

Adrian Hadley: They'd built it in a matter of days. We'd trained on the pitch soon after we arrived, and it was literally just a field. A week later, they'd knocked this breeze-block stand up. The King had to be higher up than everybody else apparently.

Jonathan Davies: After the anthems, we all had to walk up to the top of the stand to shake the King's hand.

John Devereux: We'd been there for ten days, and it had pissed down for nine of them, so the King turned up wearing ski goggles, a knee-length leather coat, and twenty-one-hole Doc Martins. He was at least twenty-five stone.

Adrian Hadley: He looked like Toad of Toad Hall, with his leather cap and ear flaps.

Robert Jones: It was the biggest fight I've ever witnessed. The referee, Brian Kinsey, was never going to be able to control it because it was absolutely brutal. Kicking, punching, the works. Devs was the only back who emerged with honour. He was hitting lumps out of his opposite number.

Jonathan Davies: He was only nineteen as well, fair play. But you had no choice but to get stuck in, otherwise you'd get beat up. Devs was probably the only one who won, if you see what I mean.

John Devereux: The first game we played in Tonga was a warm-up against a President's XV, and Jonathan Davies – our first-choice fly half – had to play, because somebody had dropped out. This nutcase of a prop with a handlebar moustache had a death wish on Jiffy. He was pointing at him before kick-off, and doing the old throat-slit gesture. Jiffy must've been thinking, 'What the hell am I doing here?' He spent the entire game hunting Jiffy down, he couldn't care less where the ball was. He just wanted to kill Jif. He never laid a finger on him though.

Jonathan Davies: I got hit with a late tackle in the warm-up game, and went off. I say tackle – the guy just launched himself at me horizontally. It felt as though my chest had caved in. I was climbing up the stand after coming off, and my chest started to tighten. I could barely breathe and had to get straight in the ambulance. Mark Titley came with me and I genuinely thought I was going to die. My breathing was getting shallower, and I was whimpering. I vividly remember thinking, 'I'm going to die in fucking Tonga. Of all the places in the world, this is where I'm going to breathe my last.' I had no way of even phoning home to say my goodbyes. Mark Titley's crying in the ambulance, saying, 'Don't die on me, Jif.' Eventually, we got to the hospital. There were no doors anywhere, and wild dogs were roaming through the corridors. Nobody was there to greet me – it transpired that all the doctors were at the game! Back at the hotel, I was given a muscle relaxant, which thankfully eased the pain. The next day, I was summoned back to the hospital by the King. He personally intervened to apologise, and had arranged an x-ray. Jeff Whitefoot came with me for moral support, and when the nurse saw that infected boil on his elbow, she insisted on treating it. The scalpel came out, Jeff grabbed my hand, and she plunged the blade in, releasing a seemingly endless torrent of pus. Jeff was clearly in pain, but it was me who was wailing the loudest, as he crushed virtually every bone in my hand. Then on the Saturday I played in the Test.

Robert Jones: A couple of key players nearly missed the Test after a misunderstanding with the police. The changing rooms were tiny, and slightly below ground so there were slats in the roof. We were all warming up and there was a bit of abuse from the fans outside.

John Devereux: They were all peering in at us. The women were leering and whistling.

Robert Jones: So Stuart Evans takes exception, and slams the slats shut. He did it so hard they shattered, and shards of glass flew everywhere. The fucking police came to the ground, with batons drawn, and tried to arrest him. This was minutes before he was due to run out for the Test match.

Adrian Hadley: I could have sworn it was Paul Moriarty who broke it. Chucking the ball around, and working himself into a frenzy like he always used to.

John Devereux: Nah, it was the Bomber, all twenty-three stone of him.

Phil Davies: It was me. I just pulled the lever to shut it, and the whole thing shattered.

Adrian Hadley: George Morgan, the WRU president, had to use all his powers of diplomacy to stop us *all* being arrested.

Phil Davies: Derek Quinnell was trying to physically restrain the coppers from coming in.

Robert Jones: Although with hindsight Stuart probably wished he had been arrested given what was about to happen. He'd have been better off in jail.

John Devereux: The violence started from the first lineout. Tulip [Phil Davies] had his eye on the ball coming in, and from nowhere, a fist smashed into his jaw. *CRACK*. It set the tone pretty early on.

Jonathan Davies: I knew what was coming. I told all the backs to keep their elbow up once they'd passed. At least then, if someone launched themselves at you they'd get a clip, and maybe think twice about doing it again. You're still going to hurt yourself, but they're gonna hurt themselves more. Get it right, and you'll see their heads split like watermelons. You knew it was going to boil over. From the first whistle, there were cheap shots going in, late tackles. Moriarty took exception to something or other, and all of a sudden it was like the Alamo. All fifteen Tongans charged in and surrounded us. The result being, you were squared up to some guy in front of you, fists clenched ready for action, and someone would clout you from behind. Down you go.

John Devereux: It was fifteen Tongans against fourteen Welshmen, because Malcolm Dacey was having a Woodbine on the halfway line watching all the fighting.

Robert Jones: Their prop, Tevita Bloomfield, who'd played against Wales in 1979, was playing. He must've been approaching forty, he was grey-haired, and had ripples on the back of his neck. He was a man mountain, and was just going round knocking everyone out.

Jonathan Davies: He was older than that. He'd played against Wales in 1974. I know because I was playing in the curtain-raiser. An under-12s game between West and East Wales.

John Devereux: He was a tough bastard. We watched the video back in the hotel. We just wanted to see this prop forward going about his business. Billy James. *CRACK*. One punch. Stuart Evans. *CRACK*. One punch. He was like a tornado roaring through a forest. Have you seen Thor with his lump hammer? It was like that. This psycho marauding around calmly picking out his victims. *BANG. You're* having it. *BANG*.

Robert Jones: Adolf [Adrian Hadley]. One punch.

John Devereux: Adolf was snoring before he hit the floor.

Adrian Hadley: All I can remember is that someone was holding Stuart Evans by the arm, and another bloke was punching him. He couldn't defend himself, so I ran in and thumped the guy that was hitting Stuart.

John Devereux: And then Bowesy [Bleddyn Bowen] comes in, my centre partner, and *SMACK*, he launches this punch at Bloomfield. It hit him on the side of the jaw, and Bloomfield didn't flinch. His jaw was made of granite. He turned around and started running after Bowesy.

Robert Jones: Bledd starts running away into the stand, trying to get away, and the crowd are pushing him back onto the pitch.

Adrian Hadley: I saw it on the video afterwards. Bleddyn vaults the fence and disappears into the crowd. And all of a sudden he comes flying back. They picked him up and chucked him back onto the pitch.

Phil Davies: They slung him back like a slingshot.

John Devereux: So he's back on the pitch now and ends up running figures of eight round the posts with Bloomfield chasing him. It was like something from Benny Hill.

Robert Jones: Mark Brown was being kicked around on the floor like a rag doll by about three or four of them. I was trying to play peacemaker by getting between them.

Robert Norster: The guy I was marking was about six foot eight, and his arms were twice as long as mine. There was a bit of a dust-up, and Adolf jumps in the middle like Batman. Then *WHACK*, Bloomfield unleashed his haymaker, and Adolf's gone. He nearly did his cruciate ligament on the way down. Poleaxed.

John Devereux: Adolf is lying face down in the mud, unconscious. They drove an ambulance onto the field. I say ambulance, it was an estate car with a cross painted on the door. It was doing wheelspins as it came onto the pitch. They picked him up and *chucked* him in the back. And then it got stuck in the mud, so they had to push it off the field. They'd have been quicker carrying him off.

Phil Davies: It was like something from *Naked Gun*. Farcical.

Robert Norster: Because it had been pissing down for ten days, the pitch was a swamp, and the 'ambulance' left two massive trenches in its wake. At the next scrum, we were packing down in the trench.

John Devereux: There was no doctor with Adolf, so guess who goes with him? Duty boy for the day, Kevin Hopkins.

Robert Jones: Hoppy's Holidays! He pulled his hamstring in the first training session, and didn't play a minute on tour. He lived in his tracksuit.

Adrian Hadley: The only recollection I have is waking up in the hospital with Hoppy holding my hand.

John Devereux: Apparently there were no doctors at the hospital either, because they were all at the game again.

Adrian Hadley: I saw a nurse, and she basically said, 'You'll be alright in a minute,' and discharged me. I had to bloody *walk* back to the game. And then some jobsworth wouldn't let Hoppy and I back in. I was still in my bloody kit, boots and everything.

Robert Jones: Unbelievably the game carried on after the mass brawl. And not long after, in front of the ref, Bloomfield hits Phil Davies again from behind. He's down on the deck, blood coming out of his mouth, and I said to Dicky Moriarty, 'Please, you've got to take us off. Someone's going to get killed.'

Jonathan Davies: It was that bad. They were all massive blokes, who didn't seem to feel pain. I've never seen anything like it. We won the match, but lost the fight. I think Devs was the only one who emerged with any credit in that regard. He gave his opposite number a tuning.

John Devereux: The crowd was going berserk. They loved to see us scrapping. That's their mentality. It was hit or be hit. The ref tried to assert his authority, warning that the next player to throw a punch would be sent off. Dicky pulled us over and said, 'Boys, next time it kicks off, I don't care who you're standing next to, twat 'em.' It's a real shame the video went missing. Everybody thought that Webby [Glen Webbe] nicked it. It was his first cap, and the rumour was that he pinched it as a souvenir.

Robert Jones: If the tape had survived, and the IRB had got hold of it, there could have been some serious repercussions.

Phil Davies: Tonga would have been banned for some time.

Robert Jones: Back at the rat-infested International Dateline Hotel, it was time for the speeches. And as Dicky Moriarty couldn't speak Welsh, they asked Jiffy if he could do something.

John Devereux: He just *slated* them.

Robert Jones: He stood there with a smile on his face, saying, 'This is the biggest shithole I've ever been to in my life, the weather is appalling, the food is worse, and you are the dirtiest team I've ever played against.' The Tongans were smiling and clapping in what they thought were the right places, completely oblivious.

Jonathan Davies: I didn't insult anyone personally, at least I don't think I did. I just said, 'You kicked the shit out of us. This is the worst place I've ever been, and we can't wait to get out of here.'

Adrian Hadley: The irony was they all gave him a standing ovation.

John Devereux: All the while the WRU committee men were sliding further into their seats with their heads in their hands.

Robert Jones: Samoa, by way of contrast, was a lovely place. Gorgeous people. We stayed at Aggie Grey's which was lovely.

John Devereux: It was *boiling*. We arrived and the commentators Huw Llewelyn Davies and Lyn Davies had already been there a few days, and their faces were like beetroots.

John Devereux: Samoa was a better game. They were physical alright, but there was no fighting. Michael Jones played for them before he switched allegiance to the All Blacks. I scored my first try for Wales, but I gave one away as well to be fair. I had a kick charged down and they scored.

Phil Davies: Webby got tripped up by a spectator at one point. He was away down the wing, and some Samoan woman stuck her umbrella out and sent him flying.

Adrian Hadley: After the post-match function, a load of local girls came back to the hotel with us, and we went skinny dipping in the pool. When we got out, all our gear had gone. Everything. Blazers, ties, shoes, socks even. They'd taken the whole lot. They're probably still walking around wearing them now.

Robert Jones: It was a brilliant six weeks, and I genuinely believe that the spirit forged there was what made us go on to have a successful World Cup the following year.

Adrian Hadley: I think that's why the WRU did it: to toughen us up ahead of what was to come.

Robert Norster: It brought us together, that tour. Because of all the fighting, we learned to watch each other's backs, and we became closer as a result. At the time, it felt like living hell. Ten days in Tonga in the pissing rain, but I look back on it now with nothing but fondness. Sometimes in adversity, you have the best times.

The fruits of such an arduous tour took a little time to ripen. The following Five Nations was particularly underwhelming. Defeats to Scotland, Ireland, and France, were punctuated by an ugly win against England in Cardiff. Phil Davies must have thought he was back in Nuku'alofa when another fist came thundering into his face at a lineout. Wade Dooley may have been a policeman, but that didn't temper his propensity for violence. Davies left the field with a broken jaw, and was denied the chance to speak to a repentant Dooley the following day. The call came through to Davies's father-in-law's house, where he and his wife were living at the time. Kenny – aggrieved on his son-in-law's behalf – slammed the phone down on Dooley. The RFU banned him and three of his colleagues for their part in what was another ill-tempered Wales–England affair, and Wales had to settle for a lowly fourth place in the Championship after losing to Ireland in the final round. They'd face the same opponents in the opening round of the first ever Rugby World Cup seven weeks later.

TEN

I BROKE LYNAGH'S NOSE

Expectations weren't especially high heading into the first ever World Cup, although the format of sixteen teams, divided into four pools of four, meant Wales were favoured to reach the quarter-finals. Topping the pool – which contained Ireland, Tonga, and Canada – would probably mean avoiding Australia in the last eight. The Rugby World Cup has since grown into a behemoth of a tournament, the world's third biggest sporting event, and the game's most lucrative cash cow. Back in 1987, times were simpler, preparations more primitive, and some of the players had other things on their minds.

John Devereux: I was still studying for my degree at this point, so I had to fly down to Wellington a day early to sit another exam. Ray Williams [WRU secretary] and myself flew down together. While the boys were in Auckland receiving their caps, I was sprawled on my bed in a Wellington B&B doing some last-minute revising. I woke up jetlagged, and covered in books and notes having fallen asleep. Ray drove me to the University of Wellington so I could sit the exam. I was in a huge room, on my own, with a woman sat at the front, knitting. That's how my World Cup began. I actually sat it before anyone in Cardiff, so I could have rung them all up and told them the answers.

Ieuan Evans: The global attention was minimal. There was barely anyone at the press conferences. The doomsayers were questioning its worth before it had even begun.

Jonathan Davies: It was all done on the cheap, but we didn't know any different. We were amateurs, most of us had to take time off work to go out there.

Ieuan Evans: There was no turning left on the plane [to business class]. We turned right, and there were some big boys folded into cramped seats. It was a long and torturous journey.

Paul Thorburn: The plane journey took twenty-four hours. When we arrived, the coaches, Derek Quinnell and Tony Gray, were so enthusiastic, they put us straight on a training pitch for the hardest session we'd ever experienced in our lives. We had six serious injuries straight away. Billy James flew home two days later.

Ieuan Evans: New Zealand were ten years ahead of us. That 1987/88 side was the best side I've ever seen. Period. Some of the finest players ever to have graced a rugby field. Michael Jones was the best all-round rugby player I've ever come across. He was a phenomenal athlete. Buck Shelford, the Whetton boys, staggeringly good.

John Devereux: Grant Fox, Joe Stanley, Warwick Taylor, Sean Fitzpatrick, Richard Loe. A roll call of legends.

Robert Jones: John Kirwan told me about a forum that was held before the World Cup, between the current players, and some of the previous generation of All Blacks. The older guys told them, 'We've always been regarded as the best in the world. Now for the first time ever, you guys have got a chance to go out and prove it.' According to Kirwan, that really sunk in. From that moment, they became professional in their approach. They trained harder, they became fitter and they became stronger.

Jonathan Davies: I remember talking to Sean Fitzpatrick, and he said the players had been told, 'You focus on that rectangle of grass, and we'll take care of everything else.' Hotels, clothing, all that admin stuff that could have been a distraction was taken care of for them.

Adrian Hadley: Our preparation was a bit less thorough. We had a 'training camp' in Tenby before we left for New Zealand. We went out on the lash on the Saturday night, and then got up on Sunday morning to do a public fun run on Saundersfoot beach. That was it. A shambles.

John Devereux: They'd have three thousand people watching their training sessions, and they wouldn't drop the ball once. They were hellbent on perfection. You never saw them going down injured either. Even if they were hurt, they wouldn't want the opposition to know.

Adrian Hadley: Back then, if we did an interview for Welsh television, we didn't get paid. A cheque would go to the WRU, but we'd never see a penny. We weren't allowed to promote anything. The All Blacks were all over the TV, doing adverts, driving cars with their names plastered all over them. They were being looked after.

Paul Thorburn: Ray Williams had us in the team room in Auckland, just before the pre-event dinner. He called us in to remind us of the amateur regulations, stressing the importance of the game's values.

Jonathan Davies: We sat down to watch New Zealand versus Italy, the opening game, and Ray brought letters round spelling out that we couldn't make any money from the World Cup. Then there are two adverts before the game starts. The first was John Kirwan advertising acne cream, the second was Andy Dalton driving a tractor. That highlighted in black and white the difference between the northern and southern hemisphere. They may not have been making money from playing the *game*, but they were being allowed to exploit their celebrity. They could have got any old farmer to do that advert – it just so happened that Andy Dalton was captain of the All Blacks, and John Kirwan was Goldenbollocks. It wasn't a level playing field.

Mark Ring: We always felt confident we could get to the semi-finals because South Africa weren't there. There was never any doubt we could beat Ireland, even though we'd lost to them two months earlier. We knew we had better players and never considered them a major threat. I scored my only try for Wales in that game. It was the first Welsh try in the first World Cup. The magnitude of that didn't sink in at the time. Years later, I was taking part in a quiz, and there was a tiebreaker question to win it: who scored Wales's first try in the very first World Cup? I said Ieuan Evans.

Mark Ring's try turned out to be the highlight of a forgettable match in Wellington, played on a day when New Zealand's capital more than lived up to its reputation as the Windy City. Atrocious conditions meant running rugby was off the menu, and Wales had to dig in to overturn a 6–0 half-time deficit. A Paul Thorburn penalty and two Jonathan Davies drop goals were enough to see off their biggest rivals in pool two.

Adrian Hadley: Wellington was miserable. It pissed down, and was blowing a gale. We didn't have much kit, and it was wet the entire time. We'd train in the pouring rain, peel our kit off, hang it on the radiators, and it would still be cold and damp the following day. The hotel staff were up to their eyeballs trying to keep on top of our laundry.

Paul Thorburn: It was that windy, the pilot had trouble landing the plane. He had a few goes at it, didn't manage to land, and then we had to go and refuel in Auckland. It was seriously windy on the day as well. There was an exposed stand at the top of Wellington Park, and my parents were right at the top of it. They thought they were going to blow away. We had a penalty longer than the one I kicked against Scotland, and it was that windy, I went for it. Completely fucked it up, though.

Jonathan Davies: One of the stands was shut because it was too dangerous. We just took our opportunities and won.

Phil Davies: My most enduring memory from the Ireland game is of Willie Anderson climbing onto the table at the post-match dinner, and giving us a wheezing, rasping recital on the bagpipes. Halfway through, he lost his balance, stacked it, and ended up in a heap on the floor, covered in vol-au-vents.

Wales beat Tonga next, thanks to a Glen Webbe hat-trick. His first score came from a searing run and a dummy in the left corner, the second from a beautifully judged Mark Ring kick-pass, and the third a solo length-of-the-field effort. It was a virtuoso performance, but he ended the game not knowing where he was, or who he was.

John Devereux: The Tonga game was billed as a rematch from the previous year.

Phil Davies: Given what had happened, we just wanted to get out of it alive with our heads still attached to our shoulders.

Adrian Hadley: The eyes of the world were on them on this occasion, so they were much better behaved. There was no all-out brawling this time.

Mark Ring: Glen Webbe got badly concussed in that game. The Tongan full back, Tali Ete'aki, flew into the tackle and knocked him out.

John Devereux: We had to pull this guy's head out of Webby's chest. He'd speared him. Literally tackled him with his head. It was a brutal hit.

Robert Jones: We found out about a year or two later that Ete'aki lost his arm in a machete attack. It didn't really surprise us. There was something of the wild man about him.

Mark Ring: Webby and I were very close, and I knew he wasn't right. I told our captain, Dick Moriarty, that he was struggling and he said, 'Just look after him, keep the ball away from him.' Tonga were causing us problems. The wind was howling, they were kicking it up in the air, and no one was fielding it. They put one up-and-under up, and I was back chasing it. It was swirling all over the place, and by the time I gathered it, I knew the defence was up so I instinctively rolled it out to one of our players. It was Webby. Having just said I'd keep the ball away from him, I've gone and thrown it to him. Moments later, he's gone and scored the most sensational individual try I've ever seen. He's gone from the middle of the field in his own half, and ended up under the posts.

Ieuan Evans: I don't think he knew where he was going, but it was a hell of a run.

Mark Ring: I had to scream at him to ground the ball because his head was in the shed. I went up to congratulate him, and he looked at me through narrowed eyes, and said, 'I know you. Where am I? It's you Ringy, who are all these other people?' Then he started crying. I'd never seen a grown man cry before. He was in a right state, properly traumatised.

Adrian Hadley: At one point, he was running in completely the wrong direction, and it was only when he saw Paul Thorburn, our full back, that he turned round.

Robert Jones: The fact we were wearing green didn't help. Glen got up from a ruck and went and stood in their defensive line. At one point someone said, 'He doesn't know who he is.' So I piped up, 'Tell him he's Barry John.'

Ieuan Evans: He took a horrific smack, and was still in serious distress in the changing rooms afterwards. It was quite unsettling. There was no way he was going to play again after that.

Adrian Hadley: I can remember Ringy crying when they said Glen had to go home. They were pretty close, those two.

Jonathan Davies: He kept asking me what the score was in the dressing room. I told him he'd scored a hat-trick, and he was just looking at me blankly and saying 'Huh?' He wouldn't have been able to tell you his own name if you'd have asked him. He broke down after a while because it was actually quite scary.

Mark Ring: There was a prize of a Mazda car for the team who scored the best try of the tournament. So we came up with a move called – originally – 'Mazda'. It was actually a variation of something France had been doing. You should never copy another team's set plays, but France had this brilliant one at the time. The ten would pass to the twelve, the twelve would turn his back, the ten would loop wide. The twelve would dummy outside to him, dummy inside to the blind-side winger, and then do a no-look pass to the full back coming into the line. You can just picture Blanco going through that hole. It looked a million dollars when they did it. But we weren't France, and Paul Thorburn wasn't Serge Blanco. He mistimed his run so badly, he ended up treading on Malcolm Dacey's ankle. The two of them ended up in a heap on the floor, and the ball bobbled harmlessly away.

Adrian Hadley: It was like something from the *Keystone Cops*.

Mark Ring: It ended up on a video of World Cup cock-ups. You could see me clocking what was happening and almost trying to pull the ball back in slow motion before it was too late. It was embarrassing.

We ended up down at the bottom of the world in Invercargill for the Canada game, and let's just say the accommodation was less than salubrious. It was all done on the cheap. We weren't in hotels, we were in *motels*. It was freezing cold down there.

Adrian Hadley: It was a proper one-horse town. We went out to the local pub, and it was deserted. But the barman twigged that we were the Welsh rugby team, got on the phone, and within half an hour, the whole town was in there. It was heaving.

Robert Norster: It was one of those places – you walk in, the piano player stops, and everyone turns to stare. Glen had his t-shirt's sleeves rolled up, showing off his guns. In the corner, they had those little arm-wrestle tables, with the handles to grab onto. The clientele all looked like extras from one of those black and white films – all naval hats and tattoos. They were pretty nasty looking, a few of them. After Webby had had a few sherbets, he challenged them to an arm wrestle. He beat them all. Left handed, right handed, didn't matter. I was worried we wouldn't get out alive because he'd wounded their pride so badly.

Adrian Hadley: The hotel had been built for the visit of the Queen in the fifties. They still had those old cast iron radiators from the period, and when the heating came on the pipes would rattle and shake and keep you awake.

Phil Davies: I was wearing my tracksuit and my coat to bed, and I still couldn't get warm.

Ieuan Evans: Despite the conditions, the pitch in Invercargill was incredible. One of the finest tracks I've played on. We were still playing on boggy pitches back home where your boots ended up covered in muck. They have the same amount of rain in New Zealand as we have in Wales, but they put so much more effort into their pitches. That helps with skill, and with the quality of the games. It suited us, we were scoring tries. We played 'wide-wide' because we had to.

Adrian Hadley: Canada were hyping themselves up. They were strutting around the streets with their mohican haircuts thinking they were the business. We battered them.

Robert Norster: They were a good side to be fair. Al Charron, Gareth Rees, Hans de Goede. Some good ball players, and they had that North American can-do attitude. Never short on confidence, those boys.

Jonathan Davies: At half-time we were only 9–6 ahead, and I said to the forwards, 'Right boys, just give us the ball. I don't care how you do it, just give us the ball.'

That was the turning point. All of a sudden, Ieuan scores four tries. We cut them to pieces.

Ieuan Evans: My four tries equalled Maurice Richards' record for a Welshman in a Test match. The only downside was that I had to drink a glass of Bluff oysters afterwards. It made me violently ill, and I've never touched an oyster since.

Robert Norster: Bluff Cove oysters, the biggest in the world, supposedly. They were *monstrous*. It wasn't just Ieuan; we got into a bit of a contest. Anthony Buchanan struggled. There was a big steel bucket full of them. You'd have to stand up, pluck one out, swallow it, all the best, have a drink. Bucs hated the thought of eating an oyster. He was coughing and retching, and just couldn't keep them down. Every time he thought he'd managed one, it'd just shoot back out like a projectile.

Ieuan Evans: Stuart Evans injured his ankle in that Canada game, and John Rawlins was plucked straight from his holiday to join us as Stuart's replacement. He tore his hamstring in his first training session, and flew straight home.

John Devereux: Straight off the plane, and into a sprinting drill. We had one doctor, and one physio. We didn't know then what we do now. Stretching was minimal, nutrition barely existed as a concept. We were all drinking gallons of Coke before games.

Paul Thorburn: Ireland did something similar, launched themselves into an intensive session after the long flight, and their coach had a heart attack. They were our first opponents, and it happened a few days before the game.

And so to the quarter-final where one of rugby's oldest and fiercest rivalries was resumed in the unfamiliar setting of Ballymore, in Brisbane. Wales had spent the previous fortnight living out of suitcases in a wintry and rainswept New Zealand. England had been based in Brisbane for the same period. It was just a short hop across the Tasman, but it was a world away when it came to climate and conditions. The travel-weary Welsh arrived to discover an England squad basking in the Queensland sunshine.

Ieuan Evans: We rocked up in Brisbane and England were all toned and tanned. We had our typical Welsh colour. Pale-skinned and rosy-cheeked.

Adrian Hadley: England thought their pack was going to destroy us, and the press agreed with them. But we were pretty confident. They didn't have anything that worried us.

Robert Norster: We weren't super confident, but we didn't fear them. Most of our boys felt individually superior to their opposite numbers.

Mark Ring: We won at a canter, 16–3. They were lucky to get three. They were really awful, we barely moved out of second gear.

Paul Thorburn: Dai Young got his first cap that day, at the age of nineteen.

Clive Rowlands (tour manager): We'd had a few injuries, so I told the union, 'We're going to get two new players in. Dai Young and Richard Webster. They're both playing up in Canberra.' 'How do you know that?' they asked. My son, Dewi had told me. And I'd been watching these two play because of him. They may have been teenagers, but they were already men amongst boys. I got a message to them both to report to the Welsh squad immediately. And when they did I thought two fucking hobos had turned up. They had holes in their trousers, and were wearing flip-flops. I'd never seen anything like it. They were like tramps. I remember saying to Ray Williams, 'Do me a favour Ray, get them down to a gentlemen's outfitters, and then a sports shop and come back with a full set of new kit.' When they came back, they looked sharp, tidy.

John Devereux: I'm not sure Webster was officially on the tour at that point, he just bummed along and kipped on Dai's floor.

Jonathan Davies: It was an awful game. The rain was heavy, the pitch was greasy, and England weren't interested in playing any football. I'm not sure the southern hemisphere crowd was particularly impressed. This was their first real exposure to Five Nations-style rugby, and we didn't exactly put on a show.

Ieuan Evans: England were highly fancied, but we won easily. Rob Jones scored a good try chasing his own kick, and outpacing Richard Harding. And Devereux sealed it with the interception.

John Devereux: It was a shitty game, but we beat them. They had booked a hotel on the Gold Coast for three days' R&R after that game, assuming they'd win. Beating them was satisfying, but not as satisfying as taking their hotel booking.

Adrian Hadley: People say it was arrogant of England to have booked the hotel in advance, but our management hadn't booked *anything*. They clearly didn't have much faith in us.

John Devereux: In hindsight, perhaps we shouldn't have gone on the piss for three days in the middle of a World Cup.

Jonathan Davies: Although we wouldn't have beaten New Zealand even if *they'd* been on the piss all week and we'd been tucked up in bed.

Wales would have been forgiven for heading into the semi-final against New Zealand with a degree of confidence. But this All Blacks side was a relentless, unforgiving machine, stacked with world class players conditioned to show no mercy. They were to a man skilful footballers, but they were also intimidating physical specimens. The pack was comprised of rugged farmers and Maori warriors, seemingly built from granite and impervious to pain. They were fitter, stronger, and hungrier than their shell-shocked opponents. The gulf in class was obvious from the first whistle, and it widened further with the sending off of Huw Richards for his part in an early brawl. Wayne Shelford had responded in kind, but escaped the referee's censure. By the time the clock ticked over into eighty minutes, Wales's try line had been breached eight times, and the mighty All Blacks were just a point shy of a half century.

Phil Davies: It was on a Sunday, which meant Michael Jones wasn't playing because of his religious convictions, so we thought we'd have a chance with the world's best player missing. But his replacement, Mark Brooke-Cowden, was awesome, and scored the first try.

Paul Thorburn: You realised when you were stood behind the posts after just a couple of minutes that it was going to be a long day at the office.

Phil Davies: DQ [Derek Quinnell] said before the game, 'I can sense something special's going to happen today, boys.' Yeah Derek, a record defeat.

Jonathan Davies: *I* thought we had a chance. We knew our backs could cause them problems if we could get some tidy ball. But they kept pushing us back, kept stealing our lineouts. The possession and territory stats were mind-blowing. They annihilated us up front. Their forwards were savage.

Robert Norster: They were streetwise too. I've still got scars on my legs, courtesy of Richard Loe, and Steve McDowall was a judo expert who could hoodwink the ref. He'd use these techniques. If he got you prone on the floor, he'd grab your shirt and pull it across your windpipe. It looks like nothing's happening, but he's choking the fuck out of you, basically. Then you get up and retaliate, and you're the villain. He was cute at that.

John Devereux: They came in waves. They were impossible to stop. It was like a runaway truck travelling downhill.

Adrian Hadley: Kirwan destroyed us. He was big and quick, and a great rugby player.

I got tied into the ruck once, and he got outside me and scored, but for his other try he came off the inside centre straight down the middle. We couldn't get our hands on the ball. They weren't necessarily better footballers, but they were better prepared physically. They'd been in camp for weeks beforehand, whereas we had to take leave from work just to go. Steve Blackmore took *unpaid* leave. That was the reality.

Mark Ring: I was on the bench. We knew it would take a colossal effort to win, but we didn't realise quite how big the gulf was until we took to the field. It was totally one-sided. It was clear that they were streets ahead in terms of professionalism. But I didn't obsess over that. I just thought about us. There's no point feeling sorry for yourself. We were just playing rugby against fifteen men, but the match was sobering. Most of us had never experienced a defeat of more than ten or twelve points, so to go down by forty was plain embarrassing.

Adrian Hadley: The changing room was a dark place. We were in a state of shock.

Ieuan Evans: I don't think you can blame the WRU in isolation. All the northern hemisphere unions were caught unawares by how quickly rugby was progressing. It was laid bare in that semi-final. Having a man sent off didn't help, mind. Buck Shelford should have gone as well. There was a sense of grievance over that. What's good for the goose is good for the gander. But it would have taken a brave referee to have sent Buck Shelford off in a World Cup semi-final. It may have been in Brisbane, but it was New Zealand's World Cup. We were on the back foot before we'd even broken sweat.

Adrian Hadley: Huw Richards didn't even know he'd been sent off. He'd been knocked out and was carried off.

Mark Ring: We got absolutely mullered in that semi-final, and yet we came third in the world. The third-place play-off was played on pure emotion. You talk about having time to think, time on the ball, there was none of that. It was highly charged and played purely on instinct.

John Devereux: People talk about the third-place play-off being a nothing game. But that was the first ever World Cup, so don't tell me it was a nothing game.

Robert Jones: We'd just been humiliated. We had a few days' drinking to drown our sorrows. And then we realised we had one chance to redeem ourselves against one of the best sides in the world.

John Devereux: Our pride was dented, and then the Aussies rubbed salt into the wound with their negative comments in the press. It amounted to 'why the fuck do we have to play a third-place play-off against this rabble, who are clearly shit?' That hurt us. And it motivated us.

Adrian Hadley: It was a chance to put things right. Let's get back on the horse.

The Wallabies, devastated by their semi-final defeat to France, were less enthusiastic about the game than Wales, but despite the sending off of their flanker, David Codey, in the opening minutes, they still found themselves 21–16 ahead as the match entered injury time. It took a last-gasp try by Adrian Hadley, and a nerveless touchline conversion by Paul Thorburn to secure the win, and cement Wales's status as the third best team in the world.

Robert Norster: There wasn't much of a ceremony about it in those days, mind. The ref just brandished the red card and you were gone. No fuss, no protest. Codey was a bit of a twat, mind. He'd been in the papers a lot, quite vocal, quite opinionated, and pretty abrasive on the pitch.

John Devereux: They were slating us during the match as well as before it. Campo was muttering about how useless we were, calling Thorby a 'fucking slug', and saying we didn't deserve to be playing rugby.

Robert Jones: Devs was just looking for fucking victims, going on the rampage with that famous hand-off of his. It was a lovely day, we had a load of support as it was in Rotorua, full of New Zealanders who hated the Aussies.

Ieuan Evans: The play-off was significant because we beat a southern hemisphere country away from home. There was a terrific atmosphere, the Kiwis were cheering us on. The stands were full of Maoris wearing red.

Jonathan Davies: The whole World Cup was geared up for a New Zealand–Australia final. France messed it up for the organisers, and Australia just didn't want to be there. They wanted to toss a coin to decide who was going to be third.
  I broke Michael Lynagh's nose. Rob Jones went on a break, I went with him, and Lynagh tugged me back, and smacked me from behind. So next time he had the ball, I showed him the outside, and smashed him with a high tackle. They knew then we were up for it.

John Devereux: Jiffy put a bomb up. I caught it, went to ground, chucked it back. Ieuan played scrum half. He slung it out to Bowesey, to Ringo, to Thorby. Great hand-off, passed it to Adolf. Adolf touches down. And Thorby nails the kick. Great kick, fucking hell.

Paul Thorburn: He could have put it down nearer the posts.

Adrian Hadley: It was the right side for a right-sided goal-kicker. I knew Thorby would get it. He was in the zone. I didn't feel remotely nervous about it.

John Devereux: I knew the moment he'd struck it, just by listening to the crowd. Everyone started running on the pitch with Welsh flags. They thought the game was over. We had to shoo them off. They restarted, and won the bloody ball back. Campese ran half the length of the field, and had he passed it, they would have won.

John Devereux: The Aussies locked themselves in a private room in the hotel after the game, and didn't come out *all* night. I thought that was poor.

Robert Jones: There was an arrogance, they didn't act in a dignified way.

Paul Thorburn: We did what we could to make them feel small. The captain Andrew Slack was very ungracious post-match. He went on to say anyone who knows anything about rugby would realise that they only lost because they were reduced to fourteen men. They weren't willing to give us any credit, they just wanted to look for excuses.

Adrian Hadley: We wanted to party, but they weren't interested in socialising. They were very sore losers. That's when they started saying they weren't interested in third place, and they claimed they hadn't even wanted to play the game. But you certainly didn't sense that during the match. To claim that afterwards was a load of bollocks.

Paul Thorburn: I think Campese was alright. I seem to remember having a few beers with him afterwards.

Mark Ring: The win banished memories of the semi-final. We felt really proud. We finished third, and that's never been bettered by a Welsh side. I felt completely drained when I came off the field. Physically and emotionally. I couldn't stop crying. I was so proud. Tony Gray put his arm around me and said, 'Ringo, you weren't that bad.' He thought I was crying because I'd had a shit game, but I didn't care about my game, I just cared about winning. It wasn't until a fortnight later, when one of the boys said, 'Yeah, but that bloke got sent off after about six minutes, didn't he?' I didn't have a clue. It completely passed me by.

On the way home, we were in transit at LA Airport, and I didn't have the patience to queue for security. How we got away with this at LA Airport, I'll never know, but I just ducked under the rope, and Ieuan followed me. We got through to the lounge, and this bloke saw the badges on our blazers and started chatting to us. 'From Wales are you, boys?' I said, 'Yeah', and asked where he was from. It was only bloody Tom Jones.

Adrian Hadley: It was surreal. He had a big bouncer with him, and his wife was asleep on the bar.

Mark Ring: I bought him a pint. Heineken with a dash of lemonade for Ieuan and me, and Tom said, 'I'll have what you're having.' His missus had a half. Within half an hour the rest of the boys arrived, and Alan Phillips took over, holding court as he likes to do, getting Tom to sign everything, so he could sell it. Typical Thumper.

Adrian Hadley: Thumper was all over him like a rash. 'Can you sign this, can you sign that, if ever you're back in Wales, come back to the hotel and have a few beers with the boys.' Later, we're at the hotel in LA, having a few beers in the bar. Ringy goes up to reception, and says, 'Can you ring Alan Phillips please, and tell him Tom Jones is in reception.' So we're all sat at the bar directly opposite the lifts. Thumper is down like a shot, and out of the lift within sixty seconds. He sees us all there doubled over laughing, shakes his head, and disappears straight back into the lift. He wasn't happy.

ELEVEN

MUNCH THE CRUNCH,
OR WHATEVER THEY CALLED HIM

The third-place finish exceeded Wales's expectations, but there was a feeling that it instilled a sense of complacency, allowing the administrators to bury the memories of the New Zealand semi-final. As Gerald Davies said at the time, 'A sense of delusion has crept insidiously in.' Put bluntly, Wales weren't as good as they thought they were. Rumours began to swirl that changes would be made, particularly in the backline. Jonathan Davies – who, by his own admission, hadn't excelled in the World Cup – felt his place was under threat. There were four fly halves vying for the jersey. When the team for the opening Five Nations game against England was announced, the fly half conundrum had been solved. Tony Gray picked them all. Bleddyn Bowen – who'd played at fly half in a 46–0 win against the USA – was named as captain and inside centre, with Mark Ring outside him. Anthony Clement, the twenty-year-old Swansea fly half, was named at full back – a position he'd never played before. In order to accommodate him, Gray dropped Paul Thorburn, who just months earlier had played a pivotal role in Wales's march to third place in the World Cup. The reason was that Wales wanted to adopt a more open, creative style, and that having a back division littered with footballing fly halves would encourage that. It was a backline brimming with vision, and with two deadly finishers in Ieuan Evans and Adrian Hadley, Wales had the means to create space, and the players to exploit it. What they needed was a pack of forwards to get them the ball.

Ieuan Evans: We were a good footballing side. We may not have had the might up front, but we could play. As a winger, when your ten–twelve–thirteen is Jiffy, Mark Ring, and Bleddyn Bowen, you know you're going to get some ball. Add in Anthony Clement at full back, and you had four fly halves on the field. The game was based more on spontaneity. Coaches would be specific on things like scrums and lineouts, but when it came to attacking, they'd let you go. You were given the space to breathe.

John Devereux: Thorby being dropped was a massive shock.

Jonathan Davies: That showed that no one's position was safe.

John Devereux: He'd kicked the bloody conversion that got us third place. Not just that, he'd never let Wales down.

Jonathan Davies: I remember being in training when the team was read out. Thorby went white.

Paul Thorburn: It was the way it happened that was the issue. It would have been nice if someone had pulled me aside and said, 'Hey Paul, bad news I'm afraid.' But it was announced in a crowded changing room in front of the whole squad. They've never been any bloody good at that though, have they? But it is what it is. They brought in Clem, a better running full back, and that's the way it goes.

Anthony Clement: I felt as though I had to apologise to Thorb, but to be fair to him, he was the first to congratulate me. I was as shocked as anyone, but I was flattered as well. I'd been six seasons at Swansea, and I'd always been a ten. They felt they needed a bit more adventure, a bit more of an unorthodox approach. Swansea arranged a game at Lansdowne three weeks before the start of the tournament, and I played fifteen in that. It was the first time I'd ever played there. The second was for Wales against England at Twickenham.

Mark Ring: I was itching to see what Twickenham was all about, so I was the first in the dressing room that day. There were loads of tele messages there in a pile, as they were called then. I picked the first one up from the top, and it said, 'Kick fuck out of the English bastards, Spike Milligan.' Brilliant. I wish I'd kept it. People ask me if it was satisfying to beat them on their own patch, but we expected to. They weren't all that good back then. I played with Will Carling for the Barbarians once, and I couldn't believe how ordinary he was. Their backs that day offered no threat. Les Cusworth, Jon Webb, they were all so pedestrian.

Ieuan Evans: They were very leaden-footed, very one-dimensional. The first four times I played England, we won. They always kept the grass really long at Twickenham. I'm convinced they did it to stop footballing teams like us getting into our stride. It used to come above your boots. You'd spend half your time lifting your feet up rather than coasting the ground. And the ball doesn't run on a surface like that.

Jonathan Davies: They'd do anything to steal an advantage. Their doctor tried to get me off the field during the game. I'd made a break and was hauled down short of the line by Jon Webb. I hurt my ankle in the process, and the English doctor was 'advising' me to go off, saying it was in my best interests. I have my doubts about his sincerity. I believe my response was something along the lines of 'get lost'.

Ieuan Evans: That game will be remembered for Jiffy's incessant taunting of Micky Skinner. Skinner was working himself up into a rage because he couldn't lay a finger on this dancing little imp from Trimsaran. I almost started to feel sorry for him, but then I thought, 'Nah.'

Robert Jones: Skinner's sole aim that day was to knock Jiffy's head off. But that only made Jif more determined to show him up. In his typical cocky way, he just said, 'Give me the ball,' and he took great pleasure in skipping around Skinner every time he lunged at him.

John Devereux: Munch the Crunch, or whatever they called him.

Robert Jones: Each time he'd left him swiping at thin air, Jif would shout, 'Da bo,' which is 'ta-ra' in Welsh. There may have been a few blown kisses as well.

Jonathan Davies: Mick the Munch. If I could occupy the flankers, our back row would have less hassle. That was part of my job, to wind up the opposition back row. But that pitch was my stage.

Anthony Clement: He had Skinner in his pocket all afternoon.

Robert Norster: He's added a bit to that over the years, mind. He claims he shouted, 'Keep up fatty,' at one point, but in Test rugby you can't hear someone shouting right next to you, let alone someone fifteen yards or more away. There's a touch of the urban myth to that now. But everyone enjoyed getting one over on Micky, because he was a loud character. I remember catching him a peach once in a lineout. I just allowed my elbow to stray downwards and caught him right on the bugle. I couldn't have done it better if I'd tried it a hundred times. Couldn't have happened to a nicer bloke.

Adrian Hadley: There was a lot of that going on. Brian Moore was their Jiffy equivalent. Always chopsing, always trying to wind us up.

Ieuan Evans: Adrian Hadley's tries were both superb. Lots of spontaneous movement. Nothing pre-ordained, just a natural affinity for that type of game. It was play-what-you-see.

Anthony Clement: Tony Gray and Derek Quinnell felt that England were big and heavy to break down, and that the best approach was to try to move them around. We had a bit more mobility in our back row, and a bit more creativity in the midfield. With four tens in the backline, we couldn't really have played any other way.

Adrian Hadley's two tries, and a trademark Jonathan Davies drop goal were enough to see Wales to an 11–3 win.

Mark Ring: In the post-match dinner at the Hilton, Glen Webbe had this pink box that made a clapping sound when you pulled a string, like a burst of canned applause with people shouting 'bravo'. Mike Harrison was doing his losing captain's speech, and it was pretty dull. He was a bland Yorkshireman with no charisma. He tried to crack a joke, with no personality behind it, and it fell flat. Webby timed his response to perfection, pulling this string under the table, and letting loose this mocking laughter. Rowland Phillips was winding Mick Skinner up, chucking cake in his face, and you sensed that things could kick off at any point.

Adrian Hadley: They hated it. Absolutely hated it. Couldn't stand losing to us.

Jonathan Davies: We were all smashed. You can imagine, can't you? Welsh boys in the Hilton. Staff Jones was bladdered.

Mark Ring: Webby did it one too many times, and got caught in the act. Skinner strode over, grabbed it off him and smashed it against the table. It didn't break, so he smashed it again. This thing was indestructible. He was so mad, he shoved it in a carafe of wine. Then it finally stopped.

Jonathan Davies: We were all laughing, going, 'Ooooohhh.' Skinner had a face like thunder.

Mark Ring: Webby fished it out, and tried to fix it, but it was kaput. He was fuming, and him and Skinner started eyeballing each other across the table. Next thing they'd gone outside, and it was all about to kick off.

Adrian Hadley: Micky Skinner's no soft touch, but Webby was pretty tasty in a fight.

Robert Norster: As I remember it, Skinner shoved a gateaux in Webby's face. And for once, Webby didn't see the funny side.

Mark Ring: It was me and Webby, and Paul Rendall and Skinner. Two backs against two forwards. But a reporter followed us out, and Webby, instead of banging Skinner, challenged him to an arm wrestle.

Jonathan Davies: Webby takes his top off, and he's cut. A real bodybuilder's physique. I think Munch kept his top on once he'd seen that.

Mark Ring: Webby smashed him. Skinner wasn't happy and insisted on a rematch left-handed. Webby smashed him in that as well.

Jonathan Davies: We were laughing our heads off.

Adrian Hadley: That wasn't the only incident in the dinner. Staff Jones cleaned out one of the committee men at the bar. He almost killed him. We were shitfaced. This poor bloke was about eighty-odd, and he was walking through the room with a ball collecting signatures, when Staff just launched himself at him, for a laugh. Next thing you know, the bloke's splayed out on the floor, with his shirt open, and a paramedic's checking for his vital signs.

Robert Jones: Johnny Price, it was. The London Welsh representative. Staff was a big, strong man who'd spent most of his life swinging a sledgehammer in the mines. I think he surprised himself when poor Johnny went hurtling into the air.

Ieuan Evans: Scotland were a sterner challenge. They were a fit and dynamic side. Finlay Calder was a fine leader of men; the finest captain I ever played against or alongside. Two drop goals from Jif. One ugly as hell, the other an absolute beauty. He could've smacked that from the halfway line and it would've gone over. And a brilliant bit of spontaneous play from him for his try. You'd probably get shouted at for doing that now, but he saw the number eight was late to come across, and BUMF, he went for it. Brilliant. Derek White wasn't a slow man, but Jif skinned him. He was blisteringly quick. The game went back and forth, back and forth. It was a case of, 'Go on then, throw your punch.'

Paul Thorburn: When you've been dropped, you watch through slightly different eyes. You want the team to do well, but you don't want the guy who's replaced you to have a stormer. We missed a few kicks in the England game, and some of my supporters in the media were lobbying for my return. As it happened Clem played very well, but then did his hamstring the following week playing for Swansea and I got back in. I'm so glad I was back in the team for the Scotland game – it was the best game I was ever involved in.

Jonathan Davies: They came to play as well, the whole game was fast, open, and breathless. They didn't have the biggest team, like us, so they liked to keep things mobile.

Mark Ring: Ieuan's try was from a set play. It was all about the early pass. When you've got players like Ieuan, you have to give him the ball in space, and he'll finish it. It was an amazing run, no one laid a finger on him.

Ieuan Evans: Fear is a very underrated emotion. When in doubt, just keep running. David Sole to this day says to me, 'Remember who tackled you on the line?' It was on the line though, it doesn't count. The defenders kept coming across, and

I kept stepping back in. It's instinctive. You see a shape and you react, go for the hole. Why run into someone when there's a perfectly good hole beside them? It was made by the backs, though. Lovely wraparound pass from Ringo to create the space.

Robert Jones: That was one of the tries of the Championship.

Ieuan Evans: Like a centre forward in football, I loved scoring tries. There's no better feeling. You want to do it again and again. It's intoxicating, it's invigorating, it's the most potent of drugs. Nigel Davies used to refer to my pout. I had the world's most theatrical pout if the ball wasn't coming to my wing.

Adrian Hadley: It was a set move off the lineout. We did the same thing against Ireland at the World Cup when Ringy scored. Brilliant try, brilliant finish.

Mark Ring: Jiffy's try came out of nothing. Pure instinct. As a backline we had immense confidence. Bleddyn was the calming influence. Me and Jiffy were a bit wild, a bit mental. If Jiffy and I were trying to cook up something daft, Bledd would calm us down.

Adrian Hadley: Bleddyn was a brilliant player, so underrated. Ringy was class, he always had so much time on the ball, but Bleddyn was outstanding. A classy player, and a very skilful footballer. He was quiet off the field, but when he spoke, it was to-the-point, and constructive. I loved playing with those two as my centres, because they would give you the ball, and then offer support. A lot of modern centres' first instinct is to step outside their opposite number and make an outside break before passing to the wing. But that just cramps up the space. Ringy and Bleddyn would pass to me in space, because I was quicker, and supposedly more powerful than them, then they'd stay with me to offer support.

Jonathan Davies: Bleddyn was like some of his predecessors in that respect – John Dawes, Arthur Lewis, Steve Fenwick. Great players who didn't get the credit they deserved. He was a superb footballer, and he had a strong left peg, which gave us options. We had space and time, and everybody wanted to play. The ingredients were simple. Great service from Rob at the base, creative midfielders, and two deadly finishers.

Although Wales had scored two tries that would go down in history as two of the finest the tournament had witnessed, Scotland surged back, and recovered from a 10–7 deficit, to lead 20–10 early in the second half. A converted Ian Watkins try and a Paul Thorburn penalty got Wales back to within a point at 20–19, before Jiffy took it upon himself to nail the victory with two drop goals.

Jonathan Davies: The first was a bit of a flapper, but the second was a peach. The biggest advantage I had was that I never played for Wales at age-grade level, so I had my apprenticeship in the club game, playing for Trimsaran Youth and seconds. That way, I developed my game management at an earlier age. It's not as clean cut as schoolboy rugby. Youth rugby was invented to cater for kids leaving school early, so I was playing against teams with big gnarly forwards who wanted to kill me. It helped me hone my instincts, and in particular, to know when to score. I soon learned that if it was going to be a tight match, in poor conditions, on a poor pitch, then all scores were crucial. I came to appreciate the drop goal as a way of accumulating points, and taking the game away from the opposition. Take your points when they're on offer. It's like chipping away at a frozen lake, chip, chip, chip, three points at a time. Eventually the lake will cave in, and you're out of sight.

If Wales relied on their innate skills and instinct to beat England and Scotland, the victory in Dublin was built on self-belief and obstinacy. They were met with the usual whirlwind of knees, elbows, and hot-headed Irish fervour. Rob Jones split his ear open after Phillip Matthews' boot came crashing down on his head at the bottom of a ruck. There was a fine line between robust physicality and naked aggression.

John Devereux: Beating Ireland was the best game of that campaign. To go over there and beat the Irish, that's the hardest place to go.

Jonathan Davies: It was wet, windy, and drizzly. We knew when we arrived it was going to be a shit fight. They had some nasty forwards then, none more so than Phil Matthews. Stay away from him. He was a madman on the field. Hard as nails.

Robert Jones: We didn't play brilliantly well, but we had real belief.

Jonathan Davies: Perhaps our nerves got the better of us because we knew the Triple Crown was on the line.

Robert Norster: It was a war of attrition.

Mark Ring: The Ireland game was the absolute worst. The scrappiest encounter imaginable. Thorby was a rock that day. He kicked the winning penalty in injury time. Four fly halves or not, that was a day when we *needed* Thorby.

Paul Thorburn: It was our first Triple Crown since 1979, and none of us were in the mood to celebrate. We were all aware of just how dire the game had been, particularly after the panache of the opening two games.

Wales were one win away from a first Grand Slam in a decade. If Tony Gray's side were to make history, they'd need to overcome title-chasing France in Cardiff.

Paul Thorburn: The build-up was good. We were staying out in the St Pierre Country Club, and there was a helicopter following the team bus into the ground. The press were anticipating a first Grand Slam in a decade.

Robert Norster: It was a bit of a novel thing at the time. We all believed we could do it. We had momentum.

Mark Ring: Up to then we'd played fantastic rugby, spinning the ball all over the field. Total rugby. But it lashed down on the day. The worst conditions. We often bang on about not wanting to play France in the spring time, but that season it was the opposite. They didn't want to play *us* in the spring time. The weather scuppered our hopes of a Grand Slam.

Adrian Hadley: Jiffy was still trying to drop goals all day even though it was pissing down. He missed about three or four. I think he had a bet on himself to drop a goal in every fucking game. It was an awful game. France had lost to Scotland, so it was up in the air who'd win the Championship.

Jonathan Davies: If the conditions had been good, that match could have been a classic.

With fifteen minutes to go, and after a period of prolonged pressure, Jean-Patrick Lescarboura dragged himself over the line despite the attentions of a number of Welsh players. It put France into a 10–3 lead. Wales hit back through a Ieuan Evans try, converted by Thorburn, but that was their final contribution. It was the closest they'd come to a Grand Slam in a decade. A 10–9 defeat gave Wales a share of the Championship, but they were denied their Grand Slam glory by the tiniest of margins.

Jonathan Davies: Look at that French side though: Blanco, Lagisquet, Lafond, Bonneval, Sella, Berbizier, Cecillon, Rodriguez. All world class. Sella and Blanco would make the best team of all time. Sella was in a different class. He could score from seventy yards – as he did against England – he could score from close range by just running through you, or he could jump higher than anyone and pluck the ball from the air to score. He was one of those freaky players that come along once in a generation. He was from farming stock in Agen. Naturally hard. When you hit him, it hurt you. No matter how good your technique was, even if you got him down, it would be painful. He was all bone and sinew. He played 111 times for

France in an era when they had an embarrassment of world class backs. That tells you all you need to know.

Robert Jones: I've got to be honest, Jif and I weren't at our best that day. But there was a mental thing with France back then. We always thought they were that much better than us.

Jonathan Davies: We were totally deflated. We'd grown up through the seventies, knowing how much it meant to the Welsh supporters, and this had been our chance to emulate those boys. If we'd have lost a high-scoring thriller, we'd have accepted it. But the whole occasion was a let-down. I ran off with the match ball as a souvenir, but Daniel Dubroca asked if he could have it, as it was his last game for France. Fair enough, I gave it to him.

Adrian Hadley: It was after that game that I went to rugby league. I asked if I could have a word with the Big Five before we all started drinking. I told them I wouldn't be available for the tour to New Zealand. It was a good one to miss.

TWELVE

EVERY DAY YOU WOKE UP,
ANOTHER PLAYER HAD GONE

Although Wales had finished the domestic season as joint champions of Europe, and were officially the third best team in the world, they returned to New Zealand that summer with a sense of foreboding. The Five Nations had given them confidence, but less than twelve months had passed since – in the words of Ieuan Evans – they'd been 'handed their arses on a plate' by the All Blacks. Those twelve months had allowed them to push the semi-final to the dark recesses of their minds. But now they were heading back to the scene of their humiliation, and the nightmares about the consuming black tide were about to become vivid and real again. By the time the torturous experience had come to an end, the press were unanimous in denouncing it as the lowest point in the history of Welsh rugby.

Wales played eight matches, losing five, drawing one and winning only two. The two Tests were horrendous mismatches, as the callow Dragons were chewed up and spat out by a cruel and merciless black machine. The aggregate score was 106 points to 12. The odds had been hopelessly stacked against Wales from the off, but a near-suicidal itinerary, and a scrimping approach to life on tour lengthened those odds further. An ill-prepared Welsh team was thrown into fixtures against some of the world's most feared and ruthless provincial sides. It meant they were demoralised, and weakened by injury before they met the full might of the All Blacks in Christchurch. They lost 52–3 – a margin of defeat that eclipsed the one they'd suffered against the same opposition at the Rugby World Cup. By the time the second Test at Eden Park rolled around, Wales were struggling to cobble a team together. Six replacements had already flown out. Captain and vice-captain Bleddyn Bowen and Bob Norster were among the injured, meaning Jonathan Davies was handed the captaincy. He ultimately put in a man-of-the-match performance – a remarkable accolade considering his team slumped to a crushing 54–9 defeat. But he led by example, tackling his heart out, throwing himself in the way of marauding monsters like Buck Shelford and Gary Whetton, and scoring a sensational solo try at the end; a try that symbolised his refusal to throw in the towel. It was a reminder to those who chided him for being a Flash Harry, that he was the ultimate team man, and that his heart was as big as his imagination was vivid.

John Devereux: I missed the whole Five Nations, and got fit just in time for the tour of death. We don't talk about that tour much. We've got to dig deep into the memory bank, because a lot of us have parked it in a very dark place, never to return. It was the worst tour I've ever been on. No one wanted to go to New Zealand. The itinerary was brutal. Every provincial match was like a Test match. They put us in the shittiest hotels you have ever seen in your life.

Robert Jones: They were very basic. Motels in the middle of industrial estates. Worse than what we'd experienced at the World Cup and that's saying something.

John Devereux: Shitholes. It was wintertime. We were going to bed with our tracksuits on. It was like being in the film, *Psycho*. All we needed was a knife-wielding maniac in the shower.

Mike Hall: I was a twenty-one-year-old student, so I didn't care. Staying in a hotel – any hotel – was a lot better than my student digs. What surprised me was that we were playing on Saturdays *and* Tuesdays, travelling all across New Zealand, from the North Island to the South Island, with barely any time to recover or to gather our thoughts.

Mark Ring: What became apparent on that tour was that we were still playing the 'old game'. We were ripping the ball to the wings, and the pack was running the full length of the field across to the far side. It was very formulaic. New Zealand were rolling their forwards into the midfield, cleaning the midfield backs out. We'd over-commit to the rucks, and leave them with space to exploit. Theirs was a modern and effective way to play.

John Devereux: First rule of any tour: win your first game. Our first game was against Waikato. Not the best provincial side, but they had the likes of John Mitchell and Warren Gatland. I remember looking up in the stand and seeing the likes of Jiffy and Bob Norster, and thinking, 'These boys should be playing.' You know, get your best side out first, lay down a marker, and beat them. We lost.

Robert Jones: Wellington were next. After the game, the local paper did player ratings. Jonny Griff [Jonathan Griffiths] top scored with four out of ten. Phil May got nought. At least he turned up. Give him one for turning up for Christ's sake.

Ieuan Evans: We played Waikato, Wellington and Otago before the first Test, and only snuck a win against Otago. As soon as we arrived we were picking up injuries, and we didn't have the players to lose. People were joining, people were leaving. There was no sense of continuity, and we didn't have the depth to cope. That erodes confidence, and you'll get nowhere in New Zealand without confidence.

Anthony Clement: In my eyes, those first three games were Test matches. I think Wellington had nine All Blacks in their side.

Mike Hall: It sounds sadistic, but I enjoyed the tour. It was my first taste of international rugby. It was bloody hard, but I got to see a part of the world I'd never been to.

Robert Norster: We weren't ready for it. After a long season of rugby, you're ready for a summer. Getting on a plane to New Zealand where it was winter wasn't my idea of a good summer. Once we got there and boys started falling over, the task became insurmountable. It was pass the parcel on the captaincy. I captained for the first Test, because Bledd was injured, then Jiffy got it when I got injured.

John Devereux: People were ducking out left, right and centre. The injury list was ridiculous. Muzzy [Paul Moriarty] went home with a shoulder injury, then Jonathan Mason arrived from a family holiday to Ibiza. Bleach blond hair, suntanned, with a guitar slung on his back. His first game was against North Auckland, they bombed him early, stuck a huge up-and-under up. He caught it, and the entire North Auckland pack ran over the top of him. He's lying on the floor in agony, and his back is just 'Freddy Kruegered'. Holes everywhere.

Robert Jones: Jiffy jogged past him and said, 'I think you're starting to peel, mate.'

Robert Norster: He's good at claiming these lines, when he's had about three months to think about them. Although he might have said that, to be fair. He's sharp as a sixpence is Jif.

John Devereux: In the night then, he's sleeping in this shitty motel, and his bedclothes are sticking to him because his back's all raw. The studs went so deep, you could see the white tissue underneath his tan.

Ieuan Evans: There was definitely a psychological hangover from the World Cup, but you either hide from it, or confront it. That's where you find out what people are made of. There are those who wallow in self-pity, and those who rise to the challenge. Who wants to take on the best, and who's just coming for the craic and the holiday?

Robert Jones: The one positive is that the tour was sponsored by Steinlager, and everywhere we stayed there was a fridge full of it. I was rooming with Steve Bowling, and after training I put the kettle on and asked if he fancied a drink. He said, 'Aye, go on then, I'll have a Stein.' That kind of set the precedent.

Robert Norster: It was everywhere, in the bedrooms, in the team rooms. We were surrounded by it.

John Devereux: We'd end up giving most of them to the maids. There was too much even for us to get through.

Jonathan Davies: We spent the Tests living off scraps, and you realised early on that there was no light at the end of the tunnel. We were just willing the final whistle to go. Tackle after tackle. Tackle a big forward, get up, tackle a back, get up. By the time you're twenty or thirty nil down, your head's gone. Once you tumble into a trough like that, it's impossible to climb out.

Mike Hall: I won my first cap coming off the bench in that first Test when we were about forty points down. I tried to take Joe Stanley on the outside with my first touch, desperate to make an impression, and he hit me so hard it felt like I'd been in a car crash.

Robert Jones: You can comfort yourself that there's no team in the world that would have come close to this New Zealand side, but that didn't stop you feeling completely embarrassed about it. We knew what to expect after the World Cup, and we knew we hadn't had enough time to close the gap. Sacking Tony Gray and Derek Quinnell was a knee-jerk reaction from an out-of-touch WRU. It put us back years, and allowed that England side of the nineties to pull away from us. They were good, don't get me wrong, but we drifted into their slipstream rather than staying out ahead.

Mark Ring: Tony Gray and Derek Quinnell were good guys, but we were lagging behind the rest of the world. We used to lead the way, in the seventies, the All Blacks were jealous of us back then.

JJ Williams: Tony and Derek asked me in before the tour to help the squad with their fitness. I was amazed at how out of condition some of the forwards were. They'd really let it slide, and the discipline which the likes of Clive Rowlands had insisted on was gone. They were just messing about during training, not concentrating, cracking jokes. The kind of behaviour that simply wasn't tolerated in my day.

Robert Jones: The Kiwis were obsessed. Satellite TV was a way off, but you could pretty much watch rugby twenty-four hours a day out there. Turn the telly on, and it's rugby. And not just the top end, they showed schools rugby, and the lowest levels of grass roots rugby played up in the mountains somewhere with one man and a dog watching. It's no wonder they were all so good, it's all they ever thought about. I was dropped for the second Test for Jonathan Griffiths. It was the first time I'd ever been dropped. I was naturally disappointed but I could understand why. He was quick, powerful, and more abrasive than me. We needed a change.

The one shining light in the second Test was Jonathan Davies' spectacular try from a move started on Wales's own try line. It was a fleeting moment of triumph in an otherwise humiliating match.

Jonathan Davies: Getting the captaincy for the second Test was an honour. Walking out at Eden Park, one of rugby's finest stadiums, wearing the red shirt, and leading your country. Only a select few have done that. But the outcome was the same. I scored our only try, and was bizarrely awarded man of the match. Maybe it was out of pity, I don't know. I think it was more for my bravery than the try. Ray Gravell praised me afterwards for never giving up, but that's just the way I was brought up. I may have been small, but I was never a shirker. That's what growing up in Trimsaran does for you.

A once-cherished rivalry had been consigned to history. Within the space of a year, Wales had played New Zealand three times, and conceded 155 points. The try count across the three matches was 26–2. It was difficult to imagine a more one-sided affair. For some, that tour served as a definitive full stop to their Wales careers. Jonathan Davies was one of a few to emerge with his reputation enhanced, but within five months, Davies would be lost to the sport, and the trough of humiliation into which Welsh rugby had sunk would take longer to clamber out of than anyone dared fear.

Wales's next fixture was an autumn Test against the touring Western Samoans, and ended in an underwhelming victory. It led to a raft of changes ahead of the next match against Romania. The Eastern Europeans were a rugged, doughty opposition, but were still minnows swimming in the choppier waters of top tier rugby. Nothing but a comfortable win was forecast for Wales.

In front of a paltry crowd of 17,000, the Romanians defeated Wales, and triggered a national crisis. The press – so fulsome in their praise of Jonathan Davies in New Zealand – decided that the finger of blame should now be pointed in his direction. He felt marooned with no support.

Mark Ring: Jiffy tried to appeal to the authorities, to persuade them that we'd need to make changes if we wanted to stay competitive. But they didn't want to listen. He might have stayed if they had.

Jonathan Davies: I couldn't have been treated with more contempt if I'd suggested planting potatoes at Cardiff Arms Park.

Robert Norster: I wrote a report with Jiffy, narrowed it down to a few bullet points and sent it straight to the WRU. The idea was to reflect on the gap between New Zealand and us. It was staring everyone else in the face, but we seemed happy to bury our heads in the sand. The letter was very polite, very respectful, certainly not a case of 'sort it out or we're off'. But it wasn't welcomed. We were seen as uppity. We didn't even get a formal response. And then the boys 'red-arrowed' out of there, didn't they? Jif, Devs, Muzz, Stuart Evans, Adolf. They all went north.

Mark Ring: There is no doubt that the exodus to rugby league was prompted by the scale of defeat on that '88 tour. We were called the worst touring team ever to have played there. Players like Jonathan Davies realised we were so far behind in terms of knowledge. He wanted to meet up with the WRU to talk about it, and he felt he wasn't listened to. We'd never seen league as a threat until that point. After the New Zealand debacle, I almost joined the exodus. I turned down Wigan a second time, and turned down a double-deal with David Bishop at Hull KR. Bish was the biggest casualty of them all. If he'd had a proper career in rugby union, we'd be speaking about him now in the same breath as Gareth Edwards. The guy was astonishing. He had an aura. He feared no one, and gave no respect to anyone. He wouldn't have been cowed in the presence of Kiwis or South Africans.

Robert Jones: That tour knocked us for six. The fallout was catastrophic. We'd gone from a team brimming with confidence, third in the World Cup, Triple Crown winners, to this. And then we were shredded by the exodus to rugby league.

Jonathan Davies: I wasn't remotely anti-establishment. I had huge respect for the selectors, the coaches, the committee men. I understood the work they'd put in, but I felt as though they didn't understand the reasons behind the gulf in class. Rob Norster and Gary Whetton were pretty much the same player. But Bob had nowhere near the support that Whetton had to get fit and pursue his goals. The only time I'd been in a gym was when I did my cruciate ligaments and had to rehab. It was some Polish guy's garage in Trimsaran, and I had to run through two council estates to get there. The All Blacks were in the gym all the time. Was it any wonder they became better athletes? The stuff we were asking for eventually came in ten years later with the arrival of Graham Henry. So it took another decade before their heads were turned as to what was going on in the rugby world. We were dismissed as 'just players'. Our input wasn't valued. We didn't want to be paid for playing, we just wanted them to invest in better facilities, and to get some sponsors on board, so we could at least be reimbursed for money lost, or our employers could be reimbursed for giving us time off. We had boys on that '88 tour, farmers, who were losing money by playing for Wales. Others were taking unpaid leave. Imagine how galling it is when you're making those sacrifices, and no one respects you or is even willing to listen to your point of view. When Phil Davies broke his jaw against England, he didn't want to go to the dinner, so he ordered a bottle of wine on room service. He had a fucking invoice for it two days later. The WRU had 56,000 people in the ground, paying good money for their tickets. And they're not willing to stump up for a bottle of wine for a bloke who's had his jaw broken out there on the pitch. I'd had a gutsful.

The sense of outrage that greeted Davies's departure was an indication of the esteem in which he was held. Despite the Romania defeat, Welsh fans believed that as long as the messiah remained, a revival was possible. The rabble-rousers who'd agitated for his removal suddenly found themselves regretting what they'd wished for. Writing in *The Times*, Gerald Davies suggested 'those who have attempted to deny him his rightful place will now ponder long and hard at the gap his departure leaves.' His self-belief was contagious; his ability a reminder to the world that Wales still produced the best of the best. But he was gone. Another spirited away by those heathens in the north of England. Money was an obvious lure – £500,000 according to the rumours – but so too was the casual indifference of the WRU. Here was the most talented player of his generation offering advice on how to bridge the widening chasm between the hemispheres; on how to rescue the reputation of the proudest rugby nation of all. And it wasn't even thrown back in his face, it was just plainly ignored.

Like Gareth Davies before him – pushed to quit Test rugby after 'AN Other' was listed in the team to play England. Like Phil Bennett – who was initially criticised for not being Barry John. It's always the number ten in Wales. Whoever wears that jersey has to balance continually on a tightrope between heroism and villainy.

His journey north was trailed by echoes of 'Judas' from the land of his fathers. But deep down, few could begrudge him his decision. It wasn't his fault that Welsh rugby had been allowed to slide into ignominy; neither was it his responsibility to drag it out of the mire. Once again, the number ten was the one to shoulder the blame.

Terry Holmes: The so-called exodus made no difference to me. I have no truck with the argument that Wales's decline was because of the lure of rugby league. They obviously lost Jonathan, and a few others. They were certainly missed, but it didn't lead to the collapse of the Welsh national side as it's sometimes painted. The Welsh public can be fickle. Maybe our mentality is more frail in Wales. We allow the departure of a few big names to cripple us psychologically. Would it happen in England or New Zealand? I doubt it.

Paul Thorburn: They all went because they'd seen the size of the gap, and knew it was widening. And after they ignored Jiffy, they realised the WRU weren't willing to do anything about it.

Ieuan Evans: It triggered a calamitous decline. We lost the core of our team. It was always going to have a negative impact. For the next few years it was like revolving doors. We lost Jif in his pomp, Devereux, Dai Young, Paul Moriarty. When we lost Dai, we didn't just lose a prop, we lost our entire scrum. He was a Lions Test prop at a ridiculously young age. He could have broken every Lions record going.

John Devereux: To play in that position at the age he did was freaky. No other word for it. Most tight-heads don't come good until their late twenties.

Ieuan Evans: And we missed his dry wit as well. Caustic doesn't come close.

Robert Jones: We struggled to hold onto possession during that period in the late eighties and early nineties. It's no coincidence that a shift to playing on the back foot coincided with Dai and Stuart Evans – two of the best props in world rugby – going north. Our scrum, so stable with those two locking it, started to retreat alarmingly once they'd gone.

Mike Hall: It seemed like every day when you woke up, another player had gone. I nearly went myself. Everything was agreed with St Helens, and I pulled out at the last minute.

John Devereux: You can't rip the heart out of a team, and expect a bunch of rookies to step in and pick up the pieces.

Phil Davies: We lost the spine of the group, went from being Triple Crown winners to having the lowest ever Welsh representation on the '89 Lions tour.

Ieuan Evans: Losing Jif was huge. He was the on-field general, the instigator of everything good that we did with that backline. He clearly saw the writing on the wall after the Romania defeat, but so much more could have been done to keep him. Rugby league had always picked players off, but this was a systematic *reaping*. The WRU was quite unprepared. Some of those on the board buried their heads in the sand, and hoped it would go away, rather than trying to deal with it. If they'd have stayed, our fortunes in the late eighties, early nineties would have been a lot different. Those players weren't just some of the best in Wales, they were some of the best in the world.

Robert Jones: Seriously, if they'd all stayed it would have been another golden era. We could have won three or four Grand Slams with that team, and maybe equalled the feats of the seventies. But the rug was pulled.

Adrian Hadley: I think thirteen of the World Cup squad went north. That's nearly a full side.

Clive Rowlands: We came third in the inaugural World Cup in 1987, and suddenly you lose John Devereux, you lose Adrian Hadley, you lose Jonathan Davies, you lose David Young, you lose Stuart Evans, you lose Paul Moriarty, you lose Richard Webster. See what I'm getting at? I wish I'd had them together again for another two or three years.

Only the lineout mastery of Bob Norster, the kicking of Rob Jones, and a disputed try from Mike Hall saved Wales from a whitewash in 1989. Captain Paul Thorburn was seen flicking the Vs up at the press box, as Wales did their lap of honour following their sole victory against England. His target was Welsh *Sunday Times* journalist, Stephen Jones, who'd suggested in his column that Wales losing to England would be a good thing. His rationale was that it would force the WRU to confront the cracks that were appearing in the national game, and that victory would merely paper over these. It wasn't meant as a dig at the Welsh team, but in these febrile and emotional times, Thorburn allowed his pent-up emotion to spill out.

The All Blacks arrived in the autumn and dished out a 34–9 thrashing, confirming that they could turn an away ground into a theatre of torture as well. It was the biggest losing margin Wales had ever suffered in Cardiff. Then, in 1990, Wales's resistance crumbled as they feebly succumbed to a Five Nations whitewash. It began with a meek performance against France in Cardiff, which was followed by a 34–6 thumping at the hands of England. Those looking for positives amid the wreckage could find none, and JBG Thomas declared the Welsh display 'so poor as to be beyond comprehension'. Nearly seventy years had passed since Wales had allowed England to breach their try line four times in a match. The coach John Ryan resigned on the spot, after just nine games in charge.

THIRTEEN

THE CIVIL WAR

The man appointed to pick up the pieces was Ron Waldron, the tough-talking, no-nonsense coach of Neath – who had undergone a renaissance under his leadership. The Welsh All Blacks were nasty, brutish, and ruthless. It was thought Ron could transfer his strong-arm approach to a rudderless Welsh team. He was either going to steer them back on course in the 1990 Five Nations, or further into the rapids. Waldron was a hard task-master, but no miracle worker, and Wales went on to lose to eventual champions Scotland, and Ireland after he took the reins, suffering their first ever Five Nations whitewash.

Hugh Williams-Jones: There wasn't much to celebrate in that tournament, but there were still a few comedy moments to treasure. Mark Jones was giving his 'war-cry' speech in the dressing room ahead of the Scotland game. He was barking and growling in his usual way. 'This is men against boys. Look at me, right. It's MEN against boys.' Right on cue, there was a knock on the door, and the ref said, 'Come on boys, let's be having you.' I wanted to laugh so hard, but I had to keep it in.

Waldron's first overseas assignment was a trip to newly independent Namibia. It was a six-match tour, to include two capped internationals. Neath hooker Kevin Phillips was given the captaincy, as one of ten Welsh All Blacks in the party of twenty-six. While Wales were never in danger of losing they made hard work of the Test series, winning 18–9 and 34–30.

Hugh Williams-Jones: Lyn Jones is the tightest man in the world. It breaks his heart to spend money. When he played for Llanelli, he used to walk round the president's lounge after the game, asking people to borrow ten pence to use the phone. Often people would only have a quid, so he'd take it and give them change. By the time he'd asked everyone in the room, he'd filled his wallet and made a tidy profit. I was rooming with him in Zimbabwe, and he wanted to buy a load of presents before we left for Namibia. There were loads of hawkers near our hotel selling stuff off the pavement. Jonesey returned to the room that afternoon, laden with ornate wood carvings and laid them out on the bed. I said, 'Bloody 'ell, butt, that's a lot of money for you to spend.' He said he'd done a bit of a deal with one of the younger sellers. Later on, we're all on the bus driving to training, and I kid you not, there on the side of the road was this little kid standing next to his near empty blanket with barely anything left on it, wearing a pair of Welsh Cotton Traders shorts that came down to his knees, a Welsh jersey, a pair of size-11 trainers, and a pair of sweaty, mud-stained socks.

The 1991 Championship began with the visit of England, who'd last tasted victory in Cardiff in 1963. But the margin of victory the previous year at Twickenham suggested a gulf had opened up between the two rivals, and the reassuring surrounds of the National Stadium were no longer a guarantee of success. Two players who would become legends were given their debuts that day. Neil Jenkins and Scott Gibbs were pitched into the Cardiff cauldron as callow teenagers, and asked to forge a ten–twelve axis against an England side hungry for Grand Slam glory. They were too young to prevent another humbling defeat, and the 25–6 reverse set the tone for another dispiriting campaign. Heavy defeats to Scotland and a tearaway French side sandwiched a high-octane draw with the Irish. That may have saved them from another whitewash, but the wooden spoon was theirs to keep for another season. This Welsh team was breaking all the wrong records. The England defeat was their worst ever in Cardiff, the Scotland loss (32–12) their heaviest at Murrayfield, and the French flogging (36–3) the biggest they'd ever suffered in any Five Nations match.

Mark Ring: A lot of people think that I don't like Ron Waldron. That's not true. I've always liked him as a bloke. But as a coach he was one-dimensional and formulaic. He'd expect you to follow pre-ordained patterns, but I operated on instinct. I would step back, consider my options, and often run in the opposite direction to what we'd been programmed. Even if it opened up space that didn't appear to be there, he'd berate me for it. I liked to keep things fresh; he preferred things stale and predictable.

Emyr Lewis: The Ireland draw was my first Test for Wales. We were staying in the Angel Hotel, and the place was heaving. I came down the stairs on game day, and walked into a sea of red. They were packed into the lobby like sardines, going insane. I remember thinking, 'How are we going to get through this?' When we eventually did, we had to walk all the way down Westgate Street, and the crowds were either side of us, chanting and cheering. When I eventually sat down in the changing room, it was like the weight of the world had descended on my shoulders. I felt absolutely *exhausted*. I was nearly falling asleep. Phil Davies was looking at me, saying, 'Are you alright?' It was all down to adrenaline. Phil said to me, 'Now, when you run out, make sure you scream at the top of your lungs,' and I thought, 'What's that going to do?' So, I started walking out. I couldn't run, I was too tired. But as I did, I started screaming. I could hear Paul Arnold screaming behind me, as loud as I was. And all of a sudden, I felt a million dollars. It was as though the energy was flooding back into me.

Mark Ring: A classic example of Ron's negative attitude came after that Ireland game. I did something naturally instinctive in that match. They'd booted it downfield and I was chasing. I got it under control, and was facing the opposite touchline. It would have been a long touch-finder, one that may not have made it, and Simon Geoghegan would have cantered in if he'd intercepted my kick. So instead, I stood stock still in the middle of the pitch. The Irish boys stopped as well, which allowed a few of the Welsh boys to get behind the ball. It was like showboating in sevens. I flipped the ball over my right shoulder, and Chris Bridges got it away to Steve Ford. He danced away down the right touchline, it goes inside, to Phil Davies, to Neil Jenkins, and we score. A counter-attack from nothing. The crowd went nuts, and the game was as good as in the bag. Later on, I get a pass off a lineout from Neil Jenkins, and my attempted kick gets charged down. The ball bobbles up, and Brendan Mullin pounces on it and scores. They end up drawing the game. The following week, we're in the team room ahead of the French game, and Waldron puts a video on. We're expecting it to be a video of France, so we can look at some potential areas to exploit. Instead, he puts the Ireland game on, and presses pause at the exact moment of my charge down. He turns to me and says, 'Ringo, you bloody city slicker. You pissed about far too long there, like you've pissed about all your career. And if you piss about again on Saturday you'll never play for your country again.' In front of the whole group. Why didn't he show the good thing I'd done that had put us twenty points up?

Paul Thorburn: Ron picked on everyone though. He didn't victimise people. That was just his way. Gruff and to-the-point.

Phil Davies: Nobody was singled out. I had it off him plenty of times. He was very passionate, and some didn't respond too well to that. Tony Gray had been a collaborative sort of coach, involving the players a lot in the decision-making process. Buck Ryan was more methodical, bringing in elements of sports science. Ron, in contrast, was old school. It was predominantly about fitness with Ron.

Mike Hall: We were doing eight laps of the field the day before the game, because that's what he'd done in Neath.

Mark Ring: I was broken-hearted over that video session, crying in the hotel room. I wrote a letter to Ron, telling him I wasn't going to play on the weekend. I didn't want to play for Wales ever again. I was about to slide it under his door when Ieuan Evans asked what I was doing. When I told him, he rugby tackled me, snatched the letter, balled it up and shoved it in his mouth. He got me back into our room, and calmed me down. I ended up playing against France, but we lost by thirty points. I just couldn't focus.

Ieuan Evans: I did take it off him. I'm not sure if I disposed of it in quite that manner though.

Emyr Lewis: The game in France was memorable for the journey to the ground. Normally when you get on the bus, the back seats are taken by the senior members of the squad. When I got on all the back seats were empty, and I thought, 'This is great,' and helped myself. The bus gradually filled up, but no one else was coming to the back. It was because they all wanted ring-side seats to witness the police escort to the ground. It was incredible. They had their truncheons out. They were kicking cars, hitting cars out of the way. We went straight down the middle of the Champs Elysees, no veering off or skirting round. Then we went careering down a load of one-way streets. Whatever was the quickest route to the ground, that's the route we took. It was phenomenal.

Paul Thorburn: Later on, when Alan Davies came in with Bob Norster as his manager, there was an appreciation of man-management. The idea that certain players needed to be treated differently, that some responded to different triggers. Ron didn't have that. It was all or nothing. 'You're a fucking twat. Sort yourself out.' It worked with Neath, but it didn't work with all the international players. He didn't have enough subtlety, enough flexibility.

Robert Jones: His philosophy was based around toughness and fitness, and guys like Ringo didn't fit into that. The best coaches I've worked under – guys like Geech [Ian McGeechan] – their biggest strength was their ability to understand people as individuals. They took the time to do it. It wasn't just about their rugby, but about who they were as people. Geech knew whether you needed an arm around you, a kick up the arse, or a tap on the back. Whatever it took to get the best out of you on the field. Man-management wasn't Ron's strength.

Ieuan Evans: We were guilty of giving short-term cameos to coaches and management teams, all of whom would come in with their own ideas, and tearing up what had gone before, all of whom had a club affiliation that would lay them open to accusations of bias. Ron Waldron wasn't the only one who favoured players because of the club they were from. But Tony Gray was got rid of far too early. He was the only Welsh coach to have won something in a decade.

Paul Thorburn: That was a disgraceful decision by the Welsh Rugby Union.

John Devereux: Sacking Tony Gray and Derek Quinnell was the start of the rot. It sent us back ten years. They'd learnt so much during their time, and weren't allowed to implement the changes they knew were necessary.

Robert Norster: They were tight with the boys as well. It wasn't a traditional player–coach relationship. Tony would sit in the team room, have a beer and a fag. It wasn't the coaches' fault we got hammered in New Zealand, but the WRU thought it was.

Paul Thorburn: And so began a lengthy period of revolving doors at the WRU. They just kept making the same mistakes.

Ieuan Evans: Ron brought in a load of Neath players he'd seen week in week out and he wanted to implement a Neath-style game plan. But that didn't work at international level. England did a similar thing with Bath in the eighties. It doesn't work. You can't take a club side and turn it into an international team. Having said that, any new coach needs to be given time to develop his philosophy. The attitude from the WRU during that period was, 'It's not working, move on, it's not working, move on.'

Robert Jones: He focused on tough farmers with a never-say-die attitude. Fitness went to another level in terms of stamina and commitment. Players were conditioned to last a full eighty minutes and beyond. He thought he could transfer that approach to the international arena, and he brought a lot of people that he knew and understood into the squad. Thorby was at the helm of it. But international level and club level are two different things.

Paul Thorburn: Regrettably, there was an anti-Neath element. You could say Ron didn't help that by picking so many Neath players, but we *were* winning trophies at the time. Ron had a manner about him that a lot of players didn't like. He told them straight, 'You're not fit enough, guys. Sort it out.'

Phil Davies: He was very honest, and very intense, and some people didn't like it.

Robert Jones: Steele Lewis [Pontypridd centre] threatened to beat Thorby up at one point. That's how deep the anti-Neath resentment became with some members of this squad. There was a level of animosity I'd not witnessed before. Stella was hot-headed, mind. He did have a tendency to wade in.

Two consecutive wooden spoons, and a raft of record defeats would have been enough to dent even the strongest player's self-belief. Add in a climate of resentment and tribalism, and you have yourself a combustible cocktail. Fly the whole party to the other side of the world to take on arguably the best side in the world, and the chances of things ending well are slim to none.

Ieuan Evans: Australia 1991 was the absolute nadir. It was far worse than the New

Zealand tour of '88, which seemed like a success by comparison. Everything about it stank of decline.

Mike Hall: We were the most underprepared, under-resourced team that had ever left Welsh shores, and we were going up against a team that would soon be crowned world champions. Their squad was loaded with world-class talent. Campese, Little, Horan, Lynagh, Farr-Jones. Australian rugby was at its peak, when we were in a trough. Everything about us was woefully inadequate. The fitness, the training, everything was way off. Australia had embraced professionalism, and were a slick, well-oiled machine. We were an utter shambles.

Gareth Llewellyn: Australia were never the most enthusiastic rugby nation, but – and this is the typical Aussie mentality – they knew there was now a World Cup, and they wanted to be the world champions. Within a few months of that tour, they would be.

Hugh Williams-Jones: We arrived in Cottesloe, a beach suburb near Perth, and it was a case of, 'Right, daps on. *Run* to the training ground.' Someone piped up, 'Where is it?' Ron replied, 'Just keep following your nose, sunshine, and you'll find it.'

Mike Hall: We were made to run *to* and *from* the training ground, that's how stupid it was. I don't blame Ron Waldron, because that's all he knew, that's what he'd grown up with. His Neath side was ferociously fit compared to the other teams in Wales, and they played a very simple game. He thought he could do that on the international stage, but it was nowhere near good enough. We were rabbits in the bloody headlights down there.

Robert Jones: The training ground in Cottesloe was a good couple of miles away, and when we eventually got there, we discovered it was an Aussie Rules pitch. It was massive, and we were made to do eight laps. Then we did some sprints and strides. We'd barely landed in Australia.

Hugh Williams-Jones: Jinks [Neil Jenkins] wanted to practise his kicking, but there were no posts.

Robert Jones: We had to run back then. Ron was in a minibus with sliding doors, and he'd be driving alongside us shouting, 'Fucking speed up, mun.'

Hugh Williams-Jones: We were running alongside a main road, with hazards everywhere, cars and taxis flying up and down, and Ron's voice booming above it all. 'KEEP RUNNING!' Jinks had had enough. It was his first tour, and he thought it might be his last, so me and him ducked down some side streets just to get away from Ron.

After routine victories against Western Australia, Australian Capital Territory, and Queensland Country Origin, Wales lost 35–24 to a strong Queensland side. What came next was to eclipse the humiliation Wales had suffered three years earlier in New Zealand.

Jonathan Davies: I was playing for Canterbury Bulldogs against Balmain Tigers the night that Wales lost by seventy points to New South Wales. I hadn't had a particularly great game, so was surprised to be surrounded by a scrum of journalists at the end, all wanting to speak to me. It was then that I discovered how badly Wales had been beaten. I drove across to their hotel and took a few of them out to my haunts in Manly, where we got fucking smashed. Me, Gibbsy, and a few others, and I tried to give them a bit of a pep talk. They were miserable. There was definitely a split in the camp; that much was obvious. Morale was low, and they'd just been taken to the cleaners. That was the moment when I realised, 'I've made the right decision here.'

Robert Jones: The build-up to the New South Wales game was farcical. In the modern day, you have half an hour out on the field warming up. We had half an hour in the *boiling* hot changing room, doing crossovers, sweating our bollocks off, slipping everywhere in our studs. It was all part of that 'COME ON!' Neath attitude. 'Let's get ourselves up for this.' It was totally misplaced.

Hugh Williams-Jones: It was getting hotter and hotter, and people started slipping and sliding and clattering into one another. The Neath boys were buying into it, because they were used to it, and that's what had got them success. It was based around this mentality of going berserk, pushing yourself to the limit, and getting yourself in the zone. But when you come from a different background, it's difficult to buy into it. Clive Rowlands pulled us all into a huddle, 'Come on in boys, for Calon, for Wales, mun, for the people back home, for your mams, for your dads, for your wives, Rob are we together? Let's do a ball coming in NOW.' And he does his usual thing of getting us to scream 'now' when the ball comes in. The only problem was there was no ball to hand, so we had to use a Vaseline tin. 'Vaseline tin coming in NOW,' doesn't have the same ring to it.

Gareth Llewellyn: I remember being asked by an Aussie journalist beforehand, 'How do you think you're going to handle Willie Ofahengaue?' and thinking, 'Who's he?' We didn't have a clue. We soon found out, but that was the point – there was no analysis. No one had looked into the opposition. Ron referred to David Campese as a 'shitty-arsed winger' before the game. He ended up scoring five tries.

Hugh Williams-Jones: We got smashed, but I'm convinced they would have beaten any international side on that day. Kearns, McKenzie, Willie O, Farr-Jones, Campo, Roebuck. It was a virtual Test side, and they were on their game.

There were, in fact, nine players in that New South Wales side who would go on to play in the Test a week later. David Campese's five tries didn't even make up half the total. New South Wales scored thirteen overall, as they romped to an eye-popping 71–8 victory. Wales approached the Test match with an understandable feeling of dread, and Ron Waldron responded the only way he knew, by cracking the whip even harder.

Robert Jones: Discipline was a big thing for him. In the week building up to the Test, he caught Gareth Llewellyn eating a lollipop and went absolutely berserk. He'd lost all sense of perspective, and was ranting and raving, poking him in the chest shouting, 'If your father could see you now, sucking on a lollipop, he'd be bloody ashamed.'

Scott Gibbs was one of his favourites, and one of the few to have emerged from the New South Wales debacle with any credit. That week he made Gibbsy get up on the table and take his shirt off. Gibbsy was embarrassed, but he went along with it, and fair play, he had quite the physique at that point.

Gareth Llewellyn: I'm sure Scott was embarrassed about that, as a young kid. But he'd fronted up against New South Wales, and Ron thought he'd set an example to us all.

Robert Jones: He was ultra-professional. Ron's pointing at him, going, 'Look at that. He's like a pocket bloody battleship. That's what you all need to aspire to. And look at you eating bloody lollipops. If I ever fucking see you or anyone in this room with a lollipop in their mouth . . .' A few days later, we were going to an ambassador's reception, and one of the boys went out and bought thirty lollipops. We made a point of walking into the reception, sucking on these lollies.

Gareth Llewellyn: It was fucking boiling outside. I was having an ice lolly to cool off, and Ron lost it. 'Fucking hell, you're about to play against the might of Australia, up against fucking "Dai" Eales, and you're eating a fucking ice cream!' I remember thinking, 'Dai Eales, who's he?'

Hugh Williams-Jones: Discipline was starting to suffer. People were turning up late for meetings, the whole thing was beginning to unravel.

Robert Jones: It was a disaster. It showed just how far behind Australia we were. I don't think we were a happy camp, and that came through in the way we conducted ourselves. I'd lost my place to Chris Bridges, so I was sat by the coaches on the bench for the Test and could hear them arguing amongst themselves. Ron would bark at Dai Richards, the backs coach. 'Dai, what's that move? What are they doing? That's rubbish. Why's he on the ball there?' Eventually, Dai lost his patience, and said, 'Fucking hell Ron, mun. There's a monitor in front of you. You have a look.' Me, Anthony Clement, and Dai Evans were on the bench laughing at the absurdity of it all. We were getting hammered on the pitch, and *none* of us wanted to go on, so whenever there was an injury, we'd shrink into our seats. At one point, Bridges went down, and the boys were all laughing. 'Bridges is down, you're on Rob.' I did not want to go on. It was that bad.

Gareth Llewellyn: We were taken to the cleaners by their backs in the Test. The game had moved on, and we were still using a very basic form of defence. Australian rugby league was way ahead of anything else in the world. We were undone by some pretty simple moves, but they were things we weren't used to defending.

All in all, the Welsh try line was breached twelve times, as the rampant Wallabies coasted to a 63–6 victory. Welsh fans were just grateful the IRB's decision to raise the value of a try to five points didn't happen until the following year.

Ieuan Evans: There were far too many schisms in that squad. Some of them superficial, others deep-seated. There were a lot of strong personalities, people who refused to back down, and that can cause fissures too. You can have the utmost respect for someone as a player while realising you're never going to be bosom buddies off the pitch. Usually that can be managed, but there was some serious animosity on that tour. One tiny positive was the emergence of Scott Gibbs. Others were scarred by the experience, and were never heard of again, but Scott went on to become a world-class operator.

Mike Hall: The Neath clique definitely drove a wedge through the squad, but it wasn't all that surprising. The club game in Wales at the time was thriving. Neath were really strong, Llanelli were strong, as were Swansea. We had our moments at Cardiff. Pontypridd were very good. So you had this ferocious tribalism which meant playing for your club was almost more important than playing for your country. Neath probably looked down on the other clubs, and it's natural that when they got together, they just wanted to stick together. I read something in the paper recently about the so-called golden age of English football, and the fact they never won anything. Apparently Rio Ferdinand wouldn't sit at the same table as Steven Gerrard, because he feared he'd give something away that would help Liverpool against Man United in the Premier League. They wouldn't even mingle so no bonds were created. Maybe it was a similar thing for us back then.

Anthony Clement: Perhaps club rugby was a bit more tribal then. You wore your heart on your sleeve.

Mike Hall: It wasn't just tribal differences, but cultural ones as well. Andy Booth and I were rooming with Brian Williams and Kevin Phillips. Boothy and I were city boys from Cardiff, and we were sharing with two farmers who were used to getting up at five in the morning to milk their cows or whatever. They couldn't shake the habit. Me and Boothy were students, and were wondering what the hell was going on. I thought the room was being burgled the first time it happened. Hearing a light go on, and seeing this shadowy figure pacing the room. In the end we swapped so Boothy and I were sharing, which just served to entrench the divide. These days that probably wouldn't be allowed. You're forced to share with people you may not choose to, to foster a sense of solidarity. For us, it seemed easier for them to go back to their default setting and act like they did in Neath. I think a lot of them struggled with the travel as well. They got homesick.

Robert Jones: I remember rooming with Garin Jenkins. He'd be up at five o'clock, having a bath filled with fucking mustard powder, because he'd heard it cleansed your body. I woke up thinking, 'What the fuck's that smell?' Looking back, it may have been curry powder or garlic. Whatever it was, it stank. Garin was a one-off.

Garin Jenkins: Richard Webster gave me the idea. As a front row forward, I always struggled with a stiff back. I shared a room with Webster once, and he put a bit of powdered mustard in my bath. I felt as though it was going right to where my back was aching.

Ian Gough: I loved Garin. When I first came into the squad under Kevin Bowring, I was just a kid. John Humphreys was captain, and captain of Cardiff, and he was the big dog. He was in charge, and didn't have much time for us youngsters. But Garin made me feel immediately welcome. 'Alright Van?' I said, 'What? Why Van?' And he said 'Van Gough, isn't it?' And I've been Van Gough ever since.

Gareth Llewellyn: He'd had his nose broken by Peter Fatialofa, and used to struggle with his breathing. I walked into the room once when we were sharing, and I could barely get across the threshold. My eyes were burning. He was flat out, fast asleep, and snoring. He'd eaten around sixteen cloves of raw garlic and emptied an entire bottle of Olbas Oil onto his pillow.

Garin Jenkins: You do what works for you, don't you? I enjoyed a cold shower in the morning, see. Someone once told me if it's cold in the morning, put your hands in freezing ice. That way when you go out, you'll be nice and warm, isn't it?

A great friend of mine from Ynysybwl once told me, 'If you have any ankle trouble, do what the horses do. Run in ankle deep water to strengthen it.' Well, I had a bang on the hip once, and he said, 'You need to get in a cold brook of water.' I remember going up the sheep dip in Ynysybwl. There was nobody up there, so I stripped off like a naturist, and sunk into the brook. It was freezing. I was squealing at the top of my lungs, and next thing you know, a bunch of ramblers hove into view. There I was, lying in the brook with no clothes on. I don't know what they must have thought. But it got me right for the game that weekend.

Emyr Lewis: It reminds me of the early ice baths, which were just a wheelie bin full of cold water and ice cubes. It wasn't too bad getting in. But try getting out of a wheelie bin when everything's gone numb.

Gareth Llewellyn: Rob Jones once arrived at training with a bandaged knee, and when he removed the bandage, a bunch of cabbage leaves fell out. One of the old boys up in Trebanos had told him that cabbage leaves would help draw out the bruise. Another old wives' tale.

It was reasonable to think that Wales's reputation couldn't have sunk any lower after their capitulation against the Wallabies. But it did. An unseemly brawl between the Welsh players at the post-match function turned a humiliating situation into a disgraceful one. One local paper summed the tour up rather succinctly with its headline: 'Whipped, Woeful Wales Wallop Each Other'.

Ieuan Evans: All the ill-will and resentment bubbled to the surface, and things erupted during the dinner. We couldn't have sunk any lower, and I felt depressed about it for a long time afterwards. There were certain players who genuinely disliked each other, and things had been allowed to ferment. I've been in plenty of situations where there have been fights on the training paddock – people care, people get emotional, and tempers fray – that's part and parcel of being involved in a contact sport at the elite level. This was different. It was ugly and thoroughly unpleasant.

Anthony Clement: It was a combination of factors. A lot of men, a lot of testosterone. Half of them were pissed off they weren't being picked, and they'd been living in each other's pockets for a month.

Robert Jones: Things boiled over between some of the Neath boys and the Cardiff boys. There was plenty of bad blood, a few players couldn't stand one another, fingers were being pointed at the Neath regime, the selection, the perceived favouritism. Some of the Neath boys were sticking up for Ron, who'd been given a hard time by certain members of the press. It was a boozy dinner, and the drink, mixed with the unhappiness and the frustration, turned out to be a toxic cocktail.

Mike Hall: Those Neath boys weren't the type to back down. I'd been playing for Cambridge University the previous season, and we'd beaten Cardiff, beaten Bridgend, before going down to the Gnoll. Neath put their full side out and kicked the shit out of us. Lyn Williams stood up off the side of a scrum and booted Rob Wainwright in the head. It was a brutal, different game then, and there were different principles that went with it.

Robert Jones: Mike Hall was headstrong as well, mind. He was quite vocal and if things weren't working, he'd be the first to point it out.

Paul Thorburn: I was on the top table thinking, 'I genuinely don't want to be here.' Things were getting unruly. Kevin Phillips started chucking food about, and arguing with one of the journalists over his treatment of Ron. Next thing a bread roll landed plum in the soup bowl of the ARU president's wife.

Phil Davies: I was applauding because he'd actually thrown it straight for once. He normally couldn't hit a cow's arse with a shovel.

Ieuan Evans: I think the story has grown in the telling. There were some skirmishes, some food was thrown, someone's hand got cut, but it wasn't quite gunfight at the OK Corral. I've seen meatier fights at a training session, where people have shaken hands and walked away. This was all about the context. It was nasty and bitter.

Mike Hall: I was the one who got cut, because I was trying to calm things down, to stop the Neath and Llanelli players from killing one another. One of them was holding a glass like a weapon, and when I tried to break them apart, my hand got really badly gashed. Then of course, it was me coming through airport arrivals a few days later all bandaged up. The press was everywhere, and there were cartoon mock-ups of me as the guilty party. I remember telling my mother, 'I didn't do anything, Mum!' She wouldn't believe me. For once I *was* the innocent party.

Hugh Williams-Jones: The behaviour of the boys was atrocious, but the incident was over in a flash.

Robert Jones: There was a bit of pushing and shoving, and what have you. You had the Australia team, who had just annihilated us, sitting quietly with their wives, drinking orange juice and enjoying the celebrations. Then you had the Welsh team, getting hammered, shouting and bawling, throwing beer cans and bread rolls across the room. Then some of them started stuffing serviettes in the empty cans, lighting them, and lobbing the flaming cans in the air. Fucking *hell*. There was a bunch of us hanging our heads in shame, thinking, 'We're better than this.' In some ways I wish someone had videoed it, because you'd never believe an international team could have behaved in that way.

Ieuan Evans: It was a total abdication of responsibility on the part of some. You're still wearing the three feathers, you're still representing your country, and much better standards are expected. You should be able to control your emotions, and resist the temptation. Let's get through this, get home, and start again.

I remember thinking, 'Is this it? Maybe I should have gone to league. They've all moved on, and I'm having to cope with this crap.' We were in the ditch. Everybody was driving past us on this beautiful road to the future, and we were scrapping in the ditch. Some of us were desperate to crawl out, others were happy to stay there.

Paul Thorburn: I said at the time that we'd become the clowns of international rugby both on and off the field. There were a lot of boys who went over the top with their drinking, which didn't help. To be critical of Ron when they were spending every spare moment slugging beer down their necks was a bit rich. That was the transition period between amateurism and professionalism, and we were at least eight years behind. There were some experienced, respected rugby players on that tour who acted shamefully. I don't want to rake up dirt from the past, other than to say they won't be at my funeral, and I won't be at theirs.

Robert Jones: It was difficult for Ron. It made him ill. He almost had a heart attack while he was out there.

The fallout was immediate and severe. Ron Waldron resigned on medical grounds when Wales returned home, and Paul Thorburn announced his international retirement. And perhaps recognising it for the anachronism that it was, the WRU disbanded the Big Five selector system – something that Carwyn James insisted should have happened back in the seventies. It meant that Waldron's replacement, Alan Davies, would have more autonomy in selecting his sides than any of his predecessors. His first decision was to appoint Ieuan Evans as the new captain of Wales. Evans led his country to defeat against France that autumn, in what was Davies's only chance to run the rule over his charges before the World Cup kicked off in October.

Ieuan Evans: You could argue that we were static throughout most of the eighties. As the nineties progressed we started pedalling backwards at an alarming rate, which was why when I was offered the captaincy it came with mixed feelings. It was an obvious privilege, and an immense source of pride, but awkward too as I'd be involved in selection. I'd have players coming to see me all the time asking if they'd been picked. I always blamed Alan and Bob if anyone got dropped. Alan brought a structure, and it felt as though there was a light at the end of the tunnel. His appointment put an end to the parochialism. John Ryan was east Wales, and had coached Newport and Cardiff. Ron Waldron was from the west, and was Neath through and through. Alan Davies was from Nottingham, so had none of those ties, and was less likely to be influenced by Welsh rugby politics. It was a breath of fresh air.

Rupert Moon: He was very theoretical in his thinking, and a big reader. Jim Collins's *Good to Great* was his bible. He knew how business worked, was a deep thinker, and he was articulate enough to be able to get his message across.

Anthony Clement: He was the closest I experienced to Ian McGeechan. It was a case of 'what do you think?' rather than issuing orders. It was a debate rather than 'we're doing this'.

Robert Jones: He was a very knowledgeable rugby man, and he knew how to deal with *people*. He came along at a time in my career when I was suffering with a bit of self-doubt. It sounds cheesy, but he'd put *Simply the Best* on the stereo, and put his arm around me, and say 'This is about you, Rob.' At the time, it worked. It was what I needed.

Garin Jenkins: That management team was ahead of its time. It had the inspirational qualities of Gareth Jenkins, together with the almost scientific approach of Alan Davies. He'd make us watch videos not just of the opposition, but of referees as well. We analysed their positioning, and the way they officiated certain areas of the game. Bob Norster was a great manager too. This was the start of us tinkering with professionalism. The diets, the fitness batteries, the analysis. It was an exciting time to be involved in rugby.

Emyr Lewis: We were trying to emulate what England were doing. They were ultra-professional at the time. They were weighing their food and everything.

Mike Hall: He was the best coach we had, and I played under five or six for Wales in a seven-year Test career. Alan understood the importance of nutrition and sports science, weight training, video analysis. We'd done nothing like that before.

Gareth Llewellyn: It was a different dynamic, and I loved it. The more professional rugby got, the more I enjoyed it. A lot of people hark back to the amateur days, the 'good old days', but I'm the opposite. I was happy to leave that all behind.

Mike Hall: He dismantled the barriers that existed between members of different clubs. It's not rocket science. We won the Championship in '94 because he managed to meld a team of the best players from Neath, Llanelli and Cardiff, and got them to play as a team. He was a very cerebral and intelligent coach, and had the man-management skills to persuade a team to play together as one. Him and Bob Norster formed quite a dynamic double act.

Rupert Moon: There was a really eclectic mix of weird and wonderful people in that squad. Crazy Rayer, Mark Perego, Nigel Walker. You couldn't have had a bigger cross section of your community, but we all got on like a family, and Alan can take the credit for that.

Hugh Williams-Jones: Up to that point, we'd train with Wales at Sophia Gardens, and you'd have to wear your own kit, whatever you had. There'd be a mish-mash of colours and styles, and at the end of the session, we'd take it home all damp and stinking. Alan said straight away that we needed uniform training kit so we were all wearing the same thing. And not only that, they'd take it away and wash it ready for next time. It would be hanging on your peg when you arrived, all nicely laundered, with a fresh towel for the shower. It sounds like a small thing, but it mattered.

Mike Hall: It was harder to get out of his squad than to get in because he'd picked the players he wanted from the start, and believed in them. He thought long-term, putting us all on fitness programmes, putting us all through psychometric testing, encouraging us to share rooms with people we wouldn't otherwise have got on with. But ultimately, he had no time to prepare us for that World Cup. He had about six weeks.

Gareth Llewellyn: When the psychometric test results came back, everyone was bunched together on a similar part of the spectrum, roughly where you'd expect them to be, and there was this one lone dot out on his own. There were a couple of categories he could have fallen into, one of which was raging psychopath. It was Mark Perego.

Rupert Moon: We got a lot fitter under Alan Davies, and he was able to manage some of the more 'mercurial' talents in the group. I'd played over the bridge in the English midlands, so knew of Alan's reputation. Him and Gareth were the yin and the yang. Gareth brought the emotion, Alan the steady hand. Davies created a 'Team Wales'. I wasn't the best player, there were better players than me that didn't play for Wales at that time, but when we got together, we'd put on our armour, and become greater than the sum of our parts. It's like being an actor. The coach is the director, and he knows what he needs. You might have the silkiest skills, but if you don't fit, you don't fit. It's rare that you have fifteen of the best, most skilful players in one team. It doesn't happen.

Hugh Williams-Jones: It was easy for Alan to introduce his methods because there was nothing left behind from the previous regime. He'd say, 'What are your lineout moves then?' And we'd shrug and say, 'Dunno.' A few years later we toured Zimbabwe again, and turned up for a session at Harare Cricket Ground the day before the Test. Alan got us in a circle, and told everybody to put their right hand across their chest. 'Get them all level,' he said, 'it's all about coordination and teamwork.' I was thinking, 'What are we doing here then?' Next thing, 'Get your left arm underneath it, get them all level. Not too high. Now, with your right hand, grab the left hand of the bloke next to you. Keep your feet shoulder-width apart. Now look around you. Look at your teammates.' Again, I'm thinking, 'Where's he going with this?' Then he goes, 'Slowly, I want you to all move your left foot followed by your right so you're going round in a circle. And we'll speed up gradually. You have to maintain your discipline and your coordination.' As soon as we start moving he starts singing, 'Ring a ring a roses, pocket full of posies, atishoo, atishoo. YOU all fall down.' We all collapsed to the floor, laughing. He clapped his hands and said, 'Okay, session over, back on the bus.' That was Alan in a nutshell. We were all buzzing on the bus because we didn't have to train. It was like a gift. He could read the players' minds – whether it was a bit of fatigue, or boredom, or whether we just didn't need it that day.

Robert Jones: At a training session before the World Cup, I'd be kicking off my right foot, and he'd say, 'Now do it off your left.' I'd do it and he'd say, 'No other scrum half in the world can do that.' He had a knack of knowing how and when to boost your confidence. He knew me, and the psychometric testing probably told him that I wasn't necessarily as confident as I came across. I'd lost a bit of my mojo, at that point. With Jiffy going – as good as Jinks and all these other players were – I probably needed someone with me who could take the game by the scruff of the neck, so I could do my own thing. Alan sensed my lack of confidence, and encouraged me to play with freedom again. This was the first time we'd spent any real time analysing ourselves, analysing the opposition. We were doing fitness testing based on the type of game we wanted to play. It was becoming more sophisticated, more organised, more professional. Alan was very scientific, and very analytical, but a certain way was never drilled into you. We'd discuss various options in various situations, but he always said that if things unfolded differently on the pitch, we should go for it. That was all new to us.

Mark Ring: The World Cup started disastrously with defeat to Western Samoa. We pushed them back in the scrums, but got drilled in the loose. I've watched it back loads of times. I had Mike Hall in the centre with me and he couldn't see anything. He was a strong runner, but had no vision. He was just a banger. Against sides like Samoa, there are opportunities to get your wingers away, to get your full back into space. It's easy for me to blame someone else, but I vividly remember moments in the game where I'd create space for Mike – set him up with a one-on-one with his opposite number, and all he'd need to do was draw his man, and put the full back away, and he couldn't do it. Key moments in the game, and any one of them would've been enough to win it. I get on with him famously now, but I didn't so well at the time.

Mike Hall: Ringo does look back at certain things through a filter. He has a very selective memory. He thinks he was a genius, and everyone else was rubbish. He was playing on one leg in that tournament because of his knee injury. I barely played with him again. He didn't get picked much after that under Alan Davies. It was Gibbsy, me, Nigel Davies, Adrian Davies. He was a brilliant player, and I can't take that away from him, but he was never a team man. I still feel an enormous sense of injustice about that game. There was a clear refereeing mistake. Vaega's try should never have stood. Robert Jones touched down before him. If we'd had a video ref then, it would have been disallowed.

Robert Jones: I definitely got there. Video evidence proves it. If there was a TMO, we would have . . . we might have gone through! That was the most physical game I ever played in. More than Tonga in 1986. The Tonga game was *nastier*, but in terms of hits, Samoa was the worst. Clem got poleaxed coming into the line and couldn't walk for days. He had a bruise the length of his body. He's a big, strong, powerful boy, but those Samoans are on a different level, and have no regard for their own welfare. They're so hard.

Mike Hall: They were no mugs either, and they had the surprise factor. These days, the Pacific Island teams are diluted because their best talent is being picked off by the richer unions. Back then, they were all playing for Samoa. Did we underestimate them? Possibly. Were we ill-prepared? Yes. Were we unlucky in the game? Definitely.

Ieuan Evans: It wasn't necessarily the surprise people made it out to be. Alan Davies had had barely any time to lay the foundations, and we'd not long come back from that disastrous Australian tour. It's a game we should have won though.

Mark Ring: There were naysayers asking what were Wales doing picking Mark Ring with his dodgy knee. We beat Argentina in the second game, and I was fine. Then we got walloped by Australia, and in the last quarter of that game, my legs were like lead, because the three games had taken their toll. Ironically, it wasn't the dodgy knee, it was the fact I'd done no training or conditioning. There was no bounce there. And then the abuse came flooding in, because when Wales lose, it's always the fly half's fault. But I was actually pleased with my personal performances. That's just where we were as a team. We only won two lineouts in that game against Australia. Says it all.

Hugh Williams-Jones: Even though we didn't get out of the group, there was a feeling that under Alan, things were beginning to click.

Given Wales's walloping at the hands of the Wallabies just a few months earlier, a final scoreline of 38–3 was seen by some glass-half-full optimists as a sign of progress. But shorn of context, it was another dreadful defeat. It was Wales's heaviest home loss in history, and the first time ever they'd conceded six tries in Cardiff. John Eales dominated the lineout to such an extent that the final tally was 28–2 in Australia's favour. It meant Wales were dumped out of the World Cup before the knockout stages, and would have to qualify for the next one.

FOURTEEN

NEIL JENKINS LOOKED
LIKE A SWAN VESTA MATCH

While the World Cup had been a crushing disappointment, it was accepted that Alan Davies had had precious little time to impose his vision. Three months later, Wales entered the Five Nations with renewed hope. The habit of lurching from coach to coach, and regime to regime had led to a loss of identity and confidence. Davies had set about restoring both those things, and the optimism appeared well-founded when the campaign began with victory over Ireland. Llanelli's Colin Stephens made his debut at fly half, and was being hailed by some as the new Jonathan Davies. But it was the Swansea number eight, Stuart Davies, who scored the winning try. It raised the nation's hopes ahead of the next game against France, but that was to end in a 12–9 defeat. It was followed by a more damaging one against eventual Grand Slam winners, England, in which Wales were nilled, before a morale-boosting victory over Scotland. Two wins out of four was a modest return, but it marked an upturn in fortunes for a team so starved of success.

Garin Jenkins: I always loved playing in Ireland. For some reason it felt like playing at home. I started four times at Lansdowne Road and never lost.

Emyr Lewis: We had a deal with Ireland. They'd win in Cardiff, and we'd win in Dublin.

Garin Jenkins: That opening game in 1992 was a massive, convincing win, 16–15. The buzz going to the ground was immense, we were playing Spandau Ballet's *Gold* on the bus, and I remember thinking, 'Flippin' heck, I've arrived.' You knew your parents would be watching, and your guts were doing somersaults. I was naive to Test rugby at the time, but the experience was intoxicating. As a hooker, you're close to the touchline, and you can smell the waft of food and cigar smoke from the terraces. You'd pick out a face in the crowd, and the excitement would grow. My father and brother were there, and the excitement of thinking they'd come all that way to watch me was overwhelming. They knew all the tricks in Dublin – the opposition ball boys were briefed to roll the ball along the ground, to make the hooker bend and pick it up. But we made an early impression – Tony Copsey gave Neil Francis a love bite around the eye early doors, and got away with it. No TMO in those days of course. Laurance Delaney, in the last couple of scrums, was out on his feet, but he was so old-school, that he stayed on. It was an era when you never came off to give your teammate a chance. And Dai Joe [David Joseph], who was a teammate of mine at Swansea, was absolutely fuming that he didn't come off. The last few scrums, Laurance was up against the Lion, Nick Popplewell, and we were literally holding him up off the ground. We clung on for the victory, and then the celebrations in the night, well, they just ran on into the next day. I don't know whether Laurance was concussed, but I remember him taking out an entire table in the after-match function. Literally falling through it and sending food and cutlery flying everywhere. It could have been the Jamesons, or it could have been the delayed after-effects of Willie Anderson's fist, I don't know.

Hugh Williams-Jones: The pleasing thing about the Scotland game was that we scrummaged them off the park, and took a few against the head. It was David Sole's last game for Scotland and I was having a pint with him after and asked why he was retiring. I thought he had plenty of rugby left in him. He was just about to answer when a WRU committee man from north Wales approached and said to me, 'Well done Garin, you had a great game today, excellent.' He turned to David and said, 'He's not a bad hooker, is he?' David replied, 'Aye, he's not a bad tight-head either.' The bloke laughed and walked off in his WRU blazer. David turned to me and said, 'That's why I'm finishing. There are so many people in Scotland like that, running the game. I just can't do it anymore.'

There was no summer tour in 1992, so Wales only had two autumn Tests to help prepare for the 1993 Championship. Italy were dispatched with relative ease (43–12), before Australia arrived. Wales thought they had a genuine chance of victory, after Swansea and Llanelli had both beaten the touring Wallabies, but it wasn't to be. For the third time in eighteen months, they failed to cross Australia's try line, and succumbed 23–6. Despite the defeat, the Swansea and Llanelli results had given the nation renewed hope, and the Australian coach Bob Dwyer admitted that Wales had improved 'out of sight'. There was a spring in their step when they jetted off to Lanzarote shortly after Christmas for a warm-weather training camp.

Emyr Lewis: That was an eye-opener. We were put through all kinds of speed and fitness tests. We shared a training base with professional track athletes and were looking on in awe at their levels of professionalism. We'd do two or three 400m circuits, and be knackered. These guys were doing it over and over again. They'd have a twenty-second break between circuits, and go again. They must have been looking at us thinking, 'What's this rabble that's just turned up?'

Garin Jenkins: The BBC cameras had come out to film a piece on Nigel Walker, who'd been an Olympic athlete, but he'd torn a hamstring, so they just filmed us fatties instead. As a hooker, I loved that stuff, I was used to chewing up the miles, and emptying the tank.

Robert Jones: We did all our serious fitness training early on, and were given a half day off. The following day we'd be focusing on the rugby side. The feeling was that the hard work was out of the way, and we could afford to go on the piss before the rugby stuff began.

Anthony Clement: The prospect of a day off in Lanzarote had us rubbing our hands with glee. About ten of us went out on the pop. Me, Rob, Jinks, Howley.

Robert Jones: We hired bikes and took off on a ride around the island, stopping at every pub we came across. We had quite a few beers. As we left the last pub heading for home, I remember saying, 'Boys, don't go fucking berserk now we've all had a few. Let's go back in our own time sensibly now.' Then three or four of them just shot off like they were in the Tour de France.

Anthony Clement: We were racing, going flat out. Somebody's front tyre clipped someone's back tyre, and then . . . carnage.

Robert Jones: I was following my own advice, trundling along with Rob Howley, as we approached the brow of a hill. I saw a Welsh peaked cap blowing back in the wind. As we got to the top, a scene of total bedlam unfolded in front of us. There were bikes strewn everywhere, upside down, buckled wheels slowly going round. Hugh Williams-Jones and Colin Stephens arguing like fuck, Mike Griffiths holding his shoulder having broken his collarbone. Clem must have skidded about fifteen metres. He didn't have an ounce of skin left on his body. There was no pavement, and there was a big camber in the road, so I pull over *pissing* myself laughing, to the point where I've stopped, my bike's wobbling, and I just tumble in slow motion into a huge fucking cactus. I'm still laughing, but now I've got these huge cactus spikes embedded in me. Bob Norster was not happy. Mike eventually came back from hospital, in a sling, and Clem comes back looking like a mummy, bandaged from head to foot. All you could see was his face.

Anthony Clement: I've still got the scars to this day. It was one hell of a crash. It's funny looking back, but at the time it was crazy. It's a wonder nobody got killed. If a car had been coming the other way, it would have been curtains.

Robert Jones: Later in the trip we had one-to-ones with Alan Davies where we were asked to outline our ambitions for the year ahead. I told him I wanted to get on the Lions tour. Clem just said he wanted his skin to grow back.

Emyr Lewis: The opening game of the '93 Five Nations was my third attempt to play against England. In '91, I was on the bench, and didn't get on. In '92, I had food poisoning, was rushed back from London in a police car and watched the game from a bed in Morriston Hospital with Lyn Jones and a six pack of beer. In '93, I finally made it onto the pitch, and I remember looking up at these monsters, these giants in white shirts. The sheer size of them. Bayfield was there, Dooley, Rodber, Clarke. They were *enormous*. I thought I was quite a big guy. I was sixteen-and-a-half stone soaking wet. These guys were eighteen stone all day long. They were all six foot six, six foot eight, six foot ten. We played that game more in hope than expectation. They had more or less a Lions team playing against us, and were going for a third Grand Slam in a row, but it was just one of those days when everything went right. The atmosphere was phenomenal. During the whole game, we couldn't hear *anything*. Couldn't hear the lineout calls, couldn't *speak* to one another. Scott Gibbs and Mike Hall in the midfield were immense. They blitzed everything, put everyone off their game. And we had a bit of luck. Dewi Morris crossed the line, and thought he'd scored. I genuinely don't think he did. Just look at the scoreboard.

Ieuan Evans was a world class player who was used to chasing lost causes during a period of famine for Welsh rugby. After a speculative kick downfield from the flank-forward Emyr Lewis, Evans turned on the after-burners, and scorched past a trundling Rory Underwood to score the game's only try. It turned out to be the winning score, as the second half played out without a single point being scored.

Emyr Lewis: What was I doing standing there, that's the question? Neil Jenkins was on my inside, and Robert Jones just passed *me* the ball. I thought, 'What on earth is he doing that for?' I was just outside my twenty-two, and couldn't go straight for touch, so I dinked it behind Underwood, and thought it would dribble over the touchline. But Underwood was caught sleeping, and Ieuan was really sharp at the time. He made the most of a bad situation.

Scott Quinnell: I was watching that game in the pub, and thinking to myself, 'I'd love to be part of that.'

Garin Jenkins: I was watching from my caravan in Porthcawl, as I was serving a sixteen-week ban after being sent off in the Swansea–Llanelli derby the week before. I missed the whole Five Nations, and the tours. The Lions went to New Zealand in the summer, and Wales went to Namibia. I came back in September stronger and sharper, but I'd love to have played in that game.

Emyr Lewis: With minutes to go, we were five yards from our line. Nigel Meek was hooker. He had forty-inch-chest-shorts – they were pulled virtually up to his armpits, and he was shouting, 'What's the call? What's the call?' We were shouting it back at him, but he couldn't hear anything. The ref was telling us to hurry up, the crowd was going bananas, and in the end, Gareth Llewellyn bawls, 'It's me coming forward, alright?', and I thought, 'Crumbs, we're going to lose this now.'

But one way or another, we won the ball, cleared our lines, and survived. The evening that followed, well, we won't go there, other than to say a few pubs were drunk dry. The whole of Carmarthen was drunk dry.

England had won the previous three meetings between the sides by an aggregate margin of 83–12, so to beat them on the opening weekend was a big statement, but it is now remembered as a fleeting glimmer of hope in another desperately disappointing campaign. Wales failed miserably in Scotland, surrendered to Ireland again in Cardiff, and were well beaten by France in Paris.

Hugh Williams-Jones: France won the Championship with that result, but we had a memorable night in Jean-Baptiste Lafond's Paris nightclub. We got the bus back to our hotel at about 4.00 a.m. to discover that some of the wives were still up and drinking in the bar with a few members of the press. The journalist Rob Cole was among them, and he bought us a beer. Then he asked me and Ricky Evans about our first scrum of the day. 'Tell me, that first scrum, with all the noise and drama, all the hype and expectation, what does that actually *feel* like?' I'd had a few, so I said, 'It feels like this, Rob,' buried my head in his chest, and drove him backwards into the jukebox. Just as he was getting back to his feet, a bit groggily, Ricky said, 'No, Pug, it's not like that. It's like this,' and BOOSH, smashes back into him again. Poor Rob had a bit more than he'd bargained for. I think he might have broken a rib.

Summer victories against Namibia and Zimbabwe were followed up with a 55–5 trouncing of Japan in Cardiff, but disaster struck a week later, when Wales fell victim to a Gareth Rees-inspired Canada. The Canadian fly half knocked over a last-gasp conversion to win the match 26–24. It marked an inauspicious debut for Scott Quinnell, and the Alan Davies regime, which had promised so much, was now having to answer serious questions. Expectations ahead of the 1994 Five Nations were understandably low, but Wales responded in spectacular fashion, demolishing Scotland in the opening game in Cardiff.

Scott Quinnell: That was one of the greatest experiences of my life, playing against Scotland in my first Five Nations game at home. Everyone talks about autumn internationals, and tours, but the Five Nations is on a totally different level. Cardiff just opens its arms and gives everybody a big hug. Taking that bus from the Copthorne into the city, and seeing the crowd parting for you, seeing the smiles, the happiness, and the joy. It's something you'll never ever forget. The heavens opened before the game, but nothing could dampen the spirits.

Ieuan Evans: It was a terrific game in the rain and the mud. We played a lot of good rugby in dire conditions. It could have been a desperate game, but we brought some life to it, and Mikey Rayer was the star with his two spectacular dives.

Emyr Lewis: He only came on because Nigel Walker went off. He'd been kicked in the head, and he was completely out of it.

Garin Jenkins: He was fighting with the physios, wasn't he?

Emyr Lewis: He was fighting with Mark Davies, the physio. He didn't know what he was doing, who he was, or who he was trying to hit. He was concussed in a big way.

Rupert Moon: Despite the awful weather, we carried on playing, carried on generating quick ball, and we backed our skills to deliver the victory. It did wonders for our self-belief.

Garin Jenkins: It was hammering it down, but it remains one of my great memories. I'd dreamt of it as a kid, from watching the old Wales–Scotland games. Seeing Gareth Edwards playing against Scotland in a lovely muddy field. Gareth Jenkins fired us up beforehand, because we'd been dealt a hiding at Murrayfield the year before. International matches in those days generally began with a bit of 'handbags at dawn' and that day began with an almighty 'all-in'. Afterwards, I got reported by a Scottish solicitor for what had happened on the field.

Anthony Clement: Mike Rayer came on as a supersub, and scored those two tries. Managing to score three tries in those conditions was remarkable. We thought it was going to be a right old slog.

Mike Hall: A fortnight before the game, after training, Alan Davies ordered us all down the pub, and encouraged us to have a skinful. The following morning, he got us up at the crack of dawn to do a 3,000m test. It sounds sadistic, but there was a sense of purpose. We bonded in the pub, and then all suffered together the next day. It's subtle psychology at play, but we became collectively stronger as a result.

Garin Jenkins: We went to Ireland after that, and I can always remember the comment from our dear friend David Parry Jones. I was pack leader, and he said in his article that putting me in charge of the pack in Lansdowne Road, was like giving a monkey a machine gun.

Scott Quinnell: That was a totally different affair out in Ireland. A hostile environment, a brutal experience.

Garin Jenkins: We did a job on them, recording another *massive* victory of 17 points to 15, and we were down to bare bones at the end. Wayne Proctor got knocked out, and Rob Jones ended up on the wing.

Emyr Lewis: Wayne had to drink through a straw for about two months.

Mike Hall: The standout game was France because they were a quality outfit at the time, with the likes of Philippe Sella leading the charge.

Garin Jenkins: We hadn't beaten them for twelve years, and we'd heard all about this monster in the second row, Olivier Merle, who'd been an Olympic shot putter. Marc Cecillon, Thierry Lacroix, Philippe Sella. They had some world-class talent, and we were up against it.

Emyr Lewis: One of the first rucks – total carnage. Garin Jenkins, Phil Davies, and John Davies went 'mountaineering'. They went straight over the top, studs flying everywhere. If that had been done in this day and age, all three would have been sent off. But it set the tone, and told the French we were ready to fight fire with fire.

Gareth Llewellyn: They were the dirtiest games you'd play in. Grabbing your bollocks and gouging your eyes was standard, part of the deal. I had a huge scar on my arm for years after being bitten by Jean-Francois Tordo. John Davies did as well. He actually named his dog after him because it used to bite him all the time.

Scott Quinnell: The reason we played in green socks was so the referee could figure out who was to blame when the feet went flying at the rucks. We wore green socks to convince the referee that it wasn't us kicking ourselves.

Garin Jenkins: We put them on the back foot early. We were coming out of that grey period, and had remembered how to win.

Emyr Lewis: Some referees are strict in the tackle area, and others are not. On this occasion, he wasn't. I remember Benetton at the bottom of one ruck looking up at the referee with this pleading expression. He'd been trampled all over, but the ref did nothing at all about it. That was it – we'd had the green light to do whatever we wanted.

Garin Jenkins: Scott Quinnell was magnificent that day. He scored an incredible try where he scattered French defenders like skittles. It was an almost carbon copy of his dad's against Scotland in 1978. He was a man-mountain.

Scott Quinnell: Philippe Saint-André says he still has nightmares about it. People still tell me they'd never seen me run so fast, and I say if you've got Benetton, Benazzi and Rodriguez chasing you, you're going to go a bit quicker aren't you? I'm surprised no one got me down. Even when I watch it now, I don't think I'm going to score.

Gareth Llewellyn: Scott virtually won us that game on his own. He was unstoppable. It was a career-defining performance. And he wasn't shy about it either. Full volume as soon as he came in the squad.

Scott Quinnell: France have always been my favourite side to play against. They wanted to beat you up, but they wanted to play rugby as well. I loved the physical side, relished it. Looking into somebody's eyes and knowing they wanted to take your head off. Them knowing that you want to take *their* head off. There's something very motivating about it.

Craig Quinnell: I was watching that game from the stand. That's got to be one of the best solo tries ever scored by a forward. Some tries get better with the telling, but he genuinely went fifty or sixty yards.

Scott Quinnell: People always remind me of my try, but the best thing for me was passing the ball to Nigel for *his* try. I didn't pass too many balls in my time. He had fifty yards to go, but as soon as he got the ball I started celebrating. The only way he wasn't going to score was if he fell over. *Nobody* was going to catch him.

Craig Quinnell: He had *proper* gas. I used to pride myself on my speed for a big man. I'd played sevens, and could run forty metres in five seconds. I once offered Walker the outside playing for Llanelli against Cardiff and it was like, 'Ta-ra.' I didn't even get a finger on him. Unbelievable pace.

Anthony Clement: As Nigel himself said afterwards – only Linford Christie or Colin Jackson could have caught him that day.

Garin Jenkins: It was another great victory and it was all roads to Twickenham for the hundredth Wales–England game, and a potential Grand Slam.

Scott Quinnell: We were all a bit worried about the etiquette with the Queen. We lined up to meet her and shake her hand, all formal, and Mark Perego grabbed her thumb, and gave her the old 'street' handshake – 'What's up, ma'am?' I was thinking, 'What the hell are you doing? She's our Queen!' But that was Pegs. A true eccentric. If we had a black-tie dinner, he'd turn up in shorts and t-shirt. If we had a shorts and t-shirt dinner, he'd turn up in black tie. He just wanted to stand out. His training regime involved strapping logs to his back and running through rivers. He had so much energy. I played in a cup final with him once, and he went for a run around Bute Park in Cardiff *after* the match.

It was the first time since 1988 that Wales entered the final weekend with a chance of winning the title. Destiny was entirely in their own hands. Beat England, and the trophy was theirs. Lose, and it was down to the maths. For the first time, a shared title would be decided on points difference. Whether the extra pressure played its part or not, Wales lacked a certain spark in the opening forty minutes.

Rupert Moon: I'm not sure we were overawed necessarily, but we were disrupted by the build-up. The police escort kept us waiting in traffic on the way there. You'd normally get an escort down the hard shoulder, but they just kept us idling, much to their delight. We arrived really late, on a day we were scheduled to meet the Queen, so everything was supposed to start earlier. We felt rushed, and were destabilised mentally. A lot of the players were put off their game because we were so angry by the way we'd been treated.

Emyr Lewis: We had to get changed on the bus. Our whole routine fell apart. It interfered with our preparations without a shadow of a doubt.

Scott Quinnell: They rushed us a bit, but I don't know if it was deliberate or disrespectful. We'd have done the same in Cardiff. You can only control what you can control, and if you let anything outside of those parameters fluster you, you can only blame yourself.

Mike Hall: We blew it. That was a good England team so we had no divine right to win, but there was a feeling we'd missed out on something special. It was a big deal for a number of reasons. They were opening the new stand at Twickenham, we'd met the Queen beforehand. I don't think anyone had played in as big an occasion as that before.

Rupert Moon: We took a while to get going, and didn't really start playing until the second half. We were inexperienced in that regard. They played a trick on us, and we let it get to us.

Garin Jenkins: I wouldn't blame the bus. In those days, Twickenham was a massive factor. It was such a vociferous arena. Alan Davies reminded us that almost all fifty/fifty decisions go their way when they're playing at home.

Scott Quinnell: I should have scored, and maybe things would have turned out differently. It was a similar position to the try I scored against France. I broke down the left touchline, ball in my left hand, so I could fend with my right. If I was ambidextrous, I'd be a Grand Slam winner now. Instead of reaching out and going for it, I got bundled into touch. Alan Davies asked me afterwards, 'Why the hell didn't you just go for it?' I was diagnosed with dyspraxia at the age of thirty-six, and I phoned Alan and told him I now realised why I didn't go for it. It was nearly fifteen years later, and he said, 'Scott, get over it, boy.'

Emyr Lewis: By the time the second half came around, we played better than them, but it took us that long to get going.

Gareth Llewellyn: It was a pretty formidable English pack. Dooley, Bayfield, Dean Richards, Brian Moore.

Garin Jenkins: They were better than us on the day. Simple as that. It was a tight game, but we didn't have it on the day. Some of their old guard pulled them through. We won the Five Nations, but we lost the Grand Slam. It was a bittersweet day.

Ieuan Evans: Lifting the trophy after losing to England was a massive anti-climax. We hadn't won anything since the Triple Crown in '88, and back then you didn't actually lift anything. To win a tournament was an achievement, but I wish I could turn back the clock, and replay that game.

England were supposed to go up first but they refused because they hadn't won anything, so we were just sat around on the pitch waiting to be summoned. The players were knackered and pissed off, and I almost had to drag them up there, which all added to the sense of anti-climax. The photos are telling. There were players holding the trophy up and frowning. It was an odd experience.

Mike Hall: Ieuan looked embarrassed picking it up. Winning a Five Nations is something to be proud of, but it would have been so much better to win a Grand Slam. Nobody wanted to go up to the podium. We wanted to send Ieuan on his own. We were all consumed by this sense of crushing disappointment.

Scott Quinnell: Yes, the Grand Slam eluded us, but to win the Championship was special. It was a good season, especially considering what had gone before. It didn't stop us celebrating. I got very drunk that night. At the dinner, all the women wanted to sit on Ben Clarke's table. He was like a god walking around the place, the handsome devil. Even my wife wanted to go and sit next to him. It was like going into the enemy camp, and finding out that they're just normal, nice guys. Although they did drink far too much port. I'd never drunk port before, and I didn't touch it for a long time afterwards.

It was undeniably an unsatisfying way for Wales to win the title, but the fact they did gave Alan Davies a little breathing space. With the World Cup in South Africa the following year, Wales's immediate priority was to qualify. They did so with ease, breaking the hundred-point barrier against Portugal, and winning comfortably in Spain. They then embarked on another tour of the South Seas.

Hugh Williams-Jones: That was a long old tour because we went there via Spain, Portugal and Canada. We were away for six weeks. There were no mobile phones and when we were away our families would write letters to us. Bob Norster would be in charge of all the post, and when it was given out in the team room, you'd be hoping that your name would come up. Bob would sift through this pile of mail and say, 'Hugh Williams-Jones?' I'd trot up to the front all excited at the prospect of a letter from home, and he'd hand it to me and go, 'Give that to Ieuan Evans, would you?' Cruel.

Rupert Moon: There was a real sense of harmony in that squad. Everyone knew how much it meant to play for your country. Your club jersey was a cloak that you wore, but that Welsh shirt was like a second skin.

Emyr Lewis: Fiji was paradise. We hung out by the ocean, living in wooden shacks. Open the door, and you're on the beach. Phil Davies went windsurfing one day. He knew how to go straight, but he didn't know how to turn around. He just kept drifting on and on until all you could see was this tiny dot in the distance. They had to send a boat out to rescue him.

Hugh Williams-Jones: The Fiji Test was bizarre. There was no noise from the crowd, and the ground was rock hard. When they kicked off, you could hear the Fijian players' studs like high heels clattering along the pitch towards you. I was fielding the first kick-off just praying there wasn't too much hang time on the ball because they weren't afraid of the rough stuff. And then I played against Tonga, and a front row containing Billy and Mako Vunipola's dad.

Rupert Moon: Neil Jenkins and I stayed up the night of the Test into the early hours drinking kava, Fiji's national drink. It tastes and looks like muddy water, but I didn't realise how strong its hallucinogenic properties were until we tried to steal Joeli Veitayaki's head. He was a twenty-two-stone prop who'd played for Dunvant, so we knew him fairly well. Neil and I were hallucinating and wanted to take back a souvenir, and he looked like a big rhino. I was on his shoulders and Neil was trying to pull his head off. Fortunately, he saw the funny side. He was a monster of a man, but he had this strange high-pitched laugh.

In Tonga, I shared a room with Robin McBryde in the Dateline Hotel, and it was as bad as I'd been led to believe. Rob Norster had been there before as a player, and arranged the itinerary so that we'd only need to stay one night in Tonga. The flight to Samoa involved crossing the international dateline, so we arrived the same day we'd left, like we'd never been there.

Emyr Lewis: The beds were far too small, so you had a choice. Either your head was exposed, or your feet. I was more comfortable with the idea of cockroaches and mosquitoes crawling all over my feet than my head, so the feet won out. We played the game, came off the pitch, and arrived at the airport, where there wasn't a cloud in the sky. The airline official met us, and said, 'I'm awfully sorry, your flight has been cancelled because of the fog.' We had to decide to either go back to the Dateline Hotel, or to sleep on the wooden benches in the airport. We voted unanimously to stay in the airport.

Hugh Williams-Jones: We were playing touch rugby one day. Skins against tops, and Garin Jenkins and Gareth Llewellyn started squaring up to one another over some disagreement or other. It turned into a bit of a ding-dong with fists flying. I wouldn't want to pick a winner there.

Gareth Llewellyn: We were the dirt-trackers that week. We went to the stadium, and there was a running track around it, and a school sports day going on, so all these schoolkids were taking part in various events while we were playing touch. For some reason, Garin short-armed me when I caught the ball. I thought he'd knocked my teeth out, and the red mist came down. I launched myself at him, knocked him to the ground, and was doing everything in my power to injure him. I had my finger hooked inside his mouth. The boys were trying to separate us but they couldn't because we were so oily and greasy. The schoolkids abandoned their sports day and just came and watched.

Hugh Williams-Jones: When we arrived in Samoa, Norster took great pleasure in reading the rooming list out. 'Gareth Llewellyn. You're with . . . Garin Jenkins.' You could hear the glee in his voice. Not long after, we had a court session in one of the round thatch-topped houses, and it remains one of the funniest things I've seen to this day. We got Garin and Gareth up to the front, put pillow cases over their heads, taped their right hands behind their backs, put a boxing glove each on their left, spun them round, and rang the bell, *ding ding*. Off you go, get stuck in lads. What they didn't know was that Mikey Rayer had a brush handle with a boxing glove attached to it. While Garin and Gareth were swinging wildly and getting nowhere near each other, Mikey was dancing around jabbing them in the face. Every time one of them got hit, they got more angry and started swinging harder. By the end they were nowhere near one another. You should have seen their faces when we took the pillowcases off. It was a picture.

Gareth Llewellyn: I was swinging like hell, windmilling, trying to catch Garin, oblivious to the fact he was on the other side of the room.

Hugh Williams-Jones: We stayed in Aggie Grey's and I was rooming with Scott Quinnell. I was sitting on the toilet, doing my business, and this huge bloody iguana sticks his head under the door. Scott came over and leapt up off the ground in fright. The two of us ran down to reception, and the guy said he could get rid of it, but if he did, the room would become infested with mosquitoes and cockroaches. And he was right. During the night you'd hear this iguana scuttling around, with his tongue going in and out, feasting on whatever creepy-crawlies had found their way in. At least I think it was him, and not Scott.

Rupert Moon: We had a few training sessions on the beach, but I don't think we realised how truly beautiful it was there until we'd left. It was paradise.

Ieuan Evans: Touring the South Seas is tough. You're not getting the facilities you're used to, travel is rarely smooth, and the heat and humidity can be oppressive. We were exhausted by the end, and suffered yet another humiliating defeat to Samoa. We couldn't play in the main stadium as it was being renovated, so we had to move to some club pitch in the middle of nowhere. We took a bus up some narrow hillside, and arrived at this place where it was 105 degrees.

Hugh Williams-Jones: It was our third Test in eight days, so we were feeling tired as it was.

Ieuan Evans: We changed in a tent which was even hotter than outside. Sweat was pouring off us before the game started, there was no running water and we ran out of bottled water. People actually sweated themselves dry, and started cramping.

Hugh Williams-Jones: It was like a marquee at the village fete. It was well over a hundred degrees, and the subs were sitting on wooden school benches in the full glare of the sun.

Anthony Clement: Rupert Moon barely made it through the anthem. He was on the verge of passing out then.

Gareth Llewellyn: From the first scrum, the ball went along the line. There was no drift defence from Samoa, they just came up and *wiped out* everyone in our back line. By the time the ball reached the wing, there was just a pile of prone players splayed all over the pitch. We were up against it from there.

Robert Norster: It was brutal. Clem came into the line from full back, like he does, all languid and casual, pops a pass to the wing, and then *SMACK*. Some bloke just 'exocets' him. It was like he'd been shot. I thought, 'Jesus Christ, he's dead.' He was all over the place when he got up. Elvis legs, the full works.

Emyr Lewis: I've never seen a bruise like it. It looked like he'd been in a car accident.

Hugh Williams-Jones: About quarter of an hour into the game, George Latu, their tight-head, knocked Ricky Evans out cold. The call came for me – 'Pug! You're on.' I was calling for the smelling salts for Ricky. But there was no way he could carry on.

Mike Hall: I was working for the BBC during the Samoa game, because I'd broken my wrist against Tonga. I watched it from the back of a boiling hot stand with mixed feelings. The conditions were brutal, but I'd liked to have played. The boys were in a lot of trouble.

Hugh Williams-Jones: Ten minutes from the end, Georgie Latu was at it again, stamping and throwing punches. I was a hopeless fighter. I was more likely to give someone the flu from the wind caused by my swinging arms. So he's stamping on Robin McBryde, and I've had enough of it, so I lined him up and hit him with my best punch. Right in the eye. *BANG*! It was a perfect connection, like a golfer hitting a driver off the tee, and I kid you not, he did not move. A few moments later, he's looking down the lineout and his eye's swollen up like a Jaffa, and my hand is swollen up and throbbing with pain. He's giving me the evil eye, and I'm thinking, 'If I've got to hit him again, it'll have to be with my left hand.' So, *BANG*, I belted him again. The game finishes, and he makes a beeline straight for me. I'm thinking, 'Oh God, here we go.' Both my hands are swollen now, so I'm thinking, 'I'm going to have to kick him.' He says, 'Fucking good shot mate, I hope to see you again someday,' and I thought, 'I fucking hope not!' A couple of years later, Samoa came over to Wales on tour, and played Llanelli. I was picked to play, and immediately scanned their team for the presence of Georgie Latu. Mercifully, he wasn't in the team. On game day, I was sat on the toilet having a read of the programme and the announcement comes over the tannoy: 'Ladies and gentlemen, there's been one change to the programme. Georgie Latu comes in for Brendan Reidy.' My heart sank. I feared that retribution was coming my way. But eighty minutes came and went, during which we got reacquainted at scrum time, face to face, and nothing happened. I put it down to two things. Either I hit him that hard that he didn't want another one, or he forgot. And I reckon the fucker forgot.

Ieuan Evans: At one stage, Pat Lam picked the ball up from the back of a scrum in the middle of the pitch, chipped over Mikey Rayer at full back, and nobody moved. We were absolutely spent.

Rupert Moon: We were like statues frozen to the spot. No energy left to chase it. We were all just standing there watching him.

Ieuan Evans: We'd given up. Ricky Evans had been knocked out, Rupert Moon was on the verge of passing out. It was getting really dangerous.

Hugh Williams-Jones: Robin McBryde was really struggling too, and he was a rock-hard, no-nonsense bloke. It was the hottest I'd ever experienced without a shadow of a doubt.

Rupert Moon: The whole of Samoa was on the pitch after the game, picking at us, poking us, grabbing hold of us. A tidal wave of ecstatic fans swamping us as we tried to get to the minibus.

Ieuan Evans: Back on the bus, people were just lying on the floor. Dehydration had set in, people had the shakes, and we were all horrifically sunburnt. Neil Jenkins looked like a Swan Vesta match. Alan Davies spoke out about it afterwards, saying it had been far too dangerous, and he was given a severe slap on the wrist for it. Those tours are fun, but they're only ever a hair's breadth away from being utter carnage.

Gareth Llewellyn: After the game, Rupert Moon was in big trouble. He'd been fitting and needed medical attention. They wanted to get a drip into him, but they didn't have one at the ground. He was retching at the back of the bus, but we couldn't get out of there because of the crowd. The bus was inching through painfully slowly as the fans all ambled back to the village.

Rupert Moon: Rattling down the side of the mountain on that minibus, I was in all kinds of trouble. I had the side door open, and was spewing and everything. The next thing you know, I'd fallen out of the bus, into a ditch. It was a low moment, curled up in the foetal position in the middle of nowhere, having a panic attack and spewing in front of my teammates. Heat exhaustion, dehydration, all of that, and it had been a physically tough game. I was in a bad way that night, but you still always find a way to go out on the piss.

Hugh Williams-Jones: That was the hardest week of my rugby career, those three games in the South Seas. I was sitting in the aeroplane coming home, and even my fingernails were hurting. We had a stopover in Hawaii on the way home, and it was all I could do to wobble out to the sunbed and drink cocktails all day.

The 1994 Championship triumph was followed by another whitewash. The panic button was pushed, and coach Alan Davies and captain Ieuan Evans were relieved of their duties a mere eight weeks before Wales left for the World Cup in South Africa. Alan Davies reportedly emerged from the meeting where he was given the news and declared, 'I've just been for a meeting with the WRU, could someone please remove the knives from my back.' Cardiff's head coach Alex Evans was parachuted into the job, and with echoes of the Ron Waldron experiment, he loaded his squad with Cardiff players he knew and trusted. Mike Hall was appointed as captain.

The 1995 World Cup experience barely lasted a week. Japan rolled over in the opening match, as Wales romped to a 57–10 victory, but then came favourites New Zealand, who had in their side a twenty-year-old winger whose terrifying combination of speed and brute force would still be giving players nightmares decades later. Jonah Lomu was the poster boy, but New Zealand's entire squad was world class. Alex Evans thought Welsh power was the only way to contain them, and picked a heavy pack with lock-forward Gareth Llewellyn packing down on the blind-side. Team manager Geoff Evans then resorted to some ill-advised boxing-style trash talk, telling the press that Wales were 'bigger, faster, and stronger' than New Zealand. The anticipated hammering didn't quite materialise. Wales lost 34–9, conceding three tries, and managed to keep Lomu quiet. The final and decisive pool game was against Ireland, and it turned out to be a stinker. Ireland full back Conor O'Shea described it as the worst game he'd ever played in. It must have felt worse still for the men in red, as they lost 23–24.

Ieuan Evans: It's a real shame that Alan Davies wasn't allowed to continue his progress into the '95 World Cup. We ended up making the same mistake again, appointing Alex Evans who had no time to prepare, and brought with him a Cardiff-centric approach. Yes, we were whitewashed the season after winning the tournament, but we had a fair few injuries, and I missed a chunk of the season. It's international sport at the end of the day, and the margins can be extremely fine. It was a huge disappointment, no doubt about that, but I think Alan Davies had earned the right to ride that through.

Mike Hall: It wasn't just because of the rugby that Alan left. He and Bob Norster could see what the future held, and were pushing for more resources, and more time with the players. It was a difficult time because players had jobs. You were working nine to five, trying to do weights sessions in your lunch break, and then training in the evenings. The demands were steadily increasing. I actually lost my job in 1994 because the company I was working for refused to let me go on tour to the South Seas and Canada. I had to quit to continue playing for Wales.

Robert Jones: Alex Evans was the opposite to Alan Davies. He was very dictatorial. It was a case of, 'This is what we do,' and if we'd stray from that approach on the training field, it'd be a case of, 'Stop! Why are we doing that?' You have to play according to your strengths. There's no point picking me at scrum half and telling me to pick up off the back of the scrum and run into the opposition back row every two minutes.

Mike Hall: It was déjà vu. Four years earlier, Alan Davies was expected to turn Wales into contenders with virtually no preparation time, and now Alex Evans was being asked to do the same. It was lunacy. There was no way the Llanelli, Neath or Swansea players were going to buy into the Alex Evans method. No chance. There was a huge sense of animosity between the Cardiff and Swansea players at the time. Stuart Davies and Hemi Taylor couldn't stand one another, but were then expected to play together in the same back row. When Cardiff and Swansea played each other back then, we were selling out club grounds and smashing shit out of each other, then the next week, you were supposed to be playing with each other. If somebody asks you to captain your country in a World Cup, you're not going to say no, but I felt under pressure to try to bring everything together in such a short space of time. Under Alex, and with Vernon Pugh in the background, there was a complete change of direction. Was it right? On reflection, no. The best thing would have been to have stuck with Alan and Bob.

Gareth Llewellyn: Mike Hall had been picked as captain over Ieuan, which I don't think Ieuan was best pleased about.

Ieuan Evans: No one has a divine right to the captaincy, but having it taken from me wasn't easy. My initial reaction was anger. I considered retiring, but I knew I wasn't ready to finish. I'd only just come back from a serious ankle injury. As an elite sportsman, you have to be able to park things and move on. You can't allow negative feelings to fester. Golfers are renowned for it. Play a bad shot, move on. I had to remind myself I hadn't been dropped. I hadn't done anything that would have been perceived as a failure. I hadn't had a bad game or a bad run of form. He obviously didn't want a winger as a captain.

Mike Hall: The World Cup in South Africa was incredible to be part of. It felt as though history was unfolding in front of our eyes. It was the first major event they were hosting since the end of apartheid, and it felt special. The crowds were massive, and the sense of anticipation was huge. But from a Welsh perspective, it was utterly forgettable.

Gareth Llewellyn: It was an eye-opener for a lot of us. You'd go into a club, and there'd be a cloakroom and a *gun* room. Hang your coat up in one, leave your gun in the other. Our hotel was attached to the Hard Rock Cafe, and one day, Keith Chegwin turned up to do a piece for breakfast TV. He wanted to be among all us Welsh lads around the pool. Steve Ford and Barry Evans picked him up and chucked him in. He spluttered to the surface and was giving it all that, 'You *boys*, what are you *like*?', trying to look all chilled on camera, but you could tell he was absolutely fuming inside.

Robert Jones: Because we were playing at altitude in Bloemfontein and Johannesburg, Alex Evans's game plan was just to boot the leather off the ball. He thought we had bigger kickers than the opposition. We tried to do it against Ireland and Conor O'Shea booted us off the park. We were training ahead of that game in a semi-opposed session and Clem got the ball in the twenty-two with a bit of space. Now, Clem's got a huge boot on him, but he's got a lot of other attributes as well. He saw some space, and ran it back. Evans immediately blew his whistle, and bollocked him for ignoring instructions. He's one of the best attacking full backs around. Allow him to run. Give him some freedom.

Anthony Clement: I'm a ball player so I always preferred playing heads-up rugby. Being over-coached dulls the senses of those around you. If your teammates are expecting you to kick every time, their instincts won't be alive to the possibility of a counter-attack. I'm not saying you shouldn't follow the game plan, but if it's on it's on.

Gareth Llewellyn: I thought Alex was an okay coach, but he couldn't pick a side to save his life. Putting me on the blind-side was a prime example. In the entire build-up to that World Cup, all through the summer, I'd only trained at six. Then in the first game against Japan, he picked me as a second row. So my first experience of playing six at Test level came against New Zealand.

Mike Hall: I played all three games in a week. Japan on a Saturday, then the All Blacks midweek, before Ireland on the Saturday. We were knackered. Alan and Bob would have had plans about how to rotate the team and manage the workload, but those plans were blown out of the water. Alex Evans was just scrambling. Geoff Evans did his utmost to lose us that New Zealand game before it had even begun, claiming that they were there for the taking.

Emyr Lewis: He stood in front of the press and told the world that Wales were bigger, fitter, faster and stronger than New Zealand. I remember being in the tunnel before the game, and Josh Kronfeld was doing shuttle runs over and over again. I was thinking, 'This guy's unreal.' Then Lomu walks past and we're all looking up at him, even our forwards. Nineteen stone, and he can run the 100m in ten and a half seconds. There was no way we were bigger, faster, or stronger than *him*. Sometimes mind games work, sometimes they backfire. On that occasion, they backfired.

Ieuan Evans: Before kick-off against New Zealand, Jonah Lomu swapped wings, so I didn't get to man-mark him. It was heartfelt gratitude from me as poor old Wayne Proctor was given the hardest job in world rugby.

Emyr Lewis: I was on the bench for the New Zealand game, but I remember being pitch-side and seeing Lomu in the flesh. You could hear his feet thundering as he went past. I felt for Wayne Proctor. People compare past and present, but there has never been and never will be anyone like Jonah Lomu. Nowhere near it. He could make something out of anything. He could demolish seven or eight players on the way to the try line, as he did against England. We played better against New Zealand than England did, but we still got heavily beaten. Lomu didn't score against us though, remember that.

Gareth Llewellyn: We were herded into the team room after training before the Ireland game, and the phone went. Garin picked it up, turned to one of the players, and said, 'You've got to go upstairs.' I forget who it was, but when he came back he told us all he hadn't been picked. Then the phone went again, and the same thing happened. It didn't take us long to figure out what was going on. Garin tried to make light of it after a while, hovering his finger over someone, before moving it to someone else, then someone else, building the suspense like the *X-Factor*. But it wasn't funny. It was an appalling bit of man-management. That's no way to let international players know they're not in the team. It just felt like they were taking the piss out of us all. I don't know what they were trying to achieve.

Emyr Lewis: We should have beaten Ireland. I've watched it time and time again, and some of the refereeing decisions were awful. There was one scrum in particular on the halfway line, where we pushed them to within two metres of their try line. It was an easy try. They collapsed it deliberately, and we didn't even have a penalty. Nothing.

Ieuan Evans: There was no passion, no hwyl. We were asleep for the first quarter of an hour, and allowed them to impose themselves. By the time we got back into it, it was too late.

Robert Jones: It was tactical naivety that lost us that. Alex Evans insisting on his flawed kicking strategy even though it wasn't working.

Mike Hall: That Ireland game wasn't the difference between success or failure though. Even if we'd beaten them by a point, we wouldn't have beaten France in the knockout stages. There were far too many underlying problems. Truth be told, none of the Home Nations were in rude health going into it. None of us had a hope of winning it.

Robert Jones: The Alex Evans appointment didn't work. It was a mirror image of Ron Waldron's Neath experiment, but with Cardiff players instead. There was a rift in the camp between Cardiff and the rest. Certain players, like Hemi Taylor and Andy Moore, had the ear of the coach. They'd talk in private and the rest of us felt excluded. He didn't seem interested in learning about what the rest of us had to offer.

Emyr Lewis: There was a lot of tugging between the coaches. You had Alex Evans, Mike Ruddock, and Dennis John. All great guys, but they all wanted their own players in the team. Alex called me in ahead of the New Zealand game, after I'd been selected on the bench, and explained that it wasn't his decision. He assured me that I'd be in any first XV he picked, but the team had been picked by consensus. They'd picked Gareth Llewellyn, a lock, at six, because they thought they needed extra bulk. I was gutted because it meant I never got to play against New Zealand in my career. Training actually went well, we were looking sharp, but we didn't come out of the blocks when we hit the field. In the final analysis, I'm so glad South Africa won, because of what it meant to the nation. At the time, I wanted New Zealand to win the final, but I've since watched the film *Invictus*, and with the benefit of hindsight I'm so chuffed they won. It was just meant to be.

FIFTEEN

ENTER THE REDEEMER

After more than a century of resistance, 1995 was the year that rugby union's amateur foundations crumbled in the face of advancing professionalism. While the World Cup was underway, the Australian tycoon Kerry Packer was paving a way towards the future and, for the players, that path was lined with dollar bills. His vision was a fully professional World Rugby Championship, and it scared the living daylights out of the game's old guard. Packer's cohort, Ross Turnbull, had been recruiting influential players to sell the dream to their colleagues. Mike Hall became the point of contact in Wales, and the Cambridge graduate used his powers of persuasion to recruit sixty Welshmen to the cause. The plan was to create two new Welsh clubs, centred in Cardiff and Swansea, with squads of thirty players each. Packer would pay the players, and offer the unions forty-nine per cent of the franchises. The Packer organisation would keep their fifty-one per cent and use the existing stadiums to build northern and southern hemisphere leagues. The winning teams from each hemisphere would then play off for the title of World Club Champions. It was to be a joint venture, but without the lightning rod provided by the money men, professionalism would never have happened. The Packer dream didn't materialise, but it frightened the game's guardians into fast-tracking the inevitable. On 27 August, 1995, the International Rugby Board declared the game 'open'.

The change came in with immediate effect, but instead of liberating the sport, it nearly bankrupted it. Unions like the WRU, who weren't awash with cash, had no idea how to cope. In the ensuing panic, committee men and volunteers, whose biggest responsibility until then had been to organise the end-of-season awards, were thrust onto the front-line of professional sports governance. You can't turn a blazer-and-cords committee man into a sharp-suited businessman overnight, and the aftermath was predictably chaotic. Smaller clubs feared they would disappear into a void if they didn't act, and their solution was to sign players they couldn't afford. The timing couldn't have been worse for Wales. Enthusiasm for the game had been dwindling because of the declining fortunes of the national side, club attendances were on the slide, and income was barely trickling in, at a time when costs were about to go through the roof.

Mike Hall: The game had been moving inexorably towards professionalism, and we had a governing body whose attitude was one of 'over our dead body'. In 1994, we were still being treated like total amateurs. If we had a cup of tea or coffee in our hotel rooms, we'd be billed for it by the union.

Ieuan Evans: The dam waters broke in '95. From being firm and rigid in their dogma, the IRB realised they had no option but to act, because they were about to lose control. It didn't seem to affect the southern hemisphere as much because to all intents and purposes, they were already 'professional'. But we allowed utter chaos to reign in Wales. It was total disarray.

Mike Hall: Before the World Cup, I'd been signing up all the Welsh players for the nascent Kerry Packer Circus. It was going to revolutionise rugby, and turn the sport professional overnight. As I'd been appointed captain, I was seen as the point of contact in Wales to surreptitiously recruit the best players in the country. I met Ross Turnbull a number of times, and after the tournament, I was running around all the boys' houses getting them to sign conditional contracts. About sixty signed up. I think Ieuan was the only one who didn't. They'd told me there were only going to be two sides in Wales. One in Cardiff and one in Swansea. I was a bit shocked at that. They were planning to lose teams like Bridgend, Llanelli and Pontypridd. Their approach was pretty dispassionate. They'd looked at the size of Wales, the population, and the GDP, and concluded that this country could only support two professional teams. So that was shocking, but I thought the blueprint was exciting, and it was the sort of thing that would raise a lot of money through broadcasting revenues. It was enormously attractive to the players because most of them were amateur, and struggling to play at the top level with all the time and effort that took. The chance to go fully professional was something they were really excited about.

Gareth Llewellyn: Mike came to my house and said Kerry Packer was going to do for rugby what he'd done for cricket, and I signed up there and then. It was £400,000 over three years, which was an awful lot of money in 1995. That was the salary for a World Cup player, but he was adamant that he wanted to take it to America, and if you agreed to go and play for a franchise out there, you'd go up to the next level of pay. The problem they had was that they asked for volunteers to go to America, and virtually *everyone* wanted to go. At the time I was a fitter in the factory at Port Talbot Steelworks, fitting training and weights sessions around my shift work. It was a no-brainer.

Rupert Moon: We'd all signed up lock, stock and smoking barrel. We'd had the promise of our golden rupees, and were ready for the promised land. I think the figure I was offered was around £90,000. I felt like a millionaire considering that when we won the Championship in '94, we got a cheque for £1,500 from the WRU trust, and a set of gold cufflinks with the trophy embossed on them. Anybody who was anybody signed up.

Robert Jones: I was off. We all were. It was a significant amount of money. But Francois Pienaar and his World Cup colleagues scuppered it by demanding more.

Rupert Moon: South Africa had won the World Cup, got greedy, and ballsed it up for all of us. I still think that's the way the game is going to go. There'll eventually be a world league, and Wales will be part of that.

Mike Hall: It all fell apart during the summer because Packer and Rupert Murdoch ended up doing some deal with one another over TV rights, and it didn't happen. But it was extremely serious at the time. The lawyer, Ross Turnbull, was flying into Cardiff for three or four days at a time, and going through things in a lot of detail. It was a very viable option. Rob Andrew was doing the English boys, Gavin Hastings was doing the Scots, and Brendan Mullin was recruiting the Irish. The rugby league boys had got wind of it, and a lot of them were interested too. It could have been amazing, and there was a real sense of disappointment when it didn't happen. But with hindsight it was the impetus we needed because Vernon Pugh and the IRB had discovered what was going on, and they knew the writing was on the wall.

Gareth Llewellyn: I came home from work one day, and Vernon Pugh was on the telly. They'd realised that their whole reason to exist had been taken away from them, and they announced that rugby union would become a professional game with immediate effect.

Ieuan Evans: There was no moratorium, no period to prepare and put plans in place. That was it. One minute we were amateur, the next we were professional. We were doing what we'd always done, except at the end of the month we started getting a pay cheque. The players weren't ready for it, the administration certainly wasn't ready for it. They got the sums all wrong. You had things like teachers signing contracts on behalf of clubs and stuff, not understanding they were guarantors. You heard all sorts of stories about people losing their houses because they'd unwittingly signed to guarantee a player's wages.

Mike Hall: If the IRB hadn't done it, Packer would have come back and had another crack. The game was ripe for it.

Ieuan Evans: Suddenly everyone thought they were *entitled* to get paid. You had people playing fourth division rugby in front of 150 people, getting paid. It was absurd. I was only professional for a year with Llanelli, but I didn't quit my job, because I didn't need to. The coaches didn't know what to do with the players. They weren't remotely organised. We were doing exactly the same thing we'd always done. Training twice a week, and playing on the weekend. No one had any real idea how to structure the working week. Do they come in in the morning? Do they come in in the afternoon? Do they come in in the morning and the afternoon? For a while it lurched to the other extreme, and they started overtraining the players to justify the fact it was now a full-time job. The consequence of that was that players were often broken down and spent before the game on the weekend. It took a while to find the right balance.

Robert Jones: I was at Bristol, and the attitude was that as it was now a full-time job, we had to be in from nine to five, but nobody had a clue how to fill the day. They looked at the football model and thought, 'Those guys only train for two hours in the morning. If we're paying these rugby guys fifty or sixty grand, we want them in *all day*.' People were coming in and twiddling their thumbs. Gyms were basic, the facilities were nowhere near what we have today. We'd end up just taking long, lazy lunches.

Gareth Llewellyn: Harlequins were the same. It was a case of, 'What can we do to fill every hour of your day?' A lot of the guys at Quins were still working in the city, and could only train in the evenings. So us boys would be in from nine to five, and then we'd have to go back in in the evenings to train with the ones who were working during the day. It was very much a suck-it-and-see situation for the clubs.

Scott Quinnell: That's ultimately why I went north. I had a good offer with Wigan, that enabled me to just train, and spend my free time with my family. Otherwise I'd have been training two or three times a week between six and nine, doing extra weights sessions, running, and combining it with a job. Prior to that, there were some weeks I would barely see my daughter. I'd often be away before she woke up, and she'd be in bed before I got home.

Anthony Clement: I was still at Swansea, and there was no way I was giving up my job, so Swansea had to arrange separate training sessions for me, Mark Taylor and Stuart Davies, because we couldn't come in during the day.

Rupert Moon: I'd just graduated from college, and I was into a nine-to-five job as a professional rugby player. A lot of the boys were still working though. Firemen, policemen, farmers. There were a few people that trained full-time during the day to start with, but they still had to have evening sessions to cater for those carrying on with their normal jobs, so some of us were at the club all day and night. It was bonkers. The attitude was, 'You're being paid a salary so you have to be in all day.'

Mike Hall: I went from being able to claim meagre expenses and having a few beer tokens to suddenly earning a lot of money at Cardiff. Where was it coming from? We were lucky in that we had a benefactor in Peter Thomas who was able to keep the ship afloat. Other clubs were spending money they didn't have.

Gareth Llewellyn: The clubs thought it was going to be like football, and all the TV money was going to come rolling in. We all did pretty well with our first couple of contracts. I signed for four years with Harlequins, but halfway through that, they realised the club was haemorrhaging money, nowhere near enough was coming in, and they were desperate to turn off the tap.

Ieuan Evans: Llanelli started signing players like Frano Botica for obscene amounts of money, and the club nearly bankrupted itself. They gave him half a million quid over two seasons. If I hadn't gone to Bath, and Llanelli hadn't got a decent transfer fee for me, they wouldn't have been able to pay their wages. It's such a precarious business. Think about it – the Scarlets crowds aren't any bigger these days than when I was playing in the amateur era. But now they've got a £5m wage bill to cover. If that revenue's not being raised, the club is sinking into a hole of its own making.

Gareth Llewellyn: My first contract was a hundred pages long and I hired a lawyer to go through it with me page-by-page, striking out anything that looked untoward. Compare that to Alfie [Gareth Thomas] who said, 'Give me fifty grand, boys, and I'll sign anything!'

Hugh Williams-Jones: I was different in that I already had a career path with the police. I'd been with them for twelve years, and I only had a couple of years of my rugby career left. I was earning about £22,000 a year. In Llanelli, we were training on Monday, Tuesday and Thursday nights. You'd play every Saturday and the occasional Wednesday. Every month, if you played in every game, and attended every session, you'd clear about £450, which pretty much covered my expenses travelling back and forth from Bridgend. Although a bunch of us used to meet at Sarn services and jam into a tiny Fiesta to save on expenses. But I never got all that money, because being a police officer, I couldn't always make every session. I was summoned in in August of 1995 when the game went professional, and asked would I be happy with £25,000 a year. I nearly fell off the fucking chair. I wasn't expected to do any more than what I was doing, and I'd be twenty-five grand better off. I took home more from Llanelli in September than I did from the police. I couldn't believe it. The October pay was good too, and my wife and I thought we'd start putting it away for a holiday. November's pay never came. A 'cashflow problem', we were told.

Anthony Clement: It was like, 'This is going to happen now, and the business plan is going to have to catch up.'

Rupert Moon: This bloke called Mel Davies had offered Llanelli a load of money and promised to underwrite all the salaries. We'd signed Steve McDowell who was due to arrive in the October, and Frano Botica was on his way. I remember coming back from a game against Sale, and Mel's accountant was on the bus. He stood up and told us, 'Mel's not going to do this anymore.' He'd only been at it a couple of months. So the money wasn't available, and it was like, *shit*. We'd promised all this money to everyone, and now we haven't got any. What are we going to do?

Hugh Williams-Jones: There was a crisis meeting. Everyone was called in and we were told the club had gone bankrupt. After two months. There had been no business plan, they'd just plucked figures out of the air. I don't know what they were basing these figures on. I was told I'd either have to take a pay cut, or the club would disappear. 'What sort of a cut?' I said. And they said £19,000! It was disappointing, but at least I had my police wages to fall back on. It was the other boys I felt sorry for. Chris Wyatt had been on about fifty or sixty grand, so his cut had a much bigger impact on his life. We're talking about a guy who, when he got his signing-on fee, went out and bought a speedboat.

Rupert Moon: Stuart Gallagher called all the supporters in, and asked them to donate money, to be shareholders. It was desperate, but they generated enough money to keep going. We still ended up signing Frano Botica, but we couldn't sign McDowell. My mum's still a shareholder to this day. It was a bonkers time.

Ieuan Evans: Wales coped badly compared to the other Home Unions. It all happened on the hoof. You're making mistakes daily, and those mistakes count, those mistakes cost, and those mistakes hurt.

In 1995, Kevin Bowring was appointed as Alex Evans' successor. The former London Welsh captain, who'd coached the Wales U20 and U21 sides, was given a four-year contract through to the next World Cup. It was an attempt to instil stability after the chaos that had preceded the two previous global tournaments. Bowring was a rugby romantic who spurned the dispassionate approach of Alex Evans, and attempted to resurrect the 'Welsh way'. He believed that Welsh rugby was strong when the players were let off the leash and allowed to express themselves. Accordingly, he picked the kind of players, like Rob Howley and Arwel Thomas, whose attitude gave a glimpse into Wales's unshackled past.

He had the easy-going, avuncular manner of a schoolteacher, which won him plenty of admirers in the squad. But there were those, like Scott Gibbs, who questioned Bowring's experience and man-management. While his overall record of fifteen wins and fourteen defeats left him in the black, just, progress was slow, and in his final campaign in 1998, Wales suffered two calamitous defeats: a 60–26 hammering at Twickenham, and a soul-destroying 51–0 loss to France. These had been preceded by a demolition at the hands of the All Blacks at Wembley. Bowring's position became untenable in the eyes of the union. In an echo of the Jonathan Davies saga a decade earlier, he prepared a dossier for the WRU, detailing exactly what Wales needed to do to keep pace with the bigger unions in the professional era. It included several recommendations that would eventually come to pass – the formation of the regions, the introduction of the Celtic League, and the need for the national coach to have more access to his players. Like Jonathan Davies, he was ignored.

Things got considerably worse after he stood down. Dennis John and Lynn Howells were put in temporary charge, and took a weakened, demoralised squad to South Africa in the summer of 1998. Only twelve of the thirty players that had represented Wales during the Five Nations were available, and others were to drop out during the tour. On 27 June, on Pretoria's Loftus Versfeld, Wales suffered the most humiliating defeat in their history. They came into the game off the back of four losses to provincial opposition, and capitulated entirely in the face of a merciless Springbok advance. 96–13 was the final score, and had Naka Drotske not dropped the ball over the line in the last minute, it would have been a hundred.

The WRU decided that drastic action was necessary and scoured the world for Bowring's permanent replacement. In the autumn of 1998, Auckland Blues coach and former schoolmaster, Graham Henry, was unveiled to great fanfare, and offered an eye-watering annual salary of £250,000. It was five times what Bowring had earned.

Garin Jenkins: I went on that South Africa tour in 1998. I had a young family at the time, and I was captain of Swansea. About twenty-odd experienced players didn't go on that tour, and a number pulled out while we were away. The itinerary was outrageous. I don't think the French Foreign Legion would have undertaken it at the time. We were ably coached by Dennis John and Lynn Howells, but we were just a young side battered by injuries. Defeat is never final, is it? The following year, we beat South Africa for the first time ever, and there were a couple of boys who'd experienced that defeat, who were then able to bask in the glory of victory. Henry came in with a boldness and a leadership, and was given free rein. It was a fresh start for many players, and we responded.

Gareth Thomas: He identified the strong personalities and leaders early on, and built the team around them. People like Gibbsy, SQ and Howlers. He made them irreplaceable rocks in the team, and built a new kind of game plan where everyone had to be in a certain place at a certain time. Had those guys not been there, and he'd inherited a squad of youngsters, he'd definitely have struggled. He used them to the maximum, and everyone else fitted in around them.

Rob Howley: He knew exactly what he wanted from the very beginning. He was determined and single-minded. I guess if you're prepared to travel twelve thousand miles, and turn your back on your homeland, you have to believe in yourself that you can do a job.

Garin Jenkins: Initially he saw me as an old has-been who was too fat and too slow. Thankfully he was big enough to change his mind, and I played about thirty times under him. That ended up being my best period, and I'm very thankful for that. That ten-game winning streak we went on was phenomenal. First win in Paris for twenty years, that epic win against England at Wembley, and becoming part of the first British touring side to beat Argentina. I enjoyed that period more, as it was a second chance. Once you've played for Wales, and been dropped, that second chance feels even more special.

Scott Quinnell: Graham came to see me in '98. I'd had a lean period when I came back from the Lions tour in '97. I had a double hernia, and it took me a while to get over it. It was a tough time. I went back to Llanelli, but failed my medical because my knees were shot to pieces. Luckily Gareth Jenkins knew what I had to offer, as I'd started with the club at the age of eight, so he knew I'd get through. Graham sat me down, said, 'Let's get you fit, and I want to make you a big part of this Welsh side going forward.' I hadn't really had that for a couple of years, so it was nice to have someone express that confidence in me. He put me in the leadership group along with Dai Young and Rob Howley. Graham empowered people, and that's important. Letting people at least *think* that they've come up with the game plan.

Dafydd James: He was undoubtedly one of the most innovative coaches in the world, but he could also be a cantankerous old fart.

Mark Jones: I got on well with him. He was a gentleman. Even when he dropped me. He called the house, my mother answered the phone, and he did it with a great deal of empathy. He told me exactly what I needed to improve, what type of wingers I needed to look at, and what I needed to add to my game.

Craig Quinnell: Graham had been told about this group of Welsh players playing in London, and he made an appointment to go and see them. The union had called Richmond, and told John Kingston that Graham wanted to meet Barry Williams, John Davies, Scott Quinnell, Andy Moore, Adrian Davies, Allan Bateman, and Nick Walne. John was like, 'What about Craig?', and he was like, 'No, not interested.' He came up and met the boys, and came to watch us training. Scott was injured so he ended up watching the session with him. At one point, he turned to Scott and said, 'Gee mate, that number four's a bit of a terror, he's awesome. Who does *he* play for?' And Scott said, 'What do you mean who does he play for?' And Graham said, 'Well what country's he from?' Scott said, 'That's my brother.' Graham asked, 'Why wasn't he in the meeting?' and Scott was like, 'I don't know, you gave out the invitations.'

Gareth Thomas: Graham was very schoolmasterly in his approach, and because I'd always struggled in school, I didn't warm to his methods. It reminded me too much of being back in the classroom. He always spoke from a pedestal, and I found that difficult. He'd pull me in and out of the leadership group, and I never felt like I was standing on solid ground. I had huge respect for him, because I could see that he was in the process of reinventing the wheel but it's my belief that you need to get *everyone* on board, not just your stalwarts.

Rob Howley: It was Jon Humphreys, David Young, SQ, myself, Jenks, Gibbsy and Shane Howarth. He'd question Dai on the scrum, Humphs on the lineout, and the rest of us on our decision-making and what we wanted the week to look like. He relied a hell of a lot on the leadership group. Sometimes you'd feel a little uncomfortable because as a player, you'd be elevated to the higher echelons, and you had to remind yourself every now and again that you were still just a player.

Gareth Thomas: Taking four or five guys into a room, closing the door and leaving everyone else outside wondering what they were talking about, only separates the group. That's a dangerous game to play. He was there to do a job of work, and there wasn't much of a sense of humour about him. But you're dealing with human beings at the end of the day, so to treat them like robots, and not take their opinions into consideration was a mistake as far as I was concerned. If you weren't high up in the hierarchy, it wasn't obvious how to climb the ladder. Did I want to be in that room with the minority, or out here with the majority? Because when it comes to the game, the majority always has the bigger say. Off the field, he was giving the minority all the power.

Neil Jenkins: It was the first time I'd experienced that kind of dynamic. As a kid, I'd come in for a lot of criticism while playing for Wales, and Graham came along, put me in this leadership group, and placed a lot of responsibility on my shoulders. I was thinking, 'Do I want this?' because I understood how things could quickly unravel. But I could see what an impressive coach he was and I realised I had to embrace it.

Peter Rogers: Henry's strength was selection. Scott Quinnell hadn't been in the squad prior to Henry's arrival for various reasons, but he was clearly a world-class player. Henry saw beyond the politics and picked him. Rob Howley wasn't number one at the time either, but Henry saw his potential. Even Jinks wasn't nailed on. Arwel Thomas was being preferred to him. Arwel was a great guy, and good fun, but Henry nailed his colours to Jenkins, because he knew all good teams needed a world-class goal-kicker, and he saw qualities in him that others hadn't. He became his lieutenant, like Grant Fox had been for him in Auckland. So he got that 8, 9, 10 combination of world class players, who'd been drifting in and out, weren't necessarily first choice, and he built the team around them.

Craig Quinnell: Two or three weeks later, he came to watch us beat Bath at the Rec, and he pulled me to one side as I was coming off, and asked if he could have a chat. He said, 'First I'd like to apologise for not inviting you to the meeting. I went back to Cardiff and asked around, and I didn't hear anything good about you. It was all bad. But if you play rugby like that, I don't care. You'll play every game you're fit for.' And in fairness to him, I pretty much did. To this day, I don't know who'd given him that bad advice, but I'd ruffled a few feathers at the union in my time. I was always outspoken, and I fell out with the WRU when they signed a deal with Reebok to supply our boots. I was already under contract with Puma. Initially I was told I'd be exempt from the Reebok deal, but then I was made an example of in front of the squad. After that I got a letter from Kevin Bowring saying he wasn't allowed to select me. Graham was straight down the line, his own man, and not afraid to stand up to the bureaucrats.

Peter Rogers: I'd been playing really well in South Africa. I was tearing tight-heads up over there, and I'd set my heart on becoming a Springbok. I just couldn't crack it.

Gareth Llewellyn: I was playing for Harlequins. I had sixty-three caps, was twenty-nine years old, and I was left out of his initial squad. I thought, 'He's got no idea what I'm like as a player, he must be taking his cues from someone else.' Then after I won man of the match against Cardiff in the European Cup, he turned up in our dressing room, and asked if I was available for the upcoming Welsh trial. I said of course I was. Then afterwards I was talking to a few of the Cardiff boys like Leigh Davies, and he already knew what team he was going to be in. Teams one and two. When I turned up, I discovered I'd been allocated to teams three and four, so I had no chance of making the cut. Even though he was very different to Bowring, my impression was that it was all about the first fifteen. If you were in the fifteen, you got all the attention. If you were a sub, you got a little bit of attention. If you were outside of the twenty-two, you were all but ignored. And I spent most of my time outside of the twenty-two.

Scott Quinnell: He was very straight. He was never one to sugar-coat anything. I'd had a shocker against Bath in the European Cup. Mike Catt took the ball out of my hands over the line at one point. Henry came up to me afterwards and said, 'Wore the wrong studs today, did you?' I said, 'What do you mean?' He said, 'Well, you couldn't get going, could you? Put longer ones in next time.' I liked that. I'd much rather that than find out he was bad-mouthing me behind my back.

Ian Gough: He turned things around very quickly. It wasn't splitting the atom, just a case of getting some of the disillusioned players back on board.

Scott Quinnell: A coach is only good if he picks you. It doesn't matter how good he actually is. From a player's point of view, if he picks you, he's brilliant. If he doesn't, he's the worst coach in the world. I got on with Graham from the word go. He was a total enigma, but he was an incredible thinker. He was superb with the leadership group. Every morning there'd be a sheet under the door with something to work on that day. God only knows when he slept. Eighteen-hour days were the norm with him.

Rob Howley: You felt so prepared going into games under him. His rugby knowledge was astounding.

Dafydd James: He was a breath of fresh air with regard to his ideas, but it's fair to say his man-management skills weren't the best. Steve Black was the go-between between the players and the coaches.

Scott Quinnell: Steve Black was a huge influence. He was brought in as a fitness coach, but he was as much a psychologist as anything else. He'd walk in and go, 'Right boys, today we've got a fitness test. How are you feeling?' We'd say, 'Good.' And he'd say, 'That's good enough for me,' and off we'd go. Done. That would lift everyone. If we were in the gym, and you'd have 150kg on the bench, he'd go, 'How's it feeling? Does it feel heavy today?' And you'd go, 'No, it's all right, Blackie,' and he'd have a go and pump out ten reps. He was as strong as any of the players. He was the most remarkable man I'd ever met.

Dafydd James: He was a Geordie, so as Celts we related to him. He'd looked after boxers, and done a bit of work with Paul Gascoigne, so he'd paid attention to sports other than rugby. He wasn't just your fitness coach, he was your friend.

Scott Quinnell: He'd always push you to think in different ways. Visualisation was a big thing with him. Closing your eyes and imagining things. Playing out scenarios in your head.

Peter Rogers: He was either a genius or an idiot, I'm not sure. Once he had us pretending to be racehorses. Snorting and whinnying, and stamping our feet.

Gareth Thomas: Some of his methods were unbelievably strange, but he was hugely charismatic and showed much more of a human side than Graham Henry did. That's important when you have a group of young players away from home for a long time.

Graham Henry's first game in charge would offer an accurate litmus test of their progress. It was against the team that had so recently condemned Wales to the most abject and miserable defeat in their history. South Africa were the visitors to Wembley Stadium, Wales's temporary home while the Millennium Stadium was being built, and with minutes to go the 'Boks were trailing 20–17. A rush of blood from Gareth Thomas in the dying moments saw a penalty decision reversed, and South Africa had the field position from which to launch their final, decisive attack. 28–20 was the final score, in South Africa's favour, but given what had happened in Pretoria, Wales could lay claim to being the moral victors.

Craig Quinnell: We should have beaten South Africa. The reason we didn't was because Darren Morris had come off the bench and desperately wanted to make an impact. We were defending, and he should have stayed blind with me. But he chased it, and went open because he'd just come on full of energy, wanting to put in a big hit. By doing that he left his pod, and they scored up the blind-side. Just one little thing, and you've lost the game.

Dafydd James: We would have beaten them had it not been for a streaker running across the pitch. Some fat bloke with a beard. That was a massive distraction at a critical point in the game. But to turn around a 96–13 drubbing and get within eight points of the 'Boks a month after taking charge showed that Graham Henry was a seriously talented coach.

Martyn Williams: Even though we lost, the headline in the *Wales on Sunday* was 'Henry's Heroes', and we all scored nine or ten out of ten in the player ratings! It was a really positive start.

Rob Howley: He brought a wealth of knowledge with him. At the time, the only southern hemisphere rugby you could watch on the TV was Super 10s. Now, you can watch everything, and it's easy for coaches to copy and paste what anyone else is doing. Back then, the southern hemisphere teams were shrouded in mystery, but Graham Henry arrived with his brain crammed full of information on exactly how the South Africans played. He knew them inside out.

Dafydd James: The hype after that result was insane. Not only was he hailed as the Great Redeemer, one newspaper had a life-size cut-out mask of his face. He must have thought we were all bonkers.

The South Africa game was followed up by a 43–30 victory over Argentina, which led Robert Kitson, the *Guardian* columnist, to declare that 'Henry has achieved more in ten days than his predecessors managed in a decade'. The plaudits began rolling in.

Craig Quinnell: Graham was very much about playing to your strengths. He saw me not just as a second row, but as one of our best ball carriers. He'd say, 'He's your best ball carrier, give him the ball.' None of this, 'He's the first one there, carry it up' nonsense. It was, 'These are your strike runners, use them! Give them the ball, get out of their way, and back them up.'

Dafydd James: To my mind, he encouraged us to return to what Wales had once been synonymous with. Free-flowing, wide rugby. He brought tempo to the game.

The build-up to Henry's first Five Nations game against Scotland was marred by the withdrawal of Dai Young and Craig Quinnell through injury. It meant the tight-five had a fairly green look to it, with rookies Darren Morris, Chris Anthony, and Ian Gough all taking their places in the pack. Scotland were looking forward to dismantling this inexperienced-looking Welsh scrum.

Scott Quinnell: The Five Nations took Graham Henry by surprise. In New Zealand, not many away fans travel, so he was genuinely taken aback to see twenty thousand Welsh fans in Edinburgh on the morning of the match. He came to love the tournament because of that, but that first one was a massive culture shock for him.

Dafydd James: I don't think he had any idea of the level of hype surrounding the Five Nations. He was blown away by how passionate we all are about rugby. He probably thought it was going to be similar to the Tri-Nations, but he soon discovered it was on another level altogether. There were twenty thousand with tickets, but at the least the same number again who'd just come up for the craic. He was gobsmacked.

Rob Howley: He allowed the boys to go out for a social beer in Edinburgh the night before. I didn't usually have a drink the night before a game, because if supporters saw you drinking, it would give them the wrong impression. But it's normal back in New Zealand. Letting us do that showed that Graham was at ease with his situation, but he probably didn't appreciate quite how many Welsh people would be there.

Neil Jenkins: He was looking out the window of the hotel on Princes Street and seeing red and white everywhere. He looked totally bewildered, and asked me, 'What's going on here?' And I told him, 'This is it, this is what it's all about. It's about more than just rugby today. This is a hundred years of history. This is what we play for.' He was taken aback, no doubt about that.

Dafydd James: That game began disastrously. They kicked off to Matthew

Robinson on the wing, John Leslie scooped it up, and scored the fastest try in Five Nations history.

Scott Quinnell: We couldn't get our game going. We'd rattled South Africa and Argentina with the tempo of our game, getting the hooker to throw the ball in as we arrived at the lineout. But Ed Morrison was a bit whistle-happy that day, and he took away that element of surprise.

Neil Jenkins: We had our chances to win it, but they were a good side, and they pulled away from us at the end. It wasn't through lack of effort though, we played some good rugby on the day.

Craig Quinnell: I missed the Scotland game, and we got bullied by them, so Graham brought me back in for Ireland and the message was, 'We won't get bullied again.' I was pumped up, thinking I was coming back as the enforcer, and we took it too far the other way. In the first twenty minutes of the game I got carded, or the white triangle, whatever it was in those days. Our discipline was awful, and we found ourselves twenty points down before the fightback began.

Rob Howley: Penalty after penalty after penalty.

Neil Jenkins: I got charged down that day as well, gave away seven points.

Scott Quinnell: We lost that one, lost to Ireland, but there was still that sense we were coming together as a team. We had some world-class players. Howlers, Neil Jenkins, Gibbsy. We had a front five that was huge and could go toe to toe with anyone. It was a setback, but we weren't about to go into our shells.

Graham Henry once compared a loss to a death in the family. He'd now suffered two in his first two Five Nations games. Wales hadn't won in France since 1975, and the French had won back-to-back Grand Slams. Paris was not the place for a team short on confidence. Knowing Wales would need to front up physically, Henry replaced his entire front row, drafting in Peter Rogers, Ben Evans, and the inestimable Garin Jenkins – a man he'd initially thought lacked the skills to play the open game he was advocating. It also marked the first appearance in a Wales shirt of the New Zealander Brett Sinkinson, a man who apparently qualified for Wales through a Carmarthen-born grandfather. Wales needed a change in their approach. Henry had noticed that the Scottish and Irish had happily stood off Neil Jenkins, considering him a slow and non-threatening kicking fly half. So Henry encouraged Jenkins to run, and it worked.

Rob Howley: Graham had arranged a scrum session against the A side that was being coached by Mike Ruddock and Dennis John. Garin and Peter Rogers were in the A team, and they pulverised us on a Monday night at Sophia Gardens. That was the changing of the guard. Jon Humphreys was a fine player, but no one understood the dark arts of scrummaging better than Garin Jenkins.

Neil Jenkins: Brett came in for Nug.

Martyn Williams: In fairness to Brett, he'd being playing really well for Neath. He'd mastered the art of coming in from the wrong side to steal ball.

Neil Jenkins: During the build-up, we'd practised restarts over and over again. Receiving restarts and playing off them. Our mindset was to go out there and play rugby. We hadn't done that in the Ireland game. It was a case of be bold, be brave, and take people on. Graham had spoken to some of the Scotland coaches who'd told him they weren't too interested in me, they told him I kept passing. He told me I had to change that, which I did. I threw a dummy early on, and went straight through. It was a shift in mindset.

Scott Quinnell: The ride in is the thing I used to enjoy the most. Their outriders got you there quicker than anyone else. They'd be kicking cars to get them out of the way. It was a genuine spectacle from the bus, watching the mayhem unfold outside, like something from *Blade Runner*. And there's something special about the French anthem. A wall of blue, the hats, the cockerels, and 70,000 people puffing on their Gitanes.

Dafydd James: My experience playing France went back to U21s and youth rugby, where you always felt as though you were chasing shadows. But Blackie gave us the belief that we could win. He broke the field down into sections, and forced us to visualise what was going to happen in certain circumstances. 'What are you going to do if you get the ball here, what are your options?' Thinking about things happening before they happened meant you felt more capable when they did. Henry gave us licence to go out and play. He said to me, 'Daf, I want you to get your hands on the ball.' And I said, 'Sure, but I'm on the wing.' He said, 'I don't care, I want you to come in, look for work, run lines off Jinks, run loops behind Gibbsy, stay busy.' It felt good hearing that. In previous regimes, if you were playing outside someone who never passed the ball you knew you were going to be stuck running up and down the touchline all day, never getting close to the action.

Scott Quinnell: The French picked five back-rowers in their back five, so they were trying to play a bit of rugby too. We felt we'd have the edge up front. It was our first time playing in their new stadium. Compared to Parc des Princes, it was like playing in a desert. It was just *huge*. An enormous stadium. On a far bigger scale than anything Graham Henry would've encountered in New Zealand.

Peter Rogers: I was pretty worried because they had Tournaire, Califano, and Ibanez in their front row, all of whom had massive reputations. The first scrum was five metres from our line, and I was shitting myself. I hadn't played international rugby but I found it really easy. I'd played against better props at club level in South Africa. Club level, not provincial. That filled me with confidence.

Dafydd James: Under Henry, we'd become so structured in our planning, and so meticulous in our preparation. The game had only been professional for three years, but it felt as though we'd advanced about thirty years. My try was from quick ruck ball. Neil Jenkins with the wide pass, textbook from our Ponty days together, and I was in at the corner against Bernat-Salles. It all seemed to open up after that. We played some sublime rugby. It was an incredible game to play in. The crowd was going mental.

Scott Quinnell: Howlers scored a brilliant try. I'd like to say I supplied the scoring pass for that one as well, but in reality my elbow hit the floor and the ball ended up in his hands. And obviously little brother got himself over for a try as well. It was an incredible atmosphere. I loved playing against the French, although it could be intimidating. The only time I've ever been scared on the pitch was against them in '97, when their loose-head gouged me, and I could feel his finger behind my eyeball. I was furious. I got up and was bleeding where his nails had scraped across my eyeball. It felt like it was hanging out of its socket. Barbaric, like something from a horror film.

Neil Jenkins: It had been a year of waiting for me. The previous year, I'd been outclassed by Thomas Castaignede. He was a hell of a player, and he'd made me look ordinary. I'd waited a year just for this game. It had been my sole focus. I was so desperate to right the wrongs of that 51–0 defeat. I needed to turn up and show what I was about.

Dafydd James: Right at the end, Dai Llewellyn came on for Howley and almost blew the whole thing. He just needed to give it to Neil Jenkins so he could welly it down the field and that would have been time. He was expecting Scott Quinnell to pick it up, and there was some confusion between them. He was tapping SQ on the arse, and Scott was looking at him thinking, 'What the fuck are you doing, just pass it to Jinks.' I remember hearing Scott Gibbs shouting, 'Fucking hell, Dai. Jinks, you have to tell him what the move is *twice*.' Dai Llew, bless him, is not the brightest boy. He didn't have a fucking clue. He was overawed by the whole situation. Cracking player, Dai, but ask him to think, and you're fucked.

Neil Jenkins: That last penalty was our own doing really, a bit of miscommunication. Dai had just come on, and our scrum was under a bit of pressure. We should have got it in, got the ball away, and cleared our lines, but we ended up giving it away and defending hard on our own line before giving the penalty away.

Dafydd James: Thankfully Castaignede put it wide, and we could celebrate.

Craig Quinnell: That game was more special to me than the England game that followed it. To score the winning try, from eighty metres, untouched. To win in Paris for the first time since the seventies. To achieve something my father hadn't, which was unbelievable because he'd done *everything* – he'd been in five winning teams against New Zealand, but he'd never beaten France in Paris.

Martyn Williams: I was bitter and angry at having been dropped, but when you see them go and win, you can't really argue with the decision.

Gareth Thomas: There was a bit of a confrontation on the bus after that one between Graham and I. I had been involved with Wales A, and he'd called me in because of an injury to Allan Bateman. I'd come off the bench towards the end of the game, and played my part, but he took issue with me celebrating on the bus. It was like he was telling me I didn't have a right to be celebrating because I shouldn't really have been there. As great a technical coach that Graham was, he didn't have the skills to be able to deal with people on a personal level. It was always professional, always on a work basis. But rugby, especially when you're away, is twenty-four/seven, and no one can be working twenty-four hours of the day. Whenever you met him, it always felt like you were addressing a sergeant. You had to be standing straight, you had to be looking good. You had to be everything he expected. It could be quite an intimidating environment.

Rob Howley: Henry was a mastermind of psychology. He had this thing about keeping the pressure on internally. He told us after that game that he respected us as individuals, but he didn't respect us as a team. Ooof. We wanted to prove him wrong. Howie [Shane Howarth] knew him best, knew when he was being serious and when he was taking the piss. It was often difficult to tell.

Neil Jenkins: He didn't allow us to get carried away. It was a case of wipe the slate clean and on to the next challenge. The nature of British or Welsh people is that you win a few games and, to coin a phrase, you think your shit don't smell. As a nation we tend to run away with ourselves, and think we're going to win the World Cup after a few good wins. Graham sensed that and realised he had to bring us back down to earth. I remember coming back and training in Swansea. I always thought I was in decent nick, but I found that session tough as hell. Doing restarts over and over again. There was no resting on our laurels. He worked us harder than ever.

The victory banished the bad memories of the opening two rounds, and inspired some hyperbole from the press. Tim Glover, writing in the *Independent*, called it the 'biggest upset in France since the revolution'. Stuart Barnes declared the victory 'epic', and proclaimed that on a Homeric scale of one-to-ten, it read eleven. Jean-Claude Skrela, Henry's opposite number, declared that he'd witnessed 'the All Blacks playing in red jerseys'. Wales's performance in the first half had been nigh on faultless, and they'd led 28–18 at the break. France came back into it in the second half, but Castaignede's kicking radar was off, and Wales survived to claim the historic victory. They followed it up with a romp against Italy in Treviso, before travelling to Wembley for the last ever game of the Five Nations. England had put sixty points on Wales the previous year, and Graham Henry challenged his team to avenge that defeat. During the build-up, Henry received a fax from a man alleging he'd been on a train with members of England's management team, and had overheard them discussing precisely how they were going to beat Wales. The tone, the man said, was one of arrogance and complacency, and there was a clear tactic to goad Wales into foul play. The England management had singled out Garin Jenkins and Craig Quinnell as two of Wales's most volatile operators, and made clear their intention to get one of them sent off. 'We'll Beckham them,' was the expression that was used.

Rob Howley: Whether or not that fax actually existed, I don't know, but if it didn't it was another brilliant mind game from Henry. He knew how to manipulate emotions and motivate his players. From an analytical point of view, he's probably the best I've ever worked with. Going into that England game we knew exactly what they were going to bring. We just had to stop it.

Peter Rogers: We trained at St Helens in the week building up to that game, and Henry got us to sit in the stand. Huddle in, huddle in. He said we'd had a good week, that we should be feeling confident, and then asked how many of us had beaten England. Only two players raised their hands. That was pretty motivational to me.

Neil Jenkins: Another thing Graham did was force you to watch yourself back, to analyse your own game. Prior to that, I used to just listen to the coach and accept his opinions, but he forced you to think for yourself.

Dafydd James: It was surreal that day. We were technically playing at home, but I remember walking into the dressing room and seeing the St George's Cross draped over the door. That didn't feel right. The buzz and the hype around the ground was phenomenal.

Garin Jenkins: There was a confidence in England. They were a better side than us without a doubt. But we had a solid pack, and a strawberry-blonde outside half that could kick goals and keep us in the game. That was one of those days when you wake up with your stomach doing somersaults and you just know something special is going to happen. Tom Jones singing *Delilah*, Max Boyce was singing *Hymns and Arias*, a lot of emotion. You're thinking of your family, and your village, about wanting to make them all proud.

Dafydd James: Everybody that was Welsh was there. I think Anthony Hopkins was the only one who didn't make it.

Rob Howley: It was fever pitch, unbelievable.

Neil Jenkins: It was quite a long distance from the changing rooms to the pitch, and you can absorb quite a bit in that distance. It was incredible.

Scott Quinnell: We had a bollocking off Graham. We were supposed to be out practising lineouts, and we turned around and started watching Max Boyce's set. Graham was fuming. Then Tom Jones comes on. He's a bloody legend. We can't not watch him. Graham marched us back to the changing rooms early because we'd got a bit distracted.

Rob Howley: I felt that we *had* to get off the field, because the atmosphere was overwhelming. It wasn't until later that I saw the Tom Jones performance, when I watched it back on video. The teams were supposed to go out together, like in the FA Cup final, but I insisted that England go out first. That way, they wouldn't get the benefit of our reception. It was a home game for us after all.

Garin Jenkins: I remember looking across at all those nasty faces. Some of the great forwards of the era – Johnson, Dallaglio, Richard Hill. This is a *real* game today. Walking down that Wembley tunnel, into an arena you dreamt of playing in as a boy. I had a job to digest the lineout calls on a good day. That day my head was all over the place. Every ball was a front ball.

Dafydd James: The adrenaline was overflowing and it got the better of us. England played the best rugby.

Rob Howley: If we'd played that game ten times, we'd have lost nine of them. Jinks kept us in it with his kicking, largely due to England's ill discipline. And their arrogance, to a certain extent.

Peter Rogers: They were all over us in the first ten minutes. Dan Luger scored a fantastic try, and they were tearing us apart. But we had them at the scrum. Henry had brought Garin back in, which helped. He was a formidable scrummager. Garin and I had been tearing tight-heads apart during that run, and we had Craig Quinnell and Chris Wyatt behind us wanting to get in on the act. The scrums were frenzied with those two involved. Wyatt and Craig would angle their drive so there'd be four of us drilling into one tight-head. Wyatt was super-fit so he pushed in every scrum. Whether Craig did or not, it didn't matter, because he was so big, even if he just leant on you, it worked.

Craig Quinnell: My hand-off of Steve Hanley is still one of the things people come up and talk to me about today. It's one of those YouTube moments. He'd come on and scored a try, and Eddie Butler proclaimed him the Jonah Lomu of English rugby. Then I ran over him, broke his arm and he never played for England again.

I know it's a sadistic thing to say, but I loved dominating people. Physically looking at someone, and thinking, 'I've got you.' I never looked at the opposition as individuals, I never thought about being up against someone with a fearsome reputation, never got scared or intimidated by anyone. But I always hoped that they would look at our team-sheet and think, 'Oh no, I'm up against this idiot.' Whenever I bump into old opponents now, the thing I hear the most is, 'I used to hate playing against you.' And I think, 'Job done.' That's the best thing anybody can ever say to you.

Peter Rogers: I'd never experienced much banter in the front row. My first Test match was against France. They don't speak English. Then we played Italy. Neither do they. So that England game was my third international, and the banter was off the charts. Cockerill, Garforth and Leonard were just relentless, if not particularly imaginative. Every scrum, there was at least one, 'Come on you sheep-shaggers.' Sheep-shagger this, sheep-shagger that. But the most telling comment came when we took the lead, and I heard one of them say, 'Shit, I'm not getting my bonus.' Wyatt always joined in from the second row. During the third scrum, he piped up 'Garforth, you're going back again, you fucker.'

Neil Jenkins: In the past, we might have been blown away and lost by thirty points, but we were full of self-belief at that time. Let's be honest, you get penalties through pressure, and we kept the pressure on. That plays on the opposition's minds. They think they're dominant, but you just won't go away. We clung on for dear life, and England just couldn't shake us off.

Rob Howley: I couldn't believe it when Lawrence [Dallaglio] decided to kick for the corner at the end instead of taking the points. We probably didn't deserve to be within a score at that point, but his decision backfired. I'm still gobsmacked when I think of it now. It's something he'll probably always regret. He lost the captaincy to Martin Johnson after that. When I went to Wasps, I never missed an opportunity to remind him of it. I still don't.

Dafydd James: The man of the match would have been Tim Rodber, but he took Colin Charvis's head off, and gave away the penalty that changed the course of history.

Scott Quinnell: When Rodber gave that penalty away on our twenty-two, Jinks picked that ball up, and he *smacked* it. Without that kick, we wouldn't have been within try-scoring range. Howlers, Jinks and myself were walking towards the lineout together trying to decide how to approach one of the most important set plays of our lives, when Gibbsy came up behind us, and said, 'Just give me the ball.' The three of us looked at each other and thought, 'Jesus, someone's made a decision here.'

Dafydd James: Gibbsy had it all mapped out in his mind. He looked across at Dallaglio as they were walking to the lineout and, using his full name, shouted, 'Lawrence Bruno Nero Dallaglio! I feel *gooooood* tonight.'

Neil Jenkins: That's Gibbsy all over.

Rob Howley: They were really good mates, Lawrence and Gibbsy. They'd been to the US together on holiday after the '97 Lions tour. But it didn't matter who he was up against, he'd happily tell you he was coming down your channel.

Garin Jenkins: My heart rate was going, and I thought, 'Dear me, a lineout. The pressure is all on me.' I used to practise my lineout throwing all the time. I wouldn't leave the training field until I'd hit the crossbar fifteen times. Five left, five middle, five right. Sometimes I'd be up there for six hours. Thankfully my one straight lineout of the game ended with Chris Wyatt just about snaffling the ball, and we pinched victory.

Scott Quinnell: We'd never practised that move before because it involved me passing the ball, so there's no point, like, innit? It was a shortened lineout. Garin, to Chris Wyatt off the top. Down to Howlers, to myself, and I genuinely thought, 'Right, look as though you're going to juggle the ball now to bring the defensive line in.' Believe that, and you'll believe anything.

Dafydd James: It all happened so fast, which was another Henry thing. Tempo was everything. Keep the opposition on their heels. The element of surprise. Take them when they're vulnerable. Little things like walking up to the lineout slowly, then bang, taking it quickly and getting it away before they've had time to organise. But that one, we'd practised over and over. It was a training ground routine. It even had a name – 'Trifecta Treviso'. SQ was there as a decoy, basically. We had *definitely* practised it. Lineout, drop Scott Quinnell out so it *looks* like he's going to get the ball. He did actually get it, and we witnessed something we'd never seen – Scott Quinnell passed the ball. And it was a deft little pass as well, fair play.

Neil Jenkins: It was a planned move, but because SQ bobbled it, we had to improvise a bit. Gibbsy saw the hole and took the short line.

Scott Quinnell: I got the ball to Gibbsy and he cut an incredible line.

Dafydd James: Gibbsy comes through like a missile.

Neil Jenkins: He's the one person you wouldn't want coming at you that fast. He's going to put you flat on your arse. Whenever I played against him, my first port of call would be to short-arm him. I'd have my forearm pad on, and make a beeline for him, and he'd be all uppity and offended. 'What are you doing?' And I'd tell him, 'Don't come down here, there's no way I'm tackling you all day. No *way*.'

Scott Quinnell: *He* did something he'd never done before, and never done again. Side-stepped! Off his left, off his left, onto his right.

Neil Jenkins: Only Gibbsy or Howley could have scored a try like that.

Dafydd James: He goes outside Dawson, who's up his own arse, inside two players, Cohen and Perry, and then under the sticks . . . well not quite under the sticks, was it? He put the old arm up in the air to celebrate, and I was shouting, 'Just put the fucking thing down.'

Scott Quinnell: The noise was absolutely deafening, but it gave way to absolute silence when the realisation dawned that we still had to kick the conversion. I was down on one knee on the halfway line having a word with the big fella upstairs. I think I agreed a twenty-five-year contract with him. 'I will do anything you want for twenty-five years, just please let Jinks get this one over.' And then of course he kicked the goal, we survived until the end, and that was that. It was quite nice to spoil their Grand Slam party, especially with a move we'd never practised before. When Gibbsy tells you, 'Give me the ball,' you give him the ball. I've never met a player with as much power, determination and self-belief. Having said that, he's never said thank you for the pass.

Dafydd James: A true enigma, Gibbsy. One minute he was your best friend, the next he'd blank you. Played to the highest level in both codes, but these days he's not remotely interested in rugby.

Craig Quinnell: Gibbsy could have gone under the posts, instead of running the other way. But nobody ever thought that Jinks was going to miss that kick.

Peter Rogers: He jogged over to Jinks with the ball, and just said four words. 'Put the fucker over.'

Craig Quinnell: I don't think anybody realised how good Jinks was. His passing was brilliant, he could tackle as well as anyone. They say Leigh Halfpenny's worth nine points a game. Jinks was worth at least twelve or fifteen.

Dafydd James: He called himself 'the radar'. He once had a run of fifty kicks at goal without missing one. It wasn't an easy kick, with the angle, and the pressure, but he was the best in the world. You'd have bet your house on him. He was cool as you like, and slotted it over. I had a huge surge of adrenaline at that point. We hadn't been in the bloody game, and suddenly . . . we're going to win it.

Neil Jenkins: As a kicker, it's what you dream of. A kick to win the game against England. That's what it's all about. I felt good, I hadn't missed all day. People ask if my heart's thumping at that point, but the reality is I'm calm. It's what you do. Once the try's scored you're into goal-kicking mode. I daren't have missed it because I'd have probably got lynched. But the position it was in, I'd have expected to nail that a hundred times out of a hundred.

Dafydd James: There were a few minutes to go, and I remember thinking, 'Stay switched on, boys.' I'd seen it so many times before. You go ahead, you have a lapse in concentration, and the other team hits back. Mike Catt very nearly broke our hearts with his drop-goal attempt. I can feel it now, I've got goosebumps thinking about it. The crowd, the noise, the roar was incredible. From both sides. The English fans were urging their team to stay in the fight, the Welsh fans were just going bonkers. It was *unreal*. It's only years later that you realise the magnitude of what you've achieved.

Neil Jenkins: Yes, Catty nearly nicked it at the death. Only me, Rob and Matt Dawson saw what happened, but Dawson illegally kicked the ball out of the scrum. He checked to see that the ref wasn't looking, and booted it towards our line.

Rob Howley: I scrambled back to dive on the ball, and was clinging on for dear life. Holding on. I was saying to Andre Watson, 'I've let it go, I've let it go,' and he gives England the scrum.

Neil Jenkins: They went for the drop goal, but thankfully, Catty pushed it right.

Dafydd James: We heard later that the English had already put the champagne on ice, and that Clive Woodward had made enquiries about where they were going to be collecting the trophy from. When we heard that, it made the win even sweeter.

Rob Howley: They'd apparently asked for the white ribbons to be put on the trophy. From a Welsh perspective, it makes it even better, doesn't it?

Dafydd James: We had a good drink that night at the Royal Gardens in Kensington. Catatonia were there celebrating with us, Tom Jones popped in to raise a glass.

Rob Howley: Neil's gran was ill. She'd had a stroke, so the hero of the hour had to go straight home.

Neil Jenkins: My mate got my kit bag, and the two of us walked all the way down Wembley Way, among the hordes of celebrating Welsh fans. I'd just played in the game, and not one person came onto me. There were people stumbling about, falling into the hedges, people laughing, people crying. It was an incredible scene to behold. I thought it was going to be hard work getting through, but not one person recognised me.

Those who knew what 'Jinks' was capable of had little doubt the kick would go over – Graham Henry later said that Jenkins' ratio would have been the same if the posts were just two metres apart. But the victory itself may have benefited from a little divine intervention. Ten days before, Henry had paid a visit to St David's Cathedral, on the westernmost fringe of Wales. During his visit, he offered up a prayer, thinking his team might need a little assistance. Ten days later, when the clock was ticking down at Wembley, Henry looked heavenward, and implored St David to intervene. Within moments, Tim Rodber had given away the fateful penalty that allowed Neil Jenkins to kick to touch, and set up that one final attack.

Garin Jenkins: After our showers we went back out on the pitch in our dinner suits, to wander round and soak it up. We didn't want to leave. I'd grown up watching FA Cup finals, watching the winners walking up those famous steps to lift the trophy. I had to walk up to see what that was like, just to stand there and take in the view. We didn't have a trophy to lift, because our victory meant the Scots won the tournament. They gave Scott Gibbs a kilt out of gratitude. I don't know what they ever gave me. It was a great day. The celebrations went on for a week.

Scott Quinnell: We got back to the hotel on the Monday, and there was a bottle of Famous Grouse for every player in the Welsh squad. A little thank you from the Scottish Rugby Union for handing them the title.

Garin Jenkins: I was playing for Swansea the following Saturday in the Welsh Cup semi-final, and the celebrations had barely stopped. I remember waking up and thinking, 'Oh, I've got a game today.' It was a good time to be Welsh. Welsh pop bands were riding high in the charts – the Manic Street Preachers, the Stereophonics, Catatonia. Welsh TV presenters were getting more prominent. The 'Cool Cymru' movement was in full flow. I'm not saying that that game had anything to do with it, but our confidence as a nation was blossoming around that time. I was getting into my red wine, and enjoying a drop of Barolo around that time. My great friend John Hughes, of the Grogg Shop fame, sent me a bottle of Barolo over while I was having a meal at the famous John's Cafe in Pontypridd. I felt like royalty. The great John Hughes, buying *me* a bottle of wine. Or I'd be in Aberdare, buying fish and chips, and someone would step in and say, 'You're not paying for those, have it on me.' It was lovely. For a couple of months we dined out on it. It made me realise that playing for Wales is an honour, and it reminded me what it means to the people, of the weight of responsibility you carry.

SIXTEEN

THE WONDERFUL WORLD OF CHRIS WYATT

The press conference on the Monday after the Wembley win lasted more than two hours. The nation was consumed by an optimism that had been absent for the best part of a decade. Graham Henry had delivered a victory of enormous significance and drama, but in front of the press, he urged caution. Wales needed to improve by twenty to thirty per cent, he said, if they were to stand a chance of challenging for the World Cup later that year. The one advantage they had, was that it was on home soil. Before that, a tour to Argentina, and a series of friendlies at the brand-new Millennium Stadium awaited.

Craig Quinnell: I was carrying an injury, and due to miss the Argentina tour, but Graham wanted to take me out anyway, to be with the boys. He said he'd run the legs off me while I was out there. The tour didn't get off to the best start, and the boys were being pushed about a bit in the warm-up games, so the Monday before the first Test, Graham tells me I'm going to be playing in it. I hadn't done any contact for three or four weeks, and it's an understatement to say the first half didn't go too great.

Dafydd James: We were 23–0 down at half-time, and Graham Henry went *ballistic*. It was the first time I'd seen him lose his rag. He went to town on us, effin' and blinding. Properly read us the riot act. He was kicking stuff around in the changing rooms, stamping his feet. He'd seriously lost his cool.

Craig Quinnell: I was playing in new boots, and they didn't feel right, so at half-time, I asked JR, the kit man, if he'd change the laces for me. Graham grabbed my boots, chucked them at me and said, 'You don't deserve anyone to lace your boots up, do 'em yourself, and pull your finger out in the second half.' We went back out, got stuck into 'em, and won the game.

Neil Jenkins: Graham got stuck into me. I'd had an operation on my shoulder, and that was my first game since the England match. I was all over the shop, rusty as anything. I'd hardly done any contact. I'd spent months just running and doing skills. I missed two penalties, had a kick charged down, and missed a tackle that led to a try for them. He pulled me to one side and asked me what the fuck I was doing. I said, 'You know I haven't played, I told you that. I'm trying to get into it.' Second half, I was a different player.

Peter Rogers: My most abiding memory of Neil Jenkins in that half was of him tackling Reggiardo into touch, and then wafting his hand under his nose in full view of the cameras. I don't think his breath was too fragrant, put it that way.

Dafydd James: The bollocking worked a treat. The forty minutes we put together in the second half was sublime. Chris Wyatt came to the fore, and we ran them off the park.

Craig Quinnell: Graham came up to me at the final whistle, apologised for what he'd said at half-time, and told me, 'Well played.' I told him to fuck off. He looked taken aback, but then noticed I had scratches all over my eyeballs and scram marks around my eyes. I looked at him through bloodied eyes, and he said, 'That's it, I'm going to get the referee, you can't have that.' And I told him, 'Fuck that, I'll sort it myself.' The second Test was going to be war.

Peter Rogers: After the game, Graham Henry announced in the dressing room that he was handing out a bonus award. And the bonus award was given collectively to the front row, because we totally beat Argentina up that day. That was manna from heaven for me. I'd always backed myself at scrum time from my South Africa days. I was nearly twenty stone, so I was difficult to shift. I'd tested myself against the likes of Frank Tournaire and Christian Califano, and now we'd humiliated Argentina on their own patch. We became known as the best scrum in the world at that point in time, which was nice. We won all our games through our scrum really. We were getting loads of scrum penalties, and we had the best goal-kicker in the world. Graham Henry was credited for transforming that Welsh team, but he might have just got lucky. He said that to me in jest once.

Craig Quinnell: We go into the second Test, and playing for Argentina are Agustin Pichot and Rolando Martin, teammates of mine at Richmond. In the first five minutes, their captain started stamping on one of our boys, and I thought, 'I'm not having this,' and I smashed him, Pich jumps on my back and we start brawling. Scott doesn't like seeing his brother being picked on, so he runs in from twenty yards, and smashes some bloke. Next thing, we're all fighting in the dugout. Fists flying everywhere.

Dafydd James: They were big buggers. Massive. Their forwards were juggernauts. We had a big pack, but they were *huge*. It was no place for the faint-hearted.

Scott Quinnell: It was one of the best brawls ever. In the football stadium in Buenos Aires, with chicken wire all round the pitch, the fans baying for blood. It was like something out of *Gladiator*. Argentina were more brutal than France. They didn't want to play rugby at the time, they just wanted to fight. It was one of their props that hit me. My brother hit the prop. And all of a sudden, everybody's in. I remember being at the bottom of a pile of bodies, not being able to move because everyone was on top of me, and among all the dirty boots, a little pair of polished brown brogues appeared in my eyeline. Their owner aimed a kick at one of the Pumas before scuttling off. When I looked at the tape afterwards, I discovered it was our team doctor, Roger Evans.

Craig Quinnell: We only knew it was him because he was wearing red socks and brogues. After that fight, they didn't want to know, and we won the game, no problems.

Dafydd James: I was right in the middle of it. Jinks had kicked long, and it was my mission to chase down the receiver and sack him. I took the winger down, and Pichot came in and stamped on me. I leapt to my feet and grabbed him, and there was a bit of a scuffle. The winger who I'd tackled got up and punched me in the back of the head, and all hell broke loose. Everyone was swinging, and the brawl tumbled into the dugout. Rob Howley pulled a billboard over himself to hide. He shit himself.

Rob Howley: That was no place for scrum halves.

Craig Quinnell: There's a lot of pointing and shouting and screaming in rugby these days. I was never into that. If I was going to hit you, I just hit you.

Peter Rogers: It kicked off because they knew they were being humiliated. They thought they had the best scrum in world rugby, and we did them in both Tests. They couldn't get their heads around the fact we were more powerful. We had better technique, and we were more up for it than they were, which sounds strange considering it was Argentina, but it was a fact.

Neil Jenkins: We'd been going backwards against the same opponents at Stradey Park in November, but our front row bossed it that day. Humph was a brilliant player, but Garin the scrum doctor took over at hooker, and he proved the missing link. The Argies were distraught.

Dafydd James: No British team had ever won a Test series in Argentina before us.

Craig Quinnell: Chris Wyatt bought a ghetto blaster out there. A massive thing that he'd carry on his shoulder as he walked through the airport, like he was in Harlem or something. He thought he was pretty cool. I put an Abba CD in there, turned the volume dial to max, and pinched his remote control. As he was walking through customs, I hit the play button, and *Take A Chance On Me* came blaring out of the speakers. He didn't know what was going on, and went bright red, bless him. I loved him though, he was an old-school amateur. When Wales first started staying at the Vale, he'd turn up with nothing but a PlayStation, and a plastic carrier bag. It always had the same things in it – a two-litre bottle of full-fat Coke, about thirty chocolate bars, and a hundred fags. That was it. He'd be thinking, 'I'm here for the week, great.'

Dafydd James: There's a bloke who underachieved for the talent he had. If he's honest with himself, he'll admit that he let himself down when he could have gone on the Lions tour and been something really special. The year before the Lions – 2000 – there was a huge billboard of him on the BT Tower in Cardiff, he had a sponsorship deal with Nike, and he thought he'd made it. You can never ever take things for granted, but he did a bit.

Peter Rogers: I roomed with Wyatt ahead of my debut in France. We stayed in this plush hotel called California and had a suite with its own lounge and staircase. The doc used to come round to give us sleeping tablets, to help us relax before the match. Wyatt never took his, and would be up until five in the morning on his PlayStation playing Fifa. Then he'd have a fag and an espresso, and in the small hours, he'd order room service. Menthols, he used to smoke. He'd call them 'fitness fags'.

Dafydd James: Wyatt was naturally so fit that he didn't need to train much. But it all caught up with him. His booze, his drinking and his escapades. He was on his own. He'd say he couldn't sleep, and then he'd be on his PlayStation at three in the morning with one hand, texting girls with the other, and sipping coffee in between. Then he'd complain he wasn't getting any sleep and felt tired in training.

Rob Howley: On a pre-match day, he'd drink nineteen cups of coffee.

Neil Jenkins: You had that variety. A big man like Craig who could carry hard and run over people, and then the athlete like Wyatt who could soar high in the lineout. It's a pity he wasn't fitter because he would have been some player. He was a great player anyway, but if he'd have had access to the kind of fitness training we have in the modern game, he'd have reached another level.

Rob Howley: We had a great blend in the back five. Those two in the second row, and then Charvis, SQ and Mr Sinkinson. Charvy was some player. He wouldn't say much before games, but he always delivered.

Neil Jenkins: You had to wake him up to go out on the field most of the time.

Rob Howley: He'd have his headphones on, be in his own space. But he was one hell of a player, one of the best back rows I ever played with.

Neil Jenkins: Before a game, when everyone else was getting fired up and in the zone, he'd be lying on the benches in the changing room 'resting his eyes'. But you knew, when the time came, he'd turn into a warrior. He was an outstanding rugby player and an outstanding athlete.

Craig Quinnell: After we won the series, we went to a nightclub called Buenos Aires News, where the world's most beautiful women hung out. There were two taxis going there, with four of us in each. Halfway there, Riot [Chris Wyatt] rings and challenges us to a race – climb out the window of the taxi, across the roof, and back in the other side. Whoever does it quickest wins. So him and Peter Rogers raced one another, going down the main street in Buenos Aires.

Dafydd James: I was in the car. Fucking idiots. You always knew something stupid was going to happen with Riot. He climbed out the frickin' window, and I was thinking, 'What are you doing?' He was standing up, surfing on the roof of the car. If the taxi driver had slammed his brakes on, it would have been, 'Goodnight, Irene'.

Peter Rogers: It was a stupid thing to do. We were celebrating being the first ever northern hemisphere side to win a series out there, and we got carried away. The car was travelling, mind. It must've been going at least forty miles an hour. I looked across and Wyatt was up on the roof of his, on all fours, with the wind flowing through his hair. The boys were all banging on the roof, cheering him on. When I got up, the driver actually sped up. They called us the urban surfers for a while after that. Buenos Aires News was a magnet for all the beautiful people. The actors, the models, and all the famous footballers from River Plate.

Craig Quinnell: There's a swimming pool in the nightclub, an ornamental thing, with a bridge over it. Riot started shouting 'Q! Distract the bouncers,' and the next thing, him and Peter Rogers have stripped off and dived in.

Peter Rogers: It was Rob Howley who dared me to jump in. Neil Boobyer said he'd give me a hundred dollars if I did. Rob said he'd give me a hundred too, as did Jinks and a few others. Overall I had seven hundred dollars promised to me.

Dafydd James: The place was rammed. And in he goes, in his suit, the fucking idiot. He stands up, dripping wet, with his hair all plastered to his head.

Peter Rogers: Water went splashing everywhere, and everyone started cheering and whooping. They were all loving it, with their Latin American temperament. They love a bit of naughtiness. A bouncer tried to drag me out, and I fought him off.

Dafydd James: I thought, 'Christ, it's all gonna kick off here.' Thirty mad Taffs, big rugby guys. But luckily a couple of the bouncers were rugby guys too, and they recognised who we were and calmed it down. Peter ended up borrowing a top off one of the bouncers, and it didn't fit him because he was a big old goose at the time. I swear to God, he might as well have put my son's top on.

Craig Quinnell: It was like babysitting at times with those two.

Peter Rogers: Six of the boys paid up, and I got six hundred dollars for my trouble. I'm still waiting for my hundred from Rob Howley. Typical Rob Howley.

Rob Howley: I do *not* remember that. Did he do it? I remember the nightclub, but not the swimming pool incident.

Dafydd James: In France, someone dared Wyatt to jump off a three-storey balcony in a nightclub. He got a bunch of us to criss-cross our arms at the bottom, and catch him. The place was packed, and everybody was smashed. Wyatt goes, 'Three . . . two . . . one,' and dived off the top. Half the boys bottled it and pulled away, the rest only just managed to break his fall. He nosedives onto the floor, smashing his head. He's lucky he's not dead. The doctor was trying to stitch him up while they were both steaming drunk. You should have seen the state of those stitches.

Within days of their return, Wales were preparing for another Test match against the Springboks. After an absence of more than two years, Wales were back in Cardiff, albeit at a partially built Millennium Stadium. Humiliated in Pretoria in June, narrowly defeated at Wembley in November, could act three of this bruising sequence really produce a victory? A year earlier, a bookmaker would have let you name your odds. Now, the fans – who'd have been forgiven for thinking Welsh rugby had breathed its last in Pretoria – were genuinely anticipating a first ever victory against South Africa.

Craig Quinnell: The atmosphere for that game was *amazing*. There were only 27,000 in there, but it felt like 150,000. There were workers up in the gantry cheering us on. They were still building the place, and they had to down tools for a couple of hours to watch us play. The rest were all rugby fans. None of the corporate crowd. Everybody *wanted* to be there. And Mark Taylor scored a phenomenal try that set us on our way to victory.

Peter Rogers: My best memory in a Wales shirt was the final whistle in that South Africa game. They were the world champions at the time. To see Gary Teichmann trudging off defeated, with his shoulders slumped, was an awesome feeling.

Craig Quinnell: People think I broke my thumb in the England game in '99 when I ran into the posts during the warm-up. That's an urban myth. I broke it in this game; bust it on AJ Venter's head off a kick-off. He carried it up, I swung a big one, and popped my thumb in half. For the first half, I couldn't grip anything, because I had my thumb taped to my hand. There was no way I was going off, though.

The series victory in Argentina, and Wales's first ever victory over South Africa – more than a century in the making – gave them every reason to be positive going into the 1999 World Cup.

Scott Quinnell: In one of our pre-World Cup training camps in Brecon School, Blackie tried to drum it into us that we were genuine contenders. After a hard session he brought us together and said, 'Right guys, gather round, close your eyes. We're going to lift the World Cup trophy.' He made us visualise being on that podium and holding the trophy aloft.

Craig Quinnell: He made Howlers climb to the top of the cricket pavilion, salute the crowd, and pretend to lift an imaginary World Cup.

Peter Rogers: It wasn't just Howley, all of us had to do it. The entire World Cup squad had to go up and lift this 'trophy'. Graham Henry and Lynn Howells were applauding enthusiastically below. Some of the boys loved it, but I was a bit cynical. I went along with it for the good of the team, but I didn't buy into it.

Rob Howley: It was bizarre, but it was always about making you feel like you were in a better place than you were when you arrived at the session. On the whole he succeeded.

Scott Quinnell: He knew everybody's personality, everybody's quirks and foibles. And he made a point of getting to know your family. I don't think there was anyone under Blackie who didn't love him. He'd always keep you thinking. For him, it was as much about getting your mind right, as your body.

Ian Gough: He was more than a fitness coach. He was a life coach, a mentor. He was everything.

Peter Rogers: He was a power lifter, an actor, a doorman, and everything in between. A renaissance man.

Scott Quinnell: He used to suffer terribly with insomnia, so he'd stay up all night, and then fall asleep in random places. Within seconds of getting on the team bus, he'd be snoring. And he'd always be sat next to Lynn Howells, so we'd taunt Lynn mercilessly about the fact it was *him* who'd sent Blackie to sleep.

Rob Howley: He'd write long, handwritten letters to every player in the squad and slip it under your door at night. Every one was individual, with a different message that tapped into your individual psyche. He really cared. It's no wonder he never slept, writing thirty-odd letters would probably take all night.

Craig Quinnell: He'd stick you in the gym, on the treadmill, and you'd never ask him how long or how many. Twenty minutes later you'd be blowing out of your arse thinking, 'When's he going to stop this bloody thing?' Then you'd look around and he'd be fast asleep.

Peter Rogers: When I joined the Welsh squad, I had to sign a contract. Part of the deal was that I had to do a fitness test. Fitness was not my forte, so I was dreading it. They arranged through London Irish for Steve Black to come and see me. I was to meet him at Sunbury, and to bring footwear – boots and mouldies. I was sitting in the dugout at about ten-to-two, feeling nervous about what lay ahead, when this cheerful Geordie bloke ambled up to me. 'Hiya, Peter, I'm Steve Black. I've just had a lovely train journey up here. Tell us a bit about your fitness regime?' I told him I did loads of weights, very little running, and that I barely ever touched the ball in games. I'd maybe make three or four tackles a game, tops. I just concentrated on power and scrummaging, and that was what saw me through. But I told him if he wanted me to get fitter in order to play for Wales, then I would. As I was talking he was taking a few notes in his little notebook. Then he said, 'How are you feeling in yourself, when you play? Do you feel good?' I said, yeah, I was feeling great. I was enjoying my rugby and on a good run of form. He put his notebook back in his top pocket, and said, 'Fantastic, you've just passed your fitness test.'

Rob Howley: I thought of him more as a psychologist than a fitness coach.

Neil Jenkins: I really liked him. He's different, off the scale. Makes you feel good. But I think he needed to be working alongside a conditioner in hindsight. There wasn't enough discipline around food and things. Sometimes there'd be a load of Cokes in the fridge, and that's my downfall. I can't resist the temptation.

Dafydd James: What he provided for me was psychological support. He knew he didn't have to worry about me training or eating right because I was obsessed with fitness anyway. I'm not blowing smoke up my own backside, but I was always supremely fit and confident with that side of things, but I used to take criticism very personally. In life, not everyone's going to like you, not everybody's going to rate you, and I used to find that hard to deal with. If I missed a tackle or knocked a ball on, he'd always be the first to say, 'Don't worry about that, let's have a look at the big picture.' He'd massage your ego just enough to get you over it. He had an amazing ability to spin things around. His phone was always on. He'd say, 'Any time you feel a bit shit, ring me.' And he meant it.

Craig Quinnell: Blackie was great for me, because I was always under pressure to prove myself. My fitness coach at Cardiff once said to me, 'You're the fastest forward we've got, you're the strongest by far, the most powerful. You can run 3km in eleven-and-a-half minutes, at twenty-one-and-a-half stone, but you need to do extra training because you don't *look* very good.' Being twenty-one stone and having sixteen per cent body fat wasn't good enough. They wanted me at twelve per cent. It's impossible. The press would always be asking about my fitness, always suggesting I was out of shape. At one press conference, Blackie said he'd just tested me, and I was twenty per cent fitter than I'd been three months earlier, twenty per cent lighter, and twenty per cent stronger. He hadn't even done a fitness test. He'd know how fit you were because he'd be there watching you train, which is exactly as it should be. Rucking and mauling, and scrummaging didn't take it out of me because it was easy.

Peter Rogers: Craig had it written into his Cardiff contract that he didn't need to do fitness. He'd arranged it through Steve Black. We'd be putting ourselves through the mill, doing bleep tests down at the university pitches, blowing out of our arses, and Craig would be standing at the side, shrugging his shoulders, going 'It's not in my contract, bro!'

Scott Quinnell: I got yellow carded in the World Cup warm-up game against France. First yellow card in international rugby. When I found out you could have a ten-minute rest for hitting someone, I thought, 'Happy days!' It was another victory, and by the time the tournament began, our confidence was sky-high. The opening ceremony was incredible. We warmed up inside, so weren't aware of the atmosphere out there. When we eventually emerged from the tunnel, the adrenaline rush was overwhelming.

Craig Quinnell: Scott and I always used to go out in our tracksuits before the game to throw the ball about, and have a look at the conditions. We jogged out, and Owen Money was there in the middle of the pitch with his band. He's warming the crowd up, getting them ready for the opening ceremony. We walk past Shirley Bassey and Tom Jones, and they're going, 'Hey Craig, how are you?' I'm thinking, 'How do they know who I am?' It's full, it's dark, the lights are going. As soon as Owen clocks us, he shouts, 'Ladies and Gentlemen, the Quinnell brothers!', and the whole crowd goes nuts. It sent shivers down my spine, and I felt a tear in my eye. That was it – I had to go straight back down the tunnel. Gibbsy's coming out, he sees us two emotional wrecks, and turns straight back around. He later said that if the *Quinnell* boys are walking in crying, you think, 'Fuck that' and walk back in with them. It was an unbelievable buzz, and that reception was just for Scott and I. Having said that I think if a Jack Russell had run out, they'd have screamed for him too.

Dafydd James: There was an expectation that we could go all the way and win the World Cup, but we played within ourselves in that first game against Argentina. The atmosphere pre-match was electric, and we were overwhelmed by the adrenaline and the emotion. It was just too much.

Peter Rogers: They'd done a bit of analysis on us after the summer tour, and in the first scrum, I had my ear bitten. I went down, and suddenly felt this piercing pain in my ear. I got up, and I was fuming. I couldn't believe it. Next thing, Reggiardo bites his own arm, and shows the referee the mark claiming that I'd done it. So I'm saying *I've* been bitten, he's claiming *he's* been bitten. I don't know whether the ref was shitting himself or what – opening game of the World Cup and all that – but he just ignored it. He'd bitten right through my ear. I've still got a scar now. He'd clearly done it to get one of us sent off early on. They knew we'd dominated them out there, and thought the only way they could beat us was if me or Dai Young were sent off. It was cynical, and calculated.

Craig Quinnell: We beat them anyway, and afterwards, I called up Agustin Pichot and invited him and Rolando to meet me for a coffee. I'd just bought a new flat, so I went out to get some Hobnobs and coffee, and they turn up with some long-haired prop called Mauirico Reggiardo – the dirtiest bastard you've ever played against in your life. We're sat there sipping our coffees, munching on our biscuits. I give Pichot my jersey from the opening game; he gives me his. We're laughing and joking, and Reggiardo goes to me, 'Hey CQ, remember in Buenos Aires when I poked my finger in your eyes?' I said, 'Yeah.' 'And then you punched me in the face and broke my nose.' And I said, 'Yeah.' He said 'Fun times, eh? Fun times?' And I had to agree with him. What other sport in the world could you say I poked you in the eye, and you broke my nose, and we had a great laugh, like?

The Argentina victory was followed up by a 64–15 rout of Japan. A win over Samoa would have seen Wales safely through to the quarter-finals. But as was the case in 1991, the South Sea Islanders sprang a surprise, outsmarting Wales, and bringing their ten-game winning streak to a shuddering end. Two key errors, including a miscued lineout, gifted the Samoans a couple of tries, and ultimately the win. The absence of the suspended Colin Charvis and the injured Craig Quinnell meant Wales were light on ball carriers able to penetrate the Samoan defensive wall. Scott Quinnell ended up taking on what proved to be an overwhelming workload.

Scott Quinnell: I had a shocker against Samoa. It was me that delivered the match-winning pass to Steven Bachop who went in under the posts. It was a tough day. I'd had a phone call in the morning from the missus telling me our kitchen had caught fire. She was calling to let me know that the kids were okay, and she was okay, but it messed with my head a bit.

Dafydd James: We just took them for granted. Simple as that. Ten wins in a row, and we thought we were invincible. We took our foot off the pedal, and we underestimated them.

Rob Howley: The conditions were tricky, the ball was slippery, and they had done their homework. They had a lot of players, like Pat Lam and Va'aiga Tuigamala who knew Graham Henry well from Auckland. They understood his philosophy, and had figured out our game plan. They stopped SQ and they stopped Scott Gibbs. And we were missing Craig Quinnell. Add in a couple of lineout errors and we lost a game we should have won.

Scott Quinnell: I got belted all over the park by Trevor Leota. He smashed me every time I got the ball. I couldn't run round him because he'd shuffle to his left and you'd have to run another six yards. Brian Lima put my bottom teeth through my lip. I've never been so battered and bruised after a game in my life. Whether you're being hit by them, or you're running into them, you get hurt. It feels as though they're wearing bricks in their shoulders. Even if they pick you up from the floor after a tackle, they try to break your hand. It's far harder than playing against the 'Boks. But after the game, they're the nicest people in the world.

Dafydd James: We were the better team on paper, but the likes of Pat Lam and Brian Lima played out of their skins. Most embarrassingly of all, I ran into the posts en route to the try line. My kids love that video to this day. Of all the things I've achieved in a Welsh shirt, that's the one they play over and over again. Even their mates at school have seen it. 'Oh, you're the guy that ran into the posts?' 'That's me, yeah.' I was dying of embarrassment. The roar of the crowd as I was charging towards the line turned quickly into a collective sigh of disappointment. We did score a try off the back of it to be fair. Scott Quinnell got over the line, and Steve Black came onto the field to ruffle my hair and say, 'See, you got us into that position.'

Peter Rogers: I was playing a round of golf with Wyatt at the Vale the day after, and the workmen who were working on the hotel bellowed out to us, 'Hey boys, tell Scott Quinnell he was Samoa's man of the match.' We had about five or six scrums on their line, where we were rolling them over. All Scott had to do was dribble it over the line, but he couldn't do it. And he threw that interception pass. We shouldn't have lost.

Allegations of spying and skullduggery dominated the build-up to the quarter-final against Australia. Graham Henry's suspicions were confirmed when the Wallabies appeared to have changed their defensive plan to counter a Welsh tactic. Wales had identified a weakness at the tail of Australia's lineout, but on game day the Wallabies seemed to know exactly what was coming. The home side also had two clear-cut scoring chances denied by referee Colin Hawke, who considered their dummy switch manoeuvre to be a form of obstruction. To add insult to injury, there was a feeling that Australia were getting away with murder at the set piece.

Peter Rogers: I maintain that if we had the technology we have now, we'd have had five or six penalties in that quarter-final. They were *living* offside. The touch judges weren't miked up as they are now, so they couldn't alert the ref. They were pulling and wheeling the scrum like nobody's business, and they didn't allow us to get our power game going. The Aussie tight-head that day was rubbish. It was like playing against a junior rugby player. If those penalties had been awarded, that could have been eighteen points with Jinks in our side.

Scott Quinnell: Australia had a try given that was definitely a forward pass. If that hadn't been awarded, things may have turned out differently. That was one of the hardest defeats I've ever had to take. I genuinely believed that we were good enough to get through. They went on to win the World Cup.

Peter Rogers: Up until the hour mark, it was 10–9, and then Ben Tune scored a dodgy try from the forward pass. They went on to beat South Africa in the semi. We'd just beaten them, and I know for a fact we'd have dominated them up front, and milked loads of penalties. We'd smashed them in July, absolutely destroyed them. Then it would have been France in the final, and we'd have beaten them twice already. Our win over them in the warm-up game was like a training ground romp. We battered them. We could have won that 1999 World Cup. I still think about that now.

Craig Quinnell: I felt as though the world had ended. A few of us left the country, we just needed to escape. Myself, Chris Wyatt, Charvy and Alfie went to New York. We didn't want to stick around. It was the best thing we could have done. Got on teletext and booked a holiday.

Peter Rogers: I spoke to one of their second rows in the Mocka Lounge after the game, and he said, 'Oh mate, we cheated like fuck.'

Rob Howley: I didn't play well in the World Cup, and I had the captaincy taken off me afterwards. I wasn't happy, and threw the baby out with the bath water. Graham thought the captaincy was inhibiting me. He phoned me during training at Cardiff, and wanted me to drop in on him at his house to deliver the news. It was two weeks before the Six Nations started as opposed to just after the World Cup. Maybe he wanted to reflect and didn't want to rush to judgement.

SEVENTEEN

IT WAS LIKE STRICTLY COME DANCING

Graham Henry may have had the alchemist's touch at the start of his reign, but two years in, the shine was coming off. The year 2000 marked the advent of the Six Nations. Wales finished fourth with victories over Italy, Scotland, and Ireland. But they were hammered by France and England. Clive Woodward's side had recovered from their Wembley wobble, to dish out a 46–12 thrashing at Twickenham. A gulf had opened up. Woodward's acute attention to detail contrasted sharply with the binge-drinking culture that was still prevalent in Welsh rugby. Wales may have evolved their style, but their fitness wasn't holding up, and it was Steve Black who carried the can. The jovial Geordie was the first to depart the crumbling edifice. He resigned at the end of the Championship after a number of articles had appeared claiming the Welsh players were overweight and out of shape. Forwards coach Lynn Howells wasn't far behind when, after a convivial dinner with Graham Henry, he was told, 'One of us is going to have to go, and it's not going to be me.' It felt as though a crossroads had been reached, and Henry was unsure whether to look forwards or backwards.

Rupert Moon: Someone had asked Graham Henry in a press conference if Rupert Moon would ever play for Wales again, and Henry dismissed the idea out of hand. But Llanelli had gone on a bit of a run in '99. We were flying. I was having breakfast in McDonald's in Cardiff, and I got a call asking if I'd come to training. Howlers was injured, and I was like, 'Fucking hell, of course I'll come.' But after that session I felt like a broken man. At that point, I'd already dislocated my shoulder, popped my sternum, dislocated my elbow, and torn my knee ligaments. I was thirty-two, and hadn't played international rugby for five years. There were a lot of injuries, and they were blooding a few youngsters like Stephen Jones and Rhys Williams. Dai Young was supposed to have been captain, but he was struggling with his leg, and Graham Henry said to me, 'Mate, you might have to lead this lot.' I said, 'Sure, whatever you want me to do.' He just needed a bit of stability. Wales had had a few bumps in the road. The World Cup had gone badly, we'd lost to Samoa again, 2000 was a comedown, and after all the magnificent stuff we'd done during the ten-match winning streak, everybody thought we were shit again. The knives were out. Graham wanted to build his side for the next World Cup, but they just needed an oldie to steady the ship. Everybody was in a bad place. We beat Scotland and Ireland, but we got battered by England and France.

Wales were to suffer further embarrassment off the pitch when it transpired that their two imported Kiwis – Brett Sinkinson and Shane Howarth – didn't have a single drop of Welsh blood in them. Sinkinson had been backpacking around Europe before picking up a contract with Neath, and when Henry made enquiries as to his ancestry, his agent replied that his grandfather was from Carmarthen. The truth, discovered after he'd won the twentieth of his Wales caps, was that Sydney Sinkinson was from Oldham, nearly two hundred miles away from Carmarthen, and very much part of England. Howarth's case was a little more complicated. He'd believed his maternal grandfather had been Welsh. But as a result of the so-called 'Grannygate' investigation, he discovered his biological grandfather was in fact Hare Matenga Popata, a Maori from the Oturu region in New Zealand's North Island. It was an upsetting episode for Howarth, with a delicate family secret being painfully revealed under the glare of public scrutiny. And it was acutely embarrassing for the WRU. There was a lot of sympathy for the players, both of whom had played vital roles during Wales's ten-match unbeaten run. But there was an element of *Schadenfreude* too, from those who felt they'd missed out on caps as a result.

Gareth Llewellyn: I got on well with Brett Sinkinson, so I was pleased for him when he entered the set-up. He was a quality player. But in hindsight it's clear there was a bit of cheating going on to try to strengthen our team. Adverts had been appearing in magazines down under looking for players with Welsh roots, trying to lure them over. It wasn't particularly subtle.

Rob Howley: As players we didn't have a clue that these boys didn't have the right qualifications. We just trusted that the governing body had done its due diligence and everything was okay.

Peter Rogers: Martyn Williams was a great player, and he couldn't get in the team. I don't think there was a lot of love lost between him and Sinkinson. He didn't consider Sinkinson to be Welsh.

Martyn Williams: I got on fine with him. He's a lovely bloke, but when you're competing for the same shirt, you never become pally-pally. That's the nature of the job. He was just a really quiet bloke, Brett. There was nothing not to like about him. No edge, no arrogance, just a quiet, humble Kiwi. And he was a hell of a player. Granted, there was a bit of bitterness, you know, 'Who's this Kiwi coming along and nicking my caps?' But you take it for granted that all the checks have been done, and that the selections are legitimate. We were winning, so nobody really cared. I was angry at the time, but I've let it go now. Henry wanted to make Wales successful, and he found some loopholes. It is what it is. I'd have been a lot more angry if I hadn't gone on to have the career I had. Boys like Jason Forster and Neil Boobyer have got far more reason to be aggrieved than me.

Rob Howley: You feel for both sets of players really. Those who missed out on caps, and those who were cast aside after Grannygate.

Ian Gough: I felt for the likes of Kevin Morgan. One of the most underrated players in world rugby. He was small in stature, but he'd throw himself into things fearlessly. He finished up with forty-eight caps, and I think Howarth had nineteen, so maybe Kev was robbed a little bit there. He was as good as Howarth, in a different way. Howie had his strengths, but he shouldn't have been there. That was time that could have been spent investing in Kev, helping him progress, but they went for a quick fix. I can understand that – Henry was under pressure to get results. He was a good guy, Howie, so it's nothing personal.

Martyn Williams: Ultimately, if you grow up in Wales, you dream of playing rugby for your country. It doesn't sit well with me when boys come over to the northern hemisphere in order to play international rugby. If you're not good enough to play for New Zealand, you're not good enough. You shouldn't have an option to move countries. It's mercenary, and it still annoys me when I see the same thing happening now.

Rhys Williams: I went on the '99 pre-World Cup tour to Portugal, and Shane Howarth took the time out to work with me on my game there. He was a good guy. Hopefully what happened will never happen again. When you consider the heritage of Welsh rugby, and the wealth of talent we produce, it's undoubtedly a stain on our history. Nothing against the guy, he was given an opportunity, and he was a great player. I was really good mates with Alfie, Kevin Morgan, and Shane, so I never felt bitter about losing caps. I'm not sure my career even overlapped with Shane's anyway.

Dafydd James: Shane was a good mate of mine. I shared a room with him, and we're still in touch, but if you're not born in Wales, or your parents aren't born here, you shouldn't be able to represent Wales. I'm big on that. It doesn't sit well with me. But Graham did what the New Zealanders had been doing for years with the Samoans and Tongans and Fijians. He manipulated the rules to suit himself.

Rupert Moon: I was in the Vale Hotel on Sunday, and by the Monday morning Sinkinson and Howarth had gone. They just disappeared in a puff of smoke. No ceremony, no goodbyes.

Dafydd James: They packed their bags and that was the end of it.

Peter Rogers: I got called in as well because there were questions being asked about my ancestry. There was a panel of Tasker Watkins, Trevor James and some other guy. I walked into the room, but before I got to sit down, Tasker said in that posh voice of his, 'I know this chap is Welsh, I know his dad.' I played for Glamorgan Wanderers before I'd left for South Africa, and my dad would often speak to Tasker because he was interested in law. 'I used to speak to his dad on legal issues. He's a West-Walian. Out.' And that was the extent of my interrogation. Who was in charge? Did they know anything?

The 2001 Six Nations saw Wales finish fourth for the second year running, although this time they managed just two victories, over Italy and France. The campaign began with a 44–14 thumping at the hands of England in Cardiff. The game in Paris was a classic, offering a glimmer of hope as Wales outscored their hosts by four tries to two, and ran out 43–35 winners. But it was the last notable victory of Graham Henry's tenure. The Ireland fixture was postponed until October after an outbreak of foot and mouth disease and the consequent restrictions on travel, so Wales didn't complete their campaign until 13 October. They were outclassed 36–6 in Cardiff by a rampant Ireland. Henry had vowed to see out his contract at the end of the previous season, but it was becoming obvious that his grip was loosening.

Peter Rogers: Henry started tinkering and making a few strange selection decisions. That had always been his strength, but he seemed to lose the courage of his convictions. Outside influences started creeping in. I won't name names, but certain people were turning up from the union, watching training, and getting in Graham's ear. There was a concerted effort by one person in particular to replace me with Iestyn Thomas. I think he came in too early. I could have had another season. We stopped concentrating on the scrum, which had been our most powerful weapon, and the game plan started getting too complicated. It started going downhill for him then.

Rob Howley: Before games, he'd spend about seven hours in his hotel room without interruption making notes. He would then distribute dossiers with about thirty-five sheets of A4 outlining plays in forensic detail to every player. We'd be expected to learn them all by heart. It was a level of detail we simply weren't used to in Wales. No disrespect to some of the forwards, but some of them struggled to take it all on board.

Peter Rogers: It did start getting a bit technical. We'd all be issued with huge sheaves of paper outlining plays. I've still got a lot of them now in my memorabilia stash. A lot of detail on the scrums in particular. It became too structured, we started to lose the spontaneity.

Neil Jenkins: You had to know every single one of them, or he'd be on to you. We were quite lucky, SQ, Howley and myself, we'd played a lot of Test football together, and felt comfortable stepping up a level. But the amount of information some of the newer, younger players had to take on board was incredible. We still use a move called the 'Highlander' with Wales now. It used to have four outcomes. It would change for specific games, specific teams, how they defended, but for it to work you had to know your roles inside out, and have the capacity to think several phases ahead.

Craig Quinnell: Chris Wyatt always struggled with it. He'd constantly be coming up to me and saying, 'Where do I go?' I'd always say, 'Go far!' I was lucky, I had a photographic memory. Other people were writing stuff on their arms, I had it all in my head.

Rhys Williams: Ben Evans wrote the moves on his arm in writing so big the opposition could read it.

Rob Howley: There were definitely a few with lower numbers on their backs that weren't able to commit it all to memory.

Ian Gough: We tried to adopt what Rod McQueen had been doing in Australia, a multi-phase system. You had to learn eight phases in advance. Ben Evans would wear forearm pads, and tape them up so he could write all the plays down. It was so structured. If a move was called, you had to know where you'd be in eight phases' time. It didn't work because if something went wrong after the third phase, you'd carry on blindly following the pattern, and ignoring what was in front of you.

The pressure on Graham Henry began to mount. His image as some kind of demigod became diminished, and was replaced by something more recognisably human. His judgement deserted him at times, his team selection became more erratic, and some of the defeats he presided over were catastrophic. Despite Wales's decline, he was still considered the best man to lead the Lions to Australia in the summer of 2001. There is no doubt his decision to accept the job contributed to his downfall. Clive Woodward resented being overlooked given his side's success over Wales in the years since Wembley '99, and Henry's selection of English and Irish players over his Welsh charges meant he lost the dressing room when he returned to his day job. Ten Welsh players were selected in the initial squad, but only three – Scott Quinnell, Rob Howley, and Dafydd James – made the starting XV for the Tests. Several of the others felt betrayed, and their exclusion led to wounds that would not heal. Alun Carter, the video analyst, recalls Mark Taylor hammering on Henry's hotel room door demanding an explanation for his omission from the Test side. Colin Charvis and Darren Morris were also among the disgruntled.

Dafydd James: There were a lot of strong characters on that Lions tour in 2001, and Graham took a lot of flak for taking all those Welshmen on the trip. Some players reacted badly to being overlooked on tour, and he lost part of the dressing room when he came back. He was mentally drained. He took a lot of the criticism personally, read too much into it, and perhaps he got a little bit stale.

Scott Quinnell: He shouldn't have gone. That Lions tour took a huge toll on him. He almost needed a year off to recharge the batteries.

Peter Rogers: There was a lot of bad feeling against him when he came home. Man-management is an important skill to have as a director of rugby, and maybe he didn't do the best job.

Martyn Williams: I was one of those players that was selected from Wales, and didn't make the starting Test team, but I didn't hold that against Graham. For me, that 2001 tour was one of the hardest tours any coach could have gone on. Everybody had watched *Living with Lions*, the video of the winning '97 tour in South Africa. That was the last 'amateur' tour. This one was a different beast, in that it had to be run like a professional operation. Henry was the Wales coach, but the best team of the home nations by some distance was England. We were getting hammered by them at the time. They were so far ahead of us off the field. So out there it was difficult to manage.

Rob Howley: There's an expectation when the Lions go to Australia that they'll win. Rightly or wrongly it's perceived as the easiest of the three countries the Lions tour. When Graham returned having coached them to defeat, he was judged – perhaps a little harshly – by a number of senior players in Wales. The criticism was in the public domain, and he took it to heart. He didn't bounce back from that.

Martyn Williams: Because I was on the bench for the Tests, I didn't feel as isolated. The likes of Dai Young and Mark Taylor probably felt a little more betrayed. Tayls was *really* angry about it all. He clearly thought he was going to be a Test player.

As embarrassing as the 36–6 loss to Ireland in 2001 was, it seemed vaguely respectable compared to the one that followed in 2002. Wales – riven by division and self-doubt – collapsed to a humiliating 54–10 loss in Dublin. It was that that did for Henry in the end. It was the opening game of the 2002 Six Nations; by the Wednesday he'd handed in his notice, with eighteen months still left to run on his contract. Steve Hansen, a few months into his tenure as Henry's assistant, seized his opportunity.

Scott Quinnell: I was captain out in Ireland when we took a tuning. Steve Hansen, who was forwards coach at that point, had called me over during the week. He'd brought the Crusaders playbook over with him, and tried to get us to play the way they'd played. We had one call with six different variations. Everyone was writing them on their hands, on their wrists. You'd call a move, and there were six different extra moves to go with it. You had to think so far ahead, it was like *Strictly Come Dancing*. You had to learn ten different dances in a week, and we tripped ourselves up. On the Thursday before the game I went to see him, and said, 'This isn't going to work.' We turned up on the Saturday and agreed to scale it back a bit, but everybody's heads were shot, and Ireland put fifty points on us.

Rupert Moon: People's heads were exploding. It was alien to most of them, and it led to chaos on the pitch. In Ireland in 2002, players were constantly looking baffled, running the wrong way. I was running on with messages. Brains were fried. We lost heavily that day, and that was the end of Graham really. He tried to accelerate our development quicker than our brains could take it in. I'm not saying we weren't a bright bunch, just that we'd played so naturally prior to that, and to play to such a structure was difficult to grasp for so many of us.

Craig Quinnell: The foreign coaches go away better than when they arrived. Steve Hansen didn't understand anything about the Five Nations. Where he'd come from in Canterbury, nobody was contesting lineouts. He'd say, 'If they stack front and middle, we throw long, if they stack middle and back, we throw to the front.' He thought that's how easy lineouts were. He'd boast that Canterbury hadn't lost a lineout the last year he'd been in charge, and we'd say, 'So you shouldn't have, no one was contesting them!' Chris Wyatt and I went to see him in his room to tell him we were worried about the lineouts ahead of that Ireland game. I said, 'Let me ask you a question. Have you ever been to Lansdowne Road?' He hadn't. I said, 'It's open at both ends. The wind whips down the middle of it, and it's always pissing with rain. They're putting Jeremy Davidson, who's taller than me, skinnier than me, and lighter than me, miles in the air. You've got Paddy Johns who's exactly the same but even lighter. So they're stacking front and middle, it's blowing a gale, pissing with rain, where do you throw to?' He says, 'To the back, mate.' He's a double World Cup-winning coach now, but he didn't have much knowledge about lineouts then. These New Zealand coaches didn't come over here the finished product. They were learning on the hoof.

Ian Gough: Scott Johnson came in as skills coach, Steve Hansen arrived as forwards coach, and looking back it was as though Henry was appointing his successors, so he could just peel away.

Rob Howley: I wonder if he had a breakdown. It felt like there was a changing of the guard, and he was fading out of the picture.

EIGHTEEN

SHANE WILLIAMS – TURBO-CHARGED

Steve Hansen and his team went on a soul-destroying run of ten straight defeats. If Hansen's approach didn't exactly enamour him to the Welsh public, he inspired an almost unbending loyalty among his players. Only those on the inside could understand the progress that was being made.

Martyn Williams: The Steve Hansen era was a transition in more ways than one. Obviously Graham Henry had gone, but so had a number of his senior players too. SQ was on his way out, Jinks was just about hobbling on.

Mark Jones: Whereas Graham had a group of senior players in or approaching their prime, Steve came in as a lot of young blood was coming through. He culled an awful lot of experience and pretty much started from scratch.

Martyn Williams: I didn't like him at first, or Johnno [Scott Johnson] for that matter. They were both really aloof, and looked down on us because we were Welsh. But when you look back on it, we were shit, so it was fair enough. They upset a lot of senior boys, going in and telling them that the culture was rotten, but in hindsight, they did what needed to be done.

Rhys Williams: I loved how focused training became under Steve. We went on to the paddock knowing exactly what we were going to do for forty-five minutes, an hour. It was intense, but when we were done, we were done. We only stayed out longer if our skills had let us down and we needed to go over and over something to get it right.

Dafydd James: Hansen and I never clicked, and I'm not sure why. He accused me of being antisocial. Not in those exact words, but he said I was a selfish player; not a team man, and all that malarkey, which is bollocks. Absolute bullshit. I looked after myself, I had three per cent body fat, was strict with my diet, and was fitter than anyone else in the squad. But it felt like he was holding that against me, like I was being penalised for being the most professional guy there. When I look back I wonder whether he was playing a game with me, to test me. But the way he treated me was wrong. He cost me about twenty caps. He brought guys like Wayne Proctor and Craig Morgan in ahead of me. I'm not criticising any player, but it felt like I was being marginalised. I feel a bit bitter about the opportunities I missed.

Michael Owen: I was part of the new breed that Hansen brought in around 2002 when he swept away the old guard. He picked five or six of us from Ponty for the South Africa tour, which was a big decision, but we'd been going really well, and the club deserved to be recognised.

Tom Shanklin: There were quite a few Ponty boys in that squad. Gethin Jenkins was one of them but he barely got a look in on tour. Steve Hansen was very keen to give players a voice, to make them feel as though their opinions were respected, and he held an open forum at the end of the trip. He wanted a squad of independent thinkers rather than sheep, so he singled out a few of the boys and asked them direct questions. He asked Gethin what he'd learned from the tour, and Gethin replied that the milkshakes in the hotel had been good.

Gareth Llewellyn: He taught us to think about the game in a totally different way. He taught us martial arts techniques to remove tacklers at the breakdown – subtle little things as opposed to just telling us to blast into the contact area. He'd have mantras like, 'One man, one bullet.' Don't waste any bullets. There's no point burying five people in a ruck, when three men, used efficiently, could do the job. He wasn't afraid to try things, but he was under no illusions that we had a long road to travel.

Tom Shanklin: He was huge on the breakdown, about turning the right way in contact, making sure your legs are out of the way for the scrum half, so Gareth Cooper and Dwayne Peel could get the ball away quickly. He'd drill into us the importance of creating quick ball, how to turn slow ball into fast ball within three quick phases.

Stephen Jones: They had a fantastic work ethic, and their attention to detail was top-drawer. They were trying to upskill us all. Steve took us as backs, and tried to improve our technique in the contact area. The intricacies of how to move someone off the ball, using technique rather than brute force. That had never been done before. It had always been considered the forwards' domain.

Mark Jones: He'd looked at all kinds of sports outside rugby. Andrew Hore, the fitness coach, had us playing netball to think about spatial awareness, hand-eye coordination, and to practise acceleration over short distances.

Tom Shanklin: He made us wear eye patches to improve our peripheral vision. For me, they were by far the best trio of coaches that I played under. And I say that as a player that wasn't always picked by them.

Gareth Llewellyn: When he first arrived, he told us all, 'You're not fit enough yet, you're not skilful enough yet. We've got a lot of work to do.' I remember doing endless, relentless passing drills, gradually getting wider and wider and wider. Initially it drove us insane, but we came to love it, because we could see where we were going with it. We could see that little by little, our skills were improving.

Tom Shanklin: Before Andrew Hore arrived, it'd be a case of going to the gym where the fitness coach would just point at things and say, 'Do a little bit of this, a little bit of that.' There was no real programme or end goal, no way to chart progression. Horey saw immediately that we weren't at the level we should have been, that we needed to be a lot fitter. I thought I was fit. I played sport every weekend, and trained every week, but when you compared yourself to the southern hemisphere boys, you realised that you weren't. Hore's fitness programmes were very structured, very specific, and tailored to our age. The older guys had bigger cardiovascular systems, so they didn't have to do as much endurance as us younger guys. We did a lot of hill runs, a lot of running up and down Merthyr Mawr sand dunes. It was hellish, but it got us into shape.

Martyn Williams: He kept things interesting. During one camp in Tenby, we had a really horrible, lung-busting fitness session and he made all the coaches and management do it with us. I remember thinking some of them were genuinely going to have heart attacks. They were playing roles, each of them. It was good cop, bad cop. Johnno was the laid-back surfer dude, who was everybody's friend. Steve was the big bad ogre that everybody hated. I used to have big arguments with Steve and Johnno about their methods and the way we were trying to play, but it was never personal, and they wouldn't hold it against you. They'd encourage you to argue and question. It was a new dynamic.

Rhys Williams: Steve Hansen was the frontman, the overseer – the ex-cop, big and brash. Scott Johnson was all about the small detail, the individual skills, and he was the best man-manager I ever came across. It wasn't just about rugby with him; he wanted to know about your personal life, your upbringing. He'd want to sit down and have a cup of tea with you and get inside your head.

Martyn Williams: He loved a debate, Johnno. About anything. Whether it be cricket, rugby, politics, the economy, he had an opinion, and he loved challenging people, forcing them to think about things they wouldn't necessarily think about, or to consider a point of view that was very different from their own.

Rhys Williams: He was big on culture and identity. He once asked me why the leek was a Welsh national symbol. I told him I didn't know, and he thought that was a disgrace. He knew – he'd read up on it. They made us proud about being Welsh again.

Gareth Thomas: We learnt so much about each other personally and professionally. What people were capable of, what people weren't capable of. Shag [Steve Hansen] deliberately put you in situations where you'd feel really uncomfortable. For example, I couldn't use a computer, didn't have a clue. I'd never needed to. He told me he wanted me to give a presentation on England, to include video clips, bullet points and stuff. A PowerPoint presentation, butt! It was way outside of my comfort zone. I was genuinely more nervous about that than about playing England on the weekend. But I knuckled down, worked on it, and pulled it off in front of the boys. I was unbelievably proud of myself.

Tom Shanklin: It was a genius decision to make Gareth Thomas captain. When I first joined the squad, him and Leigh Davies were always messing around – doing things like taking sleeping pills during the day to see who could stay awake the longest. They were proper jokers. But Hansen saw something in Alfie that no one else had seen. He was always one of our best players, but Hansen realised there was an inspirational leader lurking within.

Rhys Williams: We became more accountable for our development. We started doing our own analysis. Previously it had just been given to us. Now we were expected to go and get the information and feed back to the team. I'd be looking at the back three of whoever we were playing next, and analysing them in forensic detail. How do they like to attack? Which foot do they like to step off? Where's the threat? Do they work around the pitch or stay on their wing? Unless your players are engaged in the game plan, the ethos, the values of what you're trying to achieve, it's never going to penetrate into them. The majority of that squad had won the wooden spoon and been in the trenches. We were ready to climb out.

Gareth Thomas: The presentations became a theme. Every week, he picked someone to lead the presentation about the team we'd be playing next. Rather than it being the same voice, the same story coming from the same person, it would be somebody different each time. It adds layers to what you can give to the team, what you can contribute, and it encouraged others to venture out of their comfort zone. That eventually translated into confidence and self-belief on the field. There'd be times when we'd be doing skills and they'd say, 'Steve Jones – you're not always going to be first receiver. Let's bring in a prop, or whoever wants to be first receiver, stand up and try it.' Props became comfortable handling the ball, and we all became better rugby players. In the Graham Henry era, it was always Jinks at ten, otherwise it would all fall apart. Under Steve, it was more 'chaos rugby', but everyone at least had a chance to show what they could do. There was no hiding place, no comfort zone to retreat into.

Ian Gough: He was very innovative. Some of his ideas were great, some were rubbish, but he was always *trying* things. He had us lineout jumpers on trampettes, to help hone our skills while under stress and off balance. He had hookers throwing in with their eyes shut, although I can't remember what the point of that was. At one point he encouraged us to do away with lineout calls altogether, and to just 'throw it where there's space'. Now, Rob Sidoli was a real lineout nerd. He'd prefer the term 'strategist', but he was a nerd. He was genuinely concerned about that. Lineouts were his passion, his bread and butter, and Steve wanted to completely trivialise them and their role. Sid was calling meetings and all sorts, he was really worried. I totally agreed with him.

Gareth Llewellyn: He used to make us play touch rugby *across* the pitch, so it was a hundred metres wide, and if you didn't have someone constantly positioned in the five metre channels at each edge, you'd lose the ball. 'Use the facilities!' was his mantra. It was all about holding full width. We'd be slinging these massive passes off both hands, just to get the ball out wide. When we reverted to a normal pitch, sixty metres across, holding width became easy. It was all about stretching defences, having the confidence to get the ball into the wide channels, to get around teams who defend narrowly.

Stephen Jones: 'Use the facilities' still echoes in my head now, all these years later.

Rhys Williams: I'd been coached to play rugby since I was six years old. I'd been coached how to catch a high ball, how to try to tackle, how to pass, how to do all those technical things, but I'd never really been taught why. What happens when this happens? How does what we do in attack affect what happens in their defence? We were taught how to play rugby *holistically.*

Michael Owen: Hansen and Johnson didn't follow trends; they carved their own path. It took a while, but eventually, the philosophy became so ingrained, it became subconscious. You stopped thinking about what you were doing, and just played.

Stephen Jones: They made sure any egos were kept in check. No one was allowed to rise above their station, and if they did they were soon brought back down again. Johnno once tried to introduce this concept called 'sledging Tuesday', where everyone could get stuck into one another, and slag each other off. 'Nothing's off limits, say what you want.' I think us Welsh are a bit more sensitive than the Aussies though. We only did it once, and we had to call it off when Ceri Sweeney slagged off Hal Luscombe's hair. He may have been going a bit thin on top, and he wasn't too happy when Sweeney drew attention to it.

Despite all the positivity within the camp, Wales had slid into a trough on the field. The 2003 Six Nations ended in an embarrassing whitewash. The writing was on the wall after the first match in Rome, during which Wales were humiliated up front by a rampant Italian pack. Their lineout totally fell apart, and a minor furore erupted when Colin Charvis was caught smiling on camera in the dugout. A newspaper poll within a few days declared him the second most hated man in Wales behind Saddam Hussein. An argument between Hansen and Mefin Davies over the lineout issues led to the hooker being dropped. Days later, thirty-three-year-old Jonathan Humphreys, who'd last pulled on a Welsh jersey four years earlier, was recalled and made captain. Defeats to England, Scotland and Ireland followed. And the wooden spoon was duly delivered after an insipid performance against France that ended in a 33–5 defeat.

Mark Jones: Colin Charvis is quite a dour person by nature, so they'd done well to get a picture of him smiling in the first place. But to get him smiling when he's coming off the pitch, when his team is losing to Italy, that's quite some feat. The fact is, if you pause the TV at any given time you can catch somebody with a stupid face. Somebody probably said to him, 'Good game,' he's laughed at them sarcastically, and the snapper happened to pull the shutter at that exact moment. Charv realised the enormity of losing to Italy. He knew it was a horrendous result, but the public reaction was hysterical and bang out of order. Charvy never gave less than a hundred per cent when he pulled that jersey on.

Martyn Williams: We got pumped in that Six Nations, and even though we were enjoying training, there was inevitably a feeling developing from the outside that it was the coaches' fault, and that our methods were actually shit. But not once during that time did they change to suit the public or the press. They knew they had a plan that needed time to take shape. Personally speaking, I didn't have a great deal of faith at that point, because we were losing games convincingly.

Gareth Llewellyn: We went through that ten-match run of defeats, and Steve was public enemy number one. Everyone hated him. He was going on about performance over results, and it wasn't washing with the Welsh fans. It was a pretty sour time, and the press were getting stuck into us. But as a group of players we just couldn't wait to get back to training. We knew what we were doing and where we were going.

Ian Gough: When you wade through a load of shit, you tend to bond more closely, and I think that's what happened. A siege mentality took hold during that period and we became convinced the methods would eventually bear fruit.

Rhys Williams: He told us that if we got the process right, the results would come. That became his mantra to the press – performance over results. Understandably, they were a little sceptical, but he'd always stand up to them. At times he was quite confrontational and lost his rag on a few occasions. But all he was doing was protecting his biggest assets, which were his players. He was creating a platform for us to perform at an elite level, and wanted us to be immune from the carping and criticism.

Mark Jones: Nick Webb from BBC Wales went after him on it quite a bit, and he felt the wrath of Steve on a few occasions. But Steve's mantra remained that if you prepare well, you give yourself the best chance of winning. It sounds perfectly logical, but not everyone abides by that philosophy, they just live Saturday to Saturday.

Rhys Williams: You don't appreciate these things at the time, but he never pushed blame down.

Martyn Williams: He'd never blame the boys. He always took it on his shoulders. Him and Johnno.

Stephen Jones: He cocooned us from all the external pressures. He had a very strong belief that what he was doing was right. He'd left the Canterbury Crusaders behind in New Zealand, and that side had been full of All Blacks. He knew the style he wanted to play, and he selected his teams accordingly. He was happy to shoulder the burden of all the external pressure, knowing what he was doing was right. Ultimately if your performances improve, your results improve.

Gareth Thomas: I used to get seriously pissed off at the press. They're the 'middle man' between the team and the rest of the nation, and they were making things extremely difficult for us to stick to our plan with Steve. We knew where our destination was, and we were still on our journey towards it. International rugby is a strange old thing. He could have scrumpled everything up, gone back to basics, and we'd have pushed teams closer, and snuck a few wins here and there. But his long-term vision – which he knew he wouldn't be around to see – was worth fighting for. That whole generation of players will be forever indebted to Steve. We all knew he was not going to be around to reap the rewards of his hard work, and that's a very unselfish thing to do. The fact he didn't get the recognition from the public and the press puts him on even more of a pedestal as far as I'm concerned.

Michael Owen: The low point was the defeat in Rome in 2003 when Aaron Persico ruled the roost. He was over the ball at every opportunity, jackling and stealing possession at will. A year later we absolutely blasted them with our wide game. I was running everywhere, running lines, taking passes off everyone. At one point, I even threw an American football-style pass. Duncan Jones caught it and passed to Rhys Williams. It was just instinctive because of the way we'd been coached and encouraged to play.

Gareth Llewellyn: Even now when I watch New Zealand, there's so much of what Steve taught us in the way they play. Graham Henry had an impact when he first came in, but Steve was on another level entirely. He was painted as a dour Kiwi, but he's got a great sense of humour, he's great company around the dinner table.

Ian Gough: Famously I didn't get on with Steve. Not that we'd have stand-up rows or anything, but he had his ideas about what he wanted, and I wasn't in that mould. I was definitely more of an old-school workhorse. I prided myself on pushing, lifting, tackling, and smoking people in rucks. He preferred the skilful forwards and maybe overlooked some of the more technical areas of forward play. We'd often do scrummaging sessions indoors with trainers on. What's the point of that? Graham Henry was very good at getting the team to play together. Hansen was almost more forensic with his approach, focusing on improving each individual's skills as opposed to the overall team. That's probably why they worked well as a duo when they went back to New Zealand.

Michael Owen: He picked rugby players over big lumps, but it was fucking brilliant, because we were just *playing*. We weren't imitating anyone. I was used to being told, 'You're going to stand here, you're going to truck it up.' Painting by numbers, essentially. There was none of that under Hansen. It was all based on instinct.

Dafydd James: He was big on values and respect. He'd make sure players cleaned and tidied up the changing room, and that's right as far as I'm concerned. Everybody should be picking up their own rubbish and putting it in the bin. You wouldn't leave shit lying around in your own house, would you? He would delegate responsibility to one player after every game to make sure the changing room was spotless. Respect the changing room, respect the jersey, respect everything you've got.

Martyn Williams: He liked to keep you on your toes. When we were on tour in South Africa in 2002, I was first choice, I'd been on the Lions tour in 2001, and I'd been playing well for my club. He used to insist on an open-door policy in our hotel rooms, so no one could cocoon themselves away. Rather than announce the team, he'd just wander the corridors telling people whether they were in or out. That day, he bowled into my room unannounced and said, 'Ginge, you're playing. But you're fucking lucky mate, because Gavin Thomas is playing better than you.' I was like, 'What?!' I thought, 'You can't say that to me. I'm the man.' But before I had a chance to respond, he was gone. I thought I was the bollocks, and he taught me a bit of humility there.

Gareth Llewellyn: That was easily the most enjoyable era for me. I was thirty-four when I went to the World Cup in 2003 and I was lifting more than I ever had, I was quicker than I'd ever been, I was in the best shape I'd ever been in. I remember thinking, 'Where were you when I was twenty-one?'

When Hansen coached the Crusaders in Super Rugby, he became used to taking his club on mini-tours to Australia and South Africa. Those trips required a degree of discipline that wasn't always evident when Wales were in camp. His insistence that squad members stay within their Vale of Glamorgan training base grated on those who valued their personal space, and wanted to spend time with their families. Inevitably, some rebelled and broke the curfew. For one player, the consequences were devastating.

Dafydd James: My relationship with Hansen reached a low point during the 2002 November internationals when I was kicked out of the squad for disciplinary reasons. I'd started to feel a bit claustrophobic in the 'Jail of Glamorgan' but we'd been forbidden to leave. I only lived twenty minutes down the road, I was missing my family, and one night I thought 'sod it' and went home to sleep in my own bed. I wanted a good night's kip, and to see my young baby. I wasn't the only one. Six or seven of us did, but for some reason he was gunning for me. I came back early the following morning and bumped into him in the car park. When he asked where I'd been, I panicked and told him I'd come out to my car to get a CD. He clearly smelt a rat, and asked me to show him the CD. That's when I knew I was in trouble.

Tom Shanklin: He was very big on discipline and team ethics. Keeping things clean, keeping things tidy. Small things like taking your empty coffee cup back, taking your empty plate up, making sure you left your room tidy. We were all pretty young and keen to impress, so most of us toed the line.

Dafydd James: I went back to my room and asked Mark Jones to cover for me, to say I'd been there all night. I told him I thought something was going to go wrong for me. Hansen came and knocked on the door, and whistled at me, like I was a dog. I didn't move. I said, 'I've got a name.' He told me he'd gone back out and felt the bonnet of my car. It was a frosty morning, and he'd noticed that there was no frost on my bonnet. The old copper in him couldn't resist, he'd discovered it was still warm from the journey and knew he had me over a barrel. He called a team meeting, where he announced he was going to kick me out of the squad, and that was that. Madness. It was so upsetting and it really knocked the stuffing out of me. I was fucking livid.

Tom Shanklin: Unless you had a valid reason or an emergency, breaking curfew wasn't tolerated. Hansen expected everyone to be up-front and honest. It was harsh, but probably the right thing to do. Dafydd James took a bullet for us all, but no one did it again. It sent a massive message to the rest of us. Dafydd James was a senior player and a Test Lion.

Dafydd James: Later, when I got called back in, I was sat in a room with Hansen, Scott Johnson and Andrew Hore, and they accused me of being a big-head, of thinking I was bigger than the team. I couldn't believe what I was hearing. I started filling up with tears and I remember thinking I had two options. I could either well up and let it all out, or I could stand up and start swinging. I was that angry. Alan Phillips, the team manager, defended me and told them they'd got me all wrong. Hansen's parting words were, 'Do you want to play for Wales again?' What sort of a question was that? I lost it and shouted, 'Of course I fucking do!' He told me to go away and think about it, and I told him I didn't need to bloody well think about it. It was a no-brainer.

Gareth Thomas: Steve could be hugely brutal, but it was all to show that nobody in that team – regardless of whether you're captain, vice-captain, fifty caps, a hundred caps, whatever – *nobody* in that team was better than anyone else. Nobody has a right to that jersey. It's not just about how you play, it's about how you train, how you prepare, how you behave. It's about your commitment to the team, your constant willingness to be and do what everyone else had to be and do.

Martyn Williams: *Brothers in Arms* by Dire Straits was his favourite song. He loved that, it was his anthem for us. He played it at the start of virtually every presentation. He was big on culture, and in Wales we didn't really know much about that. He'd come from the Crusaders where they'd developed the best rugby culture in the world. It was all about creating a sense of brotherhood.

Dafydd James: Rules are rules, but it could have been kept in house. He could have just fined me. The way he did it was wrong. I felt vilified and victimised. Neil Jenkins had gone home. Jamie Robinson had gone back to Cardiff. Ben Evans walked back into the hotel just as the team meeting was about to start. To be fair, Ben confronted Hansen about it and said, 'Hang on, Shags, a few of us went home.' I'm all for rules, and I'm not above the rules, but I thought the punishment was over the top.

Martyn Williams: It was probably more the fact that Jamo didn't come clean when he was challenged about it than the actual breaking of the curfew. It was tough, having to stay there the whole time. I'd not long had my first daughter, I was living in Ponty, which was only fifteen minutes away, and my missus was expecting me to come home and help out every night. It was a test. How much do you want this? How much are you willing to sacrifice for this? We did have a really lax culture before that. The boys were making good money, and he could see that rugby wasn't the focal point for a lot of them. It was more about money and cars, and all the materialistic stuff. Coming from the outside, he knew he had to change things, to come down hard on us and find out who *really* wanted it.

Gareth Thomas: It was harsh on Jamo, but Steve's explanation was, 'I'd have loved to have gone home last night.' Everyone would have liked to have gone and seen their family, but they didn't because we were in it together. Some people lived in Llanelli, so weren't able to get home, some lived five minutes around the corner, but we're all in it together. Steve was taking all that shit in the press, and he could have just got on a plane back to New Zealand. But he didn't. He stuck around.

Martyn Williams: I felt for Jamo because he was clearly made a scapegoat, but Steve had to set an example to prove he wasn't messing about. Loads of boys used to go home and come back. Jamo was the one who got caught. I can understand why'd he'd be really bitter towards him.

Dafydd James: Maybe I should have reacted a bit differently in hindsight, but he upset me. It was the one time I'd stepped out of line. I was a consummate professional, I was never a big boozer, never a troublemaker, yet I felt as though I was being punished. It's lucky I had been home in many ways, and not scuttling about, getting up to no good. Scott Quinnell left the squad after it happened, partly in protest, and didn't play in the World Cup as a result.

Scott Quinnell: That's not strictly true. I was asked to play in the World Cup, but turned it down. I retired for a few reasons. Not being allowed to leave the Vale of Glamorgan base was just one of them.

Martyn Williams: SQ hated Hansen. SQ would never train. When I look back there'd be a lot of that. Boys claiming they couldn't train, and spending all their time in the physio room. Hansen and Johnno weren't having that. If you weren't able to train on the field, they'd expect you to do fitness instead of kicking around in the physio room. You didn't have to be as fit in the Henry era, you could get away with being naturally talented. Steve Black probably indulged that a bit, but Steve felt he had to come in and shake it up.

Gareth Llewellyn: He could be strict, but in the main, you knew he was on our side, that he had the players' backs. Never was that more evident than during a pay dispute we had with the WRU before the New Zealand tour in 2003. Steve Lewis addressed the squad to tell us he'd reviewed the pay structure. He was doing away with base payments, and making it all performance-related, as if that would make us try harder? Ridiculous. He told us that we'd all get a flat £1,500 for going on tour to New Zealand, with win bonuses coming on top. We all agreed we wouldn't be going for that amount of money. It was a pretty frosty meeting, and he walked out. I called a meeting with the players, and we agreed we were worth more than that. Scott Quinnell was the players' rep, and he tried to negotiate on our behalf, but they were having none of it. So on the morning we were due to leave, we all met at Cardiff West Services before departing for Heathrow, and agreed we wouldn't go. Carcass [Mark Davies, physio] was sitting in the hotel wondering why it was so quiet. Iestyn Harris came to tell us it was all kicking off. Scott eventually returned saying the union had compromised. It wasn't the deal we wanted, but he thought we should accept it, so we agreed, and got on the bus a bit late. There were big traffic jams going into London, we got delayed, and it became obvious we were going to miss the plane. Steve got on the mic at the front of the bus. A lot of coaches would have been fuming. He just said, 'Clearly boys, we're going to miss our plane, and there'll be a lot of shit going down over it. I just want to say one thing: good on you, well done for what you've done. It was the right thing to do. It's done now, let's put it to bed,' and he never mentioned another word about it again. That's brilliant management.

The negotiations may have strengthened the bond between the players, but that did nothing to galvanise their performances on the pitch. A defeat to Australia was followed by a virtual shutout against the All Blacks. New Zealand enjoyed nearly seventy-five per cent possession, and Wales were forced to make an exhausting 190 tackles. On one of the rare occasions Wales had the ball, Colin Charvis was knocked clean out by a brutal Jerry Collins tackle. It summed up the game in microcosm. Wales had been beaten up, and lost by a record score of 55–3. But despite the evidence to the contrary, the players were insisting things were moving in the right direction.

Gareth Llewellyn: That Hamilton game where Charvy got knocked out was relatively close until the final quarter, when they ran away with it. We went into analysis the next day, and Steve was very clear about what needed to change if we were to beat them next time. There were three mistakes that they scored off, and our fitness dropped off in the last fifteen. Steve was so confident and assured, that we left that room thinking, 'Okay, we've just lost to New Zealand by fifty points, but next time, we've got a genuine chance.' He was fantastic about putting emotion to one side, and focusing on the nuts and bolts.

During the build-up to the 2003 World Cup, Hansen decided to focus almost exclusively on fitness and conditioning. As a result, Wales entered their warm-up games woefully short on match practice, and were beaten with ease by Ireland. Next came a result that nearly proved the last straw for the WRU hierarchy. An England second-string came to Cardiff to take on Wales's first choice XV, and battered them 43–9. Hansen had already made it clear he was picking his reserve side for the final warm-up game against Scotland. Privately, he had no interest in playing these games.

They'd been added to the calendar by the WRU to make money to help chip away at the £70 million debt on the Millennium Stadium. Hansen had prioritised fitness and skills ahead of the World Cup, and saw the games as an unnecessary distraction. He was instructed by David Moffett, the chief executive, to change the side he'd picked for Scotland, and told that if he lost that match, he might not be going to the World Cup as head coach. Hansen's response was that he'd already told the boys what he was going to do, what the team was, and he insisted he was not going to let them down. He stuck to his guns, the second-string defeated Scotland 23–9, and a glimmer of hope appeared on the horizon.

Stephen Jones: Prior to the World Cup, we got smashed at home by England's seconds. No doubt a lot of questions were being fired around at that time. Andrew Hore was trying to raise the bar in a physical sense, because we weren't fit enough – that was the reality – to compete with the big boys on the international stage. Steve knew that if we didn't have that conditioning foundation then we couldn't challenge for the World Cup.

Martyn Williams: I was captain for that England game. Jonny Wilkinson didn't play, Martin Johnson didn't play. It was a second-string England against our best team, and we got absolutely pumped. Hansen called me in the next day, and said, 'Mart, tell me now – have I lost the changing room? If I have, then I'll go.' But he hadn't. The boys loved him. We really enjoyed the environment. It was a really harmonious atmosphere, despite all the defeats.

Mark Jones: What a lot of people didn't realise was that prior to that England game we'd only done one rugby session. The rest of our time had been spent running up hills outside Pontypridd and sand dunes near Bridgend. We were absolutely *hanging* going into that game.

Gareth Thomas: As much as we were aware of the pressure he was under, we were all hugely supportive of him. There were individuals who may have gone against the grain, but the majority were right behind him. They'd back him to the hilt. The only opinion that mattered to him was that of the team.

Mark Jones: He could well have gone back to his more experienced, better players for that Scotland game, but he stuck to the squad he'd picked and they went out and delivered for him. That was him all over. He wasn't prepared to compromise his values, not for anyone or anything.

Martyn Williams: Make no bones about it, if he'd lost that game, they were going to sack him. That ended up being a massive turning point. You knew he'd back himself, and he did. You never got a sense of panic from the coaches even though we lost all those games. They just kept saying, 'Trust us, it'll work. It'll come good.' We never once deviated from that path. I had so much admiration for him for that. He was getting hammered left, right and centre by the press, but he absorbed it all. He could have easily said he didn't have the tools to work with, that it was our fault, but he always took the criticism on himself.

There followed an intensive training camp in Lanzarote, during which Hansen took over the attack, and set the platform for the displays to come in the World Cup.

Martyn Williams: Steve allowed us an afternoon on the piss out in Lanzarote, and we got absolutely steaming. I can picture it vividly now. We found ourselves in this pub called the Galleon on the other side of the island. I've never seen a bunch of boys get so pissed so quickly. People were puking and all sorts.

Tom Shanklin: We were probably only out for an hour-and-a-half, but we *went* for it. We found a karaoke bar with a dentist's chair, and we were just *ruining* ourselves as fast as we could. Back on the bus, it was absolute carnage. Jon Thomas has pulled a seat head out and he's whacking people with it, water bottles are being flung around, the boys are all peeing all over the place, because they're desperate for the toilet. We pile back into the hotel, and Gethin Jenkins spews all over the reception area. Then we go on to a nightclub on the complex. The team manager, Alan Phillips, is walking to the table with a huge tray of drinks, and Alix Popham sneaks up behind him and whips his shorts and pants down. He can't pull them back up because he's got this tray in his hands. Thumper was fuming. He told Popham that he'd never play for Wales again.

Martyn Williams: Then at six the next morning, we're all hungover to hell, and there's a loud knock on the door. It's Steve calling us all out for a fitness session. It was like being in the marines. It was pitch dark, the sun hadn't come up, and you couldn't see a thing, but they said we couldn't use that as an excuse – no dropped balls were allowed. Sweeney and Shanks had plastered their faces in sunblock and kept looming out of the pre-dawn mist like ghosts.

Tom Shanklin: Steve Hansen was shouting, 'The darkness isn't an excuse!' I'd got hideously burnt on day one, because I'd borrowed Huw Bennett's suncream, which actually turned out to be oil. I don't think my room-mate, Stephen Jones, got much sleep that night, as I was up at all hours slathering myself in after-sun. So I was taking no chances this time.

Martyn Williams: It sounds horrendous, and it was . . . but whenever the boys get together now, we always talk fondly about those things. It sounds sadistic, but experiences like that definitely bring you closer together.

Tom Shanklin: After the session, Steve split the group up between those who'd misbehaved the previous evening and those that hadn't. Anyone who'd got pissed, played up, been sick, or missed breakfast were in one group, and those that had been 'good' were in the other. Only Mark Jones, Sonny Parker, and Mefin Davies were in the 'good' group. They must have been feeling smug at that point, thinking they'd escaped further punishment. But then in what Steve thought was a cunning bit of reverse psychology, he proceeded to beast those three in front of the rest of us. He thought we'd feel so guilty it would teach us a lesson, but we were just pissing ourselves. The good guys got the punishment for our bad behaviour.

Martyn Williams: In the World Cup, he had us in self-catering apartments, where we had to cook for ourselves. He didn't want us in hotels, and it was brilliant in terms of creating a great environment, looking after each other and getting close as a group. It forced us to muck in. We all complained like fuck at the time – you know, 'What is this shit?' But looking back it was a masterstroke.

Tom Shanklin: We were given a budget every day for food. Sixty quid. A few of us figured out that you could bulk-buy baked beans for next to nothing, and pocket the rest. We were young and didn't have that much money. But after a week of eating beans on toast, our weight began to plummet, so we had to can that idea.

Martyn Williams: We had Canada first up. They were quite tough then, but we played good rugby and blew them away. We scraped through against Tonga and then Italy was the big one. It sounds strange to say, but I've never been as nervous before a game as I was before that one. If we lost to Italy we'd be out of the World Cup. Win it and we were in the quarter-finals. We scored three tries and kept them just to a bunch of penalties to win 27–15. Job done.

Mark Jones: Steve said to Nugget, myself and a couple of others that he was giving us a rest for the New Zealand game, to keep us fresh for the quarter-final. It was great to hear, but I was still gutted we weren't going to be playing against New Zealand.

Martyn Williams: Iestyn Harris and I were training on exercise bikes in Canberra, when Steve wandered over and said, 'Ginge, have a rest against the All Blacks.' I was one of the main players then, and wanted to play in every game, but he just gave me the nod and said, 'Make sure you're fit and firing for England.'

Mark Jones: Shane came in and played outstandingly well. As a winger, seeing the speed of ball and the quality of ball that he was getting his hands on, I was a little envious. Wales is my country, and I was always desperate for them to win whether I was involved or not, but I started to fear a bit for my place.

Martyn Williams: We hadn't seen Shane before that. Literally hadn't seen him. Steve threw all the boys in who hadn't had a look-in. Alix Popham, JT [Jonathan Thomas], Garan Evans. They all had their chance.

Tom Shanklin: I was staying next to Shane, and he'd been ill all week. It was touch-and-go whether he was going to be fit. I said to him, 'If you're ill, you're ill, but if there's a chance you can play, you have to, because it could be your last chance in a Wales shirt.' It ended up being the game that launched him into the stratosphere. He never looked back.

Shane Williams: It was a tough World Cup for me because I hadn't figured in any of the games prior to the New Zealand game. I hadn't spent a second on the field. He was obviously resting guys for that game, but I didn't care. It was one of those where I would have done anything to get on the field, as would JT or some of the other lads. It was the last chance saloon for me. If I didn't play well, Steve would have been justified in dropping me for good. In true Welsh fashion, a lot of lads put their hands up in that game, and were difficult to ignore for the quarter-final.

Gareth Llewellyn: I was commentating during the New Zealand game, with Marty Roebuck and Gareth Charles. Steve will never admit it, but it was definitely his intention to give the fringe lads a run. A few urban myths have emerged about the boys grouping behind the posts, and saying, 'Forget the game plan, forget everything we've been told to do, let's just go out there and chuck it around,' which Welsh people love to believe, but it is absolute bollocks. It took a bit of Shane Williams magic for things to start to happen, and all the things around our structure that we'd worked so hard on actually started to crystallise.

Stephen Jones: The Aussie commentators were loving it. After a while they were just shouting, 'Give it to Williams!'

Shane Williams: It was one of the biggest moments of my career. I went out there to prove a lot of people wrong, and to play my heart out. Did I think we were going to win? No. We were playing one of the best sides in the world. Joe Rokocoko, Carlos Spencer, Dougie Howlett, these guys had been ripping teams apart for fun.

Martyn Williams: Did we see it coming? Fuck, no. The rest of us boys were sitting there watching it with our jaws on the floor. We were thinking, 'Fucking hell. What is happening?' Our first team had lost to them 55–3 a couple of months before. JT and Shane were turbo-charged, they were off the charts.

Shane Williams: The lads that played in that game were frustrated and felt that we were fielding a second team. Going out on the field, I remember saying to JT, 'We've got nothing to lose today. No one's giving us a chance. Let's go out there and play to the best of our ability.' We still had a pattern that we followed, but the pattern didn't involve the left winger – or the right winger as I was at the time – popping up on the left-hand side of a ruck and taking on the All Blacks' defence. I wanted to make a statement, so I played off the cuff and got involved. For the majority of the game, the structure went out the window. I was popping up at nine, playing ten, roaming off my wing. I was covering kicks, I was chasing kicks, and it worked for me. It was all very random and unstructured. We attacked both sides of the breakdown and played an expansive, high-tempo, offloading game, which – at times – New Zealand couldn't cope with.

Gareth Thomas: People say it was an accident, but it was the moment everything we had done finally came together. One hundred per cent. I have no doubt. That was the moment that all our hard work started to bear fruit. People say it was the B team, but we trained as a thirty. It wasn't a case of Charvy, the captain, picking his best XV and going off training separately. We were all equal, and we all did the same shit together. That was unusual for international rugby. The public perception was that it was the B team, but we were all in it together. It was like a Matrix moment where everything slows down and things fall into place. And with that came belief, because when you see these things starting to happen, you think, 'I'll try it again.' All of a sudden *everyone* is seeing the game in slow motion, *everyone* is realising that all the work we've put in hasn't been a waste of time.

Stephen Jones: It was the first time that an organised structure was breaking the defence down. All the patterns we'd put in place suddenly started reaping rewards. People say it was gung-ho and spontaneous, but what was happening was we were *shaping* the defence in our favour. You then had people with individual brilliance like Shane getting the ball with time, meaning he was able to work the mismatches. Because we were 'using the facilities', the spaces between the defenders were bigger, which provides the opportunity for people like Shane to take people on one-to-one rather than having two defenders marking him up. The plan was working. It was wonderful, and it flies in the face of the theory that it was a fluke. Saying that is a typical example of not giving coaches credit for all their hard work.

Tom Shanklin: People were giving us no hope of beating New Zealand. I'd played against Tonga, and knew I was second-string at that time. I was on the periphery, still young, but my family was out there, I was on the big stage. It didn't bother me that people were saying it was lambs to the slaughter, I just wanted to play.

Shane Williams: I had no idea we were going to put forty-odd points on the

The first Wales XV before the match at Richardson's Field, Blackheath, 19 February, 1881.
Back row: WD Phillips, GF Harding, Mr R Mullock, FT Purdon, G Darbishire, E Treharne, RDG Williams
Seated: TA Rees, E Peake, JA Bevan (captain), BE Girling, BB Mann
Front row: L Watkins, CH Newman, EJ Lewis, RHB Summers

Billy Bancroft.

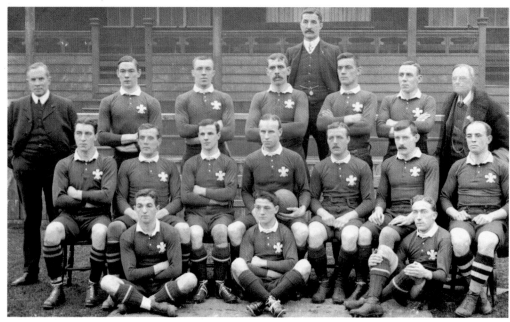

The Welsh team that faced New Zealand in 1905.
Standing at the back: Mr A Llewellin (touch judge – WRU); *Back row:* Mr T Williams (selector – WFU),
JF Williams, G Travers, D Jones, W Joseph, RT Gabe, Sir JTD Llewellyn (president – WFU)
Seated: CM Pritchard, JJ Hodges, W Llewellyn, EG Nicholls (captain), HB Winfield, CC Pritchard, AF Harding
Front row: E Morgan, RM Owen, PF Bush

Arthur Gould.

Ken Jones crosses for a try against the All Blacks in 1953.

Gareth Edwards and Barry John getting ready to play for Cardiff.

Clive Rowlands takes a forwards session on the beach in 1969.

The Pontypool front row (*left to right*): Graham Price, Bobby Windsor and Charlie Faulkner *Getty Images*

Jonathan Davies and Ieuan Evans wrap up Richard Harding
at Ballymore Stadium during the 1987 Rugby World Cup. *Getty Images*

Ieuan Evans crosses for one of the great tries of the Five Nations against Scotland at the Arms Park in 1988. *Getty Images*

Scott Quinnell rampages through Philippe Saint-André on his way to scoring in the 1994 Five Nations. *Getty Images*

Ieuan Evans lifts the 1994 Five Nations trophy at Twickenham. *Getty Images*

Scott Gibbs flies in to score a spectacular try against England at Wembley Stadium in the 1999 Five Nations. *Getty Images*

Chris Wyatt during the 1999 World Cup quarter-final against Australia. *Getty Images*

Shane Williams announces himself on the world stage with a bewitching performance against New Zealand. *Fotosport*

Gavin Henson upends Mathew Tait in the opening game of the 2005 Six Nations. *Fotosport*

Martyn Williams crosses for the first of his two tries against France in 2005. *Getty Images*

The players do a lap of honour around the Millennium Stadium
pitch after sealing the 2005 Grand Slam against Ireland. *Getty Images*

Coaching dream-team: Warren Gatland and Shaun Edwards. *Getty Images*

The players celebrate the full-time whistle at Twickenham in 2008. *Getty Images*

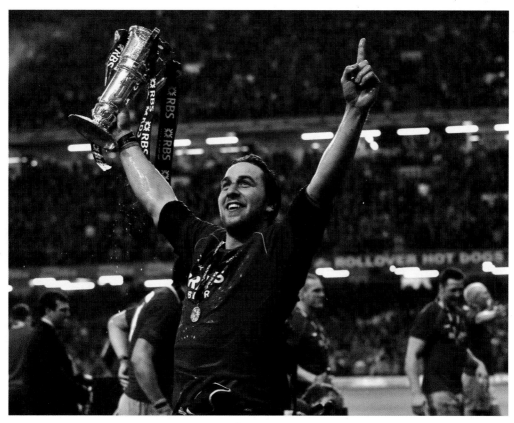

Captain Ryan Jones with the 2008 Six Nations trophy. *Getty Images*

Mike Phillips scores down the blind-side against Ireland at the 2011 World Cup. *InphoPhotography*

Game-changer – Sam Warbuton flips Vincent Clerc during the 2011 World Cup semi-final. *InphoPhotography*

Scott Williams bursts away to score the winning try at Twickenham in 2012. *InphoPhotography*

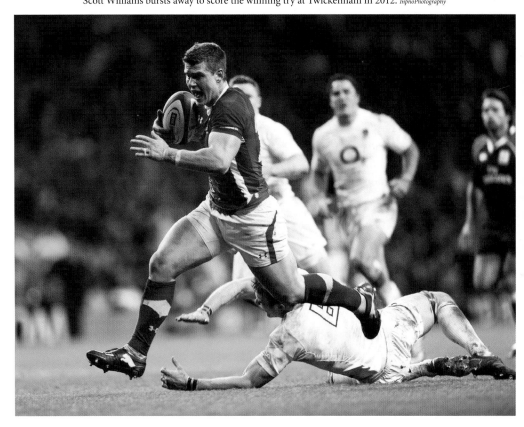

Sam Warbuton and his team celebrate their third Grand Slam of the 2000s. *InphoPhotography*

Gareth Davies finished off a spectacular attack to score against England
during the 2015 World Cup pool match at Twickenham. *InphoPhotography*

George North pounces to score from a Yoann Huget error against France in Paris in 2019. *InphoPhotography*

Josh Adams collects a Dan Biggar cross-kick to score the winning try against England at the Principality Stadium in 2019. *InphoPhotography*

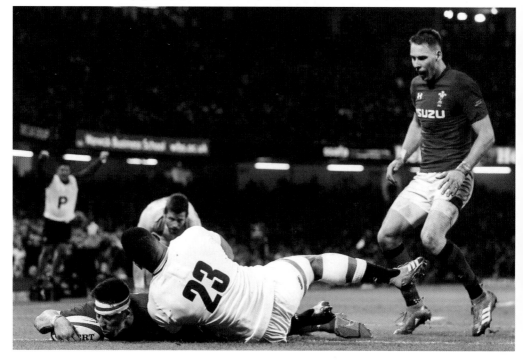

Hadleigh Parkes crosses to open the scoring against Ireland at
the Principality Stadium as Wales clinch the 2019 Grand Slam. *Getty Images*

Louis Rees-Zammit's acrobatic finish was crucial to Wales's win
over Ireland in the opening fixture of the 2021 Six Nations. *Getty Images*

Kieran Hardy celebrates scoring from a quick-tap against England in the 2021 Six Nations. *Getty Images*

Alun Wyn Jones lists the 2021 Six Nations trophy and Justin Tipuric
lifts the Triple Crown, the first silverware of the new Wayne Pivac era. *Getty Images*

All Blacks and really rattle them. I got involved in play every time I could, and I defended pretty well. I ran around and covered some mileage in that game, I can tell you. That was one of my best games in the Welsh jersey.

Stephen Jones: What Steve was doing was smart. Keeping morale high by giving everybody an opportunity. Jonathan Thomas was nineteen or twenty at the time, and he was carving it up as well. It was in the Telstra Stadium in front of a massive crowd, and all the neutrals were supporting us, the place was rocking.

Shane Williams: It wasn't until we started scoring points, and I was looking up and seeing so much space, that I started thinking, 'Do you know what, these guys aren't as good as I thought they were.' We're scoring tries against them, some of them easy tries. Tayls went under the posts untouched, and I began to think, 'If we keep going like this, we might even beat the All Blacks here.' Unfortunately we forgot we had to defend at times as well.

Stephen Jones: As a player I *never* had the mindset of thinking we were going to lose a game. I always enjoyed the challenge, and I always backed myself. With sixty minutes gone, we were winning, but they pulled away in the last quarter.

Martyn Williams: It was bittersweet watching it. It was amazing to witness from the stand, but I desperately wanted to be involved. Deep down I knew I'd lost my place. I remember thinking, 'Surely Steve can't change this team now?' He tweaked it a bit, brought Daf Jones back at eight, but JT had played so well, I was relegated to the bench for the England game. I was first choice seven before that. I'd turned down the captaincy before the World Cup. It's the biggest regret of my life not doing it. There had been a lot going on. I'd lost my brother two years before, we'd just had our first child, and I just didn't feel ready for it.

Gareth Llewellyn: Steve was interviewed afterwards and said the plan was always to play Shane in that game, which was bollocks. It was a B team, but they played out of their skins. People talked about Shane and JT, but the others stepped up, too. Ceri Sweeney was second or third choice ten, and he came off the bench and put the mighty Jerry Collins off the field. Collins was huge, but he came off second best in a collision with Ceri.

Tom Shanklin: The person I felt sorry for was Garan Evans. He'd snuck into the squad ahead of Gavin Henson. He was handed his big chance against New Zealand, and got knocked out after five minutes. Alfie came on as an emergency full back, and had a wonderful game.

Gareth Thomas: It was going to click eventually. None of us really knew when it would, or whether we'd all lock in at the same time. But it happened against the best team in the world, and we thought if we could do it against them, we could do it against anyone. I genuinely thought we were going to win. I remember looking at the clock on seventy-five minutes and thinking, 'I never want this to end.' I felt like I was playing a part in this amazing game of rugby that we were all contributing to. At half-time, we were all trying to stay calm, but you could tell we were all thinking, 'Something's going on here.'

Adam Jones: People say it clicked, but they still put fifty points on us. We still got hammered, didn't we? My memories of that game aren't as fond as some of the other boys, because I was subbed off after half an hour. I wasn't injured, and I didn't have a clue what was going on – I just saw my number come up. I was so upset. Mike Wadsworth, our masseur, handed me a blanket on the touchline, I put it over my head and bawled my eyes out for two or three minutes. I bumped into Steve Hansen in the lift the day after and he asked me how I'd found the game. I told him I felt humiliated being subbed off, and he just said, 'Well you'll have to get fitter then, won't you?' If he'd told me beforehand that he was going to do it, I might have understood, but I fucking hated him for a while after that.

Shane Williams: If it was Hansen's plan to keep the likes of me, Jonathan and Alix hungry, it was a stroke of genius. But I'd be fibbing if I said I thought that was the plan. In fairness to Steve, he rewarded us for the performances and picked us again for the quarter-final. People still ask me, 'Was that meant to happen?' and my answer is, 'I don't care.' I got my opportunity, and I took it, and I'm grateful for that.

It would come to be seen as the game of the World Cup, but despite Wales's pulse-quickening contribution, they eventually slipped off the pace, conceding twenty points in the final quarter. They'd become accustomed to losing, and didn't know how to capitalise on a winning position. Despite the defeat, they approached England in the quarter-final with understandable optimism.

Stephen Jones: The big question was, 'Was New Zealand a one-off, or are we here to stay?' We were winning at half-time, before England tightened things up.

Adam Jones: I was picked to start again, but my confidence had taken a bit of a knock after being subbed off. I'd spent the previous few days moping around, and I struggled to psych myself up for the England game, because I knew it was going to happen again. I was young and I didn't know how to deal with it.

Shane Williams: It was my job to chase everything, including the kick-offs, which was interesting, as they'd normally stick one of their big lumps underneath them. But my mindset was, if Dallaglio's catching this kick-off, or Ben Kay, there's no point me running up slowly, and letting them run at me as quickly as they can. My job was to get there and put these guys down as quickly as possible. If I could get them man-and-ball, it suited me, because it didn't give them momentum to run over the top of me. That job didn't faze me one bit, I just wanted to get involved in whatever capacity. We started as we did against New Zealand, and Stephen Jones put us into an early lead with the opening try.

Stephen Jones: Shane, Alfie, and Coops all burnt off a couple of people to set it up. I just happened to be on the end of it.

Tom Shanklin: Credit to Stephen for scoring that first try, but it was the worst finish I've ever seen. Terrible. He put it down awkwardly, almost apologetically. Where was the flamboyant Rokocoko-esque dive? I could have got into him about it but he takes such a hammering anyway, for his dress sense, and for his pale skin, that I eased off on him.

Shane Williams: I was on a high, things were going right for me. The style we played really opened England up. I remember looking up several times and thinking, 'I'm up against Ben Kay, here. I can take these guys on. I've got the confidence, I've got the pace, let's do something.' I was involved in most of the tries, and I came off the field happy that I'd played well, but devastated that we'd lost. I wanted to play in the semi-final, I wanted to get to the final. I wanted to come away with something. We should have beaten England, and anything could have happened after that. Who knows, we could have won the World Cup. I still think that now.

Gareth Thomas: England were shell-shocked. They had no idea how to cope with us initially, but that day I learned just how difficult it is to be an international full back. England realised it was only my second game there, and switched tactics. They had Jonny with the left peg, and Catty with the right peg, and they exposed me with their kicking. I was running this way and that, and I found it really difficult to figure out what was going on.

The introduction of Mike Catt at half-time was a tactical masterstroke, adding a second kicking option in the midfield alongside Jonny Wilkinson, and allowing England to dictate territory.

Stephen Jones: One person changed that game. Mike Catt. They started kicking to the corners and pinning us back. Up until that point, they didn't have an answer. Their pack decided to tighten things up, and they strangled us. We'd been winning the running game completely.

Gareth Thomas: I'm not one for regrets, but I wonder what might have happened if we'd had a more honest conversation at half-time, rather than being unbelievably excited because we were all on this fairground ride together. We were in a quarter-final against England, and we all had this gut feeling that we were going to beat them. I still believe to this day that we should have. The excitement of it all took over, and it got out of control. That was the first actual game where from the start we understood how we wanted to play, but we weren't able to contain it. You have to have some kind of structure, some kind of game plan to revert to when things are getting chaotic. It was the first snap of reality of what we were capable of, but we hadn't yet learnt to control it.

Martyn Williams: If we'd had a little bit more self-belief, we'd have won. We just had so many scars from previous hammerings, I'm not sure we believed we could actually go on and beat them. They were so far ahead of us off the field. They were doing things then that we wouldn't start doing for another five years or more. They had dieticians, specialist coaches, they were having their blood tested at Harley Street, their hair analysed to determine whether they were getting the right nutrients. I remember rooming with Phil Greening on the 2001 Lions tour. I'd make myself a cup of tea after training, and he'd pull out this big bag of supplements, and start making himself complex protein shakes. I had no idea what he was doing. They were streets ahead of us. To get within a whisker in 2003 was a hell of an achievement.

Mark Jones: There were a couple of key moments. There was a chance for me to give a pass late on, and I didn't take it. Shane was outside me, but he was marked, so I kept hold of the ball. I think it was Tindall who chopped me down about five yards short. I still look back on that thinking, 'Should I have?'

Martyn Williams: Ultimately, that England team knew how to win. They'd beaten New Zealand in New Zealand, Australia in Australia and won the Grand Slam. We'd ground out wins in the pool stages, but we didn't know how to win the big games. As a group, we hadn't beaten a big team. We'd been whitewashed in the 2003 Six Nations, and been battered in Australia and New Zealand. England probably thought subconsciously, 'We'll batter these', and they took us a little bit lightly initially, but when they realised they had a game on their hands, they had the nous and the experience to close it out.

Mark Jones: At the end of the day, they benefited from one loose kick return. Jason Robinson made the burst up the middle and Will Greenwood scored in the corner. That was the difference. Robinson was a nightmare. I didn't mind playing against the big guys like Ben Cohen; they would just try to run over you, so as long as you stood your ground, you'd be okay. It was the little guys, with the footwork that I feared. Over those first five or six metres, Robinson was phenomenal. His ability to step off both feet was electrifying. He could change direction in the air, which took some doing. He was horrendous to mark one v one.

Gareth Thomas: We were tough on ourselves afterwards for losing a game we should have won, but I was really excited for what the future held. Everyone was now tuned into the same wavelength. I felt proud because we were playing the 'Welsh way' again, especially after those Graham Henry years when everything was so structured, where you weren't allowed to play what was in front of you.

We'd found something that represented Welsh rugby. It truly did. We'd won a lot of the nation back, and world rugby had stood up and taken notice. We were suddenly a team to be reckoned with. I will always be adamant that our success was built on all those failures we'd endured together, and was a reaction to the negativity that surrounded Steve's early period in charge.

Disappointingly, the euphoria of the World Cup didn't translate into a successful Six Nations. Scotland were dispatched in the opening game, but Wales lost heavily to a Paul O'Connell-inspired Ireland in round two. The set piece was borderline disastrous against the French, with ball from the scrum invariably messy, and a lineout success ratio of just fifty per cent. Wales's most destructive scrummager, Adam Jones, had been humiliatingly subbed off again after half an hour in the opening two games. For the French game, Hansen gave Jones's tight-head jersey to Gethin Jenkins. He was a player of outstanding ability, but a loose-head by trade, who didn't have the technique to lock the scrum at Test level. Earlier accusations levelled at Hansen that he didn't take scrummaging seriously – sacrificing live sessions in favour of practising in trainers on indoor rubber surfaces – resurfaced. The 22–29 scoreline could have been worse. In the penultimate round, England again took advantage of an under-powered scrum to win 31–21. The final act of Steve Hansen's reign was a 44–10 victory against Italy, in which Gareth Thomas broke Ieuan Evans's Welsh try-scoring record, and Wales recaptured some of the vim and razzle-dazzle of their World Cup campaign. It allowed the Hansen acolytes to claim that the trajectory was still on an upward curve, but the cynics maintained that progress had been patchy, and that any evidence of a bright new dawn was far from compelling.

NINETEEN

EVERYTHING I'D DREAMT OF AS A KID

The race to become Hansen's successor had narrowed to a shoot-out between the people's choice, Gareth Jenkins, and the Harlequins CEO, Mark Evans. There were those who thought Gareth's appointment was long overdue. He'd been Wales's most successful club coach for more than a decade, and was considered the spiritual successor to Carwyn James – a rugby romantic from the west of Wales. But Mark Evans had emerged as a genuine contender, and when a roomful of journalists took their seats at WRU HQ on the day of the announcement, it was too close a contest to call. At the moment of truth, when the door adjoining the conference room swung open, there was a collective gasp, as Mike Ruddock strolled in.

Mike Ruddock: Bear in mind, I hadn't actually applied for the job. I was approached by Steve Lewis and Terry Cobner, and persuaded to throw my hat in the ring. I was asked a couple of simple questions. Wales had lost to Ireland quite badly the year before in Lansdowne Road. Shane Byrne had scored a couple of tries off the back of the driving maul. They asked what team I'd have picked, and I told them I thought there was a crack in the selection of the forward pack. I thought they were picking too many non-specialists. For example, Gethin Jenkins would often start on the tight-head, or come on there after thirty minutes. I'd learnt many years earlier at Pontypool, that if you don't get your scrum right, you go backwards. They had Michael Owen in the second row, who I thought was too much of a footballer to have buried in the scrum. You've got to *love* scrummaging to play in the tight-five. Michael was better off being a ball player. Then you had Gavin Thomas, a smallish open-side, playing at number eight. So you had a crack right the way through the scrum. I even remember Gareth Thomas packing down in the back row at one point, as part of a special move. You might have one chance to win the game off a scrum, and if you can't get the ball back, or you can't get the quality of ball you need, you've blown it. The scrum wasn't being given enough respect.

Michael Owen: He actually apologised to me when he took the job, because he'd just signed me for the Dragons from Pontypridd. Ruddock was very astute. He saw what was working, and recognised which areas needed improving. The attacking philosophy was beginning to bear fruit, so he retained Johnson and Andrew Hore. The defence needed tightening up a bit, so he brought Clive Griffiths back into the fold. Clive had been marginalised under Hansen, and had been released after the World Cup. And finally, he put a much greater emphasis on the set piece.

Martyn Williams: I got a call from Mike ahead of the Argentina tour, and he told me he wasn't going to take me because he wanted me to stay behind and put weight on. I wasn't sure what to read into that. Then I was on the bench in the autumn for the South Africa and New Zealand Tests. He'd tightened up our set piece, and clearly wanted big men in the pack. He brought the likes of Brent Cockbain in, Mefin Davies and Adam Jones. Nuts-and-bolts set-piece merchants.

Michael Owen: He picked scrummaging forwards, like Brent Cockbain in the second row, and Adam Jones on the tight-head, so I'm sure Adam would be one of those that would say Mike was amazing and Steve Hansen was shit. If you ask anyone who's played second row and number eight which they prefer, they'll say number eight, but I didn't think too much about it. I played some of the best rugby of my career in the second row. If you're playing well, you're playing well. Mike concentrated on those two areas, and made a few other good decisions, like making Alfie his captain.

Gareth Thomas: When Mike took the job, he stressed that he wasn't going to try to reinvent the wheel. He told us to carry on doing what we were doing. He didn't try to implement an entire philosophy the way Graham or Steve had done. He just said, 'Guys, I love the way you play, I love what you're doing, help me understand it, and let's carry on doing the same.'

Rhys Williams: Mike realised that the squad was on the right path. He saw what was going well, and tried to nurture and encourage it. The continuation of that open, attacking style was crucial, and it was vital that Scott Johnson hung around for that.

Martyn Williams: He didn't come in with an ego, and start ripping things up. He was smart enough to see that what we were doing was working, particularly with ball in hand.

Mike Ruddock: Wales were playing great rugby, scoring great tries, and I fully wanted to keep that style of rugby going. Scott Johnson had done a fantastic job with that – it was better than anything I'd coached. But I felt that Wales could be better if we got the set piece right, put the right players in the right places, and got more game time for people like Adam Jones on the tight-head. Other than that, I wouldn't have wanted to change the way they played, it was fantastic. But it was a bit like the Kevin Keegan footballing philosophy. They were scoring lots of points, but letting lots in too. During the World Cup in 2003, they played fantastic rugby against both New Zealand and England, but at the end of the day they lost. My view was that you'd have to bring in a specialist defence coach to sort that out.

The defence proved to be a thorny issue. Ruddock's man, Clive Griffiths, was keen to introduce a rugby league style 'blitz' system, but faced stern opposition from some of the senior players including Gareth Llewellyn and Colin Charvis, who favoured the 'drift' approach Steve Hansen had introduced. Scott Johnson voiced concerns that the blitz wouldn't work at Test level, despite the fact that Wales had beaten a talented, attack-minded Barbarians 42–0 in Ruddock's first game in charge. The blitz was all about pressurising the opposition when they had the ball, forcing turnovers, and capitalising on the ensuing confusion. Counter-attacking against a side themselves aligned for attack, would allow broken-field runners like Shane Williams to exploit the space created. Eventually, an uneasy compromise emerged, mockingly referred to as the 'dritz' because it was neither one thing nor the other.

Tom Shanklin: No one really blitzed back in 2005. South Africa had the biggest line-speed in those days, but they'd still go up-and-out. It was unheard of to go out-to-in.

Martyn Williams: Hansen had a totally different philosophy on defence. They don't really blitz in New Zealand, whereas Clive came from a rugby league background and was determined to bring it in. There was definitely a difference of opinion.

Mike Ruddock: It was one of my three guiding principles. I wanted to make us much more stubborn in defence, I wanted to get the set piece more robust and technically better – through selection, and a little bit of focus. And I wanted to retain the free-flowing attacking style developed under Steve Hansen. Do those things, and I was convinced the Welsh team would improve without huge amounts of over-coaching. Lo and behold, that's exactly what happened.

Michael Owen: Steve Hansen had been ruining Adam Jones by taking him off after thirty minutes, and Mike essentially reinvented him by making him one of the first names on his teamsheet, and the cornerstone of his pack. So I guess the likes of Adam would always judge Ruddock more favourably. But as a player, it's difficult to have an impartial view. You're subconsciously influenced by the coaches that treat you better.

Martyn Williams: We were definitely loose up front with Hansen in charge. He was a centre, wasn't he? We ultimately had two centres in charge, with him and Johnno. We didn't do much live scrummaging until Mike came in and added the northern hemisphere set-piece game. That was his obvious area of expertise.

Rhys Williams: Without a doubt, he shored up the pack. We knew if we had parity up front, we had the creativity and skills to cause havoc against anyone. Ruddock also brought a few little innovations in and around the contact area – how to make a few extra yards after the tackle, how to create a little more momentum. He thought up ways of winning collisions and making ground without necessarily out-muscling the opposition.

Martyn Williams: Training was fun under Mike, he brought a really enjoyable environment with him.

Tom Shanklin: He didn't have the same aura that Steve Hansen did, but whenever a new coach comes in you want to get their respect as fast as you can. I got on with him fine. He's a lovely bloke.

Ruddock's tweaks seemed to make a difference. In the 2004 autumn internationals, Wales scored three tries against the Tri-Nations champions, South Africa, and came close to knocking them over. They then came closer to beating New Zealand than at any point since 1953. Tries from Tom Shanklin and Mefin Davies took them within a point of the feted All Blacks, while their star man Richie McCaw was neutralised by Colin Charvis. Wales suddenly looked like a team that were on the verge of turning performances into results – an irony that wouldn't have been lost on the All Blacks head coach, and assistant coach, Graham Henry and Steve Hansen.

Tom Shanklin: We walked into the Walkabout bar through the back entrance after the New Zealand game, and were announced to the entire club by the DJ. Everybody was coming up and patting us on the back, shaking our hands and congratulating us, and we were happy enough with that. I don't think we quite realised how close we'd come to beating them. We hadn't yet developed that ruthless streak where winning was everything. We were content to celebrate a narrow defeat as though it was a win.

What was needed was a big win. And the Six Nations began with a visit from the reigning world champions. England weren't quite the team that had won the World Cup less than fifteen months earlier, but their 32–16 autumn defeat of the Springboks provided evidence that they were still a formidable side, particularly up front where they'd pulverised a strong South African scrum. Ruddock's return to live scrummaging and focus on the nuts and bolts was about to be put to the test.

Martyn Williams: I shouldn't have played in that Six Nations at all. I'd hurt my neck and Carcass had ruled me out. Then two weeks before it began, Charvy broke his foot playing for Newcastle, and Carcass decided we needed to get a second opinion. I ended up going for this Korean massage treatment called Su Jok, where your hand and fingers correspond to parts of your body. Your thumb is your head, your palm is your spine, and so on. He was massaging the joints in my fingers to try to heal my neck. I'd been on the bench for the autumns, and supposedly ruled out for the Six Nations, so I was keen to try anything I could to get fit, because I could see my Wales career slipping away. It's bizarre how things fall into place. I ended up recovering, winning my fiftieth cap against England and beating them.

Ian Gough: I watched the England game on a pouffe in Dubai drinking bullfrog cocktails. Steve 'Jabba' Jones and I had been released from the Welsh squad to play for the Dragons in a friendly against Western Stormers.

Martyn Williams: England were still considered the dog's bollocks, Sky's *The Rugby Club* was bigging them up all the time, but Stephen Jones led a presentation in the week highlighting their weaknesses, and drawing attention to the fact that they weren't as good as they thought they were. Having said that, I don't think any of us had ever beaten them. The last victory had come in '99, and there were only a few survivors from that. As a group, most of us had no idea what it felt like to beat England.

Shane Williams: We were warming up and Dwayne Peel's foot went straight through the ground, where the four pallets of grass met. Half his leg disappeared. The groundsman came over, and instead of doing what he needed to do to fix it, just put a cone over it, so no one else fell down. It was crazy. I remember thinking, 'I hope my foot doesn't go down there, I'm going to need to look out for that.' It was like when you play rugby down the park as a kid, and come across a piece of dog shit. You put something over it, to make sure no one lands in it. The pitch wasn't in the best state, and was heavy on the legs at times making it difficult to get the side-step going, but it was the same for both sides. You've just got to get out there and get on with it.

Tom Shanklin: It was around that time that my partnership with Gavin Henson really began to flourish. That was remembered as *his* game. He obviously nailed the winning kick, and he smashed Mathew Tait with those two monster tackles. Gav fed off positive feedback. When he made those big hits, I'd be in his ear, geeing him up, saying, 'You're a machine, you're a machine.' He needed to be told he was looking good and playing well. He and I were completely different. He was far more of a ball player, and had a real deft touch. I was the strike runner out in the wide channels. His job was to take it to the line, and decide in a split-second whether to miss me or hit me. We worked so well together because we had clearly defined roles. You never saw him die with the ball in his hands. It always came out of his hands, he always kept the movement alive.

Stephen Jones: That was a *really* good centre partnership. As a lead runner, Shanks used to pick excellent lines, he'd have an eye for the gap, and he'd hit hard between shoulders. Gav was a really good footballer, with a great kicking game, very much like a New Zealand-style second five eighth. And both of them enjoyed the physical side which you *have* to in international rugby. As much as Shanks loves a laugh, he took massive pride in his D.

Tom Shanklin: Gav was very particular about the way he looked. He had to have his shirt given to him the day before the game so he could sew a compression top into it. He wanted it to fit snugly, and insisted on long sleeves because he thought his wrists looked ugly. His nan would sew an extra two inches into his shorts because he liked them longer. If you looked closely, there'd be two lots of three feathers on his shorts. He was totally OCD about the way he looked. It was a little bit strange, but most players have quirks of some kind. Sonny Parker always insisted on running out last from the tunnel. Jamie Roberts *has* to run out second. We all have our superstitions.

Stephen Jones: Gav was look-good, feel-good, but jeez he could play. He took massive personal pride in his performance, and was a pleasure to play with. He's smart, his calling was on the money, and that's what you want as a first-receiver – you want the communication outside you to be clear. Your inside-centre has a better line of sight than you. As a ten, you're naturally more ruck-focused. Gav would tell me where the space was, whether or not the full back was up, where and if there was room to kick. He was very much like a co-driver in a rally car. He was constantly making the correct calls to help me steer the ship.

Martyn Williams: He was a quiet bloke off the field, but on it he'd have no qualms in bossing you around, regardless of seniority or experience. He'd always see things first. His vision was so sharp. He liked to pretend he was cool and didn't really care about rugby, but deep down he loved it. He knew the game inside out. He could kick brilliantly, his distribution off both hands was impeccable, and he could carry the ball hard as well. He was deceptively quick – a glider rather than a runner, and he was a big man as well. People forget how big he was. The most naturally talented player I ever played with, without a doubt.

Tom Shanklin: Shane's try against England was a perfect example of the things Hansen and Johnson had worked on coming to fruition. The fact that Michael Owen threw the scoring pass was evidence of that. The timing of it, and the weight of it allowed Shane to beat Cueto on the outside. It was all about forwards and backs interlinking. It genuinely didn't matter what number was on your back.

Shane Williams: We were playing open, expansive rugby, and scoring some great tries. Even though we were conceding tries, we were outscoring teams. That's the way rugby was going in 2005. I knew I had Cueto for pace, but for so much of the game, I couldn't get my hands on the ball. England just frustrated us. The one and only try came quite early on. I remember the breakdown being on the right-hand side, and the ball taking an absolute age to get to me. There were four or five passes in the lead-up to it. Great passes from Gav and eventually from Michael Owen. I remember looking up at Cueto and thinking, 'I've got him for pace, but I'm going to be close to the flag here.' I dived for the line, and immediately thought, 'Why did I go legs-first?' I had that thought at the precise moment I crossed the line. 'How close am I to the touchline? Where are my knees?' I hadn't had time to adjust. I didn't even look to my right to see who was coming over to cover, I just thought, 'Score this try, this game is going to go down to the wire and every chance will count.' Even after I scored I thought, 'Oh God, how close was I? Is he going to give it?' This wasn't a game against Tonga where we were forty points up. This was against England and I'd *better* have scored that try. Even when I look at it now, my first thought is, 'Why did I dive feet first?' Actually my first thought is, 'What was I thinking with that hairstyle?', and *then* it's, 'Why didn't I dive in the conventional way?' It could have been so much easier.

Michael Owen: One of my most vivid memories from that game is of winning a lineout. I was the front jumper in a five-man line, and I remember rushing forward to win the ball, and thinking, 'Thank God we've held on to possession.' It was probably of little significance overall, but it's funny what sticks in your memory. Most fans just remember Gav's tackles on Mathew Tait, but I've got no recollection of them happening at the time. You tend to remember your own moments, and when you're a forward no one but you remembers your significant moments!

Stephen Jones: Tait had commanded a good deal of newspaper headlines because he was so young, and so full of promise. But he met his match that day. Big time.

Shane Williams: I can still hear those two tackles now. They were brutal hits. Not only that, but he smashed Julian White as well, who was a renowned hard man. That was probably a bigger tackle. How the hell did a back hit a front row forward that hard? Without doubt, that was Gavin Henson's best game in a Welsh jersey. When you're up against a physically dominant team like England, having a back capable of making hits like that makes a difference. When Gav picked up Tait and drove him back, the whole crowd went absolutely ballistic. There was more noise then than when I scored my try. I almost felt sorry for Tait because he was being billed as the next big thing in England, and he got rag-dolled by someone who literally didn't give a shit. Gavin Henson was the reason we won that game.

Mike Ruddock: He was a perfect fit for us at twelve. He was skilful and elusive but he was *very* physical as well. He could blitz in defence *and* play a bit of football. Clive Griffiths was probably the catalyst for Gav's domination of Mathew Tait. He'd wound Gav up in the week by playing him loads of clips of this bright young talent that was coming down. There was no way Gav was going to let someone upstage him on his home patch.

Martyn Williams: We targeted Tait, no question about that. He was only eighteen, so there was every chance he'd wilt under the pressure. And he came up against a guy in Gav that just oozed class that day. He had a special tournament. He'd been awesome in the autumn against South Africa and New Zealand, and he carried that on in the Six Nations. He was the full package. He had so much time on the ball.

Henson was without peer that day – his physical domination of Mathew Tait was just one aspect of a masterful performance. He glided, he swooped, and he dazzled. And when Wales were awarded a potential match-winning penalty four minutes from time, the nation's destiny was in his hands. It was written in the stars.

Martyn Williams: It was Coops [Gareth Cooper] we've got to thank for that. He put that clever little grubber through, and won the turnover for us. Before that, we were 9–8 down, and I was thinking, 'Here we go again. Another defeat to England.'

Tom Shanklin: He had an impressive long-distance boot on him. Steve was our frontline kicker, and he was a great kicker but anything over forty-five metres was beyond his range. It was a big call from Steve to give it to Gav, very unselfish.

Stephen Jones: That kick *was* just outside of my range. It would have been full-club for me. I was tempted, I could have been the hero, but I think you've got to make a smarter decision than that. If Gav hadn't been comfortable taking it because of the occasion, no issues, I'd have done it. But you've got to realise what you've got around you. If someone's got a bigger club and is comfortable, then give them the ball. It's team first, always. And it was a wonderful strike.

Tom Shanklin: He had massive quads on him. In kicking practice, he could always kick it so much further than anyone else. He'd try to hit the giant TV screens high up in the stadium. It was a big moment for him, but a huge moment for the team. Rob Sidoli couldn't look. My job as a centre was to run hard after the kick, in anticipation of that once-in-a-blue-moon moment when it might bounce off the posts. Your gauge is the crowd, and the roar told you all you needed to know. That was a huge moment and he stepped up. He was absolutely nerveless. It was the start of the Gavin Henson phenomenon. He was seeing Charlotte Church, who was no stranger to the tabloids, so his profile began to soar after that. He had the tan, the spiky hair, and the silver boots. He became a celebrity.

Michael Owen: It was a massive kick and an incredible moment in Welsh rugby history. We'd been knocking on the door for a while, coming close to the big teams, so to finally turn one of them over was hugely significant. What pleased me was what happened *after* that kick. We didn't get tight, didn't retreat into our shells. We kept *playing*. We had the confidence to be bold and see it out.

Mike Ruddock: I'm superstitious, and for many years I've deliberately looked away when kickers are taking penalties. That day was the same. I put my head down and scribbled something in my notes, trying to quell the emotion. That's one thing I can't control. I need to see everything else on the pitch, but once a kicker places the ball on the tee, it's down to him and him alone.

Shane Williams: It was one of the toughest games I'd been involved in. After so many near-misses under Hansen, we'd finally beaten one of the big guns. It was impossible not to feel a surge of confidence after that.

Ian Gough: I got back on the Monday, horribly hungover and jet-lagged after a great few days in South Africa. I assumed I had no chance of playing against Italy, because they'd allowed me to travel with the Dragons. But as I was groggily going about my business in training, I was told Ryan Jones had hurt his back, and that I'd be on the bench. I had no idea what the moves were, and had to learn them all from scratch.

The Italy game was a week away, so there was no time to celebrate a first win over England in Cardiff for twelve years. And there could be no room for complacency against a side Wales had lost to on their last visit to Rome. But this was a different Wales. The total rugby they were building towards came together in a slick, pulsating performance that brought six tries, some of which were mesmerising.

Martyn Williams: We were nervous going out to Italy. They'd become a bit of a bogey team for us. But some of the tries we scored that day were brilliant, in fairness. We blew them away. That's the game when it clicked for us.

Shane Williams: It was like playing touch rugby at times. We knew if we were going to win a game by opening up and scoring tries it was against Italy. We started at a hundred miles per hour, made a break right from the whistle, and almost put Shanks in. I felt I had acres and acres of space, my confidence was sky-high. That game felt like a reward for all the hard work we'd put in against England. They couldn't cope with our off-loading game, Alfie was getting over the gain line every time, Nugget was on fire, Kevin Morgan was creating gaps and making breaks. I honestly felt as though I was untouchable, like I had some force-field around me. I went into the changing rooms at half-time thinking, 'How the hell haven't I scored!'

Michael Owen: By then we'd developed a true confidence. Shane Williams got his try in the second half after two unbelievable passes from Alfie and Martyn Williams. There was nothing preordained about it, it was just based on trust and instinct.

Shane Williams: Alfie made that break, Nugget did the pass, then there's another nonchalant, no-look pass from Kevin Morgan and all I had to do was finish it off. We looked like Fiji at times, doing these back-door passes, and one-handed offloads. We were just playing with smiles on our faces.

Tom Shanklin: Blind passing, living off your wits. Doing the kinds of things you couldn't plan, and couldn't do again if you tried. Things like that just *happened.* Some days the stars align, and you're dealt a perfect hand.

Stephen Jones: All the interplay and ball skills we'd been working on in training transferred to the pitch. The boys allowed themselves a few beers after that, but I barely had any time to celebrate because I had to head back to Clermont where I was playing my club rugby. I was virtually living in the airport at that time.

After the game, Italy coach, John Kirwan – who'd terrorised Wales during their tour of New Zealand in 1988 – tipped them for the title. The omens were good. The win in Rome meant Wales had won their opening two matches in the Championship for the first time since 1994 – the year of their last triumph. Kirwan went on to single out Shane Williams for special praise, after he'd punished every loose Italian kick with his counter-attacking brio. The diminutive winger had had a hand in four of the six tries Wales had scored.

Round three found Wales in Paris, and their campaign was almost derailed by a rampant, irresistible home side. France scored two tries in the opening twelve minutes, and only a heroic rearguard action from Gareth Thomas stopped it from turning into an avalanche. The 15–6 half-time score was far from an accurate reflection of France's dominance.

Michael Owen: We were getting *battered* at the scrum. I was having to pick up from a retreating base every time, and we were getting obliterated behind the gain line. Adam Jones had been quite quiet up until that point, and I remember shouting, 'Can we sort the scrum out boys or what?' He turned round, glared at me and said, 'Mikey, do us a favour. Fuck off.' He'd been up against Sylvain Marconnet who was blitzing him, and he was clearly taking it personally.

Adam Jones: Marconnet was one of the best loose-heads in the world at the time, and Mefin and I had done a lot of video analysis, trying to come up with ways to neutralise him. Sometimes though, you just meet your match. He pulverised me in the first scrum, and I went down or backwards in virtually every one after that. It was soul-destroying. My most important job was to anchor that scrum, and I was failing miserably.

Stephen Jones: Playing my club rugby in France had given me a kick up the backside. I'd never lived outside Wales, the language barrier was a struggle, and the style of rugby was completely different. Pierre Mignoni was my scrum half at Clermont, who's gone on to coach Toulon to three European titles. Playing with him gave me a true insight into their philosophy – the nine is the general as opposed to the ten. He would dictate the play, make the decisions, even call the lineouts. Dimitri Yachvili was performing the same role that day. He scored one of their tries, and was calling the shots. It was good for me to learn different styles, and play in different places. Everything was different. Even the goal-kicking. In the Pro14 there's one ball sponsor, and one type of ball. There were *seven* different balls in the French league at one time. All different pressures, shapes, sweet spots. You were constantly thinking, always adapting. It helped me in that game when the chips were down.

Michael Owen: Aurélien Rougerie against Shane was a defining battle. It was David versus Goliath. Rougerie was all over Shane in the first half, running through him, trampling over him, and chucking him around like a rag doll.

Stephen Jones: Rougerie was a hell of a ball carrier, a hell of an athlete. Him against Shane was a mismatch physically, and we were struggling to give Shane the space to get his footwork going. In defence, we couldn't slow their speed of ball down, so their momentum became irresistible. They were constantly on the front foot, and Yachvili was making all the right decisions. We were getting carved open.

Martyn Williams: When they're on, they're on. And that was a classic French performance. We were chasing shadows for forty minutes.

Shane Williams: They threw everything they had at us, and Rougerie was a big part of that. At one point, I went down to tackle him thinking, 'I've got him here.' Two seconds later, I was looking over my shoulder to see him fifteen yards further down the pitch. He'd just swatted me away. We were playing into France's hands in the first half, trying to outmuscle them, and I definitely gave Rougerie far too much time on the ball. He was having the game of his life, and a lot of that was because I was letting him have it.

Gareth Thomas: It wasn't that we were being outclassed, we were just struggling to get into our stride. We did well to contain them to the point that when we *could* start playing, we were still in a position to win it.

Stephen Jones: Alfie put a massive shot in before fracturing his thumb. He was such a fantastic last line of defence. He put an end to several of their linebreaks.

Martyn Williams: Fair play to Alfie, he made two or three crucial tackles to keep us in the game. If he hadn't made those, they'd have been out of sight by half-time. As it was, it was 15–3, and we had a penalty just before half-time to make it 15–6.

Rhys Williams: At half-time, the changing room was shell-shocked. We were completely under the pump, desperately hanging in there. I looked across and saw Alfie's thumb pointing in the wrong direction, and Mike Ruddock said, 'Right, Rhys, you're in pal.' I remember thinking, 'Oh, shit.'

Mike Ruddock: We lost Gareth at half-time, but Michael Owen stepped up and replaced him as captain seamlessly. In other circumstances, losing your captain would have been dreadful, but we had another leader that could do and say the right things and lead by example. Gareth's influence wasn't missed as much as it might have been. The half-time team talk was all about the three Ts: touch, tackles and turnovers. We'd missed touch a lot in the first half and were giving the ball back to them cheaply, and then wearing ourselves out having to defend. Our first-up tackles were not as good as they should have been, and we weren't dominating the collisions. And we were trying to play a bit off amber/red ball, and giving away a few too many turnovers in the process.

Martyn Williams: It was calm in the changing room. There were no Churchillian speeches. Despite what had happened, it was only 15–6, so we knew if we scored first, we were back in it.

Shane Williams: A few of the boys stood up and said, 'Look, we know what we've got to do. Let's play a bit of rugby and let's beat them.' Despite the apparent hopelessness, we still had faith we could do it.

Stephen Jones: I knew there'd be lapses from France in the second half. I knew we'd have opportunities. We just had to keep in touch on the scoreboard.

Shane Williams: I explained at half-time that as a winger, I had so much space in front of me, I just wasn't getting the ball. I explained that I needed the ball out on the wing and all we needed was to inject a bit of urgency. If we played with width, and spread the big French team around the field, we'd get something done.

Michael Owen: In the second half, Shane completely turned the tables on Rougerie and started running rings around him.

Shane Williams: I'd vowed to shut down the space and dive on him whenever I could. He was a big lad and he was quick, but he took a bit of time to get himself going. As the game went on, we continued playing at a high tempo, and they were tiring. It suited me, it suited Nugget, it suited Rhys, and we got stronger as the game went on. It was a game of two halves, certainly. I hated the first half, and loved the second.

The second half was just seconds old when Stephen Jones made an uncharacteristic break from his own twenty-two. He'd forged a career out of being the steady hand, the master tactician, but his decision to run with the ball caught the French defence unawares, and proved the catalyst for the unlikeliest of comebacks.

Tom Shanklin: He was no slouch, Stephen Jones. He makes that break, our tails are up, Martyn feeds Shane, and Shane skins Rougerie before passing back inside to Nug. Try time.

Stephen Jones: It was pure instinct. It opened up so I went for it. My next instinct was to look for support, look for Shane, someone quick! You want one of your wing men on your shoulder. It led to Nug's first try.

Shane Williams: We changed our game completely in the second half. We were offloading a lot more, playing with a lot more width. Adaptability is the sign of a good team. You've got a game plan, you've got to go out there and do what the coach has said. But sometimes that's not working, and the coach isn't out there on the field. Instead of trying to match France up front and trying to bully them, we decided to do something different, and get the likes of myself involved and really stretch them. That wasn't the tactic prior to the match, and it wasn't the tactic twenty to thirty minutes in to the game. But we had players who played with their heads up, we changed things as the game went on, and it won us the match.

Michael Owen: Within minutes of finishing off that try, Nugget scored again from a quick tap. It was instinctive. We weren't even thinking at that point. We'd been training the same way, with no time to question your decisions or doubt what you were doing.

Rhys Williams: We were ready to give him a bollocking for that quick tap, but he ended up sneaking over.

Shane Williams: No one knew he was going to do it. It very rarely happens that an open-side flanker takes a quick tap from five yards out, and he almost fell over so he did well to reach the try line. It was a period when we *had* to score. At times, things move in slow motion. He'd have been going over the line thinking, 'Please ground this ball otherwise I'm going to get a bollocking off everyone!'

Martyn Williams: As I was doing it, I thought, 'Fuck, I'd better score here.' It was an awful attempt at a tackle. I don't know what Fabien Pelous was doing. I sort of attempted to side-step, but he should have got me. It was an awful attempt. But that's how we played, we were frantic. It was all about quick taps and stuff. Scott Johnson's first words to me after the game were, 'You were fucking lucky you scored that, mate.' If I hadn't scored, I'd have probably been yanked off.

Shane Williams: It's surprising but those kinds of thoughts *do* go through your head. When heading for the line, I'd be conscious of support outside me, and it would increase the pressure. I'd usually ignore the support and back myself to finish, but I'd always be thinking, 'If I don't get this now, I'm going to get the piss taken out of me, and it's not going to be a good briefing tomorrow.' I like to think that I got there most of the time, although I once took on three defenders against Italy instead of passing to an unmarked Duncan Jones. He never scored for Wales, and he still reminds me about that chance now. 'You scored fifty-eight tries for Wales, and you wouldn't even let me have one.'

Michael Owen: Those were career-defining moments from Martyn. Those are the golden moments that people will remember for decades to come. Stephen Jones was phenomenal that day too.

Stephen Jones: Nug was fantastic. Taking the tap penalty was a smart decision. I managed to get a drop goal over as well, which made things a little more comfortable. I think I might have given it the old fist pump at that point. That didn't come out too often. I was a happy man.

Rhys Williams: Steve was monumental. He led us that day. You could see even then, he was going to be a coach. He was so tactically astute, and had managed the game brilliantly.

Mike Ruddock: He was an incredible craftsman. He orchestrated everything.

Martyn Williams: He was outstanding. It was a big game for him personally because he was playing for Clermont at the time, and he bossed it. Defensively, it was like having a fourth back rower alongside you. Everyone refers to it as the 'Martyn Williams game' because of my two tries, but Steve was man of the match, and rightly so. Truth be told, I didn't actually play that well!

Rhys Williams: Steve and Nugget were the most consistently brilliant players I played with. Nugget wasn't one for words or big speeches, but his level never dropped below excellent. You'd follow him into anything. Open-sides are often influential because they're always in the game, but he was simply better than anyone. Creative, determined, and strong. And I've no idea how, because he was rubbish on the weights.

Stephen Jones: The second half showed there's more than one way to play the game. Whenever Shane had the ball, it gave the whole team a massive lift because you knew he could just make something happen. At times he was on a different level to anyone else on the park. A lot of opponents probably underestimated him because of his size, but he was ridiculously strong, pound for pound. And so hard to stop, even when you managed to lay a finger on him. I loved being on the field with him.

Martyn Williams's brace of tries signalled the most dramatic of swings in fortune, but there was still time for a fourth-quarter wobble. After the hour mark, Wales's lineout fell apart, with four throw-ins going astray. They then conceded a flurry of late penalties as their discipline deserted them. Nerves were beginning to fray, limbs were beginning to ache, and demons were starting to whisper. With the clock ticking down, the French found another gear, and set up camp on the Welsh line for a nerve-jangling sequence of set scrums.

Mike Ruddock: People remember Martyn's tries, and Stephen's drop goal, but it was our defensive resilience in the last quarter that won us the game. We battled heroically in those last few minutes to repel the kitchen sink.

Martyn Williams: Absolutely. My two tries came early on in the second half. We had to defend like hell in the last ten minutes. People remember the tries, but I remember that last quarter where we put in tackle after tackle to hold them out. We were flying into contact, and holding on for dear life.

Tom Shanklin: The French knocked on, and my abiding memory is of Stephen Jones turning his back, and booting the ball over the dead ball line.

Shane Williams: My heart was in my mouth. We were right by our own try line, and the lads were all screaming, 'Jonesey, make sure it's time!' As soon as Steve got it, he turned and I thought, 'It must be time.' Steve doesn't get those things wrong.

Tom Shanklin: The ref didn't blow up. I was thinking, 'What? What? Surely not?'

Shane Williams: Hold on, what's going on? The last thing we wanted was another scrum against that French pack. Steve was always our go-to man with the laws. If something happened on the pitch we weren't sure about, we'd always ask Steve, 'Was that right? Did he call that right?' If it had been passed to me, I'd have been really worried. I wouldn't have known what the hell to do with the ball.

Tom Shanklin: We waited for what seemed like an eternity before hearing the blast of his whistle.

Rhys Williams: At the post-match dinner, myself, Martyn Williams, Tom Shanklin and Kevin Morgan were chatting about the prospect of a Grand Slam. Players always claim they don't discuss those sorts of things, that they take every game as it comes, but I'm telling you now – it's all that was on our minds at that point. We knew if we could come back and win in Paris like that, we should fear no one. There was a massive surge in self-belief.

Stephen Jones: Personally, I've never struggled with self-belief. Winning in Paris wouldn't have changed my thought process.

Rhys Williams: It occurred to me then that I'd never won at Murrayfield. I'd drawn there, lost there, but never won. And later when Mike Ruddock asked the question, 'Who among you has won in Scotland?' only Gareth Llewellyn raised his hand. That focused the mind, and kept our feet on the ground.

Martyn Williams: My mother had just been diagnosed with cancer. I rung her after the game and we both got really emotional. After speaking to her, and the boys, I think we realised, 'Shit, we could actually do something here. Something big.' When I got home, I was on the front cover of the *Sunday Times*. It wasn't just Wales that was taking notice anymore.

Stephen Jones: On the Sunday I was going back to Clermont in the car with Pierre Mignoni and Rougerie. I left the Welsh boys behind, and headed over to the French team hotel to wait for my lift. The two of them looked pretty glum as they trudged out to the car. We slung our kitbags in the boot, I got in the back seat, strapped myself in, and just burst out laughing. I couldn't help myself. It was a four-hour journey from Paris to Clermont and they had to drive all the way with a smug Welshman in the back.

Scotland may have been at a low ebb under Australian coach Matt Williams, but the statistics made depressing reading for Wales. They had travelled to Murrayfield on fifteen previous occasions with designs on the Championship, and lost every time. Form was in their favour, history wasn't. They needn't have been concerned. By half-time, their dominance was complete. Ruddock's Wales ran rings around a hapless and bewildered home side, and were 38–3 up when they returned to the dressing room. That was already more points than they'd ever scored against the Scots, and there were still forty minutes to run.

Stephen Jones: I'd been back to Clermont to play a game, so I'd been out of the bubble, but when I came back, the hype in the media was insane. They were already talking about the Grand Slam game against Ireland. We had to get past Scotland first. I'd never won at Murrayfield. Scott Johnson tapped into his psychological bag of tricks that week to help us overcome our mental demons.

Shane Williams: He came up with this speech about a Scottish lighthouse to try to inspire us. I was looking at the other boys in the room thinking, 'I hope nobody else understands what he's on about because I have not got a *clue*.' We came out of that meeting feeling very confused. I had no idea what a lighthouse had to do with beating Scotland. It was like speaking to the Riddler in *Batman*.

Stephen Jones: It was basically an iceberg theory. You see this lighthouse in the ocean, but you don't see the foundations that have been laid beneath. It was a metaphor for the Welsh team – the bit beneath the ocean was all the hard work that had gone unseen. In stormy weather, this lighthouse will get battered by waves and strong winds, but it will stay standing. He was saying that we'd have to withstand all sorts of pressure on the pitch, but like the lighthouse, we'd still be standing at the end of it all. I thought he was very clever with his motivational speeches. I wouldn't be able to do that – to get up in front of twenty-five guys, and hold their attention like he did. It was impressive. He'd been out and bought us all a keyring from the souvenir shop. I've still got it.

Martyn Williams: Stuff like that didn't resonate with me at all. I'm rubbish with things like that. It goes through one ear and out the other. He'd always lob in a curveball about something or other. Sometimes it landed, and it was brilliant, sometimes it'd leave us all scratching our heads and thinking, 'What is he on about?'

Rhys Williams: What stands out for me at Murrayfield is the bus journey. Going through the centre of Edinburgh, it was just red shirts everywhere. We could barely believe it. The buzz was incredible.

Tom Shanklin: There were a ludicrous number of Welsh shirts there that day. I'm pretty certain the Welsh fans outnumbered the Scots.

Martyn Williams: I'd been up to Murrayfield quite a few times and I'd never ever seen it like that. It was surreal. The momentum was spinning out of control. A mad, mad time. Running out, it felt like a home game.

Rhys Williams: Things clicked that day, we were scoring at a point a minute in the opening quarter. We were looking to attack from anywhere. After Ryan Jones had put us ahead, with that sensational opening try, we were defending our line for about five minutes, and struggling to get the ball back. Then the interception happened. I raced up out of the line, snaffled the ball, and pinned my ears back. I remember looking across at Chris Paterson, and thinking, 'This could be a good footrace.' But as soon as I had that thought, he slowed up and started jogging. He saw that I'd gone. When I touched down, the BBC cameras cut from me putting the ball down, to a bunch of supporters all wearing Scott Johnson masks, who just happened to all be my schoolmates from Cowbridge. It was a perfect moment.

Shane Williams: We put Scotland to the sword. Everything we did turned to gold. We had the fitness, we had the confidence, we had Rhys Williams and myself in there. That's a lot of pace and gas behind. We'd been scoring tries for fun. Offloads, angles, even Ryan Jones scored a try from thirty yards and *that* doesn't happen every day, let me tell you. When you score two or three tries, you feel like you're made of iron, like you can do *anything*, and when you're in that frame of mind, you take more risks. You *can* do that offload, you *can* throw that risky pass, you *can* try that little chip-and-chase.

Tom Shanklin: I threw one pass out the back door. I've never done that before or since, but you just felt as though anything was possible that day, that everything would go to hand. We were so relaxed.

Shane Williams: They were out on their feet after half an hour, and we punished them. We were ruthless. When you've been defending for ten minutes, the last thing you want is someone taking a quick tap. We did that, keeping the tempo up, taking quick lineouts, running everything. When you're in that frame of mind, you don't get tired, you just want the ball. Even the front row forwards were making breaks and trying to get their hands on the ball. It was *exciting*.

Tom Shanklin: I got told off at half-time for being disrespectful. Just before the whistle went, Scotland had been given a penalty. They were 38–3 down, and Gethin Jenkins and I were shouting at Dan Parks, 'Go for the posts, go for the posts!' It was a bit childish, and Mike Ruddock took me to one side and told me to show some respect.

As things happened, Wales were made to show Scotland a little respect, as they emerged in the second half a team transformed. After enjoying a glut of possession in the first half, Wales were forced to defend for much of the second. The final scoreline of 46–22 was a record for Wales against Scotland, and the ball-in-play time of forty-three minutes was the highest ever witnessed in a Test match. It was an emphatic victory, but to go from 43–3 after fifty minutes to 46–22 after eighty gave Wales plenty of pause for thought ahead of the crucial Grand Slam decider against Ireland.

Martyn Williams: They came back into it, but we'd switched off by then. Nobody wanted to get hurt because we all wanted to play in the Grand Slam game the following week. We were bollocked for taking our foot off the gas, but that's human nature, isn't it?

The Murrayfield hoodoo may have been laid to rest, but to win the Grand Slam, Wales had to rewrite history again. Cardiff was a happy hunting ground for the Irish. In a strange statistical anomaly, they'd gone twenty-two years without losing in the Welsh capital. It was the longest unbeaten run of any Championship team against another away from home. In that same period, Wales had habitually won in Ireland. Wales–Ireland was a fixture in which home advantage was a burden rather than a boost.

Martyn Williams: The coaches looked after us well that week. We flew back from Scotland the same day, because it was a six-day turnaround, and we stayed in the Vale the whole time, cocooned away from the hype and the mania. Training was fairly light because we knew all the hard work was in the bank.

Adam Jones: It was all very low-key in camp. They were keen to keep us calm. Jon Thomas and I went to Tesco the night before the game, and returned to the Vale with a car boot full of chocolate. We spent the night before Wales's biggest game for three decades slouched in the team room watching films, and stuffing ourselves with chocolate.

Tom Shanklin: There was no hiding from what was at stake. Journalists had been chucking the Grand Slam question at us since the French game, and we'd all become adept at flat-batting it. But on that day, it was unavoidable. At breakfast all the papers were laid out, and the headlines were screaming it out at us. We were being compared to the Grand Slam heroes of the seventies. The team room had to be cordoned off because the hotel lobby was full of supporters trying to get a glimpse of us.

Rhys Williams: I'd pulled my calf at around sixty-five minutes in the Scotland game and I knew it was bad. The protocol was to ice it every two hours, so I was icing it on the flight back from Edinburgh, and then getting up through the night to treat it in the build-up to the Ireland game. On the Thursday when the squad was announced, I was in it, and on that day, I tried to run for the first time. I couldn't even get out of a jog. There was no way I was going to make it, but we decided to keep it a secret. I had to pretend to warm up on the day. My replacement, Mark Taylor, hadn't played on the wing for a number of years, and we didn't want to give Ireland any time to prepare for the change.

Mike Ruddock: We didn't tell Ireland about it until the last five minutes when we had to change the teamsheet. Kevin Maggs tackled Mark Taylor about twenty minutes in, did a double take, and said, 'What the hell are you doing here?' To win a Grand Slam you've got to be able to plug the gaps when you've got injuries to key players.

Stephen Jones: Because of the way Johnno worked the backline, everyone knew their roles and responsibilities. Any player coming in would be part of a smooth transition.

Tom Shanklin: I'd said to Scott Johnson, 'I'll play on the wing, for the good of the team. Let Mark Taylor play in the centre.' But Johnno was adamant he didn't want to mess with the combinations. It was a huge ask for Mark to do what he did. I don't think he'd ever played on the wing before, and he'd only just returned from a long-term injury.

Rhys Williams: What it did allow me to do was experience the game from a different perspective. When I was 'warming up', I was actually able to look around and soak up the atmosphere far more than I would have done had I been playing.

Gareth Thomas: I was obviously on the outside looking in, and Johnno did his best to keep me involved, but I felt totally disconnected. Unless you sweat and toil, you're not part of it. The Ireland game was, for me, the 'best worst' moment ever. Any player worth his salt wants to be out there earning the right to lift the trophy. I'll always be able to say that I was part of a Grand Slam squad, but I felt like a spectator from half-time in the French game onwards. Having said that, I *always* felt a bit detached. Even when I *was* playing, I often felt like a fan who'd managed to sneak on the field without anybody realising.

Stephen Jones: What a day that was. The sun was shining, the Irish were in town in their droves. They were going for the Triple Crown, and they'd had some good results over us in recent years. They were backing themselves, but there was no way we were going to lose that game. I wasn't nervous, I was champing at the bit. I couldn't wait to get out there.

Shane Williams: It had been a long time since Wales had achieved anything big. We knew there were thousands of people watching on the big screen outside Cardiff City Hall because they couldn't get into the stadium. We were nervous, but quietly confident. The senior players stepped up and said, 'We're not winning this for the coaches, we're not doing it for the people back home, we're doing this for *ourselves*.' We'd worked so hard against England, we'd come back from the dead against France. We deserved this.

Ian Gough: I only really played a cameo role in 2005, but the atmosphere that day was incredible. I watched the Ireland game in the stadium on that amazing sunny March afternoon.

Rhys Williams: Usually you get to the Taff Bridge and the crowds begin to thicken. But on that day, the coach could barely move beyond Leckwith, three miles from the ground. I was gutted that I wasn't going to play a part. After all that build-up, I knew I desperately wanted to be on the pitch when that final whistle went, but it just wasn't to be. I'd love to have been the one on Shanks's shoulder to score that brilliant try that Kevin Morgan scored. But history is what history is.

Michael Owen: We were so relaxed during the build-up. The day before, we were just chucking the ball about, playing touch and having a laugh. We were ready to go. I didn't feel any pressure.

Martyn Williams: It's the most nervous I'd ever been. More than before Italy in the 2003 World Cup. We had a poor record against Ireland in Cardiff, and they were bringing a star-studded side over with Championship ambitions of their own.

The sense of expectation among the supporters was overwhelming. Spring had sprung in South Wales, and Cardiff was bathed in brilliant sunshine. A big screen had been erected in the civic centre, allowing those who didn't have a ticket – and weren't willing to pay the rabid touts – to watch the game. More than 200,000 fans descended on the capital, convinced that their team was about to emerge from the shadows of their illustrious forebears. But among their number was a healthy contingent of green-shirted fans, quietly confident that their boys could do the business. After all, Ireland always won in Cardiff, and if they did so again by a margin of thirteen points or more, that trophy would be heading back to Dublin.

Michael Owen: You could tell it was different, driving in. The scale of the crowd was on another level, but because there had been little in the way of expectation before the tournament, we genuinely didn't feel under that much pressure.

Martyn Williams: Because we came in the other way, we didn't see Civic Hall, and the big screen and the extra thousands of fans who'd crammed in there. We didn't appreciate the scale of it all until the Monday when we watched it back on TV.

Mike Ruddock: Reggie Corrigan said to me years later that they knew before they got to the ground they were beaten. They couldn't get through the crowd, couldn't get over the amount of Welsh people there. He'd never seen anything like it. And we fronted up really well. The forwards got stuck in, Sidoli had a bit of a wrestling match with Paul O'Connell which showed we were up for the fight. We had a bit of an edge about us up front, and we scored some great tries as well.

Shane Williams: We were on a roll, but we were aware of the calibre of player Ireland had. O'Gara, O'Driscoll, O'Connell. We had to slow the game down to win that one. It was a lot more cagey, more tactical. It was a different mindset. We were far more reserved than we'd been up to that point, which didn't suit me personally, but we did what we had to do to win. Defensively we were very good. Our line-speed was excellent, and that's what led to Melon's try.

Stephen Jones: They were wound up for it. We were expecting them to be physical, but we weren't going to bow down for anyone. There wasn't going to be a backward step taken that day, that's for sure.

Martyn Williams: They came with their usual fire and brimstone, and tried to drive every lineout like they'd done the previous year. But we were ready for it. Sid and Cobers pretty much repelled every one, and they gave up on it.

Adam Jones: They'd scored two easy tries in Dublin the year before through their driving lineout and that had seriously hurt our pride. We weren't going to let it happen again.

Shane Williams: They came to rough us up, to stop our momentum, and they definitely came to stop us from playing expansive rugby. They tried to slow the ball down, got a bit niggly in the breakdown, tried to frustrate us. It was probably the right tactic, because against Italy and Scotland that hadn't happened, and we'd run riot. They tried to put us under the pump, and at times it worked. We *were* getting frustrated, we weren't scoring tries out wide, and I wasn't getting the ball in my hands.

Martyn Williams: It got a bit feisty. Drico was wound up and stamped on Cockbain.

Tom Shanklin: The Celtic brotherhood went out the window at that point.

Martyn Williams: We'd ruffled his feathers a bit, and he was up for it. It was always our intention to target Drico. Off the first kick-off it was a case of, 'Find him, kick to him, and pile into him.' The attitude was pretty much, 'Stop O'Driscoll, stop Ireland.'

Tom Shanklin: Mark Taylor rose to the occasion. He was so solid in defence, constantly jamming in and snuffing out attackers, chopping down Denis Hickie all day long. Fair play to him for doing what he did. He's not the quickest, but he's very, very solid. And Henson was brilliant with the boot that day. He put in some monster touch-finders, kicked an important drop goal, and nailed that huge penalty from the halfway line – although he stole a few extra yards for that when the ref wasn't looking.

It was 3–3 with fifteen minutes gone, Ronan O'Gara's early penalty having been cancelled out by Gavin Henson's drop goal. The atmosphere was febrile. *The Fields of Athenry* was being sung as loudly and heartily as *Bread of Heaven*. Spirits in the crowd were soaring, but so too were the tension levels. Someone or something needed to break the deadlock. Step forward Gethin Jenkins.

Shane Williams: O'Gara had a habit of kicking through a low trajectory, and he liked to kick the ball back where it came from, as Sexton does now. We knew that was something in his game, we studied it closely. And we knew we had someone like Gethin Jenkins who runs non-stop for eighty-five minutes. He's the fittest prop I've ever seen on a rugby field. Him, Mike Phillips and 'ROG' have always had a bit of banter on the field, so you could see how special that was to Melon.

Tom Shanklin: I'd like to take the credit for that try, because I lost the ball in contact out wide. I got stripped by O'Driscoll. Sometimes that happens. You're not concentrating, or you're not holding the ball tightly enough. So he dispossessed me, and all of a sudden, O'Gara's about to kick the ball downfield. Gethin, being the player he was, charged it down and had the skill to grubber it through, and the pace to reach the line first. And then he's still not finished because he wants to chuck it at O'Gara's head. Classic Melon. He's an angry bloke. There are different ways to show emotion. Some smile, some cheer, some chuck a ball at an opponent's head.

Martyn Williams: That was pure Melon. Forget about the euphoria of scoring, just channel your anger towards ROG! He wouldn't have known him well then, because they wouldn't have toured together yet. They get on brilliantly now, but he's always been so competitive and so angry. That came at exactly the right time. It settled us down nicely.

Stephen Jones: Imagine how O'Gara must've been feeling. He's just been charged down and outpaced by a loose-head prop, and then he gets the ball thrown at his head for his troubles. Talk about adding insult to injury. Credit to Melon to get off his line and put him under pressure like that. He was a smart player. Great skills. It was a soft try for them to concede, and it put them right back on their heels.

Shane Williams: ROG didn't mind chopsing on the field, didn't mind letting the opposition know how poor he thought they were, so Melon couldn't resist a cheeky throw of the ball at him. It was Melon's way of saying, 'You can shut your face now, we've got you.' That was a huge moment. It took the wind out of O'Gara's sails.

Adam Jones: What you might not have seen was O'Gara stamping on Melon as he crossed the line. That was the reason Melon reacted. I've played with and against O'Gara. He's an angry little fucker at the best of times.

Michael Owen: Tom Shanklin can be as self-deprecating as he likes, saying he gave away the ball, but he had an *incredible* game against Brian O'Driscoll.

Tom Shanklin: Gav and I had reached a point of near telepathy by then. We'd always be anticipating the linebreak. Always running positive hard lines. A lot of that was down to Steve Hansen. I'd often run dummy lines, and Stephen Jones would either give it to me, or miss me. It's hard for a ten to make quarter-of-a-second decisions as to where the space is, but he almost always got it right. I probably made three clean linebreaks that day. We knew Ronan O'Gara was one of the weakest defenders in that backline, so we'd engineer situations where I'd be running at him. You didn't want to be running too much at Kevin Maggs or Brian O'Driscoll. You'd try and pinpoint O'Gara and Stringer.

Martyn Williams: Defensively, Shanks was a rock. He was a big strong bloke, powerful as hell, and he didn't give Drico any space to breathe. Nothing was coming down that channel.

Michael Owen: The Lions tour was around the corner, and O'Driscoll was a shoo-in for the captaincy, so what better way for Shanks to make a statement than by outplaying him in a Grand Slam decider? It inspired the rest of us to keep playing the same way, and it was his trademark break that created the second try.

Tom Shanklin: O'Driscoll still had a great game. He was a constant threat all day. I didn't run through him, I didn't run around him, he didn't miss any tackles on me. Other people missed tackles and there were holes elsewhere. It was probably my best ever game in a Wales shirt. I still think I should have got man of the match, but Brian Moore gave it to Dwayne Peel. He had a great game, but he didn't make linebreaks, did he? He didn't nail Kevin Maggs, he didn't nail Brian O'Driscoll!

Stephen Jones: Shanks was a great lead runner. He cut a great line, Kev [Morgan] tracked him, and went over for the try. He could probably have gone for the line himself, but he took the smart option. Kev bust a gut to get to him, and he got his reward for working hard.

Martyn Williams: Two Ponty boys scoring, wasn't it? Rat and Melon. Nice. Come to think of it, look at that pack – Mefin, Melon, Sid, Cockbain, myself, Michael Owen – half that side were Ponty boys originally. Good pedigree.

Michael Owen: We knew we'd won with fifteen minutes to spare. They brought David Humphreys on for Ronan O'Gara, but it felt like a last roll of the dice. We were just seeing out time by then. It was an amazing feeling.

Stephen Jones: It was a lovely situation to be able to relax in that final ten minutes. The mood we were in, and the collective spirit we had – you don't get to feel like that very often. It's very, very rare.

Martyn Williams: Every time there was a break in play during the last ten minutes, I was looking up at the clock and thinking, 'Fucking hell, come on!' We knew it was in the bag, but the clock just seemed to slow right down. Eventually, the clock ticked over, and I hoofed the ball high into the stand.

Michael Owen: I felt a huge surge of elation and relief. We'd just won our first Grand Slam in twenty-seven years, and I was captain. I kept my scrum cap on for the trophy presentation, didn't I? That was a good move. It didn't occur to me that I was picking up the trophy in front of tens of thousands in the stadium and millions watching on TV. When I saw the pictures afterwards, I was so embarrassed. It didn't fit me at the best of times, and there it was balanced on my head, half-on, half-off. I looked like a right numpty. It's all Mike Griffiths's fault – I developed a cauliflower ear after one of his ridiculous scrummaging sessions at Pontypridd, and had to wear a scrum cap until it healed up.

Tom Shanklin: We hadn't seen or heard much of the fanfare beforehand – Charlotte Church, Katherine Jenkins, the thirty thousand odd at City Hall. We didn't realise how big it was until after the match. How much it had captured people's imaginations and how much the public were behind us.

Gareth Thomas: It felt like it belonged to the nation, because we'd won it playing a typically Welsh way. All the fans were reliving the myths of Welsh rugby that our generation had never seen before. It was an amazing style of play – Welsh passion, Welsh flair. Those fans who'd not been around to witness the seventies could now say they'd seen something comparable. It felt like a renaissance.

Mike Ruddock: I was just so pleased for the Welsh public. I'd grown up thinking Grand Slams were ten-a-penny, but this generation hadn't seen one for twenty-seven years. People talk to me about coaching, but I've always said the art of coaching is overrated. The better the players, the better the coach, and those players were superb. Sometimes you actually don't do what you think you were going to do. If things are in place and working, you go with it. It's like business. If you take over a business, and the sales team is doing brilliant work, you might not agree with their strategies, but if it's working, you just let them carry on. Good coaching is often about letting players off the leash.

Michael Owen: When you're in the thick of it, it's very difficult to appreciate the magnitude of what you're doing. It's only afterwards when you reflect, that you realise that running out in front of tens of thousands of people, and enacting the dreams of your countrymen is not a normal way to earn a living.

Gareth Thomas: Seeing the boys' faces was my favourite moment. Friends of mine, like Nugget, Steve Jones, Peely – boys that had been on the front line when the flak was flying. Seeing them taking the plaudits, and drinking the champagne made it all worthwhile.

Martyn Williams: What was unique was that the families were all invited into the changing room after the game. That had never happened before, and it was special to be able to share it with our loved ones.

Adam Jones: My dad and my uncle piled in but they were more interested in getting a photo with Katherine Jenkins than celebrating with the boys. Jug Head [Ryan Jones] was roaming around looking for a TV camera as usual. Shanks was walking around naked with his bits between his legs, pretending he was a woman. But most of us were just quietly sipping on our beers, contemplating the enormity of what we'd just achieved.

Tom Shanklin: I swapped shirts with O'Driscoll without thinking things through. I look like an imposter in all the celebratory shots wearing an ill-fitting Ireland shirt, while O'Driscoll's moping around in a Grand Slam-winning Welsh shirt. Alan Phillips insisted that I put a tracksuit top over it during the official team photo with the trophy. If I'd thought about it I should have waited until afterwards to swap.

Martyn Williams: That was the only occasion when I genuinely felt like a rock star. There were hundreds of people crowding around the entrance to the Hilton where the post-match function was, so we had to sneak in through the back entrance, and wander through the kitchens in our dinner suits. It was wild. We'd never experienced anything like it before.

Tom Shanklin: The next day we were all in the Crawshays pub at the Brain's Brewery dressed to the nines and ready for a serious night out. Our captain,

Michael Owen, turned up in his full Reebok tracksuit and trainers, had two pints of Guinness and left. He was very old school. He wanted to go home and have lunch with his wife and kids. Fair play to him.

Martyn Williams: Gav was at the other end of the scale. He was absolutely steaming. It got very messy once he had a few pints inside him.

Adam Jones: He threw a glass off the top of a balcony like Begbie from *Trainspotting*. Luckily it didn't hit anyone, but that pretty much signalled the end of his night. Charlotte Church arrived shortly after to bundle him into a taxi.

Shane Williams: The celebrations rolled into Sunday. It was one of those weekends that even though you know you enjoyed it, you have no real recollection of what happened.

Michael Owen: I went to get fish and chips from Beddau on the Sunday evening, and the woman in the chip shop said excitedly, 'Did you watch the game yesterday, love?' I told her I'd seen it. 'The boys were amazing, weren't they?' 'Yeah, they done all right, aye.' I took my fish and chips and went home. Any delusions of grandeur I might have had were shattered there and then.

Martyn Williams: A three-day bender, and then Dai Young picked me to play for Cardiff on Friday night, the bastard. I was like, 'Are you for real?' Me, Shanks and Melon all played, and we were *terrible*.

Ian Gough: Ceri Sweeney didn't sober up for a month. He barely came in to the Dragons. If he did, it was with a hangover, and still wearing his going-out clothes.

Martyn Williams: I was told afterwards that I'd been voted player of the tournament, which was mad considering I'd been ruled out of contention before it had even begun. It's lovely to receive an award like that, but there were any number of contenders. Gav or Steve could easily have won it. We thought that was going to be the beginning of something special. In reality, it was the end.

Michael Owen: I'm not really one for watching games back, but we were all given a video of the troops in Afghanistan and Iraq watching that Grand Slam game. They went mental at the final whistle, and that was pretty humbling to see. But it wasn't until five or six years ago that I stumbled across the Ireland game on *ESPN Classics* and sat down to watch it properly. It felt surreal, watching myself captaining my country to a Grand Slam. I was on my own on the sofa, and I had goosebumps reliving it. It was everything I'd dreamt of as a kid.

TWENTY

HOW DO YOU GET OUSTED
WHEN YOU'VE WON A GRAND SLAM?

Those of a gambling persuasion could've cleaned up at the 2005 Six Nations. The pre-tournament odds of a Welsh Grand Slam had been 40–1. It was as unexpected as it was celebrated, which made the fallout even more difficult to take. Wales's triumph wasn't reflected in Clive Woodward's Lions squad to tour New Zealand, with just ten Welshmen making the cut in the squad of forty-four. There were twice as many Englishmen, despite their underwhelming fourth-place finish. When it came to the Tests, Woodward backed a number of his 2003 World Cup-winning squad to do the business. Gavin Henson missed out to Will Greenwood, and the Lions were subjected to a humiliating 3–0 series defeat. The following autumn, several of the Grand Slam stars were sidelined with injury. Henson, Shanklin, Peel, Gethin Jenkins, and Ryan Jones were all unavailable when the All Blacks came to Cardiff, and Wales were duly trounced 41–3. The so-called 'battle of the hemispheres', in which the champions of Europe took on the Tri-Nations champions, was a massive anti-climax. Cracks in the Wales management team began to widen. Rumours circulated that Scott Johnson – who'd never signed a contract with the WRU – was undermining Mike Ruddock from within, taking the players' side when disputes arose. Johnson's lack of contract, far from making his position vulnerable, seemed to embolden him. The cracks were papered over temporarily when Wales finished their autumn campaign with a rare victory over the Wallabies. But the end of the Ruddock era was nigh. Wales began the 2006 Six Nations with a 47–13 defeat to England, before rallying to beat Scotland. Two days later, on Valentine's Day, Mike Ruddock walked. His departure has become one of the most enduring mysteries of Welsh rugby. How on earth could the man who guided Wales to their first Grand Slam in more than a quarter of a century, be gone within a year? The reasons why are still being debated more than a decade later, as is the question of who deserved the credit for 2005's remarkable triumph.

Gareth Thomas: It was Hansen's Grand Slam, without a shadow of a doubt. I can't emphasise that enough. You ask any one of those players, and they'll tell you the same. It had *everything* to do with Steve. Nothing to do with me, or any other player – it was the outcome of what Steve had instilled in us. If he hadn't come over in 2002, that Grand Slam would never have happened.

Ian Gough: You'd have to say Scott and Steve were the ones behind the success, because they'd had that core of players for a long time, and they went through a lot together. They went through some dark times, including that loss out in Italy where Charvis was the most hated man in the world. I remember leaving the stadium, and waving to a fan who was stood by the side of the bus, and he did the wanker sign back at me. I liked Mike though, I thought he came in and controlled things well, which led to one of a number of disparaging nicknames, 'the fat controller'. Changing rooms can be cruel places.

Adam Jones: Some of the boys had started referring to him as 'the bus', because he wasn't a coach. That was out of order as far as I was concerned. He was never going to interfere unnecessarily in our attack, because Johnno had that under control. The lineouts were the domain of Sid and Brent Cockbain, but when it came to the scrum, Mike was very hands-on. He was the one that took the good elements from the previous regime, added a few extra layers, and turned us into a Championship-winning team.

Martyn Williams: The foundations were laid in 2003. You look at some of the players that were involved then – Gethin, Mefin, Cockbain, Sid, myself, Michael Owen, JT, Peely, Steve. They'd all wax lyrical over Hansen, Johnno and Horey, because we'd all learned so much from them. We were Johnno and Horey's disciples, and we were very loyal to them.

Shane Williams: It was very frustrating for me, not getting selected much under Steve. But I could see that what we achieved in 2005 was in some way down to all the work he'd put in. Wales owes him a lot.

Mark Jones: I disagree that it was all Steve. Every coach has their own style. Steve was direct, clear about what he wanted, and good at communicating that to his players. I don't claim to know as much about Mike's philosophy because I only played a short time under him, but he was much more of a hands-off coach, allowing his players and assistants to do more – and maybe that was what Wales needed at that point in time. Steve had put a lot of the groundwork in, upskilling the players and improving their mental capacity for the game. Mike came in and let them off the leash. It probably ended up being quite a good blend.

Stephen Jones: Whether it was Steve or Mike's Grand Slam is an impossible question to answer. All I know is that I'm grateful to Steve for everything he did for Welsh rugby. He broadened my horizons, and made me a better player. Even when I was first-choice for Wales, he was telling me I wasn't good enough. It would really get my back up and I'd think, 'Hang on a minute here', but he just wanted to improve my mindset. He'd say, 'What you're doing here's not good enough. Evolve. Get better.' Often the penny wouldn't drop until afterwards, and I'd think,

'He was right about that.' He wouldn't set out to ruffle feathers, but he'd hit you with the truth, and I hadn't been used to that. I had a huge amount of respect for him. Look at what he's gone on to achieve. Says it all.

Tom Shanklin: Mike wasn't technically as good. We reverted to some old-school drills, and lost some of the finer detail when he came in. That's not to say he's a bad coach, but he wasn't as forensic as Steve. He relied more on passion; 'fire in the belly, ice in the head' sort of thing. We'd become used to high standards, fine detail, and reams of video analysis. But just because Mike was different, it didn't mean I didn't like him. I thought he was a great bloke, and I've got loads of time for him. It just didn't quite work to be brutally honest. But it was his Grand Slam. The foundations may have been laid by Steve, but Mike picked the team that year, and he was in charge.

Gareth Thomas: Whenever we were training, Steve's presence still hung over us. The style of play and the way that everyone was switched into the same mindset was way more important than any crappy drills we happened to be doing.

Mike Ruddock: I heard criticism that I didn't do enough on the training field or whatever, but if it's already being done really well by one of your coaches, then let them get on with it. That's probably the way international coaching has evolved, with a delegator at the top, and a team of specialists beneath. If it's working, you'd be foolish to change it.

Ian Gough: Hansen was very hands-on, and very progressive. Ruddock was more laissez-faire, if you like. He would run some of the scrummaging sessions, but he'd leave a lot of the other stuff to the specialists. There'd be times when his assistant coaches would be running their sessions, and Mike would be sat in the car to stay out of the cold. These were little things that some of the boys picked up on and didn't like. They were used to someone being heavily involved, and Mike was more of a delegator. I could understand where they were coming from, because it was different to what they'd been used to. But what's right and what's wrong? Mike must have felt the negative vibes. He wasn't quite getting the engagement and the connection with certain players, but he wasn't completely without blame – if there was a bit of resentment, that should have been addressed early to stop it festering. Having said that, he was a confrontational guy, Mike. He wasn't afraid of confrontation. Didn't he once throw some boxing gloves at a player in Leinster, and offer him out for a fight?

Mike Ruddock: The fact I encouraged them to play with width and ambition didn't mean I always had to be on the field coaching the attack. When I took over at Worcester, the players had been told never to offload in case they made a mistake. We abandoned that immediately. My point being, I could have easily gone in and started saying, 'Don't do this, and don't do that', and encouraged a more conservative approach but that wasn't my style. Ultimately, it was a team effort. The players were fantastic, and the coaching staff made it work in the end even though there were slightly different philosophies there.

Mark Jones: At the end of the day, Mike took the job and won a Grand Slam. You don't do that by fluke.

Gareth Thomas: If he'd come in and wanted to change everything, and we'd been successful, then fine. But he understood that he was taking over a team that had gone through a transition and was in a good place, and he wanted to keep them in that place, which I think was the sign of a good coach. It showed that he wasn't driven by ego.

Rhys Williams: If Hansen had stuck around, would we still have won the Grand Slam? Yes, of course we would have.

Martyn Williams: That's a really good question, and it's impossible to answer.

Mike Ruddock: People say I'm a lucky coach. I *am* a lucky coach. It's extraordinary how lucky I've been. I won two championships with Blaina, and got the post-war try-scoring record in Cross Keys. Swansea were second from bottom when I took over, and I was very lucky to win the league with them the next year. Two years later, we won it again, and won the Welsh Cup in between. We beat Australia when they were world champions. I was lucky enough to win the Irish interprovincial title with Leinster against top coaches like Declan Kidney and Warren Gatland. I've finished top of the league four times out of seven attempts in the All Ireland League where you suffer a massive turnover of players. I've been lucky many times, but I also like to think I know a bit about the game. I'm not the best coach in the world, I'm not the worst coach in the world. I feel like I've got to defend myself a bit because a lot of people have thrown a lot of brickbats towards me. What I implemented with Wales made a difference.

Michael Owen: The idea that he was lucky is insulting. What Mike did was proof to me that he was a good guy who didn't let his ego get in the way of doing a good job. Mike was probably aware of his own limitations as a coach, recognised the good stuff that was going on, and made a decision to keep doing it.

Mike Ruddock: Clive Griffiths was very underrated. He brought the blitz back, and it didn't go down well with some of the squad and the rest of the coaching team. We were told it would never work in international rugby. It was a tough sell for us. Primarily we blitzed; we only really drifted if we were scrambling. We lost by one point to the All Blacks in 2004, because we closed them down really well. When people talk about the Grand Slam, we played great rugby, and Scott Johnson deserves huge credit for that, as does Steve Hansen for putting those structures in place. And the players that executed it deserve huge credit. But you've got to remember that we won the Grand Slam because of those last ten minutes in Paris when we repelled everything France threw at us. Ultimately it's those moments that win you Championships.

Michael Owen: The truth is somewhere in the middle. You couldn't give Hansen all the credit because we didn't have a complete game under him. Equally Mike wasn't the architect because he benefited from the foundation Hansen had laid. Hansen made a massive contribution to Welsh rugby. You look at the way we played in the 2003 World Cup, and the 2004 Six Nations. We were standing toe-to-toe to people instead of just trying to survive. It all came together under Ruddock.

Shane Williams: It definitely wasn't a case of someone forcing out Mike. I can assure you of that. I got on with him very well. I was grateful for the fact I was in the Welsh team, I was playing good rugby under his guidance, and we won a Grand Slam. Personally I didn't have a problem with him.

Gareth Thomas: I know there's a perception that there was some kind of beef between Mike Ruddock and me, but it's been blown way out of proportion. The fact was, I was very much Steve Hansen's man, and I felt a huge responsibility to the team when he left. I felt like it was up to me to keep things moving in the direction he'd taken us. It's like I was carrying the torch. I took that responsibility extremely personally and extremely seriously because I was so passionate about it.

Mark Jones: I missed the Grand Slam through injury, but when I returned to the squad in 2006, there was definitely an undercurrent between some of the players and Mike. No doubt about it. I was shocked at how transparent it was. Mike got up at the front of the bus after we'd lost the first game to England and appealed to the squad to take it easy that night. He was happy for them to have a few quiet beers, but didn't want them to go nuts. I thought that was a perfectly reasonable thing to ask. He could have *demanded* it as head coach, but he asked them politely. Quite a few players didn't take heed of that, which I was pretty disappointed with. They were senior guys who I lost a bit of respect for after that. Mike had asked them to do something in his capacity as head coach, and they'd pretty much stuck two fingers up to him. That was poor. As soon as he was off the bus, the chatter started. It was obvious there wasn't much unity in the group.

Adam Jones: It was the right call from Mike. There were some angry Welsh fans hurling abuse at the team bus as we were pulling out of Twickenham, and Alfie wanted to get out and fight them. Emotions were running high, and Mike knew he had to try to keep a lid on things.

Ian Gough: I was sad at the way it happened. He was a good guy. He'd worked brilliantly at the Dragons, cobbling together a team made up largely of rejects from other regions, and he took us to within a whisker of the title. It's easy to forget that. And the story soon became blown out of proportion, especially given the farce of Alfie's appearance on *Scrum V*, and the drama that followed. I think when Mike and the WRU agreed severance terms, he signed a non-disclosure agreement, so he never gave his side of the story, and I think that almost made things worse. He just sort of slid away.

Dafydd James: It was a mutiny. He was undermined by a number of senior players who were instrumental in his demise. No player is ever bigger than their country, and some players thought they were. It was embarrassing and it was wrong. My sympathies lay with Mike. It was horrendous how he was treated. In professional sport, whether you agree with a coach or not, you have to abide by his decisions. I had to abide by Steve Hansen, and toe the line as best I could. There should be one captain or leader of the ship. Whether you believe his training methods were right or wrong is irrelevant. He ended up being undermined, and was eventually ousted. How do you get ousted when you've just won a Grand Slam?

Shane Williams: To this day the Mike Ruddock thing is quite bizarre for us as players – the fact you're being told in a training session that your Grand Slam-winning coach has left. It happened as quickly and as strangely as that. Looking back, a lot of the training sessions and meetings *were* player-led. Colin Charvis, Stephen Jones, Martyn Williams, Gareth Thomas were all massively experienced players that had a lot to say, but there was never a period where the coach was overlooked. Gareth Thomas never said, 'Don't listen to what he says, we're gonna do this.'

Stephen Jones: The sad thing about it was that it was so messy. I was in France, and when I turned my phone on after training, I'd about sixteen missed calls from Nugget and Peely. I knew something was up. Mike had resigned. It was carnage.

Martyn Williams: It's not that the senior players didn't get on with him on a personal level. There were some who didn't think he was making enough of an impact to move us forward, but I've never known a CEO or chairman make a decision based on the opinions of players. The idea that me, Alfie, Steve and Cobers [Brent Cockbain] got rid of him is pure fantasy. We were always having meetings with Steve Lewis and David Moffett to talk through some of the money issues, about how much money we were getting paid, and I think because of that, we were the four that were accused of getting rid of Mike. *Wales on Sunday* published a photo of the four of us with the word 'guilty' underneath it after Mike went. It wasn't a nice time. My mother was diagnosed with cancer in the January of '05, and she passed in the October. She was really young, and I was really close to her, so I didn't really take much notice of the Ruddock fallout because I had bigger things on my mind.

Michael Owen: I was the type of player that always questioned my coaches, because I thought about the game a lot. I remember going to Mike with feedback from the boys, telling him about their concerns, about things we were doing they thought weren't working, and he was always open, always willing to listen.

Ian Gough: There was a loyal core of Hansen/Johnson acolytes in the squad that didn't take to Mike. I wasn't among them as I'd been in the wilderness for a few years, but there was a core group of players that remained loyal to Hansen and Johnson. It was like putting a cocktail together with the wrong ingredients, and watching it curdle. The boys had been sold a good concept, and Mike's philosophy was a different one. Some of them weren't receptive to it, and Mike was almost fighting an uphill battle from the start.

Mike Ruddock: Only one player came to me to express any dissatisfaction. And he just said he thought the preparation could be better. If there were difficulties and people had told me, perhaps we could have talked it through.

Adam Jones: Even during the Grand Slam campaign, there'd been quite a lot of sniping from certain quarters, quite a lot of sapping. 'We didn't do this with Hansen, we didn't do this with Johnno.' That sort of thing.

Stephen Jones: They had such different styles, you can't compare them. Steve had brought so many fresh ideas to the table, and with sport, you've got to evolve every year. You've got to get better. A lot of our time in the week was spent with Scott Johnson anyway. We were desperate for the union to keep Scott, or to replace him with someone with similar expertise. When you look back we were fortunate, because we had the very best. Scott wasn't putting the knife in the back because he wanted Mike's job, which is what some people suggested. It was always his plan to go back to Australia. He wasn't interested in a promotion.

Martyn Williams: Contrary to rumour I never witnessed Scott trying to undermine Mike. If he did, it certainly didn't happen in front of the players.

Gareth Thomas: There were a few of us that had been around for a while. We didn't consider ourselves any better than anyone else, but we'd had experiences and felt we could sit down and talk to coaches and other senior players about things we thought might have been going wrong. There were times when we thought we were veering off course. That senior player culture has always been there.

Shane Williams: Lively debate is essential, but there was never a chat between the lads where we said, 'We've got to get Mike out because we've got no faith in him.' He'd just won a Grand Slam. We certainly didn't feel we had the power to kick a coach out of the Welsh team, and rightly so. I'd love to find out there was some niggle behind the scenes, so I could at least make some sense of it, but I still don't know what really happened.

Stephen Jones: When we were discussing things, the big one was holding on to Scott Johnson. Do everything to keep him, and if he's made his mind up to go to Australia, get a suitable replacement in. It was a messy situation. You look back, and think would you do things differently? Yes, is the answer. Maybe I should have talked to Mike more. I'm sad that it ended like it did. We're grateful for what he did. There are no hard feelings whatsoever.

Dafydd James: Because Scott Johnson had that bond with the players, they were more likely to side with him. I liked Scott Johnson, don't get me wrong. He was an innovative coach, and a colourful character, but he ran with the foxes and the hounds.

Rhys Williams: I never saw that side to him. He was always straight with me.

Mark Jones: Me neither, I never saw him openly try to drive a wedge between Mike and the players. He was an excellent coach. Difficult to understand sometimes, because he talked in riddles. I learned an awful lot from him, once I'd deciphered what he was trying to tell me. I never saw Scott undermining Mike, like a lot of people have suggested. His strengths were relating to players, and helping them improve, and for that reason he was probably always going to be a better assistant than a head coach. As a head coach, you can't get that close with the players because at some point, you're going to need to make some tough calls.

Adam Jones: I wasn't team Mike, or team Johnno. I was just a member of the squad. Johnno definitely had his disciples, most of them backs like Stephen Jones and Dwayne Peel, but there was never anything cliquey about it. They just enjoyed working with him and could see how much he'd brought their game on. The idea that Johnno was some kind of sinister puppet-master whispering in people's ears and trying to instigate a coup sounds pretty far-fetched to me.

Gareth Thomas: Johnno was someone who the players hugely trusted, and he'd never betray that trust. He was the bridge from Shags to Mike because he was still there. There were things we were doing with Mike that were different, and there were times when Scott would question it, but it was all very diplomatic. What people who've never played professional sport don't understand is that I could be standing between Scott and Mike, and we could have a full-on heated argument about something we truly believed in, but it wouldn't affect our working relationship. I'm the type of person who'll argue my hind leg off if I believe I'm right, but if I'm persuaded to see a different side, then that's fine. Arguments are great, but you've got to be prepared to lose, and not lose face. People on the outside can't comprehend that you can have an argument and not end up hating that person. I'd have arguments with Nugget from time to time, but I'd always respect the shit out of him. I've had arguments with every player or coach I've played with, because I care. If I didn't I wouldn't have played for Wales once, let alone a hundred times.

Adam Jones: I preferred Mike to Steve Hansen. People may say that's no surprise, because Mike picked me regularly, didn't sub me off after half an hour, and treated me with a bit of respect. But I thought he was a better man-manager. He was just a straight up-and-down bloke.

Stephen Jones: Maybe there was a clash of personalities, I don't know. It's a shame people's opinions have been clouded. I don't know the truth of what went on with his contract negotiations. Did Mike think we as players had gone against him? I don't know. The 2005 season was such a wonderful memory and he was at the helm in fairness to him. He picked those teams, and organised the working week.

Mike Ruddock: The other coaches weren't to know what made me tick. I won't say we were thrown together, that's just the way it happened. It *was* difficult for us all to gel. These days the coach has the luxury of bringing in his own team. It's not a case of bagging anyone. Perhaps it was a watershed thing – people now realise if you want to give a head coach the chance to coach, perhaps he needs to do it with people of a similar philosophy, you know? I hate having to talk about it fifteen years later. It wasn't the Hollywood drama people liked to make it out to be.

Tom Shanklin: There *were* issues between Mike and Alfie. Arguments about what was best for the team. Maybe a lack of respect on both sides.

Gareth Thomas: All these rumours started circulating about clandestine meetings behind Mike's back. Fucking classic Welsh shit-stirring. I was playing in France at the time, which was probably the best place I could have been. Out of the bubble. Even now, looking back all these years later, I'm embarrassed for the Welsh Rugby Union, I'm embarrassed for Mike, I'm embarrassed for the press. It was an absolute fucking joke. The story was the first headline on the news for a week in Wales. Surely there were more important things going on in the world? The only thing that really upset me, was that Mike wouldn't actually talk. He kept very quiet about it. While that whole war was being waged, it was the people that spoke out that laid themselves open to attack. He was innocent in his silence.

Michael Owen: When I was appointed captain in the middle of the 2005 campaign after Alfie got injured, it was the best job in the world. Everyone was nice as pie, and it was all positive. Then when Mike left, it wasn't quite the same. I was in front of the world's media at the age of twenty-four, dealing with this whole farce, and I didn't have the confidence. I was fielding all these questions about player power, and I didn't know what to say.

Mike Ruddock: The crux of it all was the contract dispute. The other stuff – any coach has to deal with matters like that anyway. That was just a sideshow.

Michael Owen: Once Mike's departure had been confirmed, Scott Johnson faced the press before me, and was asked if he'd spoken to Mike. He said no. I was then asked the same question, and I felt compromised. I *had* spoken to him, but I didn't want to admit that because it would look as though I was taking sides. I said that I hadn't, and I just think it made me look more guilty. The truth was that Mike had called me and told me it had been a pleasure working with me. He insisted that it was a contractual dispute that forced him out, that it wasn't about player power.

Gavin Henson's controversial autobiography, which had been released in 2004, had caused a bit of unrest within the camp and on the day of the opening Six Nations game against England, the ghost-writer, Graham Thomas, had written an article in the match programme. It praised Henson's willingness to speak candidly at a time when other players trotted out bland platitudes. It didn't go down well with some of the players, and when Thomas appeared at the next press conference before the Scotland game, Gareth Thomas walked out. Despite pleas from Ruddock for him to return, he refused, saying he was acting out of solidarity towards the rest of the squad. Michael Owen was asked to deputise for him, and he too refused, leaving Ruddock to face the press on his own. It was an appropriate image for his increasing sense of isolation.

Martyn Williams: Alfie and Mike Ruddock had fallen out by this stage. I don't think that was a big secret.

Michael Owen: I know Alfie didn't go and speak in the press conference because of Graham Thomas. I was caught between a rock and a hard place. I didn't want to go against what Alfie had decided, because that seemed like the wrong thing to do.

At that stage, there were definitely some players questioning Mike and disagreeing with some of his methods, but I'd been communicating that to him. Questioning the coach is part of being a good player as far as I'm concerned. I did the same with Lynn Howells at Pontypridd. There were never any clandestine meetings with the WRU insisting that he had to go, because none of the players would ever have done that. They didn't have the power to do that. That was just a big conspiracy theory. I can understand it from the Welsh public's perspective though. We'd just won the Grand Slam, and then this happened. It was rubbish really.

Gareth Thomas: We'd called a meeting about Gareth Cooper suffering a shoulder injury against England. We wanted clarification that he, and the rest of us, were fully insured in the event of a serious injury. We took a stand, refusing to play until Coops's situation was sorted. We met Steve Lewis to discuss it, and that must've fed the conspiracy theory. It leaked out and people assumed we were meeting about something else.

Both Thomas and Martyn Williams admitted in their autobiographies that the subject of Ruddock's coaching had come up during this meeting with Steve Lewis, but that it was an incidental conversation and hadn't been on the agenda beforehand. Both players denied that they were agitating for Ruddock to be shown the door. Williams and Thomas were Hansen acolytes, and were concerned that the nucleus of that coaching ticket had been slowly eroded. By this point, Andrew Hore had moved on, and Scott Johnson was pondering a return to Australia. It was as much about trying to persuade Johnson to stay as it was undermining Ruddock. Johnson famously never signed a contract, saying his word was his bond. It meant that his presence was always a nebulous one, and those who rated him worried that he'd disappear in a proverbial puff of smoke.

Ian Gough: I went into the barn one day, and I think it was Nugget who told me, 'The shit's hit the fan again. Ruddock's walked.' I remember thinking, 'Oh, no', because I'd only just got myself back into the reckoning. I was on a decent run, and it all went tits-up again. Alfie famously went on *Scrum V* and went up against Eddie Butler, and the whole situation descended into utter farce.

Gareth Thomas: All I know is that Mike had asked for a new contract. Toulouse were playing in Narbonne the day before my infamous *Scrum V* appearance, and I rang Mike on Saturday morning and told him I'd be going on *Scrum V* to deal with this shit. To tell them it's not this player power thing. I asked if I had his support. He told me, yes, I fully had his support, so I asked him for a favour. I asked him to put that in writing, and send it in to the BBC, so I could produce it on the show. Just a sentence explaining he hadn't left because of player power, he'd left because of a contract dispute with the Welsh Rugby Union. He said, 'Yeah, that's fine.' So I get to the BBC, and meet Rupert Moon at the door who was working for the WRU at the time. I wasn't really briefed on anything before heading into the studio, where I asked if anything had come from Mike. Nothing had, but that was okay, because Mike was kind-of on our side anyway. Just as we were about to go live on air, the presenter, Gareth Lewis, said 'Mate, I just want to say I'm sorry for what's about to happen,' and then boom, we went live. The shitfest unfolded.

Rhys Williams: That was the worst thing I'd ever watched on telly. I was cringing. Alfie was an amazing captain. It was, 'I'm Gareth Thomas, I am who I am, and this is how I'm going to lead.' Your stereotypical captain may have been a bit more of a yes-man, someone who'd toe the line, and say the right thing in press conferences, but he was Alfie.

Gareth Thomas: I felt like I'd been pushed into a corner and had to come out fighting. The alternative was to cower away. But this fucking nation that I passionately love, and will always love, and have always given everything to, was the *reason* I was in the fucking corner.

Adam Jones: I love Alfie to bits, but he shouldn't have gone on the programme. He was too emotional, too passionate, and he came across like he had something to hide. Eddie Butler was too smart to lose the argument, and Alfie lost his cool. The Welsh public were fuming about what had happened and wanted to point the finger of blame at someone.

Gareth Thomas: I tried to get hold of Mike after to ask why he hadn't sent the letter in, but I couldn't get through. To this day, I've never spoken to him. I don't hold a grudge. I'd cross the road to speak to him if I saw him, but I'd ask him flat out, 'Why did you leave me that day? I was your captain. Why did you leave me and hang me out to dry? If it had been you being interviewed on TV that day, I wouldn't have just *sent* the fucking letter, I'd have been by your side.' Thumper rang my mate Compo, and asked him to tell me I'd done a really good job. I was like, 'A good job of what? Where were you then? Why weren't you sitting next to me? Why wasn't I prepped on anything?' I was living in France, I'd come to the UK that day, I didn't know that much about the story, all I'd heard was what my mother and father had decided to tell me, which was very selective. I was aware of some of the conspiracy theories about player power, but I assumed everybody knew Mike had left because of a dispute over his contract. I learned a lot about the Welsh Rugby Union that day. I also learned a lot about me.

One of my biggest downfalls is that I care too much. I felt it was my duty to go on there and represent the players, but I also realised that day that they are my second family. My first family are the ones that I really need to look out for.

Dafydd James: I can't fathom it. You had Alf going on telly. That whole episode was horrendous. He got all defensive, and started freaking out, and then he had a fit afterwards.

Gareth Thomas: It was a mini-stroke. I'd been knocked out playing for Toulouse a few weeks earlier and had bruised an artery, so it was that, in combination with the stress I'd been under. It happened when I got back to the house. I was sitting with my mother, when my left side went all numb, and I collapsed. They called an ambulance. The paramedics knew who I was, but they hadn't seen the show, so I had to explain what had happened. I had an ECG at the hospital, and was told nothing was untoward. They said it may have been a severe migraine. It was when I went to BUPA later on that they told me it was a mini-stroke. The following Saturday, a group of my mates were in a pub in Cardiff watching the Italy game, and I'd gone there to work for the BBC. I came on the telly, and a nurse who'd been at the hospital when I was admitted stood up and addressed the crowd in the pub saying, 'He didn't have a stroke, it was a bloody migraine, I was there in the hospital when he came in.' It was all to do with the whole bloody Ruddock thing. The nation had divided into for and against camps. My mother found out and was fuming, because she used to work in the hospital and she understood the confidentiality thing. It really hit home then – some people like you, some people absolutely hate you. You can't please everyone. It was something I knew I'd have to learn to live with.

Mike Ruddock: I switched the TV off and didn't read the newspapers for a couple of weeks.

Mark Jones: I did feel for Mike. I think whilst you're there with the Wales team, it's your job to do the best you can regardless of whether you agree with everything the coach says. There were certain players who didn't do that.

Martyn Williams: As far as I was aware, Mike was on less money than Graham Henry and Steve Hansen had been. Given that he'd won a Grand Slam, you could understand him wanting to be rewarded for that.

Mike Ruddock: People are still looking for something that didn't actually exist. The reality was, I accepted the job while I was still Dragons coach, so I literally hopped over the week before the Argentina tour. I was handed a contract about 500 pages long, and it had different sections with different typefaces so it had clearly been cut and pasted. I'm no lawyer, but I read it and didn't think it made a huge amount of sense, so I gave it to my solicitor, Tim Jones. I went on tour, did the November Tests, and won the Grand Slam, before the contract had ever been signed off. I was asked by Steve Lewis after the Grand Slam to consider a new contract. We talked about the financials and got that sorted very quickly. That was never an issue. But there was a lag then between that being put together, and it being finalised between myself, Steve, my solicitor and their solicitors. For the life of me I don't know why. The things we asked to look into were insignificant as far as I was concerned. Things like insurance – if you were away on tour and the scrum machine fell on your leg for example, were you covered? Another was that I'd asked for an international ticket post-contract, in the same way that an international player gets one. We'd delivered a Grand Slam, and it would be nice if in the future I could go and sit in the stadium and enjoy watching Wales play. Things were just never nailed down, there was no sign of this thing being finalised, more than six months later, and towards the end of January 2006, on the eve of the Six Nations, I had a letter from the WRU saying they'd withdrawn from contract negotiations. The wording was along the lines that the proposals we'd put forward wouldn't be accepted. It advised that I should just concentrate on the Six Nations, and we'd look at it again after the tournament – which was hardly a confidence booster for any coach going into a Six Nations.

I took that letter I'd received on the eve of the Six Nations as a vote of no confidence. We'd been at this 'contract negotiation' since the summer of 2005. During my time as Wales's national coach I'd never signed a contract. I went into that Six Nations very disillusioned, as you can imagine. I started to get some feedback that things weren't overly happy in the camp with some of the players. There was some friction in the coaching team, and it wasn't really an enjoyable place to be. So I tendered my resignation, and told them I wanted to move on at the end of the campaign. Instead, I was asked to stand down with immediate effect. It was simple as that. I accept that there were all sorts of rumours going round, but that's the reality. It's one thing having to deal with some difficult dynamics in your environment, things that make it less enjoyable. But when it appears that your employer doesn't want you it's difficult. My time with Wales always felt transient.

Gareth Thomas: I can't separate the euphoria of winning from what followed. The picture changed after that. I'd gone from being a guy who just wanted to be known for playing rugby, to this figurehead, this politician, this panto villain. It didn't feel like just a game anymore. It opened my eyes to a dimension I didn't want to see. Battles with the press, public mud-slinging. There was a bad smell after that that lingered for some time. It put a stain on everything. I don't think anybody really wants to know the truth. They want it to remain this big conspiracy. Whenever I go to a rugby club, I get asked about it. I'm bored shitless of it; it does my nut in. Ultimately though, I'll never lose the bonds I had with *all* my coaches, and I include Mike in that. Those bonds will endure beyond something as petty as this. Whether I've agreed or disagreed with them, liked or disliked them, they've all been my coaches. I still talk to Allan Lewis about rugby now. He's my hero. He doesn't coach anymore, and I don't play anymore, but when it comes to rugby I still speak to him as if he's my coach, and I hang on his every word. I'd like to think I'd still have that with Mike, and I'd like to think he'd feel the same about me.

Shane Williams: I still speak to Mike, we've met up a couple of times since. He hasn't got a problem with me, and I don't have a problem with him. Perhaps what he did was very unselfish and very noble.

Mike Ruddock: I'm proud of 2005 because I did what I set out to do – improve the scrum by selecting different combinations, tighten up the defence and maintain the excellent attack – but I can't say it was an enjoyable time because I was always aware that I didn't have a signed contract. For any coach, that's not a nice thing. It puts you in a disadvantaged position in terms of the power you're able to exert on the environment, to shape what you want to shape. It also makes you feel unwanted. It was a tricky time for me. I've never watched those games back. It's not a reflection of the team as they played superbly, I just can't look back too fondly on that period, unfortunately. It wasn't great having TV cameras outside my house the morning after my resignation when my kids were trying to go to school. It was tough on my family. My kids and my wife were constantly being asked, 'What did he do, then?' It was such a mess. It doesn't do me good to reminisce. I don't have a smile on my face when I remember those days. I felt isolated and pretty depressed for some time afterwards.

TWENTY-ONE

GARETH JENKINS DESERVED BETTER

Scott Johnson's caretaker role lasted until the end of the 2006 Six Nations, and he left without a win. Under his stewardship, Wales lost to Ireland and France, and drew with Italy, confirming the suspicions of many that Johnson was not cut out to be a number one. The vacancy was filled by Gareth Jenkins, the man who'd lost out to Ruddock two years earlier. While Gareth's pedigree was unquestioned, and his knowledge unrivalled, his regime lacked some of the rigorous attention to detail of his predecessors. An autumn campaign that began promisingly with a 29–29 draw against Australia, ended in another thumping by the All Blacks.

Jenkins' first and, as it turned out, only Six Nations was a disappointing one. Early defeats to Ireland and Scotland put Wales on the back foot. The Scotland game was particularly farcical, with Rob Sidoli playing in what Adam Jones referred to as 'clown shoes' after his prototype Reeboks came away from their soles, hampering his ability to jump in the lineout, or establish any grip in the scrums. A number of fans wrote angry letters to the WRU in the wake of the defeat, having seen a number of Welsh players out drinking that evening. A small band of supporters made their point by collectively turning their backs on the Welsh squad when they arrived en masse at Edinburgh Airport the following morning. Defeat to eventual champions, France, was by a more respectable margin, but disaster struck in round four when Wales lost in Rome again. For the final match against England, James Hook started at fly half in place of the injured Stephen Jones, and turned in a virtuoso performance, guiding Wales to a morale-boosting 27–18 victory.

A tour to Australia followed during which Wales came close to a victory in the opening Test, before capitulating in the second, losing 31–0. It was not a good portent considering the Wallabies were in Wales's World Cup group later that year. If Wales needed an excuse, they'd rested a strong core of their first-choice players with the World Cup in mind. Jenkins did something similar for the first World Cup warm-up game against England at Twickenham, giving a number of fringe players a run out. It backfired spectacularly. An experimental England battered Wales all over the park, scoring nine tries and ratcheting up a record score. When the final whistle blew, the Welsh fans could barely bring themselves to look at the scoreboard, which bore the grisly legend 'England 62 Wales 5'.

Gareth Thomas: Gareth was a bit loose in what he allowed us to do. That was his style. Shags was very strict, so was Graham Henry. 'Gyppo' was more like one of the boys. Things were nowhere near as professional. Standards started to slip, discipline became a bit lax, and there was no one in the management group who was willing to crack the whip.

Tom Shanklin: With him and Rowland Phillips [defence coach], you had two comedians. They were so much fun to be around. We'd never laughed so much, but the flipside was that they weren't strict enough with us. I was twenty-six, twenty-seven, and still quite immature. When you're that age, you're always testing boundaries, seeing what you can get away with. They were happy to keep us on a long leash, and they weren't as professional as we were used to.

Stephen Jones: Gareth Jenkins is a brilliant man, but it's about the whole package, isn't it? The support staff in place, it's not just about one man. He was surrounded by inexperienced coaches and wasn't given the chance to make a decent fist of it.

Tom Shanklin: He had a terrible short-term memory. He'd forget people's names all the time. I did a press conference with him once and he kept calling me Jim.

Gareth Thomas: The build-up to the 2007 World Cup wasn't particularly encouraging.

Tom Shanklin: Gareth Thomas and I played in the centre through all the warm-up games bar one when I was resting my knee. Then the first game up against Canada, we weren't selected together. Alfie, who was squad captain, was picked on the bench. It just seemed a bit muddled, a bit strange. I'm not sure there was a coherent strategy.

Martyn Williams: That was how chaotic it was. There was a big debate about who was going to be captain. He wasn't really sure, but he went with Alfie. Then in the first game, Peely was captain, and he'd never been captain before. Everyone was like, 'What the fuck's that about?' Peely didn't have a clue he was going to be captain. It was absolute chaos.

Mark Jones: It was a busy week for Peely. He'd been testing our patience at times with his constant pranking. He used to put bikes and baked beans in people's beds. We were staying in a chalet complex in Pornichet, and there was a family of sheep there to eat the weeds and the grass. One was quite friendly, but he could be a bit nasty as well. I asked the owner if I could have a lend of him, and he told me I was welcome if I could catch him. That was a bit of a challenge, but being a farmer's son, I managed it, and put him in Peely's room while he was doing a press conference. The conference ran on, and Peely got delayed. The sheep was only meant to be in there twenty minutes, but he ended up being in there for two hours. By the time Peely got back it had shat everywhere – all over his bed, on the floor, it had chewed some of the bedding and he *claimed* it chewed his brand-new watch. I'm not so sure about that. I'd arranged for the S4C TV crew to film him going back to his room, as though it was a guided tour of the complex. He was tamping! We then had a screening of the video in the team room later. It was pure gold dust – and it was the gift that kept on giving because we found out afterwards that the sheep had fleas, so Peely was itching and scratching for days. He never pranked me again.

Stephen Jones: I came on against Canada, but my first full game was against Australia in Cardiff, which was bizarre. You're in a World Cup in France, and you have to come back to Cardiff to play. We lost fairly comfortably.

Gareth Thomas: Because we'd lost to Australia, Fiji was essentially a knockout game. I could feel the tension among the players, and sometimes as a captain you hold the responsibility for creating an atmosphere. Often it's as much about bringing some humour as it is about firing people up. That day I felt as though I needed to relieve some tension. Changing rooms can quickly go from a place of relaxation, to a place of unbearable intensity. Everyone felt under enormous pressure.

Tom Shanklin: It was Alfie's hundredth game for Wales, and he'd had these special boots made, with '100' embroidered into them. He gathered us together in the huddle, and locked us all with his steely gaze. He knew we were feeling nervous, knew we were feeling the weight of expectation. And fair play to him, he was normally brilliant in those circumstances, he could always read the mood. He was a real leader. So he pulled us all together and in a solemn voice he said, 'Boys, I know what you're thinking,' then he left this dramatic pause, and allowed his gaze to wander over each of us. We were all waiting for the inspiring speech he was about to deliver. Then slowly, he lifted up his leg, pointed to his special boots, and in this exaggeratedly camp voice, he goes, '*Fuckin' luussh*!'

Stephen Jones: We felt really good with the ball that day, but defensively, we were dreadful, just dreadful.

Martyn Williams: We were dritzing again. We were all over the place, leaving gaps everywhere.

Stephen Jones: What did they score against us? Thirty-eight? If you concede thirty-eight points, then you've got no right to win. Yes, they had good footwork and were good athletes, but there was no excuse for conceding that amount. I remember our training team carving us up on the Tuesday and the Thursday, so the warning signs were there in advance. There were obviously flaws in our game.

Tom Shanklin: There was a bit of confusion over the application of the blitz defence again. It was the right thing to do to try to implement it, but we couldn't grasp it as a team. We had people calling for a blitz when they weren't in a position to call it. You can't call blitz from a ruck, for example. You have to call it from out wide where you have a better view.

Stephen Jones: If you're scoring thirty-four points, you're doing something right with the ball, but to concede thirty-eight – unless they're all from interceptions or loose play, there's clearly an issue with your structure. Or your commitment. If a team like Fiji is working you through phases, and scoring that amount of points, something's not right, is it? We should have won comfortably with the talent we had. Fifty per cent of our game was decent that day, fifty per cent was poor. That's how I'd sum it up.

Mark Jones: Fitness-wise, in terms of strength, speed, and skills, it's the most prepared I'd ever been going into an international tournament. There was a good harmony in the squad, everyone was pulling in the right direction. We just got it wrong in one game.

Ian Gough: We got ahead of ourselves. On the day of the game, we were given the sheet for the following day which had our travel itinerary for Marseille and a quarter-final against South Africa. We took our eyes off the ball, and got sucked into their way of playing. We'd had a belting night on the piss in Paris the week before that which probably didn't help. We'd been to Longchamps racecourse and had one of the best days ever. In retrospect, the week before a crunch game in the World Cup probably wasn't the best time to have one of the biggest booze-ups of your lives. But we'd been misfiring going into that game. We'd had a close game against Canada, and lost to Australia, before beating Japan.

Martyn Williams: The night out got a bit messy but it didn't cost us the game. We should still have won.

Tom Shanklin: We'd been staying in a hotel where there was literally *nothing* to do. Alan Phillips had been out for a recce in the summer, when it was packed and really lively, but when we arrived in the autumn, it was *dead*. The whole town had shut down, and we were miles from anywhere. You can't use the surroundings as an excuse, but it didn't help. Morale was low.

Martyn Williams: It was a massive cock-up. There was nothing there. The environment wasn't great at all. The most exciting thing you could do as a team was go and have a pancake or something.

Tom Shanklin: So if you're told you can go out to Paris for the day, you're not going to say no, are you? It was a phenomenal trip. I look back on that as one of the best days we'd ever had as a squad. Had we beaten Fiji, no one would be talking about it, but people always want to find a reason, don't they? When we went to the World Cup in Australia in 2003, we went diving with sharks, we went surfing in Manly Bay, and we all bonded as a result. In 2007, we spent half the time in the Vale of Glamorgan, and the other half in some dead one-horse town in France. It didn't really feel like a World Cup, so we *needed* that Paris trip. We wanted to do something *different*, something *French*. We went to Lido afterwards, to a cabaret show, and I'm not sure we fitted in entirely. People kept telling us to 'sshh', because we stayed by the bar throughout acting like typical Welsh boys on tour. Half of us were dressed properly with blazers and shirts, the rest were way too casual. Ian Evans had a yellow sequinned t-shirt on. There'd be a quiet part of the show, and you'd hear Ianto [Ian Evans] go, 'Five sambucas please, butt,' at the top of his voice, as a row of angry faces turned round in unison. We met the dancing girls after the show, and Colin Charvis – thinking he was all sophisticated – tried to speak to them in French. One of them turned round and said, in a broad Yorkshire accent, 'We're from Leeds, luv.'

Mark Jones: We got lured into too loose a game. We scored thirty-four points, and we lost. You shouldn't be scoring thirty-four points in an international game and end up losing. I didn't feel that was a fair reflection of the players and the coaching group at that time.

Tom Shanklin: We'd had decent wins against Canada and Japan. Yes, we'd lost against Australia in Cardiff without offering much, but we weren't in too bad shape going into the Fiji game.

Ian Gough: We gave Fiji gaps, allowed them room, and they came alive. I thought Martyn had won it for us with that cracking try just before the end, but then they scored at the death. The final whistle went, and the realisation dawned that we were in a world of shit. Another World Cup we'd bombed out of before the knockout stages.

Tom Shanklin: We weren't very good at defending their pick and go. They scored a lot of tries from that, which was actually quite un-Fijian. We gave them way too much space. We had so many opportunities to put it to bed. I made a break off Stephen Jones, and should have given the ball to Mark Jones earlier. I gave it to him too late, and we didn't score. Martyn Williams went over for that intercept try and we thought Fiji would fold.

Martyn Williams: We thought we'd done it then, thought we'd dug ourselves out of a massive hole.

Tom Shanklin: But they refused to roll over. Delasau scored that freak try when the ball bounced backwards over the heads of Mark Jones and Gareth Thomas. The gods were smiling on them that day. That try would never be scored again in a million years.

Martyn Williams: They had some magnificent players. Delasau, Rabeni, Little. They were just awesome that day. It's easy to say we were sucked into an open game, and to ask why didn't we target them at the scrum? But it's not as simple as that. Sometimes there just aren't many scrums in a game. Every time we did have a scrum, we destroyed them, but they were few and far between. You can't just knock the ball on on purpose to get a scrum.

Gareth Thomas: I maintain that virtually no team in the world outside of the top three would have beaten Fiji that day. They were phenomenal. I realise we're a bigger rugby nation, and we're expected to beat Fiji every time we play them, but I had to tip my hat and say, 'It may have been my last game for Wales, and my hundredth cap, but I wouldn't want to take that win away from you. You fucking deserved it, so it's yours to have.' Everybody who played knew Fiji were the better team, and anything that's been said about it afterwards is irrelevant. In rugby, the team that deserves to win should win, and that's how it'll always be.

Martyn Williams: We've got to take a lot of responsibility as players. Gyppo was a great man, and we let him down. Defensively we were disorganised, and as a group we just didn't click. We had some bloody good players there who'd go on to win a Grand Slam a few months later, but at that time we were far too loose and chaotic.

Michael Owen: If Wales had won that, who knows what might have happened? Fiji nearly beat South Africa, who went on to win the whole thing.

Tom Shanklin: I've never been as disappointed at the end of a game as I was that day. The changing room was like a morgue. We'd had a poor Six Nations, where we'd only beaten England, and to prove we were a better team than that, we had to at least get through to the knockout stages. It didn't happen.

Mark Jones: Ultimately, Gareth Jenkins had said, 'Judge me on the World Cup.' We didn't win that key game, and he had to fall on his sword. I felt for him, he was a hell of a good coach, and a great man-manager, and an honourable man. The best in the business.

Tom Shanklin: He was a brilliant bloke. He was universally loved, and had a great rapport with the players, but maybe he was a man out of time.

Martyn Williams: He probably got the job ten years too late.

Dafydd James: He was poorly treated. We've got a way of doing things in Wales, and it's often the wrong way. The way he was dismissed was a joke.

Martyn Williams: The day after we lost was horrible. We had a meeting that morning where Roger Lewis stood up and told us he was sacking Gareth. He was always going to lose his job, but they could have waited, couldn't they?

Ian Gough: He was a good guy, a passionate guy, but he got it wrong. Yes, we'd failed to get out of the group, but the way it ended was cruel. In the team room in Pornichet, he'd given an impassioned speech about not giving up, wanting to carry on. And then the next morning, he was sacked.

Martyn Williams: I rang the missus straight after and said, 'Book us a holiday. Anywhere.' I didn't want to hang around in Wales any longer than I needed to, because I knew how ugly the backlash was going to be. I wanted to get the hell outta Dodge. When we landed in Cardiff, there were a load of Welsh fans there waiting to fly out to Marseille to watch us in the quarter-finals! I pretty much stepped off one plane and onto another.

Tom Shanklin: Gareth was so harshly treated, and what made it worse was the manner in which he left. We arrived back at the Vale hotel, and he asked to get off the bus before we reached the entrance. He didn't want to deal with the press, so he walked to the front of the bus, said, 'Boys, it's been emotional,' and disappeared down the steps. Our last image of him was of this solitary figure, shoulders hunched, walking down a country lane on his own with a bag of duty free. We all felt for him.

Ian Gough: Cigarettes and booze. He cut a pretty forlorn figure as he walked away on his own in his cream suit. We all liked him, and it felt really sad.

Dafydd James: No one deserved to be treated like that. No one goes out to lose, no one goes out to mess things up. Everybody deserves a bit of respect.

Stephen Jones: You can make that decision a couple of weeks later when the guy's in his own home. There was a real lack of respect, and if you ask most of the boys they'd say the same. Seeing him walk off the bus felt plain wrong. It was so unpleasant to witness. This was a man who'd given his life, heart and soul to Welsh rugby, and he was just cast aside. What were the learnings from it?

Mark Jones: He was never given the credit he deserved. He did a hell of a lot of work behind the scenes. He completely remodelled the analysis department, he was committed to developing Welsh coaches, he brought in Robin McBryde and Neil Jenkins straight out of their playing careers. He wanted to bring in Mike Ford who he'd worked with on the Lions tour, but the WRU wouldn't sanction that, so he had to turn to less experienced coaches like Nigel Davies and Rowland Phillips. Those guys were learning international rugby on the job. Nigel had only ever worked at the Scarlets, and Rowland was coaching in the Premiership at the time. Gareth, for the right reasons, was trying to develop a Welsh ethos, but perhaps it needed some outside influence in there as well. I wouldn't say, as others have, that Gareth was a man out of time. He wasn't a stupid guy, he understood rugby inside-out. In terms of looking holistically at the rugby programme, forging a team dynamic, figuring out what you need rugby-wise and style-wise, he was excellent.

Adam Jones: The assumption that Gareth Jenkins wasn't as sophisticated in his methods as a Steve Hansen or a Graham Henry was a lazy one. He may have been looser in his approach to discipline, but his attention to detail, his rugby knowledge, and coaching ability was as good as anyone's. The players were as much to blame for any failing as he was.

Ian Gough: Nigel Davies took over for the one game against South Africa after that, and I was dropped. Not that Duncan Jones knew. He phoned me the day before a squad session, and asked if I wanted a lift to Tenby. I said, 'Ordinarily, I'd take you up on that, Dunc. But I haven't been picked.' He was mortified. A week later, we got smashed by South Africa.

At the end of his tenure, Jenkins could look back on a win ratio of six games from twenty. Whether that was a fair reflection of his abilities or not, it wasn't good enough for a union that had celebrated a Grand Slam two years earlier. The WRU was about to begin its search for its thirteenth coach in nineteen years. Any potential candidates would have understandably paused before choosing to swig from an increasingly poisoned chalice. Wales's early exit from the World Cup gave the WRU a head start on other nations looking for a change at the top. The chief executive, Roger Lewis, flew to New Zealand with Gerald Davies and David Pickering to sound out a number of candidates. John Mitchell, Robbie Deans, and Steve Hansen were all in the mix. Jake White – whose South Africa were about to lift the World Cup for a second time – was also a target. But the man who was eventually anointed was Warren Gatland – the former Ireland coach who'd enjoyed considerable success with Wasps, before returning to his native Waikato. Conscious that any incomer would be wary of Wales's revolving-door policy, the WRU offered him a four-year contract that made him one of the highest-paid coaches in world rugby. His predecessors, Mike Ruddock and Gareth Jenkins, had been offered two years each. A Kiwi accent, it seemed, carried more weight than a native Welsh one.

TWENTY-TWO

WARREN GATLAND – HE MAKES YOU FEEL INVINCIBLE

Tom Shanklin: Everyone liked Warren Gatland straight away. He had that Steve Hansen vibe – a commanding sense of authority. It came through in the way he spoke. He was very specific about what he wanted, there were no grey areas, and in those early days he didn't bend when senior players questioned things. That's just what we needed after Mike Ruddock and Gareth Jenkins. A bit of structure, a bit of purpose.

Ian Evans: At the first ever squad meeting, he stood up and said, 'This is what we'll be doing. It works. And if you're not willing to jump on the train, you won't be playing in my team.' If you weren't willing to toe the line, you weren't going to be a part of their plans. They set the fear factor high, and we hadn't been used to that. Previous regimes had encouraged the players to speak their minds; these guys were looking to rule with an iron fist. 'This is the way we're doing it, and it's not up for negotiation.' It's what we needed at that point.

Adam Jones: There was a clear hierarchy from day one. Shaun Edwards sat us all down in the team room, and said, 'From this point onwards, we're a blitzing team. And if you don't like it, you can fuck off.' Everyone nodded in agreement. There were no murmurings, no dissent.

Martyn Williams: You couldn't have had a starker contrast to what had come before. Fucking hell. When Gats and Shaun came in, it was totally, totally different. We could only go in one direction after that World Cup because we'd hit rock bottom.

Ryan Jones: There was a lot of uncertainty after the World Cup. There was a big question mark over the squad. Were we going to be competitive? Were we over the disappointment? Was there going to be a hangover? Warren came in and from the word go, was pretty direct with his game plan, and wanted to put strong foundations in place. We'd played some brilliant rugby between 2005 and 2007, but there was a sense that we'd flown by the seat of our pants. He questioned whether we had the discipline, the defence, the set-piece foundation, and the fitness to be a truly successful international side.

Warren Gatland: We were starting from a pretty low base after being knocked out of the 2007 World Cup by Fiji. There was only really an upward curve as far as I could see. I knew from my time with Ireland that the Welsh were all really skilful, so it was an exciting challenge.

Martyn Williams: I'd retired from international rugby after the World Cup, so I wasn't expecting to hear anything. I was thirty-two, and was just hoping to get a few more years of club rugby before I had to hang up my boots. I played for the Barbarians against South Africa in the December. We won, I got awarded man of the match, and I came off thinking, 'Have I been a bit premature here?' Next thing, I've got a voicemail from Gatland inviting me for a coffee. The conversation lasted less than ten minutes. He told me I still had a bit to offer and asked if I'd consider coming back for the Six Nations. He guaranteed me two things: that I'd train harder than I'd ever trained, and that we'd be successful.

Gatland's opening assignment was a Six Nations match against England at Twickenham. Two decades had passed since Wales had last won there. During that period, they'd suffered five shattering defeats, the worst of them the previous summer when they'd shipped sixty-two points. England's HQ had become a forbidding fortress for Wales, but not so for Gatland. He'd won three Premiership titles and a European Cup there with Wasps.

Ian Gough: Gatland had about fifteen days to prepare us for that campaign. He wasn't able to split the atom at that point, so he just changed a bit of the detail, upped the intensity in training, and things clicked. We wouldn't train for longer than an hour. If we nailed something, we'd move on. We'd become used to long, boring, plodding sessions where you'd be constantly looking at the clock, desperate for them to end.

Martyn Williams: You switch off mentally when training sessions go on too long. This was different; it was new, it was refreshing, and we bought into it en masse.

Ian Gough: We'd finish sessions knackered but feeling confident. For him to transform that squad in the amount of time he was given was unbelievable.

One of Gatland's must-haves was Gavin Henson. The mercurial playmaker had hit several career roadblocks since his 2005 heroics, including missing out on the World Cup in 2007. He'd been suspended, spent months on the sidelines injured, and had been marginalised for a time after releasing a controversial autobiography that upset some of his teammates. But Gatland's Wasps had always been a home for wayward players, and the Kiwi was confident he could push the right buttons to resurrect Henson's ailing career.

Warren Gatland: There are a lot of people out there who don't really know him or understand him. Fundamentally, he's a very quiet, shy person. That whole extrovert persona – the tan, the boots, and the hair – was a facade that wasn't really him. People saw that image and thought that was exactly what he was like in real life. The truth is that he was a very good professional who trained hard, prepared well, and understood the game. He flourished in our environment, and I think we got the best out of him.

Tom Shanklin: Sometimes Gats would ask him, 'Gav, how long do you want to train for?' Gav would say forty-five minutes, so we'd train for forty-five minutes. Bang, bang, bang, no hanging around. It empowered Gav, and it sharpened our focus. If we trained well, and concentrated hard, we knew we'd be off the paddock within the hour. For those of us that hated training, that was awesome.

Ian Evans: The irony is, Henson's a really shy bloke when he hasn't had a drink, so he seemed the least likely candidate to get into trouble off the field. He was unbelievably single-minded. He always brought his own food in, measured out precisely in little tubs and pots. Normal porridge wasn't good enough for him; he had these super-fantastic, low GI protein oats that he used to whip up himself. You'd often look across and see him munching on a red pepper like it was an apple. He was so disciplined that every now and again, inevitably, he'd have a blowout. And because he was normally so healthy, he just didn't have the tolerance for booze. Unsurprisingly, it often ended badly.

Martyn Williams: There were a few loose boys in that set-up.

Shane Williams: He'd gone through this period where he was out of the team, had lost a bit of form, and started to question himself. Gatland had brought him back into the fold, nurtured him a bit, and got him playing some of his best rugby. Gav could have been one of the best ever, if he'd stuck purely to rugby and avoided all the other distractions. He started to find form again under Gats, and it was no surprise that Wales started to play very well with him exerting his influence in the midfield. Shaun Edwards and Gats knew he was one of the most gifted players out there, and our team was a good deal better with him in it. He needed to be handled sensitively. Sometimes he needed a bit of gentle encouragement instead of a kick up the arse. For someone so fundamentally shy, he always responded well to responsibility. Gats and Shaun made him defensive captain, and he thrived on that.

Ian Evans: Gatland immediately picked up on Gav's incredible work rate. As a forward, it was the kind of stuff I'd never have noticed if it hadn't been highlighted in a debrief. He was a really intelligent rugby player, and he'd work so hard off the ball, trying to find mismatches. His work rate in defence was unbelievable, too. Don't let his pretty boy image fool you, he was hard as nails.

Gats knew which buttons to push with Gav. He realised how good he was, and that he was in a different category to the rest of us. His profile was much bigger, he was going out with Charlotte Church, he was a proper celebrity, and the papers were constantly hounding him, waiting for him to slip up so they could have a story. Gats protected him from all that, and gave him the space he needed to be himself. It was a masterstroke in terms of man-management.

Martyn Williams: Some days, you'd come into a team meeting, all strapped up and ready to go, and he'd say, 'Right boys, go home.' He was one of the first to use GPS and really monitor our fitness and well-being. If the conditioners had told him they weren't going to get anything out of the boys, he'd call training off. He was a genius at reading the mood of a group, and reacting accordingly.

Tom Shanklin: It would only last longer if our execution was poor, and there were always punishments for that. One of his favourites was making us do a figure-of-eight sprint around the entire field if anyone dropped a ball. I remember one particularly sloppy session before the Italy game in 2009, when we were doing multiple figure-of-eights, sprinting flat out. That's how Tom Prydie got his first cap. He was like a whippet, lapping the rest of us.

Shaun was huge on centres and back rowers doing extra drills after training. Tackle, up, jackal. Tackle, up, jackal. Over and over again. In those early days, he'd always have to remind us. One day he didn't make training and was reviewing the footage afterwards. He saw a group of us doing that of our own accord, and was so proud that he'd instilled that work ethic in us.

Martyn Williams: I'd loved Shaun as a player, watching Wigan. The opportunity to work with him was one of the reasons I came out of retirement.

Mark Jones: He was a proper character. We toured South Africa in 2008, and he was late arriving because Wasps were in a final. He turned up one day towards the end of a training session wearing a white formal shirt, a pair of tracksuit bottoms, and black suit shoes. Training had virtually finished but he was desperate to get involved. He wanted to do some clean-out work, and within minutes he was down on the ground jackling Rhys Thomas, rolling round on the floor, getting stinking dirty. He got up off the floor, his shirt all ripped and stained, and said he wanted to do some cross-field kick work with me and Shane. He didn't have any boots, so he was asking the players if he could borrow some. Someone asked what size he was, and he said, 'I'm six, seven, eight, nine, ten boys. I don't care, just give me some boots.' Ian Gough gave him his size thirteens. They were like clown shoes – his toes didn't reach the end, and his kicks were going all over the place. Shane and I were falling about laughing.

Ian Evans: You'd go into the gym at eight in the morning to do some sly weights, and he'd be there on his own, with his massive headphones on, shadow boxing. He'd always be wearing his regulation uniform of a vest, tracksuit bottoms and black shoes.

Scott Baldwin: I once walked into the team room and saw him playing imaginary darts. I watched as he slowly and methodically threw three darts, went to check where they'd landed, mentally added up his score, and removed them from the board. But there were no darts and no board.

Mark Jones: He was old school, it was all about getting down and dirty on the paddock. He's not the most proficient on a laptop, but he's got an incredibly sharp rugby mind. He's very precise, knows what he wants, and is one *hell* of a coach.

Martyn Williams: Craig White, the fitness coach, had a big influence as well. He'd often come onto the pitch in the middle of a session and go, 'That's enough now, Gats.' The gym sessions were full-on. There was no cruising around doing a few bicep curls here and there, it was really intense.

Stephen Jones: The sessions were shorter, sharper and more intense, which came as a shock. They were physically harder on the body and the lungs. Lots more contact, lots more ground covered, lots more metres run. They judged us a lot on what happened on the training pitch. Once people realised that, they started to raise their game.

Tom Shanklin: It was intense. There was a lot of full-on contact. Before, certain players used to shy away from that – myself, Martyn Williams, Gethin Jenkins. We'd have little winks between us, gentlemen's agreements to pair up in tackle practice. We'd fall over convincingly just before contact while shouting, '*Good* tackle.' You couldn't get away with that under Gatland. He noticed *everything*.

Ryan Jones: They secretly filmed one of our early training sessions to find out who were the workers, and who were the shirkers. We had cones laid out, and were doing sprinting drills. There were members of that squad that weren't the most dedicated of trainers, and would happily cut corners if they thought they could get away with it. Later that day, without any fanfare, they stuck the video on in the team meeting. It showed players deliberately stopping short of the cones, trying to get away with doing less while the coaches' backs were turned. It was a horrible moment. No voices were raised, but you could sense how disappointed they were. The guilty parties felt like naughty schoolboys. No one ever shirked again.

Martyn Williams: I was a bit longer in the tooth by then, don't forget. That's not what I'd signed up for, coming out of retirement. I used to try to hold things back, to save myself for the Saturday. Gats had promised he'd look after me, that I wouldn't have to do contact, but that soon went out of the window. In hindsight, it was the right thing to do. It wouldn't have sat well with the other boys, if I was taking time off, sitting on the sidelines while the rest of them were being put through hell. There was no walking between sets. You had to sprint everywhere. But we soon realised that Gatland based a lot of his selection decisions on what happened on the training paddock. You could be on fire for your region, but if you didn't give it everything in training, you wouldn't get picked.

Warren Gatland: We were very basic in what we did. We had an attitude of working hard and we pushed the boys right to the limit. One of the things I've learned about the Welsh boys is that they hardly ever complain about how hard they're made to train. You get some bitching and moaning now and again, but in general, they're fantastic.

Martyn Williams: He had a knack of making you feel invincible. 'You're fitter than anyone else, you're stronger than anyone else, no one can beat you.' He was brilliant at that. That kind of man-management was his major strength. That, and team selection, which he rarely ever got wrong.

Warren Gatland: I was constantly saying, 'Do you think Ireland are training as hard as this? Do you think England are training as hard as this? There's no way they are.' I had no idea how hard anyone else was training but I just kept reinforcing that message. In the end, the players picked it up themselves, and it snowballed. I'd hear them shouting it to each other: 'There's no way anyone's training as hard as this!' My work was done.

Martyn Williams: Before that first game against England, even though we hadn't won there for twenty years, he had us believing we could. 'Boys, you'll be fitter than them, you'll outlast them, and we'll win it in the last ten minutes.'

Warren Gatland: Everyone was talking about twenty years of misery for Wales at Twickenham, but I was trying to take away the fear. It had been a really lucky stadium for me, and I tried to use that as a positive.

Ian Gough: Gats picked thirteen Ospreys in that first game, which was very astute. We were the only team in Wales using the blitz defence that Shaun favoured.

Martyn Williams: Nobody saw that coming, but they were the best team at the time so I guess it made sense. They knew how to blitz. Not with the same intensity or level of detail that Shaun brought, but they had that 'off-the-line' mentality. We weren't blitzing at Cardiff. Boycey [Mark Jones] and me were the only non-Ospreys. In hindsight, it was a smart move. It was so left-field, and it flummoxed everybody.

Warren Gatland: There was a period during that first half when Shaun Edwards was looking increasingly uncomfortable.

Martyn Williams: We were getting dicked.

Warren Gatland: Shaun didn't say anything but I could tell from his body language that he was thinking, 'Jeez, have I made the right decision coming to Wales?'

Martyn Williams: They were blowing us away. None of us had experienced winning in Twickenham in a red shirt. I'd done it with the Baa Baas, but never with Wales, and that begins to play on your mind. If Benny [Huw Bennett] hadn't got underneath Paul Sackey like he did, we wouldn't have won. Simple as that. Typical Benny, that. He was unbelievably fit, and he'd leave it all out there. He'd empty the tank every time.

Warren Gatland: If England had scored then, and gone 23–6 ahead at half-time, there's no doubt they'd have won the game, maybe run away with it. That was a critical moment.

Ian Gough: We were on the ropes, just absorbing the punches and hanging in there.

Mark Jones: At half-time, we were actually told to play a bit more rugby. We were kicking too much ball away, and Gats was frustrated that we'd defended for as long as we had. The message was: 'More of the same without the ball, but let's see if we can be a bit more positive with it.'

Adam Jones: One of England's big weapons was their driving lineout. Rather than coming up with a way of stopping it gaining momentum, Warren told us to stop it happening altogether. The way to do that was simple – kick infield or keep hold of the ball. Do that, and England wouldn't *have* any attacking lineouts, and wouldn't be able to form any rolling mauls. Sometimes the solution is simpler than you think. Even though we were ten points down, Shaun persuaded us that England had fired all their shots. The game was now ours to win.

It worked. Wales re-entered the fray with renewed hunger. They started to turn over England ball, and their defensive intensity forced their hosts into mistakes. The penalty count began to mount in Wales's favour. Gatland had lobbed a few verbal grenades in England's direction during the week, and suggested that Iain Balshaw might be a weak link at full back. It would be a Balshaw mistake that would provide the catalyst for the unlikeliest of victories.

Before that, it was Mr Reliable, Jonny Wilkinson, who'd shown signs of England's fallibility. Receiving the ball on his own ten-metre line, he threw a speculative pass. Danny Cipriani wasn't expecting it and had to run backwards to retrieve the bouncing ball. He was consumed by a pack of marauding Welsh forwards, and Wales were awarded a scrum. Several phases later, Wales went to the blind-side, and James Hook floated through the first line of defence, before delivering a scoring pass to Lee Byrne. Hook's conversion brought Wales level.

Tom Shanklin: Lee Byrne used to get so nervous before games. He'd get flustered on the pitch, and was forever coming up to you asking which move we were about to run. Shaun Edwards advised him to start reading before games to calm his nerves. He gave him a copy of *Hurricane*. Four years later he was still reading the same book. He just used to pick it up and pretend when Shaun walked into the room.

From the restart, Mike Phillips kicked deep towards Balshaw. The full back hesitated for a fateful second, long enough for Phillips to launch himself skywards and charge down his miscued clearance. Gethin Jenkins scooped up the loose ball and passed to Martyn Williams, who found Phillips on the outside. It was their second try in two minutes and proved the knockout punch. England still had ten minutes to mount a comeback but Wales hung onto the ball. Opportunism had got them back into it; pragmatism won them the day.

Martyn Williams: Phillsy's try was *unbelievable*. He kicked the ball, made the charge-down, and then scored in the corner. It was one of *the* best tries. I used to love playing with him. I'd end up playing scrum half more than him because he'd be carrying all the time, and tearing it up. We had a good little combo going. He's a serious competitor, and you'd go to war with him any day of the week. In Wales, we've often lacked that strut and that confidence, but he had it in spades.

Warren Gatland: He epitomised what the game was about and what we were trying to achieve. Constant pressure, and a never-say-die spirit. There was an inevitability about that try.

Shane Williams: He still lives off it, he really does. It was an eighty-yarder by the end of the night. I'd have loved for anyone else to have scored that because ten years on, I still have to put up with him bragging about it. Credit where it's due, if you need someone to power over the line when you've got two defenders in your path, Mike's your boy. It was a great try, and it summed him up. He put the opposition under relentless, suffocating pressure and eventually they cracked.

Ian Evans: Alun Wyn Jones twisted his ankle with about two minutes to go, and I was sent on with one message – 'Don't do anything stupid.' I remember feeling so inhibited. I was terrified of doing something wrong, so I just told myself to stay in the defensive line, stay as square as I could, and to smash anyone who came towards me. Without giving away a penalty, of course.

Tom Shanklin: I think we won the second half 20–3, which was a real point of pride. It became a theme throughout that tournament. The games would be fairly close until the last quarter, when our fitness would become the deciding factor.

Adam Jones: Gatland and Edwards had such a winning mentality that it immediately rubbed off on us. They told us we had nothing to fear, and we believed them.

Ian Evans: Traditionally, Wales had run out of steam at sixty minutes, and Gats wanted to reverse that. He wanted to make *us* the team that kept on going. During some of those brutal training sessions, that would be the message – 'This may hurt now, but when you reach the final quarter of a Test match, the opposition will crack, and you'll keep going.' It was all about staying in the arm wrestle until the point you could cut loose. When that came through in the England game, we realised the coaches had been right all along. We *were* fitter than them. If anyone had doubted it up to that point, they didn't afterwards.

Martyn Williams: That was a big part of Gats's motivation. I'm pretty sure it's physiologically impossible to get that much fitter in ten days, but he had us believing that we had. It's the placebo effect, isn't it? Mind games.

Warren Gatland: As I was walking down the steps towards the tunnel, one of the Welsh reporters came up to me and said, 'Warren, Graham Henry was known as the "Great Redeemer", what are you going to be known as after this?' I looked at him and said, 'The lucky bastard.'

A victory against England used to be the most important yardstick of success for Wales. But the 'as long as we beat the English' attitude was becoming a tired and tedious refrain. The triumph over England the previous year was Wales's sole win that campaign, but it had sent fans into raptures. After Ieuan Evans burned past Rory Underwood in 1993 to beat England in Cardiff, they went on to lose every other match, a fact that is conveniently forgotten. Gatland knew better than to bask in the glory of a Twickenham win. As in 1993, it was the first game of the campaign and Gatland was determined to keep his players grounded. Rather than showering them with praise, his debrief focused on their first-half deficiencies. He told his victorious side that each and every one of them would need to prove their worth in training that week, and made it crystal clear that no one's place was safe.

Ian Gough: Pops [Alix Popham] had had a decent game when he came off the bench, but he hadn't followed Shaun's instructions to the letter. For the Scarlets, he'd do this thing where he'd chase down the opposition scrum half off the ruck, and try to sack him. He'd get his hands on him maybe one time out of four, but that wasn't a Gatland/Edwards policy. Shaun outed him in the week for going against the system, and maybe a few other little things, and he didn't play again. He fell out of favour over that one small thing and he never pulled on the red shirt again. And he was a bloody good player, Pops.

Ian Evans: Warren explained to us why he didn't always start Rob Howley when he signed him for Wasps, even though he was one of Europe's best scrum halves. It was because he knew he could get more out of him by pushing and challenging him. When he criticised you, it was for a reason. You couldn't afford to take it personally – it was all about making the *team* better.

Shane Williams: It was horrible at the time, because it really deflated your ego, but then you thought, 'Actually, I didn't do that well, did I? I made three mistakes, I dropped a ball, I missed a tackle, I lost the ball in contact twice. Who was I kidding saying I'd done all right?' I liked that your job wasn't always safe, that you weren't considered perfect. It was a kick up the backside to have your coach tell you that, but I'd make sure I didn't make the same mistakes the following week.

Ian Gough: Poor old JT [Jonathan Thomas] had been knocked out by a Jonny Wilkinson swinging arm, gone off concussed, and missed the victory. On the Monday we were all given our assessment sheets with the coaches' verdicts on our individual performances. He got a nought out of ten, and Gatland had written a comment along the lines of 'you ignored our instructions, so you got what you deserved'.

Ian Evans: That was it, yeah. 'Serves you right.' Thanks for that.

Tom Shanklin: We basically had a policy of running off nine in the fifteen-metre channels, and running off ten between the fifteen-metre lines. He'd run off nine instead of ten, got knocked out for his troubles, and then got a nought out of ten for his performance on the Monday. Brutal.

Adam Jones: There we were, thinking we were the dog's bollocks after beating England, and we were immediately brought back down to earth. It was obvious that victory alone wasn't enough; our performances were being scrutinised to the nth degree. There was no room for complacency.

Ian Evans: The sheets were all pinned up on a board called the 'wall of fame', but more often than not it was the 'wall of shame'. You'd see it first thing in the morning after breakfast. It didn't half puncture the ego.

Martyn Williams: They didn't hold back at all, which was good when it was in private, but I think they criticised players publicly a bit too much in those early days. Alun Wyn was once called out for a trip that got him a yellow card against England, Ryan was made a scapegoat after a draw against Fiji. You expect to get rinsed in the changing room, but publicly you want your coach to back you. I'm sure he was doing it for the right reasons, but I think it was ill-judged. The changing room's a funny old place, and it's hard to let go of a grudge.

Ian Gough: I was on the receiving end of it in South Africa that summer. Next to my name on the whiteboard were the words, 'Will the real Ian Gough turn up next week?' It was pretty biting.

Tom Shanklin: Ian Evans always got the worst comments. The two I always remember were, 'Discipline. Discipline. Discipline,' and, 'You are a complete liability to this team.'

Martyn Williams: Shaun rinsed me in the debrief as well. I was slouching in my seat thinking I was golden bollocks, having just come out of retirement and beaten England, and he called me out for one incident where I hadn't taken my place in the defensive line. That made me sit up straight. It was a rocket up my arse. He made a point of singling me out for one error. Nothing came of it – they didn't score, but it showed that they were perfectionists.

Ian Gough: That was Shaun Edwards' way. He'd always say, 'If we're not being critical, it means we don't care.'

Martyn Williams: As much as it hurt, it was their way of making us all harder. We weren't mentally weak necessarily, but it was a soft sort of environment. They raised the levels of accountability and introduced a fear factor. I never went onto the pitch after that without the spectre of Shaun Edwards over my shoulder, and it worked. It made you put that extra yard into it all, to make sure you were in position. It was painful when you were outed, but as long as it's not you every time you can handle it. It's always easier to accept a bollocking if you still get picked. If you have a bollocking and you're dropped, that's a double whammy, isn't it?

Mark Jones: That's what happened to me. Our first win at Twickenham in twenty years, and I was dropped like a stone.

Ian Evans: Boycey and Pops got dropped. We knew then that no one was safe.

Warren Gatland: I don't know if that was part of my psychology. I don't think having thirteen players from one team was the healthiest thing. It was what we needed for that game, but it wasn't sustainable. I was thinking about how I could reduce that number because I wanted the other teams to be represented. That was more at the forefront of my mind than keeping the players on edge.

Mark Jones: There were two reasons I was dropped. One was for not blitzing hard enough, and the other one was because I stayed down when I was injured. Unless you were knocked out, or had broken your leg, Shaun expected you to get back in the defensive line. This was long before the introduction of HIAs, and I'd been short-armed in the face by Lesley Vainikolo. He caught me a beauty and I was down for a few minutes, getting treated by Carcass while play was going ahead. I actually got rid of Carcass, and got back into the line, before dropping down again, and they weren't happy with that. Shaun showed the clip of me going down in front of thirty of my colleagues in the team room. He asked, 'Were you knocked out?' I said, 'No, not completely.' He said, 'Had you broken your leg?' Again, 'No.' 'Well you should have been in the line, then.'

Tom Shanklin: He was big on that. Even if you'd broken your arm, he'd expect you to get in the defensive line. If you can stand up, it looks like an extra body, and that's all the opposition is going to see unless they're really clever. If you stay down, all they'll see is a hole.

Shaun Edwards could not be accused of not practising what he preached. Ten minutes into the 1990 Challenge Cup Final, he took a severe blow to the face, fracturing his cheekbone and his eye socket in three places. He played on for the rest of the game, never once shirking a tackle or avoiding contact.

Mark Jones: It was only the third time I'd met him. I didn't know him from Adam, but I remember thinking, 'I don't like this.' This guy was questioning the cojones between my legs. I was sat at the front of the room, and I could feel thirty pairs of eyes drilling into me. It was England–Wales at Twickenham, I hadn't been lacking for motivation – if I *could* have got back into the line I would have. You're not exactly going to take a rest and leave your mates to it, are you? I pulled Shaun aside a few days later and told him he'd got his point across, but he'd embarrassed me, and that he wouldn't be doing that again.

Tom Shanklin: Mark was always a bit more sensitive to criticism. He'd drop the ball, and immediately start stretching his hamstrings, like that was the reason he'd dropped it. Moments later, he'd be firing down the wing.

Ian Gough: The night of the England game was the start of the Fab Four.

Shane Williams: Me, Phillsy, Hooky and Byrney. There was always some kind of issue with one of us. We had our own little clique without realising it. Alan Phillips started calling us the Fab Four. He'd say we were the rock stars.

Ian Gough: Normally we'd stay over, and sneak out to Richmond for a few drinks, but we had Scotland the following week, so a decision was made to head back to the Vale for a quiet one. Gav, Shane, Phillsy, Hooky, and JT had other ideas.

Martyn Williams: The cans were flowing on the bus and we were all watching *Predator*, for some reason. Then we put the Eagles on the stereo. Henson loved 'Busy Being Fabulous' so that got a few spins, with him singing along. We got back to the Vale at about midnight, and it kicked on from there. Most of us went into the champagne bar, and it got very messy.

Tom Shanklin: Getting a bit loose on the piss is one thing, but when Shane Williams offered Gats out for a fight at one in the morning – that probably overstepped the mark.

Shane Williams: Now, my recollections are a little hazy, but apparently I offered him outside for a fight. It was a ridiculous thing to say, not least because we already *were* outside.

Warren Gatland: He was the worse for wear, whereas I'd had a fairly quiet night.

Shane Williams: To this day, I don't know what I was thinking. It was probably fifty per cent trying to be funny, and fifty per cent trying to act tough. I do suffer from small man syndrome at times.

Warren Gatland: Before I'd arrived in Wales, I'd stopped off at the Dubai Sevens and done an interview there. I'd said that I was going to train Wales hard, push them, and break some of them. It came across aggressively and that must have rankled with some of the players. I wanted to breed a mental toughness in them, and I think Shane's behaviour that night was in reaction to those comments. He'd read it, didn't like it, and wanted to prove something to me.

Shane Williams: I woke up in the morning with a pounding head, thinking, 'Oh God, I'm never playing for Wales again.' After taking a bit of advice from the boys, I went and knocked on Gatland's door with my tail firmly between my legs. He immediately put me at ease, and told me to relax. He said, 'It's all good, it's all a bit of fun. Thank you for apologising, but there's no need to worry.'

He told me a bit of niggle was good, that we had a big game against Scotland next week, and he wanted me to have a bit of fire in my belly ahead of that. I remember thinking, 'This guy's a legend.' He's pretty much told that story for the last decade on the after-dinner circuit, so at the very least, I gave him some decent material.

Warren Gatland: Look, when you've been involved in sport all your life, as a player and a coach, those kinds of thing happen. It was fine. It was a one-off situation. Everyone makes mistakes. They're young men who get a bit exuberant. If it had happened again, there would have been different consequences. Two strikes and you're out. It's so important to have a balance. If you work hard, you've got to enjoy yourself and celebrate your victories. We talk about going to the edge of the cliff and having a look over. You know, have a peek but don't jump, whatever you do. We've had players that have jumped in the past, let me tell you.

Ian Gough: In the team room the next morning, the main culprits were all a bit sheepish, bracing themselves for a bollocking. Gats walked in with a face like thunder and said, 'Boys, I'm really disappointed.' He left a dramatic pause for it to sink in before saying, 'You forwards are rubbish. The backs were all drinking and fighting until two in the morning. You boys had three pints and went to bed. What's the matter with you?'

Ian Evans: Gats is old-school at the end of the day. If you put in a good shift, you deserve a few beers, as long as you front up the next day. And the boys always fronted up.

Martyn Williams: Scotland were poor at the time, but we were conscious of the fact we had to back up the England win. Slip up against Scotland, and it would count for nothing. It would be a different sort of game because we knew we'd have a lot more ball than we'd had against England.

Shane Williams: There was huge pressure because we'd just beaten the tournament favourites away from home, and no one had expected that to happen. We loved playing in Cardiff, we enjoyed the whole atmosphere, and we believed we were going to win that match. We knew we had them fitness-wise, and we had a really good set piece that would get clean, quick ball to our backline. I felt I had a lot to offer personally and that I was going to go out there and enjoy myself.

Scotland had lost 27–6 to France in round one, and their head coach, Frank Hadden, was under pressure. Unlike the previous week, Wales were clear favourites, although memories of the previous season's heavy defeat in Murrayfield were fresh enough to focus the mind. They needn't have worried. After his boxing bout with

Gatland came to nothing, Shane Williams delivered the knockout blow against Scotland – his brace of tries steering Wales to a comfortable victory.

Shane Williams: There was no question over my first try, but the second was pretty controversial. I'm sure if you ask any Scottish fan, even now, they'll say I was in touch all day long. In fact, *I'm* still torn fifty-fifty about whether I was in touch.

Martyn Williams: It wouldn't be allowed now. He was in touch.

Ian Evans: Regardless, Shane had this infuriating ability to find space where there was none. After training, Shaun and Gats used to get the forwards to try to tackle him one-on-one, in a five-by-five square box. We'd have five goes each and we had a licence to hit him as hard as we could, but it was irrelevant because no one ever got near him. It was a moral victory if you just managed to scrag him as he danced around you. Getting a clean shot on him was a pipe dream.

Martyn Williams: I know for a fact that if there'd been another winger playing well in Wales, they wouldn't have picked Shane for that game. Wingers are really important for the blitz defence, and they thought he was too small. But then he scored those two tries against Scotland, and a year later he was officially the best player in the world. It's funny how things turn out.

Shane Williams: At times during that game, I felt like there was *no one* that could touch me. I know it sounds big-headed and a bit weird, but everything I did, I did it so well. Every time I stepped, I felt really powerful. I was leaving players for dead. I felt really sharp and pacy. I was at the very top of my game.

Jamie Roberts: I played on the wing against Scotland, we won, and I didn't play again. It was a bit of a rocket for Mark, but he went on to play really well in the last three games. I was gutted when I got dropped. I was like, 'Fucking hell, we've just won!' I was twenty-one and I thought I was going to be a one-cap wonder. I didn't have the courage to go and knock on the coach's door and ask for an explanation. They never made players feel comfortable. We were constantly reminded how intense the competition was.

The final score was 30–15, Wales's biggest victory over Scotland in Cardiff for fourteen years. But as was the case after the England game, Gatland's perfectionism didn't allow much room for self-congratulation. Wales dominated the game territorially, were far more fluid in attack than Scotland, and made eleven clean line-breaks. Gatland thought they should have won by more against a side so bereft of confidence and creativity. The one overwhelming positive was the defence. As Shaun Edwards' system had had longer to bed in, so the players had become more proficient at working in unison, flying up in a line, and suffocating the Scottish attack. No tries were conceded, and at one point the crowd were chanting 'Wales, Wales' as they defended their line. Shaun Edwards was as excited about stopping tries as he was about scoring them, and it was rubbing off on the fans.

Adam Jones: We had a two-week gap between the Scotland and Italy games, and weren't due to report back to camp until the Wednesday. The forwards were summoned to the barn, and I was expecting a light session to get the limbs moving again. Instead, we were subjected to one of the most horrendous experiences of my rugby career. We were introduced to a small, northern bloke called Paul Stridgeon, who proceeded to beast us with one of the most horrible, punishing fitness sessions of our lives.

Ian Evans: Three times in my life, I've had an out of body experience, and that was one of them.

Adam Jones: 'Bobby' as he's universally known, is outwardly cheery, but inwardly he's an absolute sadist. He introduced us to this method of his called 'power endurance'. It was absolutely savage, and there was no resting between sets. It was utterly relentless.

Ian Evans: There were about five stations for chin-ups, squats, shoulder-presses, step-ups and bench presses. One was a clean bar with different denominations of weights on it. All the older heads had figured out what was coming so they gravitated to the lighter weights. Me, being young and naïve, ended up with the heaviest weights, and I didn't have a partner so I ended up being paired with Robin McBryde, our forwards coach and one-time 'strongest man in Wales'. It was a *horrendous* experience. My back went into spasm by the end. I couldn't lie down, I couldn't stand up, and I was spewing everywhere.

Adam Jones: That was just the first phase. After that, there were shuttles, wrestling matches, and tug of war. The Muckers [Robin McBryde] vs Ianto [Ian Evans] tug of war was the only bit of light relief. Ianto is a huge bloke – six foot eight and around eighteen stone – but he was just being tossed around like a rag doll. Muckers showed him no mercy.

Ian Evans: He was completely ragging me around. I didn't have *anything* left in my body. Gats obviously felt that we weren't fit enough. We hadn't been to hell and back, or been mentally tested before he arrived. I can laugh at it now it's in the past, but at the time I was close to tears.

Adam Jones: Virtually everyone was staggering around spewing and shaking uncontrollably. By the end, Ianto was virtually comatose. All the boys were taking the piss, but he didn't even have the energy to open his eyes. He was gone, dead to the world. That was when the backs arrived. They strutted into the barn looking all fresh and eager, and were confronted by the sight of us forwards splayed out all over the floor retching, groaning and begging for mercy. Alun Wyn Jones had his head in a bucket. Even in my state of extreme discomfort, I took a small amount of pleasure in knowing they had it all to come.

The response against Italy was what Gatland had been looking for. While he was rotating his squad, selections remained pragmatic. Unlike some of his predecessors, he didn't select on sentiment and he didn't experiment with players out of position. Where Steve Hansen might favour a footballer over an out-and-out specialist, Gatland picked the best man for the job, and told him to stick to what he knew. Ian Gough was a case in point. Gatland charged him with the responsibilities of your classic warhorse lock. Tackle, hit rucks, smash people. If you can't be creative, be destructive. Gough lived up to the billing against Italy, hitting an astonishing forty-seven rucks, and losing five kilograms during the game through sheer effort. All in all, Gatland made six changes from the team that beat Scotland, dropping Mike Phillips and James Hook, and recalling the experienced duo of Dwayne Peel and Stephen Jones. Hook had provided some jaw-dropping moments of skill during the opening two games, aligning himself with some of his fleet-footed predecessors in Wales's most romanticised jersey. But Gatland knew he needed to curb his attacking instinct on occasion, and picked the more reliable Jones. Another notable selection was the return to the wing of Mark Jones. Gatland was wily enough not to underestimate Italy. They'd lost their opening two matches narrowly to Ireland and England, and were being intelligently coached by Nick Mallett. Furthermore, Wales had a chequered recent past against the Azzurri, and hadn't beaten them since their Grand-Slam-winning season three years previously. A gritty, attritional first half gave way to a free-flowing second, during which Wales scored an unanswered 34 points. Results elsewhere meant that with two rounds to go, only Wales could win the Grand Slam.

Tom Shanklin: It was my fiftieth cap, and Warren asked if I'd like to lead the team out. Before we got on the bus to the stadium, we gathered in a horseshoe for Gats to deliver his last speech. He said they had a big heavy pack, and reminded us to keep the ball on the field as much as possible to tire them out. He finished up by saying it was my fiftieth cap. I readied myself for a little tribute, maybe a video montage, and some heartfelt words to mark the milestone. Gats went on, 'When Tom was at Saracens, and I was coaching Wasps, we always used to target him because we thought he was the weakest link.' Some of the boys started sniggering. I thought he was gearing up to apologise for having made such an outrageous error of judgement, and to admit how wrong he'd been, but he just wrapped it up with

'But somehow, against all the odds, he's made it to fifty caps. On the bus then, boys.'

Martyn Williams: That was brilliant. Shanks is quick enough to take the piss out of the boys, and to swoop on people's weaknesses, so he got a taste of his own medicine there! We were laughing all the way to the ground. Your fiftieth's massive. Mine was against England. It's a big, big day for you, a huge milestone. That meeting before you get on the bus, when you're all in a horseshoe, that's the big emotional one. The one in the changing room is usually done by the captain. We all knew it was Shanks's fiftieth, and were expecting a little tribute, and Gats just rinsed him. I don't know what hurt him more – that, or getting voted into the world's ugliest rugby XV in the *Sun* before the 2007 World Cup. That was gold. We've never let him forget that.

Shane Williams: At least he got to lead the team out, and score one of our tries, bless him. We beat Italy with ease, thanks to people like Goughie keeping them quiet up front, and allowing us backs to capitalise.

Ian Evans: Goughie's work-rate was absolutely berserk. His stats were off the charts. He wasn't an athlete, he was a grunter, and Gats loved players like that. He fitted perfectly into the game plan. He did the graft which allowed the likes of Alun Wyn or myself to get around the field a bit more.

Martyn Williams: He was a ruck-hitter, Goughie. A piano pusher, and they're worth their weight in gold. He'd hit a million rucks, and would never stop grafting, doing the unseen dirty work to make everyone else look good. From that point of view, he was the perfect lock for Gatland's set-up. Gatland struck gold with Goughie. 'Don't touch the ball, Goughie, just hit the rucks.' He couldn't catch the ball without sliding on his knees.

Shane Williams: It was telling though, that despite the emphatic win, Shaun Edwards was furious that they'd scored first. It was a lucky try from a botched lineout, but Shaun hated it when our defensive line was breached. That's his job. If your leg's broken, you've got another leg, you can stand up on that one. That was his attitude, and you know he'd do the same thing himself. There were so many occasions in games when I'd be out of position or miss a tackle, and think, 'Oh no, Shaun will have spotted that.' We may have been thirty points up, but it wouldn't matter. He'd take it personally. If I missed a tackle, he'd have me back on the pitch half an hour after the game throwing big rubber inner tubes at me, making me judo flip them and doing God knows what else. I'd be thinking, 'Come on Shaun mate, I only missed one tackle,' but at the same time, I'd be thinking, 'Fair enough, I deserve this.'

Warren Gatland has always been a man to keep his own counsel, but those who know him can detect emotion in the slightest of gestures. The anger in a narrow-eyed glare, the frustration in a clamped jaw, the delight in an upturned lip. Imperceptible shifts that only a keen-eyed observer will notice. He did well to keep his emotions in check during the build-up to the Ireland game. He'd coached Ireland for three seasons from 1998 to 2001, but his tenure had come to an acrimonious end amid allegations of player power, and Machiavellian machinations. His assistant, Eddie O'Sullivan, became his successor, and the game at Croke Park marked the first time they'd locked horns as international adversaries. There was little love lost between them. Gatland showed his proclivity for mischief by dropping some verbal bombs into the discourse during the build-up. He suggested that Brian O'Driscoll had lost a yard of pace, and that Rory Best had handed Wales a team talk by claiming they'd yet to face a decent opposition. Eddie O'Sullivan tried to take the moral high ground, defusing the bombs with his own brand of passive-aggression. He dismissed Gatland's tactics as amateur-era nonsense. Subplot aside, Wales hadn't won in Dublin since 2000, when the respective coaches of the national sides were Graham Henry and Warren Gatland. That meant only three players in the XV – Stephen Jones, Ian Gough, and Shane Williams – knew how it felt to win in the Irish capital.

Shane Williams: We used to call them 'the grenades'. Warren used to love dropping something controversial into a press conference, and watching the aftershocks play out in the media. It was his way of taking the focus off the players. Week in, week out, we'd be saying, 'What's he done this week?' But we never looked too deeply into things. We knew it was all fun and games. We knew him and O'Sullivan had a rivalry, and we just left them to it. The players went and did the job on the weekend. People always wonder whether Gats planned these things or whether they just came to him off the top of his head. It was almost always calculated. I'm sure there are things he knows he wants to say, and he picks a time to say them. It was almost always tongue-in-cheek though.

Warren Gatland: I've always just given honest answers to questions. You can't win. If you express an opinion, you're accused of being controversial, and if you don't, you're accused of being boring.

Martyn Williams: As players, we didn't really know what had gone on in Ireland. We knew he'd left, but we didn't realise it was as bad as it was. To be fair to Gats, he didn't bring it up. I know it's a cliché, but you've just got to concentrate on the game, haven't you?

Ian Evans: Gats didn't make a big issue of it, he certainly didn't bring it up with us players. He's actually quite a reserved bloke behind the scenes.

Tom Shanklin: For the whole of his career, Gats has looked for moments when he can wind people up. He'd often come out with a controversial comment to ramp up the tension. Most of the time, I don't think it is premeditated; it just comes out. Everyone knows he was a little bit bitter about the way it ended with Ireland, but he's gone on to bigger and better things, hasn't he? It was actually the following year when he lobbed the biggest grenade, saying we disliked Ireland more than any other nation. I remember reading in the paper that we hated the Irish, and thinking, 'We don't, do we?'

Martyn Williams: I felt really privileged to have the opportunity to play at Croke Park. When you read up about the history of it all, it's a special place to go and play. I'm fascinated by that side of things. Going there for the team run, I was overwhelmed by the sheer size of the place. I've played in some big stadiums around the world, but that place is on another scale.

Adam Jones: They were being dubbed the golden generation on that side of the Irish Sea, and playing at Croke Park elevated them to another level as they'd shown when they destroyed England the year before. There wasn't much love lost at that point. Early on, after an Irish kick-off, I was running a lazy line to protect Ryan Jones from the onrushing Tommy Bowe when I was suddenly caught by a stray elbow and poleaxed. Looking up from the turf, I heard Tommy shout, 'Get out of my way, you fat bastard.'

Martyn Williams: It was another niggly game, because we knew each other so well through the Pro12, and most of us knew one another through Lions tours.

Tom Shanklin: That Ireland game was really tough. They were 6–3 up at half-time, and it would have been more were it not for Mike Phillips holding up Shane Horgan over the line.

Martyn Williams: That was a hell of a tackle from Phillsy. I think they'd have been a couple of scores clear if they'd have got over the line then. He was over for all money, and Shaggy's a big strong bloke, and a great finisher. The strength and determination Mike showed epitomised what we were about.

Shane Williams: I spent a lot of the game at nine thanks to Mike Phillips, who got sin-binned *again*. We were under massive pressure. There were a number of times during that game where we could have lost hope and given up.

Stephen Jones: Mike apologised at half-time but we actually survived comfortably when he was off the field. We tightened things up and kept hold of the ball for most of the ten minutes he was off. That was a clear sign of our improving maturity.

Tom Shanklin: Martyn Williams took a yellow card in the second half for tripping Eoin Reddan, but that was as a sacrifice. Gatland didn't mind that. Better to concede three points than seven.

Martyn Williams: He said mine was a 'smart' yellow card, and Phillsy's was a dumb one. I'd made a defensive error, and they'd bust the line. There was no way I was going to catch Eoin Reddan and I just thought 'do something' and went for the subtle trip. Fair play to Wayne Barnes, he spotted it. I remember thinking, 'How the hell did you see that?' He pulled me straight away, and I felt like a naughty schoolboy. I was shitting myself while I was off, hoping nothing bad would come of it. They got the three from the penalty, but no more. We were down to fourteen men twice, in Dublin against a team that would win the Grand Slam a year later, and we still found a way to win.

In a game as niggly and tight as this, it was likely that the outcome would be decided by a single score, and it came as no surprise that that moment of inspiration would come from the team's talisman, Shane Williams. The game's deadliest finishers have a habit of spotting a gap where there doesn't appear to be one. With the game in the balance, Williams spied the narrowest of openings, and accelerated through it, dumping Andrew Trimble on his backside en route to the try line.

Martyn Williams: We hadn't done a hell of a lot with the ball that day, but it just needed one bit of magic from Shane.

Stephen Jones: That was probably my moment of the tournament, when Shane fended off Trimble and broke down the touchline to score. He had no right to score it – there was no overlap, and very little space. He just beat the defence with pace and power. Good fend, great feet, and lightning acceleration.

Ian Evans: It was a great hand-off. People see Shane and assume he's not very strong, but his power and strength are unreal for such a little guy, as is his drinking ability for that matter. Someone of his size has no right being that strong, or having that capacity for alcohol. Defenders rarely got a clean hit on him, but even when they did, he had the strength to ride the tackle. It must be something to do with coming from Ammanford.

Tom Shanklin: But who was keeping the width to allow Shane to do that? Ask yourself that. If I hadn't been there hugging the touchline, someone would have just jammed in on him. It was a piece of genius from me. It had nothing to do with the fact I was knackered.

Shane Williams: It was the first time I've ever handed someone off successfully.

I didn't feel that I had much space, but I just about had the pace to get between Trimble and Tommy Bowe, and flop over the line. I probably covered more yardage that day than in every other game combined. One, I was playing nine quite a bit, and two, I was keeping my eye on Tommy. I really didn't want him to have the better of me, because he was an Osprey. I came off that pitch absolutely shattered.

Stephen Jones: It was such a hard-fought win. We were a point ahead with about ten minutes to go, and we knew that one mistake could mean the difference between victory and defeat. Luckily, it was them who made it.

With the game finely poised at 13–12, Ireland's reserve hooker Bernard Jackman launched himself into the back of Ryan Jones, whose legs were tangled in the bottom of a ruck. It was a fleeting moment of madness, with enormous consequences. The referee didn't hesitate in awarding the penalty.

Martyn Williams: I don't know what he was thinking. He almost broke Ryan's back. I was virtually KO'd in the ruck next to them when it happened, but I remember coming to, and watching it on the big screen. Ryan was trapped, and nowhere near the ball. It was a brainless challenge.

Mark Jones: These games turn on such small margins. Bernard Jackman's shoulder charge in the dying moments ended up being the difference. Hooky kicked the penalty, and that gave us the cushion we needed to win the Triple Crown.

Tom Shanklin: Two things stand out from that game. The first is Adam Jones's hair – I still have no idea why a tight-head prop thought it was acceptable to have braids put in. And the second is how long we kept hold of the ball at the end. Ten minutes of picking-and-going. We did a lot of that in training. It was called 'the minute drill'. Three players against three defenders going from ruck to ruck to ruck. To do that in Croke Park under that kind of pressure was first-class game management.

Warren Gatland: Was there an extra layer of satisfaction in winning that one? Absolutely. I made some noise coming down from the boxes for sure. Niall O'Donovan (Ireland forwards coach) came out of there, he saw me celebrating, and I jumped up and down a bit more and let out a few f-words. I'd tried to play it down to the press and the players, but on the inside it felt pretty special. It was the Triple Crown game, it was the first time I'd been involved in a match at Croke Park, and there was the history with Eddie O'Sullivan as well. I got up during the dinner to go and see Billy and Margaret Glynn. They were great friends of mine from Galway where Billy had been on the board at Connacht. It was one of those situations where it felt as though every pair of eyes in the room was trained on you, wondering what you were going to do. But the fact was, I still had a lot of friends within the IRFU. I still knew people from the board and got on with them well. The decision to get rid of me wasn't made by the board, it was made by about four individuals, which was the way the Union was being run. There were four senior guys who called all the shots. Eddie approached me and asked if we could have a beer. He basically tried to say that he hadn't been responsible for putting the knife into me. I have no doubt that he did try to undermine my position to some extent, but that's in the past. When I reflect on it, I realise that I'm indebted to the IRFU for giving me the opportunity to coach there. But if I'd stayed on another year, which is what I wanted to do, I wouldn't have ended up at Wasps, and I wouldn't have ended up with Wales. My path would have been completely different.

Victory over Ireland meant only France stood in the way of Wales, and a second Grand Slam in four years. Flamboyance and flair were at the core of 2005's triumph. This campaign had been largely about pragmatism, precision, and patience. The final act in Cardiff would be as much about quelling the passion, as igniting it.

Martyn Williams: On paper, they had a hell of a team.

Warren Gatland: I was convinced we were going to beat France.

Adam Jones: By the time Friday rolled around, we were all in a pretty zen state of mind. Nugget and I went on a chocolate run to Tesco, and filled up the boot. You'd never have thought we were all about to play one of the biggest games of our lives the following day, as we lounged around in the team room, watching *EastEnders* and gorging ourselves on jumbo-sized Galaxy bars.

Seven of those who'd started the Grand Slam decider in 2005 were to start this one. After rotating his squad through the tournament, Warren Gatland had some big selection calls to make, most notably at half back. James Hook was preferred to Stephen Jones, and Mike Phillips got the nod over Dwayne Peel.

Martyn Williams: It was very different to 2005, when Cardiff was bathed in warm spring sunshine. In 2008, it was damp, drizzly, and overcast, but it was a hell of an emotional day. Goughie led us out for his fiftieth, and he was accompanied onto the field by Ray Gravell's daughters. Grav had always been there during my career, waiting at the top of the stairs once the coach had arrived to shake every player's hand, and give us some words of encouragement. He had the strongest handshake I've ever experienced. It was odd to think he wasn't around anymore. Come game time, we were struggling. Gav got yellow carded towards the end of the first half, and it developed into a real arm wrestle.

Adam Jones: We were 9–3 up, but we conceded six points while Gav was off the field. Things got a bit twitchy at that point.

Martyn Williams: They'd won the Championship two years in a row and were going for the triple. And they had a good team, too. Jauzion, Clerc, Skrela, Dusautoir, Thion, Nallet. We were going to have to play well to beat that lot.

Shane Williams: They were blowing out of their arses after forty minutes.

Stephen Jones: Shaun had identified that Yannick Jauzion was their danger man; the one that needed to be neutralised. He's six foot four inches tall, rangy and incredibly strong. They used him as a battering ram to get over the gain line, but his one potential weakness was that he carried high. Shaun recognised that, and we worked all week on gang tackling – one low, one high – to stop him offloading. It was drummed into us during the week. First guy: stop him dead, second guy: kill the ball. So much of their attacking shape revolved around him, and we pretty much kept him wrapped up all afternoon.

Martyn Williams: Jauzion loved an offload. All week it was about doubling up on the tacklers, wrapping him up, preventing that offload. He was one of several big, big carriers, all of whom could offload.

Shane Williams: I knew the Welsh try-scoring record was up for grabs. I'd drawn level with Alfie with my fortieth against Ireland, and the press were constantly reminding me about it. I tried to put it to the back of my mind, but I'd be lying if I said it stayed there. It happened fairly early after a defensive error from them. I managed to dot down after a bit of dribbling to get over the line. You can probably see in my reaction how surreal it felt. I'm the all-time Welsh top try-scorer. We'd been under pressure, doing all the defending, but our pride and joy was our line-speed – getting up in the attackers' faces. If you weren't making a tackle, you were spooking someone, putting a player off. France made the mistake, we capitalised, and they went into their shell after that.

Martyn Williams: Skrela had a shocker at ten. As a young outside half, we deliberately targeted him. Gav and Shanks were rushing up on his outside, forcing him to turn inside, where the likes of Goughie and Ryan were waiting to dump him on his arse.

Warren Gatland: It's using defence as a form of attack. Line-speed and aggression was our core focus.

Adam Jones: The only moment I remember with any clarity was that scrum around the hour mark. It was their ball, they were five metres from our line in a prime attacking position. Their scrum half was whispering behind the ball, calling some kind of back row move. Our backline was set, fanned out and ready to defend for their lives, but us lot in the front-five had other ideas. We decided that this was *our* house, *our* try-line, and no one was going to cross it. The ball went in, our entire pack aligned perfectly, driving hard and straight, and splintered them to pieces. It was nigh on the perfect scrum.

Ian Evans: We drove over the top of them, and split them apart. The crowd went absolutely berserk. We'd been under the pump, and we'd just smashed them in their area of strength. Ryan Jones mopped up the loose ball, and Phillsy cleared our lines. They seemed to physically deflate after that, like we'd taken away their manhood. I didn't often get the chance to score tries, so that was as close as us tight-five forwards got to glory.

Adam Jones: Too right. It's the equivalent of a winger scoring a fifty-yarder. There's no better feeling for a front-row forward than to drive your opposite number into the dirt. That was a big old French pack that prided itself on its strength and power. I felt like running into the stands and high-fiving everyone in the crowd.

Martyn Williams: It was as much a turning point as Shane's try.

Ian Evans: It was 19–9 at the time, and it felt then as though we'd snuffed out their last attack. That'll do. Job done.

Mark Jones: Nugget got over the line for another try.

Martyn Williams: Jauzion tried to tackle me and I went to fend him. Often with a hand-off, you mistime it, but on that occasion, I planted it right in the sweet spot, and put him on his backside. I remember putting the ball down, turning round, and seeing *all* of the boys running towards me. Within seconds, I was enveloped. That was the moment we won the Grand Slam, and I'll cherish that memory forever.

Adam Jones: The feeling at that point was indescribable. We knew we wouldn't have to go through another of those nail-biting finales. We were home and hosed.

Martyn Williams: Running back, I knew where my daughter was sitting, so I turned and waved to her up in the stand. She was only five, but she knew what was going on. She does remember Dad playing a bit.

Tom Shanklin: I don't remember that game anywhere nearly as clearly as the

Ireland Grand Slam game in 2005. I had less of an impact. I remember winning, obviously, but I don't remember that much about the eighty minutes. I can recall the Ireland game play-by-play. I can still map out the whole thing in my mind.

Adam Jones: It felt like the beginning of something as opposed to an unexpected one-off like in 2005. The coaches had instilled this winning mentality, and within a couple of months, the Fiji debacle had been banished.

The crowd was going absolutely insane, and the excitement levels went through the roof. Mark Jones picked up one of the corner flags and started playing along to 'Rocking All Over the World' like it was a guitar. I think he even tried to do a Chuck Berry duck walk as well. If I thought my daffodil hat was ill-advised, it was nothing on Jamie Roberts' pink cowboy hat.

Ian Evans: Grand Slams are rare, aren't they? I'd been brought up by my old man worshipping at the altar of Gareth Edwards, JPR and all those boys. The 'golden era', or whatever you want to call it. I so badly wanted to achieve what they'd achieved, but when I did, I got lost in the moment. It took a couple of weeks for it to sink in that we'd actually done it. A few weeks passed before I woke up one morning, and thought, 'Hang on. We've won a Grand Slam.' It's not an easy thing to do. During the week leading up to it, we felt under so much stress, that the overwhelming emotion at the final whistle was relief. As mad as it sounds, we were just *relieved* to have pulled it off. We were physically drained after a brutal eighty minutes, and a long campaign, but mentally drained as well, because we'd been carrying all that pressure on our shoulders. To win it was beyond any fantasy I could have imagined. Growing up, all I wanted to do was play for Wales, but to win a Grand Slam and become part of history was beyond my wildest dreams.

Martyn Williams: 2008 was all about defence. It was a very English way of playing. I should have been sitting in the pub or watching it on TV at home, so to actually be there with the shirt on, and to score the winning try made it that little bit more special for me. I've never been more tired at the end of a game. There's a shot at the final whistle which I'm quite embarrassed about. It's me, Melon and Ryan, and we're on our knees, heads bowed feeling absolutely knackered. After '05, I wanted to go straight out on the smash. This time, after the function, I got on the bus with the trophy and my missus, and I just wanted to go home to bed. The rock stars were all kicking on into Cardiff, and I just slumped back to the Vale. I was exhausted.

Adam Jones: We all were. Shaun led a rendition of *Saturday Night at The Movies* in the changing room, and Prince William popped in to offer his congratulations, but it wasn't particularly raucous in there. I just remember cracking a few cans with Jug Head [Ryan Jones] and Alun Wyn and quietly toasting our success.

Ian Evans: A bunch of us went out in town. We had the keys to the city that night. Shanks was the ringleader, getting us into all the VIP bars, and doing his David Brent impressions. It was a great night, but it's all a bit of a blur now to be honest. After that, I just wanted to get back to normality, as boring as it sounds. You have to be so focused for six-to-eight weeks, you get a bit alienated from reality, from your own life. As soon as it was over, I just wanted to go back to Aberdare for a quiet pint, and let my mates just rip into me.

Shane Williams: It was my best-ever season. I'd had a long pre-season, recovering from injury and operations, I'd trained really hard, and got myself into peak physical condition. I was bouncing in training, and couldn't wait to get involved in the Six Nations. I hit it at full pace. I scored in every game apart from England, broke Alfie's try-scoring record, and came away with player of the tournament, so for me it was even more enjoyable than 2005.

Warren Gatland: He was the kind of player that could score three tries from nothing, but also concede three tries as well. But attacking-wise, pound-for-pound, he was undoubtedly one of the best players in the world. He deserved all the accolades that came his way.

Stratospheric highs are often followed by soul-searching comedowns. The euphoria can only last so long. If you reach the top of a steep and precipitous mountain, the descent can be as tricky to negotiate as the climb. Warren Gatland had set the bar impossibly high, and the weight of expectation lay heavily on his shoulders the following season. Wales came fourth in 2009, but that doesn't tell the full story. They began with back-to-back victories over Scotland and England before losing narrowly to France in Paris. A close-fought 20–15 win over Italy left them needing a handsome win over the Grand Slam-chasing Irish if they were to retain their title.

Ahead of that game, Gatland declared that the Welsh hated the Irish more than any other of the Home Nations. It was patently untrue, and had the opposite of its intended effect. It left supporters feeling baffled, handed Declan Kidney a convenient team talk, and convinced neutrals that Wales were the ones feeling the heat. The match was as tight as its counterpart the previous year, and its tense denouement was unbearable for both sets of supporters. With five minutes remaining, Stephen Jones dropped a goal to nudge Wales ahead. Three minutes later, Ronan O'Gara responded in kind. As the clock ticked into injury time, Wales were awarded a penalty on the outer edge of Jones's range. The crowd watched in agonising silence as the ball sailed towards the posts . . . before dropping inches short. Slim are the margins on which fortunes swing. Ireland prevailed, winning their first Grand Slam for sixty-one years; Wales slid into the bottom half of the table, a lick of paint the difference between second place (and a Triple Crown), and fourth place and nothing at all.

Fourth was their fate in 2010 as well, though this time it was where they belonged after convincing defeats to England, France and Ireland. They would have lost to Scotland too, had it not been for the mother of all comebacks. The euphoria of victory was such that Andy Powell spent the night in a police cell after stealing a golf buggy and chugging down the hard shoulder of the M4 in search of a midnight snack.

In 2011, they entered the final weekend needing to beat France by 27 points to take the title. They were condemned to a 28–9 defeat and ended up fourth again. So although they'd entered the final round twice in three years with a mathematical chance of winning the Championship, the record books read that they were the fourth best team in the Six Nations for three years running. The Grand Slam was receding in people's memories as the 2011 World Cup approached. Not many were rushing to the bookies to lay a bet on Wales.

TWENTY-THREE

KICKED IN THE NUTS BY STEEL TOECAPS

Your lungs are screaming for air, your head is thrumming with pain and your heart is thudding against your chest. Your body has been pushed to the very edge of its limits, your limbs drained of energy. The smallest task seems insurmountable. Overwhelmed by fatigue, you're reduced to a crawl, barely able to lift a bottle to your parched lips. You're broken, physically and mentally, and wondering if anything is worth this. Here there is no glory, no hero-worship, no fame nor celebrity. Here, you're just a puppet in a twisted theatre of torture, being pushed to the boundaries not just of your physical capabilities, but of your own sanity.

This is what the fans don't see. A rugby team is judged by what happens on a rectangle of turf over the course of eighty minutes. That is when the eyes of the world are watching.

For the player, that's the end of the road. For Wales, the journey to the 2011 Rugby World Cup was a long one with a torturous diversion to the remote, nondescript town of Spala in central Poland. It was there that Warren Gatland's squad experienced the most brutal and unforgiving training regime in the history of Welsh rugby.

Martyn Williams: Off. The. Charts. It was like boot camp. Five sessions a day, every day. A relentless, punishing regime. We'd be in the pool at six in the morning before breakfast, and then we'd have a full day of fitness and rugby, before topping it off with a weights session in the evening. There were about forty-five of us, and we knew only thirty-odd would make the cut for the World Cup, so there was no let-up. You're under the microscope in every session, and you know you can't drop off. You can't pace yourself like you sometimes can with your club. If you gave anything less than a hundred per cent, you'd be putting your World Cup chance in jeopardy. And bear in mind, I was thirty-six at this point.

Sam Warburton: Those camps were *savage*. I couldn't do it now. I didn't enjoy them at all, but hindsight proved that it was worth it. We fitness-tested a couple of months afterwards and everyone was off the scale. Even little guys like Shane and Richie Rees looked massive. We all had bodybuilders' physiques.

Dan Lydiate: They toughened us up mentally, especially the younger boys like me who'd never been before. Nugget told me he'd never trained as hard as he did in

Poland. On day one, I was thinking, 'Jesus, is *this* what it's about?' Nugget assured me that it had *never* been that bad before. By the time the World Cup began, we'd already been to the darkest of places.

Shane Williams: The confidence amongst the youngsters out there was something I hadn't seen before. The Sam Warburtons, the George Norths, the Dan Lydiates were all saying, 'We're going to win the World Cup.' It was contagious, and after a while, I started to agree with them.

Jamie Roberts: We had a good age profile. Experienced guys like Adam Jones and Gethin Jenkins, who were in their thirties. The youngsters like Sam Warburton and Taulupe Faletau. And guys like me in their mid-twenties, who were closing in on fifty caps. It was a good blend of youth and experience.

Jonathan Davies: It was our ability to recover that surprised me the most. We'd go to bed every day feeling wiped out, and drained of every last ounce of energy. The thought of having to go through it again in the morning was too horrendous to contemplate. But when the sun came up, we'd feel fresh and ready to go. It was surreal. Whether it was the cryotherapy or not, I don't know, but I remember feeling shocked that my body was capable of receiving so much punishment.

Dan Lydiate: Even though the games at the World Cup were tough, we *knew* that we wouldn't drop off. We *knew* that in the last twenty minutes of any game we could keep playing at the same intensity, whereas other teams might not be able to. It was part of Gatland's strategy to publicise the fact we were training so hard, and using the cryotherapy chambers for recovery. He never missed an opportunity to mention that to the press. It was a calculated move to put doubt in the mind of the opposition, to make them know that Wales was a team that would just keep going and going.

Shane Williams: It was the toughest training I'd ever done, but I went into that World Cup feeling supremely fit, supremely confident, and believing we were going to do something special. Going into ice chambers at minus 140 degrees takes some bloody willpower, let me tell you. By the end we felt mentally invincible, and physically indestructible.

Sam Warburton: The cryo allowed us to do up to five sessions a day. When you do that for three months, it's no surprise we got ourselves in the condition we did. I can't say it categorically, but I can't imagine any team trained as hard as we did.

Dan Lydiate: The early morning sessions were split into three groups. If you weren't in the first group, you'd wake up to the sound of the whistle blowing, knowing the boys were being run ragged out there. You'd be lying there dreading it, thinking, 'What the hell have they got in store today?' It was difficult to drag yourself out of bed at that point. There was a lot of bitching and moaning at times. You certainly asked questions of yourself. It was a test of character as much as anything. Gats was watching intently to see if any boys wanted to give up. If you were behind with your fitness, but you kept going, he was happy. That's what he was looking for. He could handle you struggling, but he wouldn't tolerate you giving up. During the strong man endurance circuit you'd be paired with someone in a similar position to you. The coaches would be walking around laying £5 bets on who'd win. I was doing tug of war with Andy Powell, and Gats was backing him. Howley put his fiver on me, and at the back of my mind, I was thinking, 'This is the selection meeting. This is a trial.' I think it was a draw in the end.

Sam Warburton: I was against Jonathan Thomas, and Gats and Howley were whispering to one another in the background. Gats gave Howley a tenner and said, 'My money's on JT.' He crouched down next to me and whispered, 'Remember you'll be up against Richie McCaw in two months. Do you really want to get beaten by a number six, by an older man? You're meant to be the young, fit guy. You should be all over him.'

Dan Lydiate: There were hideous punishments. If you were late for training, missed monitoring, or wore the wrong kit, you had to do a sandpit session with Dan Baugh.

Adam Jones: Jamie Roberts and I were the first to suffer at the hands of Dan Baugh after failing to 'self-monitor' on day one. You're supposed to weigh yourself, and answer a few questions on how you'd slept and that sort of thing. I'd not long become a father, and had been looking forward to Spala as an opportunity to catch up on a bit of sleep. I couldn't have been more naïve. After a few months of sleepless nights at home, I decided to have a lie-in on day one. Big mistake. Into the pit, I went.

Jonathan Davies: Dan would be barking orders at you, 'Crawl! Tuck jumps! Press ups!' The first victim only had to do five minutes, but as the fines accumulated, the time increased, so the next person to screw up got fifteen minutes, then twenty and so on. I think the longest session was forty-five minutes. That was *brutal*. I can't remember who did it, I've erased it from my memory. I did mine with Andy Powell and Rhys Priestland, and we had a king-of-the-ring wrestling match, which Powelly won easily. We were there for twenty-five minutes. By the end of that we could barely move, our lungs were burning and our muscles were screaming for mercy. And then we had to do another weights session in the evening.

Adam Jones: The whole thing was put into perspective when we took a day-trip to Auschwitz. As anyone who's been there knows, it's an incredibly humbling experience. Any gripes and moans we had about our training camp in Spala suddenly paled into total insignificance. We realised then that we were just pampered sportsmen being paid to do what we loved.

After the second Spala camp, Wales returned home to prepare for three warm-up games. They were to play England twice, home and away, and Argentina in Cardiff. Previous World Cup warm-ups against England had ended in disaster, but this time, things felt different.

Jonathan Davies: The first indicator of where we were at was the first warm-up game at Twickenham. Normally before the first game of a season, I'm bricking it, thinking, 'Will I be able to last?' and that's usually ahead of a friendly for the Scarlets. This was a Wales–England *international*. We lost the game because we were rusty at the start, but we finished so strongly compared to England. That ability to outlast teams became our defining theme in the tournament. We beat them the following week, beat Argentina, and should have beaten South Africa in the opening game of the World Cup.

Sam Warburton: I had a phone call from Warren the day the final squad was due to be announced. Maybe it was the day before. I was in my house, sat in the lounge, and he just came out with it: 'Do you want to be captain for the World Cup?' No small talk, no preamble, he just hit me with it. I immediately felt terrified and thought, 'I can't do this.' I was looking at myself in the mirror during the call, and despite the fact I was shitting myself, I heard my voice say, 'Yes.'

He asked if I could come down within the hour to prepare for a press conference. It was that quick. I had to go and dig out an un-ironed WRU polo top from upstairs. I rang my Dad en route because I was panicking and needed a calming presence on the other end of the line. When I met up with Gats, I asked, 'Why not Alun Wyn? Why not Gethin? Why not Stephen? Why not Shane?' He just said, 'Because I want *you* to do it.' When I asked why, he opened his laptop, and clicked on a clip of us beating England in the warm-up game. I'd made a tackle, and won the turnover, which led to the winning penalty. I was punching the air, going nuts, picking guys up off the floor, and rallying the team for the final flourish. Gats folded his laptop back down, and said, 'That's leadership. That's what I want you to do,' and I thought, 'Oh right, I can do *that*.'

Warren Gatland: I recognised early on that Sam was a guy who hated losing. He was so competitive, so determined, and he set his standards so high. I knew that he'd raise the bar for others to follow.

Sam Warburton: I was never going to be a captain that gave Churchillian speeches, I was just me – a competitive animal who hated losing, and never took a backward step. I always wanted to be authentic. People often asked me what player I'd most want to be like, and I always replied, 'Myself.' I've never looked at another player and thought, 'I need to do that because he does it,' or 'I need to say that because he said it.' I did what I wanted. Andy McCann, the squad psychologist once told me to be true to myself, and that's what I always did. I never tried to be anybody else.

Jamie Roberts: I didn't use Andy McCann much. I know him well and I like him, but didn't feel the need to use him. It's probably because of my academic background. I'm a keen problem-solver, and I like to think that that's helped my rugby. Whenever I've had issues mentally, I've solved the problem in my own head. I've always tried to manage that myself. Whether that's a good thing or a bad thing, I couldn't tell you.

Sam Warburton: He was a really important part of that squad in 2011. He didn't get much credit, but that was how he liked it. He was very much under the radar. I know there are people who think that using a sports psychologist is a sign of weakness, but it's not. In the modern game, it's really important. There are a lot of really talented guys in the squad who find it hard to deal with the pressure of being an international rugby player. It's not just therapy for people who are low on confidence, it's advice on how to manage your life outside of rugby, so that you can perform to the best of your ability when you put the shirt on. There was an awkward moment before the World Cup. There was room for about twenty support staff on the trip, and the final spot on the plane was a toss-up between Andy and an extra video analyst. The team manager stood up in a meeting and called a vote in front of the two guys in question. He said, 'Video analyst . . .' and a couple of people put their hands up. He said, 'Andy McCann . . .' and all the rest raised their hands. It was a pretty big majority.

Andy McCann's presence offered Warburton solace at a time of immense pressure. It's said that the captain of the national rugby side has a higher profile and is subject to greater scrutiny than the First Minister of Wales. For an inexperienced twenty-two-year-old, new to captaincy, it was a heavy load to bear.

Sam Warburton: I doubted myself and I was conscious that there were a lot of senior players who didn't agree with the decision. There were older, more experienced candidates who could have been given the job. Andy came up with a 'leadership compass' which I lived by. I kept it on my phone, and in my notes, so I could always refer to it. It was really simple, just four broad bullet points: be positive, be professional, develop relationships with everyone in the squad, and above all, *perform*.

When the squad arrived in New Zealand, they quickly became darlings of the Kiwi press, charming the locals with their impromptu choir sessions, and impressing with their politeness and professionalism. The lens of the media was focused sharply on the hosts – who'd developed a reputation for underachieving at World Cups – and England, who seemed intent on self-destruction. As stories of England's dwarf-throwing, late nights and excessive drinking began to fill the front and back pages, Wales's exemplary tourists were being held up as paragons of virtue.

Jamie Roberts: We're no angels but we were very aware we were in a country where the press would look for anything to disadvantage the opposition. You might think you have rhino skin, but if an article appears in the paper about you or one of your teammates doing something out of hand, it does affect you. Campaigns can derail pretty quickly when things like that happen. Gats made it clear that no transgressions were going to be tolerated, but that didn't mean we couldn't have a few beers from time to time. After that Samoa win in Hamilton we had a hell of a night out. It's what it's all about, isn't it? Being on tour, having beers with the lads.

Sam Warburton: The boys *were* going out, but there was a line they knew they couldn't cross. There was a group of players that weren't involved in the match-day twenty-three that went 'off tour', and started going out drinking quite a lot. Rob Howley sat them down at the end of the trip and told them they'd never play for Wales again because of the way they'd conducted themselves. Ninety per cent of the squad were on board, and super strict, but there's always a minority who are a bit rebellious.

Jonathan Davies: We weren't monks, but it was a perfect scenario for us. The English boys were getting slated, and we were all perceived to be squeaky clean. Our 'front-of-office' person was Sam Warburton, whose only vice was having a bar of chocolate after a game. People thought we were *all* Sam Warburton. I'm not knocking him for wanting a chocolate bar, everyone's different, but some boys prefer to go for a drink.

Warren Gatland: You've got the Sam Warburtons on the one hand, then on the other you've got the likes of Mike Phillips, Shane Williams and Lee Byrne getting smashed back at the hotel where no one can see them. We never wanted them to be monks, we just wanted to strike a balance.

Sam Warburton: Someone suggested the idea of a drinks chart to monitor who was wet and who was dry. It was agreed by the senior players' group. Everyone put a tenner in, and whoever had stayed dry by the end of the tour got to share the kitty. It was the easiest investment I've ever made because I knew I wouldn't even be tempted to have a drink. Everyone started on dry, then you moved over to the wet as soon as any alcohol had passed your lips. The chart was in a prime position in the gym so everyone could see it. It was all about willpower, not giving in to temptation, and was based on honesty. Two days in we were all asked 'Has anyone had a drink?' and to be fair, Andy Powell put his hand up straight away and said he'd had a glass of wine with his steak the night before. In the end, there were only a few of us left. Me, Leigh [Halfpenny], George [North] and Dan [Lydiate]. All the youngsters, basically.

Jamie Roberts: Having a few beers and letting off steam is part of Gatland's creed, but he's not a schoolteacher about it. He trusts the players not to take advantage. That attitude empowered us because if you accepted responsibility off the field, you took responsibility on it. We enjoyed ourselves, but we knew there was a line, and stayed on the right side of it. England crossed it. They were playing in a country that would examine their behaviour under a microscope. And we're talking about an era when not everyone had a smartphone. You have to be squeaky clean now.

Sam Warburton: I didn't drink because I needed to know that on match day I was the best possible version of me that I could be. Mentally, that put me in the right frame of mind to play. I never felt like I was missing out. I always saved it for the end of a tour, or the end of a championship. Would you see Jess Ennis going on the piss a week before the Olympics? No. Playing for Wales was my Olympics.

Jamie Roberts: Everyone's different. Some will abstain completely from alcohol before or during a tournament. Some, like myself, like to celebrate the wins with a few beers. Some will come out and not drink, some won't come out at all. That's their choice. They'll get the piss ripped out of them, but it's their choice. You have to respect each individual's ways of preparing for games.

Jonathan Davies: A lot of fuss was made about the England team, their nights out and their drinking. We went under the radar, and we were comfortable with that.

Warren Gatland: There's no doubt the New Zealand press were closely monitoring England, looking for any indiscretions. Other teams did similar things but none of it was reported.

Sam Warburton: Because they're England everything's magnified by ten so I felt a little sympathy for them. But there's a line and they crossed it. Our boys wouldn't have done that. We wouldn't have jumped off a boat in the harbour (like Manu Tuilagi did). That was stupid. We were going out, but were maybe a bit cuter about it. We stayed local, kept a low profile, and behaved ourselves. I say 'we', but personally I never went out. I was religious about my preparation.

Jonathan Davies: You've got to be smart and box clever. If you put yourself in situations you shouldn't be in, you'll get found out.

Warren Gatland: We had a curfew after our night games of one a.m., and we expected everyone to be back at the hotel by then. But the hotel bar was open until around three or four, so we were pretty relaxed about the boys carrying on if they wanted to. It was all about perception; we didn't want them seen out on the town at that time. We might not get back to the hotel until gone eleven on a match night, so I had no issue with the boys going out for a quiet drink, as long as they were back within the curfew.

Jonathan Davies: Gats had knowledge of the culture and he used it. By the end of the pool stages we were everyone's second team. There were photos and videos of us singing, hanging out with the locals, and we were playing good rugby, which helped.

Warren Gatland: A lot of teams who visit New Zealand don't do their homework, in terms of preparing culturally. We understood the importance of embracing the Maori culture, and of having our own responses to the haka and the welcomes we received. We were probably better prepared than any other team in that respect.

Jamie Roberts: We embraced the country. We visited Maori tribes, mingled with the locals, and did all the outdoor stuff. Huw Bennett, Byrney and myself did a bungee jump over Lake Taupo. Prof. John Williams came with us for that, and I distinctly remember thinking, as he was being strapped in, 'Is his ticker going to hack this?'

Warren Gatland: It wasn't just the off-field stuff that endeared us to the New Zealand public, we were playing some pretty good rugby as well. Two of our games were in my home town of Hamilton. Waikato people are pretty loyal, and they decided to get behind one of their own. We got massive support for those two games against Samoa and Fiji, and I think that surprised a few people.

Dan Lydiate: It was the best tour I've been on, because we got looked after off the field, and really got to experience the country. A lot of rugby tours these days are money-oriented. You're there to do a job, you're whisked around between games and various corporate commitments, and it's hard to really embrace the culture of the place you're visiting.

Wales's first pool game was against the defending champions, South Africa. It was a daunting opening encounter, but after Spala, Wales felt ready for anything.

Adam Jones: We dealt with their physicality comfortably, and I kept the Beast [Tendai Mtawarira] quiet. We were the better team and should have won. But they were the defending world champions, and they were streetwise. They knew how to get over the line.

Jonathan Davies: They were a hugely physical side. Schalk Burger, Pierre Spies. Victor Matfield and Danie Roussow in the second row. All big men, but our boys stood up to them. Lyds was chopping them down, and Warby was winning turnovers. They just couldn't get him off the ball. We outmuscled them, which very few northern hemisphere sides had done to the Springboks. There were far more positives than negatives, just a couple of switch-offs in defence. Those things could be sorted, no problem. It was a tough game but we never felt pushed off the ball. South Africa knew they'd been in a Test match.

Sam Warburton: We should have beaten them. We gifted them the match through the most trivial defensive error. And James Hook's disallowed penalty didn't help us.

Hook's kick in the fourteenth minute sailed high over the posts, and appeared to travel between the uprights. But the flags stayed down, and referee Wayne Barnes didn't refer it to the TMO. Hook was adamant it had gone over, as were the thousands of Welsh fans inside the Wellington Regional Stadium.

Jonathan Davies: I chased the kick, and was convinced it had gone over, but I didn't kick up a fuss like I would now. I'd throw my toys out of the pram now.

Sam Warburton: I blame myself for that. If I'd been a more experienced captain, I'd have asked the ref to check with the TMO. That could have been the game. We had the making to beat anyone that year.

Warren Gatland: We were adamant it went over. At half-time, Neil Jenkins approached the ref and said, 'That kick went over,' and Francois Steyn, who was nearby, said he thought it had as well. To this day, I don't know why they didn't go to the TMO. He may well have stuck with the original decision, but at least ask the question.

Jonathan Davies: In terms of the overall draw, losing was the best thing that could have happened. It was obviously disappointing, but we gained a lot from it. Deep down there was a quiet confidence among us. If we could replicate that physicality, and be a bit more clinical with the ball, we knew we could do well.

Sam Warburton: The night before our second game against Samoa, Ireland had beaten Australia, and blown the draw wide open. I remember looking at Rob

Howley at breakfast, and we had these massive beaming smiles on our faces. If we won our remaining games, we'd probably face Ireland in the quarters instead of Australia. We knew we could beat Ireland. It wasn't arrogance, it was confidence. We had the northern hemisphere route to the final, and we knew we could beat all those teams. There was this weird aura of excitement in the room. We all started to think this could be our year. We could win the World Cup.

Stephen Jones: I didn't think about the route to the final. We were just living in the moment. But we knew we could beat Ireland.

Before they could think of the quarter-finals, Wales had to negotiate their way out of the pool. Next up were Samoa, Wales's World Cup bogey side. They'd played them twice in previous tournaments – in 1991 and 1999 – and lost on both occasions. Both were seismic upsets. The first was arguably the biggest in world rugby, the second brought a ten-game winning run to an end. The Pacific Islanders were not to be taken lightly.

Warren Gatland: There was a bit of pressure on us because if we didn't beat Samoa, we were out of the World Cup.

Adam Jones: Our tactics going into that game were interesting. Robin McBryde encouraged us to 'T-bone' them, which essentially meant running straight into them rather than around them. Given that they're the most aggressive defenders in world rugby, it could have been foolish, but we were so confident in our physicality that we were happy to take them on at their own game. Jamie laid down the gauntlet early on by smashing into his opposite number, Seilala Mapusua, and knocking him back. He was a talisman for them, and to see him crumple gave us a big psychological boost.

Warren Gatland: We were behind at half-time, and that was the moment that team grew up. I didn't have to say anything. Sam Warburton stood up and said, 'We're not going home. We haven't worked this hard, we haven't trained this hard, we haven't gone to hell and back in Poland, to go home now.' From a coaching perspective, that's gold. I didn't need to say anything after that. Sam wasn't one of these players who spoke for the sake of it, but when he did speak up, when he did lose his rag, it was very effective. That's why we made him captain.

For all Wales's physicality, their performance was uninspired. Only a Shane Williams try separated the two sides, and it took a bit of front-row skullduggery to secure the win, as Samoa launched a series of attacks in the closing stages.

Adam Jones: Having studied their loose-head, I thought I could put pressure on him by scrummaging a bit higher. It allowed me to push down and put more weight on the back of his head, forcing him to hinge. It's technically cheating because I was aiming down rather than straight, but if you're cunning about it, you can make it look like your opponent's collapsed the scrum. I hoodwinked the ref, and got away with it. It won us a penalty, we cleared our lines and snuck home 17–10.

Given the history of the fixture, and the context of the game, the victory was significant. A routine win followed against minnows, Namibia, before Wales faced another Pacific nemesis. Fiji had dumped Wales out of the previous World Cup, and the memories remained vivid in the minds of those involved. But this Fiji side didn't have the pedigree of its 2007 counterpart, and meekly surrendered to a rampant Wales. They coasted into the quarter-finals on the back of a 66–0 win.

Warren Gatland: On the day of the quarter-final, Ireland were meant to be travelling to the ground first, but they were late. Apparently their hotel was jam-packed and they'd struggled to get on the bus. It meant we had to wait for their police escort to return to our hotel to take us in. We were all sat on our bus impatient to leave, and eventually I told the driver to just go. En route to the ground, we saw the police escort travelling the other way. As soon as we arrived at the stadium, the copper in charge boarded our bus in a rage and yelled, 'Liaison officer off the bus now!' Moments later, him and Alan Phillips were nose to nose having a massive argument. The copper was furious we'd left without the escort, and Alan was insisting it'd been late so it wasn't our fault. It wasn't the best preparation for a World Cup quarter-final, so I made a complaint to Neil Sorenson, New Zealand Rugby's general manager. We ended up with a formal apology from the New Zealand police.

Sam Warburton: Ireland knew what was coming in the quarters, but they couldn't stop it. That was typified in the opening few minutes, when Jamie Roberts ran straight through Donncha O'Callaghan. He was one of their biggest, most abrasive players and Jamie absolutely *flattened* him.

Adam Jones: When I think of that game, I think of that moment. Donncha hit the deck hard. It was like he'd tried to tackle a freight train. When that happened, I knew it was going to be our day.

Jamie Roberts: That was a pretty cool moment. I'm a glorified second row anyway!

Warren Gatland: We *were* a big team, we *were* physical, we *were* fit, and we wanted to impose that on other teams. We knew we were capable of beating anybody.

Jonathan Davies: The work rate in the first half of guys like Luke Charteris, Warby, and Toby, was off the scale. They were phenomenal.

Luke Charteris: It was a hell of a defensive shift in the first half. Ireland liked to keep hold of the ball and send their big carriers into contact, but we kept smashing into them, knocking them backwards and thinking, 'We can do this all day.'

Warren Gatland: It was the first time we went for a two-full back strategy, using the open-side winger as a second full back to counteract O'Gara's kicking from hand. He ended up kicking the ball out about three times on the full. We shut his kicking options down, meaning they couldn't kick so much for territory. We'd named Shane on the left wing, but as we ran out onto the field, we switched him to the right to help negate some of their kicking strategy. We knew they'd have planned to kick a lot to Shane, so that tactic had gone.

Jamie Roberts: It was just an amazing game. Shane got that try early on, then Phillsy dummied and went over in the corner with his swallow dive. It was one of my proudest moments in a Wales shirt. It was mega.

Jonathan Davies: Ireland probably went into it a bit too confident after beating Australia, and we just blew them off the ball.

Warren Gatland: They believed a bit too much in their own hype.

Jonathan Davies: It was a special day, especially for me, as I scored the last try. I received the ball and looked up to see their prop, Cian Healy, in front of me. I went round him, and then no one else laid a finger on me. Pens [Leigh Halfpenny] was outside me in space, and apparently all the coaches were up in their box, yelling, 'Give it to Pens! GIVE IT TO PENS!' Seconds later, they were all shouting, equally enthusiastically, 'Keep hold of it, keep hold of it!' It was a special moment in my career, that. Something I'll always treasure. I'd shown for the first time what I could do on that stage.

Sam Warburton: It was Shaun Edwards who masterminded that win. Sean O'Brien was European player of the year off the back of some barnstorming displays in the Heineken Cup. He was a one-man wrecking ball who was so hard to stop once he'd got some momentum. But in that quarter-final, he made a total of about two yards with his carrying, because of one reason: Dan Lydiate's chop tackling. He revolutionised tackling in that tournament, and it was Shaun's idea – chop him at the ankles before he gets into his stride.

Players have spoken of the disorienting effect of a Dan Lydiate chop tackle. There was an element of stealth to it. One minute you were upright, braced for contact. The next, you were on the deck, dazed and wondering if a sniper in the crowd had taken you out. It's little wonder Lydiate earned the nickname 'Silent Assassin' during the tournament.

Dan Lydiate: Our defence was the best it had ever been in that game. Their back row was highly rated and hugely physical. Their reputation was enhanced even further after they beat Australia, especially when Stephen Ferris picked up Will Genia and ran him back about twenty yards. Shaun sat down with Toby, Warby and me before the game and said, 'Everyone's talking about this back row, but hand on heart I wouldn't change any one of them for any one of you.' You knew he was being genuine, and that meant a lot to us. It was a *hell* of a battle. One of the best we've had. Sean O'Brien, Jamie Heaslip and Stephen Ferris *were* probably the best back row unit in Europe at the time, if not the world.

Sam Warburton: Our game plan suited Dan Lydiate to a tee. He was the perfect six for the way we wanted to play. He'd be brilliant in the NFL. He fulfilled a really niche role in rugby, like a safety in NFL, I guess. Because he had to be fit to play rugby, it took away some of his raw power. If he *only* had to be a power athlete, he'd be nineteen stone, and an absolute monster. No one would have come close to him.

Dan Lydiate: There was a moment when Sean O'Brien took a ball off a five-man lineout, and Warby and I were lying in wait like two predators. We pincered him and chopped him down at the same time. Back then, you didn't have to release in the tackle, so Warby mauled him into the jackal position and I won the turnover. We went hammer and tongs at them. It was probably the most physical we've ever been as a Welsh squad.

Warren Gatland: There were a few things they didn't see coming in that game: the chop tackle, the two-full backs strategy, and our attacking shape. Brian O'Driscoll was really effective at shooting out of the line and shutting teams down in defence. To counter that, we played with our ten standing flat, but maintained the depth behind him. Because we held our depth really well, O'Driscoll was rushing up quick, realising he was in no-man's land, and dropping back, which allowed us more room to play. Over time, their line-speed dropped off dramatically.

Jamie Roberts: Ultimately, we blew a very experienced Ireland side off the park. Paul O'Connell, Ronan O'Gara, Brian O'Driscoll, they were all playing. Howlers had said before the game, 'I want O'Gara off the park by sixty minutes,' and lo and behold on fifty-nine minutes, he's getting subbed off, and we knew we'd done a job.

Dan Lydiate: You speak to the Irish boys now and they say they never thought they were going to lose. You could tell that by looking at their faces on the final whistle. They were genuinely shell-shocked. Johnny Sexton told me as much when I played with him out in Paris for Racing.

Shane Williams: It felt like it was our destiny to win that game.

Luke Charteris: I went off injured at half-time, and I remember being so relaxed watching the second half. It wasn't a massive winning margin but it felt like it was never in doubt.

Warren Gatland: I went down onto the field afterwards, and Roger Lewis, the WRU chief executive, was heading straight for me with a beaming smile on his face. He could barely contain his joy, and he looked as though he was about to burst. When he reached me, I said, 'Roger, whatever you do, *do not* kiss me.'

Wales were through to the World Cup semi-finals for only the second time in their history. Their performance against Ireland confirmed them as serious contenders. There were four teams left – New Zealand, Australia, France and Wales. France had beaten England but their coach Marc Lievremont was struggling to quell an internal Gallic mutiny. They'd already lost twice – to New Zealand and Tonga – and held no fear for Wales.

Warren Gatland: There was another administrative bungle before the semi-final. We headed back up to Auckland, and France were made to move out of the big Sky City hotel so we could base ourselves there. We didn't want to go into Sky City, we'd have preferred to stay in a quieter, smaller place with a bit more anonymity. Neither team was happy. It was so dumb. The night before the game, Sam and I went to see the referee, Alain Rolland. It was a pretty short meeting. We weren't sure whether to be aggressive with him in terms of demanding certain things, or to take a more softly-softly approach. We went softly-softly in the end, and I'm not sure it did us any favours.

Sam Warburton: I always went to see Andy McCann during the build-up to big games to try to calm my nerves. After fifteen minutes with him, any doubt would have disappeared, and I'd be ready to take on the world. The semi-final against France was undoubtedly the biggest game of my life but I felt totally chilled beforehand. Half an hour before I jumped on the bus, I went to see Andy and said, 'No offence, but I don't need anything. I feel the best I've ever felt.' It was the shortest conversation I'd ever had with him. I was just consumed by this supreme sense of confidence.

Dan Lydiate: We didn't think we'd be going home after that semi-final. We genuinely thought we were going all the way.

Sam Warburton: I told the players to be brave, to not worry about taking risks. 'Don't go into your shells, express yourselves as if you're playing in front of no one. Think about what you can achieve, not what you might lose.'

Jonathan Davies: There were more people in the Millennium Stadium watching it there than were at Eden Park. Seeing those photos was amazing.

If ever an illustration was needed of how passionate Welsh rugby supporters are, that was it. 61,543 fans poured into the Millennium Stadium to cheer on their heroes who were 12,000 miles away in Auckland.

Shane Williams: I was a hundred per cent confident we would win that match. I didn't expect we'd be going home with our tails between our legs. We *should* have won. Losing that game is one of the biggest regrets of my career.

Sam Warburton: Things started superbly. During the opening quarter, Imanol Harinordoquy picked up off the base of a scrum, and I *melted* him. It was brilliant. Then the red card happened. I'm going to be asked about that until I'm seventy.

It's an image indelibly stamped on the brain of every Welsh rugby supporter. The diminutive Vincent Clerc being upended and dumped by Wales captain, Sam Warburton. One of the most disciplined and even-tempered players in world rugby was facing the ultimate on-field sanction.

Sam Warburton: I knew Clerc was coming, because Ireland had tried the same move with their winger in the quarter-final, and I'd mis-read it. We knew France would have picked up on that, and would try something similar.

Warren Gatland: We'd prepared for it. We'd seen them use that move as well, and agreed that Sam would ignore the ten and focus on the winger.

Sam Warburton: I had a chat with Dan and told him, 'If they run this move, you take the nine [Dimitri Yachvili], and I'll take the winger.' As a seven, you learn to read body language. When you look at the back line, you develop a sixth sense as to who's going to receive the ball. Just by looking at Vincent Clerc, I could tell he was preparing to get it. Our attitude back then was to physically dominate the opposition, so I lined him up and went in as hard as I could. He twisted in the air to try to present the ball, which is what made him go down on his head. As soon as he was on the deck, I went for the jackal, thinking to myself, 'This is a hell of a turnover.' It never occurred to me that I might be in trouble. I just thought I'd absolutely mullered him. I was more than happy with it. Next thing, the French second rows were swinging upper cuts at me, and I thought, 'Hang on a second . . .'

Dan Lydiate: It was *how* he hit him that made it look bad. It kicked off a bit, and tempers started to flare. To the letter of the law these days, what he did was a certain red, but at the time everybody thought it was going to be a yellow.

Shane Williams: I remember thinking, 'Ooof, that's a yellow, but we'll be alright for ten minutes.' When the red came out, I thought, 'How the hell are we going to do this now?' Looking back, the tip tackle had been a massive focus in that World Cup. It was a new directive, and the referee had no option but to make a statement, but that didn't stop us feeling terribly hard done by. It was the semi-final of a World Cup, for goodness sake. Give us a break.

Jamie Roberts: I was defending at twelve, and saw it happen. I thought, 'Oh God, he's dropped him on his head, this could be a card.' I never thought for a second it would be red.

Warren Gatland: I was amazed. The red card just came straight out of his pocket. It was instantaneous. I didn't see it at first. Someone said it was red, and I said, 'What!?' It was one of those situations where I thought the referee would blow the whistle, calm things down, maybe talk to his touch judges, and take a bit of control. A red card in the semi-final of a World Cup seemed so extreme, especially considering Sam's record. It wasn't a malicious act of violence; it's not like he punched someone from behind. I think a yellow card or a penalty would have been a fair outcome.

Sam Warburton: Some people have suggested I was pumped up and overly aggressive because of the occasion, but that's nonsense. I did exactly the same tackle on Ronan O'Gara in the quarter-final. And Stephen Ferris, for that matter. I picked them up and dumped them, and didn't even get penalised. I'd done it throughout the World Cup. Within two seconds the red card had been shown. There was no time to process anything. I've always hated seeing footballers protest a referee's decision, so I thought 'button it up', and walked straight off. For the rest of the first half, there was a camera stationed six feet away from me, waiting for me to slip up and show some emotion. I wanted to grab it and shove it in the cameraman's face.

Warren Gatland: He was probably the worst person on the field for us to have lost. Not only was he our captain, but he was an absolutely pivotal player. The form he'd shown up to that point, the way he was playing, the way he was competing on the ball, the amount of turnovers he was winning, he'd been outstanding.

Jonathan Davies: I watched Warby run off, and thought he was going to the sin bin. It was a good few minutes later that I looked up at the big TV screen and saw a red card underneath the Wales badge. I turned to Jamie, and said, 'Was Warby sent off?!' He looked at me in disbelief. 'Are you serious?' he said.

Jamie Roberts: All everyone remembers was the red card, but Bomb going off was a major blow as well. He was the cornerstone of our pack, and we were up against one of the best scrummaging teams in the tournament. That moment proved just as pivotal.

Jonathan Davies: At that point in his career, Bomb was unstoppable. He was our rock. It was a huge loss. We went into our shells a bit there.

Adam Jones: I was getting a bit sick of it, to be honest. How many times had I had to leave the field in career-defining games? The World Cup quarter-final in 2003, the second Lions Test in 2009, and now this? Barely seven minutes had been played, but I knew I was done for. I felt a strange thud in the back of my leg during a scrum, and Carcass came on and told me I'd torn my calf. Game over. I collapsed onto the subs' bench, pulled a coat over my head and started bawling my eyes out. I was still lost in my own world when I felt someone sitting down next to me. I peered out from underneath my coat, and saw Sam. I was confused. I asked him, 'What the hell are you doing here?' He looked a bit vacant and said, 'I've just been sent off.' I thought he was taking the piss until he pointed at the big screen where his tackle was being endlessly replayed in graphic slow motion. Oh, shit.

Sam Warburton: He was a massive figure for us, particularly against France. His scrum penalties could win us games. It will bug me forever. You'll never ever know what would have happened, but I think if Adam had stayed on, and I hadn't been sent off, we'd have won the game, and potentially the World Cup. It will always haunt me.

Warren Gatland: Sam felt a huge amount of responsibility and guilt for being sent off, but he definitely wasn't the reason we lost.

Jonathan Davies: No one blames Warby. We blame ourselves for not winning the game.

In adversity, Wales summoned a remarkable, stirring response. In the driving wind and rain, they erected a red wall that France were unable to penetrate despite their superior numbers, and surfeit of possession.

When it seemed Wales had nothing left to give, Mike Phillips – as he'd done against Ireland – seized the initiative. After a couple of hard carries from his forward pack, Phillips spied a mismatch, threaded himself between Pascal Papé and Lionel Nallet and sprinted twenty-two yards to the try line. It brought the score back to 9–8, with the conversion to come, but Stephen Jones's characteristic poise deserted him and the ball shaved the left-hand upright.

Warren Gatland: He rushed the kick, and it's one he'd normally nail with his eyes shut.

Moments later, Jones missed an attempted drop-goal, but as the game entered its final quarter, it was the French who were hanging on. With six minutes to go, Nicolas Mas strayed offside on the halfway line, giving Leigh Halfpenny a shot to win it from fifty metres out. He was a distance specialist with an impressive range, but despite an almighty thump, the ball fell agonisingly short.

During the final five minutes, Wales launched a sustained assault, chiselling away at the French defence, finding a dent here, a hollow there. Patiently, they made their way from the halfway line to the ten-metre line. Twenty-six nerve-jangling phases took them so far, but never close enough for Stephen Jones to drop back into the pocket for an attempt on goal. Eventually, the ball was spilt, and the match was lost.

History has softened the pain, not only of defeat, but of raging injustice. In the fullness of time, Warburton's punishment has been accepted as justified, but when emotions were as raw and tender as they were at the final whistle, the red mist over the red card was clouding every Welsh fan's vision.

Warren Gatland: Realistically, losing our captain to a red card so early, we should have lost by 15 to 20 points. But the fact is we should still have won. Mike Phillips went over for that try, but Stephen Jones missed the conversion. Towards the end, we had a lineout in their twenty-two, Jamie Roberts made a great bust and gave us the perfect opportunity for a drop goal but we didn't do it, we just played through phases, and Stephen eventually lost the ball in contact. Leigh Halfpenny's kick fell short. It just wasn't meant to be.

Stephen Jones: The reality is that we had chances to win that game despite the red card. I don't reflect on the moment with Sam, I think of the chances we blew after that. There were sixty minutes left to play when he went off. We had so much possession at the end, but we couldn't get close enough for the drop-goal. We just needed someone to get their nose through, and we could have gone for it.

Warren Gatland: The first time that Jamie went through, we were close enough. That was the moment. We were in the best possible position. We didn't drop back into the pocket to look for that opportunity.

Stephen Jones: The prospect of a drop-goal was definitely on my mind. I was thinking, 'Just give me half a chance.' I wanted that one little half-dent, that one little gap, but credit to the French for their discipline. They weren't contesting the rucks, they were just filling the front line. There was never a clear and obvious moment.

Luke Charteris: France defended brilliantly and just didn't give us that extra ten or fifteen metres we needed to take the risk. The feeling in the changing room after the Ireland game was the best I'd ever felt after a rugby match. The feeling after the French game was the worst I'd ever felt.

Jamie Roberts: Losing that match is the biggest regret of my career. To fall short by such an agonising margin on that stage is brutal. It will always haunt me. It's my biggest failure in rugby.

Luke Charteris: I was rooming with Jamie and when we got back to our room and shut the door, the two of us just burst into tears. It suddenly hit us, three hours later, that the dream was over.

Shane Williams: My heart sunk to the floor when the whistle blew. I knew that was my last opportunity. The finality of it was difficult to digest. I was *never* going to get to a World Cup final. I'd had a conversation with Warren about retiring at the end of it because I'd wanted to go out a World Cup winner. Had France been the best team on the field then fair enough, but they weren't. It was like being kicked in the nuts with steel toecaps.

Jonathan Davies: I broke down. There's a photo of me in floods of tears, with Andy Powell trying to comfort me. I was absolutely devastated. I got back into the changing rooms and got myself together, then I walked out and saw my parents and burst into tears again. You put so much into it, you invest so much of your life in it, and then it's gone in an instant. And you know deep down you might never get that opportunity again. France didn't offer anything. They were just big heavy men. I haven't ever watched it back. I couldn't bear to. The only bit I've seen since is Mike Phillips's try because he keeps showing it to me on his phone!

Shane Williams: When Mike did anything positive, you never heard the end of it. If he did anything bad, it never happened. That's Mike Phillips for you. He'd probably have gone on to score the winning try in the final and *then* we'd never have heard the end of it.

Jonathan Davies: I've never seen the final and I don't want to. I was in the air at the time, and had no interest in watching it. I think we would have won the World Cup. We'd have missed Warby for the final, no doubt. But we still had Jug Head,

Lyds and Toby. By all accounts, New Zealand were there for the taking.

Dan Lydiate: New Zealand didn't play that well in the final because they were so scared to lose. That only deepened the pain of not being there.

Warren Gatland: I had two tickets for the final, and I gave them to Sam Warburton and his dad. I went to the beach and watched it with my son. At half-time, I said to him, 'Let's watch this game how I might watch it as a coach. Let's watch it from a French perspective.' In the second half, he was going, 'That should have been a penalty against the All Blacks. Richie McCaw should have been penalised there.' He started seeing it through different eyes. I've had conversations with top referees who thought New Zealand were fortunate on the day. That's not to say I wasn't supporting them. Obviously when I coach against them, I'm desperate to beat them, but at the end of the day, I'm a proud Kiwi who played for the All Blacks, so if they're playing anyone else, they've got my support. I wanted them to beat France and create some history.

Sam Warburton: That's why it kills me. I could be sitting here now as a World Cup winner. You'll never know for sure, and that's what's so gutting.

Jonathan Davies: I was rooming with Leigh, and he was distraught over that missed kick. He carries so much responsibility on his shoulders. That's the way he's wired, and he'll never change. He takes such pride in his game, and he *expects* to make the big kicks. No one blamed him. That's what I was trying to tell him. We should have put that game to bed long before the penalty was even given. He just wanted to hole up in his room, and shut the world out, but I refused to let him. I told him I wasn't leaving without him. It took a bit of persuading, but I got him down to have a beer with the boys eventually. A couple of beers helps any situation, but it was really difficult. We spent the next couple of days walking around Auckland wondering 'what if?'

Sam Warburton: I'd swap the drawn Lions series with New Zealand for that World Cup. It was great to have beaten New Zealand in a one-off Test, but we didn't win the series. It's more difficult to win a World Cup with Wales, and no one's ever done it.

Warren Gatland: Does it keep me awake at night? Not really. I can't change it. If you dwell on it too much, it would just consume you. You've just got to park it.

Sam Warburton: After Gats did his debrief in the changing room, he asked Neil Jenkins to speak, but Neil was too emotional. He turned to me, and I returned to my earlier theme of being brave. I told them they had been, and that's all we could have asked for. It took every ounce of emotional energy I had left not to break down in front of the boys. After I'd finished my speech, I walked into the toilet cubicle, sat down, and bawled my eyes out for a quarter of an hour. I was devastated. I thought about how Beckham had been crucified when he got sent off in the World Cup, and I thought I was going to get killed when I got home. I genuinely thought people were going to hate me.

Adam Jones: There was barely any anger towards Warby from the fans. It was Alain Rolland who bore the brunt of their rage. I understand that emotions were raw, but the amount of hate directed towards him was wrong. It takes balls to be an international referee, and he was just doing his job. Once all the emotion had subsided, most sensible people had to admit that it was a fair decision.

Sam Warburton: I was given the option of missing the post-match press conference, but I wanted to front up. It was one of the hardest things I've ever done. The disciplinary hearing on the Sunday was walking distance from our hotel down a busy street lined with bars and outdoor cafes. I was dreading the reception I was going to get. Within minutes, someone clocked me and Gats, and I braced myself for a barrage of abuse. The bloke stood up and started clapping. Others soon followed suit, and it set off a Mexican wave of applause. I'd been sent off in a World Cup semi-final, yet here I was getting a standing ovation on the streets of Auckland. I was overwhelmed with emotion. I'll never forget that.

Warren Gatland: It was surreal. I think it showed that the Kiwis had embraced Wales. History played its part. Wales had always been seen back in the thirties, forties and fifties as one of the major rivals, and we're similar countries in terms of our love of the game. We'd been playing some good rugby, and a lot of Kiwis had been hoping for a New Zealand–Wales final.

Sam Warburton: I didn't say anything to Alain Rolland, and I didn't speak to him for more than two-and-a-half years. In 2013, I was on the bench against Italy, and he came in to check the boys' studs. I said hello to him, and he ignored me. I wanted to be the bigger man, and shake his hand but he didn't seem interested. In hindsight he was probably in the zone, and didn't realise it was me, but it felt a bit odd. Twelve months later he refereed his final game, and it was Wales v France. It's probably the most enjoyable game I've had as a captain. We got on throughout, the banter was flying, and we spoke afterwards. I presented him with a Welsh shirt at the dinner and we hung out for a bit. People expect me to say he's my least favourite referee, but he's actually one of my favourites. I saw a clip of him sending someone else off for exactly the same tackle as mine on Clerc, which made me realise it wasn't personal.

Warburton received a three-week ban after admitting he'd committed a 'dangerous tip tackle'. It prevented him from playing in the third-place play-off against

Australia, which Wales lost 21–18. Unlike its counterpart game in 1987, it lacked spirit, as both sides were smarting from semi-final defeats and thinking of what might have been. For Warburton, there was one more farcical moment to endure before he could leave New Zealand.

Having stayed behind longer than the rest of the squad to attend the IRB awards ceremony, he found himself in the airport departure lounge with the entire French squad. After enduring the unrelenting glare of publicity in the preceding few days, he kept a low profile, pulling his hood up, and avoiding conversation. A little while later, as he wandered wearily up the aisle of the plane, he encountered a familiar face in the seat next to his.

Sam Warburton: It was only bloody Vincent Clerc. What are the chances of that? Just think of how busy that flight route is? How many hundreds of planes, and thousands of passengers were leaving for Europe that day, and I happened to end up not just on the same flight as Vincent Clerc, but in the seat next to him. It was unbelievable. Our eyes met as I was putting my bag in the overhead locker. There was a brief moment of tension, before he cracked a smile, and said in heavily-accented English, 'You owe me a massage.'

Any concerns Warburton may have had about returning home to an angry reception soon dissolved in an outpouring of sympathy and affection.

Sam Warburton: The fallout when I returned couldn't have been more different to what I expected. Middle-aged women were hugging me in supermarkets, strangers were knocking on my door to wish me well. At one point, a car-load of strangers pulled up outside my house, wound down the windows, and started blasting that 'Sam, Our Captain' song from their speakers. It was like I'd returned home a hero. It was my first taste of genuine fame. I couldn't go anywhere for weeks. My wife and I agreed to go to a breast cancer benefit at St David's Hall in Cardiff, where most of the guests were seventy-year-old women. I thought we'd be able to blend in and nobody would know who we were for a change. After thirty seconds, there was a queue of around thirty women waiting to speak to me at the bar. A week or so later, my wife and I had been treated to a weekend away in Claridge's in London, where I was *convinced* I'd be anonymous. We checked in and made our way up to our room along with the concierge. He dropped our bags in the corner of the room before saying, 'Enjoy your stay, sir,' and as he was closing the door, he added, 'By the way, it was never a red card.'

TWENTY-FOUR

THE REAL SAM WARBURTON

Shane Williams bowed out of international rugby in the most appropriate manner – with an acrobatic try in the last minute of his final Test match. It wasn't enough to win as Wales slipped to another defeat to the Wallabies, but it was a fitting finale for Wales's most prolific try-scorer. When Wales reassembled for the Six Nations, it would be without their Roy of the Rovers. The man who replaced him couldn't have been cut from a more different cloth. Alex Cuthbert was tall and rangy, but shared Shane's electric pace and eye for the try line. A late convert to rugby union, he'd prove to be an influential presence in the upcoming campaign.

Wales were suffering from World Cup burnout, with several key figures sidelined. Second row was the worst affected area, with Alun Wyn Jones and Luke Charteris both crocked. It led to a recall for the popular Ian Evans, who, while delighted by his return to the fold, was also a little anxious about what lay in wait.

Ian Evans: I'd heard all the gruesome tales about Spala from the boys. I'd been texting them while they were out there, and the responses always came back along the lines of 'brutal', 'horrendous', 'savage', and 'counting down the days until we're out of here'. Before the 2012 Six Nations, I received a letter from the WRU congratulating me on my selection. The pride I felt upon opening it quickly turned to dread when I read the last sentence: 'We'll be assembling for a trip to Gdansk, for a pre-tournament training camp.' I thought, 'For fuck's sake.' As much as I was chuffed to be back, I was horrified about what lay ahead. Luckily, because the weather was so bad, we could barely train.

Adam Jones: We had Ireland first up in Dublin, and they were obviously fuming about what had happened in the World Cup.

Ian Evans: Most of the pundits on both sides of the Irish Sea were predicting a handsome Irish win. No one seemed to be giving us a chance out there which annoyed me. People seemed to have forgotten that we'd just beaten them in the World Cup.

Warren Gatland: We thrived on that underdog tag. Being written off suited us. We were so determined to banish the memories of the World Cup, and to really go out and do something in this campaign.

350

Adam Jones: We had a bit of an injury crisis in the lead up to it, and picked a side with a few untested combinations. Alun Wyn, Charteris, Melon, Smiler [Matthew Rees] and Dan Lydiate were all out, so the front five had a different look about it.

Jonathan Davies: My grandfather had passed away on the Thursday, and I didn't know if I was in the right frame of mind to play. Rob Howley told me they wanted me in the side, but said he'd understand if I didn't want to travel.

Sam Warburton: No one knew. He kept it to himself.

Jonathan Davies: I decided to play, but I was on the edge emotionally. Trying to sing the anthem was the worst. It's always meant a lot to me. I always think about the people that mean the most to me when I'm singing, and that's invariably my family. I decided not to sing that day, to close my eyes and think of something else, but you just can't help yourself. Normally I have a heart of stone, but if I'm in the stadium, and I clock a member of my family, I well up with emotion. My grandfather was at the forefront of my mind that day.

Sam Warburton: It didn't occur to me that Ireland might be looking for revenge after what happened in the World Cup. I didn't care what they thought to be perfectly honest. They were just one hurdle out of five.

Adam Jones: Just like we'd done in the World Cup, we started brilliantly. We stacked the short side off a scrum, creating a five-two overlap, and Rhys Priestland delayed his pass superbly to put Foxy in at the corner.

Jonathan Davies: When I scored, I was walking back with the ball in my hand and for some ridiculous reason, I kissed it and held it up to the sky.

It was an explosive start from Wales, but a riposte from Rory Best saw Ireland head for the sheds 10–5 in front. Johnny Sexton extended the advantage with an early penalty in the second half, and it looked as though Ireland were headed for victory before Wales exploded back into life. Leigh Halfpenny bagged three points from the tee, before a perfectly executed set-move sent Jonathan Davies over for his second.

Jamie Roberts: Foxy's second try came from some nice tight play off the left-hand side lineout. I ran a decoy line, North steamrollered through McFadden, and Foxy finished it off.

Jonathan Davies: It was a magic bit of skill from George, and he sent McFadden into the middle of next week.

Warren Gatland: That's what an x-factor player can do for you. He had the ability to not only get through the tackle, but to get the offload away as well. It's those things that set you apart. He won the collision convincingly *and* got the pass away. That's pretty special.

Sam Warburton: It was a perfectly executed set-move. George swayed his hips to get beyond the first defender, before he put the hammer down. It was freakish. The fact that we had backs that powerful gave us a sense of invincibility. Most of our backs were at least a stone heavier a man than their Irish counterparts, and several of them – Jamie, Foxy, George – were bigger than me. I can confidently say that no team in international rugby was as physical as us back then. Not even South Africa.

Ian Evans: We knew that as long as we got the ball to those boys, they could do something with it.

Jonathan Davies: My grandmother was so pissed off that I wasn't man of the match. She rang me up to complain about it. I told her Mike had played really well, but she wasn't having any of it.

Sam Warburton: George was my man of the match that day. He was an absolute freak, and the Irish couldn't contain him.

Davies's second try on fifty-five minutes levelled the scores at 13–13 and Leigh Halfpenny's conversion nudged Wales ahead. But unlike the World Cup quarter-final there was never a comfortable margin. Ten minutes later, Ireland were back ahead courtesy of another Sexton penalty, before Bradley Davies saw yellow for a reckless tip tackle on Donnacha Ryan. The consensus from the stands was that it should have been red. The pendulum had swung decisively back in Ireland's favour.

Jonathan Davies: There was a ruck, the ball was coming back on our side, and Brad was acting as scrum half. Bomb was over the ball, and I heard him warn Brad that Ryan was coming through on the counter ruck. Bradley clearly thought, 'Right, he's having it,' and chucked him on his head.

Warren Gatland: That made me angry. It was just dumb. I wasn't angry at all about the Sam Warburton sending off in the World Cup – that was unintentional and he was unfortunate, but I get frustrated with players who make silly errors and do things that are inappropriate. I can't stand foul play in the game. It was just a brain-freeze from Bradley, and I thought he was lucky to only get yellow.

With Bradley Davies off the field, Ireland exploited the one-man advantage to send Tommy Bowe over in the corner after a sumptuous pass from Rob Kearney.

Wales refused to give up, and moments later Bowe was rocked back on his heels as one of several defenders George North dragged over the try line. Ireland 21 Wales 20.

As the clock ticked into its final minute, Wales were in possession, using their powerful runners to punch holes in Ireland's defence, making steady progress into their half. All the home side had to do was make their tackles and keep their discipline. As Ian Evans prepared to carry into the heart of the home defence, Stephen Ferris grabbed one of his legs and drove him into the ground. Wayne Barnes didn't hesitate in brandishing another yellow card. The booing from an incensed home crowd reverberated around the stadium as Leigh Halfpenny lined up the match-winning penalty.

Ian Evans: It wasn't really a spear tackle, but I milked it, and the referee bought it, to be fair. I was howling in pretend agony, shouting, 'Fucking hell, ref?' and giving it the big one.

Adam Jones: Ianto's performance was worthy of an Oscar. He was like a bloody footballer, rolling around. Get up, mun.

Ian Evans: It was a fair tackle. As soon as Wayne Barnes awarded the penalty, I jumped to my feet, tapped Ferris on the head, and said, 'Cheers, mate.' Even I couldn't believe I'd got away with it.

Dan Lydiate: Leigh Halfpenny had missed that kick in the semi-final against France, and that really hurt him. He put so much time into his kicking, spending hours out on the paddock on his own, long after everyone's gone home. An unbelievable level of commitment. After the World Cup, he made a vow to himself, that in the big games, he'd nail the big kicks. And he nailed that one.

Warren Gatland: He carries a lot of responsibility on his shoulders, and dwells on his mistakes more than anyone else. He was incredibly nervous taking that kick. He admitted that to me afterwards.

Sam Warburton: Without a doubt, he was thinking about that same situation against the French. He had to wait three months to have a kick as big as that, and knowing Leigh, he'd have thought about it every day. He needed to exorcise those demons. He's renowned for his bravery, for putting his head where it hurts and we've seen him do that hundreds of times. But for me, his goal-kicking is just as brave. That single-minded determination to step up and nail those big moments when every pair of eyes in the stadium is boring into you. I don't know how he does it. My knees would be trembling if I was in his position. He was desperate to make amends for the semi-final rather than hide away and risk the same thing happening again. And he did.

Jonathan Davies: I was having a pint of Guinness after the game with Andy Powell and Bradley Davies and the game was being played back on the screen in the bar. When it came round to Bradley's yellow he says, 'Boys, have a look at this now, I don't think it's that bad.' We all watched in silence. After he'd seen the multiple replays, Bradley turned back to his pint, had a sip, and said, 'See you in five weeks then, boys.' He was banned for the rest of the tournament. It was worse than Warby's in the World Cup, and he knew it.

Ian Evans: We had a few injuries leading into the Scotland game. Warby was out, so was Alun Wyn, and Brad was obviously banned. Bomb was concerned because he likes a beefy second row behind him. I'm taller than Alun Wyn, but he's heavier.

Adam Jones: Having Ianto behind you was like having a wasp up your arse.

Ian Evans: When he was going forward, everything was alright. When he went backwards it was always the second row's fault.

Dan Lydiate: Winning man of the match was a massive honour. I wasn't scoring the tries or doing the fancy stuff; I was just trying to do my job to the best of my ability. It's surprising how the media can alter people's perceptions. If someone on *Scrum V* highlights the unseen work, the non-glamorous stuff, it gives people in my position a bit more credit. It's not as rock'n'roll as the backs scything through and scoring spectacular tries, but it's important. And it's often stuff the ordinary fan wouldn't have a clue about. Everyone knew about Alex Cuthbert's contribution because he was scoring all those tries. I never go looking for praise, but it's always nice to get a pat on the back.

Ian Evans: Lyds was on fire at that time. He could single-handedly kill an attack dead with one tackle. As soon as he made the hit, one of our jacklers, whether it was Warby or Melon, would be over the ball slowing it down or turning it over. In some ways Alun Wyn's injury made us more dangerous in that area, because Jug Head came into the side as an extra back rower.

If George North stole the headlines for his barnstorming performance against Ireland, it was the turn of Wales's other hulking winger to step into the limelight in Cardiff. After a stodgy first half, Alex Cuthbert exploded onto a delicate pass from James Hook, swatting away Greig Laidlaw on his way to the line. Scorer turned creator for the second, as Cuthbert's arcing run sucked the defence in enough to let Halfpenny canter in. Within moments, Halfpenny had snuck round the blind-side of a scrum to bag his brace, and Wales were out of sight. In the space of sixteen minutes, the score had moved from 3–3 to 27–6. Leigh Halfpenny had scored 22 of Wales's 27 points. From that day on, he became Wales's undisputed first choice goal-kicker. England, like Wales, were unbeaten after two rounds. When the two sides met at Twickenham, something had to give. Wales rarely need any extra motivation to perform at Twickenham, but on this occasion, the Triple Crown was on the line.

Sam Warburton: I was walking through the Twickenham car park with my headphones on, but I didn't actually have any music playing. I wanted to take the atmosphere in, to hear the sounds, but I didn't want any distractions. I wanted it to look as though I was in my own world. As I was walking through the crowds, I heard an English fan shout, 'Warburton, you're fucking shit, and it was a red card.' It's fair to say that that motivated me a bit.

Adam Jones: These days, we're made to park the bus at the back of the car park. Instead of making a surreptitious entrance, we're forced to walk through the car park past all the posh fans in their mustard chinos and boating shoes. I'm sure it's a ploy to try to unnerve us, but believe me, when you've walked into places like Loftus Versfeld, where the home fans actually want to rip your head off, it's not that intimidating.

Ian Evans: Twickenham, and that whole experience – the Barbour jackets, the prawn sandwiches – represents a totally different set of values to what we're brought up with in Wales. Whether you like it or not, we're brought up to actually hate them. The reality is that off the field, most of them are top blokes. They're just people, but for some reason, that hatred of the English is instilled into you from an early age. Playing England always gives you an extra edge, an extra layer of motivation, and that will forever be the case, whether it's grass roots rugby, or international rugby.

Sam Warburton: I got pretty fired up in the team talk for this one. Shaun Edwards told me afterwards that I'd reminded him of Lawrence Dallaglio. Before the warm-up, the messages are all tactical, it's always quite detached and unemotional. But in the dressing room, that's when you go into war mode. The public perception of me is that I'm chilled out and laid back, but most people haven't seen me in a changing room environment. When the 2013 Lions DVD came out, there was a clip of me ranting and raving before a game. My brother's parents-in-law refused to believe it was me. They were like, 'I don't like that. *That's* not the Sam we know.' My brother Ben had to explain, 'No, that's *exactly* who Sam is.'

Jonathan Davies: It was a physical game that one, and a quick one. At one point, we were bending, but we weren't breaking.

Adam Jones: We were supposedly underdogs for this one as well, but Twickenham no longer held any fear for us. Having said that, it was a tough old game, with plenty of niggle and backchat.

Sam Warburton: They were getting into us verbally from the off. I remember one breakdown when we gave away a penalty for not releasing, and I stood up to a chorus of 'Have some of that, you Welsh c***s.' I realised then that they did not like us, and they wanted to beat us badly. It's all handshakes at the end of the game, but it was serious business out there. That kind of sledging just fuels the fire. I love it.

Dan Lydiate: Manu Tuilagi wasn't that far from the line, and Warby just chopped him by his laces. It was the best tackle in the game. Gatland chose it as his favourite moment, full stop. When Manu shifts, he's a hell of a threat. Warby and I joked about it sometimes, referring to tackles like that as 'defensive tries'. Test matches are often lost by a margin of a try or less, so moments like that are as significant as scoring at the other end.

Sam Warburton: The myth goes that I broke my nose making that tackle. It's not true, although it did cause a gash below my eye that required stitches. What I do remember is that I was outrageously offside. They made a big line break off their lineout, and rather than retreating behind our ruck to get onside, I slyly ran through all the England players and turned around just as Manu got the ball. It wasn't strictly an illegal line, but it was the shortest route to get onside, and get in position to make the tackle. It was a cute bit of play, but I didn't realise the significance of it at the time.

Early in the second half, Rhys Priestland had a kick charged down by Mouritz Botha. In a bid to make amends, he made a tackle from an offside position at the next ruck. He was sin-binned, and Owen Farrell slotted the penalty to put England into a 12–6 lead.

Sam Warburton: While we were under the posts for Farrell's penalty, the message was to get the ball back, and keep hold of it. And that's what we did. England didn't touch it for eight of those ten minutes. It was a massive psychological boost.

Jonathan Davies: As Priestland was going off Mouritz Botha said to him, 'Well done mate, you've lost your team the game.' Rhys waited until the final whistle before asking him, 'What did you say again?'

Two years earlier in the corresponding fixture, Alun Wyn Jones had been sin-binned for tripping Dylan Hartley with the scores tied at 3–3. England scored 17 points while he was off the field. This year, Wales worked their way back up field and were awarded a penalty which Halfpenny kicked to reduce the deficit to 12–9. Crucially, they'd survived the ten minutes without losing any ground. Gatland later praised Wales's maturity for the way they handled the sin-binning. With Priestland back on the field, they were awarded another penalty for English hands in the ruck. As the match entered its final ten minutes, Leigh Halfpenny levelled the scores at 12–12.

Adam Jones: We were into the last ten minutes and England were in possession. They shipped it out to Courtney Lawes whose game is based around physicality and aggression. He saw Scott Williams in front of him, tucked the ball under his arm and dropped his shoulder.

Sam Warburton: I went in to tackle Lawes. We were being coached to tackle one low and one high. I went low, and Scott went high.

Adam Jones: Pound for pound, Scott is one of the hardest, strongest blokes I know. He stood firm, soaked up the tackle, and then – like Houdini – emerged with the ball in his hands. In the blink of an eye, he'd robbed Lawes of the ball, and booted it downfield.

Dan Lydiate: He came off the bench in a massive game, ripped the ball off a guy twice his size, and then produced an outrageous bit of skill with the kick-and-chase. We always practised jackling and ripping the ball, but Scotty's renowned for having the knack. It's one of his strengths. He was only a young kid, but to show the composure to follow up that kick and get over the line said a lot.

Jonathan Davies: I don't think Scott realises how good he can be. I've seen him play with my brother since age grade level. He is an unbelievable rugby player. That was just something you expect to see from him. That bit of skill, the rip, the vision, the kick, and then that pace. He's so quick.

Adam Jones: I was convinced that England had enough numbers in defence to scramble back, but Scott accelerated so smoothly, he left them all trailing in his wake.

Sam Warburton: When I looked up and saw Scott legging it after the ball I was just praying he'd get there first. We're coached to always get up off the floor, chase and support, but on that occasion, I knew there were only two outcomes: they'd get it and kick it into touch or we'd score. It was like staring into busy traffic and squinting to see the three things that mattered: Scott Williams, a white jersey, and the ball.

Adam Jones: The ball bounced perfectly into his bread basket, and with that, he was over the line. It was one of the most dramatic tries the Six Nations has ever seen.

Warren Gatland: Some of Scott's biggest impacts for us have been coming off the bench. He's had some big moments coming off the bench, and that was a prime example.

Adam Jones: Obviously I hadn't chased the kick as enthusiastically as the backs, so I was still on the halfway line, and overheard Ianto abusing Lawes on the floor. It wasn't quite up to Australian cricket standards of sledging, but he can't help himself. He loves to chirp up.

Warren Gatland: The ironic thing about that was that a rugby website had just commissioned Courtney Lawes to do a presentation about the art of taking the ball into contact. It was a bit of a disaster for them. I think they canned the idea.

Sam Warburton: Other than that initial burst of emotion, no one went overboard with the celebrations. Gats and Howley always coach 'critical moments' – there were times in training when they'd go, 'Right, it's the seventy-eighth minute, you're 15–12 down, here's the ball, go. Build something.' Because there was time left, we were all locked into that mindset. No one was celebrating, we were just focused on getting the next thing right. There'd been times in the past, against the likes of New Zealand, when we'd follow something great with a vital error. Gats would drum it into us – 'Always think about what's next. Don't allow something good to upset your concentration.' We snapped straight back into the moment. We knew we had three minutes left to defend like hell. No one really said much back on the halfway line. It was more the looks in our eyes that said 'we are *not* going to let this slip'. Nothing summed up our will to win better than that defensive effort at the end. Leigh Halfpenny deserves huge credit for getting across and hurling himself at Strettle, and Jonathan Davies then manoeuvred himself underneath to stop the grounding. You can't coach scramble defence like that. You've either got that desire within you, or you haven't.

Ian Evans: Once I heard the words, 'He hasn't grounded it,' I flung my arms up in the air in triumph. That was it. We'd done it. Beaten England and won the Triple Crown on English soil for the first time ever.

Jamie Roberts: The England game was a strange one from a personal point of view. I'd come off at half-time with that knee injury after tackling Manu Tuilagi, and Scotty Williams came on and scored that brilliant try. I was delighted we'd won the Triple Crown, and delighted for Scotty, but I felt a bit detached.

Jonathan Davies: Just before half-time, Jamie had told me he'd blown his knee, and I'd said, 'Come on mate, dig in.' But he had to go off. After the game, we posed for the photo, and next thing, Jamie's frantically hopping over trying to be the first stood next to Warby. I said, 'Knee's alright now, is it, pal?' He'd got the whiff of a Grand Slam and was back running by the next Thursday! 'Lazarus', that's what the boys called him.

Dan Lydiate: Everyone was like, 'It's a miracle. He's back from the dead!'

Jonathan Davies: It was a hell of a night, and I nearly missed the ride back after sleeping through my alarm. I woke up in a panic, slung all my stuff in a bag, crawled onto the bus with my hood up, and slept all the way back to Cardiff. When we got back to the Vale our press guy told me I had some TV interviews to do. I said, 'Are you serious? You're putting me in front of a camera?' My eyes were like pin-holes. I was feeling pretty dusty.

Sam Warburton: Once we'd beaten England to win the Triple Crown, we knew the Grand Slam was on. No disrespect to Italy but we expected to beat them at home. And then it was revenge time against the French.

Jamie Roberts: Gats will tell you when you're under pressure. He has a way of pushing little buttons. He'd walk past you in the corridor and mention how well one of the other centres had trained. It might seem innocuous, but it's definitely designed to get a response. He'd drop it in and just walk off without giving you a chance to respond. You'd think, 'Cheers for that.' That kind of approach might not work with Warby, or Adam Jones, or Alun Wyn but it worked on me. That's part of the art or the science of coaching. Knowing which methods will motivate which players.

Ian Evans: About four hours before the Italy game, the boys were quite relaxed. We'd had our walk-through, discussed our roles, and everyone was wandering about quite chilled. Shaun called a meeting and went nuts, saying, 'We're not on edge. Everybody should be on the fucking edge! What's the matter with you?' There was a stunned silence in the room before Gethin Jenkins piped up, 'To be fair, Shaun, there's four hours to go before kick-off.'

Jamie Roberts: I was relieved to keep my place, and felt I owed the shirt a game. I was nervous, especially after Scotty's cameo. We played Italy and won comfortably. Now it was all about France.

Dan Lydiate: A lot of us had been involved in that World Cup semi-final. We'd been in that situation once before, and we were not going to let it happen again. A hundred per cent it was about revenge.

Jonathan Davies: Momentum had built so strongly towards that point, that we felt invincible. Personally, I never felt we were going to lose any of the games at any point. We knew we'd finish stronger, with the fitness work we'd done and the talent we had. We knew that someone would make something happen. We were in a much better place than all the other nations.

Jamie Roberts: We felt confident, but the coaches were desperate to keep a lid on things, to keep our egos in check. Shaun Edwards once told me, 'You play your best rugby when you have a point to prove, and that's why we don't give you very much praise.' They knew that if they showered me with praise, I'd get stuck in a comfort zone.

Sam Warburton: Shaun thought we were all too sensitive when it came to accepting criticism. He said we should be worried if he *stopped* critiquing us because that would mean he didn't care anymore. He was always thinking of small ways to make us all better.

Jamie Roberts: Everyone has a different level of emotional intelligence. Some players need to have their egos stroked, to have their break or their big tackle shown in the debrief. Some need to have their egos punctured, to be pulled up on things they've done poorly. That's the art of coaching – knowing which buttons to push to get the best out of the individual.

Dan Lydiate: I was quite wound up in the week. Shaun Edwards pulled me to one side and said, 'Look mate, I know you're really keen for this game, but don't overthink it, don't get wound up. Just go out and do what you know you can do.' He could see I was quite edgy. You don't just take the next game as it comes, no matter what people say. This was a Grand Slam game, and not many of us had been in that position before.

Sam Warburton: That was the most nervous the squad had been, more so than the semi-final. The Thursday session – which is usually a pretty heated affair – was an absolute disaster. One of the worst I'd been involved in. The standard was terrible. Balls were being dropped, moves were being bungled, passes were going astray. Adam Jones pulled all the boys in and calmed everyone right down.

Adam Jones: The session was completely chaotic and everything was falling apart at the seams. All the youngsters had played brilliantly throughout the campaign, but the pressure of a Grand Slam game was clearly affecting them. I've never considered myself a leader, but I'd been through this twice already. Melon, Jug Head and me were the only survivors from the 2005 Slam, and we just gathered everyone together and told them to calm down a bit.

Sam Warburton: That was a perfect example of the power of experience over youth.

A lot of the younger boys didn't know what to do, how to handle the pressure. Their nerves were getting the better of them. After Bomb's speech, everyone relaxed, we finished the session off fine. You had the energy and exuberance of the youth, and the cool heads of Adam, Gethin and Stephen Jones. It was the perfect blend.

Jamie Roberts: Less is more when you go into a game. You don't want your head crammed with too much knowledge. Shaun was good at breaking down the defensive strategy to two or three key messages. That week there were two main messages – we decided not to contest the rucks in the middle third of the field, instead we'd just makes our tackles and fan across the field in defence. And secondly, we would gang-tackle certain individuals like Louis Picamoles, because he carried quite upright. Stop him in his tracks and prevent the offload. That hard work is done in the week, and you go into the game with complete clarity of thought. Everyone becomes a cog in the machine.

Jonathan Davies: The bus ride in was a memorable one. We left the Vale, and by the time we reached Canton, hordes of people were walking down the street into town. As soon as they saw the bus, they started roaring and pumping their fists. I got quite choked up because it's hard to believe that you're on this bus, and all those thousands of people want you to win so badly. When we turned into Westgate Street, the crowd was unbelievable. The sheer volume of people and the noise they were making was difficult to comprehend. We all took our headphones off and tried to soak it up. These moments don't happen too often.

Sam Warburton: That's why home advantage is so important. This was my thirteenth game as captain but the first time I'd captained Wales at home in a Six Nations match. The fans are amazing. That kind of hype and atmosphere really helps to spur you on.

Adam Jones: It dawns on you then that the whole nation is behind you, but there's only twenty-three of us who actually get to wear that jersey. It's a massive privilege.

Warren Gatland: Wales are a real 'momentum' team. More so than any other team in the tournament. We get on a roll and the confidence grows, and by the final round we've become really tough to beat. That's how we felt going into that last game against France.

Ian Evans: Lyds was on fire again that day, chopping people's kneecaps for fun.

Jonathan Davies: We weren't brilliant, but we were comfortable. Our defence won us that Championship. It wasn't just a revenge mission for me, because we had a lot more to gain than just revenge. There was a Grand Slam on the line. We knew we were better than them, but we wanted to be better than them *and* Grand Slam champions.

France had requested that the roof be kept open and the steady drizzle that fell for much of the day made conditions tricky for running rugby. Wales took a suitably pragmatic approach, kicking the proverbial leather off the ball and pinning France back into their own half.

Adam Jones: It was a pretty cynical move by them. By the time the game kicked off, the pitch was soggy, and the ball soon became greasy and difficult to handle. There was a fair bit of kick tennis in the opening exchanges.

Warren Gatland: Traditionally, France have always possessed a real attacking threat, but that day they didn't really pose any threat at all. We contained them fairly comfortably.

Dan Lydiate: We were relentless. We just kept going and going. That match was a culmination of all the hard work we'd put in. It was tough, though. There are times in the game when you relish those big collisions, but jeez there are times when you make a tackle, and you're struggling to catch your breath. You're trying to wind them, but you're knocking your own wind out every time you make a hit.

As he had been throughout the tournament, Dan Lydiate was a one-man wrecking ball. Blessed with a gargantuan physique honed through years of hard graft on his parents' farm near Llandrindod Wells, Lydiate was every ball-carrier's nightmare. Time after time, he'd hurl himself at the feet of an attacker, with scant regard for his own welfare. Time after time, they'd be swept to the deck in a disorienting jumble of limbs. At one point, the BBC cameras zoomed in on 'the chopper' as he sat bowed on one knee, chest heaving, gulping huge drafts of oxygen into his lungs. It was a defining image. He was the epitome of the selfless servant to the cause; a relentless defensive machine. He wasn't just man of the match, but man of the tournament.

Dan Lydiate: Do I love tackling? It depends. I'm always on a ceaseless quest to make the perfect tackle. If you get the timing and the execution right, tackling doesn't hurt. But that only accounts for a small percentage of the tackles I make. In that France game there were a lot of tackles where my timing was slightly out but they *looked* almost perfect. Wesley Fofana for example, stepped away from me, well past me, but because he jumped in the air, and I got fingertips to him everything fell into place and it looked spectacular. On another occasion Jean-Marcellin Buttin hit the hard line, and I blind-sided him with Ianto and caught him sweet. When it's like that it's great, but ninety-five per cent of the time it's not like that, it *does* hurt, and you can hear the impact up in the commentary box.

That's not so much fun. The pleasure I get is from watching it back. At the time you're blowing out of your arse and afterwards your body's in bits, but if you've put in a good shift, those aches and pains don't feel half as bad.

Sam Warburton: Dan's one of the most popular guys in the squad. He is so mild-mannered and laid back, and gets on with absolutely everyone. But once he crosses that white line, he's a machine. I've never seen a more aggressive defender in my life.

Lydiate made twenty tackles that day, nearly all of them significant, but the most important was the one on Thierry Dusautoir after twenty minutes. The ball was swiftly turned over by Alun Wyn Jones and Wales snapped into attack mode.

Dan Lydiate: Dusautoir was stepping away from me, so I felt like I was sliding into him. Rob Howley had said to me, 'It's great making all these big tackles, but you need to get back into the game as quickly as you can.' I stood up and saw the ball there on a plate, and with Howlers' words ringing in my ears, I played it away to Priest who put Cuthy in to weave his magic and score the try. It was an incredible finish – he turned the defence inside out – but it was a genuine team try because without Alun Wyn Jones turning the ball over, and Priestland timing his pass to perfection, Cuthy wouldn't have had the space to do what he did. Everyone was a cog in the machine. I like to think of my involvement as a try-assist!

Adam Jones: There was some slick handling to get it out wide, but Cuthy absolutely shredded the French defence. There was no better finisher in world rugby at that time.

Sam Warburton: Cuthy was awesome back then. He was big and fast, and he suited our gameplan to a tee. He was the quickest guy in a straight line I'd ever played with. He still had a lot of work to do with that try, to step in and go under the posts. People underestimate just how hard it is to change direction when you're six foot five and moving at that speed. I certainly can't do it. He was one of the first names on the team sheet back then.

Dan Lydiate: We've all had abuse from trolls on social media, but no one's had it as bad as Cuthy. It's difficult not to bite sometimes. People think you're world class one week, and then slag the arse off you the next. Too many people focus on the negatives. All players get it these days, even Warby.

Warren Gatland: There have been two or three players in my time that really suffered at the hands of the social media mob. Alex was one, Rhys Priestland was another. When things were going well, they got all the plaudits, but if they had a poor performance, they were slated. The way that the tide turned was unbelievable. It had a big impact on them. A really negative impact in terms of lack of confidence, lack of self-belief, and whether they even wanted to be here anymore.

Ian Evans: Everyone's entitled to their opinion, but the rise of social media has made it harder to ignore what people are saying. It's not like the old days when you could just avoid reading the newspapers.

Warren Gatland: I've noticed a big change in recent times with regard to social media. Six or seven years ago, when it was a new thing, players used to read everything, and would be weighed down by all the negative comments. It had a massive influence on their confidence and performance. But nowadays, they've learnt that that way madness lies, and if they see something remotely negative, they'll just keep scrolling.

Sam Warburton: It only really resonates when someone says something that a player is already thinking. If there's an aspect of your game you're feeling insecure about, and some 'fan' brings that up on social media, it reinforces your negative thoughts, and starts to make you paranoid. What you've got to worry about is when the press says something, and the casual fan treats it as gospel. Having said that, these people that pay their money to come out and support you have got a role to play, and if I'm playing crap, they've got a right to point that out. At the end of the day, I wouldn't have a job if these people didn't keep paying to come and see us play. But you need to mature a bit to arrive at that conclusion. I used to get really riled when criticism was directed my way. By the end of my career it became like water off a duck's back.

Adam Jones: France didn't buckle like they sometimes do when they concede. They kept coming at us, and Harinordoquy was only stopped from scoring by a great smother tackle from Ianto. Moments like that don't linger as long in the memory as Cuthy's try, but were just as significant.

By half-time, Sam Warburton had succumbed to his third separate injury of the tournament, and didn't re-emerge for the second half. Gethin Jenkins assumed the captaincy, and Ryan Jones entered the fray as Warburton's replacement. At that point Wales were 10–3 ahead. It could have been more but for two missed kicks, both of which hit the post, but Wales were comfortable. Their territorial tactics were working.

Dan Lydiate: At half-time, I'd split my eye open, and bust my nose, so I can't remember what was said in the changing room; I spent the entire twelve minutes getting stitched up. Warby was so unlucky with injuries, but it's the nature of the beast. The position he's in and the way he played. It's such an attritional position. You can have the best back row in the world on paper, but once you start picking up bumps you're down to your second and third choices. He could barely lift the trophy at the end of the game because of the nerve damage in his shoulder.

The second half saw fewer points scored, but was no less absorbing. France's replacement full back Jean-Marcellin Buttin set Welsh nerves jangling with a few silky interventions, but the Welsh defence held firm, Dan Lydiate again chopping him down as he hared towards the Welsh line. It was all about penalties. Beauxis kicked one, narrowing the gap to 10–6, and Halfpenny responded, giving Wales some breathing space at 13–6.

France were not rolling over, though. Lionel Beauxis continued to launch high, hanging kicks into Welsh territory, and when Leigh Halfpenny spilled one, panic ensued. Harinordoquy and Picamoles both punched holes in a scrambling Welsh defence, as France sniffed an opportunity. After several frantic phases, the ball spilled loose, and Ryan Jones dived theatrically on top of it. Craig Joubert called a scrum for an earlier knock-on, and France got the shove on. Yachvili kicked the resulting penalty to reduce the gap to 13–9.

Adam Jones: Jug Head could not have been more melodramatic with that dive. It was like something from *Die Hard*. He launched himself through the air, with his arms flailing, and his face all contorted in pain. It was like the ball was a ticking bomb, and he was sacrificing himself to save the lives of everyone in the stadium. And I swear to God, he looked around afterwards to see if one of the TV cameras had caught it. Suffice to say, he didn't get away with it. Foxy and I rinsed him after the game.

Moments later, Halfpenny was pirouetting his way upfield, before Rhys Priestland threaded a kick through for Cuthbert to chase. Francois Trinh-Duc was back to cover but was tackled into touch. Petulantly, he threw the ball into the stands. Penalty Wales. Leigh Halfpenny – the man who'd tortured himself over his miss in the World Cup semi-final – stepped up to widen the gap to seven points. 16–9.

Ian Evans: The seven-point cushion felt safer, but we were still at the edge of our nerves. Ken Owens came on late in the game, and was properly fired up for it. At one stage, when France were in possession, he started counter-rucking aggressively and giving Harinordoquy a load of verbals, mouthing him off. He was eager and desperate to make an impression. For the first time in my life, I was the one trying to calm someone down. I told him, 'Ken, we've got to stay squeaky clean, here, mun. Don't give the ref any reason to penalise us.'

Sam Warburton: Ianto was amazing that day. He'd come back into the side after almost four years, to plug an injury gap, and was one of our best players. He could easily have been man of the match if Dan Lydiate hadn't put in his ridiculous, career-defining performance. There's no greater feeling for a Welshman than lifting that Six Nations trophy in the Millennium Stadium, but I felt guilty receiving it because there were boys around me who had been through more pain, suffered more hurt, and shed more blood than I had. I felt a bit like a thief. Warren suggested I lift it jointly with Gethin and Ryan, who'd captained the side in my absence, but they refused, telling me to crack on and do it myself. It was a lovely gesture from the two of them.

Adam Jones: Ryan's one of my best mates, so it was extra special to be able to share that moment with him. We'd joined a pretty elite group of Welshmen who'd won three Grand Slams. If you'd have told me I'd have been enjoying this moment during the Hansen years when I was being subbed off after half an hour, I'd have thought you were insane. All three of them were won on home soil as well, which makes it extra special. It's impossible to pick a favourite, but if I had to, I might just go for this one, because I was still on the pitch at the final whistle.

Dan Lydiate: Walking around the field afterwards, they were playing that 'Titanium' song, and whenever I hear that on the radio it takes me right back to that moment in time. It was an unbelievable experience, to see everyone staying in the stadium dancing and celebrating. Obviously all the Frenchies started slinking away, but there were still around 60,000 Welshies there, loving it.

Adam Jones: After the presentation, I set off on a lap of honour, swigging from a bottle of champagne. Someone in the crowd threw me their daffodil hat, so in most of the photos, I'm wearing an enormous daffodil on my head, glugging champagne, and awkwardly raising three fingers to signify my three Grand Slams. I did that on Shaun's suggestion. I do whatever he tells me to.

Sam Warburton: You never think it's going to happen to you. It only seemed like a few years ago, I was playing there for my school in front of thirty people. Now I was celebrating a Grand Slam in front of 75,000. It was completely, utterly, surreal. To win it on home soil made it extra, extra special.

Jonathan Davies: Back in the changing rooms, we were having a big team photo and I had to take myself away and sit on my own to let it sink in, to think to myself, 'You lucky bastard.' You've got to have that moment to yourself, to emphasise what you've achieved. Then Lyds came over and put his big arm around my shoulder, and I don't remember much of the night after that.

Sam Warburton: That was the last time I went out in Cardiff. I was walking with my wife over to 'Revs' past the castle, and I bumped into George coming the other way with his girlfriend, Becky James. He said, 'Mate, don't go in there, it's absolute carnage.' The place was heaving but we braved it. The whole team was in there, but so were a load of my mates from school. We managed to get a private table with them, and have a proper session until two or three in the morning. I hardly ever drink but I had a good old swig that night.

Jonathan Davies: We carried on into 'Super Sunday' in Cowbridge. Not everyone made it, but the hardcore were there. People were constantly coming up to congratulate us, to chat, and to ask for photos. They were all insisting on buying us drinks, because of all the joy we'd brought them. It can be easy to forget the wider impact you're having when you're in the bubble, so focused on training and performing. There are three million people in Wales, and countless others around the world that take as much pleasure from Wales winning as we do.

Sam Warburton: People talk about how amazing we were in that campaign, but I always remind myself never to get too carried away. Look at the facts. It was a controversial penalty against Ireland, an isolated moment of brilliance against England, and an individual score from Cuthy against France. The three biggest games were all decided by single, decisive moments. That's the difference between a Grand Slam and finishing in the bottom half. Tiny margins. You can finish fourth in a Six Nations having played the best rugby. Winning tournaments is about having big players in big moments. Gats always says that. Most top teams are pretty level these days; it's about which team has the most x-factor players who can produce those defining moments. We had a fair few of them in that tournament.

Warren Gatland: If you can get three or four players in your team with genuine x-factor, that can be the difference between mediocrity and doing something a little bit special.

TWENTY-FIVE

I APPROACHED HER GRAVE
AND SAID, 'THANKS, MAM'

When Australian fly half, Berrick Barnes kicked a penalty five minutes from time at the Sydney Football Stadium, on 23 June, 2012, Welsh hopes of a first victory down under since 1969 were crushed. It sealed a 20–19 win, and condemned Wales to a 3–0 whitewash in a series they'd had serious ambitions of winning. It had been the Grand Slam champions against the Tri-Nations champions, and a chance for Wales to confirm their burgeoning reputation as world beaters.

After deservedly losing the opening Test, they'd lost the next two by a combined margin of three points, both to agonising late kicks. Rob Howley – in charge of the team while Warren Gatland recovered from two broken heels – was left to rue what might have been. If the Australia tour was disappointing, the autumn series that followed was devastating. Miserable defeats to Argentina and Samoa were followed by a routine loss to the All Blacks, before Australia compounded the misery with another narrow win, this time by 14 points to 12. After scaling the lofty peaks, Wales were now scrabbling around in the foothills, lost and disoriented. Welsh fans, giddy with excitement after the Grand Slam triumph, were wondering what on earth had gone wrong. Was Gatland the alchemist? Was his absence the issue? Whatever the reasons for the decline, negative energy began to thrum within the squad, and confidence became increasingly fragile.

Sam Warburton: I came back from my shoulder injury too soon at the end of the Grand Slam, and didn't do myself justice at all on the Australia tour. I went out there against David Pocock, who was the best open-side in the world at that time, and came off second-best by some margin. It set me back, and I was under pressure for the next six months to get on the Lions tour. I went from being, in my opinion, one of the world's best sevens, to wondering whether I was good enough to get into the Welsh team. I'd suddenly lost all confidence in jackalling, which had been my point of difference. It disappeared from my game, because I started getting paranoid about getting injured. Instead of being that rock-solid presence over the ball, I was getting cleared out way too often. I let it eat away at me for six months, because I thought I was big enough and old enough to deal with it myself. Eventually I picked up the phone to Andy McCann and told him I needed his help.

Andrew Coombs: There was a second-row injury crisis ahead of the 2013 campaign. Alun Wyn, Bradley Davies, and Luke Charteris were all sidelined, so I got my first call-up at the age of twenty-eight. I saw guys in the squad talking to Andy McCann, and I couldn't see why they needed to. In my head I was thinking, 'You're in the best place you could possibly be, you're playing for your country, earning all this money, what have you got to whinge about?' I found it really difficult to understand at the time, and I frowned upon the boys who did it, to be honest. There's a much bigger focus on mental health in sport now, and I can understand the need for it, but at the time, I thought they were soft. I'd be looking at my teammates and thinking, 'What's wrong with you?'

Sam Warburton: I sat down with Andy and told him that when I was jackalling, all I could imagine was my ankle dislocating, which was really weird because it had never actually happened. He'd dealt with professional golfers whose swing had just gone for no reason whatsoever, and he could see comparisons in what I was going through. He helped me pull that image out of my brain, by getting the video analyst to clip up every single jackal attempt I'd ever done. He clipped more than 250 of them and encouraged me to watch them over and over again. Not once did I get injured from it. I'd been the most competitive, confident player since I was fifteen. I always thought I would play for the Lions, and six months out from the Lions tour, I was consumed by self-doubt. I'd never suffered a crisis of confidence like it. All these demons were in my head. I'd retired in my mind about five times that season. I was sick of rugby and, mentally, it nearly got the better of me. I remember being on a plane going to Leinster and seeing the guy on the runway with the paddles, directing the plane, and thinking really clearly, 'I want his job. I want to have a job with no pressure, I'll drop all the salary, I don't care about money. I want a job outdoors, where there's no pressure, where I'm not getting scrutinised and slagged off in the press every week. I want a normal life, with a normal job, I'll drive round in a nice little two-door car. I don't care. I want to give it up.' I had a bad eight or nine months, but luckily I came through it.

Dan Biggar: I remember speaking to Leigh Halfpenny. He'd won the Grand Slam in 2012 and then gone pretty much a full *year* without a victory for either club or country, which is extraordinary for a player of his calibre. Going into that 2013 Six Nations campaign, a lot of players were really low on confidence, and that was reflected in the nightmare first forty minutes we had against Ireland in Cardiff. It summed up where we were at.

Andrew Coombs: On the morning of the game there was a letter under the door. I thought it was a bill. I imagined my roommate, Ianto, had gone a bit mental on the room service. I opened it up, and it was a letter from my father, telling me how proud he was of me. I lost my mother when she was forty-three, and had fought hard for everything I'd achieved. He talked in the letter about how much I'd deserved it, about the value of hard work and self-belief. I hadn't been fast-tracked or gone through an academy system. I'd dealt with the setbacks and fought tooth and nail to prove my worth. It was a really powerful gesture. I had to go into the toilet to read it because I knew I'd well up, and Ianto would rip the piss out of me. It had been Gats's idea. He'd encouraged every parent to do the same when their son was winning his first cap. Little things like that make a hell of a difference.

It was a remarkable match. If Wales's collective confidence was fragile coming into it, it was surely shattered by an Irish display that combined verve and panache with guts and brutality. It was 23–3 at half-time, and within moments of the restart, Brian O'Driscoll burrowed over for a third try to take them clean out of sight at 30–3. Warren Gatland was watching from the stands as a neutral, having been appointed Lions coach for the summer tour to Australia. He was probably inking in several names on his squad sheet, and they'd all have been wearing green.

Andrew Coombs: I'm quite a grumpy person. It's hard to make me smile. But on the bus into the ground that day, I had to face the window because I couldn't stop giggling to myself. Everyone else had their game face on, but I was giddy with excitement about the fact I was about to play for Wales. There was nothing anyone could do to stop me. Unless the bus crashed, or I got a freak injury in the warm-up, I was going to fulfil my dream. We rounded the corner of Westgate Street, and the first sight that greeted me was a bare belly with 'Come on Coombsy' written on it. It was Big Brett, one of my butties from Nelson.

Jonathan Davies: We were terrible in the first half. I was terrible, I think I passed two balls into the stands. My kicking wasn't any better – Bomb still jokes about me kicking drop goals into touch.

Ian Evans: He's an absolute class player, Foxy, but I was convinced he was playing for Ireland at one point. After that game he got ripped to bits by the lads. He more or less put an end to my hundred per cent winning record on his own. I don't hold a grudge, though. It's the only Six Nations game I've ever lost. I've only played in three campaigns, mind. We beat them in the second half though, does that count? I've only lost one half of Six Nations rugby.

Andrew Coombs: I got stripped of the ball on my first carry. My first international, my first carry, and I lose the ball in contact. I was questioning myself on the floor at that point – did I belong here? Was I out of my depth? I had to have a word with myself, and say, 'Right, you've got to carry harder, you've got to be better, because these boys are better than anyone you've ever played against before.'

Adam Jones: They were all over us in that first half. Simon Zebo was a nightmare, popping up everywhere. He scored their first try, and then showed the kind of footballing skills Maradona would've been proud of to keep the ball alive for their second. We were on the ropes, big time.

Andrew Coombs: We were way off the boil. There was one opportunity for Phillsy to put me in for a try, I cut a line right back towards the ruck, and there was nobody in front of me, but it was just as though the lights weren't on for most of us. It was all too slow and laboured. Throughout the game I felt like I was at least a metre behind where I needed to be. In a drift defence, when you're drifting across together, I was drifting as I would in a regional game, but the gap outside me would open up so quickly that the player I was marking was gone. The step up in pace was a real eye-opener. We couldn't get close enough to them to tackle them. They were that sharp, just way too quick for us.

Sam Warburton: They were pretty sharp in that first half, no doubt. But we gave a pretty poor account of ourselves.

Andrew Coombs: For the 2005 Grand Slam, I was on Westgate Street with my wife, with my Welsh top on, a big Welsh flag on my shoulders, and dragons painted on my cheeks, cheering the bus in. So I'd watched these players win Grand Slams, and now I was on the field with them. But during that first half, I felt nothing but disappointment. We weren't remotely in the game. I knew those players were better than that. Nobody was talking, it was really quiet. I was used to being part of a really vocal side at the Dragons; there was always a chorus of voices at Rodney Parade shouting, encouraging, barking orders. I couldn't believe how quiet it was out there on the Millennium Stadium pitch. I felt quite alone out there. We were a bunch of individuals rather than a team.

Ireland's first-half dominance made Wales's second-half comeback all the more remarkable. If the crowd sensed a capitulation, the players had other ideas. Cuthbert ran a hard line off Biggar to go under the sticks, before some slick passing saw Halfpenny score in the corner on the hour mark to make it 30–15. It was another fifteen minutes before Wales struck again, Craig Mitchell crashing over from short range. It was too late to prevent an eighth consecutive defeat, but it appeared that the Dragon had awoken from its year-long slumber.

Adam Jones: When Drico scored at the start of the second half, something weird happened. It was the catalyst we needed. All of a sudden, we remembered how to play, the swagger returned and we started scoring. Cuthy went over, then Halfpenny, and Craig Mitchell scored in the last few minutes. The final score was 30–22, but I swear we'd have won if the game had gone on five minutes longer. It was a total transformation.

Jonathan Davies: It felt as though we'd turned a corner psychologically. It drew a line under the previous ten months.

Andrew Coombs: When I came off the field, the changing room was like a morgue. It was just dead. The comeback didn't make a difference to me. The fact was, we'd lost. Howley was feeling the pressure, and the senior players were as well. I went to the ceremony to receive my first cap, but the mood was so low, it was a total non-event. I had a song prepared – Billy Joel's *We Didn't Start the Fire* – but I wasn't even asked to sing.

Sam Warburton: A BBC reporter told me that no team had ever won the Six Nations after losing their opening game. I replied that records were there to be broken.

Dan Biggar: It was France next, and going to Paris is difficult at any time, let alone to try to end a long losing streak. We just went out there and rolled our sleeves up. It wasn't about playing fancy rugby or expressing ourselves. It was about getting stuck in and grinding out a victory.

Andrew Coombs: I didn't really know any of their players if I'm honest. I didn't follow the French league, so I wasn't sure what to expect. We'd had a better week in training after the Ireland game. The senior players really took a grip of it. Melon and Ryan spoke up and drilled it into the boys that what had happened the previous week wasn't acceptable. I'd roomed with Ryan that week, and he was great in terms of offering advice and showing me the ropes. He was a big improvement on Liam Williams who I'd been paired with the previous week. Sanjay's just a ball of nervous energy who snores like a train.

Adam Jones: There was nothing in the way of razzle-dazzle that night in Paris. It was the ugliest of wins, dominated by kicking and defence.

Andrew Coombs: Our defence won that game. I was worried going into it having spent just a few weeks in camp, and constantly hearing Shaun Edwards repeat his mantra about getting up off the floor. With Wales, you're not allowed to stay on the floor, but that was what I'd always done. For most of my career, I'd been lying on the floor, trying to hold players back, to tussle with them, and start a bit of a ruckus. At the Dragons, I felt like I was being paid to piss people off. My defensive duties with Wales were so different, I was worried I wouldn't be able to contribute. It was all about tackling low, and getting back into the defensive line – two things I'd never done.

Jonathan Davies: After the victory, we were walking around saluting the fans and I asked George, 'Was that your dad?' He said, 'No way.' I said, 'Are you sure?' He said, 'Yeah, yeah, hundred per cent.' In the changing rooms afterwards, I was two seats down from him, and all I could hear was George on the phone going, 'You what? He's where? Are you serious?' Turns out I was right. It was his dad, and he'd been locked up in a police cell ever since.

Ian Evans: Fair play to him, he was obviously proud, wasn't he? You can't control that emotion, can you?

Sam Warburton: George doesn't like to talk about it.

Adam Jones: A few journalists got all high and mighty, saying it was an irresponsible thing to have done, but I loved it. I've met George's dad on a few occasions and he's a character. Your son's just scored the crucial try in a must-win game in Paris – why wouldn't you go a bit nuts?

Dan Biggar: It was such a relief to finally get a win. That eight-game losing streak affected our friends and family as well as us. The criticism and the bad press is as painful for them as it is for us.

Sam Warburton: More so, sometimes. I'd go out of my way not to read the press, but my dad would always read it, and the criticism would get to him. It then stresses me out to see *him* stressed out. If a player has a bad game, 99.9 per cent of fans will have forgotten about it by the following Saturday, but as a player you live and breathe it, every second of every day, and you can become paranoid. There were times I'd be driving in the car, after being slagged off in the press, and I'd feel as though everyone was staring at me, judging me. It's only now I'm outside of that bubble that I realise they weren't. As much as fans feel down after their team loses, no one feels the pain and disappointment more than the players and their families.

Jamie Roberts: It was my fiftieth cap and I got a bit emotional at the end. It was the grittiest of wins, but we didn't care. All that mattered was that we got over the line. It was the first time Wales had won in Paris since the Grand Slam in 2005.

Sam Warburton: We were pleased for Rob Howley because he was starting to feel the heat. People were speculating about whether Gats was actually coaching from a distance, but he was barely there at all. He'd watch the occasional session but the boys didn't really speak to him because they didn't want to be seen to be sucking up. Rob was in charge, no doubt.

Andrew Coombs: The after-match function couldn't have been more different from Ireland. The atmosphere was lively and there was a good bit of banter with the French boys. We were trying to get Richard Hibbard to pose with Dimitri Szarzewski for a photo, saying they were lookalikes, and Szarzewski was absolutely furious. He was mortified that we thought they looked alike. A suave Parisian and a valley boy from Taibach. He pretty much told Hibbard to fuck off. Because my first cap had been a bit of a washout, the boys decided to toast my introduction to international rugby on that night instead, and I was royally tucked up by the Scarlets boys. Sanjay, Scott Williams, George North, Aaron Shingler and Jon Fox all plied me with booze. Within an hour, I was outside in the bushes being sick. I was nervous about being seen because I didn't know if I was allowed to get drunk. Was it going to be frowned upon by the coaches? As those thoughts were going through my mind, the French team started leaving, and they were all staring at me, shaking their heads in disgust.

Jamie Roberts: I'll never forget Phillsy getting on the coach. He drew level with Howlers, and said, 'We saved you your job there,' and carried on walking. It was genius. There was a lot of heat on Howlers in the press, and that broke the tension completely.

Ian Evans: He was always pretty good with the one-liners, Phillsy. 'Howlers? Howlers? Aren't you going to say thank you?' 'Why?' 'I've just saved your job again, haven't I?' I don't think Howlers was best pleased.

Dan Biggar: Only Mike could have got away with that. He was fearless. He didn't care what he said or who he said it to, but he always had that twinkle in his eye. We needed a bit of humour in those situations. We bonded as a squad over things like that.

Sam Warburton: Standard Phillsy, that. On another occasion, after he'd been subbed off against Italy, he shouted from the back of the bus, 'What the hell were you thinking, taking your best player off the pitch?'

Andrew Coombs: One of the main lessons I learned that weekend was to never sit next to Mike Phillips at breakfast. He's worse with a hangover than when he's drunk. Really loose. He was absolutely steaming from the previous night and he came and sat next to me. The coaches were on the next table when he started shouting, 'Where's Rob Howley? Where the fuck is Rob Howley?' Rob said, 'All right Mike, I'm here.' Mike said, 'Oh, you're still here are you? Still got a job have you?' At this point I was sinking into my seat, praying they wouldn't consider me guilty by association. He carried on, 'You know who should be coach of this country? Me. Mike Phillips.' He turned to me and said, 'Innit, Coombsy?' I'd just won my second cap and was thinking, 'This isn't where I want to be.' It was so awkward, I just wanted the ground to swallow me up. The natural reaction would have been to laugh, but that would have looked like I was agreeing with him. Looking back, I think Howley was glad he was behaving like that because we hadn't seen that side of Mike until then. You have to worry about Mike when he *hasn't* got that swagger and arrogance about him.

Jonathan Davies: It was Italy in Rome next. It had been lashing it down all day before kick-off, so we knew it wasn't going to be much of a spectacle. It was tight at half-time, but we pulled away in the second half. I scored a try off a box kick from Phillsy, and Cuthy scored another. Two out of three. Not so bad. We weren't talking about winning the Championship at that stage, just going to Scotland and putting on a good show.

Adam Jones: I'd been suffering a bit of a confidence crisis ahead of the Italy game. The scrum had been under the pump against France and I genuinely thought I was losing my mojo.

Andrew Coombs: There was a sense that all was not right in training. Rob Evans had been invited in to train against us, and he was a man on a mission, with unlimited reserves of energy. There were quite a few scuffles in the scrum that week because Bomb and Melon were trying to focus on their technique, whereas Rob was doing whatever he could to make it a complete mess. I was begging him to stay square because all he was trying to do was beat Bomb. Bomb was getting really, really pissed off. You can tell when he's annoyed, because he just looks up to the sky, rolls his eyes and huffs and puffs.

Adam Jones: I'd done a lot of soul-searching, and Robin McBryde and I had spent hours analysing my technique, trying to come up with little tweaks to reinvent myself. Alun Wyn was back from injury, and on the bench. I'd missed having his strength and power behind me. Coombsy had been amazing in his first campaign, but he was a converted flanker, and didn't have the same ballast. He was scrummaging on the loose-head side, and Ianto was behind me. Much as I love Ianto, scrummaging is not his strong point. If Alun Wyn's behind you and you win the hit, there's only one way that scrum is going.

Ian Evans: He didn't have many complaints about my scrummaging at the end of that game though, did he?

Adam Jones: We absolutely destroyed them up front. They couldn't handle our scrum. Every time we connected, they splintered and collapsed. It really hurt their pride, and things very nearly boiled over. Andrea Lo Cicero came up swinging a few times. That forward dominance won us the game, and completely restored my self-belief.

Sam Warburton: Ahead of the Scotland game, I told Andy McCann I needed to drop the captaincy. I needed a big game at this point, and didn't want the extra burden. At half-time, we were 13–12 up, and I'd been mediocre at best. I went to the toilet in the changing rooms, and slapped myself across the face. I looked at my reflection in the mirror, and said to myself, 'You're ruining your Lions ambitions; something you've dedicated your entire life to.' It was a line in the sand. I'd had enough of this self-doubt. I went out like a man possessed in the second half. I won three turnovers and ended up man of the match. I got a big hit on Stuart Hogg, drove him back five or six metres, and turned the ball over. That was the turning point. Without exaggerating, it was one of the most important moments of my career – the exact moment that I mentally put all that negativity to one side. I knew then that I could kick on to become one of the world's best.

Adam Jones: Hibs scored the only try, and fair play, old 'Fatrick Sleazy' took it well. He just had to hold on and batter his way to the try line which isn't actually that hard when you weigh as much as he does.

The match set a world record for the number of penalty kicks in a game. Eighteen were attempted, thirteen were successful. Seven for Leigh Halfpenny, six for Greig Laidlaw. Not a record to be proud of necessarily, but regardless of how it was achieved, this was Wales's fifth consecutive away win in the Championship. They may not have been setting the tournament alight with dazzling rugby, but their defence was as mean and impenetrable as at any time under Shaun Edwards' stewardship. Three away victories, no tries conceded. Did they really have a chance of retaining their title? If they did, it seemed a slim one. If England put a big score on Italy, they'd be travelling to Cardiff the following week in search of a Grand Slam. Wales's chances of defending their title would depend on the maths – England's points difference could be unassailable by that point.

Jonathan Davies: It all depended on how England went against Italy the following day, so Howley gave us a strict curfew that night. Two hours' drinking was all we were allowed, and he made it pretty clear he wanted no dramas. We got back to the hotel two minutes before the curfew ended. There was a sense that now we were back in the hotel, we could still have a few more drinks, so I went to the bar and ordered twelve bottles of Peroni. As I was walking back with the tray, I realised that the bar had emptied. Everyone had disappeared. Rhodri Bown, the analyst, came down and said, 'I know you're having a good time, but I reckon it's a good idea if you call it a night. None of the players are here, Howley's sent them all to bed.' I left all twelve bottles there, untouched, and did as I was told. I put the round on Thumper's tab.

England laboured to an 18–11 win over Italy on the Sunday; a scoreline nobody had predicted. The result made the equation simple for Wales. Beat England by eight points or more, and the title was theirs. Their previous two Tests against England had resulted in seven-point and ten-point victories respectively. After all the sniping, Rob Howley now had a big shot at redemption.

Sam Warburton: Howley was one of the best coaches I worked under. I'd find it hard to say anything negative about him. I had a lot of coaches in my time and not all of them were easy to speak to, even when I was captain. That was never the case with Howley. Because he'd been a Wales captain as well, he understood what was involved; he got it. He's honest and up-front and I liked that. He'd get stuck into me a lot over my game. I wasn't spared the criticism as captain, far from it.

Jonathan Davies: In the week of the England game our target was to win. Simple. It was a case of, 'Whatever happens after that happens.' It was a short week but everyone felt good.

Adam Jones: That's not how I saw it. We were going for the eight-point margin. We may have trotted that line out to the press, but privately we wanted the title. Denying England the Grand Slam and finishing second wouldn't have been enough, not for me anyway.

Jonathan Davies: Ryan wasn't fit, so Melon was given the captaincy after missing the Scotland game through injury. When the team was announced he declared that Wales were 'bringing the main man back for the big one'. That was quite funny for Melon.

Jamie Roberts: The Monday before the England game was the week of my final medical exams. It was brutal. I was getting up at five o'clock most mornings at the Vale, and doing three hours' work before training. Then I'd cram in another few hours before going to sleep. It was really tough. When I look back, I can't believe I did it, but when you're that age, you're a ball of energy aren't you? I never questioned it. The test for me has always been how can I achieve in both fields without failing in either. I've always had a fear of failure. If I had the chance to succeed in both then why not? Working my body hard in rugby and my mind hard in study was a nice balance. Each one gave me an escape from the other. Those three hours in the morning were actually an escape from the pressure of the rugby. If things are easy, and you're cosy, you're not really living as far as I'm concerned. You never really know what you're capable of achieving unless you test yourself.

Gats came up to me early in the week and said, 'Are you gonna be all right?' I told him I'd be fine and walked away thinking 'Fffuuuuuuck!' It was one of the biggest games of rugby in my life and I also had my finals. If I failed them I'd have to resit the entire year. But I'd prepped for it, I'd worked bloody hard on both fronts, and I just needed to deliver.

Ian Evans: On the Monday morning, Shaun said to us, 'Look here, lads, this is the biggest week of your lives. If you have got a missus, or a partner, give them whatever they want. Tell them to go and buy whatever they need, and to leave you alone for the week. This week you have to be the most selfish person in the world. Just do what you need to do to make sure you've got the space you need.' It was a great pep talk. Mrs Evans got a new pair of shoes. I didn't speak to anyone outside of camp for the whole week, not even my parents.

Jamie Roberts: We trained terribly. We were shit. It was greasy, we couldn't win a lineout against no opposition. All the lads were dropping balls. I'd done an exam in Cardiff at eight o'clock on the morning of the last full session. I'd got in my car, driven to the Vale, past the hotel and straight to the field. I got my kit out of the boot, put my boots on, and did that last unit's session before the game against England. It's nuts looking back. The coaches gave me a bit of extra time to warm up, to make sure I didn't pull a hammy.

Sam Warburton: On the way to the stadium, the bus is normally silent. This time, when we were around halfway there, the monitors dropped down and a motivational video started playing. It was all about what we'd been through as a squad. The World Cup semi-final, the Grand Slam. The agonising defeats in Australia, and our run of three away wins up to that point. We didn't know it was coming, but it was just what we needed to focus our minds and bring us all together.

Andrew Coombs: That was pretty powerful. I looked around the bus and saw the focus in the players' eyes. The belief and the hunger was there. I was so proud to be part of it.

Jonathan Davies: There were quotes from the English players through the week. Ben Youngs saying, 'We're coming to Cardiff to win the Grand Slam,' someone else saying, 'We're not afraid of the big Cardiff atmosphere.' 'We can beat Wales on their home patch. We're not scared.' It finished with a montage of our boys making huge tackles, going on big powerful runs, and scoring some great tries. It was set to the soundtrack of Eminem's *Until I Collapse*. My jaw clenched, my veins starting popping, and I just thought, '*Right*. Here we go.'

Sam Warburton: We walked into the changing room and slap bang in the middle was the Six Nations trophy. It hadn't been there for the other games because they'd all been on the road. Everyone walked past and touched it. Psychologically that was the moment we knew it was on. That was *our* trophy, we were *still* champions, and we weren't about to relinquish that.

Jonathan Davies: The Welsh dressing room is always very quiet. We haven't got any ranters or ravers in our squad. That day, there was a bit of chat about what we needed to do, but otherwise there was an almost eerie silence.

Dan Biggar: It was very difficult to see us losing that game. I can't comment on the mindset of the English players, but we were so focused and determined that I didn't foresee any result other than us winning.

Sam Warburton: It was the easiest pre-match chat I had to do. Sometimes things get so tough in a game that if someone had a gun to your head telling you to run faster, you couldn't. I said to the boys, 'If you're out there on the floor, spent, struggling, feeling as though you can't do any more, just remember that feeling from 2012 when we lifted that trophy. Remember what it was like to be with each other that night.' From that point on, nothing could stop us. We walked out feeling invincible.

Andrew Coombs: Sam really surprised me in that campaign. I'd known his family before I turned professional, and I'd played against him a lot. I always thought he was a bit soft, because off the pitch he's such a gentleman. I'd once put him in a choke hold on the floor, and he was tapping out. I'd given him a few digs in matches over the years and never had anything back from him. I didn't think he had much of an edge, but I couldn't have been more wrong. With Wales, he really surprised me with his physicality in training and on the field. The way he carried himself, and the way he talked were impressive too. I vividly remember his first captain's speech. I've heard so many over the years, it's difficult not to be cynical, and I was thinking, 'Here we go, what's he going to say to inspire me?' He was phenomenal. You get your shouters and screamers, and you get your guys who deliver a quality message. He was both. He could deliver a message with passion and aggression and it really hit home what a quality captain he was. He's a smart guy; he knows what to say and when to say it. He'd dropped the captaincy by this point to focus on his own game, but he was still vocal, still a leader.

Sam Warburton: The English anthem was impressive. I thought they'd cocked up the ticket allocation, and allowed too many English in.

Jonathan Davies: *God Save the Queen* comes on, and you're thinking, 'Christ, the English have bought up all the debentures. The rich English guys have come down in their masses and paid over the odds for their tickets.'

Andrew Coombs: It was so noisy, I remember looking around and thinking, 'Hang on. Am I in Wales?'

Jonathan Davies: But then *Hen Wlad Fy Nhadau* starts and nearly blows the roof off. It was incredible, and after that, there was no doubt that we were at home, that this was our place, and we were in the midst of something special. That atmosphere will beat anything I've ever experienced.

Sam Warburton: It was the most powerful rendition I'd heard in my entire career. I don't normally get goosebumps, but I did then.

Jamie Roberts: Best atmosphere ever, period. Best rendition of the anthem. You watch it on YouTube now and it gives you goosebumps, it was mega. The atmosphere that day surpassed that of the Grand Slam twelve months earlier. Not to do that any disservice, but 2013 was epic.

Adam Jones: When the chorus began, the band dropped out, and the whole stadium sung 'Gwlad Gwlad' a cappella. If anything, it got louder. It was incredibly emotional – 75,000 voices singing the anthem in unison. By the end, a few of the boys were biting their lips, and the tears were streaming down Leigh Halfpenny's face. At that point, I knew we were going to win. The English boys had no chance.

Jamie Roberts: The sheer thought of losing that game, and having to walk the streets of Cardiff afterwards, was one none of us were willing to contemplate. We were well aware that the result would sit with us forever, as the 2009 game against Ireland in Cardiff has done, when *they* won a Grand Slam on *our* turf. I've never experienced emotion like that, seeing Ireland parading the trophy around our ground. It hurts deeper when it happens on your turf. An England Grand Slam in Cardiff? I don't think so. That is such a no-no. It simply can't happen.

Andrew Coombs: You could definitely see that England were nervous.

Sam Warburton: I looked across at the English lads and thought, 'They have not got a clue what's hit them.' They were like rabbits in the headlights.

Jonathan Davies: The first half was so fast. You're sucking it in from every hole in your body. At one point I ran past Ianto and Hibs on the way to a lineout, and I thought they were both going to pass out. Ianto's mouth was wide open, like a frog's – he was desperately trying to get oxygen into his lungs.

Adam Jones: It was nervy and tense out there, but we felt like we were edging them in the small battles. Steve Walsh seemed to be giving us all the fifty-fifty calls, particularly in the scrums. Our first scrum had been rock-solid – we engaged cleanly, pushed them back, and the ball appeared at Toby's feet. England's first scrum was messy – Melon got underneath Dan Cole, and both front-rows popped up. The decision could have gone either way, but it seemed as though Walsh had made his mind up that our scrum was stable, and theirs wasn't.

Jonathan Davies: Running in at half-time, you could tell that England were knackered. Apparently Alex Goode was delirious. He was that tired, he didn't know where he was. That's the rumour, anyway. The coaches were pretty pragmatic, pretty level-headed. We were 9–3 up, but we hadn't really got much out of the half. They assured us we'd get our reward in the second half.

Adam Jones: It was a very calm changing room. We were told to keep the pressure on, to keep building the scoreboard. I don't think anyone knew what was about to happen.

Sam Warburton: It was so nip-and-tuck for fifty or sixty minutes, but it was the one game when every single player was at least nine out of ten.

Adam Jones: About fifteen minutes into the second half, Ken Owens ripped the ball from Tom Wood in contact, it spilled loose, and Tips [Justin Tipuric] was the first man there. We switched into attack mode, it went through the hands, and we worked it to Cuthy out wide on the right.

Sam Warburton: Mike Brown was scrambling across and had the angle on Cuthy, but he barely got a fingertip to him. It was a sensational finish.

Andrew Coombs: Sitting on the bench, I felt like I'd travelled back in time eight years. In 2005, I was a fan in the stands cheering Wales on to a Grand Slam. Honest to God, I was celebrating on the bench with the same enthusiasm as in 2005. I remember thinking, 'This is one of the best games of rugby I've ever seen.' I was so taken aback by the performance, I forgot I was sat there in a Welsh kit.

Jonathan Davies: Not long after, Bigs slotted the drop goal that took us to 20–3. I ran past him and said, 'We're in for a good night tonight,' and he laughed. We had that moment together, because at that point it was 'job done' and we could relax. That's rare. Normally you're hanging in there, with your backs against the wall, and you're desperate not to make a mistake or concede a turnover. It's only usually when the whistle blows that you get to relax and think, 'Phew, thank God for that.'

Dan Biggar: Foxy's got a better memory than me because I can't remember that at all. I do remember the feeling of being relaxed, though, which is very, very rare in international games against top-tier opposition. It wasn't just a rugby match, it was an occasion, and at that point, I was able to sit back and enjoy it. I could be a spectator and a participant at the same time.

Adam Jones: With that drop goal, Dan slammed the door shut and bolted it. He's had his critics over the years because he doesn't conform to the romantic ideal of a jinking, dancing Welsh ten, but his game-management is superb. His decision to drop back into the pocket and slot that was absolutely the right one.

Jonathan Davies: At that point, we're thinking, 'This is probably an unassailable lead now,' and then, *boom*, turnover, Tips puts Cuthy in for the second try, and all of a sudden, you're like, '*What* is going on here?'

Adam Jones: Tips is a genius. He can see several moves ahead like a chess player. He took the ball and sold Mike Brown the sweetest of dummies before cutting back inside. Anyone else would have pinned their ears back and hoped for the best, but Tips is always thinking. His dummy had created a two on one, but he delayed his pass until Brown had committed to the tackle. Only then did he offload, giving Cuthy the simplest of run-ins. It was an absolute masterclass in three-quarter play – from a bloody flanker.

Sam Warburton: I was still on the floor when he touched down, punching the ground as hard as I could, not in anger, but in euphoria, knowing that was it. There was no way they were going to come back now.

Dan Biggar: Everyone speaks about how good Tips was that day, but I actually don't think he was *that* good, by his standards. I mean that as the ultimate compliment. He was man of the match in a Six Nations game against England, but for me, he was *always* that good.

Scott Baldwin: Andrew Hore once told Tips that he'd never be a starting seven for Wales. He said he'd eat two raw eggs in front of the whole squad if it ever happened. At the start of the following season, Tips turned up in great shape. I mean, he still had a body like a bag of custard, but his results were off the charts. Not long after, he was picked as a starting seven for Wales, and Horey was forced to keep his promise. He stood up in front of the boys, swallowed two raw eggs, with the shells on, the whole lot . . . and spewed everywhere.

Jonathan Davies: Once Cuthy gets into his stride, he's one of the quickest I've ever played with. He's quicker than George. George has got the pace *and* the power, but Cuthy has serious wheels. He's been so unfairly treated by the public. He's played nearly fifty times for Wales, and scored countless crucial tries, but because he had a dip in form – like everyone does – people thought it was acceptable to lay into him. Social media is a double-edged sword. When you play well and win a Championship, you're deluged by positive tweets, but if you do something like miss a kick to touch, you get hate mail. You get slated. You've got to take the rough with the smooth, I appreciate that, but it's a sorry world when people feel the need to kick someone when they're down. Ninety-nine per cent of people who send you bad stuff would probably ask for your autograph if they saw you in the real world. They're just acting the 'big one' behind their keyboards. Cowards. It's never nice to read a nasty tweet, but it doesn't bother me anymore. Later that year when I was selected for the third Lions Test ahead of Brian O'Driscoll, there was all this 'justice for BOD' stuff. I hadn't even played and I was getting negative tweets. I remember one that said, 'Just arrived in Sydney, going to look for @JonFoxDavies so I can break his legs. #JusticeForBOD.' Every Friday on tour, I'd meet my parents for coffee in the afternoon somewhere. Leaving the hotel that Friday my mum joked, 'You go on ahead, and we'll walk a hundred yards behind you!' Even she was getting on the bandwagon. After the game I wanted to get on Twitter and hurl abuse back at people. But I knew I had to rise above it.

Sam Warburton: My agent sent me a quote once which summed it up quite nicely: 'Do Lions really care about the opinions of sheep?' I was watching Man United play with a mate, and Wayne Rooney missed a shot on goal. My mate pipes up with, 'Rooney's shit!' I couldn't help but be amused. This was a fat, out-of-shape guy who played parks-pitch level, and he was calling Wayne Rooney shit. It was at that point that the penny dropped for me. All these people on social media who contact me and criticise my performance are essentially people like him. It's all just noise.

On that day, Alex Cuthbert could do no wrong in the eyes of the Welsh public. Born in Gloucestershire to a Welsh mother and English father, he could have turned out for either country. He chose Wales, and once he'd dabbed down for his second try, he was being hailed a national hero.

Sam Warburton: Normally, when you walk back after a try, not many people are talking to each other. On that occasion, everyone was acknowledging each other and spurring each other on, grinning from ear to ear. We just knew we'd reached another level; a level England couldn't get close to.

Jamie Roberts: A lot of us got on the Lions tour to Australia off the back of that result. If you can't deliver in the big moments, your reputation suffers. England were tipped to win that game and the Grand Slam, but when it really mattered, they didn't deliver.

Jonathan Davies: When the whistle blew, I jumped up and hugged Cuthy. Then we both turned and saluted the crowd. It was pretty special, I have to say. When I'm old and fat and I walk into a pub showing the rugby, I want to be able to say, 'Oi, I used to do that, and they aren't as good as I was.'

Adam Jones: The contrast between our players and the English players couldn't have been more pronounced. We were in seventh heaven, and they looked as though their entire world had caved in. It had been ten years since they'd last won a Grand Slam, and their dreams had been shattered. I made a point of putting a consoling arm around both Joe Marler and Dan Cole. We'd definitely had some marginal calls go our way at scrum time, and I told them that.

Sam Warburton: They dropped the lights for the trophy presentation, which heightened the drama. The players had no idea it was going to happen. We were called up one by one, and felt like rock stars. They'd call out your name, you'd walk into the spotlight and 75,000 people would roar at the top of their lungs. Players were bouncing up and down like kids waiting for their medals. During the lap of honour, I punched the air, and everyone in all three tiers threw their arms in the air in unison. It was unreal, unbelievable.

Adam Jones: I wandered over to chat to Graham Rowntree at the post-match function, and he greeted me with: 'Adam Jones, you're a fucking prick.' I think he may have taken some of those scrum decisions personally.

Sam Warburton: Back at the hotel piano bar, we were physically and emotionally spent. There were no wild celebrations; just a bunch of mates having a few quiet beers together, and barely moving. Even I had a beer . . . or was it a vodka-cranberry? We were too tired to go out, but it was such a special night. No experience, including the Lions, will ever top that.

Adam Jones: I'm not sure Warby did have a drink, you know. He certainly turned down my offer of one. I'm pretty sure he just had his protein shake and went to bed. That's why he was on media duty the following morning. He was the only one who surfaced before midday and didn't look like a corpse.

Andrew Coombs: Driving home from the Vale the following morning, I approached the junction that leads to where my mam is buried. Without thinking, I took it, and drove straight to her grave. I lost her just before my twenty-first birthday, when she was forty-three. I had an eight-year-old sister, and my parents were separated, so it was literally just me and my sister at home when I found her. It was a lot to take in. I'd just lost my Dragons contract at the time as well, so it all came at once. That's why I wasn't really nervous getting my first cap. I just felt blessed to have had the opportunity. Maybe I wasn't a frontline player, maybe I wasn't as good as the other boys, but if you're going to give a cap away for hard work and dedication, no one deserved it more than me. My mam had always been so supportive of me, it just felt like the obvious thing to do, to go and share it with her. I approached her grave, laid my Six Nations winners' medal over it, and said, 'Thanks, Mam.'

It was a record victory against England and the first time Wales had retained the title since 1979. Had it been pitched as a film script, it would have been rejected on the grounds of being utterly implausible. How could a team so riven with doubt, so psychologically crippled, recover from an eight-game losing streak to win the title?

It served as a final Lions trial, and ultimately changed the complexion of Warren Gatland's squad. Chris Robshaw had been the bookies' favourite to captain the Lions during England's charge towards the Grand Slam. In the final reckoning, he didn't even make the cut. There was a case for the entire Welsh first fifteen to stride in when the squad was announced six weeks later. Fourteen of them did, with only fly half Dan Biggar left on the sidelines.

Dan Biggar: I won't lie, it was tough to take, but I can understand the reasons why. I'm not saying I'd have been rivalling Jonny Sexton for the Test jersey, not by any stretch, but I think I could have done a job in the squad. I watched one or two games where Stuart Hogg stepped up at ten in one game and started in another. I don't think I could have done too much more in that Six Nations, but in a sense I was lucky to have had the opportunity because of Rhys Priestland's injury. But considering so many other Welsh boys went on that tour, of course it was disappointing. I haven't dwelt on it over the years, though. Gats's career has been defined by making big calls, and nine times out of ten he's got them right.

Warren Gatland: As Lions coach, I knew there were players who'd played consistently well all year, and had a certain amount of credit in the bank. And then you've got players where it's a fifty-fifty call with someone else. There's no doubt that that game was a trial match. Justin Tipuric was outstanding that day, and his performance probably got him on the tour. And he wasn't the only one – there were players on the pitch who played themselves onto the tour, and others who played their way *off* the tour during that eighty minutes. Absolutely. It was probably one of the best Welsh team performances of all time.

TWENTY-SIX

YOU KNOW WHO I AM NOW

The phrase 'Warrenball' was coined to describe Wales's relentless, physical approach under Gatland. It's an epithet he's always despised. Complimentary at first, it soon morphed into a pejorative description of a supposedly limited, unsophisticated game plan based around big men blasting away at defences until gaps appeared. Modern Welsh rugby had always been viewed through the prism of the seventies, when jinking feet and snaky hips held sway. What's often forgotten through the fog of nostalgia, is that this was made possible because of teak tough forwards like Derek Quinnell, Charlie Faulkner, Graham Price, and Dai Morris, not to mention hard running centres like Ray Gravell and Arthur Lewis.

If Gatland's detractors wanted a stick to beat him with, it was that 'Warrenball' didn't work against the southern hemisphere superpowers. During his tenure to this point, Gatland could only boast one victory over the big three in twenty-seven attempts, and that had come in the November after the 2008 Grand Slam (nine defeats v South Africa, eleven v Australia, seven v New Zealand). Customary defeats to South Africa and Australia followed the 2013 Championship win, despite the fact an overwhelmingly Welsh XV had thrashed the Wallabies in the deciding Lions Test the previous July.

The failure to match glory in Europe with success against the big three was becoming an albatross around Gatland's neck. Media suggestions that the psychological hurdle had become too high to clear were summarily dismissed, but the facts suggested otherwise. Wales finished third in the 2014 Six Nations in a topsy-turvy campaign that included a heavy defeat to Ireland, and a record 51–3 victory over Scotland.

That autumn, all three southern hemisphere giants came to Cardiff. Australia extended their winning run over Wales to ten in a row, while New Zealand extended theirs to twenty-six in a row. On 29 November, the Springboks rolled into town with victories over England and Italy under their belts. They were defending an unbeaten run against Wales that stretched back to 1999. An underwhelming crowd of 55,000 passed through the turnstiles hoping that Wales would finally break their duck. Eighty minutes later, after a match of unbridled ferocity, no tries and precious little sparkle, Wales emerged bloody, bruised . . . and victorious at last.

Sam Warburton: That was one of my best moments in a Welsh jersey – the relief of finally beating one of the big three. I always knew we could, but we'd never got over the line, despite all our success in Europe. Once we did that, it was a massive weight off my shoulders. I *do* think it's a mental thing. There are twenty-three guys in a squad, and perhaps fifteen of them genuinely think they're going to win. That means there are around eight that don't. They'd be happy to get within seven points. I can't pick out who those players are, but there *are* players like that in Wales. Glass half-empty types, who haven't got that extra level, that unstinting self-belief that I've always had. That's the difference between Wales and the Lions. With the Lions, you have thirty-two guys climbing the walls, desperate to get out of the dressing room to beat the opposition. That's why we beat New Zealand in 2017. You need twenty-three guys who have no mental chink whatsoever, no room for self-doubt. It's the only explanation I can think of.

Jonathan Davies: Our poor record against the southern hemisphere sides winds us all up. When we finally beat South Africa, it was a massive relief, and to all the people who kept saying we couldn't, it was a case of 'have that', and sticking two fingers up to them. It was such a scrappy end, but crucially after surrendering leads to New Zealand and Australia, we held it together to cling on. We tried everything we could to lose that game, but in a perverse way, it was nice to go through it, play shit at the end, and still win, because on so many occasions, we'd played well and lost.

Scott Baldwin: We had a good drink that night and we deserved it. Everyone but Samson Lee, that is. He asked to be excused from drinking because he wanted to get up at five in the morning to go ferreting. We said that was fine, but for every alcoholic drink we all had, he'd have to bolt a glass of tomato juice. He was more sick doing that than any of us. His nickname for a while after that was 'Ketchup'. He was up and away by five though. He loves his outdoor pursuits. He claims he can kill a rabbit from a hundred yards with a slingshot. Bollocks.

Ian Gough: I came through during the late nineties, when we got beaten by ninety points, and we were sacking coaches every other week. Gats has given us success and he's given us hope. We go into World Cups now expecting to make quarter-finals, expecting to make semi-finals. To criticise him because we're not flinging the ball around like they did in the seventies is ridiculous. The old rugby romantics are still looking for the fairy and the unicorn. They don't exist. We've got a lot of armchair critics in Wales.

Ian Evans: It's nice to play attractive rugby, but if a coach has brought in a method that works, then as a player you just follow orders. It takes a strong person to stick to your guns the way Gatland did, and you can't argue with the results.

Scott Baldwin: He's always encouraged us to have a go. 'If you see something, play it.' The forwards knew that our role was almost always to get up off the floor, and get around the corner, but that's not to say that if there was an overlap the backs couldn't call something. If you're getting round the corner quicker every time than the opposition, you're going to get gain-line, and you're going to get tries. Yes, we've always backed ourselves physically and fitness-wise, but that's just one aspect of our success. 'Warrenball' is a myth.

Sam Warburton: Over a four-year period, he masterminded two Grand Slams, a World Cup semi-final and a Lions series win. You can't argue with it. Those things don't just happen by accident. We recognised, after 2013, that our game plan wasn't as effective anymore, because the game had evolved. But back then it was irresistible. People want to see flashy, glamorous rugby, they want to see breath-taking tries being scored, but there's only one thing that *players* care about, and that's winning. We had a team debrief ahead of the 2014 tournament after we'd won two Six Nations in a row. In the past, those things had gone on for hours, and you normally hear all these buzz words like 'belief', 'honesty', and 'determination', which I think is a load of rubbish. It goes in one ear and out the other. That year, Gats sat us down and asked what we wanted to achieve in the Six Nations. One of the boys put his hand up and said, 'Win it.' Everyone nodded. Gats said, 'Anyone else?' No one else said a word, and that was it. Meeting over. We don't care about scoring tries, and playing attractive rugby, we just do whatever it takes to win Test matches.

Dan Lydiate: It's crazy to think that we were getting criticised for our style of play when we were winning things. Would our fans rather we scored length-of-the-field tries, and lost games? I know you've got to develop and evolve, but you still have to stick to your strengths. When we played Ireland in 2011, they knew exactly what we were going to do but they couldn't stop it. No one was complaining then, were they? 'Warrenball' for me was as much about the work ethic as anything else. No team's going to work harder than us, or be fitter than us. That was always a massive Gatland message.

Sam Warburton: I really like Warren. We never had much of a relationship beyond rugby. We'd call one another when something needed to be sorted, and that was about it. It was a very efficient, very laid-back relationship, and there was a lot of mutual trust. We didn't live in each other's pockets. Some coaches would probably have hated me as a captain, because I was so laid back. And some captains wouldn't like him as a coach because he's so laid back. But for me personally, he was the best coach I worked under, without a shadow of a doubt.

The 2015 World Cup draw was made nearly three years before the tournament began, during Wales's ignominious slide to eight defeats in a row.

That losing run had seen them drop out of the world's top eight, relegating them to the third group of World Cup seeds. It meant they'd be paired with two rugby giants in the so-called 'pool of death'. There was a sense of resigned inevitability when their nemesis, Australia, was drawn from the hat. Their other tier-one opponent in pool A would be the host nation, England. It was as mouth-watering for the fans as it was daunting for the players.

The 2015 edition of the Six Nations made for intriguing viewing. Ireland, England and Wales all finished on eight points with four wins apiece, with Ireland taking the title on points-difference. Their differential was only ten points better than Wales's, who wound up in third place. Their only defeat had come in their opening match against England.

Jamie Roberts: We knew the draw three years in advance, and the equation was simple. We had to beat Australia or England to emerge from the pool of death. All eyes were on the England game for obvious reasons. It was sexed up everywhere. We worked very hard for that tournament, the training camps out in Switzerland and Qatar were incredibly tough.

Gareth Davies: We had to do our main conditioning sessions obscenely early in Qatar before it got too hot. Even at seven in the morning, it was pushing thirty on the thermometer.

Sam Warburton: They were even more brutal than 2011. We were doing insane running drills in fifty-degree heat, with paramedics on standby at the side of the pitch. It was right on the edge, straddling the boundary of what was safe and dangerous. As soon as the first session was over, we all made a beeline for the air-conditioned changing rooms. All of us except Tom Francis, who'd passed out. He had to be carried off the pitch, and laid out on ice towels while oxygen was pumped into him.

Gareth Davies: It was like a scene from *Casualty*. Once we got him safely back into the changing rooms, he came round, and the boys immediately started taking the piss out of him. I think it was his first Wales training camp, and he'd probably never had to train that hard in his life. No offence, but he didn't really look like a professional rugby player, did he? He's come on leaps and bounds since, but when he first arrived, a lot of us were like: 'Who's *this* guy?'

As horrible as they were, we left those camps feeling invincible. Some people suggested afterwards that the reason we had so many injuries during the campaign was that we'd been over-trained, but I don't believe that. I felt fitter and more powerful than I'd ever been.

Dan Biggar: During the summer, we lost Jonathan Davies, Leigh Halfpenny, and Rhys Webb. Three world-class players who were as good as anyone in their position in the world. It could have broken the spirit of a weaker squad, but to his credit, Gats kept the place as positive as I've ever experienced it. He'd always slip positive comments into the meetings, always make sure morale was kept high. He never doubted that we'd beat England, or that we'd qualify from the pool.

Scott Baldwin: We accentuated the positives after every session. We talked about what we'd done well rather than what we'd done badly.

Gareth Davies: Those camps really did pull us together as a squad, and helped tighten the bonds. We had the utmost belief in one another, even when all those key players kept dropping out. We knew that whoever ended up in the jersey would do a job.

Dan Biggar: We're a country where the easy option is to be negative, to look for excuses, and to come up short. Gats refused to accept that. He kept drumming it into us that we were going to qualify. Whatever the circumstances, whatever the injury situation, however much time was left on the clock, we were *going* to find a way to win.

Scott Baldwin: There was a genuine sense of camaraderie between the boys. Everyone got on brilliantly, and Gats helped to foster a club mentality. I was rooming with Samson Lee, which was an experience in itself. He liked to go to bed at eight o'clock and told me to get up and turn him on his side if he snored. It didn't really work, and I was down on my sleep after a few nights. He was up bright and early every day and on our first day off, I attempted to have a lie-in. It was ruined by a loud knock at the door. It was a DPS delivery guy with a parcel for Samson. A big brown box. When he came back later and opened it up, it was full of money. Reams of it. I said, 'Sams, what the hell is that?' 'Money, butt.' 'What for?' 'I ran out didn't I, so I had the missus send it up.' It turned out they only had one bank card between them, and he'd never used it because he didn't know how.

Gareth Davies: He's clean off, Samson. One of a kind. Every away trip, whether it's with the Scarlets or Wales, he's always had his bath and is in bed by eight o'clock.

Scott Baldwin: His missus looked after the finances, and would just dole out the money as and when he needed it. When he got his first pay cheque at the Scarlets, he went into the chairman's office to ask what '*tax*' meant, and why it had been deducted from his wages. He didn't have a scooby.

Lloyd Williams: I was rooming with Phillsy, who I got to know really well. He's a really good mate of mine now, and I saw a different side to him during that campaign. Before I roomed with him, I thought he was arrogant, but I got it wrong. He's very dry, very intelligent, and great company.

Luke Charteris: I was with Brad Davies for most of it. He's special. I love him to bits. One minute he's moping about, and complaining about being homesick, the next he's leaping around naked, and trying to jump on me. The hotel was supposed to be haunted and Brad was convinced he'd seen a ghost. Him and Lyds wouldn't stop going on about it. He was genuinely spooked about it.

Gareth Davies: I roomed with Rhys Priestland throughout. He's a bit of a secret trainer, and would be working on his abs every night. He got me into it too, doing a few extra sets before bed. He got me into decent shape, fair play. It was nice to start against Uruguay in Cardiff. We played some good stuff, and had plenty of confidence going into the England game.

England, like Wales, had opened their campaign with a bonus point victory. So after nearly three years of hype and anticipation, two of the biggest predators in the pool of death were ready to bare their teeth in a potentially career-defining game. England head coach, Stuart Lancaster, gave the headline writers plenty to scribble about when he reshuffled his midfield, opting for Owen Farrell over George Ford at fly half, and selecting the rugby league convert Sam Burgess at inside centre.

Sam Warburton: I'm not pointing my finger at the RFU, but our changing room was *boiling hot.* So much so, that I was starting to feel drowsy and lethargic. You're usually in there for about an hour, so we thought someone was deliberately trying to mess with our heads. Then the lights went out, leaving us in pitch darkness. I thought, 'Someone's trying to pull our pants down here,' and we were straining at the leash by the time we stepped onto the pitch.

Dan Lydiate: I don't remember that. Maybe Warby just had the sweats that day. I do remember running out and seeing the likes of Billy Vunipola and Sam Burgess, and thinking, 'Jesus, these are big lads.'

Lloyd Williams: I was so focused on the game, I was oblivious to anything untoward going on. But if the game had been in Wales, we'd have done exactly the same, if not worse.

Gareth Davies: It was Wales–England in their home World Cup; the biggest fixture you could ever imagine. It was an unbelievable place to be. There was a good buzz in the changing room, and I couldn't wait to get out there. From the moment we woke up that morning, we were ready to go.

Lloyd Williams: It felt quite eerie inside the stadium. The whole occasion was overwhelming. There were eighty thousand people there, but it was actually quite quiet. The suspense was difficult to bear.

Sam Warburton: When you're Welsh, you pride yourself on the fact you're all working-class lads. You're not from the private schools like them, and we thought, 'If we're going to need to roll our sleeves up, and go toe-to-toe, we've got twenty-three boys who can do that.' Tough lads. With that side of things, we'll always back ourselves against any team. We pledged there and then that any chance we had to put that kind of marker down, we'd take it. They'd been putting us off with their changing room antics, and it was winding us up. They'd poked the bear and some of our boys were getting seriously angry. England were going to have it.

Scott Baldwin: Warby does get on edge. He's such a calm character normally, but before a game he turns into a completely different person. He's like the Incredible Hulk. 'Who are you and what have you done with Warby?' There's a side to his personality the public will never see. Lyds is exactly the same.

Sam Warburton: When I was younger, I was never intimidated by another player. I always thought about the opposition, 'I'm more determined than them, more professional than them. Athletically, I'm probably better than them.' I used to assess my opposite number and think, 'He hasn't prepared himself as well as I have, he hasn't eaten as well, trained as well, slept as well. And he hasn't got my genetics.' Without wanting to sound arrogant, I always thought, 'He can't be better than me.' That day it all came boiling to the surface when Dan Lydiate chopped Tom Wood down around the twenty-minute mark. It erupted into a big brawl, and every single Welsh player flew in. That was a big psychological turning point. England suddenly realised there were fifteen lads there who were mad keen for it and would not, under any circumstances, be backing down.

Scott Baldwin: That suggested to me that they were vulnerable, that they were starting to break under the weight of expectation. The fact that Chris Robshaw got involved was significant. He was their captain, their rock. You always expect the fiery ones like Mike Brown to come out swinging, but when the likes of Robshaw lose their cool, it's quite telling.

Sam Warburton: I love that kind of confrontation. That won the game for us. England realised what we were about. We were a lot tougher than they thought we were. That was our way of saying, 'It doesn't matter how many people are cheering for you from the sidelines. We don't give a shit, we're here to beat you.'

Dan Lydiate: It wasn't long after that that they scored. They had this play where Billy Vunipola peeled off the lineout. I was in the back line so I had Billy running at me, and Sam Burgess running short, so I had to stick on those two otherwise it would be try-time. They ended up going out the back and scored anyway.

Scott Baldwin: My head never dropped. Because of those camps in Qatar and Switzerland, we felt really tight, like a club team. We reacted well and didn't go into our shells.

Gareth Davies: I shouldn't admit this, but I started to feel vulnerable at that point. I was thinking the worst. We'd had all those injuries, and here we were at Twickenham, ten points down and under severe pressure. You have to banish those negative thoughts from your head.

Jamie Roberts: I turned to Bigs a couple of minutes before half-time after England had put in a clearing kick to the halfway line. Burgess was walking slowly back into place, and I called a play involving a tunnel ball between the twelve and the winger. I knew we could fix ten and twelve at the end of a tiring first half. Lo and behold, we hit Scotty Williams on an out ball, made fifty metres, got a penalty and kicked three points. We clawed it back to 16–9, and were within a converted try at the break. Little moments like that can change the momentum.

Sam Warburton: When Lancaster picked Burgess in the centre, it was a sign they wanted to fight fire with fire. They knew what game plan we were coming with and were worried about stopping it. It's my firm belief that you should pick a team to implement your game plan, not to try to stop the opposition. That selection made us think they were worried about us, which gave us a huge confidence boost. It put us in the driving seat. Twelve is a tough position to play, especially for a rugby league convert.

Dan Lydiate: I was surprised they picked him at twelve, because he'd been playing as a flanker for Bath, and he'd been phenomenal there. He's a lump, mind, and his YouTube show reel is pretty special, so wherever he played, we wouldn't have underestimated him.

Scott Baldwin: Nothing against Sam Burgess, because I thought he played well, but it struck me as a defensive selection. It meant they were more worried about us than we were about them. We didn't have to change *our* defence to allow for Sam Burgess, because we had Jamie in that channel, and he wasn't going to get through him.

Jamie Roberts: I knew as soon as they picked him that we had a great chance. He was a fantastic athlete and a great player, but he hadn't played in union that long. To pick him in a game of that magnitude was a risk. I saw it as a weakness for England rather than a strength. I walked past Howlers in the hotel corridor after their team had been announced, grinned and said, 'Happy days.' He grinned back, and was clearly thinking the same thing.

Dan Lydiate: Before the game they interviewed Burgess about Scott Williams. Scott had said something about preferring to play against big centres rather than fast, nippy ones. Burgess misheard the question and said, 'Who's that?' He obviously knew who Scott was, and actually tweeted him after the game to say, 'Well done,' but I'd be lying if I said that that didn't get Scott well revved up for the game.

Lloyd Williams: He insinuated that he didn't know who Scott was, and as soon as I heard that I knew there was only going to be one winner in that duel. Scotty's not the type of player to go into his shell, and that would have really fired him up.

Gareth Davies: That pissed Scott off privately, and the two of them had words during the game. Scott wouldn't bow to anyone on the pitch, regardless of their size or reputation. That quote motivated him even further. He tackled him hard early on, forcing a knock-on, and as he was getting up, he said, 'You know who I am now.'

Wales had enjoyed a brief period in the ascendancy as half-time approached, but England were still in overall control. They had a dominant scrummage, were aggressive in defence and dangerous in possession.

Scott Baldwin: England were getting away with scrummaging illegally because it was in England and it was such a big game. We were getting frustrated with the ref and with ourselves. There were a few we lost legitimately, mind. Franny's arse went right up in the air during one. I turned to my right and saw Alun Wyn's head next to mine in the front row. That's not where it was meant to be. His eyes rolled heavenward, and he screamed 'FRRRANNNYY!' Although we were behind, the messages at half-time were clear: 'Just relax, we've got a good bench, we just need to be ten per cent more clinical in what we're doing.' We tidied up some detail around the lineout. They weren't mirroring us in terms of their marking, they were just going zonal, so we could figure out where the space was. At scrum time, we knew we had to stay tight and win clean ball, rather than contest and look for penalties, because we weren't getting any. These may seem like obvious things to point out, but believe me, there's so much going on on the pitch, sometimes you can't see the wood for the trees. You might feel as though you've absolutely drilled the opposition in a scrum, but you look up and find out you've been penalised. It's only when you watch the video back that you realise what went on. Having clear direction at half-time from someone who's been observing at a distance is vital.

Soon after the break, Farrell and Biggar exchanged penalties. Every time England widened the gap, Wales narrowed it. It was turning into a who-will-blink-first duel between the two fly halves, and with Jérôme Garcès's strict officiating, the penalties were coming thick and fast. With the game approaching the hour mark, England conceded their tenth, and Dan Biggar chipped away further at the deficit. It was now a four-point game. Gradually Wales began to grow in confidence, a shift signified by two surging runs from George North and Liam Williams which took Wales to within metres of the try line.

Dan Biggar: Everything went England's way during the first hour, but as the second half progressed we got a foothold in the game and started to play a bit of rugby.

Gareth Davies: I remember certain things like they happened yesterday. Around the middle of the second half, we had an attacking lineout in their half. We were jogging towards it with a pre-call ready to go, and Billy Vunipola took a knee to try to slow things down. We were jogging to the lineout, pumped and ready to go, whereas they looked – excuse my French – fucked. I told our forwards, 'They're on the ropes here. They're looking vulnerable. If we raise the tempo now, we're going to be all right.'

But just as Wales began to sense a shift in momentum, the twisted hand of fate intervened. The sporting gods are often cruel, but here they appeared downright sadistic. Wales would have been forgiven for thinking some vengeful rugby god was gleefully jabbing pins into voodoo dolls of their players. Already crippled by injuries, their team began to disintegrate in front of their eyes. Four minutes after Biggar had kicked them to within four points, they lost three of their three-quarter line. Scott Williams was the first to depart, stretchered off with a damaged knee. He was followed by Hallam Amos, who dislocated his shoulder handing off Owen Farrell, and then by Liam Williams who suffered a suspected concussion after a boot to the head from Tom Wood. With less than fifteen minutes to play, Wales were forced into a desperate reshuffle. George North moved to the centre, Rhys Priestland came on at full back, and Lloyd Williams – the reserve scrum half – came onto the left wing. Three players playing out of position in one of the most important games of their lives.

Dan Biggar: It was ridiculous. We had two options: roll over and let England run away with it, or front up. That's when people earn their money, not when you're winning games comfortably and playing all your fancy stuff. Everyone's got skills and can do that, but you find out just how good you are when the heat is on. That day we all looked each other in the eye, and we all stepped up. Everyone earned their pay-cheque.

Lloyd Williams: I never felt like our luck had run out. I'd played them three years earlier at Twickenham when Scotty scored that wonder try, and that teaches you that it's never over 'til it's over. As long as we were within ten points, we were in with a shout. We just needed to get our hands on the ball.

As Wales were wondering quite what they'd done to displease the rugby gods so, Owen Farrell kicked his fifth penalty to put England 25–18 ahead. With eleven minutes left to play, it felt like the final nail in the coffin. But what the capacity crowd at Twickenham was unaware of was that it was about to witness a final act that not even Shakespeare could have conjured in its audacity and daring.

Gareth Davies: Our pattern was to go through the phases, from one side of the pitch to the other, to tire them out, and get to the edges. We'd hit the right-hand touchline and were on our way back. I passed to Alun Wyn, who dummied to carry and pulled it out the back to Priestland. Priest passed to Bigs, who fired a miss-pass to Jamie on the edge. Jamie had a two-on-one, drew his man, and fed Lloyd on the left-hand touchline.

Lloyd Williams: I pinned my ears back and went for it. I didn't know who was inside me, but I could sense that the support was there.

Gareth Davies: Lloyd's decision to kick infield was pure instinct. It was a very scrum half thing to do.

Dan Biggar: There was nothing pre-planned about that. When you have to reshuffle as much as we did, it's difficult to put too many set-plays together. The structure goes out of the window.

Dan Lydiate: What are you on about? We trained that move all week. Obviously we knew Lloyd was a left-footer, so we put him on the left wing, and the move was called. It was a lovely chip through, and Gar followed up beautifully.

Dan Biggar: The last ten to fifteen minutes were a bit looser, a bit more off-the-cuff. Fair play to Lloyd and Gareth – it was a brilliant bit of skill, and it dragged us back into the game.

Lloyd Williams: I was running out of space and there was an open expanse of grass in front of me. Kicking the ball felt like the only option. There was a big gap, and I knew there would be quicker lads than me inside, so I went for it. Thankfully, it was a bit of a perfect kick.

Scott Baldwin: The irony was that Lloyd was playing out of position. We'd probably never have scored that try if anyone else had been on the wing.

Lloyd Williams: Toby had come into my peripheral vision, and I expected him to be the chaser, but as soon as I put boot to ball, Gar pegged onto it.

Gareth Davies: A couple of years earlier, I wouldn't have run that support line, but having been in the Welsh squad for eighteen months, I'd learnt a lot off Rob Howley. That was one of the main things he'd taught me. If he hadn't encouraged me to run those lines, I wouldn't have been there. I would normally have followed my ten and tucked in behind him, but we were taught to always anticipate a line break.

Lloyd Williams: I watch a bit of rugby league, and that sort of kick happens quite a lot in league. When I did it, Jamie thought I'd taken the wrong option, and shouted, 'NOOOOOOOOOOOO!' A nanosecond later, he was shouting, 'YEEEEEESSSS!!'

Luke Charteris: You've got to take your hat off to Lloyd, to have been thrust into an unfamiliar position, in such a high-stakes game like that would have been daunting. To pull off what he did was phenomenal.

Gareth Davies: When Lloyd kicked it, I thought, 'There are still a few defenders in front of me, there's still a bit to do here.' The bounce of the ball wasn't kind. I caught it with my two middle fingers, just about gripping onto it. If I tried that a hundred times, I'd probably knock it on ninety-nine of them. Something or someone was on my side that day, and I held on to it.

Scott Baldwin: He's a poacher, Gareth. He scores from anywhere.

Gareth Davies: The ref wanted to check the grounding and the offside line. I knew the grounding was good, but I wasn't a hundred per cent sure about the offside. I was praying no one had been ahead of the ball because I knew that if the try was awarded, it would go down in history. As soon as I saw the first replay, I was confident I was onside. The ref still took a few minutes because they checked two or three angles, but I knew for a fact it was a try. The conversion levelled it, but at that point all I was thinking about was winning.

Lloyd Williams: My dad [Brynmor Williams] was in the stand with his mates, but he was in the toilet at the time. He gets nervous and doesn't like watching me, so he was under the tunnels when we scored. All his mates ran down to tell him what had happened, and he came back to watch the rest of the game. He wants me to do well, obviously, but he can barely bring himself to watch me live.

Dan Biggar: With the conversion, we got level, and for me there was only one winner from that point. The difference in body language was obvious. There were still two teams out on the field but only one looked like they were going to go on and win it.

Lloyd Williams: I was over the moon that I'd got to play a part in such a massive moment, but I was conscious that we still weren't winning. I knew we had some boys who were great over the ball, and we had a great chance of forcing a penalty in the last few minutes. It's easy to re-focus as a scrum half because you know that after a score, you're going to be touching the ball again within a few minutes. But as a winger, I was just watching the game from the touchline, trying to stay focused, trying not to get carried away.

With eight minutes left, Dan Biggar launched a high, hanging kick into England's half. Mike Brown caught it, and was immediately set upon by a horde of rampant Welsh tacklers. Sam Warburton did what he does best, planted his feet, got his hands on the ball, and prevented Brown from releasing. A shrill blast from Jérôme Garcès's whistle indicated a penalty for Wales.

Dan Biggar: The kick was forty-nine metres out, just inside England's half. It's amazing how much of a psychological difference that metre makes. As I was lining it up, I told myself, 'You've waited so long for the opportunity to be Wales's first choice kicker. Don't mess it up.' It was the sweetest of connections, and I knew it was good. It sailed over, and had a couple more metres in it as well.

Gareth Davies: I was stood right behind him and he nailed it. The rest is history.

Lloyd Williams: If Biggar hadn't knocked that over, I wouldn't have been asked about the try ever again. I owe Bigs a lot for that. He probably thinks me and Gar have taken all the credit.

Jamie Roberts: It was ballsy to knock that penalty over from fifty metres. I remember his 'macarena' routine from back then. A sweep of the hair, little shuffle, a touch of either shoulder, another sweep of the hair, a few deep breaths and boom. Over it goes. I still rib him about that. I'm convinced he came up with it to get a bit more publicity.

Gareth Davies: He was milking it a bit, wasn't he? But the more he did it, the more he came to rely on it. And it worked a treat.

Lloyd Williams: He was actually really self-conscious about that. He didn't like doing it, but it became a crutch. If he kicks as well as he does though, he can do whatever dance he wants.

Jamie Roberts: He's changed it now, but he was on fire that World Cup with the boot. It was so reassuring to have a kicker of his quality, because games like that are often decided by a single score.

Lloyd Williams: I play golf with Bigs and he's exactly the same before every shot. It takes six hours to play a round with him. I guarantee that he definitely doesn't do it to seek attention. He's a modest guy and does everything he can to stay in the shadows.

Dan Biggar: I wasn't really aware what was going on in the moment. It's all quite mechanical, trying to stick to a process. You don't want to snatch at it or rush it; you want to make sure you're composed and in the zone. I had plenty of belief despite the distance, but you never know until you've actually made contact.

With three minutes left on the clock, England were pummelling away at an increasingly belligerent Welsh defence, when Sam Warburton was penalised for an almost identical jackal attempt to the one that had led to the Biggar penalty. Mike Brown was again the man in possession, but this time the decision went England's way. Warburton was adjudged to have been involved in the tackle, and should have released the man. It was a kickable penalty that would have salvaged a draw.

Jamie Roberts: All of us assumed they would go for the sticks. Chris Robshaw looked to the corner and told George Ford to kick it out. I thought, 'That's ballsy.'

Sam Warburton: They turned down the kick at goal and were going for the win.

Luke Charteris: I thought, 'Brilliant, we've got a chance here.' We were confident in our lineout defence.

Sam Warburton: I was walking up and down the lineout absolutely screaming at my players, 'Don't you fucking dare let them score.' I was borderline hysterical. I wanted to appear physically intimidating to England, to get inside their heads. It was as much a message to them as it was to my players. I was so desperate not to let the game go.

Scott Baldwin: As soon as they went to the corner, I thought, 'Happy days.' Our driving lineout defence had been superb and I knew for a fact that we'd blitz them into touch. They weren't going to risk throwing long, and spreading the ball wide, so we knew we'd be able to contain them. It's the easiest place to defend because you've got everyone coming from one side to smoke them. It was ballsy going for the lineout, but pretty conservative to then throw to the front.

Lloyd Williams: They'd made the big call going for the lineout, so you'd think they'd just go for broke and throw to the back.

Gareth Davies: They obviously backed themselves, didn't they? The worst-case scenario was that they'd score from the driving lineout, and we'd lose after all that hard work. I'm sure everyone was thinking about all the hard work we'd done at those training camps in Switzerland and Qatar. *This* was the time to put all that hard work into practice.

Sam Warburton: Luckily most of the boys were in the same frame of mind as me. It wasn't the time for negative thoughts. We just had to bury that driving maul into touch. I told them, 'I don't care if you injure yourself, if you break an arm, if you *finish* yourself, this maul is going straight into touch. They *cannot* win.'

Gareth Davies: I was doing my best to gee up the forwards to snuff it out. My role was to guard the short side and make sure no one snuck through.

Scott Baldwin: That moment was a culmination of everything that had gone on that year. Our pack was getting better and better. We'd beaten South Africa the previous autumn and pushed them off their own ball when they had an attacking scrum on our line. We'd been in those type of situations and won, and we knew we could do it again.

Jamie Roberts: Luke Charteris was on the field by then. There can't be many better defensive maul players in world rugby. He's a real unsung hero.

Scott Baldwin: Charts was one of the best lineout defenders in the World Cup.

Jamie Roberts: I was the defensive captain, and I thought, 'Right, *this* is a test.' Whether they maul the lineout, whether they come through the midfield and punch, this is the biggest set we've done in a long time, probably since that England game in 2013. Big games, big moments. Seventy-eight minutes on the clock, Wales v England, World Cup, they've gone to the corner. *This* is where we bring it. We'd lost three of our back line. Lloyd Williams was on that left wing, and I had him coming up to me saying, 'What do I do? What do I do?' I made sure he was clear on his roles.

Gareth Davies: Wingers have got really important roles in defending driving lineouts. They've got to be plugging either side of the maul, and even if the opposition get the shove on, the winger's got to be in place to get under the ball in case they drop over the line. Shaun Edwards has always emphasised the importance of the wingers in that situation. Lloyd would have been vaguely aware of what he was meant to do, but he wouldn't have known the specifics.

Luke Charteris: We laid a trap and they fell into it. They did exactly what we wanted them to do when they called the front option. We managed to get through,

break up the maul, and isolate the carrier. Then everyone piled in and killed it off.
Jamie Roberts: Fair play to Alun Wyn and Charts. They were the glory boys who got their hands everywhere to disrupt the maul, but the buy-in from the entire pack to smash that maul back into touch was incredible. On the biggest stage of all, we'd repelled their last desperate attack, snuffed out the chance, and neutralised their strongest weapon. Those are proud moments for us backs, who get to stand back and admire the work of the forwards. You're the product of your preparation and I've no doubt they'd have practised and practised that. England are a side who take enormous pride in their forward power, in their maul strength, and our boys totally dismantled it.

Luke Charteris: England are renowned for having a strong set piece and driving maul. They'd had a few rumbles early on and got a bit of joy out of it, but when it mattered, we smoked them.

Dan Biggar: That summed up our campaign in terms of the attitude of the boys. My penalty kick may have grabbed more headlines, but there's no difference between what that pack of forwards did, and what a goal-kicker does to win the game. They had to produce their best when it really mattered, and it was more difficult because the eight of them had to do it together. They deserve huge, huge credit.

Dan Lydiate: When Biggar thumped the ball into the stands, you could feel the elation. It was only two games in, and we hadn't won anything yet, but it was the group of death and momentum had massively shifted in our direction.

Scott Baldwin: Gethin Jenkins said afterwards that it was the best win he'd ever had. When you consider he's our most capped player and he's won three Grand Slams, that's some statement.

Gareth Davies: Any of the boys who say it was just another game are lying. There is an extra buzz about a Wales–England game, without a doubt. And the context of this one made it extra special.

Dan Biggar: Ninety-nine per cent of our fans will tell you that beating England means everything. I don't see it like that. Don't get me wrong, I enjoy beating them, but if you offered me one victory against the All Blacks in return for losing every match against England for the rest of my career, I'd take it. We need to be bigger than just beating England.

Scott Baldwin: I saw the interview Mike Brown gave afterwards when he was fuming, and everyone was rinsing him for it. I felt sorry for him. He just lost in a home World Cup against Wales, and he was gutted. I'd have given exactly the same interview to be honest. What do you expect him to say? I had more sympathy for him than anything else.

Dan Lydiate: Gethin grabbed Lloyd after the game and asked if he could have his boots. Lloyd panicked and said, 'Yeah, yeah no worries.' Once Gethin had them in his hands, he said, 'These will make a lot of money for my testimonial.'

Lloyd Williams: There's no guarantee he got the actual boot. I wore three pairs during the World Cup, and I gave him *one* of my three left boots. I still have the other two pairs. I didn't mark the ones I'd worn on particular days, so no one will ever know if he had the actual one. Either way, he gave the proceeds to charity, so it was for a good cause.

Scott Baldwin: Back in the changing room, everyone was bouncing around the place, the atmosphere was buzzing, and in the midst of all that, I slumped down in my seat and thought, 'I played fucking shit today.' The lineouts hadn't gone well and the scrum had been under pressure. I'm really hard on myself with lineouts, whether it's my fault or not. Gethin was to my right, Franny to my left. They were both having a beer, laughing, joking, and loving life, and I was sitting there silently fuming. It had been the biggest game of my life, we'd just beaten England, and I felt miserable about my own performance.

Dan Lydiate: Geoff Parling came into the changing rooms and admitted that we were better than them. For him to lose in such a big game but still come and have a beer with us, spoke volumes. Fair play.

Scott Baldwin: Gats sat next to me and asked what was wrong. I told him I wasn't happy with the way I'd played, and he said, 'Better to have a game like that and still win. I know you'll put it right on Wednesday.' It wasn't much but it was a real confidence boost. I'd been unofficially told I'd be starting against Fiji, and that I was still first choice. To know he was backing me really lifted my mood. He's always been really good at knowing how to get the best out of people.

Luke Charteris: The changing room afterwards was one of the best I can remember. The atmosphere was incredible. Yes, it was only a pool game, but it was England at Twickenham, and the result meant we were almost certainly through to the quarter-finals. It was a big release from all that pressure that had built up.

Dan Lydiate: We had to get on the bus back to the Vale of Glamorgan to do a session in the cryotherapy chamber. The coaches were all on the beers at the front of the bus and we were in bits at the back. There was no time for us to celebrate –

we had Fiji in four days' time. We needed to pick ourselves up and go again.

Gareth Davies: We were going through the tolls on the Severn Bridge in the early hours and there was a minibus in front full of Welsh fans. They pulled in on the hard shoulder, waiting for us to catch up, and as we drove past, they were all stood there whooping, cheering and jumping up and down. Our driver was tooting and waving and they were going mental. They were so, so happy. All the way back, people were leaning out of car windows, waving flags and going insane. We were on cloud nine. We couldn't believe what had happened.

Scott Baldwin: From the bright lights and euphoria of Twickenham to a dark, freezing cold cryo chamber in the space of four hours. It isn't all glamour.

Gareth Davies: I was rooming with Rhys Priestland and neither of us could get to sleep. Even though I was exhausted, I couldn't wait to get up in the morning. I was so excited.

Scott Baldwin: When we returned to our English base in Weybridge, someone had clambered up during the night, and taped a big 'G' over the 'O' on the hotel sign. The Oatland Park Hotel had become the 'Gatland Park Hotel'.

Luke Charteris: To this day, no one has claimed the credit for that. I'm pretty sure it was Thumper.

Gareth Davies: Weybridge was a lovely spot, but other than wander round and drink coffee, there wasn't a great deal to do. We filled the void with a poker club which quickly got quite competitive. There was a bit of cash involved. Melon, Charteris, and Dan Biggar were the big dogs. They'd rarely ever lose, and they were pretty strict about it. During another camp, Foxy joined in for one night, won a bit, cashed out and refused to play another round. Those three were fuming, and they banned him from ever taking part again. Bad etiquette, apparently.

Scott Baldwin: The Fiji game was actually the most physical game I played in in that World Cup, and there were times when it was in the balance. It was only our scramble defence that got us over the line. Personally, I felt much more positive off the back of that. I carried really well, I put some good shots in, our lineout functioned really smoothly, and I scored my first and only try for Wales. Our scrum got hammered, mind.

Lloyd Williams: They were a strong side. All their players were playing in the French Top 14, and they were really athletic lads. But we had a lot of confidence and even though it was a sticky first forty-five minutes, I never thought we were going to lose.

A 23–13 victory over Fiji meant Wales were three from three and sitting pretty. England had to beat Australia if they were to have a chance of making the quarter-finals.

Jamie Roberts: I went to watch England–Australia at Rosslyn Park. I had a few mates playing there, and I was the only Welshman in the clubhouse, celebrating everything Australia did. I felt like a bit of a knob, but the result meant we went through and England were kicked out. Don't get me wrong, I don't hate England, but if, as a Welshman, you help dump them out of their own tournament, it feels pretty special.

England's defeat gifted Wales a passage through to the last eight. Their match against Australia would determine who would top the group. The winners would face Scotland in the quarter-finals; the losers would take on the Springboks.

The opening quarter saw Wales dominate territory, with eighty-two per cent of the game being played in Australia's half. The Wallabies felt their way back into it during the second quarter, using their superiority in the scrum to establish field position, and nudge themselves into a 9–6 half-time lead.

Bernard Foley extended that to 12–6 within ten minutes of the restart before the Wallabies felt the wrath of referee, Craig Joubert. Within two minutes, Will Genia and Dean Mumm had been sent to the sin bin. For thirteen minutes, Wales had a numerical advantage. For seven of those minutes, it was fifteen against thirteen.

What followed was a defensive display of extraordinary courage and discipline. Outnumbered and outgunned, Australia continually hurled their bodies at the advancing Welsh tide, and managed to repel everything that was thrown at them. Wales laid siege to the Australian line. Taulupe Faletau crossed it, but knocked the ball on. George North carried three defenders over it, but was held up. Liam Williams came within inches of it on a crash ball. Jamie Roberts thundered towards it, but was hauled down short. All of these determined attacks floundered in the face of a Wallaby rearguard that was as frantic as it was fearless. A man light, the Australian scrum began to buckle, but refused to break.

Gareth Davies: We got a bit over-eager, and fell into a trap. We should have been a bit more patient rather than going too wide too early. We were camped in their twenty-two for that entire period, but they were flying up out of the line and shutting us down. We got held up a couple of times. On another day, with a bit more luck, we could have won.

Scott Baldwin: To be fair, they used the yellow card really well. We had scrum after scrum, but they kept getting reset. They were being smart, deliberately conceding penalties, and trying to hoodwink the ref into thinking it was our fault. Stephen

Moore was talking to Joubert after every scrum, wasting vital seconds. It was pretty smart captaincy. We could have gone for the corner just to speed things up, but by this point, we were so dominant in the scrums, we were convinced we'd reap the rewards eventually. They ate up around seven minutes, and rode their luck. In my opinion, we should have had a penalty try, but they got away with it. Eventually they brought Tatafu Polota-Nau on, who's a stronger scrummager than Stephen Moore, and they had a lot more solidity after that.

Luke Charteris: I've no doubt Stephen was trying to influence the referee's interpretation of things, but if I'd been captain, I'd have been doing exactly the same thing. I'd never have a go at a player for doing that. You want the ref to be strong in those situations, but if our advantage wasn't obvious, then it was down to us to have dealt with it better. Australia didn't bring anyone into the scrum, so we should have had a clear advantage, but when it was obvious we weren't going to get the rewards, we should have gone out the back, or called a back-row move to exploit their lack of scrum half. We just weren't canny enough.

Dan Biggar: Straight afterwards, a few of us spoke up about how disappointed we were with our attack. We'd created all those chances and blown every one. We knew we hadn't played as well as we could have. We could either beat ourselves up about it all week, or we could say, 'We're in a quarter-final of a World Cup against South Africa with a chance to get to a semi-final and take care of some unfinished business from four years ago.' That's the attitude we took. We parked the Australia game and looked ahead.

Scott Baldwin: We'd have preferred Scotland in the quarter-final because we'd never lost to them under Warren Gatland. But we backed ourselves against South Africa anyway. We backed ourselves against anyone.

It had taken Wales a hundred years to register their first victory over South Africa, but the last two matches between the two countries had seen the momentum shift in Wales's favour. In Nelspruit the previous summer, they'd raced to a 17–0 lead, before losing in the dying moments. That autumn, in Cardiff, they'd bludgeoned their way to a 12–6 win. Psychologically, they were in a good place. Physically, they were falling to pieces. The latest raft of injuries led to yet another backline reshuffle, with Gareth Anscombe playing out of position at full back, and twenty-year-old rookie, Tyler Morgan, picked at centre.

Gareth Davies: George nearly scored in the opening few minutes and it was obvious we had them rattled. Bigs knocked a few penalties over and he chipped and gathered to put me through for my fifth try of the tournament. We were 13–12 ahead at half-time and looking comfortable.

In what had become a trademark move, Dan Biggar hoisted a high up-and-under into South African territory, beat Willie Le Roux to the catch and cantered into the twenty-two before releasing Gareth Davies. Wales were supposed to be on their last legs, decimated by injuries, but they were refusing to play the victim. On the stroke of half-time, Biggar dropped a goal to nudge Wales ahead.

Dan Lydiate: Bigs had an absolute stormer in that game. His high balls were on the money and his chase and regather for Gareth's try was timed to perfection.

Luke Charteris: Whenever there was a penalty, you knew he'd knock it over, and he was dictating play brilliantly, bossing the boys around the park. That's exactly what you want from a ten. He was at his peak in that campaign.

Scott Baldwin: Things went a bit downhill in the second half. I got knocked out on the pitch and we got knocked out of the World Cup. It was in the fifty-third minute. I came flying out of the line to hit Eben Etzebeth, and my head smacked directly into his hip. Boom. I sprung back to my feet and thought I was fine, but our physio, Prav, told me I'd been out cold for two minutes. I had no option but to go off. It was weird, I had no loss of memory other than the two minutes I was out. I remember everything that happened up to that point in vivid detail. They made me go off on the buggy as a precaution and everybody took the piss out of me afterwards saying I was milking the applause, waving like the Queen.

Dan Biggar: That South Africa team was a star-studded side. Victor Matfield, Schalk Burger, Duane Vermeulen, Bryan Habana, JP Pietersen, Willie Le Roux. My biggest regret is not hanging on to that lead. We kicked a penalty with ten minutes left, to put ourselves 19–18 ahead, but then we succumbed to a single moment of brilliance from Vermeulen.

In an act of dexterity that belied his bear-like physique, Duane Vermeulen picked up off the back of an attacking scrum and drew two defenders before releasing Fourie du Preez with the most delicate of offloads. Alex Cuthbert had come off his wing in an attempt to shut down Vermeulen, leaving du Preez with a clear run to the line.

Lloyd Williams: They couldn't have prepped for that on the training field. It was completely random.

Scott Baldwin: I wasn't allowed to watch the rest of the game because I was on gas and air to try to stop any swelling, and the doctor said the stress of it would have affected my heart rate and blood flow. At that stage, we were still on course for the semi-finals, and if I had any ambition of playing in that, I'd need to pass all the concussion protocols. It was torture not being able to watch. All I knew was that we were winning. Then I heard the stadium erupt and asked the doctor, 'Have we scored?' He said, 'No. They have.'

Lloyd Williams: I went low to tackle Vermeulen and Cuth came in to stop the offload, but it was way too good, and Fourie du Preez waltzed in at the corner. It was a bit of magic.

Luke Charteris: I was watching from the bench, quietly confident that we were going to see out the last few minutes. South Africa aren't known for their trickery; they almost always take the direct route, and our defence was equal to that. Nobody saw that offload coming. It's certainly not what Vermeulen's renowned for.

Scott Baldwin: The only thing that stopped us getting to the semi-final of a World Cup was that one piece of genius from Duane Vermeulen.

Dan Lydiate: The pass was virtually unplayable.

Luke Charteris: Cuthy would have seen Vermeulen running at Lloyd and assumed he was going to try to run over him. His instinct was to come in and get the double shot. To knock the big man over before he built up a head of steam.

Scott Baldwin: It wasn't Cuthy's fault. He had to come in.

Lloyd Williams: He tried to stop the offload, but the offload beat the man. You'd never practise defending that because it's impossible to anticipate. I didn't know what had happened. One minute I was wrapping my arms around Vermeulen's legs, the next Fourie du Preez was running in at the corner. It was absolutely heart-breaking. All the boys were gutted. We felt like we deserved a spot in that semi.

Sam Warburton: The stars weren't aligned for us. We'd suffered so many injuries, and it had disrupted us so much. If we'd beaten South Africa, we'd have played New Zealand in the semis, who were better than they were in 2011. That could have been a game too far, and we could have really unravelled.

Scott Baldwin: That try was only the third we conceded in the entire tournament. That's not bad going considering we were in the so-called pool of death. But the injury curse had struck again. I came off, Tyler came off, Bigs came off.

Sam Warburton: In hindsight, we probably went out at the right time. We had a historic win over England, got out of the most competitive pool in the competition's history, and came within a whisker of beating South Africa. We emerged with credit, and it leaves a bit of unfinished business for 2019.

Dan Lydiate: It felt weird because we genuinely didn't think we'd be going home, despite all the injuries. Our self-belief was unshakeable going into that. It never entered our minds that it would be our last game. We were thinking it would be tough, but that we'd get through to the semis and go again. The following morning, we were packing our bags.

Scott Baldwin: Heyneke Meyer came into the dressing room afterwards to congratulate us on a great game. He admitted it was decided on a single pass; that was it. At the time it was of no consolation, but now that the pain has subsided, it was a really nice gesture.

Gareth Davies: Maybe our luck ran out. All those injuries were bound to take their toll, but even with a patched-up back line, I'm convinced we'd have given New Zealand a run for their money.

TWENTY-SEVEN

A RARE, PRECIOUS MOMENT

In November of 2015, Warren Gatland announced that he'd be standing down after the next World Cup. By then, he'd be the game's longest serving coach by some distance. His twelve-year reign seems even more remarkable considering how unstable the post had been before his arrival.

The door to his office had been a revolving one, with nine men taking charge of the national side in the preceding twelve years. He'd transformed a frothing whirlpool of chaos into an ocean of relative calm and put paid to the Welsh tendency towards feast and famine. In a nation where wild optimism, and withering pessimism are comfortable bedfellows, he imbued Welsh supporters with an unfamiliar self-confidence.

Under his command, Wales have become ferociously competitive and, more importantly, they've become winners. He may have replaced some of the misty-eyed romanticism with a dose of hard-nosed pragmatism, but Wales are no longer a side content to bask in the glory of a one-off victory or to console themselves in the wake of a 'heroic' defeat. They've risen from being the tenth best team in the world, to the second best. They expect to win every time they take to the field.

England's World Cup triumph in 2003 was preceded by a Six Nations Grand Slam and summer tour victories over New Zealand and Australia. To be the best, you have to beat the best, and that year England arrived in Australia on a tidal wave of belief and positivity.

With the 2019 World Cup looming, Wales had an autumn programme of four Tests – against Scotland, Tonga, South Africa and their long-term nemesis, Australia. They duly swept the board, winning all four November internationals for the first time in their history. The victory over the Wallabies was a dour, turgid affair. It was 3–3 as the match entered its final quarter, 9–6 by the time the final whistle blew. But it mattered not a jot. The symbolism of the victory far outweighed the spectacle. Wales's thirteen-match losing streak against the Wallabies had finally been snapped, less than a year before they'd face each other again in the World Cup.

The 2019 Six Nations would provide Wales with their last competitive action before their journey to Japan. They flew into a rain-soaked Paris on the opening weekend with the confidence of a team who'd forgotten how to lose. Warren Gatland declared that if his team won in Paris, they'd go on to win the Championship.

Rob Evans: We prepared really well for that France game. We felt ready and full of confidence – but they took us by surprise.

Hadleigh Parkes: It was the first time I'd played a Test match on a Friday night, nine o'clock local time in Paris. I'm normally in bed by nine o'clock, so that was different. You have to change your whole schedule, especially as it's an away game. With a home game, you have your home comforts, you go out to your local coffee shop, catch up with friends, and the time passes quickly. Away from home, time passes much more slowly. It's a very long day.

Rob Evans: They raced into a 16–0 lead, but we only had ourselves to blame. The tries we conceded were down to individual errors. Louis Picamoles just seemed to waltz in, without anyone touching him. Then George [North] made a wrong read that led to a soft try for Yoann Huget. Liam Williams had a try disallowed. Nothing was going our way.

Liam Williams: I considered taking a quick drop-goal to convert it because I knew I hadn't scored, but that would have been obvious, so I said to [Gareth] Anscombe, 'Take it quickly, I think I've lost it over the line.' But Neil Jenkins came on and was encouraging Anscombe to relax and take his time. While that was happening, the ref decided to have a second look. I knew the laws; I was just trying to bend them.

Gareth Anscombe: The French crowd were starting to rise up and get loud and we were so flat when we came in at half-time. For the last few years, for whatever reason, we haven't started the Six Nations well. We didn't have any discipline about us. We were doing things that were totally against our defensive nature. We were so inaccurate. You can't even say we were overplaying because literally every time we got the ball we dropped it.

It had been an abject opening half for the travelling support. Wales's insouciant swagger had deserted them and in its place was a stuttering anxiety. France, for so long a team much less than the sum of its parts, were beginning to click. The 16–0 scoreline flattered Wales. Morgan Parra had missed three kicks at goal, which would have taken France out of reach. Sixteen points was daunting enough – no team had ever recovered from a half-time deficit that large in Six Nations history.

Rob Evans: Gats told us there was no need to panic, that they'd only scored because of our mistakes. We just needed to shut it down a bit, put boot to ball a bit more.

Liam Williams: We hadn't looked after the ball. We'd given away a couple of knock-ons and made a succession of sloppy errors. One individual error let them score in the left-hand corner and that set the tone for them. The message was simple: 'Look after the bloody ball.'

Gareth Davies: We hadn't played *that* badly. We'd trained for two weeks in good conditions in the Vale, and hadn't had a single day of rain. When it came hammering down in Paris, we weren't clever enough in adjusting our tactics. We tried to overplay, when realistically we should have played a more territorial game.

Hadleigh Parkes: We were still confident at half-time. We thought that if they could score sixteen points in weather like that, surely we could as well.

Liam Williams: We knew we could still win; we'd just have to do it the hard way. If you put the French on the back foot, they don't like exiting from their own half. In the second half, we played more of a territorial game and stopped conceding all those knock-ons and stupid penalties.

Josh Navidi: We realised that we had to make the conditions work for *us*. Kick the ball long and force *them* to make the mistakes.

Rob Evans: Everybody had been talking about the size of the French pack. They were all absolute monsters and people thought we'd be overwhelmed by them, but in the second half the scrum was only going one way. Was that evidence that technique trumps size? I doubt it. I don't have much in the way of technique. It was just pure Spittal-strength. 'Agricultural strength' as my old man likes to call it. I've played against Uini Atonio quite a lot and I like to cramp him up because he's such a big man. If you do that, he doesn't have the space to get the hit that's such a big part of his game. We knew if we cramped him up his back would go and he'd crumble, so every scrum we punched in so we were all tight and ready to go. To be fair to Adam Beard, he was brilliant. He's a big man and adds a lot of weight from the second row. And Ken Owens was class. When Demba Bamba came on, I told Ken to make sure he got his head under his left shoulder so I could get a good angle under his chin. At one scrum we got it spot on, I came across, and he popped up and started squealing. I'm not very good at speaking French so I wasn't really chopsing that much in that game. I just had to let my actions do the talking.

Gareth Anscombe: The second half was a mirror of the first. We started getting the rub of the green and Josh Adams created something out of nothing.

Jonathan Davies: Josh has got unbelievable acceleration. He spied the gap and scorched his way through. Tomos [Williams] was on his shoulder, running a support line, and that was it . . . we were back in the game.

Hadleigh Parkes: Tomos Williams's try pretty much lit the touchpaper that led to the Grand Slam.

Gareth Anscombe: And then Parkesy got his shin to the ball to set up George.

Jonathan Davies: The ref was playing advantage and we were running a set move. I was preparing to receive the ball and Parkesy just spoons it off his shin. As I started chasing it, I was thinking, '*What* was he thinking?' George was coming up quickly on the inside, but the kick was too far and the ball was bobbling harmlessly over the try line. Then, in a split-second, Huget commits the mother of all howlers and George pounces.

Rob Evans: A big thing we talked about was chasing lost causes. Because it was so wet, the message was, 'If there's a ball on the floor, put a boot to it and chase.' We knew France weren't good at getting down on the ball, and they had at least a mistake or two in them.

Jonathan Davies: They just do it, don't they? The previous year we grubbered it through François Trinh-Duc's legs and nutmegged him for a try. We knew that whenever we kicked the ball, we had to put pressure on them and chase hard, because they were vulnerable covering back. We knew they had the capacity to implode. They really lack urgency when it comes to getting back into position. If they make a mistake they'll look around for someone to blame rather than getting back into the right defensive shape to prevent them compounding the error. We'd never be accused of doing that because we're all too afraid of getting a bollocking from Shaun Edwards.

Gareth Davies: That was a lifeline for us. Not many top-class internationals make those kind of mistakes. Even in those conditions, you'd back most Test players to look after the ball in a situation like that.

Hadleigh Parkes: We'd actually previewed that. Not necessarily the kick itself because it wasn't a great kick. It came off my shin and probably my knee before that. A number of teams have scored tries against France like that over the past few years. They've conceded easy tries because of stuff-ups at the back. We had a different move called, but after we got the penalty advantage from the scrum, I thought, 'Bugger it, I'm going to put a kick through.' All credit to George North, he kept chasing that hard, Foxy was right there as well, and luckily the bounce of the ball went our way. Foxy and I exchanged relieved glances after George scored. There was a real sense that we'd got away with one there. My shocking kick had turned into a peach of a try. I did feel a bit sorry for Huget, but it was happy days for us, eh?

Liam Williams: To come back the way we did was a reflection of the spirit in our squad. We've become so close and tight-knit over the last eighteen months, and our self-belief – even in the most hopeless looking situations – has dragged us through more than once.

Gareth Anscombe: After that, George got a freakish intercept, and the turnaround was complete.

Jonathan Davies: I played with Seb Vahaamahina in Clermont, great bloke, very nice guy. It was his pass that George picked off. After the game, I went up to him to console him in my best French. We've all made mistakes, and I felt gutted for him personally. I knew he'd have taken that to heart.

Gareth Anscombe: Getting out of that hole in the second half was a big deal. It really felt like we'd dodged a bullet. That gave us the belief that we could go on and win the whole thing.

Hadleigh Parkes: There's a heck of a lot of belief in this squad, and a lot of young boys who've come in and don't know what it feels like to lose a Test match. Adam Beard has played fourteen, won fourteen. That's *insane*. There aren't many players who can say that in any team in the world.

Jonathan Davies: I can't believe that. If he retired tomorrow, he'd go out on a hundred per cent. Christ, I'd be happy to get fifty per cent!

Hadleigh Parkes: We had a lovely week in Nice between the France and Italy Tests. When that was suggested, we were all rubbing our hands together thinking, 'This could be amazing.' Thirty-one of us went and the management was deliberately trying to replicate the feel of being at a World Cup. The weather was terrible in Cardiff that week, as my wife kept reminding me via text, whereas in Nice, it was gloriously warm and sunny. We were swimming in the ocean every day.

Gareth Davies: It couldn't have been a bigger contrast to Paris. The sun was out and we were strutting around in shorts and t-shirts.

Gareth Anscombe: We watched the England–Ireland game the following day at an Irish bar in Nice, and I was really impressed by the quality of that Test match. I was looking at two teams playing at a really high level, and I thought we'd have to massively raise our levels just to compete with, let alone beat, those two sides.

Gareth Davies: There were loads of English and Irish fans in the bar, so we stayed in the corner minding our own business. After a while, they all clicked that we were the Welsh team, and when the final whistle blew, all the English fans started piping up that they were going to win the Six Nations. We had a good bit of banter between us.

Hadleigh Parkes: It was an awesome trip and a great interlude in what was always going to be a pretty challenging eight-week campaign. Don't get me wrong, we trained hard, but it was so refreshing to be in a different environment. I'd never been to that part of France and I was blown away by it. We took a day trip to Monaco, and I've never seen so much wealth and privilege. Yachts sitting in the harbour worth £250m! Everything was so clean and shiny, you could almost eat your lunch off the floor.

Liam Williams: We'd go out and get coffee, play cards, have some food, all as a team. Being out there in the hot weather, and training in the spring sunshine, was brilliant. It's during moments like that when I have to pinch myself. Only a few years earlier, I was playing lower league rugby for Waunarlwydd and working as a scaffolder. I never imagined it would one day be my job to train and play for my country.

Hadleigh Parkes: People want to work hard and train hard because we're all mates. There are no cliques within the squad which is pretty rare. You just sit down over lunch or breakfast with whoever's there. Everyone gets on really well. There's no one I wouldn't want to have a beer with, and that extends to management as well. It hasn't always been that way with teams I've been involved with.

Liam Williams: We were all desperate to play against Italy because we didn't feel we'd given a good account of ourselves in Paris. Gats told us early in the week that he'd probably make a few changes to give some of the squad players a chance.

Jonathan Davies: I was lying on the treatment table having a massage when Gats wandered over and said, 'How do you feel about being captain of your country?' I was like, 'What? We're making *that* many changes?'

Gareth Davies: Gats would never have referred to it as his second string. We're at a point now where we could put two XVs out and they'd virtually be as good as each other.

Hadleigh Parkes: There's great squad depth and everyone's pushing everyone else for places. Gats made ten changes for the Italy game. I was happy for Owen Watkin to get a chance, but at the same time, I wanted to play every game. Personally speaking, I know I don't have a huge amount of time in the jersey. I started when I was a bit older than most of the other boys, so I want to play every game I can.

Josh Navidi: There was a four-year gap between my first cap and my second, so I've learned never to take anything for granted. I want to play in every game because you never know when it will be your last. I have the same attitude with my club. I'd always rather play, because there's always that fear someone might come in, play a blinder, and take your place.

Gareth Davies: I'd been carrying a bit of a quad injury, so I'd struggled to train during the first two weeks in camp. I was on the treatment table three times a day. With Wales, you've got to be training and you've got to be fully fit to be considered. If you miss a few sessions, it counts against you. I was so relieved to make the thirty-one-man tour party for France and Italy because if I hadn't, I'd have missed the first two games completely.

Liam Williams: I was one of the five that was retained for the Italy game, and I was chuffed because I wanted to get straight back on the horse. Gats stressed that we shouldn't read too much into selection. He was just keen to rotate the squad, to try to replicate the feel of a World Cup.

Gareth Anscombe: The performance against Italy wasn't anywhere near as good as it should have been. But we knew we'd take care of things, and it set us up for a big game against England. To use a cricket analogy, we were like an opening batsman starting our innings, defending the first ten balls and surviving. Those two games away from home were us feeling our way into our innings. We were always going to get mentally up for a big game against England, especially as it was back home in Cardiff. Hopefully by then, we'd knock a few out of the blocks, get into our stride and start aiming for the boundaries.

Liam Williams: Italy on their home turf are a decent team. Every game at this level is hard. You can't just turn up and expect to score four tries. Don't get me wrong, we weren't thrilled with our performance, but we weren't that bothered about not getting a bonus point. The win was the important thing, and by the end of that block we'd won twice on the road.

The final scoreline of Italy 15 Wales 26 served as a warning to Wales. The victory was their eleventh in a row, equalling a record that had stood for more than a century, but the manner of it was far from reassuring. Warren Gatland admitted that if Wales performed like that against England, it would be 'embarrassing'.

Jonathan Davies: The way the fixtures were arranged, we knew that to win the Championship, we'd probably have to win the Grand Slam, so we weren't really bothered about bonus points.

Rob Evans: The competition for places against England was intense and it spilled over a few times in training. Samson Lee and Ross Moriarty came to blows that week. Samson was desperate to start and was putting himself about a bit. We were practising our lineout drives, eight on eight. He was in the reserves, and they were giving us a bit of a tuning to be fair. Ross is a bit of a hot-head, and after one maul collapsed, he gave Samson a dig in the ribs. It flared up a bit and the fists started flying. I don't know who came off best, because I ran off to hide in the sheds.

Gareth Davies: That was one of the hardest weeks I've experienced in rugby. It took me back to the dark times of Qatar before the 2015 World Cup. We knew it was going to be tough, but we didn't expect it to be that bad.

Hadleigh Parkes: You like to think you're pretty fit, but we were *buggered* at the end of some of those fitness sessions. Gats brought in a couple of old-fashioned drills to put us through the mill.

Gareth Anscombe: That week was a hell of a lot harder than anyone expected. They took it a bit old school, and it certainly revved a few of us up in terms of how fatigued we felt. There were a few drills that weren't really about skills, just about digging deep and seeing how much punishment we could take. We knew it would stand us in good stead further down the line, but a few of us were wondering if we were going a bit too far.

Jonathan Davies: It was the worst week of my life! I was wishing I was still playing in France where I'd have been eating baguettes and enjoying a glass of red wine.

Gareth Anscombe: A few years back everyone used to feel sorry for the boys playing in England because they had to go back to their clubs during the fallow weeks, but I'm telling you, these days, during the fallow week, you're wishing you were at an English club.

Hadleigh Parkes: We did a lot of flat out running to test our aerobic fitness and then went straight into skills games to test our ability to perform under fatigue. They'd go on for about five minutes non-stop to replicate that continuous period of possession in a match.

Rob Evans: Gats had identified that five minutes was the target. We had to prepare for five minutes of continuous activity because that's often what you have to do in a game scenario.

Jonathan Davies: That was my fault. During the third Lions Test in New Zealand, there was a sequence of play at the start when we were attacking their line. There was an interception, we chased the guy down, turned the ball over and kicked it back to them. They kept on playing and eventually scored off a cross-field kick. That entire sequence lasted about five minutes. If you watch it back, I'm supposed to work for the tap-down of the cross-field kick, but I turn far too slowly, and the All Blacks centre gets there before me. I knew instantly that I should have been there, but I was absolutely knackered. Gats showed me afterwards and asked what I thought. I admitted that I was blowing through my arse and didn't think I'd last until half-time. I remember being over the ruck after we got the ball back, and thinking I just wanted to walk off the field. I was that exhausted. When we were next in camp with Wales, Gats had decided that five minutes was the new threshold we'd have to reach. He showed the clip to the boys and asked me to explain what I'd been feeling. The 'game blocks' became five minutes after that, and I think a few of the boys have resented me for it ever since!

Gareth Davies: I'm glad Foxy brought that up because I wasn't going to mention it. Gats says we can blame him for the games going from three minutes to five, but the reality is, I wouldn't be sitting here as a Grand Slam winner now if we hadn't trained as hard as we did.

Jonathan Davies: The week was way worse than a pre-season. We had double-days on the Wednesday and Thursday, and another savage session on the Friday morning. A few of the boys were close to breaking down. While it's horrendous at the time, you know it's all credit in the bank, and that you'll reap the rewards come game time.

Hadleigh Parkes: Often to finish up, we'd have eight or nine in defence, with fifteen in attack, and you'd have to score three tries on the bounce before you could wrap up. Full contact, without making any mistakes or dropping any balls.

Jonathan Davies: That was an old drill of Gats's that had lain dormant for years. It was cruel of him to bring it back.

Hadleigh Parkes: If anyone dropped a ball, you'd *all* have to go off and do a 'Heini Müller'. To the uninitiated, that's a figure-of-eight, starting on the halfway line, sprint diagonally to the try line, jogging across the try line to the other corner, then sprinting diagonally back to the halfway line.

Jonathan Davies: You wouldn't be going full pace, but you certainly didn't want to finish last. I missed the Thursday afternoon session with a tight hamstring, and they did a fair few Heini Müllers. I was standing on the sidelines doing my best to motivate them, shouting, 'Come on, boys, you can do it.' At one point, Alun Wyn turned round and gave me one of his death stares, and I thought, 'Okay, I'll pipe down.' He told me afterwards it wasn't a death stare, but a look of absolute desperation from a man who could barely put one foot in front of the other any more. You know that if *he's* struggling, everyone else must be in a world of pain.

Hadleigh Parkes: Then you'd have to start again from zero, and score three tries. The first time we did it, I was on the defensive side, and we made them do three Heini Müllers on the bounce. Then they scored two tries, before Wyn Jones stole the ball, and they had to go and do *another* Heini Müller. It was full on.

Gareth Anscombe: The standards in those five-minute games during the first week was pretty poor. Balls were being dropped, boys weren't really talking to each other. Six weeks in we'd reached a drastically different standard.

Gareth Davies: After three or four weeks, the games were getting noticeably easier. You could feel yourself getting fitter and stronger.

Hadleigh Parkes: The build-up to the England game was intense, everybody wanted to be there.

Gareth Anscombe: I may have been born and raised in New Zealand, but I'm under no illusion how important the England game is to the Welsh public. You knew it was a much bigger deal because there were about twenty more journalists in every press conference. Boys in the squad who don't often speak up suddenly become really vocal, there's a real emotional connection there. There's the same big brother-little brother rivalry that there is between Australia and New Zealand. Little brother always wants to smash big brother, and that will never change.

Liam Williams: Being the underdogs suited us. We knew we had our own house in order. I was champing at the bit, desperate to get out there. I could have played the game on the Thursday.

Gareth Anscombe: Technically and tactically, I don't think Gats has reinvented the book, but he's got this incredible way of creating a winning environment. Going into the England game, he just slowly built us up and got us to the edge. Once we were at that edge, he trusted us to take over and deliver. He always made us feel that we were going to win that game. He's a master of pressing the right buttons at the right time, of getting a reaction out of certain players. A quiet word here, a quiet word there.

Gareth Davies: Gats loves it when people are talking up the opposition, and not paying any attention to us.

Gareth Anscombe: The captain's run was superb, Gats said it was one of the sharpest sessions he'd been involved with. There was a real steel and belief about us and I felt supremely confident we were going to get the job done. Alun Wyn said to me afterwards that he was worried the captain's run had been *too* good, that we might have jinxed it and played the game a day early.

Jonathan Davies: You could tell that the boys were on another level completely. The energy in training, the volume, the intensity, the pace, the look in peoples' eyes.

Rob Evans: England didn't have any kind of radar on us. We hadn't shown our true colours in Paris, and we then made ten changes in Rome, so they had no idea what to expect. They had obliterated Ireland and France, but we hadn't hit our straps yet.

Gareth Anscombe: The way England dismantled Ireland was probably their best performance under Eddie Jones, but in a strange way, I think that worked in our favour. We hadn't played well but we'd won twice, and could only get better. England had been unbelievably good in those first two games, but when you're at that level, it can be difficult going back to the well and pulling out more of those performances.

Hadleigh Parkes: It felt like we were playing most of the rugby in the first half. They scored a lucky try, but other than that I didn't feel like they were threatening us at all.

Gareth Anscombe: Their try came out of nothing.

Jonathan Davies: I initially thought there had been a knock-on when Ken [Owens] was stripped of the ball in the maul. Then in the confusion, Tom Curry just popped up and scored. It wasn't a case of us being out-manoeuvred, or of our system letting us down.

Gareth Davies: Our guard just took his eye off the ball, and Curry picked up and went over. It was a pretty disappointing try to concede, but our heads didn't drop.

Jonathan Davies: It was just a freak thing, so we didn't panic. That showed the maturity of the squad. In the past we might have thought, 'Oh, here we go,' but we all knew that it was a cheap try. They hadn't had to work for it, and they didn't deserve it. For the rest of the game, they didn't get close again.

Hadleigh Parkes: England based their attack around their kicking game, but our boys did a superb job putting their nine and ten under pressure, forcing them to hurry their kicks, and the forwards did a great job of making the breakdown a complete mess.

Jonathan Davies: There were times when I'd be standing in the defensive line watching the forwards going about their business with a sense of awe. They'd be clattering into rucks, smashing people back in the tackle, and chucking their heads in where it hurts, and I'd be thinking, 'There's *no way* I'd have ever been an international rugby player, if I'd been a forward.' The work those guys get through is unbelievable. There is no way I could do what they do; that's the god's honest truth. My defensive secret is flying up and applying pressure on the ball carrier to try to turn him back *into* the forwards. I made ten tackles in the Scotland game which is the most I've made for a long time. Josh Navidi made twenty-eight on his own in the Ireland game!

Josh Navidi: A lot of my attitude comes from my dad, who runs a gym in Bridgend. He was a wrestler back in Iran, and he trained me when I was younger. You need a completely different type of engine as a wrestler, and there were a few times when he nearly made me sick. He'd climb on top of my shoulders, and make me do ten squats, then I'd have to do ten laps of the training mats, with him still on my shoulders, followed by press-ups with him on my back, before we got into wrestling bouts. If he'd stayed in Iran, he'd have probably gone on to take part in the Olympics. He lost to the Iranian champion once by a single point. He still thinks he should have taken him!

Hadleigh Parkes: The forwards were putting themselves about, and Sanjay was gobbling up every high ball that came his way.

Liam Williams: That's my job. I'm the bomb defuser. With Scarlets, with Wales, with Saracens, it's always been my calling card. In modern rugby the ball is kicked a lot, as teams try to unpick organised rush defences, so you have to have a full back who relishes the aerial battle. I *love* it, it's what I do.

Josh Navidi: There's not many better in the world than Liam at what he does.

Liam Williams: Against France, England had kicked away possession *fifty-two* times, which is an insane amount. France had players playing out of position; Yoann Huget was a winger playing at full back, and Gaël Fickou and Damian Penaud were centres playing on the wing. England exploited that by kicking the leather off the ball, so we knew that they'd be coming down the M4 with the same game plan. That said, I still didn't think they'd kick as much to us as they had to France.

Jonathan Davies: Their entire game plan was about kicking behind us, pressuring us into mistakes, and capitalising on them. But we weren't making any mistakes, so they realised they had to *play*, and they weren't comfortable doing that. Yes, they scored some good tries against France, but most of them were down to French errors. When they were forced into a situation where they had to create, they couldn't do it.

Gareth Anscombe: There was no space for them to kick to. There'd been a couple of times when Ireland played England that Ireland pushed up and left space in the backfield, as had France. Myself, Sanj [Liam Williams], Bigs [Dan Biggar] and George [North], made sure we held our position in the backfield so they had to constantly check themselves. A few times, Henry Slade shaped to kick, saw us all there covering the space, and realised they'd have to run, they'd have to play. That suited us, because we backed our defence to swallow them up. The more they kicked, the more possession we gobbled up, the more they ran, the less ground they made.

Hadleigh Parkes: Sanj and Bigs are renowned for their ability under the high ball; they're two of the best in the world. Everyone was talking about the tries England had scored against France, but France had had fifteen men in the front line half the time, and Jonny May's pretty quick, so he got through. We knew we'd be able to cope with that.

Liam Williams: Everyone said I was very good at the back, defusing those bombs, but that all comes down to the guys in front of me. They were filling the field, running good blocking lines, and preventing England's chasers from getting close to me. Added to that, England were kicking too long half the time, so most of their kicks were going straight down my throat.

Gareth Anscombe: When the kicks were fifty-fifty contestable we generally won the battle.

Rob Evans: Our pick-and-go strategy caught them off guard as well. We'd done it in training a lot. Under John Mitchell, their defensive line-speed had improved a lot. But us picking and going around the fringes meant they couldn't get off the line, and it upset their rhythm. They hadn't seen that coming.

Gareth Davies: We'd noticed that England hadn't been committing many defenders to the breakdown, and thought we'd have an opportunity to go through them rather than around them. When you have powerful runners like George North and Josh Adams, it makes sense for them to come infield and make easy yards around the rucks. Eventually, that will narrow the opposition defence, as they tighten up to fill those gaps. That's the time for us to have a crack out wide.

Rob Evans: Some have accused England of not being smart enough to change their approach. In fairness, it's immensely hard to read the game while you're on the field.

Gareth Anscombe: We won the penalty count 9–3, and had a more controlled element to our discipline. We wanted to get under their skin. There were guys we wanted to annoy, to provoke, and we did a particularly good job on one of them.

Gareth Davies: We definitely targeted a few of their key players, there were a few in their pack we knew we could wind up.

Josh Navidi: We were almost zen-like in our calm. There was nothing you could have done to wind *us* up.

Rob Evans: We'd talked about winding Kyle Sinckler up because he's a hot-head. As we packed down for an early scrum, Ross Moriarty was yelling from the back, 'Come on Rob Evs, you're gonna hammer him.' Alun Wyn was telling him to 'stop crying', just to rub it in. Then as we were about to go down, Gar Davies turned to me and said, 'Gats was right, Rob, he *is* fucking shit.' He was getting it from all sides.

Josh Navidi: We'd seen him get aggravated a fair bit against Ireland, and we knew he was an emotional time bomb.

Gareth Davies: Every time I was about to put the ball into the scrum, Rob would pipe up with something or other. I couldn't help but laugh. You know what these props are like, they're quite proud and they don't like giving an inch. I can remember a few things Rob said to Kyle that day, but none of them are repeatable.

Gareth Anscombe: Sinckler had a bit of a lesson that day in how to hold yourself.

Rob Evans: During one scrum in the first half, as he came up, he back head-butted Ken in the chin. I gave him a bit of a push, but Ken was calm as ever and shouted at me to back off. 'Leave him to it, it's not worth it.' Eventually, Sinckler lost the plot, and ended up being given the old shepherd's crook, didn't he? He was one more offence away from a yellow card. After the game, he came up to us in his London accent and said, 'Fair play, you boys dusted me.' He's all right off the field.

Liam Williams: We were on the Lions tour together and he's a lovely lad, but for those eighty minutes we were sworn enemies. He's not so lovely on the pitch, but then neither am I. There are a lot of people out there who think I'm a knob on the pitch, that's just the way it is.

Gareth Davies: There's no one I know in rugby that I don't get on with off the field. What's said on it is just banter. We'll always shake hands and have a beer afterwards.

Gareth Anscombe: There's a fine line between playing close to the line and maintaining your discipline. We never want to back down in terms of the physical or psychological battle, but we were conscious of the need to stay within the laws. Anyone can throw a punch, but it's only going to hurt your team in the long run.

Josh Navidi: There were several flashpoints during the England game where things could have kicked off, and I'd be thinking, 'Get in, and get the boys out of there before they do anything stupid.' The difference in attitude was summed up when Alun Wyn and Sinckler had each other by the collars. Sinckler was on the edge, ready to erupt, and Alun Wyn was just looking down and laughing at him.

Liam Williams: They were rattled, big time. They knew we were getting on top of them, winning the aerial battle, starting to get the nudge in the scrums, and they were getting more and more wound up. It all accumulates, and their frustration started to boil over. When Manu Tuilagi had me round the throat, a voice in my head just told me to stay cool.

Gareth Anscombe: Liam's matured a hell of a lot in the last few years.

Jonathan Davies: Manu had a good grip on him as well, which probably would have hurt, so he did well not to retaliate. When that kicked off, I didn't get involved. I just walked back into position. Owen Farrell appeared alongside me and said, 'You don't want to make him angry.' I couldn't agree more. Tuilagi's the last person I'd want to make angry, because he can *kill* you with a tackle.

Liam Williams: Back in the day, maybe I'd have started swinging, but I'm in a different place now. A few years ago, Gats took me aside and told me I needed to calm down a bit, and I've become a lot more focused ever since.

Gareth Davies: Discipline is massive in international rugby. One cheap penalty can easily lead to three points, or against a team like England, a kick to the corner and a try off a driving lineout. We knew there would be some heated exchanges because we were deliberately trying to wind up some of their more volatile players. When we saw them losing their cool, we knew we'd done our job. We just had to step away, and let them self-destruct.

Gareth Anscombe: There was only one side in it in the last thirty minutes. Sinckler gave away two penalties in that third quarter, one for the late challenge, another for a high tackle on Alun Wyn. We were clawing away at their lead.

Liam Williams: Owen Farrell had had an armchair ride against France. We weren't going to give him that same luxury.

Gareth Davies: One of my main jobs was to put as much pressure as I could on him. To fly up and spook him, get in his line of vision and shut down his space. The game plan was spot on and we executed it to perfection.

Hadleigh Parkes: Owen's a very good player, but Cawdor [Gareth Davies] put him under immense pressure and rattled him. He's so quick coming off the line, and is the king of the intercept. That kind of pressure can really put doubt into a fly half's mind.

Josh Navidi: When you've got a nine that quick leading the defensive line, it makes your job as a flanker that bit easier. If Farrell tries to kick, chances are he'll be charged down, and if he tries to step, he'll be running into one of us. That's meat and drink for me. It's what I do week-in, week-out.

Hadleigh Parkes: So much of the play is dictated around the fly half, so if you can pressure his pass, or put him on the ground just after he's made it, take him out of the game for five or six seconds, you can really upset the rhythm of their attack. Eventually he'll start to lose his head. We knew how influential Owen could be, so if we could just put him off his game a little bit, it would help us hugely.

Rob Evans: At one point in the second half, he kicked the ball out on the full. In isolation, it was just a clumsy mistake but, in my mind, that was the moment the match turned. It was a massive momentum-changer. It was a weird feeling. I knew right then that we were going to win.

Liam Williams: It's not like him at all, is it? He's normally so composed.

Gareth Anscombe: Owen was chatting to our coaches after the match, and he was questioning whether England were fit enough in the closing stages. He probably had a point. I don't think any team works as hard as we do on fitness.

As one fly half was fading from the picture, another emerged to play his part with vivid, illuminating clarity. With England clinging on to a 10–9 lead, Dan Biggar entered the arena. The veteran playmaker strode onto the pitch with his chest puffed out, and his jaw locked in steely determination. There were twenty minutes left. Biggar wasn't content with being a 'finisher'; he was to prove the executioner.

Hadleigh Parkes: What Bigs did when he came on was superb.

Liam Williams: He was like a caged animal. A few of his touches were out of this world. Not long after he came on, we were under pressure in our twenty-two after Gareth Davies was charged down. As England came rushing through, Bigs casually scooped up the ball and belted it seventy yards into touch. It was an incredible bit of skill under pressure. An old-fashioned torpedo kick that you rarely see these days.

Jonathan Davies: I was calling to Bigs to shift it to me, so we could try to play ourselves out of trouble down the right-hand side. I was yelling, 'Bigs, Bigs Bigs!' and then he just casually smashed that kick to touch. I thought, 'Yep, do that instead.'

Gareth Davies: He's a world-class player, no doubt about it.

Rob Evans: He doesn't get flustered in situations like that. He's calm, and he controls everything. He came on against France to close it out as well in similar conditions. Those games suit him down to the ground.

While England had been content to kick away much of their possession, Wales chose to tuck it up the jumper. Trailing 13–9 with around quarter of an hour left, Wales crunched into top gear, driving relentlessly into England's twenty-two. For phase after punishing phase, they recycled the ball, chipping away at England's defensive wall. It was an almost masochistic display of endurance. Eventually, after thirty-four continuous phases, George North spied a gap on the right-hand side. He drew the attention of three defenders, and when the ball appeared at the back of the ruck, Dan Biggar was in the scrum half position. Cory Hill, one of Wales's more athletic forwards, whose lungs would have been ready to burst, cut an incisive line, took Biggar's pass without breaking stride, and lunged for the line. Wales were in the lead for the first time.

Hadleigh Parkes: That's where those games we were playing in training really came to the fore. Thirty-six phases amounts to about five minutes of continuous aerobic exercise, and it allows you to maintain high levels of skill under extreme fatigue. To hold onto the ball for that long and not make a mistake takes some doing.

Gareth Davies: In years gone by, we'd have probably dropped it or knocked it on after that many phases, but we're at a different level now.

Jonathan Davies: Our previous mentality when we were that close to the line had been to tighten up, and pick and go. But we'd developed the confidence to go wide and try to get out there.

Rob Evans: In between the five-minute blocks in training, we'd do skills sessions to test our skills under stress. We'd practise things like passing the ball into a tyre.

During the last week, our accuracy under pressure had increased by forty per cent, because we were fitter, and our heart-rates were lower when we were executing critical passes in pressure situations.

Jonathan Davies: If you're physically fitter, you're mentally sharper. You're not thinking, 'Oh my God, I'm so tired', you just do it.

Liam Williams: You're knackered, you're out on your feet, and then someone crosses the line. It makes all that effort worth it. The horrors we'd been through in the week soon fade in your mind when you score a try against England in the Six Nations. What an unbelievable feeling, oh my God.

If that felt good, what followed would send the team, and the 75,000 fans inside the stadium, into raptures. With three minutes to go, Wales again found themselves ensconced in England's twenty-two. Josh Adams had stationed himself on the right-hand touchline and was trying to get Dan Biggar's attention. The fly half had already read his mind. Displaying the kind of Midas touch that had characterised his performance since he'd come on, Biggar caught a pass one-handed, and in the same fluid movement sent a high, hanging kick skyward. Adams timed his jump to perfection, soared above Elliot Daly, and juggled the ball in the air before landing and burrowing his way over the line. It was a remarkable act of composure from the Test rookie.

Liam Williams: England's ten, twelve, thirteen and open-side wing all stand quite flat in their defensive line, and the fifteen is behind on his own. We'd been working all week on our kicking strategy to test that formation, to try to land kicks that would stress the fifteen. And with virtually the last play of the game we pulled it off to perfection. It was *exactly* what we'd worked on all week.

Jonathan Davies: I could see Elliot Daly was tight, so I called the kick. Bigs was on the money and Josh finished it off magnificently.

Hadleigh Parkes: Josh is superb. He's fast, he's got good footwork, he's pretty strong, and he's obviously got good hands in the air. To have the presence of mind, not only to win the ball, but to juggle it in mid-air, and then scramble the last few yards over the line, was impressive. That'll always be on his highlights reel.

Josh Navidi: The noise in the stadium when Josh went over was unbelievable. The crowd went ballistic. I just remember looking up and seeing pint glasses flying everywhere.

Liam Williams: The final whistle against England was probably my moment of the tournament, because I play with half of those boys at Saracens. They were the favourites, they came down with a kicking game to beat us, and our back-three boys completely nullified it. It was topped off by me getting man of the match.

Rob Evans: In the huddle at the end of the game, Alun Wyn gathered us round and said, 'We've got two choices. We can either go nuts out here in front of everyone. Or we can go back inside and keep it to ourselves.' It was all about staying grounded.

The victory brought to an end Wales's five-game losing streak against England in the Championship. More significantly, it set a new record. Wales had now won twelve Test matches in a row; more consecutive victories than any other Welsh side had ever achieved. Eddie Jones may have had his tongue in his cheek when he'd claimed pre-match that this was the best Welsh side ever, but now – statistically at least – it was true.

Rob Evans: I'm in lift club with Ken, so the following Monday morning I met him at seven, as I usually do, at Cross Hands service station. The first thing he said when I got in the car was, 'Scarlets and Ospreys are merging, it's a done deal, and it's being signed off on Tuesday.' I was like, 'You what?!' Somehow Ken always seems to know what's going on; he's not called the Sheriff for nothing. It just seemed insane to me. The rivalry between the Ospreys and the Scarlets is one of the biggest in sport. I *hate* the Ospreys. The thought of some of them coming across to us, and some of our Scarlets mates losing their jobs as a result just didn't sit right.

Jonathan Davies: We hadn't had an inkling of it until that Monday. Julie [Paterson] and Martyn [Phillips] from the WRU came in that day to explain to us what was going to happen.

Gareth Anscombe: It was up there with some of the craziest scenes I've seen in professional rugby, ever.

Jonathan Davies: Someone summed it up pretty succinctly by calling it 'an absolute cluster fuck'. It was a huge distraction, but thankfully we were still good enough to beat Scotland.

Gareth Davies: It wasn't the best time for them to stick that on us.

Rob Evans: When we arrived, the rumour had spread like wildfire and it was all the boys were talking about. Martyn Phillips came down a bit later and told us all what was going on. As far as he was concerned it was a done deal and just needed to be signed off. The boys weren't happy. They felt as though they were being shafted.

Jonathan Davies: There was another WRU board meeting scheduled for the day of the Scotland game and they were going to call us all into the Vale on the Monday to explain the outcome to us. I said that wasn't right. That could be the first day of a potential Grand Slam week, and we hardly wanted it to start on that note. I requested that we all meet on the Sunday in the hotel before we left Edinburgh. That way, we could digest whatever was said, allow it to sink in, and hopefully clear our minds ahead of the working week.

Rob Evans: A lot of boys were coming out of contract and they were trying to introduce a new pay-banding system which might have seen lots of them take a pay cut.

Josh Navidi: You're talking about professional people who have mortgages to pay and mouths to feed. I was lucky in that I'd signed a new contract before Christmas, but the boys who were out of contract realised they might only have two or three pay cheques left.

Rob Evans: The first few days of training that week were absolutely shocking. You can't blame the boys because their heads were all over the shop. You had mates from the regions constantly ringing up trying to find out what was going on, WhatsApp messages were getting leaked to the media, and boys were falling out over that. It was a mess. Especially when we were approaching leg four of a Grand Slam campaign. It was a strange atmosphere.

Gareth Anscombe: Monday and Tuesday were crazy, it really was nuts. We didn't train well at all. Our minds were elsewhere. We were frustrated and disheartened by what was being said and done. We were finding things out through the media rather than through the official channels. I spoke to the boys and said, 'Let's go away on Wednesday, think about it, digest it, and come back Thursday and get our minds back on the job.' We got to Thursday and said, 'Right. That's that. We can't do anything about it now. Let's park it and focus on Scotland.' Being away from home and out of the bubble helped. It felt like escapism of sorts. A group of thirty-five of us up in Edinburgh with our backs against the wall. Had we been in Wales, we'd have been having more conversations, more meetings, and it would have been a major distraction. Ken spent the whole of Wednesday in a board room. It was insane.

Rob Evans: Gats was really sympathetic. He backed the players all the way. By the Thursday, Alun Wyn got the boys together and said, 'Look, whatever bullshit is happening behind the scenes, we've just got to pull together now, put it to the back of our minds, and go and beat Scotland.'

Liam Williams: He's class. The bloke's a different animal. He speaks so well. Him, Ken and Foxy are the leaders of the squad. They'd all come and speak to us in turn to try to set our minds at ease.

Jonathan Davies: Alun Wyn and Ken went through a lot of shit that week. For them to still perform on the weekend was a testament to just how mentally strong they are.

Gareth Anscombe: Alun Wyn is the glue that holds us all together, and keeps us honest. He's going to go down as one of, if not *the* greatest Welsh player ever. He's one of the hardest trainers I've ever come across. Week after week, he turns up and puts his body through the wringer. He's set the tone and standard for Welsh rugby for the last decade, and hopefully we can give him a bit more success before he hangs up his boots.

Hadleigh Parkes: We had a huge amount of respect for Scotland. They're a creative side, and they're exciting to watch. They can score tries from anywhere. They're one of the more inventive international sides, and that's down to a couple of players who aren't afraid to chuck the ball around. When they're on fire, they're on *fire*.

Gareth Anscombe: The Scotland game was harder than the England game because we were on such a high, and everyone was expecting us to beat them and set up a Grand Slam showdown against Ireland. That made me really nervous. I was worried about the mindset of the team. I was worried that we weren't going to have the same edge, the same sense of desperation. The public were already talking about the Grand Slam, thinking Scotland was a formality, and booking their hotels in Cardiff. It was the perfect storm for us to slip up.

Hadleigh Parkes: Murrayfield has become a tough place to go. They'd beaten Ireland there in the opening round a couple of years earlier, they'd beaten England the previous year, not to mention us in 2017. There was no complacency whatsoever.

Rob Evans: The off-field politics ended up having a galvanising effect. We wanted to take our anger out on the Scots. Instead of just going up there to beat them, we wanted to batter them. We were confident in the set piece, and in the first half we totally dominated them.

Jonathan Davies: We were winning the collisions, we were powerful, we were accurate; all those key things we build our game on.

Hadleigh Parkes: Josh scored another great try with amazing footwork and precious little space against Blair Kinghorn. Wales are pretty blessed with outside backs at the moment. We've got the big powerful ones, and the quick, nippy ones. Foxy put Josh away, and he made mincemeat out of Kinghorn. Stepped one way, stepped the other, and then boom, he was away. A classic winger's finish.

Jonathan Davies: I passed Josh the ball and got taken out in the process. I just remember looking up and thinking, 'Jesus Christ, he's scored!' I watched the replay up on the big screen, and thought 'Jeez, that is *world* class.' A lot of these youngsters arrive in camp with real confidence and just back themselves. I don't think I'd have had the confidence to take defenders on the way he does when I first came into the squad. I'd have been a bit cagier, but this new generation don't give a damn.

Wales's second try owed more to power and precision. After multiple phases, the ball arrived in Jonathan Davies' hands, and he was able to step through what remained of a splintered Scottish defence.

Rob Evans: It was similar to the one against England with Cory. We just built phases, tired them out, and scored on the edge. Parkesy made a good bust just beforehand to get us over the gain line, and Foxy pretty much waltzed in unopposed. It almost felt too easy.

Jonathan Davies: Just before half-time we had a scrum on their five-metre line, and we didn't get anything out of it. That would have been a bit of a momentum changer. Jogging in, I was really angry about that. If we'd got seven points there, or even three, they were done.

Gareth Davies: Scotland came out all guns blazing in that second half.

Rob Evans: It was like fifteen different blokes emerged from their changing room.

Gareth Anscombe: Under Gregor Townsend they play a really attacking brand and as a team they're at their most dangerous when they go behind. Their game is based around risk and, crucially for them, they're *allowed* to take risks.

Jonathan Davies: Our second half performance was disappointing, but it was nothing to do with the off-field stuff. Alun Wyn had made it clear before the game that we were not going to use that as an excuse. We just couldn't get hold of the ball, and we were making far too many mistakes.

Rob Evans: At one point, Alan Dell tried to counter ruck me, and he just bounced off. I couldn't resist chirping up, and said, 'Bloody hell mate, how the hell did you get on the Lions tour? You're shit.' Five minutes later he's making a fifty-yard break down the field, beating defenders for fun. I felt smaller than my left toenail.

Dell's break was a microcosm of Scotland's second half approach. Unlike Wales, Scotland looked to run into holes, not bodies. In Finn Russell they had a conjuror capable of unpicking the most stubborn of defences. A trademark no-look inside pass released Byron McGuigan on an arcing run, McGuigan linked with Adam Hastings, and Darcy Graham sprinted over for Scotland's opening try.

Rob Evans: The biggest thing Shaun talked about was concentration in defence. Finn is quite loose with the ball, but if he runs out of options, he'll start doing crazy stuff. It was all about staying alert if we conceded penalties, because he's the sort of player who'd shape to go for touch, then kick across to the wingers. The message was, 'Whenever he's got the ball, *nail* him. Just *nail* him.'

Jonathan Davies: Hamish Watson came on not long after, and went into full-on beast mode, skittling some of our defenders for fun. I was thinking, 'Boys, what the *fuck* is going on here?' He's always gone well against Wales for some inexplicable reason. He's *so* dynamic and difficult to get down.

Josh Navidi: When you see someone good on the bench, and you know they're coming on, you're conscious that you'll have to raise your level even further. He's a top-quality player. He's so hard to shift over the ball, and he's such a strong carrier. He made a *mental* impact.

Gareth Anscombe: I was in the backfield and I was praying someone was going to drag him down before he got to me! He's not the biggest, but he's *so* powerful, and he fights hard in contact, pumping his legs, scrapping for those extra few yards. He was like the Hulk when he came on, the crowd lifted, and they started to believe they were going to win.

It was an astonishing cameo. Throughout the entire Six Nations campaign, Wales missed ninety-five tackles. Ten of those were on Hamish Watson during those fifteen minutes. It was the one time that Wales's defence looked vulnerable.

Liam Williams: That aside, our defence was phenomenal for six weeks. It's what won us the Grand Slam. As Shaun Edwards likes to remind us, attack sells tickets, defence wins Championships.

Hadleigh Parkes: We put in a good attacking performance for forty minutes and a good defensive performance for forty minutes. It turned into a real dogfight in the second half. We made something like 160 tackles, which takes a real physical toll. When you've got the ball, and you're running into someone, it's a lot easier than having someone constantly run into you. You're taking a lot more impact when you're defending, and they just kept on coming in that second half.

Gareth Davies: Adam Beard went off for some stitches, Parkesy went off for stitches, and he came back on with a massive bandage and a black eye. It got pretty brutal out there.

Rob Evans: Scotland complained afterwards because we got penalised a few times in our twenty-two, and the ref didn't get his yellow card out. They would say that after losing the game, but I actually thought *we* had a raw deal from the ref. There were some scrum decisions that confused me, and Scotland had a few blatant knock-ons that went unpunished. It was swings and roundabouts.

Gareth Anscombe: We got a couple of tough calls against us, but we were guilty of sloppy discipline, whereas against England we'd given away nothing. Our silly penalties gave them some easy outs, and put us back in our twenty-two. We were hurting ourselves.

Jonathan Davies: When we eventually got back into their twenty-two and got a penalty at the end, I thought, 'Thank God.' That's why I went for that stupid drop goal that barely got off the ground. Jinks came on fuming and said to me, 'Are we the dumbest team in world rugby or what? *Why* did you go for that drop goal?' I reminded him we'd had a penalty advantage. 'I know that,' he said, 'but what if you'd got it over? There'd have been time left on the clock for them to go for the draw.' I grinned and said, 'Jinks, there was *no way* I was ever getting that drop goal over.' He smiled despite himself, but he could barely contain his anger.

Hadleigh Parkes: Credit to Scotland, they threw caution to the wind in that second half, and knocked us back on our heels. When Chicken [Anscombe] knocked over the last penalty, and the clock ticked into the red, we were mightily relieved.

Jonathan Davies: That was definitely the day we played our 'get out of jail free' card. We may have been 16–0 down against France, but the Scotland game was a hairier experience. Once we'd got ahead against France, we were comfortable we were going to win, but against Scotland, we were living on the very edge of our nerves.

Gareth Anscombe: Martyn Phillips came into the changing room after the game to apologise to the players for all the unrest and upheaval in the week. I felt a bit sorry for him because I like him as a bloke, and think he's genuine. I don't agree with the way it was handled, but you can't place the blame solely on the man at the top. He was sincere with his apology, and he seemed hurt that it had threatened us as a group.

Without much fuss or fanfare, Wales had navigated four rounds of the Six Nations and entered the final week as the only team capable of winning the Grand Slam.

England may have shown more attacking élan and accumulated more bonus points, but the destiny of the title was in Wales's hands. Win, and they would be Grand Slam champions. Their final opponents were the defending champions, conquerors of the All Blacks, and officially the second-best team in the world. But in the preceding six weeks, Ireland's crown appeared to have slipped.

Gareth Davies: They'd played France in the previous round and battered them, so we knew the real Irish team was back. If felt as though they'd recovered their mojo after losing to England at the start of the tournament.

Jonathan Davies: I looked around the changing room before the game and everyone was in the place they needed to be. Rob Evans was bouncing off the walls, Ken was silent and pensive, but you know he's strictly business, Ross Moriarty was staring into space, looking like he was ready to run through brick walls, Sanjay was on one. We were all about ready to explode.

Rob Evans: Often before a game, you get an instinct about whether you think you're going to win. Before that game, I just didn't know, and it wasn't a nice feeling.

Jonathan Davies: Alun Wyn is a very good speaker. He holds the attention of everyone in the room. His intelligence comes through, possibly too much for some of the boys. I don't know whether he plans his speeches, but they're always very structured and focused. Sometimes his message is a technical one, but often it's pure emotion.

Rob Evans: Alun Wyn's last words were, 'Remember, your families are watching, remember your dads are watching. Mine won't be here to watch, so make sure you go out there and do *your* dads proud.' We all knew Alun Wyn's dad had passed away the previous year, so that was a big moment, we all got a bit emotional. We'd have run through a fucking wall for him after that.

Jonathan Davies: Al's line was, 'Do it for someone you love, someone who means the world to you.' He loved his dad, and I'm sure if he could have chosen one more game for his father to have seen, it would have been the one where he captained his country to the Grand Slam.

Rob Evans: The way he's led this group has been unbelievable. He's been awesome. When he speaks *everyone* listens. He's just a fucking great bloke. Probably the greatest player Wales have ever had.

Gareth Anscombe: He's learnt how to relax a little bit more, I've definitely witnessed that. He can relate to the boys a bit more. He's the ultimate professional, and deserves a special place in Welsh rugby.

Liam Williams: Even now, at the age of thirty-three, he trains like a teenager. He's always sprinting between drills, always the first to arrive, shouting, hollering, and dragging everyone else along in his wake. I don't know what his secret is. We'll be walking around gasping for breath, and he'll be fresh as a daisy. Honestly, he's a *machine*. He gives one hundred per cent at *every* session.

Jonathan Davies: He doesn't *have* to sprint between every drill, but it makes the younger boys think, 'If he's doing it, I'd better do it.' And that raises everyone's standards. As a leader, he's an inspiration. I honestly don't know how he does it.

Gareth Davies: He's the oldest in the squad, but he's never missed a single session. Often on a Monday, some of the boys who've had a big game on the weekend will just do a bike session to loosen up for the big day's training on the Tuesday. But Alun Wyn would do every session regardless. If anyone has a bit of credit in the bank in that regard, it would be him, but he never shirks or cuts corners.

Josh Navidi: He's just got an old-school mentality. He's a dying breed. A lot of youngsters coming through now have never had a real job, so they don't have the same work ethic.

Jonathan Davies: During a game, Alun Wyn looks exhausted by about the third minute, and you're thinking, 'He's never going to make it to the second half.' By the eightieth minute, he still looks the same, but his energy levels haven't dipped at all.

Gareth Davies: If you asked him to play another eighty, he would.

Josh Navidi: He was player of the series by some distance. It was a no-contest.

Hadleigh Parkes: The game could not have begun more perfectly. Chicken's kick off was judged to perfection, and George did fantastically well to get there.

Liam Williams: Alun Wyn had won the toss, so we chose to kick to put them under immediate pressure. Jacob Stockdale was underneath it but it was an unbelievable chase from George to put him into touch.

Hadleigh Parkes: There was a great drive off the lineout from the forwards, Ken broke off and made about ten yards, fending off Sean O'Brien in the process. The forwards won the collision again, there was a good clear-out.

Gareth Anscombe: We had an advantage so we knew we had a free play. We knew with the way that Ireland's back three worked that we might get some kicking space, and we had the luxury of being able to take a risk.

Liam Williams: Anscombe stuck it on the toe, Parkesy scooped it up and touched down under the sticks. That's what dreams are made of.

Jonathan Davies: Fair play to Chicken, he put it on the money. Right in Parkesey's channel. If he'd kicked into my area, I think Ringrose might have got across to cover it but it was such a precise kick and Hadleigh finished it well.

Rob Evans: Can you believe that we won the Grand Slam and not a single Welshman scored a point in that last game?! We take the piss out of Parkesy all the time. 'Parkesy, how the fuck are you Welsh? Is it your grandfather's sister's dog or something?' I've got to give it to him though, he's a top man, he's fully bought into the Welsh culture, learnt the anthem and everything. He's a great bloke.

Gareth Davies: He gets more shit about it than Anscombe does. Anscombe's always quick to point out that his mother's Welsh, so he's a more authentic Welshman, even though he's got the strongest New Zealand accent I've ever heard.

Hadleigh Parkes: Those little dinks over the top are becoming more prevalent in the game, especially against the likes of Ireland who bring a lot of line-speed. The fifteens heading across to get to last man, drifting towards the wing.

Jonathan Davies: Kearney does tend to defend a bit wider, which leaves a bit of space in the back field.

Hadleigh Parkes: I talked to Chicken about the chance. It's Foxy's and my job to be the eyes and ears for the ten, because he's looking at the breakdown. I was yelling out for the chip kick, so we had to back it up. Sometimes in the stadium, it's incredibly hard to hear what's being said. Talking is a skill, but listening is a skill as well, and thankfully Chicken listened to us on that call, and it worked out perfectly. We've always told our tens, 'Listen to us, trust us.' If it's the wrong call, I've got no problem putting my hand up in the team meeting and saying so. We'll always front up to Rob Howley and say, 'Sorry, that was our decision, not the ten's.'

Gareth Anscombe: After six weeks together, things become a little more telepathic. You're working with each other every day, and you can start to sense things before they happen. You start to read body language, and anticipate each other's thoughts. Would we have been able to pull that off against France in round one? Probably not.

If Hadleigh Parkes had already won the affection of the nation's hearts with his try, what he did next would elevate him to the status of national hero. Ireland were awarded a penalty just outside their twenty-two, and Jonny Sexton shaped to kick to touch. Instead, he swivelled round, and sent a cross-field kick skyward and into the grateful arms of Jacob Stockdale on the opposite wing. Stockdale palmed off an unbalanced Gareth Davies and gave himself a clear run to the Welsh line. Irish fans were already on their feet celebrating when the grim-faced Parkes hoved into view, gobbling up the yards, and hauled Stockdale down.

Rob Evans: That was one of the biggest moments of the Six Nations. Full stop. If they'd scored then, the game would have been a lot tighter. Parkesy isn't the quickest of guys, but you could see the sheer desire in his face and his body language to get there. It was a case of, 'I can't let this guy score.' It was pure heart.

Jonathan Davies: We were well aware of that threat. We *know* that when Ireland get a penalty on the right-hand side, Jonny Sexton *expects* his left winger to give him a cross-field kick option. We'd said it all week, and previewed it, so when the whistle blew, Parkesy and I started fanning out in anticipation. It was then I noticed George was down. I was shouting, 'George, get up, get *up*!' I started running straight across. Cawdor was chasing him down but he missed him.

Gareth Davies: My heart was pumping at that point. Stockdale caught it and handed me off. I started chasing him down, but I was thinking, 'I'm never catching him. I'm in serious trouble here.'

Jonathan Davies: I was thinking, 'Jesus, Shaun's probably about to jump out of his box and rip our heads off.' I was convinced he was going to score – and then Parkesy appears out of nowhere, like Roadrunner or something.

Gareth Davies: Hadleigh Parkes, the hero of the hour.

Josh Navidi: That tackle was *outstanding*.

Hadleigh Parkes: I was winding back the years there! It's been a while since I've run that fast. I just got a little roll on and managed to reach him. George North was down with a broken hand, so Jonny exploited the space. His kick was pinpoint. Fortunately I managed to be in the right place at the right time and was quick enough to get there. It was really more about timing than speed. Of knowing exactly *when* to commit to the tackle. If I'd have given it another couple of metres he might have got away from me. It was knowing in the heat of the moment 'now's the time'.

Gareth Davies: I definitely owe him a few beers, because he saved my arse there.

Gareth Anscombe: Every time I watch that tackle, it gets better. It was a potential game-changer. If they'd scored then, it would have been 7–7, and momentum could have swung back in their direction. You never know how a team is going to respond to something like that.

Jonathan Davies: I arrived seconds later and watched the ball bobble into touch. That was a massive moment. It was one of those moments when all that fitness and conditioning work we'd been put through came to fruition. At times like that, you don't think about what you're doing, you just do it. Parkesy and I had gone through all of their backline beforehand noting their strengths and weaknesses. I write things down for each player and we compare notes the night before. Next to Stockdale, I'd written: 'Left hand carry, right hand fend.' That's exactly what he tried to do, but Parkesy was equal to it.

Hadleigh Parkes: To put him down was really satisfying. If he'd scored, it might have changed the complexion of the game. I took more pleasure from the tackle than I did from the try.

Rob Evans: I rang him a couple of days after to tell him how proud I was of him for that. He said, 'Cheers mate, the scrums were good too, boy.'

Hadleigh Parkes: Our scrum was superb that day. We got a lot of penalties from it. The lineout was the best it had been all Championship. The forwards did a wonderful job.

Jonathan Davies: They won a scrum penalty straight after that tackle, which completely killed off the attack.

Rob Evans: Gar Davies loves chopsing at the tight-heads when we're packing down. I think he just does it to try to make me laugh. At one point, Tadhg Furlong went down on his knee, and Gar asked, 'Rob, why's he always on his knee?' I said, 'It's cos his drum's too big, isn't it? He can't support his own weight.' I felt bad afterwards because he's a really nice bloke, but in the heat of the battle, I'll say anything.

Jonathan Davies: The two of them were talking about the scrums after the game. I don't know what they were on about, it all sounded alien to me. But Tadhg was getting into Rob about something he'd done, some abuse he'd given him and then he says, 'Next thing I know, Rob was whooping in my face. Rob Evs was whooping and hollering right in my face!' Rob grinned and said, 'I only did that cos I like you, pal,' and I told him, 'Stop backtracking now, Rob. Climb out of his arse.'

Gareth Anscombe: Rob wears his heart on his sleeve, and he's an entertaining bloke. His photo with Prince William pretty much sums him up. Alun Wyn and Adam Beard are both smiling respectfully, and there's Rob, gurning. He just doesn't care.

George North's hand injury ended his involvement, forcing Wales into an early positional change. Dan Biggar came on at fly half; Gareth Anscombe switched to full back.

Gareth Anscombe: We've been good at adjusting our tactics to suit our team selections. If I'm ten, I prefer to counter attack, whereas one of Bigs's greatest strengths is chasing the high ball, so we'd be silly not to play to that. Bigs likes to chase them so we encourage him to do that, whereas I prefer hanging back and having a crack from deep.

Hadleigh Parkes: Gareth hadn't trained much at full back that week, so to shift there when Bigs came on at ten and play as well as he did, shows what a class act he is. It was a shame to lose George, but you've then got two kickers on the field to play for field position. Two game-drivers who do a lot of calling, and that's no bad thing.

Gareth Anscombe: There's always a little bit of awkwardness between rivals for the same shirt but, ultimately, you're there to help the team out. This group has grown and developed so much that everyone just wants the team to perform well. I'd say this is the closest Welsh squad I've been involved in. The tens spend a lot of time together at kicking practice, so we're constantly rinsing one another, and giving each other shit. But ultimately, we're all learning from each other, too. I can't speak highly enough of Dan, Patch or Jarrod. They're all top men.

Rob Evans: After about twenty minutes, we got awarded a penalty quite far out on the right-hand side and Chicken lined up to take it. I turned to Dan and said, 'Bigs, why aren't you taking that?' He told me, 'Chicken started the game, he's kicking it.' There's a mutual respect there.

Gareth Anscombe: To get that big one really settled the nerves. It was wide out, from forty metres, and the rain was teeming down. That set me up for the rest of the game. Bigs coming on actually helped me relax a bit because I thought, 'If this one goes next door and hits someone in the head, Dan will be there to step up and take over.' Subconsciously, it helped me. When Dan came on, he told me I was going to move to full back, but that I'd still be taking the kicks, and that's exactly what I wanted to hear.

Josh Navidi: Sometimes when you score early, you feel the other team raise their levels. But the opposite happened with Ireland. Twenty-five minutes in, they looked as though they didn't want to be there, and they didn't know what the hell was going on. Their heads were down, and they weren't talking to each other.

Jonathan Davies: After that it was just a case of keeping the scoreboard turning over. Chicken wasn't missing, and we went in 16–0 up.

Hadleigh Parkes: It was thanks to Chicken's accuracy that we were so far ahead at half-time. Ireland made a big mistake leaving the roof open. It backfired on them. They're a team that like to grind out wins, but it's hard to come back from a 16–0 deficit in conditions like that. Weirdly, that was the exact same margin we were down against France in the opening game, but we were confident we wouldn't make the silly mistakes France had.

Jonathan Davies: Alun Wyn reminded us of that. We'd mounted a comeback against the odds against France, and we knew Ireland were a quality side, so there was no room for complacency. We were still a score away from genuine safety. We knew that if we got the first shot on goal after half-time, we'd be okay. There was no way our defence was going to concede twenty points in forty minutes. No way.

Hadleigh Parkes: There were a few conspiracy theories going around afterwards that Gats actually wanted the roof open, and he'd tricked Joe Schmidt into keeping it open. I'm not so sure. He certainly didn't reveal that to us if that was the case.

Rob Evans: Gats wanted it shut because of the weather, but privately he told us he didn't really mind either way. I spoke to Tadhg Beirne after the game and he admitted they thought they were going to beat us up up-front. They thought the rain and the soggy pitch would play into their hands, that they'd outmuscle us. It bit them on the arse a bit.

Jonathan Davies: I'm not sure where they got that idea from. They must not have watched the England game. Having spoken to a few of their coaches afterwards, I think they realised that keeping the roof open was a bad decision.

Liam Williams: It was absolutely soaking out there, from the start of the warm-up, to the trophy lift, it was peeing down and we adjusted our tactics to suit the conditions. We squeezed them and squeezed them, forced them to concede penalties, and the scoreboard just kept ticking over.

Jonathan Davies: Because our defence is so good, it puts less pressure on our attacking game. If you're letting tries in for fun, you know you have to make every attacking opportunity count. We know we can take control of games territorially and strangle the life out of teams. We're in the business of winning and we've got into a habit of doing it through a very shrewd defence and a precise attacking game. We might want to tweak the balance a little bit, because we all like playing a bit of rugby, but I'd much rather win a game ugly, than score forty points and lose.

Gareth Anscombe: There's a bit more of a Barbarians feel to the autumn internationals and the summer tours, but the Six Nations feels like a mini World Cup, and things are a lot tighter. You'd be silly to play too loosely – you've got to earn the right to play. Over the course of the last eighteen months, we've shown we can win rolling our sleeves up, and we can win moving the ball.

Liam Williams: Sometimes a game just unfolds in a certain way. Because of the pressure we exerted on Ireland, they kept giving stupid penalties away, and we were chalking up the scores. 3, 6, 9, 12, until we were out of sight. If that's what's working, that's what you do. Other games will be more conducive to running rugby, but when you've got the squeeze on, and the rain's hammering down, you do what you need to do to win.

Seven minutes into the second half, Ireland conceded their ninth penalty. Discipline under Joe Schmidt had been woven into the very fabric of their identity. It was coming apart at the seams.

Jonathan Davies: Alun Wyn turned to me and asked if I'd like to go to the corner. I said, 'No way, keep that scoreboard ticking over.' There's nothing more demoralising than standing behind your posts seeing that ball sailing over again and again and again.

Hadleigh Parkes: From the restart, Johnny Sexton put the ball straight out, handing possession back to us. Five minutes later, Ireland gave away another penalty, which Chicken nailed again. 22–0 with about twenty-five minutes to go. That's when I felt we were home and dry. There was no way we were losing that game from that position.

Jonathan Davies: Johnny got really frustrated out there.

Josh Navidi: When you see someone visibly rattled, they become an even easier target. You just pile more pressure onto someone who's already feeling the heat. It's a difficult spiral for them to recover from.

Not long after Sexton's miscued kick-off, he passed a ball behind Jacob Stockdale directly into touch. The 2018 World Player of the Year was looking increasingly fallible.

Gareth Davies: He's one of the best tens in the world, so you'd think he'd be used to dealing with the pressure, but we were so relentless that he couldn't get his game going at all.

Liam Williams: I'd become quite close to Johnny on the Lions tour, where a few of the boys started calling him 'coach' because he was so influential. We knew that to beat Ireland, we had to make sure he had no time or space to take control.

Rob Evans: Sexton completely lost his head, didn't he? Gats has coached a lot of the Ireland players, and he can read a situation really well. He knew that if we got in front and they had to chase the game, they wouldn't be able to, because Sexton would lose his head and get frustrated. That's exactly what happened.

Jonathan Davies: Gats is extremely good at reading people. I've always said he'd be a great poker player. He doesn't give away much, but he takes a lot in. His stints as Lions head coach have allowed him to build up a mental dossier of the best players from all the home nations. He knows what their strengths are but also their weaknesses and how to exploit them. Obviously he wants to win a Lions series as a coach, but I'm sure he's mentally making notes on the non-Welsh players, on the way they might react to certain things, to be exploited later down the line.

Gareth Anscombe: For the last five years, the Irish half-backs have been among the best in the world, so it was an undoubted tick in the box to see Sexton's game start to crumble, to see that our plan to put him under pressure had worked.

Jonathan Davies: Gats told us beforehand, 'Sexton and Murray don't like playing against Wales. Make sure they still feel that way at the end of the day.'

We neutralised their strike runners as well. Bundee Aki wasn't really a threat. We took his time and space away. Neither he nor Ringrose could get into the game.

Josh Navidi: We were up against a pretty impressive back row – all of them Test Lions, but from an early age, my coach at Bridgend Athletic had taught me never to worry about the other team, only worry about yourself. Obviously, you have to do your analysis, but I never bow to anyone on the pitch.

Gareth Anscombe finished up with a perfect record from the tee with seven from seven. Every time he swung his right boot towards the uprights, Ireland's sense of desperation increased. They continued to fight valiantly, but Wales were disappearing over the rain-lashed horizon. Deep into injury time, Ireland launched one last frenzied attack, hurling their bodies at the Welsh line. Eventually, with the result long since decided, Jordan Larmour shimmied through a gap. Rarely has a try-scorer looked so disconsolate. It prevented a whitewash, but that was all.

Jonathan Davies: I was genuinely gutted we didn't nil them. I lunged at Larmour, and I was really annoyed when he snuck over. Then I saw all the boys lining up to try to charge down the conversion, and thought, 'Ah, sod that, I'm ready to celebrate.'

Josh Navidi: Alun Wyn made a point of telling us all, 'Don't celebrate yet. Make sure we all line up and chase this kick.'

Jonathan Davies: I spoke to Al about that when we were waiting to go and receive the trophy. He was gutted that we didn't nil them.

Gareth Davies: That is classic Alun Wyn. You'd think that having captained his country to a Grand Slam he'd be happy about it, but he'd wanted to keep that line intact. That shows how much of a competitor he is, how much of a legend he is.

Jonathan Davies: We know that will come up when we reconvene in the summer – the fact that we conceded a try in the eightieth minute. Had it been a one-score game, we'd have lost it at the death. Everyone was a bit gutted, but when you realise you've won a Grand Slam, you quickly get over it.

Any disappointment over conceding the try quickly dissolved on a tidal wave of emotion that swept through the stadium in the moments that followed. As the rain continued to fall, the crowd rose as one to salute their heroes. In the seething cauldron of noise, the BBC television cameras captured a tender moment between Jonathan Davies and his captain, with the former declaring, 'Thank you, mate, I love you' as the two embraced.

Jonathan Davies: It was an emotional moment. I was on one hell of a high, because not only had we won the Grand Slam, my horse, Potters Corner, had won the Midlands National. A few of the non-playing subs ran on after the final whistle shouting, 'Potters Corner, boy!' and I was saying, 'What happened? What happened?' They told me he'd won. I was over the moon. I went over to Rob Evs and Cawdor, who'd both put a bet on him at 20/1, and they went nuts as well. We were like kids at Christmas. Grand Slam champions and that on the same day.

Gareth Anscombe: Forty-five minutes after the final whistle, it's still teeming down with rain, it's starting to get pretty cold, and not a single person has left the stadium. Even the Irish stayed. That sticks with you as a player. It was a mark of respect that they stuck around for us. You do remember those things. The Irish are great people, we had a good few beers with the players in the after-match function, and they were pretty gracious losers. They've won a fair few trophies in recent times, and Joe Schmidt's a good man, so it was nice to chat to him afterwards. I've no doubt they'll be World Cup contenders in Japan.

Hadleigh Parkes: A couple of players on that Irish team were my mates. I caught up with Tadhg Beirne after the game. He was crucial to us at the Scarlets, and it's so great to see him doing well back in Ireland. You get to know these guys pretty well in the Pro14, so there's not much in the way of animosity. You can still go into an opposition changing room afterwards to chew the fat and have a beer. That's the beauty of rugby.

Liam Williams: Alun Wyn delivered a very gracious victory speech at the dinner. It was very humble and came from the heart. He knew the Irish boys were feeling low, and he judged the mood perfectly. That's just the way he is. Ireland are one of the hardest teams to play against. We had a good few beers and a catch-up with them afterwards. Johnny Sexton told me that we did to them exactly what they'd wanted to do to us. We had a laugh, we had a giggle, and we had a pint. That's what rugby's all about.

Hadleigh Parkes: We had a cracking day out in Cowbridge on the Sunday. Ireland's forwards coach, Simon Easterby actually lives there. When I found out he was a local, I invited him out with us for a few beers. 'Come and have a couple of quiet ones mate, you're more than welcome.' Unsurprisingly, he wasn't too keen.

Rob Evans: We all met at 12.30 in the Bear Hotel in Cowbridge and we didn't pay for a drink all day. All the locals were insisting on getting the rounds in and the landlord came over and said, 'Have whatever you like.' It's easy to forget how much pleasure Wales winning brings to the masses. You spend eight weeks encased in this bubble, training hard and keeping your head down, and then you emerge with a Grand Slam to find the whole country's been going absolutely nuts.

Jonathan Davies: It was a good turnout on the Sunday, even Ken Owens – who'd gone back to his fiefdom in Carmarthenshire – got himself in a cab and showed up. My uncle had texted me to say he was in my parents' pub in Carmarthen, then a few hours – and one expensive taxi ride later – he turned up in Cowbridge with Josh Turnbull in tow. It was a good effort from the boys.

Josh Navidi: Late that afternoon, I had one of those moments where I thought, 'Flippin' heck. Did that actually happen?' I'd watched Wales win Grand Slams growing up and had dreamed of being a part of it one day. I couldn't quite believe it had actually happened to me.

Hadleigh Parkes: After the Ireland game, I was face-timing my brother and he said, 'Who would have thought five years ago, you'd be playing for Wales, in a Grand Slam-winning side, and you'd be having a beer with Prince William after the game?' He had a point. I wouldn't change anything in my journey to this point. I know my time in the jersey is short. I'm not going to have a ten-year Test career like a lot of the boys. I might get three or four years in the shirt if I'm lucky.

Gareth Anscombe: You're on such a high, partying and celebrating, then you wake up on Tuesday and think, 'What's just happened?' It's one that I'll look back on in a few years' time and get chills when I watch it. I'm just glad I got to give something to Welsh rugby, and gave the fans something to be really proud about.

Jonathan Davies: Having won two in a row in 2012 and 2013, and then going a good few years without a trophy, I was beginning to wonder whether I'd ever have another crack at it. It's like a drug. When you're standing on that podium, there is no feeling like it. That's all the hard work, all the shit you've put up with, the things you've given up, sacrificed, missed out on. You don't care about it at that point because you know that it's all been worth it. Moments later, I had the trophy in my hand, and as I was lifting it up, I could hear the noise swelling around me. It felt incredible. You've got to enjoy it; it's such a rare, precious moment.

Warren Gatland's time in charge had been both euphoric and agonising. More than a decade of reassuring stability punctuated by moments of ecstatic triumph, and gut-wrenching defeat. The curtain would fall on his tenure in the land of the rising sun. His last few years were spent tinkering with his tools, and priming his engine. He was accused of being disrespectful when picking an under-strength side against Italy in 2018, but it was phase one of bolstering his squad, of ensuring that he'd have a battalion of able reinforcements in the event of another injury crisis. The process was accelerated on the summer tour when a young squad denuded of its Lions returned home undefeated after wins over South Africa and Argentina.

And in March of 2019, Gatland's Six Nations journey with Wales ended as it began. With a Grand Slam. It confirmed him as the most successful coach in the tournament's history.

TWENTY-EIGHT

I DON'T LIKE TO TUMBLE INTO THE WORMHOLE

Warren Gatland's two World Cup campaigns with Wales had left lingering questions in the minds of Welsh supporters. A feeling of unfulfilled destiny swelled with the passage of time. Time didn't heal; it only encouraged glassy-eyed ruminations on what might have been. What if Sam Warburton hadn't been sent off? What if Adam Jones hadn't torn his calf? What if the injury curse of 2015 hadn't lain waste to Wales's squad? What if Fourie du Preez hadn't come out of retirement? In his final act with Wales, Warren Gatland had one more chance to consign these questions to history. One more tilt at glory, and the ultimate prize.

As the 2019 World Cup approached, Wales's talent pool was deeper and better stocked than it had ever been before. Its defence was as stubborn and unyielding as a concrete wall, and its attack was discovering new ways to shimmy and shake. Wales had climbed steadily up the rankings since 2015, eventually reaching the coveted number one spot after defeating England during a World Cup warm-up match in August. The Webb Ellis Trophy remained the only piece of silverware Warren Gatland had competed for, and not won. Could it have been, as the country bathed in the glory of another Grand Slam, that Welsh rugby's most triumphant chapter was about to be written?

Tomas Francis: There was a lot of hype surrounding us coming into the World Cup, particularly after getting to number one in the world and all that, but we still ended up coming in under the radar to some degree, which suits the Welsh, doesn't it? We don't want to be put up on a pedestal.

Any sense of serenity in Wales's camp disappeared swiftly in Japan when it emerged that Rob Howley, Gatland's loyal lieutenant for the previous twelve years, had been sent home under a cloud. An investigation later revealed that he'd made more than three hundred bets during the previous four years, several of which involved the Welsh national side. This obviously amounted to corruption under World Rugby's regulations. It was a tragic story of human fallibility; during the investigation, Howley explained that he had turned to gambling in the wake of his sister's death, and had actually lost rather than made money. Howley was held in high regard throughout the rugby world, and while the story generated a degree of shock and outrage, the overwhelming reaction among those who knew him was one of sympathy. Public rehabilitation would follow, but back in Japan, with the tournament just three days away, Welsh plans had been thrown into disarray.

Dan Biggar: I'd be a bare-faced liar if I said it didn't have an impact on the squad, because it was obviously big news on the eve of the first game. It overshadowed his contribution, and I don't think Rob got enough credit for what he had put into place in the lead-up to that World Cup.

Owen Watkin: We were all genuinely surprised and couldn't get over what had happened.

Tomas Francis: He's a top bloke, one of the nicest guys in rugby, and what happened to him was savage. No one saw it coming. Everyone knew he liked a bet, but a lot of people like a bet on the horses and the stuff you're allowed to bet on. Obviously he went a bit further.

Jake Ball: It was bizarre. I suppose you give credit where it's due in how they [the WRU] dealt with the situation. They dealt with it as well as they could have done in terms of it not disrupting our preparation. We only got told what had happened shortly after he'd gone.

Dan Biggar: The evening the news broke, Warren called a senior players' meeting and a couple of options were discussed to replace Howley. We all agreed that Steve [Jones] was the right man. He was coming in anyway after the World Cup, and his personality was just what we needed. Steve always brings loads of energy and enthusiasm, and we knew he would just crack on with the job. At that point, his character was almost more important than his coaching ability. I think his positivity really helped.

Tomas Francis: Steve came in with no expectations. He couldn't change much, and there wasn't time for him to implement much of his own vision. It was more about soaking up the vibe and getting to know people.

Jake Ball: The majority of the squad were told the news the morning after Rob had boarded the plane home. The management said, 'Look, this isn't going to affect our preparation. Steve's going to come in and take over.' It was pretty regimented, the way they did everything. There wasn't much room for sentiment. Obviously players were disappointed, but at the end of the day you're out there to play in a World Cup.

Dan Biggar: As soon as you get on the training pitch or the match field, external distractions get pushed to the side. We're all driven individuals who want to do well, so without sounding callous, you focus on what you need to do to be successful. The media made a lot of it, but we put it to one side and concentrated solely on getting the job done. And despite all the furore, we started the tournament really well.

Jake Ball: It's probably just as well the World Cup wasn't in Wales, where the story would have blown up much further. In Japan, we were in a tight bubble, and it was up to you whether or not you looked at your phone. There wasn't really anyone who could get to us in the hotel, so we parked it and moved on. We were just there to do a job.

Dan Biggar: A lot of the stuff we did, particularly in the first two games against Georgia and Australia, was according to Rob's blueprint. He'd set us up really well for those first two games, with Australia as the main focus.

Tomas Francis: Yeah, it was a nice homage to him to be able to execute some of those plays he'd devised. I just wish he'd have been out there to see it come together. It was Gats's swansong, and he'd been there with him throughout, so it would have been fitting if he'd been there to finish the journey.

Dan Biggar: The World Cup had started on the Friday and we didn't play until the Monday night, so we watched all the games on the Friday, Saturday and Sunday almost like fans, getting swept up in the hype. It was quite a wait before our game which probably added a bit to the nerves.

Wyn Jones: We had Georgia first in Toyota. They're renowned for their scrummaging, and as a pack we agreed that we'd really try and go after them there. If we could get a few penalties or push them off the ball, we knew we'd have them.

Tomas Francis: Georgia were a big potential banana skin. They had a strong, heavy, physical pack.

Jake Ball: We obviously talked beforehand about their strengths at scrum time and the fact they'd look to get some dominance there.

Tomas Francis: Are they as fearsome as they're made out to be? One hundred per cent. I'd been talking to some of the English lads who'd done training sessions against them, and they told me that they get more fired up for scrums than for the game itself. It's in their nature, isn't it? It's where they're from, their history, their culture. The scrum is a proper man test to them.

Jake Ball: It was a physical encounter, I remember that. I managed to break my nose trying to tackle someone with my face. I ended up with two tampons up my nostrils for most of the game. There were some big lads in their pack, all right.

Wyn Jones: We did quite well in the first half, and their heads dropped a little bit. They knew they had nothing to come back at us with. We picked on their strength, went after them there, and it paid off. We gave the backs an easy ride that day.

Jake Ball: We'd spoken about the fact their backline wasn't as strong as their forward pack. We knew if we could win some good ball off the lineout, we had some good set plays, and sure enough we managed to do that.

Tomas Francis: We wanted to get the ball in and out quickly and we scored two tries off first phase. The third one, they kicked out on the full and gave us a scrum on halfway. We said, 'Right we're going for it now, double shove.' Sure enough, we got the penalty out of it. We executed our plan to a tee.

Jake Ball: It's always nice when you do your homework and it pans out exactly as you'd planned. We'd done our prep in the week and everything we'd spoken about and put in place came to fruition. It doesn't always work out that way.

Dan Biggar: It always helps when you start well against a team like that who want to drag you in to a bit of an arm wrestle. We came out firing, and got to about 22–0 with twenty minutes gone. We scored a couple of good first-phase tries off set piece which was pleasing. We'd identified a weakness off the tail of their lineout; I think they had a hooker or a prop off the tail, and Josh Adams went through on an inside ball to finish one off. It helped that we got the scoreboard moving because it meant we could control the game and avoid any hairy moments. We got the game won quite early.

Tomas Francis: In the first game of a tournament, you want to paint a good picture of your set piece. That might not mean getting twenty penalties in the game, but if every scrum has an outcome, referees then perceive your scrum to be better. That gave us more opportunities as the tournament progressed, to play around and take advantage, whereas if we'd have scraped through and taken a hiding up front, it might have affected perceptions of us later on in the tournament.

Hadleigh Parkes: I thought my World Cup was over because I'd broken a bone in my hand just after half-time. After the game everyone was bouncing but I was really down because I thought I'd be going home. In the changing room, the physio and the doctor asked if I was alright, and I lied to them, telling them everything was sweet. Prav [Mathema, medical manager] wasn't buying it, and said, 'Are you sure?' I confessed that I'd done something to my hand. They x-rayed it and thankfully, they said, 'We can work with that. It's gonna be all right.' After sinking into a trough of despair at the thought of going home, I was suddenly jubilant again.

Dan Biggar: We all knew that Australia was the pivotal game in the group. If you win that, you give yourself a little bit of leeway, whereas if you lose, with Fiji to come, you put yourself under a hell of a lot of pressure. In terms of the build-up we were all really excited to get to Tokyo because we'd been in Kitakyushu for our training camps which was a little bit out of the way. The stadium and infrastructure there was brilliant but like Toyota, where we played Georgia, it was a quiet, remote place with not much going on.

Jake Ball: The Japanese were a pretty crazy bunch. Kitakyushu was just mental; like Wales away from Wales. They'd converted the whole town into Wales. There were Welsh flags everywhere, and locals wandering around with our kit on. It was pretty strange, to be honest, to see that halfway across the other side of the world.

Rhys Patchell: We had this group of kids who followed us everywhere. They were relentless, always asking for pictures and bits of kit. They wanted my hat. It was the first week, forty degrees and boiling hot and clearly I don't go well in the sun. I tried to explain that to them: 'You can't have my hat. I need it!' It was the only hat I had. This was the start of hopefully nine weeks away and I can't be giving away my hat in the first week. I'd be burned to a crisp. I didn't get hassled anywhere near as much as Bigs though. They *loved* Bigs. I couldn't tell you why.

Dan Biggar: We trained in a 15,000-seater stadium there and, for that one session, they packed the place out and were belting out the Welsh national anthem. It was a really special moment.

Tomas Francis: They sang it better than I can, to be honest.

Dan Biggar: To have 15,000 rammed in for a training session . . . you'd struggle to get that back in Wales. It's a time in my career that I really enjoyed, and I'm sure when I retire I'll look back on it as one of the absolute highlights.

Hadleigh Parkes: The Welsh Rugby Union had done a good bit of work forging ties with Kitakyushu for about eighteen months before the World Cup and it really showed. The town got right behind the boys.

Rhys Patchell: We had this welcoming dinner, and as Welshmen we were obviously expected to sing. We were intending to sing *Calon Lan*, and had been practising down in the lobby in front of this big Yamaha piano. I was coaching the lads, making sure we had our timing right and stuff. It was our time to shine. Then during the ceremony this group of six-year-olds walked on to the stage and sung this beautiful, note-perfect rendition of *Calon Lan*. The melody was perfect, the pronunciation was spot on, and they were breathing in all the right places. We all looked at each other and thought, 'We can't follow this.' We'd have been a million times worse. We got introduced, and I explained that there was no way we could compete with that, so we bottled it and did *Ar Lan y Mor* instead. In my role as choirmaster, I'd come up with this jazzy arrangement of *Calon Lan*, but after being shown up we had to ditch it.

Jake Ball: We'd been told there'd be a few people down to watch training but we had no idea how many. As we were driving in there were queues of people – *long* queues, mate – and they were waiting there just to get into the ground. About a kilometre's worth of people all waiting patiently in single file. We got absolutely *beasted* that day as well. Gatland saw it as an opportunity to show them how hard we worked and we ended up copping an absolute flogging. 'This is Team Wales and we work harder than anyone else.'

Tomas Francis: That's Gats to a tee. He likes to put on a good show. He extended the session just for them. Bloody marvellous.

Dan Biggar: We got to Tokyo and got a real buzz straight away from the city. We stayed in the New Otani Hotel which is literally the best hotel any of us have ever stayed in. It was absolutely top drawer. That's part of the World Cup as well: experiencing different cultures, different cities, going out for food in different restaurants, things like that. Those cultural experiences contributed to a real sense of excitement within our camp, and the significance of the game coming up on the weekend only added to that.

Owen Watkin: Compared to Bridgend, Japan's a different kettle of fish. I'm a home bird who doesn't like to be out of his comfort zone, but I knew I had to make the most of it. Not just rugby-wise, but in terms of seeing and experiencing something different. It was a long time to be away, but I thoroughly enjoyed it.

Dan Biggar: It was absolutely awesome. It was such an adventure, and so different to any other tour we'd been on. The only downside to staying in the poshest hotel in Tokyo was the hit to the wallet. My wife came out for the first week, and we sat down for a club sandwich and two cokes, and it cost me forty-six quid! I had to get the currency translator out to make sure they'd got it right. I couldn't have stayed there on my own account, that's for sure.

Hadleigh Parkes: We were constantly trying to convert everything back to pounds in our head, and we were struggling. Sitting there with a coffee, thinking, *how much is this?* You can easily get stung in some of the more expensive places.

Owen Watkin: I was with Nicky Smith, Beard, Tips, Bigs and Franny in this Japanese restaurant trying to order Katsu curry. They didn't have a clue what we were on about so we loaded up the old Google Translate, but whatever we typed in wasn't translating into the right thing. We were there for about half an hour and everyone was getting really wound up. All we wanted was a Katsu curry but they didn't have a scooby what we were on about.

Rhys Patchell: I look back and wish I'd made more of it, but having said that, I wasn't there to be a tourist, I was there to work.

Owen Watkin: We went to Disneyland in Tokyo and it was absolutely heaving. Adam Beard wasn't happy because he couldn't fit his legs into any of the rides. They're probably not used to having a six-foot-eight giant trying to squeeze into them.

Rhys Patchell: A few of us went on the bullet train to Hiroshima, and that was pretty sobering. I went around the museum with Leigh Halfpenny who's got a kid, and you sit there and read about all the schoolkids who died, and you realise there are different levels to it. I was there thinking, 'Gosh this is terrible,' but he's looking at it through the eyes of a parent.

Dan Biggar: Tokyo is the best city I've ever been to by a country mile. The buzz of it, the infrastructure, the training venues, the stadiums, the crowds, the people, everything was just incredible. You could go to the most expensive steak restaurant and spend hundreds of pounds or find a funky little backstreet place that was just as good and cost a tenner. It was a seriously impressive place, and it made the World Cup for us.

Rhys Patchell: That's what I liked: proper Japan. Exploring all the little side streets and eating where the locals ate rather than making a beeline for the nearest big chain.

Owen Watkin: I roomed with Tips for the entire eight weeks. He's similar to me: very tidy, neat and organised. We both love our pop and chocolate so I brought a bag full of shit food with me, and we'd share it in the evenings. We started watching *Walking Dead* on Netflix, and over the course of eight weeks, we pretty much binged the entire thing. It was all quite romantic. I think his wife was getting a bit worried at one point. Nicky Smith and Adam Beard shared a room, and Nicky is the messiest bloke you'll ever meet. You can understand why just by talking to him; he's a bit of a drip. The first time I went to visit them, I opened the door and stepped straight into his suitcase. His clothes were strewn everywhere. How can anyone be that messy? Beard's the only one who's willing to room with him, the only one who's willing to put up with his snoring. He sounds like a choking pig.

Hadleigh Parkes: Before the Australia game, I had to get used to catching a ball again. We only had a six-day turnaround and for those first three days I couldn't catch anything. People talk about the power of the mind, and I haven't always been a huge believer in that, but as soon as I got it moving the pain just went away. I was walking around with a rugby ball in my hand the whole time, even around the hotel, just trying to get that grip back. To be honest, it got me out of contact training, which was quite nice. It's interesting knowing what the human body can actually do when you put your mind to it.

As has been documented, Australia were Wales's bogey side for most of Warren Gatland's tenure. The 9–6 win over the Wallabies the previous autumn may have been low on quality but it was huge in terms of psychological significance. Dan Biggar had been the man who'd kicked Wales to victory. Eleven months later, he was primed to continue where he'd left off.

Dan Biggar: We always do a walk-through of our moves and defensive set-ups about two or three hours before kick-off, and that day Shaun Edwards approached me on the way back to the hotel and said, 'A drop goal or two would be nice today.' When Shaun speaks, you listen, otherwise you're in for a bit of trouble on Monday morning, so I suppose that stuck with me. We turned the ball over off the kick-off, and I knocked one over after thirty seconds. We got off to a flying start.

Hadleigh Parkes: It was outstanding. Everything we'd trained for in the week just came off. Ken smashed into contact, turned the ball over, and Biggsy kicked that drop goal. It was a great way to start a Test match.

Jake Ball: The prep had been really good, and we'd come off the back of that good victory against Georgia. We'd spoken a lot about the importance of the Australia game. Lose that one and you're under pressure. We were pretty wary that we still had Fiji to come, who on their day can produce special things.

Owen Watkin: We'd spoken a lot about how this was the one to win, how it was pretty much our final. We knew that victory over Australia meant we'd be in with a good chance of going deep in the competition.

Wyn Jones: We set our stall out early and built a convincing lead which really bolstered our confidence.

Dan Biggar: Parkesey scored in the corner from a cross-field kick. We had an advantage from a penalty, and I had a fifty-fifty shot to put the ball in the corner. Fair play to Parkesey; he got up ahead of Marika Koroibete and the confidence just flowed from there.

Hadleigh Parkes: Biggsy still gives me grief about it. He says, 'I can't believe you managed to get off the ground, Parkesey!' Jinks is the same. He told me afterwards that he'd been shouting from the sideline: 'Yes, Biggsy, kick it,' followed by, 'Oh no, it's Parkesey out there on the wing. What the hell's going on?' It would have been nice if one of the wingers had been there to finish it, but it's always nice to get a try, isn't it? I play that one back in my mind quite a bit.

With just over a quarter of an hour on the clock, Biggar found himself on the receiving end of a reckless shoulder charge from Michael Hooper, which was greeted with a chorus of outrage from the red-shirted hordes. Despite a lengthy TMO referral, the Australian captain avoided a yellow card.

Dan Biggar: It's strange; when you look at it compared to what's going on now, there may well have been a stronger sanction. It was a bit late and he led with the shoulder, but I don't think there was any real intent in it. Sometimes it's better to just get on with it and not make a fuss, but he'd probably be looking at a harsher punishment for that nowadays.

Another cross-field kick produced the game's second try; Australia's Adam Ashley-Cooper was the beneficiary this time, as the Wallabies' first meaningful attack bore fruit. Meanwhile, within the claustrophobic confines of the breakdown, a ferocious battle was unfolding, with the much-vaunted pairing of Michael Hooper and David Pocock seemingly having met their match.

Jake Ball: In the week we were constantly being shown clips about what the Aussies were good at, and Pocock and Hooper's faces were appearing in virtually everything. Our back rowers would probably have been fed up seeing their faces, and would have been fired up to prove a point. Rugby's a game of respect and it was a big opportunity for those guys to take on some world class opposition and do a job on them. I think it's fair to say they did that. Those boys are now world class in their own right. We'd talked about how many turnovers they were getting and how they like to launch attacks from turnover ball. Their turnover stats were a lot lower in that game; they didn't get much joy out of the breakdown.

Before the game was half an hour old, Dan Biggar found himself on the end of another bone-crunching collision. After Marika Koroibete had rounded Jonathan Davies on the left-hand touchline, Biggar was the last line of defence. His try-saving tackle would prove his final contribution as he was forced from the field with a head injury. With the game delicately balanced at 10–8 in Wales's favour, it was a huge moment for the replacement fly-half, Rhys Patchell.

Rhys Patchell: You're aware at a time like that, that there are a lot of eyes on you. The cameras are all trained on you, because a ten going off early doors in a game is not a regular occurrence. I hadn't played that much rugby in the previous twelve months, so I knew I had to look like I was relaxed, and confident, and that everything was going to be okay. I was confident that it *would* be okay, but I was acutely conscious of how I would be perceived. Alun Wyn is going to watch you walk on the field and is clearly going to say something to encourage you, or Jon Fox is going to explain what we're planning to do next and to tell you to get your head around it. You've got to look calm and assured. You've got to come on with a bit of a strut and a swagger.

My first involvement was a kick-off, which was nice because as long as you don't kick the ball dead, you're straight in the game. They're either going to kick the ball off the field, or back to you, so you're going to get a possession and you're going to get into your rhythm. The next time I touched the ball, Gar Cawdor [Gareth Davies] passed it directly at my feet off a lineout and I managed to catch it. After that I was like, 'Yeah, sweet, I'm going to be okay.' Then we had a penalty and as I was lining up the kick, Sanj came running over and told me HIA subs weren't allowed to take kicks at goal. I was the only recognised goal kicker on the pitch, and the ref didn't seem to be paying much attention, so I told Sanj to sling his hook. I just wanted to stick it through the posts and worry about the consequences after.

Within moments, Patchell too was feeling the full force of one of Australia's powerful ball carriers. Cue more howls of outrage from the Welsh supporters, as Samu Kerevi appeared to drive his crooked forearm into Patchell's neck.

Dan Biggar: In fairness, Patch probably tackled him a bit high, but Kerevi did lead with his elbow. It could have gone either way. Look at it now, and you're looking more at the actions of the attacker – whether they're leading with their elbow or their wrist. There was certainly no shortage of drama in the game. You couldn't take your eyes off it.

Jake Ball: At the time, all of us were thinking yellow, and a yellow there could have been handy, but looking back it was probably just a bit careless from both sides. Patch got his tackle tech all wrong, and it was just one of those things: a rugby collision.

It was decided that Kerevi's forearm had initially made contact with Patchell's chest before riding up towards his neck, and that a penalty was sufficient punishment.

Despite Michael Hooper's audible protestations that Patchell's 'terrible tackle technique' was to blame, referee Romain Poite stood by his decision. Patchell duly slotted the three points, stretching Wales's lead to 16–8.

Rhys Patchell: I didn't think there was anything in it, to be honest, but I'm glad they came back for it because I'd missed one of their players down the wing and they were in for seven points. At one stage I thought *I* was getting penalised for going too high.

Hadleigh Parkes: Yeah, Patch came on and knocked over a few big kicks. He's got a hell of a boot on him. Whether it's his right foot or his left foot, he practises enough so it's almost guaranteed to go over. I'm sure Jonny Wilkinson is one of his heroes, and he understood that repetition and practice makes you a better player. He certainly has a great work ethic.

Rhys Patchell: It was a close call that I'd even got on the plane to Japan, and a lot of it was down to *Sliding Doors* moments in other people's careers. Chicken [Gareth Anscombe] blew out his ACL against England in the warm-ups. I knew I was in the mix, but I'd had a few injuries and Jarrod Evans' star was rising.

Dan Biggar: He just kept nudging us ahead, fair play. Then off the restart, Gareth Davies scored the intercept, didn't he? He picked off Genia. That's one of his specialities.

Rhys Patchell: Genia is one of those scrum-halves who pulls the ball back to his hip and takes steps before he passes.

Jake Ball: That try stands out for me as the key moment in that game. For whatever bizarre reason, when the scoreboard's tight, and one team intercepts, that team generally tends to win. It's a real deflater for the opposition. It can suck the life right out of you.

Wyn Jones: Once he caught that ball, you knew no one was going to lay a hand on him.

Jake Ball: I don't know how he does it. His timing is unbelievable, to intercept a ball from a nine passing to a forward is just crazy. It was a huge swing in the game.

Rhys Patchell: Shaun Edwards always talks about wanting his scrum halves to make an absolute nuisance of themselves, and that's what Gareth was doing. He reads things that much quicker than anyone else.

Tomas Francis: That's the moment you remember, isn't it? He was on fire during that World Cup. He turns up for the World Cups doesn't he? He likes the big stage.

Wyn Jones: Rugby's a game of small margins. If he doesn't catch that ball, and we don't get the seven points, it might have been a completely different game. With a bit of luck on your side, those small margins make a big difference.

Like he'd done in the 2015 World Cup, the unassuming scrum half – whose shy off-field demeanour is a stark contrast to his strutting on-field confidence – produced a moment of individual brilliance. With his synapses firing more quickly than anyone else's, he anticipated Genia's pass and scorched past the scrambling Australian defence like a Ferrari accelerating smoothly through the gears.

Rhys Patchell: At half-time, we were thinking, 'We're in the driving seat here.'

Jake Ball: Patch's drop goal at the start of the second half took us 26–8 ahead.

Rhys Patchell: The ugliest drop goal you're ever likely to see.

Jake Ball: Looking back, you realise how big a margin that was, but you don't really have time to reflect on those things in the heat of the moment. You're always just thinking, 'Next job, next job,' and trying to see it out, but occasionally, when there's a break in play, you have a chance to gather your thoughts. That's when you think, 'Wow, this is a World Cup and we're doing an absolute job on Australia.'

Rhys Patchell: Shaun Edwards loved a drop goal. He couldn't believe that it was one point in league and three points in union. I was convinced we were out of sight at that point, that the game was dead.

Wyn Jones: We were kind of thinking, 'Game, set and match,' after the drop goal, but the messages coming on were pretty clear: keep playing, don't park the bus. Don't wait for them to attack you.

Dan Biggar: Australia came back into it, as you'd expect. We never thought for one minute we'd have it all our own way.

Rhys Patchell: We always knew the Aussies would have a purple patch. We just didn't think it would last as long as it did. We barely touched the ball in the second half.

Wyn Jones: Yeah, they scored a few tries then and started to creep back into it and you're thinking, 'Oh god, we're not going to chuck this away are we?' Sometimes it gets more difficult to play when you're ahead, as opposed to chasing a game down. It's a different mindset. When you're behind you tend to play with more abandon.

Tomas Francis: I remember thinking, 'Fuck, they're coming.' They were relentless, carrying into us, knocking us back on our heels. Crucially though, we'd beaten them 9–6 in that terrible game in Cardiff, so the belief was there. We'd got over the hoodoo of not beating them.

What followed was a nightmarish period for Wales who saw their seemingly unassailable lead begin to crumble. As the second half progressed, Australia's swagger returned in earnest. Dane Haylett-Petty's try kick-started the comeback, and the indomitable Michael Hooper emerged from the bottom of a pile of bodies to claim the Wallabies' third on the hour mark. Once Matt Toomua's kick had bisected the posts following a scrum offence in the sixty-seventh minute, Wales's 26–8 lead had been whittled down to a paper-thin 26–25.

Hadleigh Parkes: We knew that was coming. The Aussies never go away, and they got a hell of a roll on in that second half. Before then we'd had some really close games against them so we knew full well what they were capable of. The first half had been all about attack, whereas the second was all on defence. It was proper backs-to-the wall stuff.

Dan Biggar: It was a tough watch. That second half felt a hell of a lot longer than forty minutes, that's for sure.

Tomas Francis: They *never* know when they're beaten, and they always turn up in a World Cup. I don't know what happened at half-time, but after the kick-off, they were rolling us on every carry. They just wrestled the momentum back, and I started to worry a bit. Ultimately though, you've got to have the belief in the boys. I was thinking, 'Keep putting them down, they're big men, keep making them get back up. They'll get tired and we'll get our chance.'

Jake Ball: We still felt pretty confident. We'd been through a hell of a spell and won a lot of games. There's no doubt that in good teams that shines through. You remember how to win when you really need to. That was a key factor.

Hadleigh Parkes: We'd been on the roll where we'd won fourteen games on the bounce, but during that run we didn't really blow the score out did we? We never really smashed anyone. Our defence was always very strong and we played to a well-drilled system. All the boys believed in it and we all did our jobs. We knew we were one of the fittest teams in international rugby and that when games got close, our defence would invariably get us over the line.

Rhys Patchell: People talk about the demons creeping in, and the run of defeats we'd suffered at the hands of the Aussies, but I'd not played in any of those games, so that didn't bother me in the slightest. I don't know how much that history really plays on people's minds. You're engaged in what you're doing in the moment, you're not thinking about what's happened in the past.

Wales struggled during the second half, with Australia enjoying an astonishing eighty-two per cent possession. The players may not have been thinking about the run of last-gasp defeats they'd suffered at the hands of the Wallabies, but you can guarantee the supporters were. When Rhys Patchell struck another penalty to extend Wales's lead to 29–25, the relief was palpable.

Rhys Patchell: Even when I knocked over the penalty to put us ahead, I couldn't relax. You're aware that a try still wins it for them.

Owen Watkin: I came on for Parkesey with ten minutes to go, and I was thinking, 'You can't fuck this up now. *Don't* fuck it up.' The boys had worked so hard to get to that point and I didn't want to do anything to jeopardise the team. One of my earliest contributions was to rip the ball off Kerevi and snuff out an attack.

Rhys Patchell: It was a big defensive play. He was one of the best in our team at that.

Owen Watkin: From a young age, I've always been quite good at it. My older brother, who plays for Newport, is the same. I don't know how we do it, but it comes naturally to us. I didn't realise how important it was until we'd played Tonga a few years earlier and Shaun gave me the defensive player of the week award for winning five turnovers. Then against France in the 2019 Grand Slam, I ripped the ball off their hooker in the eighty-first minute just before we kicked it out. Gats approached me during the week and told me he was going to ask me what my point of difference was in the team meeting. He wanted me to say, 'We wouldn't have won the game in France if it wasn't for me.' I just couldn't do it. It sounded too big-headed, so I bottled it and said something like, 'My ability to rip the ball in contact really helps the team.' He was clearly trying to instil a bit of confidence in me, but there was no way I could stand up and boast in front of the boys like that.

Dan Biggar: There's no doubt we were absolutely hanging on by our fingernails at the end, but I think it was just about the right result. We deserved it on the basis of the game overall and we'd shown a hell of a lot of resilience to get the job done. When you're two from two at the start of the journey, you build that excitement and energy from that point.

Owen Watkin: It's hard to explain, but from the 2019 Six Nations through to the World Cup, it literally felt like we were unbeatable. If we'd played the All Blacks ten times, we'd have beaten them ten times. That's how we felt. Everyone was so tight, we were in the best condition we'd ever been in and Gats convinced us we were invincible.

Tomas Francis: We knew we were going to come through in the end. We had the superior fitness, and that's what Gats's game was built on. Shaun would always show clips of UFC fighters bleeding everywhere and choking someone out, and he'd say, 'That's us.' We'll take the hits all day, we'll suffer, and we'll bleed, but we will suffocate them in the end. Gats instilled that attitude. It's similar to Exeter for me; you never feel you're going to lose a game in an Exeter shirt. It doesn't matter what the score is, you never feel you're going to lose the arm wrestle. That day against Australia, even when they came back at us, we felt we had their number.

Jake Ball: I suppose it's not until you finish the game that it sinks in what's gone on, and that often takes a good few hours or even a day, once you've seen the fans and your family, and you're going, 'Wow, it's pretty special what we've just done to a quality outfit.'

Wyn Jones: Once we'd won that game, we knew our route to the final was probably going to be a lot easier. It gave us the confidence to beat anyone.

Tomas Francis: It was a really hot night in Tokyo. I got drug tested and it took me five hours to piss after the game. Some little Japanese man wouldn't let me have more than two bottles of water which amounted to one litre. I tried to explain that I'd lost six kilograms in the game, which was the equivalent of twelve bottles of water, so unless he let me drink more than two bottles, we'd still be there two days later. I ended up getting a lift home in a random taxi, because everyone had left without me. I've been drug tested three times in my international career: Ireland at home after the 2019 Grand Slam, that Australia game, and then England home in 2021, so I've missed some big changing room celebrations. I must be jinxed.

Rhys Patchell: The boys had a quick high-five, bowed to the crowd, and moved on to the next job. Our aim from the outset was to get to the World Cup final, and the mantra in camp was always: 'X number of days until the final.' We didn't go nuts after beating Australia; we just saw it as one step closer to our ultimate goal.

Dan Biggar: We had three days off afterwards and went to Beppu down on the coast for some rest and relaxation. There wasn't much to do but we stayed in a lovely hotel on the front and enjoyed a bit of time away from the training pitch. It had been so hectic; two games in six days, lots of training and media and intensity around the place, so it was nice to go down there and switch off for a couple of days before getting our heads right for Fiji.

Jake Ball: It was an eight- or nine-day turnaround before our next game. We didn't get ahead of ourselves, which probably shows you the mindset of the squad. Beating Australia was just part of the process of getting where we wanted to be. There wasn't a huge amount of celebrating going on and there wasn't a huge amount to do. Warren deliberately kept us away from the limelight and encouraged us to relax and look after our bodies, which was a smart move. My father came down at that point, and I spent a lot of time with him and Aaron Shingler. We hung out in this arcade together which sounds a bit weird, but they had table tennis in there and all manner of crazy games which were a welcome distraction. It gave us an opportunity to escape the madness for a bit before the Fiji game.

Hadleigh Parkes: Fiji had lost to Uruguay the week before so they were kind of out of it, but they definitely wanted to target Wales. Their coaches told me as much after the game.

Dan Biggar: I've played against New Zealand, South Africa and Australia, England and Ireland countless times, but those two games against Fiji in the 2015 and 2019 World Cups were the hardest games of international rugby I've *ever* played. You just look across the park and there's not a single person in their team who isn't an athlete. Their second rowers and back rowers are as quick and skilful as their centres.

Tomas Francis: The hardest game I've ever played in was the Fiji game in the 2015 World Cup, but this one was a close second.

Owen Watkin: It sounds bad but if I could have picked one game *not* to have played in that campaign, it would have been the Fiji game. They're all so big, fast, and strong, and they're incredibly awkward to tackle.

Jake Ball: I remember standing in the tunnel and glancing back thinking, 'Christ, they're all the same size.' Their backs were as big as their forwards. They were a *huge* team, absolutely massive.

Rhys Patchell: They were enormous. I'd played on the sevens circuit so I knew from first-hand experience that those boys hit hard, and when they get on a roll, they're almost impossible to rein back in.

Jake Ball: They came out like raging bulls and it was bloody hard to deal with.

Hadleigh Parkes: I'd have to agree. It was the hardest I've ever been hit in my life, and it hurt just as much when *you* were running into *them*. You look across their backline and you're running at guys who could be loose forwards or even locks. Josua Tuisova on one wing, Semi Radradra on the other. They belted us. We may have beaten Australia but we knew after a few minutes that this wasn't going to be easy. They started really well and got their tails up.

Tomas Francis: They'd had a ten-day rest, it was their last game of the tournament, and they had nothing to lose. We knew what was coming. They're physically intimidating, and they can literally score at the drop of a hat. It's tough to have them in your group.

Dan Biggar: Back then they had Radradra, Tuisova, Murimurivalu, Botia; everywhere you looked there were threats across the park. Radradra produced one of the best individual performances I've ever witnessed. None of us could lay a finger on him all night.

Hadleigh Parkes: I remember racing up in a line to chase a kick, looking at the guy receiving the ball and thinking, 'Okay, this guy: he can run around me, he can step inside me, he can step outside me, or he can go over the top . . . oh shit, he's gone past me.' They're phenomenal athletes, the Fijians.

Within three minutes, Fiji had lain down the gauntlet. Receiving the ball in space down the right flank, Josua Tuisova crashed through the attempted tackle of Josh Adams before dragging Dan Biggar and Josh Navidi with him to the try line. His nickname of 'The Bus' had never seemed so apt.

Jake Ball: I got up from the scrum and they'd scored in the corner. I remember thinking, 'What the hell just happened?' Josh Adams is a brave rugby player who always puts his body on the line. He chucked his head into the spokes, flat-out, fully committed, and it didn't make any difference. Tuisova just bowled him over. He had three players hanging off him as he went over the line.

Hadleigh Parkes: Tuisova steamrollered me as well in a move later in the game. I reckon he was actually Patch's man on that occasion, but Patch has just jammed out and said, 'Parkesey, there you go.' I've literally gone arse over end and backwards. Yeah, cheers Patch, thanks for that, mate.

Dan Biggar: I had to laugh, we played Fiji under a roof on a beautiful warm evening, on the firmest pitch we'd played on to date. We couldn't have teed it up more perfectly for them. Then we went 10–0 down after ten minutes and had Ken Owens sent to the bin.

Jake Ball: To this day, I don't know how he didn't get a red card. Every time I bring it up with him, he goes, 'Nah, it was never a red card.' *One hundred* per cent it was a red card, especially in that tournament when they were clamping down so much on dangerous tackles.

Tomas Francis: I don't actually remember it, but he tackles with his head, doesn't he, the Cannonball.

Jake Ball: Ken's got pretty good chat, so he probably convinced them it wasn't that bad. Like the Lions decision in the third Test in 2017. It was a Jedi mind trick. If that had been me, I'd have had a red card *and* an eight-week ban.

Within minutes of the yellow card, Fiji had scored another in Josh Adams's corner. This time it was Kini Murimurivalu making his presence felt as he swatted both Adams and Liam Williams away en route to the line.

Dan Biggar: We were standing around under the sticks, looking for someone to take the game by the scruff of the neck. We were battling at that point, no doubt about it. We were well under the cosh.

Jake Ball: Talk about things not going to plan in the first twenty minutes. Our meticulous pre-match prep had gone completely out of the window. Everything that could have gone right for them, went right for them.

Owen Watkin: I was thinking, 'Fiji are looking shit hot here,' but if I had to lay a bet, I'd have put my life on it that we'd come back to win.

Jake Ball: It wasn't panic stations, we were pretty organised. 'We need to do this, we need to do that.' The key message was: 'Calm down, get our breath back and stick to our game plan. They've scored a couple of one-off tries, that's all.' We still had faith in our system.

Rhys Patchell: We knew we were a very fit team and as long as we were accurate with what we were trying to do, we'd eventually squeeze them. They're good players, but if you put good players under pressure, they'll struggle to get territory and they'll struggle to execute.

Wales referred back to their script towards the end of the opening quarter as Dan Biggar launched another of his pinpoint cross-field kicks, allowing Josh Adams to soar above Ben Volavola to claim the ball and touch down. Then, with half-time approaching, some crisp passing across the backline saw Adams bag a second. After his nightmarish opening twenty minutes, the winger from Hendy had redeemed himself.

Jake Ball: We had a lineout and everything panned out in that area. They defended in exactly the way we thought they would. Our driving maul started to function pretty well, we got a couple of openings and scored some good tries.

Dan Biggar: Thankfully, we managed to stem the Fijian tide. Josh scored a couple of good tries in the corner, and we went in 14–10 ahead at the break.

Jake Ball: Shaun Edwards spoke to Josh at half-time.

Tomas Francis: He was raging, telling us all to make our 'fookin' tackles', and then he looked at the replay of Tuisova's try.

Jake Ball: After seeing it again, he softened slightly and said something like, 'Fair play lad, there's not a whole lot more you could have done there.' The guy was shifting. It's not like Josh had shit himself and put his head somewhere else. He'd gone all at it, full metal jacket. Tuisova's just a hell of a specimen and, one-on-one, not many players would have stood a chance.

Tomas Francis: It's the laws of physics, isn't it? It doesn't matter how good a defender you are, there's no way you're going to stop that guy.

Owen Watkin: It's like tackling a bus isn't it?

Jake Ball: Josh has been on the end of plenty of bollockings from Shaun – like every player has. If you get it wrong you're going to cop it, but he was good the other way, too. If you played well he wouldn't blow smoke up your arse necessarily, but he'd let you know in his own way. He's a good-hearted bloke which a lot of people probably don't realise. I loved working with him. You were always clear where you stood. If he had a problem with something you weren't doing, or with something you *were* doing but not well enough, he'd just come and tell you. It sounds pretty simple but it's something a lot of rugby coaches struggle with – communicating effectively with their players. Shaun had his own way of doing that.

Wales may have thought they'd weathered the storm, but Fiji emerged from the sheds like a raging tornado, striking back with a penalty try from a driving lineout. James Davies had been sin-binned moments earlier, so Wales now found themselves behind on the scoreboard and a man down. Within moments of the restart, Dan Biggar took another head knock.

Dan Biggar: There was a bit of a kick which went into no-mans land. I was coming back to claim it, and Sanj was coming on to it from full-back. Typical Liam, not wanting to bale out of anything, he absolutely clonked me.

Rhys Patchell: As soon as it happened, I was like: vest off, here we go again.

It was an ugly collision, with Biggar's head clashing first with Williams' shoulder in the air, then his knee on the ground, and then with the turf itself. He appeared to be out cold for a number of seconds. For the second match running, Wales's general was forced from the field, and Rhys Patchell entered the fray at a critical moment.

Rhys Patchell: It was a bit edgy when I came on. We were behind on the scoreboard and they had their tails up. It was no use us beating Australia and then undoing all the hard work by losing to Fiji. You don't go to a World Cup to sit on the bench, or not be involved, or maybe get five minutes at the end when a game's won. You want to be there, competing at the sharp end, so I was glad to get on and prove my worth. Soon after I came on, we had a penalty straight in front from forty yards out. Funnily enough, it was the only spot I'd struggled from during the warm-up. I've no idea why, because it was bang in front, but I'd been stroking them a bit thinly. Fortunately, on the night, it went straight through the middle and drew us level.

Tomas Francis: Jaddsy's third try settled the nerves a bit. He's a world class finisher.

Owen Watkin: A proper finisher. One of the best in world rugby.

Tomas Francis: He only needs a sniff of a chance. He's a pretty chilled character, so those two tries down his channel in the first half wouldn't have fazed him. He'd have just wanted to get back on the horse and take every chance he got. Thankfully for us, he got the hat-trick and finished everything that came his way.

It was the most Fijian try Wales could have scored: slick handling, a monster Jonathan Davies hand-off, a no-look offload and an acrobatic finish.

Owen Watkin: Foxy's hand-off to set up Jaddsy's third was awesome.

Rhys Patchell: The classic Jon Fox fend and chicken wing offload.

Tomas Francis: That's a Jonathan Davies special. He could have a highlight reel just of those.

Owen Watkin: Foxy's just got massive forearms. They're like pistons. It was a brilliant fend and offload, but after he gave it, he went down. As he tried to stand up his knee kept giving way, so I instinctively started stripping off. I knew this was my moment. But then, after Patch missed the conversion, Foxy limped back into the line and it looked like he was going to carry on. I was all anxious, and I was saying to Bobby [Paul Stridgeon], 'Look at him, he can barely stand up. Surely I must be going on?' Bobby kept telling me to wait, and the boys started lining up for the kick-off. Eventually it was obvious that Foxy couldn't carry on, so I was given the green light. There was no panic when I came on, I immediately felt quite comfortable out there. I was just hoping Semi Radradra wouldn't run at me. In a one-on-one battle, I would have been a massive underdog because he's physically a lot more gifted than I am. He's a much better athlete, but I quite liked the thought of going up against him and showing people what I was made of. I tackled him once or twice but didn't do much damage because he's massive. I carried the ball once and their centre just picked me up and hammered me into the ground. That aside, I had a few nice touches and got into the game quite quickly. I really enjoyed it.

Dan Biggar: We settled down and ground a result out in the second half. We were relieved to get off the pitch without any more injuries. A couple of the boys had lumps and bumps and we were hanging on a little bit, but when you're in a team that's winning, it's easier to hang on and close games out. If you've already lost a few, doubt starts to creep in. It was our mindset that got us through.

Tomas Francis: I didn't play in the Uruguay game. A few of us went out to the karaoke bar the night before and enjoyed a few beers, which was nice. I didn't have a go-to song like some people, I just sang along to whatever they put on. It's a weird culture over there. There are all these little buildings that have got karaoke bars where the beer's brought to you, they put on the songs and away you go. It was nice to experience some of that.

Rhys Patchell: Although Uruguay had beaten Fiji, we knew we'd have too much for them. That said, it was quite emotionally draining getting ourselves up for it. After the Fiji game, we barely had fifteen bodies to train with. We'd been really battered. I didn't appreciate how much the travelling actually took out of you. Constantly packing your bags and moving from place to place.

Dan Biggar: There was a bit of concern in the media as I'd had two head knocks in two games, but I felt absolutely fine. I spoke to some specialist guy in Australia over Zoom and I was back in training after a few days. A lot was made of it, but I choose to play the sport and I'm a realist; I know that there are going to be collisions like the ones I was involved in. There'll be some where you're required to rest, and others where you can crack on. It's obviously a very, very serious part of the game and head injuries aren't something to be taken lightly, but the medical staff we have in Wales are exceptional. Prav Mathena, who heads it up, is comfortably the best physio that I've ever worked with, so we've got a brilliant team who wouldn't have taken any risks if it hadn't been the right thing for me or the team. We played Uruguay four or five days later, which I missed, and I just got myself right for the quarter-final against France.

Hadleigh Parkes: I tore a ligament in my shoulder during the Uruguay game, so both Foxy and I were serious doubts.

Owen Watkin: I trained all week in the thirteen position. The plan was for Foxy to just do the team run and play but then he wasn't able to do the team run, so I did that at thirteen as well. On the morning of the France game, there was a message in the group WhatsApp chat from Prav saying Foxy was out, and I was starting at 13. That's how I found out. I was like, 'Oh, alright then.'

Dan Biggar: Foxy trained all week in some shape or form, but we were constantly looking at him and thinking, 'He's not right here,' do you know what I mean? He was nowhere near the same level he'd been at a couple of weeks before.

Owen Watkin: Starting in a Rugby World Cup quarter-final was something I'd dreamt of as a kid and while I was incredibly nervous and excited, rugby-wise I knew I was ready. I was confident on the one hand, while still thinking, 'Flippin' hell, it's happening.' Tips was a reassuring presence. He's the most laid-back man in the world. Ten minutes before a team meeting, he's running a bath and putting some music on to chill out. On the day of the game, I was getting ready, doing my hair, making myself look pretty, trying to contain my nervous energy, and he's sliding into the bath. He's so chilled out.

Tomas Francis: Losing someone like Foxy is always a big deal, but there were people to step in and step up. We were a very tight group. We'd done some work before going out there around restructuring the payments so they were split more equally across the whole squad. It made things more inclusive, and there was a good buy-in from everyone. The non-playing twenty-three were a key part of our success and that was a massive thing because everyone was buying into a common goal. The size of the pot didn't change; it's not like we were saying, 'Give us another million pounds so we can have loads of money,' it was more like, 'Is there a fairer way to dish out the money we've got?' It was mainly about the prize money, so it was the bonus money that got split.

Owen Watkin: Yeah, when you're not involved and the other boys are getting match fees and bonuses, it can be quite disheartening. You're arguably putting in more work than them because you're training with the first-choice boys *and* then having extra conditioning. Splitting the payments equally meant everyone was focused purely on winning, whereas your motivation might not be quite as high if you're on the outside looking in.

Tomas Francis: Rather than being based on how many games you'd played, it just got split equally. If we'd reached the final and won, the squad members who hadn't made the twenty-three would still have got a massive part of the reward because they would have been a massive part of the reason. It creates a much better environment.

Owen Watkin: Going up against Virimi Vakatawa was the biggest test of my career. He's shorter and more powerful than someone like Radradra, who's more tall and rangy. Vakatawa's stockier, and has the potential to run over the top of you whereas Semi's more likely to use his footwork, hand you off and go round you. Vakatawa can offload *and* run over the top of you. Luckily I didn't have to tackle him one-on-one too much.

Dan Biggar: in fairness, Owen Watkin had a really, really good game in that quarter-final. I don't think he'd slept all night knowing Foxy was 50/50, and getting the call at breakfast gave him no time to prepare. Given the circumstances, he was really solid and played well, so fair dos to him.

Tomas Francis: France started that game on fire. They hadn't played the week before because the typhoon had cancelled their last pool game, so they were fresh and playing some really good rugby.

Hadleigh Parkes: We had a pretty good record against France [Wales had won seven of their last eight meetings] so the belief was there, but we knew how good they *could* be.

Dan Biggar: We didn't play very well at all in that game. Speaking to a few of the lads afterwards we felt quite sluggish considering we'd had so much energy and bounce about us during the pool stages.

Hadleigh Parkes: There was a fair bit of doubt within our ranks after they started so strongly.

Tomas Francis: It was one of the worst performances in the run we'd been on. For eighteen months, we'd been in the form of our lives, but that day we weren't firing any shots. If we're honest, we were lucky to progress.

France had enjoyed an extra week of rest after Typhoon Hagibis had forced the cancellation of their fixture versus England, and questions abounded about whether the break would leave them fresh and energised, or undercooked. The answer was apparent within the opening ten minutes as they surged into a two-try lead. Sebastien Vahaamahina crossed first, before Charles Ollivon completed a sweeping move begun by a trademark Vakatawa break.

Owen Watkin: I was thinking, 'Fuck, how are we going to come back from this?'

Dan Biggar: Perhaps they took us by surprise. France in that World Cup weren't what France are now. Back then you genuinely didn't know what you were going to get, whereas now, with Shaun Edwards involved, you know exactly what's coming. Perhaps there was a little bit of complacency in our ranks. Perhaps we thought it would just happen because we'd been in good form and won all of our games up until then.

Jake Ball: We needed to impose ourselves on them, to show them we weren't going to be shoved around. I wanted to make a statement, and I did so with my tackle on their hooker, Guirado, which Wainwright scored from.

Tomas Francis: That got us right back into the game. It came out of nothing. Wainwright was on fire in that World Cup. He brought the energy in that game, when a few of the boys were looking sluggish.

It was an opportunist score from a man who'd first picked up a rugby ball just six years earlier, joining his mates at Newport's Whiteheads RFC after being released from Cardiff City's football academy. After Ball's shuddering hit on Guilhem Guirado, Aaron Wainwright swooped on the loose ball and cantered forty yards to the line.

Jake Ball: Sometimes you need one-off moments to create something. We certainly had a team full of players that could do that; guys that could score tries from nothing. It was nice because me and Wainwright had been the ones who'd let Vahaamahina through for his try. I'd hit him too high and Wainwright had fallen off the tackle, so it was redemption of sorts that it was me that put the shot in on Guirado, and Wainwright who scored the try.

Owen Watkin: It really settled the nerves, that try. I remember thinking, 'Right, we're going to be okay now.'

Jake Ball: It was intimidating for Guirado. He stayed down and didn't move for a while, which told me everything I needed to know. For forwards who trade on their physicality, an incident like that gives you a real mental edge. The fact he was hurt and getting treatment really spurred me on. I certainly looked at it as a big turning point in that game. Everyone always speaks about Wainwright running fifty metres to the line, and quite often the footage is cut before my tackle, but that's rugby. I don't play the game to stand out and be glorified; that's not my role. The reason I don't often get seen in the wide channels is because I've always been so effective in close. Even though I could do a perfectly fine job out there, I've always been used in close because there are a lot of people who can't do that job. You've got your piano players and your piano pushers in life and in rugby, and you need one to make the other work.

A Dan Biggar penalty narrowed the gap further, but on the half-hour mark, Wales were reduced to fourteen men after Ross Moriarty saw yellow for a high tackle on Gael Fickou. France took immediate advantage, with Vakatawa stepping inside Liam Williams to stretch France's lead to 19–10. With the French playing some of their most beguiling rugby of the tournament the margin could so easily have been wider. Several opportunities had either been squandered or snuffed out by a desperate, scrambling Welsh defence.

The game's defining moment came seven minutes into the second half. Still nine points ahead, and with a muscular maul advancing ominously towards the Welsh try line, Sebastien Vahaamahina, inexplicably, launched an elbow into Aaron Wainwright's exposed jaw. It was as blatant an act of foul play as you're likely to see, and the referee, Jaco Peyper, wasted no time in brandishing a red card.

Hadleigh Parkes: That was a huge brain explosion!

Tomas Francis: That was the turning point. It was him who'd thrown the miss-pass in the first match of our 2019 Grand Slam campaign that George North intercepted.

Hadleigh Parkes: Yeah, he's been very kind to Wales, hasn't he? He's a great man for that.

Owen Watkin: I think his grandmother must be Welsh or something.

Tomas Francis: He helped us out a lot that year, to be fair to him. We needed that one hundred per cent.

Wyn Jones: I remember looking up at the big screen and thinking, 'Oh, they could be down a man here.' It was a moment of utter madness and it definitely helped us. Once you see that red card come out, it gives you a bit more hope.

Hadleigh Parkes: You've got to ride your luck a bit sometimes. Fortunately, we were good enough to take advantage.

Owen Watkin: You could hear all the wives and girlfriends, and mums and dads cheering in the stands when it happened. They'd been a bit quiet up until then, but that moment gave all the Welsh fans a huge lift. Everyone was thinking, 'Here we go now.' The crowd really lifted the team.

Dan Biggar: The red card made a big difference. It got us back into it, and we managed to sneak a try close to the posts at the end of the game.

Rhys Patchell: When we were still behind with about five minutes to go, the thought entered my head that I hadn't packed. If we'd lost it would have been a case of bags on the bus and head straight to the airport. It's that cut-throat. Mentally, we'd all been counting down the days to the World Cup final, so prior to the game we were all thinking in terms of being in Japan another two weeks. But with five minutes left on the clock, my mind wandered to my hotel room, and the fact my clothes were still strewn all around the place.

Hadleigh Parkes: You need a bit of x-factor and fair play, Tomos Williams delivered the goods off the back of that scrum, ripping the ball in contact, and Tips was in the right place at the right time.

While Justin Tipuric made the initial surge for the line, it was Ross Moriarty who stooped to collect the ball and touch down.

Hadleigh Parkes: It was Ross, was it? I thought it was Tips who scored. Are you sure?

Owen Watkin: Ross is an angry, powerful bloke and he's pretty hard to stop from that sort of distance.

Tomas Francis: It was off their scrum, too, which made it all the more impressive.

Rhys Patchell: I've never been so excited about a scrum.

Tomas Francis: Fair play to Dillon Lewis and Rhys Carre. There'd been a lot of talk about their scrummaging not being up to standard, but that day they won us the game. It's as simple as that. They attacked the French scrum, gave Tomos the room to apply pressure, and that was the try.

Charles Ollivon scooped the ball up from the back of the retreating scrum and looked up to see Tomos Williams in his grille. The feisty scrum half ripped the ball from his grasp, sending it skywards before Justin Tipuric gathered and lunged for the line. He was held up just short, but Ross Moriarty was on hand to provide the last powerful surge to send Wales into the last four of the World Cup.

Wyn Jones: I was on the bench watching with our conditioner, Bobby, and a huge sense of relief washed over us. Bobby went absolutely nuts and started throwing bottles of water everywhere. He spent the next five minutes picking them all up. The lids had fallen off and all sorts.

Tomas Francis: I was off getting a head knock assessment at the time after Alun Wyn headbutted me in the ear. I was peering round trying to watch the TV as they were showing the endless replays.

After a lengthy debate with the Television Match Official, Jaco Peyper was eventually satisfied that the ball hadn't gone forward off Williams, and that the try was good.

Rhys Patchell: France had succeeded in keeping us at arm's length all afternoon, but when we scored that try, I knew we'd hold on to win.

Wyn Jones: We always knew that in that last ten/fifteen minutes, we could turn it on and win the game. We always had that belief. We knew we were the fittest team there, and we knew we had guys on the bench who could come on and do a job. That's what happened in the French game.

Rhys Patchell: It was that nuisance factor again from one of our scrum-halves. That's why Shaun Edwards used to make us do all those post-tackle extras after every session. I remember asking him why once. Not in a moaning way but in a genuinely inquisitive way. I've got an interest in coaching and he's one of the world's best so I'd always pick his brains when I had the chance. Tomos's intervention there was the answer. If he hadn't been made to practise that over and over, maybe we'd never have scored that try. That would have given Shaun a real buzz.

Dan Biggar: There was an overwhelming sense of relief when the final whistle blew. We hadn't been ready to go home. We managed to find a way to hold on, but we knew there was a lot more in us.

Jake Ball: I don't know whether we'd have won if they hadn't had the red card, but that's rugby, isn't it? There are always what-ifs. We did everything in our power to win that game, and at the end of the day they got a man sent off and we showed enough nerve to close it out. What did Gats say afterwards? The best team lost? He was right.

Rhys Patchell: That was one of the few games where the post-match fitness session didn't feel so bad. We were still beasted, but you don't mind it so much because you're on such a massive high.

Dan Biggar: We were definitely lucky in that game, no doubt. But to find a way to win – albeit against fourteen men for the last twenty minutes or whatever it was – shows a lot of courage and grit. It typified what we'd become under Gats and Shaun. We just managed to grind results out when we needed to. I think everybody realised we were better than a quarter-final team in that World Cup and we'd have been kicking ourselves if we'd not got over the line in that game.

Wyn Jones: Often when you're down to fourteen men, you change the way you play. You kick a bit more, and work a bit harder, and it can sometimes have a galvanising effect. It didn't seem to affect them that negatively. Ultimately though, it boils down to the last ten minutes; if you play long enough with a man missing, there'll eventually be a lot of tired bodies out there, and it's in that last ten minutes that you usually make them pay.

Tomas Francis: It was a weird atmosphere after that one. We were obviously happy to have won, but we knew we'd have to play a hell of a lot better if we were to stand a chance of winning a semi-final against the Boks.

Dan Biggar: Gats and Shaun and the coaching staff deserve a huge amount of credit. When they took over after Wales had been knocked out of the pool stages in 2007, nobody had really high expectations of that team. What they instilled was a grit, a determination, a strong work ethic and a will to win. Look at their CVs; they're winners, aren't they? The whole coaching team were winners and that culture just spread through the whole team. By the end of Gats's tenure, we felt almost invincible.

Hadleigh Parkes: France played better than us in that game and we got away with it, but if you can win ugly, you know you're in a decent place.

Dan Biggar: When the chips were down we knew we had to roll our sleeves up and get to work. Again, we found a way to win and set it up for a huge semi-final against South Africa. That's where you get to the real business end.

Tomas Francis: When you start a game, and come off, it's no fun to watch. It's worse than being a supporter. Especially with horribly close games like that one.

But to know you're going to get to a semi-final is amazing, especially having been knocked out in the quarters four years earlier. My dad, my sister and auntie were already over, but my girlfriend was only willing to fly over if we got to the semis. She was watching back home with the game on one screen and booking.com open on another, ready to cancel her flight if we lost.

Rhys Patchell: I went straight back to the hotel and got on the phone to my parents, asking if they were coming out. Along with thousands of other Welsh people, they ended up paying through the nose to jump on last-minute flights to Japan.

Owen Watkin: I thought there was a chance I'd start in the semi too, as Foxy was still struggling. That week, if we did a double day in training, he'd do the morning which was quite light and I'd do the heavier session in the afternoon, so I was convinced I was going to be involved somewhere. Then Gats started picking Halfers to train in the starting XV. He'd been travelling reserve up until then while I'd been on the bench covering the midfield and the back three. All of a sudden, I was thinking, 'Shit, I'm not going to be picked here.' Bigs was telling me, 'Don't worry, it's just Gats playing mind games with us.' Thankfully, when they named the team it was exactly the same as the quarter-final pretty much, but with me on the bench and Foxy starting. I couldn't really argue with that.

Jake Ball: Foxy did well to get back from that. It was a nasty injury, it really was.

Dan Biggar: Four years earlier had been really disappointing. They'd had a ridiculous team that day: Fourie du Preez, Victor Matfield, Bryan Habana, JP Pietersen, Willie Le Roux. Given the injuries we'd had back then, to be in the lead with five minutes to go was heart-breaking. There was a sense of . . . not revenge as such, but certainly unfinished business.

Four years on from that quarter-final defeat, this South Africa team was no less formidable, but if Wales could take a positive, the Springboks' most potent attacking weapon, Cheslin Kolbe, had been sidelined with injury. Wales too, were without one of their talismanic backs: Liam Williams having fallen victim to one of Gatland's infamous no-holds barred contact sessions.

Tomas Francis: If we could have picked a team to play in the semis it would have been South Africa, because you always know what's coming. They play a similar style to us and we back ourselves in an arm wrestle with anyone. There was a lot of optimism going into to it. It felt like this was our chance.

Hadleigh Parkes: We'd suffered a few injuries up to that point. Sanjay was out. Josh Navidi was out. Not many of the other teams suffered too many injuries so the impression was that they were in better shape than us. But I think we'd beaten the Boks the last four times we'd played them, so we backed ourselves nonetheless.

Jake Ball: Sanj got injured during a contact drill in training. No one likes to see anyone get injured, let alone in training when there's nothing on it. It deflates the whole session. The whole time I was just thinking, 'Shit, is he alright?' You're desperately hoping that it's not too bad because you know how much he's put in to get there. He was a key player, and it's devastating to come so far, and then be denied at the final hurdle.

Wyn Jones: That week the boys could hardly sleep. You knew there was something huge coming. Training went up another level, and you could really feel the tension in the squad. We couldn't wait for the game to come, if only to get it over with!

Dan Biggar: You're better off calling a spade a spade; it was a pig of a game of rugby, but quite often those games are. If we'd got over the line by three points, everyone would have been saying how brilliantly the plan had worked.

Rhys Patchell: In terms of the style of play, and its nip-and-tuck nature, the game unfolded exactly as we'd expected it to.

Tomas Francis: I was up against the Beast [Tendai Mtawarira], and he was on fire. I'd played him before in Cardiff but I'd always thought Kitshoff was the better player to be honest. That day though, Beast was on song. He'd been playing brilliantly throughout the whole World Cup.

Wyn Jones: You want to test yourself against the best, and there's no bigger stage than the World Cup semi-final against South Africa. As a scrummager, you knew you had to get your job right or you'd have lost it for the whole team. They're a big physical eight who pride themselves on their power, and that's a challenge us front rowers relish.

Tomas Francis: We were in the arm wrestle all day. We weren't getting dominated like England did in the final. We weren't getting hosed in the set piece. We managed to hold onto our own ball. There were a few penalties here and there, which was always going to be the case against a side like that; we were never going to dominate them, but I thought that tactically, we played the game really well.

Owen Watkin: I look back now, and think, 'Fuck, I played in a World Cup semi-final!' As a kid, I'd never have dreamed I'd end up doing that. Because we hadn't had a back-three player on the bench up to that point, I'd been covering twelve, thirteen and wing. I'd had a lot of homework to learn defence and attack for all three positions and, as it happened, I went on the wing when George came off a few minutes before half-time. Shaun Edwards came up to me in the changing room, and said, 'I'm not panicking, are you panicking?' I said no. And he said, 'Good. You've got this.' I remember thinking, 'I'm glad someone's got faith in me.' He'd been doing extras with me on defence after training to prepare myself for the unlikely scenario that I'd have to come on as a wing, and in the biggest game of my career, that's exactly what happened.

Wyn Jones: It was one of the biggest physical challenges I'd come up against. We knew what they'd bring. I think they'd won every lineout up until the Welsh game, which was very impressive, and their set-piece dominance, both scrum and lineout, had been the bedrock of their victories. They had the six-two split on the bench, so you knew at some point that they'd be bringing a whole new front five on. The 'Bomb Squad' as they liked to call it. You knew what the challenge was; you knew the game could be won and lost in the front five.

Owen Watkin: As a twelve, there's a lot of movement on you, a lot of things happening right in front of you. You've got to be able to step in, adjust and think on your feet. At thirteen, you're more like the glue that holds the backline together; the one who has to fix things when they go wrong. You're worrying more about someone going round you than through you, because if they do you look a fool. I was familiar enough with my defensive duties in both midfield positions, but as a winger, my attitude was just, 'I'm going to copy Foxy. If he flies off the line, I'm going with him.' That was the best course of action.

It was almost a dream start for Wales as, after just eight minutes, Jonathan Davies put Josh Adams away down the left-hand side. The winger had already bagged five tries in the tournament and appeared in the clear before the referee called him back for a forward pass.

Jake Ball: There was a lot of kicking, which we expected, because we kicked a lot as well. We knew the territory game was going to be key, but the game itself is now just a blur of memories. I remember bits and bobs but nothing with any real clarity. The only thing that lingers is the sense of crushing disappointment.

Tomas Francis: I didn't last that long, did I? I got my shoulder obliterated by Duane Vermeulen, so it was a bitter day for me. I have no idea how long I was on the field. Half an hour at the most, I'd say. I try not to think about it. It was off a kick-off and when it happened it was like being knocked out. I don't remember anything for those first few minutes, apart from the searing pain. Then it suddenly disappeared, and I said to Geoff [Davies, WRU doctor] 'Oh, I'm fine.' He just shook his head and said, 'No, you're not. Dillon Lewis is stood at the lineout, you need to get off.' I thought, 'Shit. I must have been down for a while.' I was deluded to think I could have carried on. I could swing my arm around in its socket but there was nothing left to hold it in place. The initial pain was clearly nerve pain; it was like an extreme stinger as all the ligaments were ripped out. Once that had subsided, it *felt* alright, but it clearly wasn't.

The kicking duel intensified as the match progressed, with both sides testing the patience and aerial skills of their opponents. The place kickers, Dan Biggar and Handre Pollard, confirmed their status as world-class marksmen, nailing any opportunities that came their way. Fifteen minutes into the second half, both try lines remained intact, and the score was deadlocked at 9–9.

Wyn Jones: That's roughly when I came off, and I distinctly remember thinking, 'We'll win this.' Because we'd been behind and come back against France and Fiji, we always had that belief that we'd get through it in the end. There was such a confidence in the squad.

Owen Watkin: I remember the De Allende try because that was on my side. There was a voice in my head saying, 'Don't fuck up here.' I desperately didn't want to be the one at fault.

On a night when Pollard had kicked virtually everything, as the game was about to enter its final quarter, he chose to run. His angle took him back against the grain where he managed to splinter the first line of Welsh defence. The referee signalled for advantage at the ensuing ruck, giving the Springboks a free play. The ball came to Damian De Allende, who managed to bulldoze his way over despite the presence of an organised Welsh defence.

Owen Watkin: I think Bigs missed a tackle and Tom [Williams] tried to get him down, but he's a big strong bloke, isn't he? He had enough power to get over the line.

Hadleigh Parkes: I'd played against him a fair few times and he's a really powerful runner. He's known predominantly as a direct ball carrier, but he's skilful as well. He took that try really well. You can't just focus on one player though; it's all about the guys around him as well. [Lukhanyo] Am had a great tournament outside him too. It was a really well-balanced midfield.

The try spurred Wales into life, and they responded with a relentless sequence of phases near the South African line. Like a wrecking ball crashing repeatedly into a brick wall, the Welsh forwards were starting to make cracks but the South African foundations showed little sign of crumbling completely. Eventually, the

Springboks conceded a penalty, and Wales executed a crisp strike play off the back of a retreating scrum. After Moriarty had reached in to retrieve the bobbling ball, Tomos Williams and Jonathan Davies combined to deliver it to Josh Adams who dived over for his sixth try of the tournament. Leigh Halfpenny's touchline conversion brought the scores level at 16–16.

Rhys Patchell: It came from a penalty. I was well happy with my kick to touch. I was aware that it had to go five metres from the try line to give us a chance to score. We got down there and drove the lineout, and eventually got the opportunity to score from the scrum. It was a really nice play down the short side, and a really brave decision.

Owen Watkin: It was a lovely pass from Foxy and you'd put your mortgage on Jaddsy to finish that.

Rhys Patchell: And, of course, Pens bangs over the touchline conversion. Of course he does, it's Leigh Halfpenny, isn't it? Why would you think anything else would happen? Not long after, I went for a drop goal. I remember thinking it was a shot to nothing and, if I missed, they'd kick it back to us. I got a bit thin and it drifted wide. It didn't have the distance or direction.

Owen Watkin: I thought, 'Why's he gone for that?' He was quite far out, wasn't he? I didn't see the logic behind it personally, but obviously he's a ten and a game manager, and he thought it was the right decision. As a teammate, you've got to back the decisions of your colleagues. I'd never shout or criticise or do anything like that, regardless of what they'd done. If he'd kicked it, he'd have been hailed a hero.

Rhys Patchell: That's life as a ten. Those are the confines in which we operate, and that's where we are judged.

Tomas Francis: We were controlling the game really well after Jaddsy's try, until they got a turnover penalty and kicked for the lineout. We were dominating their half, keeping them hemmed in. We had the territory, we had everything. It was Alun Wyn's carry wasn't it? We were trying to get a penalty, weren't we? That's where the game was at. We were playing in the middle third, trying to milk a penalty, but sadly Francois Louw did his job as supersub and got the jackal. It was properly heart-breaking.

Rhys Patchell: That had been my concern when I went for the drop. The more phases we go through, the more opportunities we give the referee to award a penalty at the ruck. It's a real catch-22. We were trying to milk a penalty and ended up giving one away.

Hadleigh Parkes: When they got that penalty, they were only going to do one thing. Boot it deep into our half and drive the lineout.

That's exactly what happened, and as the driving maul picked up momentum, Rhys Carre lost his footing, and Dillon Lewis entered illegally from the side.

Dan Biggar: It was a big moment. If you're wearing a red jersey you're thinking it's not a penalty and if you're wearing a green jersey you're probably thinking it is. It's one of those things. We weren't undone by a refereeing decision in that sense; it was one of those where it could have gone either way, and unfortunately for us it just went against us.

Wyn Jones: It is what it is. There's nothing you can do about it now, so there's no point overthinking it; no point dwelling on it.

Hadleigh Parkes: I'm not going to get into that argument.

Owen Watkin: They penalised Carre, didn't they? I think it was a South African guy that went to the deck and pulled it all down on top of him. I remember thinking at the time, 'That's a bullshit call.' I've watched it back loads of times and I still think that.

Hadleigh Parkes: Referees – you've got to take your hat off to them because they do an outstanding job and everyone's watching them. Unfortunately, on that occasion, it just wasn't to be. Very political answer that, wasn't it?

Owen Watkin: The ref's decision is the ref's decision. I felt sick when Pollard lined up that kick. I'd genuinely felt that we were going to win the tournament, and all my dreams were crushed in that moment.

Rhys Patchell: After that they put a stranglehold on us and we couldn't get out of our twenty-two. When you can't get out of your twenty-two, you have no choice but to kick the ball away. It was pretty heart-breaking.

Wyn Jones: A few little things went against us, and it could have been a different outcome. We'd worked so hard to that point, and to be so close to the final only to lose like that is disappointing. But it could have been worse. You wouldn't have wanted to make the final like England did and then lose in that fashion. We at least put up a good fight, and on a different day it could have been a different outcome.

Dan Biggar: Because we lost by three points, it left us with a feeling of 'did we really fire enough shots? Did we go for it as much as we could have?'

Hadleigh Parkes: Maybe we played within ourselves a little bit, or went a bit too direct and played into their hands. I think we only took it wide once or twice and we made decent yards when we did. Our attacking kicks probably weren't as good as they had been; we didn't use them quite as effectively as we previously had. Looking back there were a couple of occasions when we could have taken it a bit wider and tried to shift their big boys around.

Rhys Patchell: I can see where Parkesey's coming from, but ironically my biggest regret is that we didn't box kick from an attacking lineout when we were thirty yards from their line. Our wingers were great in the air, and I wonder why we didn't just stick the ball up there, put a load of heat on their back three, and make it a competition five yards from their try line.

Dan Biggar: If we'd won by three then everyone would be praising the performance and wouldn't give a damn about the strategy we'd had, or the way the game was played. It was a really tough defeat to take, and the boys took quite a bit of time to get over it.

Owen Watkin: The final whistle went and I was standing on the sideline with my hands on top of my head thinking, 'What the fuck's just happened?'

Hadleigh Parkes: We were five minutes away from winning that game. It's so much tougher to take when you lose by just a few points, and you know what they did in the final as well. If it had have been a penalty to us, it might have been 19–16 to us with three minutes to go, so . . . look, it wasn't to be.

Jake Ball: You could spend your whole life wondering, and it's like a big wormhole you don't want to go down. It's easy to say if we'd won that one, we'd have fancied our chances against England in the final, but for whatever reason it wasn't meant to be that day. It's a bloody tough one.

Owen Watkin: It was the worst feeling of my life. I felt like crying.

Tomas Francis: I've never lost to South Africa. Apart from in World Cups.

Rhys Patchell: I've never felt that low. I still think about it now on my drive to work. Not necessarily every day, but more frequently than you'd imagine. At the time I wanted the ground to swallow me up, and I didn't want to talk to anybody for hours after the game. I was just stuck in my own head with my own thoughts.

Dan Biggar: We just couldn't really get our game going that day; it was a game for the purists and we came up just short which was frustrating because in all our other close games we'd found a way to get over the line. It hit the boys really hard. We were staying in Tokyo and the game was in Yokohama which was an hour away on the bus. It was a pretty quiet journey back.

Jake Ball: All that was going through my mind was the fact that all the work we'd put into it, and all the sacrifices we'd made, had ultimately came to nothing. A lot of people probably don't think about that, but the training we went through was absolutely brutal. The stuff that we put our bodies through to get that far was pretty horrific to be honest.

Owen Watkin: You think of the weeks and months of relentless hard graft, and all the time we'd spent away from our families and loved ones. What was it for?

Jake Ball: Switzerland, Turkey, all the training camps. I don't think people fully appreciated how hard they were. The step up from 2015 to 2019 was crazy. I thought 2015 was tough, but we were blasting numbers that we'd been doing in 2015. I think back to images of the boys being sick while running, and that just sums it up. Think about that – boys were being sick and running *at the same time*. Talk about effort, and the blood, sweat and tears that goes into it. To get that far and not quite cut it really hurts. Everyone had been so pumped up, but on that journey back to Tokyo, we all felt entirely deflated.

Rhys Patchell: Alun Wyn is clearly going to go on forever, but I remember looking around and thinking, 'There are some proper warriors here who may never get another chance.' There was Ken, there's Foxy – absolute warriors for the cause – and you had the coaches who were all moving on. It was so much more than just our personal ambitions as players. It was the end of an era.

Owen Watkin: My job on tour was to always tell a joke of the day. Travelling back on the bus after the game, I said to Sanj, 'Mate, I can't do this now, can I?' He said, 'Come on mate, it'll pick the boys up.' So I did it, and the tumbleweed just blew across the bus.

Hadleigh Parkes: She was a pretty quiet bus, to be fair.

Owen Watkin: There was a horrible awkward silence. I thought Alun Wyn was going to knock me out. I sat back down fairly quickly.

Rhys Patchell: I felt like I couldn't look anyone in the eye afterwards. I felt absolutely devastated. I went to see my parents and I just kept apologising profusely, telling them over and over, 'I'm so, so sorry.' They didn't know what to say. What could they have said? Nothing they could have said in that moment would have made it any better.

Dan Biggar: If we could have jumped on a flight the day afterwards it would have been great because playing in that third/fourth place play-off was mentally difficult to get back up for.

Tomas Francis: I thought I'd be fine to play in it. I said, 'Start me up, and I'll be fine to play,' but by the Wednesday I couldn't even pick up a cup of coffee. I'd lost all the power in my shoulder.

Dan Biggar: Hands down that's the toughest defeat I've had to take in my career. Can you imagine if we'd managed to set up a Wales–England World Cup final? The press would have dined out on that for the next twenty-five years.

Jake Ball: It was gutting, absolutely gutting. Their masterstroke was their bench. The 'Bomb Squad' as they were called, and the impact that they had. I honestly believe that they changed the game in the way in which they approached the subs' bench. Picking out-and-out impact players, big humans to come on and do a job. Looking back that was a revolutionary approach, and probably what made the difference.

Tomas Francis: When they got tired, they just brought six brutes off the bench to finish the job, and fair play to them, it worked. I saw clips from the documentary *Chasing the Sun* where Rassie Erasmus was saying, 'We're going to break them, we're going to beat them up,' and they did, repeatedly, to every team they played.

Rhys Patchell: There was one lineout I can't get out of my head. If we'd won it and held on to the ball, there may have been a different outcome.

Dan Biggar: We watched the final and saw South Africa dismantle England in terms of ruthless power. They negated England's set piece and blew them off the park. They'd have beaten anyone that day, and you have to take your hat off to them. What was frustrating for us watching was that they probably didn't play at that level the week before, when we couldn't get over the line. It would have been easier for us to take the defeat it they'd steamrollered us like they did England.

Tomas Francis: Gats nailed it with his quote: 'England played their final against New Zealand.' They really, really did. They spanked New Zealand [in the semi-final] and thought the final was a foregone conclusion. They thought they were just having a procession to lift the trophy.

Jake Ball: I guess the difference between our performance against South Africa and England's came down to the way we'd been training. We felt better equipped to cope with their onslaught. I honestly believe that no other nation had trained anywhere near the level we had, certainly under Gatland. We were *beasted*. Every session was seriously tough and while it was horrible at times, it built this unshakeable sense of belief that we could withstand anything. That was Gatland's thing: almost conning you into believing you were superhuman. Some of the stuff was right on the edge and sometimes players got injured, but those are the risks you take. We're not always blessed with the biggest people or the most genetically gifted players but one thing Welsh players don't lack is heart. They'll stick their heads where others don't want to. Like Rassie Erasmus said afterwards, 'The Welsh are just generally a nuisance that won't go away.' That's a compliment in itself, isn't it?

Dan Biggar: To have beaten them in 2015 would have been a bit of a bonus considering everything that had happened, but 2019 was utterly heart-breaking.

Owen Watkin: Even now, I don't get how we lost that game.

Rhys Patchell: I've never watched it back in its entirety. I've watched my clips and the bits from the team review, but I can't put myself through the whole game.

Tomas Francis: Handre Pollard said it was the hardest game he'd played in because he just could not go off script. He had to just keep kicking the ball, and kicking the ball and not get excited or give us a sniff.

Jake Ball: There was part of me that felt like we possibly trained too hard. I couldn't help thinking that when Sanjay got injured. It's a tough one in hindsight. We did need to be doing the contact during the World Cup, but for me, Sanjay was a player that could have won us a game on his own. He could create something from nothing. Yes, he could have got injured walking down the street, but I would probably have erred on the side of caution and not exposed us to the risk of injury in training. Having said that, Gats had been doing what he'd been doing for a long time, and it had worked for him so he wasn't going to change it. Maybe he'll look back on those moments and learn from them. The likes of Sanj and Foxy were key cogs. If we'd had a fully fit-and-firing Fox and Sanj back on the field, would that have been enough to get the job done? I'm in danger of going down that wormhole again. It's easy to get sucked back into it, especially when you've had a couple of beers. That's why I don't like to talk about it.

Tomas Francis: I was devastated about my shoulder, and I was devastated that the journey was over. You might only get to play one World Cup semi-final in your life. To only last one half was frustrating personally, but then to watch the boys fight that hard against a world class South African team, only to come up short was gut wrenching. Especially to see the game decided by such a fine margin. Absolutely *gut wrenching*. After the 2019 Six Nations, we'd all thought the fairy tale ending was coming. It was Gatland's last dance, and when we beat Australia and mapped out a route to the final, we genuinely thought destiny was on our side. The realisation afterwards, that that group would never have that chance again was devastating.

Hadleigh Parkes: We had a bit of a swill that night. We had Monday and Tuesday off, so the pressure was kind of off. The tournament wasn't over; both us and the All Blacks were happy to play the third-place play-off, but we both knew we were playing in a game we didn't want to be. We weren't going to the big dance.

Rhys Patchell: I couldn't even bring myself to have a beer with the boys. I just went straight up to my room. I couldn't stop thinking about my missed drop goal. I could have hit that better, I *should* have hit that better. Faf de Klerk made an unbelievable read, coming round the outside of the ruck and he saw it happening. Maybe I could have pulled the trigger a bit earlier. I felt like I'd let the team down.

Wyn Jones: If we had made the final, God knows what would have happened. We didn't really think too much about that. Once we'd lost our semi-final, it was tournament over.

Rhys Patchell: We had a day off afterwards, and I didn't want to look at anybody, I didn't want to talk to anybody, I didn't want to be around anybody. My girlfriend, Heledd, and I went for a coffee and I was horrific company. I had to apologise to her in advance. I said, 'I'm really sorry, but I'm going to be terrible company,' and I was. That's what the fans don't see: the pressure that's brought to bear on your friends and family. My character is such that I don't park things quickly, and it takes me time to process disappointments like that.

Tomas Francis: I didn't actually watch the final. We were on an all-dayer in some underground bar. Some of the boys were looking on their phones and shouting out the score every now and then, but it didn't matter to me at that point. It would have been awesome for northern hemisphere rugby to have had an England–Wales final, but it's all what-ifs isn't it?

Rhys Patchell: I've never watched the final. I had no interest in actually sitting down and watching it. By then I was sick of rugby. If you'd have told me after that tournament that I'd never have to play rugby again, that wouldn't have sounded too bad. That's not to say I hate rugby, but in that moment I felt so emotionally defeated by it all. It's a silly career choice when you think about it. Genuinely. The lows are always lower than the highs are high. I don't think that's just me, you'd find a lot of players would have a similar outlook. The highs last for a few hours after the game, and then it's on to the next job. The lows stay with you for a long time. I'm still carrying the disappointment from that semi-final with me now, two years after the game.

Tomas Francis: People always say to me, 'If you'd have made it to the final, you'd have beaten England.' It's not that simple.

Rhys Patchell: It doesn't work like that.

Wyn Jones: You can't keep looking back and wondering what might have happened, because you could do that all your life. I wouldn't say I've moved on necessarily; I'd love another pop at it. If you could have that day back, it'd definitely be one you want to try again.

Rhys Patchell: I have this deep, deep disappointment in my bones which will probably never completely fade. It will always be there. I hope it doesn't fade completely, because it fuels me. When that chance comes around again, in that type of scenario in a game, I'll nail it. I'll get it right next time. I struggle with the fact that I didn't get it right that time. I had an opportunity to win the game, and I didn't take it.

TWENTY-NINE

WAYNE'S WORLD

The battle to succeed Warren Gatland came down to a straight shoot-out between two fellow Kiwis: Wayne Pivac and Dave Rennie. Pivac had been Scarlets coach for five years, transforming them from mid-table plodders to swashbuckling champions. In 2017, they romped to the Pro12 title, running rings around a leaden-footed Munster in front of a capacity crowd at Ireland's Aviva Stadium. Pivac managed to channel the spirit of the Scarlets sides of yesteryear, which prized skill and dexterity over power and strength. It was a refreshing reminder that rugby could be beautiful as well as brutal. The following year, they travelled to Scotland in the semi-finals to take on Dave Rennie's Glasgow, who hadn't lost at home all season. Both coaches had been interviewed for the Wales job that week. Once again, the Scarlets ran riot, outclassing the Warriors to reach their second consecutive final. The WRU bigwigs may have already made up their minds, but as final auditions go, it was an encouraging one for Pivac. Within six weeks, he'd got the job.

It hadn't always been so harmonious. When he first took the reins in 2014, Pivac faced an internal mutiny which may have dented the confidence of a less steadfast operator. His countryman, Mark Hammett, had recently been ousted at the Cardiff Blues after a number of senior players had objected to his manner and methods. Fortunately for Pivac, the Scarlets' board backed their man, the mutiny was quelled and the revolution began in earnest. Pivac, it became apparent, was not one to suffer fools. His avuncular demeanour and easy way with the press concealed a steely inner resolve. A former life as an Auckland policeman dealing with robberies, muggings, rapes and murders had given him a perspective many career coaches will never have. Compared to being a beat cop in an often-violent neighbourhood, rugby seemed a glorious folly. While many saw his appointment as Gatland's successor as the equivalent of drinking from a poisoned chalice, Pivac saw it as an opportunity. He knew from experience he was able to withstand the weight of significant pressure bearing down on his broad shoulders and, as he was about to discover, he'd need to.

Dan Biggar: I don't think Wayne had an easy job, did he? You look at the managers that have tried to succeed after Fergie at Man Utd, and you get an idea of the scale of the task. Gats left such big shoes to fill, but what I immediately liked about Wayne was the fact he was very much his own man. We'd all loved playing under Gats and Shaun because we'd been so successful, but it had been a very serious environment. When Wayne came in, it became a bit more chilled. His manner was more relaxed, and that vibe quickly spread to the team room and the hotel. It was different for us because we'd never experienced anything other than the previous regime.

Owen Watkin: When Gatland and Shaun Edwards were there, you'd always be a bit on edge, looking over your shoulder, and wondering if they were watching you. If I'm honest, it was hard to relax, even when you were on your break, whereas with Pivac it's a bit more chilled. You can have a bit more of a laugh and piss about.

Wayne Pivac: There are a lot of similarities between club coaching and international coaching, but at Test level you have a much smaller window of time to implement your vision. We haven't nailed it yet, but the improvements are there to see. I had the same experience with the Scarlets; you start to see little bits of the puzzle coming together but it takes time to get the skillsets where they need to be under pressure. That was the biggest thing for us at the start, and we knew we might have to endure a bit of pain at first. The year the Scarlets won the Pro12, we actually lost our first three games. People forget that. Internally we knew that those defeats were down to mistakes *we* were making, and that once we got those right we would start to win those games. You need to put yourself in a position of control, so that it doesn't matter what the opposition does. It's all about getting you own game right. If you look back at that first Six Nations where we lost four out of five games, there were things we were doing that were actually quite good, but there were lots of little things that didn't go our way.

Dan Biggar: We played Italy first and played really well, but then we played poorly and lost against Ireland. I actually thought the rugby we played against France and England was exactly what the Welsh public had been crying out for the previous six or seven years, but we just fell short of victory.

Wayne Pivac: We were travelling in the right direction, and started scoring more tries in that tournament. On the face of it, it was a poor return, but we could see improvements and we could see them on a daily basis in camp. The record books say one win, and four losses, but we only lost 33–30 to England, and would have won the French game were it not for a penalty try decision that went against us. France have now beaten us twice since I've been in charge, but we should have won both of those games. Psychology plays a big part; the French mindset is, 'We can beat Wales now,' but we know we've got their number. From a confidence point of view, we were never frightened of France. We knew if we got certain things right, as we did for the majority of the game in 2020, we weren't far off where we needed to be.

Dan Biggar: Wayne didn't get enough credit for the way we played. We lost to France 29–25 and to England 33–30 in really entertaining games but we didn't get over the line as perhaps we would have done under Gats. Wayne put his stamp on how he wanted to play and we knew that things would definitely get better.

Wayne Pivac: I've always taken on jobs where there is work to be done, and you know that takes time; experience tells you that. When I got the Welsh job, things were nowhere near broken. They'd come off the back of sustained success with Warren and the last eighteen months had been very successful. But we felt that it was one thing to win a Six Nations or a Grand Slam, but to be successful in a global sense, we needed to be beating the southern hemisphere teams on a regular basis. Statistics will tell you that we don't have the best record against those sides.

Owen Watkin: Everything was new. There was a completely new structure, new moves, new everything. For a coach, that's difficult and the situation with Covid wouldn't have helped.

Wayne Pivac: When Covid hit, we were trying to add to our attack. The defence had been great, discipline had been great. The set piece was a bit wobbly, but the main focus was our attack. To be able to attack, you've got to have a strong base to work from, so we put a lot of work into our scrum and lineout in the first couple of campaigns.

Tomas Francis: The more times you run a pattern in training, the better you get. In club rugby, it's easy: you have eight weeks in pre-season to run a shape before going out and executing it. In internationals you have one week and you're into a game. So you could say they used the five weeks of the Autumn Nations Cup in 2020 as a kind of pre-season. 'This is how we're going to play.'

Dan Biggar: It takes a bit of time for the team to gel because we were so used to what was required of us in the game plan under Gats's regime, and we were all finding everything a little bit new and a little bit different.

Tomas Francis: Wayne quickly came to realise that you can't play the way him and Steve [Jones, backs coach] played at the Scarlets at international level. There was a realisation that you can't constantly throw the ball around, make risky breaks, or play off ten from your own forty-metre line, because there are too many opportunities to get turned over or find yourself on the end of a big shot. Jenks had a pivotal role in changing that mindset. He encouraged a balance between heads-up attacking rugby, and a more strategic kicking game that Gatland had favoured. We've now reached a point where we can transition between the two, and it's ultimately made us better as a team.

Wyn Jones: It was probably easier for the Scarlets boys to change and adapt, knowing Wayne and Steve as we do. For the rest of the boys, it took a bit of time to bed in.

Dan Biggar: We play a lot more through ten under Wayne and Steve than we did under Gats, and it takes time to adjust when you're slightly outside your comfort zone. Do I relish the fact that more of the play is now coming through the fly half? Yes and no. Even though I quite like taking command, and bossing a game, I also like to have a bit of time when I'm *not* fully in charge, if that makes sense; a bit of time to assess what else is on, to take a little bit of pressure off. Having the ball played through ten was something I had to get used to because it wasn't necessarily something I'd done a huge amount of. It was a case of finding out how tight I needed to stand to the rucks, how much extra time I needed, and how much flatter to the line I needed to be to bring people into play. During that first Six Nations, I felt like I attacked the line better than I'd done for quite a few years, but because we finished fifth maybe that wasn't shown up quite as well as I'd have liked.

The coronavirus pandemic brought the 2020 Six Nations to a premature end, meaning Wales's final game against Scotland was postponed until the autumn, where they sunk to a dispiriting defeat in a blustery, empty Parc y Scarlets. A week later, on the eve of the Autumn Nations Cup – a one-off tournament devised to keep the cash-strapped unions afloat – defence coach Byron Hayward was sacked. Three weeks earlier, Sam Warburton had stepped away from the Welsh coaching ticket, citing personal reasons. The optics didn't look good. The fifth-place finish in the Six Nations was Wales's worst since 2007, a challenging autumn fixture list was looming on the horizon and now two influential members of the coaching team had gone. The impression was very much of rats leaving a sinking ship. The real story, as if often the case, was more nuanced. Warburton had simply decided that coaching wasn't for him, and Hayward's departure was a hard-nosed business decision taken by a man who's never been afraid to make the big calls.

Wayne Pivac: It was the hardest thing I've ever had to do in rugby, without a doubt. You're dealing with careers, and you're dealing with people's livelihoods. That extends to the players as well. There are five match-day squads to be selected during a Six Nations, and if a player doesn't get in the match-day twenty-three he doesn't get the extra money. There were two guys in the 2021 Six Nations campaign – Jarrod Evans and Ryan Elias – who didn't achieve that, but when we make our selections we've got to put the team first and we always do. It's no different with a coaching decision. Byron is a very, very good coach – you don't become a bad coach overnight. He'd been very successful at club level, but his style, and the way he was operating just wasn't as effective with the national group.

Tomas Francis: I had nothing to do with Byron. My first week was his last, sadly. Melon [Gethin Jenkins] came in and changed the defence immediately. He brought that Shaun Edwards-esque physicality back. It's not particularly sophisticated; it's all about collision dominance. Attack is built on defence. You can have the best attack in the world, but if you don't get the defence right it doesn't matter. In the autumn it didn't fire, but in the Six Nations that followed, it did.

Wayne Pivac: Those Wales players had done things a certain way for a long period of time and been very successful. It wasn't about Byron's lack of knowledge or experience, it was more around delivery and getting the buy-in. Things like tone and body language. All those things are really important, more so at Test level than club level. So it wasn't knowledge-based, it was a decision around what was best for the team at the time, and it was certainly the most difficult thing I've had to do because I'd worked with Byron since I'd arrived in Wales. His was the first appointment I made at the Scarlets, and he's such a wonderful man, which made it even harder. The way he handled that conversation was admirable. He stepped aside, put the team first and I'll always respect him for that.

Melon had worked under Shaun for so long, I guess you see him as a bit of a Shaun disciple. That's all he has seen at Test level, and it's been pretty successful. Also, it's personalities. If you look at Gethin's personality, people may call him Mr Grumpy, but that also means he doesn't suffer fools easily. He's been there, done it, and he knows what it takes. Byron's style was more suited to the club environment where you've got a lot of young players – middle-management sort of guys who aren't Test players but are good club men – and your senior statesmen. He had to pitch it at a level where the weakest cog was, and that's usually at the younger guys. Unfortunately that didn't transfer into the national scene.

Wyn Jones: The autumn that followed wasn't the easiest of campaigns. We were told from the outset that it was to develop and try new combinations and try new people. It was tough though, especially with Covid and the bubble.

Owen Watkin: Mentally, I found it really draining because of Covid. We had to stay in camp through the week, meaning we were stuck in the Vale the whole time. I'd rather get away and see my family and forget about rugby for a night or two. That's what keeps me sane.

Wayne Pivac: We had to completely change our working practices and adapt to all the restrictions, from the medics that put in all the extra hours, to the S&C staff that had to operate in a different way than they were used to. There were limits to the number of people who could be in the gym at any one time for example, so our days became much longer. We had to learn to be very clever with our schedules and everybody played their part in that.

Wyn Jones: It was the first campaign where we were stuck in the Vale and couldn't do anything. There were no crowds, there was no atmosphere at the games, so it was a uniquely challenging campaign, but at the same time we were building towards the future, the next World Cup, and he did blood a lot of youngsters.

Wayne Pivac: We were always going to try things and involve new players in that tournament, but what gave us even more confidence to experiment was World Rugby's decision during the pandemic to freeze the world rankings where they were after the World Cup. That meant that regardless of results between then and the next World Cup, we knew we'd be seeded fourth. That gave us a lot more freedom to mix things up and experiment, and to worry less about winning those autumn games and climbing the rankings. It became all about taking the opportunity to further develop and build depth in the positions we thought were the weakest.

Dan Biggar: Wayne was quite specific in saying he wanted to use the autumn to develop some new players and a new style of play.

Wyn Jones: I think that campaign has probably underpinned a few campaigns moving forward. It gave some vital experience to a few young boys.

Wayne Pivac: We put in some young players; Louis Rees-Zammit, James Botham, Kieran Hardy, those sorts of guys we knew would be big players come 2023. We always knew we'd be judged on the 2021 Six Nations; that was part of the development plan we'd signed off with the WRU board, so we knew by the time that tournament rolled around we'd have to pick our strongest team and look to win every game. But in the autumn, we had that freedom to experiment.

Tomas Francis: Those were the foundations that the 2021 Six Nations was built on. Pivac always said that and no one believed him. He'd said from the start, 'I'm testing combinations, I'm looking at players, seeing what I've got.' If that meant discovering a few players, like a Sheedy or a Louis Rees-Zammit, then it's worth it, isn't it? There was no real prestige to the Autumn Nations Cup. It was just a warm-up to the Six Nations, really. I would say England got it wrong, because their priority was to keep on winning. They didn't care about their performance or the brand of rugby they were trying to develop. All that mattered to them was winning that tournament, whereas for us all that mattered was winning the Six Nations. That's what you're judged on in the northern hemisphere.

Wayne Pivac: Those experiences I'd had in the past, of building something, and understanding that it takes time, were invaluable. I was trying to use the media to get that message across to the fans, because understandably, our fans want victory every time we take to the field. It gives them something to look forward to, and it lifts productivity in the country when we win. You look at what rugby does to the country without a pandemic, and then you look at what everybody's had to deal with, with devastating effects in so many cases; families losing loved ones, businesses going down the drain, incomes taking a big hit. To be able to have success and give something back was a big driver for us.

Wales's forward platform during the Autumn Nations Cup was a serious cause for concern. An alarming amount of possession was lost due to a malfunctioning lineout, and the scrum was looking increasingly powder-puff.

Wayne Pivac: In New Zealand, you have Mike Cron, the scrum guru, who's been there for a couple of decades. All the scrum coaches in New Zealand work under him and his teachings, so when you come into a New Zealand campaign it's just a case of tweaking what you've already been doing. That's not the case here. We've got to get the guys in, they've got to change methods, and adapt to new techniques they're not always comfortable with. It takes time for these guys to develop the confidence to do that, and when they're under pressure they tend to revert to old habits.

Wyn Jones: It's just a case of fine tweaking, to be honest with you. It depends who you play with. I'm quite fortunate in that both Ken [Owens] and Ryan [Elias] are at the Scarlets with me so the hookers are pretty consistent. It's only Elliott [Dee] that's a bit different. For me, it's just about constantly talking to your back-rowers. You expect the same from every second row really: just to push, so it's quite straightforward from that point of view. I'd say we tweak from week to week anyway depending on who we're playing. Yeah, it's a little bit different everywhere, but I wouldn't say it's a massive issue. Sometimes you pick little things ups from other props, find out what they do with their region, and it makes you a better player.

Wayne Pivac: Also in the autumn when we trialled so many new players – eleven new caps I think it was – you're changing your hookers, you're changing your lineout callers, and changing your jumpers and your lifters. There are a lot of moving pieces that have to come together for a lineout to function at ninety per cent plus, as you'd want it to. We took it on the chin knowing that the chopping and changing we were doing to build depth wasn't giving us continuity in selection, and wasn't helping our game. If you look at the Scotland game that finished the 2020 Six Nations, we were all over the shop. The conditions weren't great, we didn't play well, and that transferred into the autumn performances.

The Autumn Nations Cup failed to fully capture the public's imagination. Fiji's participation was limited to one game in the final round after a Covid outbreak saw them confined to their team hotel for most of the month, and much of the rugby on show was turgid and unimaginative. Wales lost to both Ireland and England and stuttered to victory over Georgia before finishing with a slightly more convincing win over Italy. It was a forgettable contribution to a forgettable tournament.

Wayne Pivac: The start of the 2021 Six Nations signified a line in the sand. That was where we knew we had to deliver, where people would see what our identity was, and what our game actually looked like. That's where the consistency in selection bore fruit. The pack was more settled, and with the likes of Ken Owens back in the mix, things were a lot better, a lot smoother.

Owen Watkin: Because of the way it had gone in the autumn, everyone was pretty sceptical about the Six Nations, but the majority of boys there had been there during the 2019 Grand Slam campaign. We trusted each other and knew that something good could happen. Despite the results, we knew there was a good rugby team in there somewhere.

On the Wednesday before Wales's tournament opener against Ireland, it emerged that Josh Adams had broken strict Covid protocols to attend a 'gender-reveal' party for his unborn child. In order for the Six Nations to proceed, the players had all agreed to form Covid-secure bubbles and as draconian as this may sound to future generations, breaking these protocols could easily have resulted in the tournament collapsing in on itself. The winger, Wales's most potent attacking weapon and a player they could ill afford to lose, was issued with a two-match ban. Liam Williams' suspension for a red card offence while playing for the Scarlets over the festive period meant Pivac was without two of his first-choice back three.

Wayne Pivac: The talk was one week or two, and it was an internal choice to go two weeks; it wasn't the WRU's decision, it was the coaching team's. Nugget [Martyn Williams] and myself discussed it, and we notified the others as to what we wanted to do.

Owen Watkin: At that time, it was literally the law, wasn't it, so it was hard to not punish someone who'd broken the rules.

Wayne Pivac: We felt that so much time and energy had been put in by so many people to allow the tournament to go ahead. Literally *hundreds* of hours on researching Covid and what we could and couldn't do just to get rugby back on the park, so we felt we needed to send out a strong message and we were prepared to take that pain. Josh put his hand up straight away, admitting he'd done something wrong and had put himself ahead of the team. In our group the team always comes first.

Tomas Francis: It was tough on Josh, but he knew he'd broken the rules and had to take it on the chin.

Wayne Pivac: There are plenty of coaches who'd have a rule for one, and a rule for another, but I've always believed you'll get the respect of the players if you treat them all equally. On that occasion it didn't matter if it was Josh or the youngest player in the group; they were going to be sanctioned, and we were going to send out a strong message because there was so much at stake. If we'd had games called off, if he'd brought something back in to the camp and it had spread to another squad, the consequences could have been devastating. We were very mindful of how we could negatively influence the tournament like that, and we didn't want to be the ones at fault. We were comfortable punishing Josh, and he took it well. He was sent home that night, we notified the team of our decision, and cracked on.

Callum Sheedy: Everyone had written us off, were saying we'd be in a battle for the wooden spoon, so to come out the way we did and get that early win against Ireland was massive. Then we pushed on week by week, chipping away, and chipping away and before we knew it, we had a Grand Slam decider against France. It was a crazy few weeks for me personally, but as a team I think we really showed the bite and the passion that comes with being a Welshman and being a Welsh rugby player.

Wayne Pivac: Going into the Ireland game, we felt we were in a great position because we'd done a lot of work behind the scenes and knew where we were at. The Irish were pretty cock-a-hoop in terms of the media and the ex-players that were being interviewed. They were all predicting a handsome victory for their boys, and we didn't get given a show at the start of the series.

Callum Sheedy: Even in the autumn you could see we weren't a million miles away from clicking. Results didn't go our way, it was scrappy at times, and we weren't putting in eighty-minute performances, but on the training pitch you could see things were beginning to gel. The five or six weeks we'd had together in the autumn were invaluable in terms of getting rid of the cobwebs, and understanding Wayne's philosophy. There was an underlying feeling that when things eventually clicked we were going to hammer someone. It didn't happen in the autumn for whatever reason, but none of us came into that Six Nations thinking, 'Oh God, this is going to be a long campaign.' We were all super confident and knew if we got it right we could beat anyone.

Wayne Pivac: There wasn't a lot of expectation on our shoulders, and there were no crowds, so it was just us against them. Twenty-three on twenty-three. We went in confident of our ability, but not overconfident.

Callum Sheedy: My dad's Irish and just because I'm Welsh and I've played for Wales doesn't mean I'll forget my Irish heritage. I've still very proud of my Irish links, but for me it was always Wales. You can tell by my accent; I'm Cardiff through and through, and it's a tough one because when there was chat in previous years about where my loyalties lay [Sheedy was also eligible for England and appeared for them in an uncapped international against the Barbarians in 2019], I didn't want to be the guy perceived as coming out and sticking two fingers up to a particular nation because I would never disrespect any country in that way. Deep down though, I knew when Wayne rang me that it was Wales, because my heart was going at a million miles an hour and I was almost crying. It's always been red for me. My first cap in the autumn had been against Ireland too, and that was out in Dublin. I spoke to my mum afterwards and she told me it was the first time in Dad's life he'd wanted Wales to beat Ireland. It was the same story in the Six Nations, so I think we've converted him. They were both so proud; it was just a shame they couldn't be in the stadiums to see those games, but fingers crossed there will be a time in the near future when they can.

Dan Biggar: Expectations weren't that high on the outside but we were quietly confident, especially as our first game was at home. All that matters in the Six Nations is winning. Scotland finished fourth and they can say that they'd have won the Championship if they'd conceded six fewer points or scored six more points, but that doesn't win you anything. In the Six Nations, you're solely judged on whether you've won a game or whether you've lost a game, and for us we got off to the best possible start in terms of winning at home.

Wayne Pivac: We knew we were ahead of the page in terms of what other people had seen, so the red card was almost irrelevant to me. People like to frame it retrospectively as the turning point, but we were already doing really well in the game. The score might only have been 6–0, but we felt we were building into it quite nicely.

Thirteen minutes in the Ireland flanker, Peter O'Mahony, led with his elbow as he flew into a ruck, clattering the unfortunate Tomas Francis in the face.

Callum Sheedy: I was on the bench and I thought, 'Jeez, that's a big clear out.' When it's happening in front of you at 100mph you don't actually see where the shoulder's hit, but when you see it slowed down on the big screen there couldn't have been any argument. He charged in with force, with a shoulder to the head. When those challenges are being clamped down on as much as they are, if you're even a millimetre above head height, you're going to have to walk.

Tomas Francis: Nigel Owens had come into camp to speak to us before the tournament, and he'd said that English refs won't look at head collisions as much as they should. They'll try to push it off as a 'rugby incident'. He told us to make sure we stayed down if we got hit in the head, so they'd at least come back to have a look at it.

Wyn Jones: I didn't see it happen in real time, but I looked up at the big screen and saw Franny get hit, and it immediately looked bad. It was probably just a bit reckless, especially as we'd all been warned before the tournament about how strictly any head contact was going to be refereed.

Tomas Francis: I got stepped by Josh van der Flier and ended up on the wrong side and as I tried to get back to my feet, Jonny Sexton piled me back into the ruck. When I tried to roll out again, O'Mahony just came straight at me with a cocked elbow to the face.

Wyn Jones: As a player, if you're a bit late arriving to clean out and you see someone there you just panic and try to hit him. He was probably a bit unfortunate to have caught Franny on the head but it was a definite red card.

Owen Watkin: If you touch someone's head with any kind of force these days, it's going to be a red.

Tomas Francis: I looked at Barnsey [referee, Wayne Barnes] and said, 'Come on, that's ridiculous,' and he just said, 'Fair clean out.' At that point I was like, 'Fine, I'll just stay down for a second because that's not fair game to me.' It was a cheap shot. I wasn't jackalling, or trying to slow the ball down, I was literally just trying to get out. I'd made my tackle, and just wanted to get out of the ruck and get back into the game. O'Mahony had done exactly the same thing a few weeks earlier playing for Munster so he had a bit of form for it.

Wayne Pivac: Red cards can change things and not always to the detriment of the offending side. Leading into half-time, I think there was maybe a mental lapse of five per cent, a little lapse on concentration; a feeling perhaps that we had the result wrapped up, which at any level of the game can be dangerous. I thought back to the Scarlets-Leinster match [in 2017] at the RDS when Steff Evans got sent off in the thirty-eighth minute, and we went on to win the second half 6–5. As a coaching group we'd had first-hand experience of winning a big game with fourteen men, so we knew Ireland were still a dangerous opponent. We just had to reset things at half-time, and make sure we didn't stop playing.

Callum Sheedy: If anything, it rejuvenated them. They played better with fourteen men. Jonny Sexton really tried to control that ship, and they put us under a lot of pressure. We needed that half-time whistle to come, so we could regroup and discuss what we needed to work on.

Tomas Francis: Until the sending off, we were by miles the better team. The red card flipped the momentum in their favour.

Wayne Pivac: We felt that whether they had fifteen or fourteen players on the field, Ireland would still play a certain type of way and that wasn't going to change. They just kept on doing what they do; pinging you in the corners, looking to build pressure and either get their drive going or force penalties. They get in to your twenty-two and grind you down, and it's very hard to stop. For us it was about controlling some possession. I think we'd given away something like five penalties on the trot from 6–0 up to 6–13 down, so we emphasised the need to get our discipline back and impose ourselves on them.

Callum Sheedy: All credit to the boys. We came out and scored a couple of quick tries and put ourselves right back in control.

Eight minutes into the second half, Wales finally took advantage of the extra man. Turning the ball over near the Irish twenty-two, Wales snapped into attack mode, recycling efficiently before Josh Navidi offloaded brilliantly to George North. The barnstorming winger – wearing the thirteen jersey on this occasion – did the rest, sucking in the defence with a deft show-and-go, before accelerating swiftly to the line.

Wayne Pivac: I've always thought he was a big, powerful man who might benefit from a move infield. With midfielders these days, it's about having a power game as well as having the silky skills; you've got to be able to bring both elements to the game. George can do that hard close-contact work, but he's also got footwork and an ability to offload. Our plan in the autumn had been to more work on his skills, and give him a bit of time in the saddle at centre, but unfortunately he wasn't getting opportunities at thirteen with his club. There was a point where he got a red card for the Ospreys, which had ruled him out of a few games at the start of the season. As a result, he didn't play well in the autumn, so we sent him back to his club. We had a good long conversation in my room before sending him back where we discussed what he needed to do. It was all framed as a positive; he'd come into camp in the autumn undercooked, and just needed to go back to his club and sharpen up. George is a confidence player, and I'm convinced that that was a turning point for him. He knew he hadn't been dropped as such; he'd just come in unprepared, knowing he wasn't quite ready, and it was showing up in games. Fair play to him, he did all the hard work, and came back looking much sharper. As Foxy was sidelined with injury, we made the decision that he should start against Ireland at thirteen. There was an opening for him and he took it with both hands.

Ten minutes later, Wales struck again. With advantage being played, the ball was fizzed across the backline with North and Halfpenny showcasing their slick passing game to get the ball to Louis Rees-Zammit, who executed an audacious, acrobatic finish in the corner.

Wyn Jones: Sometimes a bit of luck comes into it, doesn't it? When you get those chances, you've got to take them. To be fair to both of them [North and Rees-Zammit], they took them and we ended up winning. On another day, the bounce of the ball or a fumble might have changed things and it could have been a very different story.

Wayne Pivac: To go from 6–13 down, to 21–16 was encouraging. We played pretty well.

Wyn Jones: We'd run that pattern for six weeks in the autumn and the boys had had more time to think about it over Christmas. By the time the Six Nations rolled around, we knew the pattern a bit better, and it was easier to execute than it had been in the autumn. It probably helped that we were back in the Principality Stadium by then, and that the weather was definitely better. People who'd criticised our performances in the autumn had probably forgotten how dreadful the weather had been at Parc y Scarlets. It was wet and cold, and windy which had stopped us from really throwing the ball about.

Whether or not the red card was a major factor in the outcome remains a matter of conjecture, but two incidents in injury time certainly helped Wales's cause. The first was a heroic diving tackle by Justin Tipuric on Garry Ringrose, the second was an overcooked touch finder from Billy Burns. With four minutes of injury time played, Ireland had an opportunity to put the ball deep into Welsh territory and launch one final assault.

Callum Sheedy: It was really tough on Billy Burns when he put the last kick dead but these things happen. Billy had to chase the five-metre line for that kick, and I know what it's like for tens. Sometimes they go your way and sometimes they go the other side of the flag. If it had landed the other side of the five-metre line he'd have been the hero. We rode our luck there, but we'll take it and we definitely needed that victory to set us on our way. I played against Billy Burns a lot over the years when he was at Gloucester and he's a really nice guy. Whenever something like that happens to a fellow ten, you put yourself in their shoes. In the last minute, you've got to go for the five and if you don't catch it perfectly it's game over. Listen, I'm grateful it happened because we got the win, but I would never wish for a game to end like that and I do sympathise massively with him.

Dan Biggar: Was it a complete performance? Absolutely not. Was it riveting to watch? No. It was a bit similar to what we produced under Gats to some degree. We rolled our sleeves up, defended for long periods, scored points when we needed to and came away with a win. If your team wins on the opening weekend, you get a bit of confidence and it often leads to a snowball effect.

Wayne Pivac: A lot was made retrospectively of the red card, but we just banked those points, focused on a six-day turnaround and moved on. I think it's the first time in the modern era we'd had a six-day turnaround going into an away game.

It wasn't just the short turnaround coupled with an away trip that Wales had to contend with. Pivac's side had suffered a litany of injuries during what had been a bruising encounter, and had to completely rethink the composition of their midfield.

Wayne Pivac: It had been a very attritional game against Ireland. We lost Dan Lydiate within minutes after he did his ACL. Josh Navidi replaced him, but then he was ruled out with a neck injury, so we lost both our sixes in the same game. Midfield was our biggest concern. Johnny Williams and George North were both casualties of the Ireland game, and Foxy was already injured.

Willis Halaholo: We'd done backs units at the Blues in the morning and were in the middle of running some strike plays when Dai Young came onto the field. Dai hardly ever comes onto the field, so I suspected something was up. He walked right in and called my name. I genuinely thought I was in trouble. It felt like I was getting arrested. I thought there must have been a complaint about something I'd done, but he pulled me over and said, 'You've got to stop training. You've been called into Wales camp. Go and get changed, get tested, and off you go.' It was all a bit of a shock.

Owen Watkin: After that Ireland game, the boys were absolutely battered. We'd gone home on the Sunday, and when I woke up on the Monday, my girlfriend had a sore throat. I was paranoid it was Covid and rang to say I didn't want to come in just in case. They were worried because Johnny and George were both injured, and Foxy was still sidelined. They only had me and Nick [Tompkins] fit, so that's when they called Willis in. I took my girlfriend for a test, and did one myself from the car. Thankfully they were both negative, but it meant I didn't go into camp until the Tuesday evening. I didn't train on Monday or Tuesday, did just a little bit on Thursday and then a walk-through on the Friday. Considering it was a new group with quite a few changes from the Ireland game, we barely had any preparation at all.

Wyn Jones: We didn't have many boys training that week. It had been a physical one against Ireland. A lot of the boys were just lying around on the physio beds and icing up. There were a lot of walking wounded, and a few of the boys in the backline didn't recover in time. Lyds obviously hurt his knee and he was out for the whole tournament.

Wayne Pivac: It was about modifying our training week and having more walk-throughs and light sessions, about getting things right mentally as well as physically.

Wyn Jones: That six-day turnaround with travel was tough, but we knew if we beat Scotland away, it would set us up nicely for the run-in. It was just one of those weeks you had to get through knowing there was a fallow week after and a bit of time to reset. Just put your head down and get through it.

Wayne Pivac: Those first two weeks were critical to us. We *had* to win those if we had any chance. To get the four points against Ireland was great, box ticked. To get the result against Scotland was always going to be tough with the injuries, the Josh Adams suspension, the travel and the turnaround time.

Tomas Francis: We'd never done that before and you could see that in the first half. The legs just weren't there.

Owen Watkin: Despite the lack of preparation, I wasn't nervous; more excitable if anything. I like to relax and enjoy it. My attitude is always that I've worked hard my whole life for this, so why stress and get nervous? I was looking forward to proving a point. I desperately wanted to play against England in the next round, and this was my chance to show I was ready for it.

Callum Sheedy: We travelled to Murrayfield the day before and it was all snow blizzards and traffic chaos.

Wayne Pivac: There was snow coming down in the warm-up, and it was bitterly cold.

Wyn Jones: I'm sure on the day of the game the weather cleared, and it actually turned out quite nice, meaning we could throw the ball about a bit. Scotland want to play a lot more now under Gregor Townsend, and it was end-to-end stuff. It was probably an exciting game to watch, but it was definitely a difficult one to play in. As a front rower it was, anyway.

It proved to be an absolute classic for the fans. A heart-stopping, lung-busting thriller of a contest that held the attention until the final, dramatic moments. After an opening quarter of an hour in which neither side seized the advantage, Scotland sparked into life. Ali Price, a continuous threat at the base, created their first try, chipping over the Welsh defence for Darcy Graham to gather and score. Their second came from a brilliantly worked move off the back of a scrum, which led to a chip-and-chase for captain, Stuart Hogg. In the space of ten minutes, Scotland had opened up a 17–3 lead and the entire complexion of the game had changed.

Kieran Hardy: It's easier being on the bench in those scenarios. If you're on the field you tend to get frustrated and confused and you tend to overdo things. On the bench you've got a much clearer focus; you see the game with much more clarity.

Willis Halaholo: I was expecting to get about ten to fifteen minutes off the bench, but the unexpected happened; Pens had to go off with a concussion, and I got on quite early. We were 17–3 down at that point, but I wasn't panicking. There was plenty of time on the clock. The boys were playing some good rugby. I knew I'd be able to go on and create moments; that's probably my point of difference: my feet, my vision and all that, so I was just thinking, 'Go on and play your game.' When I got on the field it was almost like I was having fun out there.

Kieran Hardy: We just needed to be more accurate. There wasn't any need to panic.

Willis Halaholo: I relish the big stages and the big occasions which can be a weakness of mine. I'll often slack off a bit if I'm not playing the big teams, but when the bright lights are on, I tend to step up and embrace the challenge. Although it was my first international, I'd been around the block, and at the age of thirty I had a good bit of experience under my belt. The intensity levels may have been a bit higher, but ultimately rugby's rugby and that's how I express myself. I came on on thirty-two minutes, so there were a solid forty-eight minutes left to create some stuff and turn things around.

As half-time approached, things did indeed begin to turn around. As Wales applied pressure near the Scotland line, the ball was spread wide, Nick Tompkins pirouetted, offloading basketball-style to Liam Williams whose final pass fizzed across the defensive wall and into the hands of Louis Rees-Zammit. It was a crucial score, keeping Wales in touch at the interval.

Callum Sheedy: About forty-eight minutes in, I got the message to warm up because I might be going on soon. You kind of think, 'Yeah right, they're just trying to keep you warm, whatever,' but then they said to me and Kieran Hardy, 'Strip off, you're going on.' We were like, 'Jeez, okay.' To be honest, the game was a bit of a blur at the time. I've watched it back since and it was amazing, we threw the shackles off, and started playing some expansive rugby.

Wayne Pivac: Changing the half-backs wasn't preordained. No, we were talking as a group at half-time, and we agreed that class players sometimes have games where it doesn't go their way. Sometimes coaches will leave them on the field because they're their number ones or they're Lions, they're this, they're that, but we wanted to win the Championship, and at 17–3 that game was slipping away from us. We were talking about changes that we might make, and what saved us from doing it at half-time was the try just before the whistle. Sometimes a player doesn't need to be told they've underperformed. Often they just need a bit of a *cwtch* and to be told, 'Flush that, get back on the horse and away we go.' We decided to give them [Gareth Davies and Dan Biggar] ten minutes after half-time. They were given directives as to where we wanted to be on the park and how we were going to achieve that, but the nine and ten axis just wasn't delivering it. I think you saw a Gareth Davies pass back to Nick Tompkins which was the wrong pass to make, the wrong decision, and it showed that there was a lack of communication. After that it was just: 'Got to be done, bang.'

Dan Biggar: I'm always open and honest, and it wasn't one of my best days in a Wales shirt. I found it a bit of a struggle. Sometimes it just happens that way. You can't be free-flowing and brilliant all the time.

Wayne Pivac: It was one of those occasions when myself, Steve and Melon were all on the same page at the same time. We had to do it. Sometimes if I get told 'we should wait a minute', I might hold on and reconsider, or I still might think, 'Bugger it, we're doing it', but that day all three of us were in agreement. We didn't wait the extra two minutes, we just thought, *do it.*

Kieran Hardy: I could see it from both sides. I've obviously been in the situation those boys [Gareth Davies and Dan Biggar] were in, when you feel like you can't get a foothold in the game, and things just aren't going your way. When it goes like that, the half-backs are always the ones who get the blame, so I sympathised with them, but from a personal perspective it was my first game in the Six Nations and I wanted to prove that I belonged on that field. I was third choice coming into the campaign, but I saw this as my opportunity to jump above the others.

Dan Biggar: There were no issues on my part about being taken off. I think it was the right call at the time. You know when you're playing well and you know when you're fighting things a little bit.

Wayne Pivac: Biggsy had taken a couple of knocks, and he's the type of player who's so physical that he'll sometimes be playing at seventy/eighty per cent because of the hits he's taken. He's a tough cookie, so he'll always play through it.

Tomas Francis: Biggsy's a warrior. Even when he's behind a pack going backwards he's still a world class ten.

Wayne Pivac: Those were big decisions at the time and we were so pleased it worked out, because a young Dan Biggar once got a chance in a big game at some stage. Kieran Hardy did really well; his box kicking, his communication, and his game management all went well, as did his partnership with Callum. It had been going well in training, so we knew they'd developed a good understanding.

Kieran Hardy: Callum and I had been watching the game together in the stand and we'd been chatting about what we'd need to do to get us back into it. We felt that if we kept the ball for long periods, we'd be able to cause Scotland problems, but we needed to play in the right areas to be able to do that. Initially when we came on, we just spoke about territory, bringing in our kicking game, and maybe going to the air a bit more. Then as soon as we got in their half, we were clinical. We scored two tries pretty quickly.

Tomas Francis: It was the right decision by the coaches. One hundred per cent. The first half hadn't gone great, and they just added a bit of tempo. It was a combination of things that turned the tide: our maul started functioning, which opened up some space, and we had two attack-minded half-backs who could play the moves off it. You give Sheedy and Kizza front-foot ball and they're some of the best half-backs out there. Those two were on fire that day.

The decision bore fruit almost immediately, as the re-jigged backline found the keys to unlock Scotland's increasingly stubborn defence. A well-orchestrated rolling maul saw Wales advance to within ten metres, before Hardy released the ball to Halaholo. Sheedy ran a loop around before taking and giving to Rees-Zammit, who punctured the defensive line, creating the space for Liam Williams to trundle in. At 17–15, Wales were right back in it.

Willis Halaholo: Sheedy and I worked well together; we both have that attacking instinct. I've been playing outside Jarrod Evans for years, who's a very similar sort of player, so it was pretty natural to feed off everything and be ready to go, because guys like that are willing to attack from anywhere.

Callum Sheedy: I get to play alongside the likes of Charles Piatau, Semi Radradra, John Afoa, Stephen Luatua, and Luke Morahan every week at Bristol. These guys would all be in a World XV and I'm fortunate enough that I can run the game around them week-in week-out. It really gives you confidence and self-belief, and because of that, I didn't feel overly intimidated stepping up to Test level. During the autumn, I automatically felt like part of the group, and although Alun Wyn Jones, Jonathan Davies and Liam Williams were like heroes to me, when you're in that bubble together, you just feel like they're your mates. When I came on against Scotland I wasn't thinking, 'I can't tell Al this because he's going to shout at me,' because he makes you feel so comfortable. If I want to be making the big calls as a ten, he backs me one hundred per cent. There are no egos in that squad and as a youngish fly-half, the way they all supported me gave me a huge amount of confidence.

Kieran Hardy: There was a sense then that we were on the front foot and they were easing off a little bit. The confidence surged through the team after we scored that try. I remember speaking to the boys on the ten-metre line while Callum was taking the conversion and saying the next part of the game was to rebuild, get the pressure back on them, and repeat the process.

The fifty-third minute brought arguably the game's most decisive moment as, for the second week running, Wales's opponents saw red. Zander Fagerson was the transgressor this time, his shoulder smashing clumsily into Wyn Jones's head at a ruck.

Callum Sheedy: I don't think it was as clear cut as the O'Mahony one but, letter of the law, it's still a red. Two years before, it wouldn't have been; it would have just been a penalty, but the way they're clamping down on it now, if you're even slightly high, you're running a risk.

Willis Halaholo: I don't get into looking at decisions after the event. That's what refs are paid for. If that's what they saw, that's what they saw. I've never looked at any replays of it. Even during the game, I won't look up at the big screen. I just focus on what I've got to do.

The decision was greeted with derision by certain sections of the Scottish media, many of whom considered it harsh. Zander Fagerson's brother Matt didn't mince his words a month later on the Rugby World podcast, accusing Wyn Jones of gamesmanship by rolling around on the floor and trying to influence the referee.

Wyn Jones: It hurt, I can tell you that much, so any reaction was genuine. He caught me square on top of the head, so I did feel it, but I couldn't stay down too long because my mates from Llandovery would get stuck into me and I'd never hear the end of it. He basically missed the jump on the clear out and had to make up time. He couldn't really pick where he was going to hit because he was a bit late. It's just one of those things that happens, but it did help us out a bit, aye.

Tomas Francis: I didn't think that was a red, if I'm honest. How else are you supposed to clear out? Wyn was trying to jackal for the ball, he'd put his head in there. I understand the importance of player safety, but that seemed like an overreaction to me.

Wyn Jones: He was unfortunate in that Stuart Hogg had half got me out, and I'd got a bit higher when he came in and hit me. You can't get away with anything now, though. There are cameras everywhere and with any contact to the head, you're running a risk.

Kieran Hardy: I wouldn't say that he went in to deliberately hurt Wyn, but it was a bit reckless, and the ref was left with no option. It was a big turning point for us. In the Ireland game, Peter O'Mahony had gone in with a clear intent; he knew what he was doing, whereas Zander Fagerson's intention was to clean out. Wyn just happened to stand up at the wrong time and he caught him in the face.

Tomas Francis: The entry point for bans is so high now. It used to be clear cut: someone would take someone's head off. Some Samoan would fly straight out of the line with a shoulder to the head and that would be an obvious red card. They're the ones they're trying to stop, but these 'rugby incidents' are frustrating and they're ruining good games. It's like being a boxer; when you sign up to being a professional rugby player, you sign up for that life, you sign up for that risk.

Wyn Jones rubbed further salt into the wound by burrowing over the try line two minutes later to put Wales into the lead, but Scotland – who'd opened their campaign with a statement victory over England – weren't about to roll over. Within ten minutes Stuart Hogg had conjured a bit of magic to weave between Owen Watkin and Nick Tompkins and reclaim the lead.

Owen Watkin: I missed that tackle on Stuart Hogg, but the majority of rugby players would have missed him one-on-one five yards from the line, so I wasn't too disheartened. Without being cocky, I don't miss too many tackles and he's probably the best full back in the world. That was my only disappointing moment. Apart from that I thought I played well.

Callum Sheedy: We'd built a bit of momentum in the last thirty minutes and despite Hogg's try, we almost felt unstoppable. Rees-Zammit's second try down the wing was incredible.

Kieran Hardy: It was a ridiculous try. Such a big play from such a young kid. For him to stand up and seize the moment like that was outstanding. He had no right to do what he did, but he's one of those players who can make something happen at any given time.

Wyn Jones: His pace is something else. Once he kicked that ball I think he overtook four Scottish players to get there. He made it look effortless. Sometimes when you're inside him in the defensive line, you're thinking, 'God, he's giving this bloke a lot of room,' and then he shuts him down so quick. That's when you realise how fast he is. He doesn't seem to be trying but he's *flying about* the place. He's got something special about him.

Wayne Pivac: All the clips people had seen of him scoring tries for Gloucester were wonderful, but when we first brought him in for training during the 2019 Six Nations, he was so unfit. He just couldn't repeat the speeds, so he'd have one big moment, and then you wouldn't see him for another ten or fifteen minutes. He wasn't doing the work off the ball that you'd expect from a Test-class winger. He wasn't the greatest under the high ball, and defensively he wasn't the most accomplished, but he had these *moments*, which everybody saw. We brought him into the environment to see him up close and when we did some testing, he was the poorest by a long shot. He was way off the pace. In terms of the outside backs, he was embarrassed. We sat him down for a chat, and to his credit he went away and thought about it. He was naturally disappointed not to get any game time in that campaign, but we told him, 'You're just not ready.' He worked really hard back at his club and when he came into the next camp in the autumn, he showed glimpses that he was ready to go. Again fate came into it: Foxy got injured and against Georgia, the young fella got his chance. We knew he was going to sink or swim, and of course he swam, didn't he? Very, very well.

Dan Biggar: He's just got that ridiculous raw pace, hasn't he?

Callum Sheedy: It looks like he's jogging but he's absolutely flying. I don't know whether he's got a sprinter's background or he's just naturally a genetic freak, but it always looks so bloody effortless.

Tomas Francis: He's got the confidence to do it, and the ability and pace to pull it off. That try got him on the Lions tour, I'm sure of it. He out-chased Stuart Hogg to a loose ball. Not many people can do that, so fair play to him.

Callum Sheedy: It's embarrassing when you're next to him, and your head's bobbling everywhere while you're trying to keep up, and he's just gliding smoothly across the turf. I'm very jealous because one thing you can't defend is speed and he has that in abundance.

Dan Biggar: He's an excellent rugby player, there's no doubt about that, and he's not short on confidence either, which is great to see. You could swear he's got about fifty caps already, the way he is around the place.

Tomas Francis: He saved our bacon at that point.

Willis Halaholo: There's no use having that freakish speed if you're not going to use it. My job as a centre is to draw in defenders and create space for our speedsters to finish. We do it at the Blues all the time. Our outside backs are always scoring for fun because of all the hard work we do on the inside. That's one of my best attributes; seeing shapes, creating space and letting the speedsters do the rest.

Dan Biggar: He's a good boy, fair play, a natural finisher.

Callum Sheedy: He's got it all, hasn't he? He's quick, he's tall, he's good looking, he's a British and Irish Lion. But he's a good lad and that's what makes him as good as he is; he always wants to learn and no matter how much people are blowing smoke up his backside, he stays humble. He's always doing extras with Jenks on his kicking, and working with Sanjay on his high balls.

Dan Biggar: We had a casino night after the Scotland game in which he'd announced himself to the world as the golden boy of Welsh rugby. We were on the roulette table, and I'd had a decent run. It reached a point where we were the last two there, so I said, 'Shall we just go red or black for the final winnings rather than split it fifty/fifty?' I should have known that there was no way the golden boy of Welsh rugby, who's on the run of his life, was going to come out

PLAYING RUGBY FOR WALES

on the losing end of that, and true enough he cleaned up. I walked away with nothing.

Kieran Hardy: He just couldn't do *anything* wrong in that campaign. I think everyone was sick of him by the end of it! Whatever he did, he did really well. Everything seems to come pretty easily to him.

Tomas Francis: When your luck's in, your luck's in.

Dan Biggar: I saw him a few months later when Northampton were playing Gloucester, not long after the Lions squad had been announced. A few of the Gloucester boys were talking the piss, saying he'd 'completed' rugby at the age of 20. It's pretty depressing for the rest of us.

The drama wasn't quite over. With the clock in the red, Scotland roused themselves for a last desperate siege, rolling a maul ten metres over the half-way line before releasing the ball to a jinking Finn Russell. Like a slippery eel, he managed to evade the tackle of Owen Watkin and offload to Duhan van der Merwe on the right. With acres of space in front of him, and just one defender to beat, the South African-born winger looked odds on to score a dramatic winner.

Callum Sheedy: During the last ten minutes we'd been feeling really comfortable, but we were only a point ahead, and when Finn Russell and Stuart Hogg are on the field anything can happen.

Owen Watkin: When Finn Russell chucked it out the back door, I remember panicking and thinking, 'Oh fuck, I better run by here.' When I'm chasing back in defence I feel like I can run faster than when I'm trying to go around someone, so I got motoring, but after the first five yards, I remember thinking, 'I'm not going to be able to tackle him here.' He thought he'd got round me because he stepped back in a bit, didn't he?

Callum Sheedy: Ows' tackle there was massive. I thought van der Merwe was in, and was thinking, 'Noooo!' when Ows came out of nowhere. His arm extended about ten metres outside of its socket, and he managed to clip his ankle.

Owen Watkin: I just thought, 'You're not going to chase him down, so just hit his ankle as hard as you can.' I dived and hit it, and thankfully he went down. It showed I had a bit of grit in me, that I was willing to keep going until the end. My tank was empty by then, mind. I winded myself as I went down.

Callum Sheedy: It's easy to remember the worldie try that Zammo scored, and maybe that ankle tap won't be remembered in years to come, but those of us who saw it will definitely remember it, and I'm sure Ows will keep reminding people about it.

Kieran Hardy: It's a moment that's probably been forgotten, but make no bones about it, that tackle absolutely saved the game for us. It was perfectly executed, and Owen deserves a lot of credit.

Willis Halaholo: A lot of people were talking about the red card afterwards, making out we'd been lucky, but we had England next and that's where my focus was. I just wanted to flush that game and get on with it.

Wayne Pivac: A lot was made of 'lucky Wales', but what about the guys that know the laws, and the coaches that focus on eliminating dangerous play from your game?

Callum Sheedy: We were well-disciplined all tournament apart from the last twenty minutes against France, so it's not our fault if teams are going to fly recklessly in to contact and get red cards. We can't control that. We can only control what we can control. At times it's harder to play against fourteen men. It gives you an extra ten per cent when your backs are against the wall, and you need to come out and fight.

Wayne Pivac: I didn't see any of our players going in recklessly because we made it a real point of focus. Week after week, we drew the players' attention to the red cards that were being issued and said, 'This is not us, we can't afford to do this.' Discipline is everything.

Wyn Jones: We trained tackle heights and ruck entries all the time, and knew if we could keep fifteen on the field we had a better chance of winning games. That was definitely a focus of ours and Wayne was driving that. It probably paid off by the end of the tournament.

Owen Watkin: Melon drilled it into us; if you get a yellow or red card, you're letting the boys down.

Dan Biggar: This narrative developed that Wales could only win games if they had a member of the opposition sent off, and a fair few people jumped on the bandwagon saying we'd been lucky. I couldn't really have cared less if I'm honest. It was amusing more than anything. You know, I probably want to say something a bit different which you couldn't put in the book.

Wyn Jones: That was always going to be the case when you've had two red cards against you in the first two games. You don't tend to read too much online stuff as a player. You're aware of it and you get asked about it in interviews and stuff, but it's ultimately something that's out of your hands.

Dan Biggar: Some of the players that were coming out and saying it, considering the lack of success they'd had, we thought it was a bit of a cheek to be honest. They had the audacity to question our credentials when we'd been consistently successful for years.

Owen Watkin: It didn't bother me in the slightest. We still won, didn't we? It's their fault for doing it.

Kieran Hardy: You can't control what the opposition do. In international rugby, you find a way to win games. It doesn't matter *how* you do it.

Wayne Pivac: Scotland were coming off their win over England, and we'd gone through a tough game against Ireland where both teams had been battered. Look at it in context, and we thoroughly deserved our win. We'd recovered from 17–3 down, and got back to 17–15 when it was still fifteen on fifteen. Things were going our way before the red card happened.

Dan Biggar: We all had a good laugh about it. In twenty years' time when I look back at my Six Nations medals, I'm not going to think, 'Do you know what, Ireland and Scotland had a man sent off so I'll throw that one in the bin.' I'm going to look back at all those medals and think there aren't going to be too many players who've won more of them than me. We kept *our* discipline, we were disciplined throughout the tournament, and we got the rewards from that in the end.

Wayne Pivac: We knew we were building nicely, so we were quite happy with that 'lucky Wales' narrative. We were quite happy for England to think 'same old Wales, they've just had a bit of luck'. It allowed us to stay under the radar.

Dan Biggar: In the opening two games, we didn't play anywhere near how we'd wanted to in terms of performance levels, but we won both those games and, all of a sudden, we were sitting on top of the table alongside France. We had plenty of stuff to work on ahead of the England game, but we were unbeaten, and that's all that mattered.

Kieran Hardy: We probably didn't deserve to win the Scotland game, particularly if you look at the first forty-five minutes, but our luck was in, and we did what we needed to do to get over the line.

Willis Halaholo: I hadn't even been in camp a week and was still in a whirlwind, but you could feel the good vibe among the boys ahead of England. We'd bagged two wins on the bounce, and you could feel something was brewing. It was one of those weeks where you could really feel the intensity and vibes in training. We were ready to pull off a big one.

Kieran Hardy: I found out I was starting against England about ten minutes before our backs unit session on the Castle pitch at the Vale. Given Gareth's [Davies] experience and it being a big game against England, I'd expected him to start so it was a genuine shock. Wayne spoke to me afterwards and said he was looking for the same sort of performance I'd put in against Scotland. He said, 'No pressure, just enjoy it and do what you do.' I was over the moon and couldn't wait to seize my opportunity. There wasn't any awkwardness with Gareth. As a player, you know as much as anyone whether you've played well or not. The reality, whether it's with Wales or the Scarlets, is that if one of us doesn't play well, the other is ready to step in. You've got to be performing well every week to keep your place. Gareth came over to me and said, 'Congrats, Kizz. You deserve it,' and that was pretty much it. If the roles had been reversed I'd have done the same thing, because there's a huge amount of mutual respect between us. Sometimes it's a case of 'let the best man win'.

Willis Halaholo: The mood among the senior players who'd been there before was infectious. You could see their attitude switch; they really meant business that week. Alun Wyn was awesome, one of those leaders you're willing to go into any battle with. Even though I'd only met him that week, I felt like he was one of those captains I'd played under for years.

Kieran Hardy: I was more nervous than I'd ever been before that game. Yes, there was no crowd there, but they're one of the biggest teams in the world, and they'd played in the World Cup final six months earlier. I'd grown up watching players like Owen Farrell, Maro Itoje and Ben Youngs, so to play against them in such a pressurised environment was huge. All week I had that nauseous feeling in my stomach, and would find myself constantly thinking about the game. It was always on my mind, even when we'd finished training and were playing Playstation or whatever. It was always there, dominating my thoughts.

Wales–England games rarely unfold without incident, but this one was absolutely littered with controversy. After a cagey opening quarter of an hour, it exploded into life with an episode that still sends diehard England fans into a state of apoplexy. Wales were awarded a penalty inside England's twenty-two, and the referee Pascal Gauzere instructed Owen Farrell to warn his team about their increasing levels of ill-discipline. While Farrell gathered his charges under the posts, his opposite number, Dan Biggar, launched a high, hanging kick towards the left touchline where Josh Adams was waiting. The predatory winger out-jumped a scrambling George Ford to secure the ball and touch down. Cue scenes of unadulterated joy from Wales, and absolute fury from England. Farrell remonstrated at length with Gauzere, claiming he'd not been given sufficient time to speak to his players, but his protests fell on deaf, unsympathetic ears.

Dan Biggar: The way I look at it, the right-hand side of England's defence – Jonny May and I can't remember who else – were ready to go, no problems whatsoever. So if I'd kicked it to Jonny May, messed it up, and he'd then booted the ball seventy metres downfield, would England still be asking for the referee to put his clock back on or to let them have more time? We're always encouraged to do what I did. Jinks, in particular, wants us to be alert at penalty kicks, and to ensure our wingers are alive to any scoring opportunities. Josh is really good at claiming those cross-field kicks; it's one of his main strengths.

Tomas Francis: It was a bad refereeing decision, wasn't it? You can't tell a captain to go and speak to his players and then let someone kick to the corner. You just can't do that. Having said that, I'm not complaining.

Wyn Jones: In international rugby you've got to be on the ball every second of the game. They took their eye off the ball for literally two seconds, and we scored.

Callum Sheedy: I'm with Biggsy on that one. I thought it was fine. You listen to the ref mic and Bigs clearly says, 'Can you tell me when time's on?' As soon as time's on, it's *game* on. I think it was Elliot Daly who managed to cover the other side, so why couldn't they have covered Jaddsy's side?

Kieran Hardy: Dan's obviously going to push the limits because he's one of those guys that plays on the edge the whole time. He's a real competitor and if he feels like he's going to get one up on England by sneaking in a cross kick, then he's going to do it. I'm pretty sure if the circumstances were reversed, England would have done exactly the same thing.

Tomas Francis: Yeah, and if the shoe had been on the other foot, Biggsy would have been absolutely livid. He'd most probably have been sent off, do you know what I mean? Actually, a hundred per cent he'd have been sent off. He'd have literally got up in Pascal's face and called him a cheat, or something along those lines. He's my roomie in camp and I get on really well with him, but he's a completely different bloke on the pitch. He has this insane competitive edge.

Callum Sheedy: Biggsy will always push it to the limit and that's what makes him the player he is. He was the in-form ten in Europe at the time, if not the world. He's an unbelievable player and has that unshakeable will to win. Not many tens in the world would have seen that chance and executed like he did. For me it's a definite try. They should have been ready.

Fifteen minutes later, with the rage still boiling in the England camp, they were victims of what was perceived to be another gross injustice.

Dan Biggar: If I'm honest we probably got a bit lucky with the second try, the one where Zammit knocked it on.

Callum Sheedy: That one was a bit more contentious. Whether it was a try or not, it's one of those where if it's against you, you're frustrated, but if it's for you, you take it.

It was an incident that had all the armchair fans reaching for their law books. Wales were on the attack, and in the act of trying to catch the ball, Louis Rees-Zammit knocked it forward. As it dropped towards the ground, it hit the back of his leg and bounced backwards. Liam Williams was the quickest to react, gobbling up the loose ball and diving over the line.

Wyn Jones: When Sanj dived over, everyone had half-stopped, thinking play was going to be called back.

Kieran Hardy: It looked like a knock-on to me at the time, but when I looked at it on the replay, I wondered if we might have a chance.

Tomas Francis: The defining image of that game is Zammo's face, isn't it? When they eventually gave the try, the TV cameras caught his expression perfectly. It was a cheeky look that said, '*How* has he given that?' He was as astonished as anyone.

Wyn Jones: It was a bizarre one. Once it was given, we kind of knew it was going to be our day. We were getting the bounce of the ball, the fifty/fifties were going our way, and destiny seemed to be on our side.

Callum Sheedy: Throughout the game, there are so many of those calls; with this one Sanjay just happened to be there to finish it off which blew it out of proportion. That's seven points in the bank and who knows how the game would have gone after that. I'm confident we'd have won anyway.

Willis Halaholo: I was watching almost as a fan in the first half, and I was just happy that the boys were taking every opportunity that came their way. Against a team as good as England, you have to. At the same time, me and Sheedy were chatting on the bench, identifying weaknesses and coming up with a plan of how to exploit them when we got on. We were chatting throughout that first half, spotting who was getting tired, who was taking longer to get back to their feet, and thinking about how we could create mismatches. We talked about upping the tempo when we got our chance. We could see their pack running out of steam.

England struck back through Anthony Watson and landed a penalty on the stroke of half-time, to keep them in touch at 17–14.

Tomas Francis: It was Kizza's quick thinking that swung the momentum back in our favour in the second half. Everyone thought we were going to go for the posts, but he had other ideas.

Kieran Hardy: I don't remember why I tapped it; I just remember the ball falling into my path and instinct took over. I picked it up, and thought, 'There's no one here.' They'd definitely switched off, and I just seized the moment. We'd spoken in the week about the way we wanted to play, and the structure we wanted to operate within, but on the rugby field you make certain decisions purely according to what's in front of you. On that occasion, I saw the opportunity and went for it. If I hadn't scored we might be having a very different conversation.

Tomas Francis: It was great presence of mind from Kizza, fair play.

Kieran Hardy: It's a real blur. I can't really tell you how it happened, I just remember leaping up, and screaming at the top of my voice into an empty stadium. All I heard was my own voice echoing back at me, which was pretty strange. Looking back, I wish there'd been 75,000 people in the stadium cheering along with us, but at the time I wouldn't have changed anything. The opportunity to start my first Six Nations game against England, with the Triple Crown on the line was amazing, and then to score a try at that particular moment was like a dream come true. In those strange times, I didn't know any different.

On the hour mark, Hardy's opposite number, Ben Youngs, proved equally adept at snaking through a gap, darting between three defenders to bring the scores level at 24–24. As the game entered the final quarter it was as good as a reset. Who would seize the initiative in the last twenty minutes?

Wyn Jones: We felt we were winning the game quite comfortably at that stage, but then you look at up the scoreboard at 24–24 and think, 'Wow, we need to step it up here now.'

Willis Halaholo: I'd come on not long before that Ben Youngs try, and Wayne had given me licence to back my instincts, and have a go. I didn't get too many instructions beyond that. It was more a case of, 'Bring some energy to the boys. Go out there and communicate clearly, and be an extra set of eyes for those boys who are tired.'

Wyn Jones: It goes back to how we were feeling at the World Cup. We knew we were a fit team that had some big players like Zammo, who could conjure something out of nothing. We knew we could always go on and win the game. We never panicked. It was just a case of doing your next job, doing it well, and getting more points on the board.

Kieran Hardy: When they drew level, that could have put the pressure on us, but it probably did the opposite. It was the nudge we needed to crank through the gears. We felt as though we were dominating the game and knew we could turn it on and score when we needed to. The boys that came off the bench made a real difference. Callum Sheedy was superb.

Wayne Pivac: During the last twenty minutes, we had some young fellas on the field, including Sheedy who'd missed a couple of kicks up at Murrayfield. For him to have the confidence to go for the posts spoke volumes. Quite frankly I'd have been happy to go for the corner at 24–24, and to build more pressure on them in the twenty-two, but the kid stepped up – Mr Cool – and knocked over three from three. Again, who was the ill-disciplined team?

Wyn Jones: We knew coming into the England game that their discipline wasn't the best, and they were giving a lot of penalties away. It was a focus of ours to try to frustrate them because if you get under their skin they tend to give penalties away. That early try when Biggsy kicked to the corner really annoyed them, and over time those frustrations started to accumulate, and their discipline started to unravel.

Callum Sheedy: After that Scotland game, where I'd missed a couple of kicks, my Twitter feed had gone mad. It was full of trolls telling me I couldn't kick, that I'd never be an international goal kicker. It was quite nice to prove them all wrong.
Kieran Hardy: There's always someone who has an opinion on the way you played, who likes to fixate on the things you didn't do well. Callum showed people exactly what he was capable of that weekend. He nailed every kick, and essentially won us the game.

Dan Biggar: Sheedy proved he had real bottle in that game. He'd been quite down in the week about missing those kicks against Scotland, so to do what he did against England showed a lot of character. It was a good blend we had, in terms of competition between me and him and him coming on and producing the goods when he needed to. It was a proper twenty-three-man squad effort.

Tomas Francis: Willis Halaholo came on too, and came of age in that game. He pretty much cemented his place in the team.

Willis Halaholo: Our pack was applying tons of pressure and breaking them down. While their discipline was falling apart, we were making all the right decisions, keeping cool heads and being accurate in everything we did.

Kieran Hardy: I remember feeling a twinge in my leg during the last quarter and I hit the deck. I managed to get up and trot a little bit, but something felt wrong. I'd done my hamstring the year before, playing for the Scarlets, but this one didn't feel as bad. I was hoping it was only a minor injury, but I was taken off as a precaution.

Wyn Jones: That last try from Cory Hill gave us the bonus point which probably ultimately won us the tournament. You only realise in retrospect how significant that try was in the scheme of things.

Wayne Pivac: A lot was made of our luck, but we came on strong in that last twenty minutes, and put them under real pressure. The English boys made mistakes and they were punished for it. To finish with that try and a bonus point just underlined our credentials as far as I was concerned. I only wish we'd had 75,000 fans in there to help us celebrate it.

Callum Sheedy: Everyone got carried away with those couple of decisions, but two or three refereeing decisions aren't thirty-point swings. We ended up beating them really convincingly. The refereeing decisions took over in the media but we knew deep down in our hearts that we'd dominated them. Going into the tournament they'd been fancied as favourites whereas everyone had written us off. That's what made it so special.

Wayne Pivac: The ongoing discussion over the tries was a moot point given that we won by more than two scores. We left a few out there too: a more favourable bounce, and Louis Rees-Zammit would have scored another from seventy metres. I look at that game as a real marker of progress. In the autumn and the previous Six Nations, it had felt like everything had been against us. We'd suffered a bit at the set piece, and I think the perception among the referees had been that we had a weak scrum. We knew we'd have to work hard to change that perception in the minds of the referees. We did a heck of a lot of work on our scrum and lineout in the build-up to the Six Nations. Jon Humphreys did an amazing job, and by that England game we were becoming the real deal. I think the referees were beginning to understand that.

Dan Biggar: Sometimes you've got to ride your luck, haven't you? Even though we didn't necessarily feel like it was luck, when the cards fall in your favour, it's amazing what can happen. If we'd lost our first two games, maybe we wouldn't have beaten England. It's a funny thing, momentum and confidence.

Wayne Pivac: To come out of the England game with forty points and a Triple Crown, we were over the moon. If you look at the last twenty minutes when it was 24–all, if England were that great, then they win that game.

Tomas Francis: That was the most satisfying result of the campaign because it's England, isn't it? They rate themselves a lot; they think they're better than the rest of us. That's how I feel anyway, and it's always good to get one over on them especially in that fashion, scoring that many points. The controversy makes it better in my opinion. They're just whiny aren't they, the English? It was a good day, that one.

Callum Sheedy: It was one of the most special days and nights I've ever experienced in rugby.

Kieran Hardy: I'd played the biggest game of my career, beaten England, scored a try and won the Triple Crown, but at the back of my mind I was thinking about my injury and praying it wasn't going to rule me out for the rest of the campaign.

Wayne Pivac: It was very difficult to celebrate much at all in our bubble. We had a couple of beers in the changing room, and I think we probably had a couple at the hotel, but it wasn't like the good old days because we had covid rules we had to abide by.

Tomas Francis: I was being drug tested again, so that's another celebration I missed out on.

Wayne Pivac: Our head of medical, Prav, was always stressing during his presentations that the pandemic throws up chaos. With chaos comes change and with change you have to adapt. We hammered that slogan the whole way through. 'Hey boys, if we win this thing, there'll be time to celebrate.' It's not going to be a Grand Slam or a Championship of old, but these are the times we're in and we change and adapt. That's what we had to do all the way through.

Tomas Francis: Playing for Exeter made it even sweeter for me, because I had the bragging rights when I went back, and not just after the England game. I gave Hoggy and Jonny Gray a load of grief after the Scotland game too.

Kieran Hardy: That Sunday and Monday, waiting for the results of my scan, were the longest two days of my life. I was moving well, and felt pretty good, but the worst-case scenario came back. It was a grade-two tear, and I was out for six weeks. I desperately wanted to enjoy the occasion and celebrate what we'd accomplished, but I couldn't really do that because I didn't really know how to feel. It was the agony and the ecstasy of professional sport wrapped up in one.

Wayne Pivac: Things were a lot tighter for us than they'd been previously. The boys stayed in camp a lot longer so we'd only go home on a Saturday as opposed to on a Tuesday and back in on a Thursday as we used to. Over that eight or nine weeks we were in a lot longer than we'd normally be, which represented a big sacrifice. But by the sounds of what was happening in England – our players talking to their players – we may have managed what we did internally slightly better than they did.

Willis Halaholo: It was very strange having to abide by all those Covid protocols, but I just took it on the chin and cracked on. Everyone was in the same boat and I was just grateful to be there. It was a dream to play international rugby.

Wayne Pivac: We did some fun things as a group. Before the pandemic, we used to have a barber come in to camp. That obviously got canned, so Prav became our barber. We all took it in turn to have a trim, and there were some pretty dodgy ones at the start as you can imagine. He's entirely self-taught, but once he got his eye in, he was fantastic.

We also had 'Covid Caff' in the Vale, which we ran ourselves. There were no external people involved so we weren't breaching any Covid regulations. We sourced everything we needed, and the boys slipped pretty easily into their roles. George was the barista; he's got his own coffee business so he was the obvious choice. Dillon Lewis was head waiter, and when he came back into the camp, Jaddsy had to pick up all the dirty dishes as his penance. Foxy was always the man on the till; he's good at taking money off the boys. We had music playing, the barber's seat was there, and we had some good times.

Dan Biggar: This should give you some idea of the confidence of the new breed. Every day off, every Wednesday afternoon, we had George – who's got a hundred caps – sweating behind the counter making coffees for all the youngsters, Foxy, who's on eighty-odd caps, waiting tables, and my job in camp has always been laundry boy. I've got ninety caps, but I've never been able get out of laundry duty. Us so-called elder statesmen have definitely gone wrong somewhere along the line.

Callum Sheedy: George, Foxy and Dillon Lewis were in charge. I was just the phantom croissant eater. I was enjoying the wide range of croissants on offer. It's tough enough being stuck in a hotel for five or six weeks straight, so doing stuff like that helped break up the monotony. In normal times we'd all have gone out for a walk and a coffee but it wasn't possible during the pandemic, so things like that were great for breaking up the week and bringing a bit of normality to strange times.

Kieran Hardy: Even though we were in a strange environment, it made it feel a bit more normal because we were able to socialise with each other. Everyone looked forward to the Covid Caff on a Wednesday. It was a chance to socialise, to switch off, have a pastry and a coffee and play cards. We did a casino night and a horse racing night as well, both of which were superb. Wayne built a brilliant environment which brought us much closer as a squad, particularly when you were hearing how strict it was in England's camp. We were strict enough with each other, wearing masks and making sure we sanitised regularly but we also had fun with it and I think that showed on the field.

Willis Halaholo: We all got to go home for a couple of days after the England game and spend a bit of time with our families. Obviously we had to be squeaky clean after what had happened with Josh, but it was great to see the family. My daughters were so proud. The younger ones don't really know what's going on, but the older ones had seen me cope with some of the darker times when I was laid low with injury, so they understood how emotional it was for me to win my first international caps.

Wayne Pivac: We made a statement with our selection for the Italy game, resisting the urge to make lots of changes. By then, we were focusing on France and a Grand Slam and we wanted to keep the momentum going. We also wanted to challenge the boys to get the job done as early as they could. That was by not being airy-fairy and forcing the game; it was about setting a good platform, keeping our discipline, and being really ruthless with our opportunities. We got the upper hand early on and rather than go for the posts, we went for the knockout punch nice and early, scoring four tries within thirty minutes. The gas came off a little bit after that, but we achieved everything we'd wanted to.

Wyn Jones: When you play Italy, with no disrespect, you usually make a few changes, and rest a few boys, but Wayne named his strongest side. It was a real statement of intent.

Willis Halaholo: Maybe if we'd done well in the autumn and the flow of the team had been good for a couple of campaigns, he'd have made a few changes, but the flow was just starting to come to us so I guess he wanted to keep hold of that and keep pushing forwards.

Wyn Jones: We'd had a fallow week prior to Italy and some of the boys didn't want to go two weeks without a game. We started with a bang, and ran in some good tries.

Tomas Francis: The more games you play the better you get. I don't like the Irish system of playing once every six weeks. I like to warm into it. That victory served us well and rolled us nicely into the French game.

Callum Sheedy: It was a romp. We got the five points, but more crucially we had a big winning margin. The tournament ultimately came down to points difference. We kept them out at the end, and those seven points could have been crucial in the shake-up, as France eventually needed to beat Scotland by twenty-one points to take the title off us. If they'd needed to beat them by twelve, or fifteen it would've been a lot more doable for them. We knew we needed to rack up the points, and we went out there and hammered them. On a personal note, I scored my first international try too, so it's definitely a game I'll remember fondly.

Jake Ball: I genuinely didn't expect to get picked for the Six Nations. I know there were murmurs and rumblings, and people saying I shouldn't have been selected and I totally understood that. I'd made my decision to return to Australia in the autumn and I knew what the consequences were. I'd no longer be eligible for selection, and I understood that I'd made things very awkward for Wayne and the coaching staff. Wayne told me he didn't want to be the guy who left me hanging on forty-nine caps. He said I deserved fifty and that it was his intention to give me my fiftieth during the tournament. He didn't have to do that, but I'm grateful he did because it was a great note to go out on. I didn't have the biggest part to play like I'd had in previous years, but I left Wales as a Six Nations champion.

Dan Biggar: It was similar to the Georgia game in the World Cup, in that you don't want it to be 10–6 or 10–all at fifty minutes against Italy because then they're in the game. Their performance probably wasn't up to scratch, but we managed to put the game to bed after thirty minutes which meant we could bring a few of the boys off for some rest. It was a really professional performance to set up something much bigger the following week.

Wales crossed the whitewash seven times en route to a 48–7 victory, with tries coming courtesy of Josh Adams, Taulupe Faletau, George North, Callum Sheedy, Louis Rees-Zammit, and evergreen hooker, Ken Owens, who bagged a brace.

Wyn Jones: I think he's a bit annoyed he didn't get the hat-trick, but two was more than enough for a front-rower. I was happy enough that he didn't get his third. He kicked the ball down the wing as well, didn't he? He had a few stern words for his troubles, and he had to apologise all the way back to the halfway line. He gets reminded of that one quite regularly. No need for a hooker to be doing that.

Tomas Francis: He always gets stick, the Sheriff. He gets it every day, and he loves it. That's his role in the team, and he takes it to be fair. He takes the heat well. I'm glad he didn't get the hat-trick too though. You'd never have heard the end of it.

Wayne Pivac: We had a plan to get certain players off the park as early as we could: George North, Alun Wyn Jones, Ken Owens, Toby. There were several key players we wanted out of there, and even though it got a bit disjointed at the end, we achieved our aim. It would have been nice to have nilled them; that was one of the things we'd wanted to achieve from a defensive point of view. Certain games are all about winning. Other games are about – and this is not being disrespectful to Italy because we *should* beat them with the firepower we've got – giving your team challenges to meet. We ticked all the boxes that day. Seven tries, five points, job done.

Jake Ball: It was difficult for me because I'd been a starting player in previous campaigns, so I certainly had a different role, but that didn't mean I didn't do everything in my power to help the boys out. I don't have any regrets as to what's gone on. I'm pretty proud of what I've achieved since moving to Wales. It's been a crazy nine years and sometimes you have to pinch yourself a bit. It's been a hell of a ride.

Wayne Pivac: As the momentum was growing, the thought of a Grand Slam was always in the back of my mind. You win the first game, and you're still on track for it whereas Ireland aren't. It's then down to three teams, then it gets down to two, and eventually it was down to just us. It was a satisfying position to be in. While we never got ahead of ourselves, by the final round, we knew the maths were in our favour. It would have been a disaster if we hadn't won the Championship. Scotland would have had to be awful against France, but we weren't thinking about staying within range; it was all about how we were going to beat France.

Willis Halaholo: I was still buzzing just from being in the environment. The thought of being Grand Slam contenders was unbelievable. It was awesome. You could see the belief grow in the boys after they'd been doubted earlier in the campaign. It was just a case of, 'One more win, to prove them all wrong.'

Wayne Pivac: We'd lost to France the previous year in Cardiff, but we'd blown a try at half-time; we could have walked in under the sticks if we'd gone right, but we went to the left. We'd replayed that game so many times, and felt that we were much better than the French. We were happy to let the media sing their praises, while remembering that, internally, when the opportunity came, we knew we could beat them. We went into the final game firmly believing we were the better team.

It was the final game of Super Saturday – traditionally the last day of the tournament, but an earlier Covid outbreak in the French camp had forced a postponement of their match with Scotland. The rescheduled game would take place a week later. Wales though, had destiny in their own hands. If they beat France in Paris, the Grand Slam was theirs and whatever happened between France and Scotland would be irrelevant.

The game began at a frenetic pace that was maintained throughout as both sides dished up a dizzying exhibition of thrills and spills. The home side started with greater urgency and were ahead within five minutes after the towering Romain Taofifenua crashed over from short range. Dan Biggar responded, running a sharp inside angle to break through and level the scores. Antoine Dupont then reclaimed the lead, running a brilliant support line after Brice Dulin's chip had wrong-footed Taulupe Faletau. The match wasn't even twenty minutes old when Josh Navidi burrowed under the French defence for the game's fourth try.

It then fell to Navidi's namesake, Josh Adams, to put Wales into the lead for the first time, capitalising on a delicate grubber from Justin Tipuric. Tipuric had been put into space by a sumptuous pass from the giant lock, Adam Beard. This was Pivac's Wales in motion: ball-handling forwards loitering in the wide channels, looking for space rather than contact. The conversion took Wales into a 27–17 lead.

Dan Biggar: It's really easy with Josh, because he's such a natural finisher and he has a radar to the try line. If there's a sniff of a ball coming to him he's going to be in with a shout of scoring. We're encouraged to play to the space, especially with Steve. He's been brilliant in terms of getting us to back our skills and play what we see. If that means chucking a long pass, taking a quick penalty, or threading a grubber through, then we're in good business.

What happened just before the hour mark still causes Pivac's brow to furrow with frustration and regret. After a lineout on the French twenty-two, Wales's forward pack formed a bristling, powerful maul that began to accelerate rapidly and irresistibly towards the try line. Advantage was called when it was illegally collapsed by the French tight-head prop, Mohamed Haouas, and Wales spun the ball swiftly to the right where Louis Rees-Zammit found the narrowest corridor of space. Soaring gracefully through the air, reached at full stretch, and planted the ball over the try line. After a lengthy referral to the Television Match Official, Wayne Barnes, he was adjudged to have touched it down against the base of the flag and the try was disallowed. The referee, Luke Pearce, then issued a yellow card to Haouas for his earlier offence, but declined to award a penalty try, telling Alun Wyn Jones he wasn't convinced a try would have been scored.

Callum Sheedy: It was a penalty try all day long. We were warming up behind the posts when the maul was powering forward and there was no way the French were going to stop that legally. But Luke Pearce is one of the best referees in the world. He's a really good guy and he's obviously seen what he's seen and that's fine; it's out of our hands.

Tomas Francis: He's from Devon. I know him quite well. We have some mutual friends. I went to a thirtieth birthday party the following August and I knew he was going to be there. On the way there, my wife warned me to bite my lip and not say anything.

Wayne Pivac: There were probably three or four big moments during the game that went against us that on another day may have been refereed differently. I believe – and it's just my view – that we won that game comfortably, but hey, it's in the record books as a French win.

Tomas Francis: I think Zammo nearly scoring in the corner took the attention away from the maul offence. If we'd just left the ball in that maul, it would have been a penalty try all day. If that guy [Haouas] isn't there, the try's being scored, no doubt about it. He went to the TMO for the try didn't he, but we didn't go back to check the maul.

Callum Sheedy: We still should have ended up winning the game. There were other decisions in the championship that went our way, so it's swings and roundabouts, I guess. We probably can't blame that one incident for us not winning. It just wasn't meant to be and we have to take a look at ourselves rather than placing the blame on something external.

Wyn Jones: It's the sort of thing that frustrates you, though. I was on the ball at the back thinking, 'There's no way I'm not scoring here,' and the next minute he [Haouas] hits me straight from the side. If the maul had been stopped there and the penalty given, I think he would have given a penalty try, but because we tried to play and Zammo nearly scored in the corner, it's taken attention away from the collapsed maul. Our intent to play actually went against us on that occasion. Perhaps we could have been a bit more street-smart.

Wayne Pivac: If we'd scored there, it would have been 34–20, which would have been hard to come back from.

Dan Biggar: That's the decision that rankles the most in hindsight. We basically mauled it all the way from the twenty-two, and he's given a yellow card for the prop coming in from the side, but not the penalty try.

Wyn Jones: All that said, my overwhelming memory of the game was the red card to be honest. I was thinking, has this really happened again?

France were dangerously close to scoring, pummelling the Welsh defence with a series of short-range carries when the French lock Paul Willemse appeared to gouge Wyn Jones in the act of clearing out the ruck. Luke Pearce was left with no alternative but to brandish a red card. It was the third time in five games a member of the opposition had been sent off against Wales.

Wyn Jones: We were under the cosh a bit when I felt his finger go in my eye. As soon as it happened, I knew there'd be a good chance of a red card, and when I watched it back I thought, 'Yep, he's gone.' I felt for him a bit because, like Zander Fagerson, he was just a bit late and had to grab whatever he could. I genuinely think it was unfortunate timing, and I'm sure he had no intention of poking me in the eye. There's no way he would have done it intentionally, because he couldn't see my face from where he was.

Intentional or not, it was a bona-fide red card offence, and appeared to have put paid to any notion of a French comeback. Wales were now ten points ahead with twelve minutes to play.

Willis Halaholo: I'd been really nervous watching from the bench, especially during that period when France were attacking our line. I desperately wanted to be out there, helping. You always think you're going to be the guy to make a difference.

Halaholo was one of four substitutes called into action in the immediate aftermath of the red card. He and Callum Sheedy replaced Jonathan Davies and Dan Biggar respectively. The two Lions had 176 caps between them compared to eleven shared by Sheedy and Halaholo. Up front, Elliott Dee and Leon Brown came on for Ken Owens and Tomas Francis who between them had 137. The spine of the side suddenly appeared a good deal less experienced.

Willis Halaholo: I'd already warmed up three times before then. A couple of the boys had gone down, so I'd been up, down, up, down, full of nervous energy. I was so happy to finally strip off and get on.

Tomas Francis: I came off thinking, 'We've done it.' It would have been two Grand Slams in three years, or two in two for me because I'd missed the 2020 campaign with injury.

Kieran Hardy: I was commentating on the game for S4C, and I was on the edge of my seat at this point.

Wayne Pivac: The belief was very much there; we were a very experienced team, with a lot of guys who'd been in a Grand Slam match before. The French hadn't won anything for a long time, so as good as this French team was, we knew that if we built pressure in the right areas of the field, we could come away with it. We also had the knowledge that in the previous Six Nations game against them, we felt we'd been the better team.

Tomas Francis: Willis came on and in retrospect you have to ask, was it the right game for him? We'd just withstood their onslaught, and the red card had reversed the try. It was an absolutely pivotal moment. All we needed to do was clear our lines.

Willis Halaholo: As soon as I got on, there was a miscommunication and I got caught offside from a kick. I gave away the penalty that brought them right back into our corner.

Tomas Francis: Willis went early and we weren't able to relieve the pressure. If we'd executed that, the game was done. But then all of a sudden, you're back in your half on a final warning and the pressure's right back on you.

Within a few minutes of Halaholo's accidental offside, Charles Ollivon was held up over the Welsh line by some heroic scrambling defence. Luke Pearce had been playing advantage and, as well as awarding the penalty, he sent Taulupe Faletau to the sin bin, nullifying Wales's one-man advantage. A minute later,

Liam Williams was also despatched for diving off his feet at a ruck. France had pulled a thread in Wales's tightly-woven tapestry, and it was beginning to unravel alarmingly. The ten-point margin suddenly felt less of an unscalable Mount Everest, and more of a Mount Snowdon. Difficult, but within reach.

Wayne Pivac: I agree that the Liam Williams incident was a penalty, but there was no ruck formed, so it wasn't a yellow card in my view. If he'd stayed on, we'd have had fourteen on fourteen. That was a big call.

Tomas Francis: It was a penalty at best. It's not like it was a try-scoring opportunity or anything. They were about forty yards out.

Wayne Pivac: These are undoubtedly big moments in games, but you have big moments go your way and big ones that don't. They seem to even themselves out over tournaments and careers.

Dan Biggar: The first thing I will say before going off on one is that we imploded in the last ten minutes. It would be wrong to whinge and moan and say we lost through no fault of our own. For the first seventy minutes our discipline was excellent. We were clinical and precise and didn't allow them to come into the game, but we made some basic errors in that last ten. There's no doubt that some key decisions went against us, and I suppose some people will say that's karma for some of the decisions that benefited us earlier in the tournament and that's fine, but we felt we did enough to win. Playing the best French team for the last twenty-odd years in Paris, with a Grand Slam on the line was always going to be difficult.

France remained in Wales's twenty-two, piling on the pressure, and eventually, Ollivon got his just rewards, making no mistake with the grounding on his second attempt. The conversion brought France back to within three points.

Wyn Jones: Once the clock turned red, we were still winning. We only had to kick it out. Unfortunately, that one decision went against us [Cory Hill slipped and went off his feet at a ruck giving the penalty to France] and they came back to win the game in all fairness. They executed really well in the last two or three minutes and scored in the corner. We'd definitely done enough to win it, but it wasn't to be.

Viewed through the filter of Welsh heartbreak, it's easy to forget just how courageous France were in those fraught final exchanges. Despite the enormity of the occasion, they continued to play with an admirable Gallic swagger. Brice Dulin's clinching try was wondrously crafted and, when the opportunity arose, it was taken with a cold-hearted precision. It was utterly soul-destroying for a Welsh side who'd defied pre-tournament predictions to come within a hair's breadth of the unlikeliest of Grand Slams.

Wayne Pivac: If you look at the stats, we won every facet of the game except the scoreboard. There was an intercept which could have been a fourteen-pointer, a three-on-one that we didn't exploit, and a nailed-on penalty try that wasn't given.

Willis Halaholo: I don't know, man . . . at the end of the game when we lost, I took it quite badly. I was pretty hard on myself. Back at the hotel, there was a group of us replacements sitting at one table away from the rest. We were looking at each other and admitting that we hadn't done our jobs as impact guys coming on to see out that game. We'd all made a mistake each that had led towards the defeat. Just little things that us boys on the bench felt like we'd contributed to the loss. I couldn't stop thinking about my offside for a while. That's what people don't see; the emotional toll these things take on us rugby players. Even days later at home, my wife was like, 'Are you all right?'

Tomas Francis: In Scotland, Wayne won the game with the subs, but I honestly think it had the opposite effect in that game. *I* was ready to come off because sixty minutes is enough for me and I was cooked, but the likes of Biggsy and Ken should have stayed on. There was no game the following week. There was nothing to save them for.

Callum Sheedy: When you come off the bench and you're twelve points up and you end up losing – even though it was nothing you were directly involved in – you blame yourself. I'm a perfectionist and my own biggest critic, and I found myself thinking, 'I wish Biggar had stayed on because if he had, we would have won.'

Tomas Francis: The experience Biggsy and Ken would have offered could have made the difference. I don't think it was a game for Sheedy to come on. I know it's nice to play in a big Championship game, but there was nothing to bring him on for at that point. We weren't chasing it, we just needed to close it out, and Biggsy is the best controlling ten in the world, or at least in the northern hemisphere. You can argue that the Saffas are better at it if you want, but up here he's unrivalled for the way he controls a game so I don't think making those subs at that time was the best idea. I'm not saying Callum did anything wrong, but Biggsy was in his rhythm, he wasn't tired, and he's not unfit. Not like me. Fresh legs for me was the right decision all day, but him and Ken are going to carry on doing what they're doing. You don't need to make a change for the sake of a change. That's nothing against Sheeds, because he was class against England and Scotland when he came on and he won us those games.

Callum Sheedy: It was an absolute killer. When I think back to that game, it makes me feel sick because we were so close to a Grand Slam. When I got back in the changing room and saw Alun Wyn, Foxy, Bigs and Sanjay all crying, it was devastating.

Willis Halaholo: It was the most depressing changing room I've ever been in. You could see how much the boys had wanted it. Just sitting in there felt yuck. It just felt *yuck*. You can't help but think you contributed to losing a game like that. If you make a mistake in those last ten or fifteen minutes, it's just one of those things you can't stop thinking about. When I came on I caused the penalty straight away for being in front of the kicker, so . . . yeah, that was my fault. At the time I was happy to get on and be involved in what could have been a bit of history, but I guess there was a whole lot of us that came on at the same time and maybe just upset the rhythm a little bit. Just before we did, the boys that were playing – Foxy and all those – had dug in on our try line and kept them out. That's when the changes were made and maybe the connections and stuff weren't quite there between us. I understand what Sheedy's talking about, wishing he'd stayed on the bench. Maybe we just came on and got a bit of stage fright. All credit to France, they played right until the final whistle. They took their chances and eventually got over the line.

The result left Wales in limbo. The Grand Slam dream may have evaporated in the chill Parisian night, but they were still top of the table. Whether or not they remained there depended on the outcome of the rescheduled match between France and Scotland the following week. It was a tall order, but if France won with a bonus point and a twenty-one-point winning margin, they would snaffle the Championship from under Wales's nose.

Wayne Pivac: I was so disappointed for the players because it would have been nice to have gone out there on the pitch, get into a huddle and say, 'Fellas, we gave it everything, but we've just got to live with it, take it on the chin and be a better team in the future. But now, let's get back in the changing room. You'll be a Championship-winning team when you walk through that door, we can open the champagne, and celebrate a Championship victory.' We were robbed of that moment.

Tomas Francis: It was the biggest anti-climax ever.

Wayne Pivac: Having to wait another week was the biggest frustration. There were so many potential scenarios and I'd imagined them all. Grand Slam champions; that's an easy scenario. Missing a Grand Slam, but at the same moment winning a Championship; that was less satisfactory but I had to think about how I was going to deal with that, and motivate the boys to actually enjoy it. We'd desperately wanted that Grand Slam for so many reasons. For the pressure we'd been under as a team, for ourselves as an ambitious, competitive group, for our families and friends and all the people back home who'd been suffering through the pandemic. We know how important rugby is to the Welsh people, and we knew how much a Grand Slam would have helped lift the nation in the midst of a pretty dark chapter.

Tomas Francis: It was a very dark drinking session after that to be fair.

Willis Halaholo: We needed each other's company more than ever. No one could bear to go to their rooms.

Tomas Francis: Some of the boys went all the way through until the next morning. They just couldn't get their heads around what had happened. It was a really tough one to take. I couldn't pull an all-nighter myself because I wasn't sure if I'd have to go back to Exeter and play the next week. Who pushed on through? Toby as always. He's a different bloke on the piss, a far cry from the mild-mannered gent everyone sees in public. Once, when he was absolutely steaming, he told Gats he should be captain. In the next meeting, Gats stood up in front of everyone and said, 'Right, Toby, you want to be captain, do you?' Toby literally didn't speak. Didn't say a word. He was mortified. So yeah, he went all the way through until dawn in Paris. Sheedy did too, and Biggsy. Biggsy isn't normally one to pull an all-nighter, but it really got to him. It was still bothering him weeks later. He was just devastated. We all were.

Wayne Pivac: We all wish we could turn back the clock. We won it up until the eighty-second minute, didn't we? It was a great game of rugby to be involved in, and for the Championship to have been won that day would have been a fantastic end to a great series. There had been a lot of fantastic matches, and everyone had played their part in a tournament that had been a great advert for rugby and the Six Nations. We were just a few seconds away from the dream.

Dan Biggar: The week that followed was really tough. We had to wait a week to watch France play Scotland on the Friday and honestly, I've never been more nervous for a game. It was really hard work watching it. I had to go out of the room and change the channel a couple of times. I've never experienced that as a player.

Wyn Jones: It was a bizarre feeling watching the Scotland game in the house knowing everything hung on the outcome. Normally, you're in control of your destiny, but we just had to watch on helplessly.

Tomas Francis: The maths were totally against France, but you never know with Scotland, do you?

Dan Biggar: My wife and little boy stayed back home in Wales, so I was on my own watching it in Northampton. I was FaceTiming my wife during the game and for some reason her telly was ahead of mine, which only added to the drama. She was reacting to things that had happened before I'd seen them. It was a bit of an emotional rollercoaster. I know what my family and friends go through now when they're watching me play. At least when I'm on the field I'm in control.

Wayne Pivac: They needed to score four tries and have a winning margin of twenty-one points and, at one point, it was on track to happen. I was sitting here with my wife, Michaela, the girls and the dog watching the game. I knew if it went our way, I'd have to do TV interviews afterwards, so I had to limit myself to one glass of red wine. It was so nerve-wracking.

Dan Biggar: I was due to play the following day so I was stone cold sober unfortunately.

Callum Sheedy: It was awkward because I had a game the next day for Bristol against Quins. We were top of the league and they were third, so it was a huge game. I'd told myself that I wasn't going to get emotionally invested in it. What's meant to be is meant to be. I wasn't even going to watch it, then I was lying in bed and made the mistake of turning on the telly. The next thing you know, my hands are sweating, my heart's pumping, I'm chucking the remote at the pillows and I'm the most invested man in the world! One of my best mates from school, Adam Hastings, came on for Scotland. I'd texted him in the week saying, 'You need to do this for me, bro, please,' and fair play, the Scots turned up and did us a favour, so we owe them one.

Wayne Pivac: I was cheering every French knock-on, every lineout to the Scots, and riding that wave just like a fan does, probably more so because our WhatsApp group was going wild with messages.

Callum Sheedy: It was horrible, I hated it. I hate things being out of our control and that French team is so good. I was glad when I saw the rain coming down because it is tough to score more than four tries in the rain, especially against that Scotland defence. That said, that French team can score from anywhere. Thankfully the Scots dug in for us.

Willis Halaholo: I was at home with the family with my kilt on!

Wayne Pivac: Scotland would score, the margin France needed would increase and you'd start to feel good about yourself, but then just before half-time, France got back in the game, Scotland got a yellow card, and things got twitchy. The French went to the corner and if they'd scored then, they'd have had two tries in the bank. You'd have backed them to get four then, and it was game on. We knew how they'd finished against us, and what they were capable of. It was a massive moment when they didn't score there.

Willis Halaholo: I was yelling at the TV and all sorts. I've never actually done that before; rooted for another team like that, but it just proved to me how much it meant.

Tomas Francis: Luckily the French are French and the Scots turned up.

In the end, the calculators weren't required as Scotland emerged victorious following a late Duhan van der Merwe try. A week after their heart-breaking defeat to France at the same ground, Wales were officially declared Six Nations champions.

Wyn Jones: It softened the blow a little, seeing Scotland beat France in the last minute. I'll always be able to say I'm a 2021 Six Nations winner, but being so close to the Grand Slam took the shine off the title in some ways.

Willis Halaholo: As a professional sportsman, you want to go for gold. You don't aim for silver. The Grand Slam is the real gold, so you don't want to settle for the Championship.

Kieran Hardy: The championship felt like second-best to most of us. All eyes had been on the Grand Slam from the third game onwards, and when you don't quite reach that pinnacle, it feels like you've wound up in second place, even though we'd actually topped the table.

Callum Sheedy: It didn't really ease the pain of missing out on the Grand Slam, if I'm honest. It was bittersweet because winning the Six Nations is definitely something to be proud of, but I'd love nothing more than to have those twenty minutes against France back.

Dan Biggar: We scored more tries than any Welsh team had ever scored in a campaign and ended up winning it. I think it was a case of finding our feet a bit as opposed to recalibrating from Gats's way to Wayne's game plan. Although we scored some really nice tries and played some nice stuff, I wouldn't say it was a vintage campaign for us. We knuckled down and rolled our sleeves up. Ultimately, we won games of rugby which always helps. If we'd lost those two opening games, people would have been calling for heads and all sorts, wouldn't they?

Wayne Pivac: We've got some very experienced people in the back room who do a great job, some fantastic young players coming through and we've got some senior players who've found a new lease of life; guys that some had written off in terms of making another World Cup, but I think everybody in the current squad has the ability to get to the next World Cup. It frustrates me when people from South Africa or other countries have an opinion on Alun Wyn and ask, 'What does he bring?' We see it on a daily basis, and believe me it's significant. I'm a little bit old-school in my coaching and I believe that age is irrelevant; whether you're a Louis Rees-Zammit or an Alun Wyn Jones, if you deliver the goods, you'll get picked. Someone has to be the oldest player to play at a Rugby World Cup, someone has to be the most capped player of all time, and who's to say it's not going to be Alun Wyn Jones? This thing up here, the mind, the brain, the experience; that doesn't go, it only gets stronger and stronger, so the crucial aspect is how we manage people's bodies, because it's an increasingly brutal sport. It's a different game to the one I played.

POLARIS

PUBLISHING